INTRODUCTION TO CANADIAN SOCIETY
Sociological Analysis

S0-CCD-886

Introduction to Canadian Society

Sociological Analysis

EDITED BY

G. N. RAMU

STUART D. JOHNSON

Macmillan of Canada
Maclean-Hunter Press

© The Macmillan Company of Canada Limited, 1976

All rights reserved—no part of this book may be
reproduced in any form without permission in writing
from the publisher, except by a reviewer who wishes to
quote brief passages in connection with a review written
for inclusion in a magazine or newspaper.

Canadian Cataloguing in Publication Data

Main entry under title:
Introduction to Canadian Society

Bibliography: p.
Includes index.

ISBN 0-7705-1375-1 bd.   ISBN 0-7705-1410-3 pa.

1. Canada—Social conditions—Addresses, essays,
lectures. I. Ramu, G. N., date   II. Johnson, Stuart D.
1925–

HN103.5.158   309.1'71   C76-017061-4

Printed in Canada for
The Macmillan Company of Canada Limited
70 Bond Street, Toronto
M5B 1X3

Contents

1   Introduction   1
Stuart D. Johnson and G. N. Ramu

Part I   SOCIAL STRUCTURE   **9**

2   Canada: A Demographic Analysis   11
Warren E. Kalbach

3   The Sociology of Communication   77
Thelma McCormack

4   Class and Status in Canada   111
Alfred A. Hunter

Part II   SOCIAL PROCESS   **155**

5   The Sociology of Power and Politics:
An Introduction to the Canadian Polity   157
Rick Ogmundson

6   Intergroup Relations: Ethnicity in Canada   212
Rita M. Bienvenue

7.   Criminal Justice and Corrections in Canada   252
Stuart D. Johnson

Part III   SOCIAL INSTITUTIONS   **293**

8   The Family and Marriage in Canada   295
G. N. Ramu

9   The Sociology of Religion in the Canadian Context   349
Harry H. Hiller

10   The Sociology of Canadian Education   401
Jane Synge

11   Bureaucracy in Canada   438
C. R. Santos

Part IV   DISCIPLINE   **479**

12   Toward a Canadian Sociology
G. N. Ramu and Stuart D. Johnson

References   495

Author Index   519

Subject Index   525

Acknowledgements

A book of this type cannot be written without the co-operation and assistance of a number of people. In recognition of this fact the editors wish to acknowledge their debt to the contributing authors who almost always responded quickly and effectively to editorial suggestions and requests. Also, we owe a debt of gratitude to our publishers, especially Patrick Meany, Virgil Duff, and Kathy Johnson, with whom we found it a pleasure to work. In addition, we wish to recognize the support and constructive criticism which we received from colleagues Ray Currie, Ric Linden, and Emily Nett. Finally, we would be remiss if we did not recognize our debt for the skilled efforts and diligent attention which Jean Anazia and Kathy Wolf applied to typing the manuscript.

Winnipeg
June 1976

STUART D. JOHNSON
G. N. RAMU

INTRODUCTION TO CANADIAN SOCIETY
Sociological Analysis

Introduction

STUART D. JOHNSON

G. N. RAMU

;

This collection of essays is designed primarily to be used by literate, intelligent persons who want to know something about the sociology of Canada. It is not an introduction to sociology in the usual textbook sense of the word. Nor is it a treatise on sociological theory or on social problems, although functionalist theory, conflict theory, and other theoretical positions are introduced at appropriate points, along with a discussion of the various difficulties that have plagued Canadian society throughout its history.

The main emphasis in this work is upon informing the reader how the major components of Canadian society are put together, what these components do to maintain Canada as a national society, and how such a national society is changing through time, with particular emphasis on historical development within the society. The effort to offset the blatant ahistorical bias that has characterized much of sociological writing will, it is hoped, help the reader obtain a perspective of the society as a growing and developing entity, evolving through time, but exhibiting certain trends or themes that provide it with a set of uniquely Canadian characteristics not duplicated in any other society in the world.

To achieve these goals, we have eschewed the usual practice of editing a reader whereby short excerpts from governmental reports, papers read at professional meetings, and articles previously printed in scholarly journals are assembled to cover the substantive areas in question. In contrast, the present work presents original essays solicited from scholars, each of whom is a specialist in some aspect of Canadian society. These contributing authors have drawn upon their extensive knowledge of the technical literature of their topics—in many cases knowledge based upon the contributor's own research—to the end that every chapter represents

an informed overview of one aspect of Canadian society especially prepared for readers who, in all likelihood, will not themselves be trained
social scientists.

As an encouragement for readers to pursue each topic further, most of
the contributing authors have appended a list of important sources to each
chapter. These references for further reading were selected on a basis of
their general availability in most college and university libraries, as well
as for their relevance to the subject areas. We believe that serious students
will find this feature of the book of considerable value.

In this introductory chapter, an attempt has been made to draw together
some of the main themes and trends presented by the contributing authors,
to help the reader relate them to the ideas of social organization and
change in Canada.

Among the trends which have received much careful scientific study
are those relating to the demographic transition through which the Canadian population has passed and the fact that Canada has nearly reached
the upper limit for urbanization of its population. In the chapter on
demographic transition, Kalbach has presented the Canadian experience
as characterized by improving standards of living, declining mortality,
and increasing life expectancy—all of which, combined with generally
high fertility, have produced a high rate of natural increase and population
growth throughout most of Canadian history. Recently, however, Kalbach
has noted that the population has begun to age, with a decreasing proportion under the age of fifteen years and an increasing proportion over
the age of forty-five years. The significance of this observation lies in the
growing possibility of a population which may, perhaps, be stabilized at
some level compatible with whatever quality of life and standard of living
the Canadian people may desire. Together with a policy of controlled
immigration, this factor may indeed make population a stabilizing element
in Canadian society.

Canada—historically more British and French than Canadian—is currently in considerable danger of losing its national identity and becoming
Americanized. In fact, the struggle for a national identity may be an
impossible struggle from the outset. National identity assumes a *consensus*
based upon a core of common shared values. Hunter, Ogmundson, Mc-
Cormack, and other contributors to this volume have stressed profound
cleavages along the lines of class, ethnic group, race, and sex which may

make consensus, and hence national identity, a chimera. The point is not that American influence undermines Canadian identity. Rather, given the internal schisms and conflicts which take place within Canadian society, a national identity apparently cannot emerge which could conceivably resist the Americanizing influence increasingly felt in all areas of Canadian life.

This point is graphically illustrated by McCormack with respect to communications, an area where Canadians seem to be committed to cultural autonomy, and at the same time to *laissez-faire* economics and a capitalist economy. Cultural autonomy in the media requires heavy government subsidy and involvement, while *laissez-faire* economics requires a free market. The conflict may represent attempts to achieve both the goal of Canadian content and the goal of economic profit for the business interests that own and control the communications industry. McCormack describes Canadian content as appearing to lose out, and American programs increasingly to dominate television, the cinema, and commercial radio. At the same time, American wire services and syndicated columnists seem more and more to be used by Canadian newspapers, and American textbooks are used with increasing frequency in Canadian colleges and universities.

Developing the theme further in the chapter on power and politics, Ogmundson suggests that Canada has an internal problem of maintaining its unity, and at the same time an external problem of maintaining its independence. He has illustrated this thesis by an analysis of the leadership élites from several sectors of Canadian life. The business élite, although very powerful in internal Canadian matters, is unique in as much as it is controlled from the United States. Ogmundson considers the labour élite to be much less powerful than the business élite, yet also controlled from the United States, since most Canadian unions are affiliates of American international unions. Further, in the chapter on Canadian polity, Ogmundson discusses the problem of American influence among the intellectual élite, most of whom are professors in Canadian universities. In some arts and science faculties, he found Canadians in the minority. Finally, and most ominously, growing American influence with respect to direct intervention in Canadian political life through large contributions of American-owned corporations to all major Canadian political parties was noted. All in all, several of the contributing authors have described the omnipresence of American influence in nearly all areas of Canadian life as one of the greatest sources of change and, at the same time, a great threat to the orderly development and stability of Canadian culture.

Turning now to what is clearly one of the major themes in Canadian life, several of the contributors have devoted considerable attention to the question of *multiculturalism*. Bienvenue, Hunter, and Synge have each stressed the importance of social differentiation in a multi-ethnic society where stratification exists within group and, more importantly for present purposes, between groups. Of all the variables related to stratification, occupation is one of the most important. Ethnicity, however, has been shown by the contributing authors to constitute the basis for recruitment into the most prestigious positions in the society. The reader is presented, therefore, with a stratification system perceived as a vertical mosaic, with groups arranged in a hierarchical system of ethnicity as well as social class. Given this structure of inequality, a conflict situation is delineated, in which areas of discontent were found to focus around welfare programs, power and influence disparities, educational opportunities, and the area of interpersonal values or life-styles. Some native people and the French in Quebec have defined themselves as deprived minorities. As the distinguished sociologist William I. Thomas long ago noted, "If people define situations as real, they are real in their consequences."

Among the consequences of this situation, the reader is helped to examine the development of organizational structures and the emergence of leaders, some of whom are reformist and others of whom are radical. Native land claims in various parts of the country constitute examples of conflicts which are largely settled through conventional procedures. When change is slow, however, Bienvenue suggests that it is under these circumstances that militant behaviour by minority groups often results. Indians in Ontario, Acadians in Moncton, and Blacks at Sir George Williams University have provided examples of the more militant type of demands. The usual response of Canadian society to the claims of inequality by various groups has been through the mechanism of *enacted change*. Attempts to stabilize the rate and direction of change and to avoid secessionist movements and more localized disorders have included the establishment of human rights commissions, the Federal Language Bill giving equal rights to both French- and English-speakers, and an official government policy of multiculturalism in which each ethnic group is encouraged to retain its own cultural distinctiveness to the extent it may desire. There remains, however, a very real question of whether these acts and policies will be able to meet the growing demands of organized groups such as those in Quebec who see themselves as an industrial society rather than as an ethnic group within the Canadian society, and of some native groups whose claims seem to include almost the entire North American continent.

With respect to the family—that most basic of social institutions—Ramu has discussed a number of important trends which seem to be developing. Canadian census data indicate an increase in the number of single-member households made up of unmarried young persons, separated or divorced persons, and the aged. Along with this demographic change has developed a number of feminist movements and the concept of *universal permanent availability* of individuals in the marriage market. This represents a profound departure from the model of orderly population replacement and the institutional family in a situation of declining importance of kinship and family life in general. Ramu suggests, however, that while endogamy remains the main form of mate selection in Canada, there is a growing trend toward a more open system in which mate selection across lines of ethnicity and religion seems more common and more socially accepted. These changes are presented in conjunction with profoundly important structural changes in the ways sex roles are patterned and in the manner in which they are presently being performed.

Additional developments are identified by Hiller, who in the chapter on the sociology of religion presents a view of Canadian society as polarized along linguistic, ethnic, religious, and political lines, with the religious dimension adding intensity to the cultural divisions produced by the other factors. In this sense, religion may be viewed as either a conservative force in opposition to change, or a disruptive force which may stimulate social change. Hiller discusses both as being present *latently* in the society and emerging from time to time in response to social conditions.

In describing the Canadian educational system, Synge has presented it as an area of structural diversity. Perhaps the education of native people provides the clearest illustration of this viewpoint. For many years the federal government remained aloof from Indian and Eskimo education, leaving it to a variety of religious organizations whose emphasis was often directed toward evangelizing for their various denominations and imposing the values and behaviour patterns of the dominant society through a policy of cultural replacement. One of the most highly criticized structural features of the educational system has been the use of boarding schools for native children. The criticisms have focused principally on the poor academic results achieved through boarding schools and because the children were isolated from their families and emerged unqualified to function well in either native culture or the dominant society. In discussing the attempts of Canadian society to cope with this problem, Synge has included the introduction of native teachers and new, culturally oriented curricula and, perhaps of greatest importance, the integration of native education into the provincial educational systems where the people happen to reside. Preservation of language and cultural differences among ethnic groups is clearly the national policy, but as yet no consensus has been reached on what form the schools will take.

Another area of structural diversity characterized by systematic and pervasive change is noted by Johnson, who presents a discussion of the Canadian criminal-justice system and its attempts to achieve what may be the antithetical functions of protecting society and, at the same time, of rehabilitating or resocializing criminal offenders. To achieve the changes necessary to perform these functions in a controlled manner, a variety of policy statements have been formulated and a growing number of programs implemented. Conspicuous examples include the Bail Reform Act, the increasing availability of free legal aid for the indigent accused, a permanent Canadian Law Reform Commission to revise the legal codes in accordance with the changing needs and practices of the Canadian people, and a growing tendency to use community correctional programs and diversion as an alternative to incarceration. To date, however, none of the measures which have been undertaken has achieved any notable degree of success in protecting society from dangerous criminal behaviour or in rehabilitating criminals so that they will become law-abiding, productive citizens.

In one of the most important chapters for the study of structure, function, and change in Canadian society, Santos has discussed the Canadian parliamentary system and governmental bureaucracy. The parliamentary system provides for a clear division of powers but with an undisputed primacy of the federal cabinet in the task of governance. In addition, the Canadian government is characterized by federalism, which provides a division of governmental powers and functions between the central national government and the regional provincial governments. Neither level of government can dictate to the other, but must bargain with and persuade the other. Especially useful for present purposes is the discussion of the Treasury Board and how it has developed a structure over the years which enables it to perform several vital functions in the context of Canadian governance. As Santos indicates, this federal division of powers which was set down in the British North America Act of 1867 has become vastly complicated by the existence of two founding linguistic, cultural, and religious groups and by the special interests and problems of different geographical regions of the country. Ogmundson's contribution, however, suggests that the present Canadian political system may be relevant to maintaining Confederation through a political brokerage system, but many groups and individuals are beginning to question the relevance of Confederation if the goal to be achieved is social justice rather than merely political stability.

In the final chapter, Ramu and Johnson have attempted to acquaint the reader with problems related to the origins and development of academic sociology in Canada. These authors necessarily distinguish between the development of two kinds of sociologies: *sociology of Canada* and *Canadian sociology*. It is argued that the substantive chapters of this book clearly demonstrate the presence of not only a strong sociology of Canada but also the beginnings of a truly Canadian sociology. This is not to deny that much work remains to be done and many questions remain to be asked about Canadian society: rather, what is being asserted is that considerable work has been accomplished in the last few years in Canada and about Canada, and that sociological patterns, needs, and problems of this society are now quite well identified. This work has been done not only by the contributors to this volume who come from the east and the west, from both sexes, and from a variety of ethnic backgrounds, but also by many other professional sociologists whose work the present contributors have drawn upon. Together, this means that a great deal of expert knowledge has been combined to delineate a sizable body of facts and observations which constitute a genuine contribution to the growth of Canadian sociology.

In conclusion, we seem to have a society beset on all sides by problems relating to national identity, ethnic and linguistic diversity, regionalism, and social inequality. In each of these areas social change is being demanded with varying degrees of militancy, and sometimes with social conflict. In response, Canadian governments, both provincial and federal, have developed policies and implemented a wide variety of programs to provide stability and maintain some measure of control over the inevitable alterations in interpersonal relationships and in the social structure within which these relationships take place.

A prediction of whether cultural stability or disorganization will be the eventual outcome is beyond the scope of this work, but providing the reader with a clear sociological perspective concerning the structure of Canadian society, an appreciation of what the various parts are designed to accomplish, together with some understanding of the problems which have arisen and the changes which are taking place at the time of writing is very much our concern. Although it is asserted that the contributing authors have provided a vast amount of scholarly information about Canadian society, in the final analysis it remains for the reader alone to decide how well the task has been accomplished.

PART I

Social Structure

To undertake a systematic study of any society one must examine the social characteristics of the people who make up its population, the ways they communicate to give meaning to their behaviour, and their relationship to one another in terms of power, prestige, and wealth. These aspects of social organization become patterned into relatively fixed relationships which sociologists refer to as *social structure*. The first three chapters of this book consider the social structure of Canadian society.

Warren Kalbach of the University of Toronto has analysed the population of Canada in terms of numbers of people, their social characteristics, and the historic patterns of mobility and change which have given the Canadian people their rich diversity and unique demographic profile. This chapter helps us to understand both the demographic transition through which the Canadian people are passing, and the population basis for the problems of biculturalism and cultural diversity which have been so much a part of Canada throughout its history.

Thelma McCormack of York University has presented an essay which examines the sociology of Canadian communications and its central struggle for a national identity when faced with the danger of becoming Americanized. A basic conflict is examined: the value of cultural autonomy and Canadian content of communications is contrasted with a commitment to *laissez-faire* economics of a capitalist system based upon economic profits. Enormous tension is generated in attempts to achieve both goals simultaneously. The structures of various kinds of mass media are examined and the phenomena of social change are discussed with respect to a nation that needs but has no social policy relating to communications.

In the final chapter on social structure, Alfred Hunter of the University of Waterloo has presented an analysis of social class and status relationships in the context of Canadian society. The contributions of race and ethnicity to positional stratification and social mobility are described and related to the élite structures and problems of poverty. Finally, unique features of Canada's stratification system have been developed out of the interaction of migration, social mobility, and the social-class system over a lengthy time period.

Canada: 2

A Demographic Analysis*

WARREN E. KALBACH

Fortunately for the social scientist, patterns of social interaction are not random, but highly differentiated on the basis of the individual's position in the social system. Thus, we can begin to understand human societies as we acquire information on the characteristics of their members and the social and economic networks within which they carry out their daily routines, and analyse both the processes by which their numbers grow or decline and their positions within the social-structure change.

The dynamics of social structure can also be observed from a demographic perspective by tracing new age and sex cohorts—which are continuously entering the system through births and immigration—as they move through the various stages of the individual and family life cycles. Ultimately these cohorts are depleted through mortality or emigration and are replaced by the younger generations following them. Thus, populations can age or grow young, as the size and character of successive cohorts vary through time, and at any stage they retain the potential for reversing the process.

Canada has experienced its demographic birth and transition to a highly urbanized society. How this came about, the nature of its demographic evolution, and its consequences for the character of the population together constitute the subject of this chapter.

Canada and the Demographic Transition

Canada's present demographic situation cannot be fully appreciated without some discussion of the larger picture of which it is a part. Yet at times

*Where specific sources have not been cited, the data incorporated in this paper have been taken from official census and vital statistics publications released by Statistics Canada, or its immediate predecessor, the Dominion Bureau of Statistics (DBS).

Canada appears to be oblivious of the urgency implicit in the continuing rapid growth rates of the world's population. Canada, in fact, has been alluded to as "a fat cat in a suffering world" (*Globe and Mail*, September 30, 1974, p. 7), sitting in spatial splendour with a relatively small population, abundant resources, and a high level of economic productivity. It has the second largest land area of any in the world, a density of only six persons per square mile, and in estimated per capita gross national product in 1973 it ranked fourth among all nations (Population Reference Bureau, 1973). As a developed country, its annual growth rate of 1.2 per cent in 1973 placed it well below the estimated world rate of 2.0 per cent, yet still above the rates of the United States and of all the major European countries.

These facts, combined with Canada's popularly accepted image of a "vast land of prairies and mountains, stretching from sea to sea",[1] have continued to make this country look attractive to potential migrants throughout the world. Its problems of rapid growth, urban crowding, pollution, and poverty, relative to conditions elsewhere in the world, do not detract from Canada's mystique as a land of opportunity. Canada, as a part of the New World, has always offered a second chance for a better life for potential emigrants all over the world.

THE GROWTH OF WORLD POPULATION

In the Beginning

Attempts to reconstruct man's demographic history are, of course, subject to considerable error. There is a general consensus among scholars, however, that for most of the time that man has been on earth his numbers have been small, irregularly dispersed, and subject to considerable fluctuations through time. Civilizations have come and gone, but from a global perspective, during almost the entirety of man's first million years of existence, his numbers have varied from between two to three million to a possible maximum of five. Between 8000 and 5500 B.C. there is reason

---

1. As sung in the words of "Oh, Canada!"
Oh Canada! Where pine and maple grow
Great Prairies spread and lordly rivers
flow.

How dear to us, thy beloved domain,
From East to Western sea,
Thou land of Hope for all who toil
The True North, strong and free!

to believe that the population may have increased to somewhere between 5 and 20 million, that it passed the 200 million mark by A.D. 250, and thereafter slowly increased to 300 million during the span of 1250 years up to the threshold of the modern population epoch. (For a more detailed summary and discussion of world population estimates see Hertzler, 1956: 9–27.)

The increase in human numbers and their dispersal throughout the world have been significantly related to a series of technological revolutions and the development of increasingly complex social, economic, and political structures. The post-fourteenth-century revolutions in commerce, science-technology, economics, communication and transport, agriculture, and industry, while bringing a new golden age, may also have brought man to the point of no return—where population growth accelerates out of control until the earth's capacity to sustain human existence is irrevocably impaired.

The Population Explosion

The phenomenon of "population doubling" in successively shorter time periods began to be noticed retrospectively in the data for the period following the mid seventeenth century. It took the whole prior history of mankind to reach a population of a half billion. It appears to have taken just two hundred years, following 1650, to add the next half billion; a figure just over one billion was reached in 1850. The next doubling required less than one hundred years, and the next only fifty. The growth rate, during this same period, increased from approximately 0.3 per cent per annum to about 2.0 per cent in 1971. If maintained at the latter rate, the world's population would require only thirty-five years to double its numbers (Hertzler, 1956). With an estimated population of 3.86 billion in 1973, there is some hope that the world's population may still be stabilized at around 12 billion by the year 2125 (Astrachan, 1974: 58).

A closer look at historical data reveals significant continental and regional variations in the patterns of accelerating growth rates. Between 1650 and the beginning of the twentieth century, the European populations benefited most from the social and technological changes and experienced more rapid growth. In the three hundred years following 1650 the population of Europe increased from approximately 100 million to around 800 million, while non-Europeans increased only fourfold (Woytinsky, 1953: 36). Consequently, the Europeans' relative share of the world's population increased, reaching about 34 per cent of the total in 1920.[2]

By the beginning of the nineteenth century, Europeans involved in the agricultural-industrial revolution were entering the first stages of the demographic transition characterized by more stable mortality conditions. As mortality was successfully held below the level of fertility, population grew rapidly (Wrigley, 1969: 164–65). Those who couldn't be absorbed into the industrializing urban centres became potential emigrants.

Between 1600 and the Second World War an estimated 45 million persons emigrated from various parts of Europe to North America, and approximately 25 million settled there permanently.[3] Of the 40 million estimated to have come after 1821, approximately 5 million were immigrants to Canada and Newfoundland (Woytinsky, 1953: Table 33).[4] Canada's share of this flood of immigrants, while relatively small compared to the other immigrant streams, was sufficient to establish in the New World the foundation for a modern industrial society patterned after the European model. New France was the infant Canada, born of the European demographic transition during the first phase of the world's population explosion.

TRANSITION IN THE NEW WORLD

It is perhaps ironic that the immigrants, who were themselves the product of the onset and continuation of the demographic transition in Europe,

2. These estimates relate only to the combined populations of Europe, U.S.S.R., North America, and Oceania. If Latin America is included the proportion increases to 39 per cent in 1920 and 1930. In either case, the proportion has since continued to decline as the growth rates of Asian and African populations have increased relative to the others. Following the Second World War, growth rates for many of the Asian and African countries have shown significant increases.

3. The other major stream involved an estimated twenty million who emigrated to Central and South America, primarily from Spain, Portugal, and Italy. Of these, some two million were estimated to have returned. Similar estimates for the lesser streams of British and Dutch emigrants who settled in Africa and Oceania were not provided. (See Woytinsky, 1953: 69.)

4. Between 1821 and 1932, a total of 54,000,000 immigrants came to the Americas, with 32,200,000 entering the United States, 5,200,000 coming to Canada and Newfoundland, and the balance going to Central and South American countries.

found themselves living under pre-industrial conditions characterized by lack of dependable transport and communications, uncertainties of climate, harvests, and supplies. In addition, they were vulnerable to unpredictable epidemics and to hostilities between the French, English, and the native Indians.

In one sense the settlers in New France had regressed demographically. Birth rates were very high, hovering around 50 to 65 per 1000, between 1665 and 1765. Death rates, also like the pre-industrial pattern in Europe, often exceeded the level of fertility but generally appeared to fluctuate between 10 and 40 deaths per 1000 population. (For a more detailed discussion and references to historical sources, see Kalbach and McVey, 1971: 11–14.)

By the end of the Seven Years' War with England, the population of New France had shown amazing growth, under the circumstances. From a handful of settlers in 1608 the population increased to 3215 at the time of the first census in 1665, and in the next one hundred years it reached approximately 70,000 (Langlois, 1934: 75–76; *Census of 1871*: 166).

During the period of British rule, from 1765 to 1867, population continued to increase. As conditions improved, death rates tended to fluctuate less violently and the areas of settlement grew and expanded. By 1861 the population of Quebec had passed the one million mark (Langlois, 1934: 262). Other non-French settlements had been established and were developing, but the lack of censuses and records commensurate with those established in French Canada makes it more difficult to assess the broader picture.

It is quite clear, however, that the British have had to rely on immigration for both settlement and growth. Their presence in Upper Canada was insignificant until the United Empire Loyalists arrived from the former British colonies after the American Revolution. In 1784 the population of Upper Canada was 10,000—hardly one-tenth the number in Quebec. By 1824 it had reached 150,000, and, supplemented by heavy immigration during the post-Napoleonic era, it finally exceeded that of Lower Canada, reaching 950,000 by the mid nineteenth century (Kalbach and McVey, 1971: 13–15). The emphasis on the contribution of immigration during this period is not meant to imply that fertility was not an important component for the growth of population outside of Quebec. In Upper Canada, immigration *did* play a relatively more important part than it did in

Quebec, where natural increase assumed the more important role as early as 1670 (Kalbach and McVey, 1971: 13–15). Nevertheless, the high rates of population growth in Upper Canada, which enabled the British population to surpass the French, cannot be explained in terms of immigration alone.

What is of interest here is that the population of British North America had apparently begun its demographic transition prior to Confederation in 1867. Data for the Catholic population between 1830 and 1860 show a drop in mortality rates from 30 to 20 per 1000, while birth rates were declining from 60 to 45 (Kalbach and McVey, 1971: 13–15). This pattern is typical of the early transition stage, and the excess of births over deaths under these conditions is sufficient to produce very rapid growth. The Catholic population did, in fact, double in this thirty-year period. It would not be unreasonable to assume that the same declines in vital rates were occurring in the non-French population at about the same time and producing the same high levels of natural increase.

POST-CONFEDERATION TRENDS

Confederation was perhaps more of a consequence than a cause of economic and political events. Yet the act itself was another step in the evolution of a more efficient socio-political organization which would in time exert its own independent effects on the economic and political events to follow. As most of the demographic trends to be discussed were well underway at the time of Confederation, its main demographic significance, in addition to being a historical benchmark, was its long-term contribution to the improvement of provincial and national data-collection systems.

Urbanization

The concentration of population into urban places was a concomitant process to industrialization in Europe and the development and expansion of trade. That this process was operative in Canada is borne out by Stone's discussion of urbanization in Canada: he provides ample evidence that urbanization had proceeded somewhat beyond the level estimated to have been reached by the world as a whole in 1825 (Stone, 1967: 14–24).

Perhaps this was so, in part, because unlike European cities, which drew population from the surrounding rural areas, the settlements in New France were founded by immigrants in a relatively empty land. These communities were the points of destination and employment for many immigrants, while others moved on to the land or to other settlements where work or land could be found. In serving as shipping, financial, trading, communications, and even protective centres, the new settlements occupied strategic positions in the flow of capital, goods, and people. Stone makes the important point that the specific developments which occurred in agriculture, transportation, world trade, and political organization produced an expansion of those activities most suited to, or requiring, the concentration of populations into relatively small geographical units. Specific Canadian examples include the expansion of wheat production for export, expansion of the railroads and telegraph systems, and even political union in Confederation itself.

Perhaps the greatest impetus for industrialization and urbanization was the need to mobilize the nation's resources in order to increase the production of foodstuffs and war materials during the two world wars. By contrast, the most effective deterrent to continuing urbanization was the cessation of economic activity during the Great Depression of the 1930s.

The net effects of factors underlying urbanization in Canada are summarized in Table 1. Just prior to Confederation, in 1851, only 13 per cent of the population resided in incorporated cities, towns, and villages of 1000 or more population. It is interesting to note that urbanization in Canada increased markedly during the last three decades of the nineteenth century, at the very time the rate of population increase was declining, and considerable outmigration to the United States was thought to be occurring (Kalbach and McVey, 1971: Table 1:4, 21).

Between 1901 and 1911 the proportion urban jumped from 35 to 42 per cent. Even the rapid settlement of the prairies increased the relative numbers living in urban places. Paradoxically, while the rural population was experiencing its greatest growth, the proportion urban showed its greatest increase. The net result was that rural population decreased in relative size from 65 to 58 per cent (Kalbach and McVey, 1971: 95). The balance between rural and urban populations was reached during either the decade of the Great Depression or the one just prior to it,

Table 1 Per cent of population urban,[a] Canada and regions 1851–1971

Region	1851	1861	1871	1881	1891	1901	1911	1921	1931	1941	1951	1961	1971
Canada (incl. Newfoundland)											62.4	69.7	76.1
Canada (excl. Newfoundland)	13.1	15.8	18.3	23.3	29.8	34.9	41.8	47.4	52.5	55.7	62.9	70.2	76.6
Newfoundland											43.3	50.7	57.2
Maritimes	9.0	9.9	11.9	15.3	18.8	24.5	30.9	38.8	39.7	44.1	47.4	49.5	55.5
Quebec	14.9	16.6	19.9	23.8	28.6	36.1	44.5	51.8	59.5	61.2	66.8	74.3	80.6
Ontario	14.0	18.5	20.6	27.1	35.0	40.3	49.5	58.8	63.1	67.5	72.5	77.3	82.4
Prairies						19.3	27.9	28.7	31.3	32.4	44.5	57.6	67.0
British Columbia			9.0	18.3	42.6	46.4	50.9	50.9	62.3	64.0	68.6	72.6	75.7

[a] From 1851 to 1911, the urban population figures refer to incorporated cities, towns, and villages of 1000 and over only; from 1921 to 1951, the percentages are estimates of the percentages which would have been reported in the respective censuses had the 1961 Census definition and procedures been used; for 1961, the figures are those published according to the 1961 Census definition of "urban", and similarly for 1971.

Source: Stone, 1967: 29. *1971 Census of Canada*.

depending upon which definition of urban is used.[5]

The economic revival which accompanied the Second World War boosted the urban population to 70 per cent of the total in 1961, and by the time of the 1971 Census the proportion had reached 76 per cent. With only 6 per cent of the population left in rural farm areas, it would appear that Canada is approaching the upper limit of the urbanization process. Continued growth of the large urban centres can occur only at the expense of the rural non-farm population and lesser urban places.

The data clearly show that urbanization has not occurred uniformly in all provinces. Along with Saskatchewan, the Atlantic provinces have lagged; Prince Edward Island was the least urbanized of any province in 1971. Clearly, the extent to which the various regions in Canada have completed their own transitions from "rural-farm" to "urban-industrial" varies considerably. According to demographic transition theory, they should also exhibit similar variations in the extent of their transition from high to low levels of vital rates.

Natural Increase

Vital rates indirectly reflect a society's values, its environmental hazards, and its manner of coping with them. These rates also indicate the society's degree of modernization, and changes in ratio are crucial determinants of population growth. Each stage of the demographic transition has a typical pattern of vital rates, and the significance of each growth component is variable, depending upon the particular stage of transition. For example, as has already been mentioned, fluctuating mortality is the crucial factor in the pre-industrial stage. During industrialization and modernization, mortality declines and fertility becomes the significant factor for growth.

Early records were inadequate for determining natural rates of increase with any degree of certainty. Even if they had been satisfactory, the statistical instability inherent in small numbers would still create a considerable degree of uncertainty in any analysis. The following birth and death rates, however, gleaned from vital statistics reports and the analyses of scholars, have been used to provide estimates of the rates of natural

5. According to Stone, this point was reached during the 1921–31 decade, using the definition of urban employed in the 1961 Census. Using the incorporated places definition, that is, populations of 1000 or over, the urban population didn't surpass the rural until the following decade.

Table 2   Rates of natural increase based on estimates of
birth and death rates for selected periods, 1665–1971.

Period	Birth Rate	Death Rate	Rate of Natural Increase
1665–1765	50–65	10–40	10–55
1851–1871	40–45	21	19–24
1891–1920	29–31	18	11–13
1921	29	12	18
1937	20	10	10
1957	28	8	20
1971	17	7	10

Source: Kalbach and McVey, 1971: 12–58.
Statistics Canada, *Vital Rates, 1971*, Vol. I and II.

increase in Canada. Note that high rates of natural increase can occur and
have occurred throughout the entire period of increasing urbanization and
economic development. Note also the high and variable levels of vital
rates prior to Confederation, in contrast to the lower levels of recent years.
In both periods high rates of natural increase occurred, but in recent times
they were primarily due to fluctuations in fertility while mortality remained
low and relatively stable.

Neither urbanization and industrialization nor the demographic transition has occurred uniformly throughout Canada's regions. While most
regions appear to have benefited generally from reductions in mortality,
some, notably the Maritimes and the Northwest Territories, still exhibit
relatively high levels of fertility characteristic of the earlier stages of
transition. Whether or not these areas can tolerate a continuation of high
levels of natural increase depends in part on the prospects for economic
development, or opportunities for out-migration. In any event, it is clear
that these regions, unlike the other areas, have not benefited to the same
extent from economic development. Perhaps it is not possible, within an
interdependent set of economic relationships such as exists in Canada, for
all regions to achieve the same degree of modernization and industrialization. A test of the demographic transition theory on data for twenty-one
different nations showed that some appeared to have achieved an equilib-

rium in their vital rates short of the low levels expected during the latter stages of their demographic transition (Hatt *et al.*, 1955: 14–21).

Immigration

Demographic transition theory assumes no emigration or immigration. The European experience upon which the theory was based, however, included large-scale emigration, both during the pre-transition stage and during the actual period of transition when the rate of industrialization and economic expansion sometimes lagged behind the rates of natural increase (Drake, 1969: 150–60). In the New World the major impetus to growth came from this European emigration; but once settled, the immigrant population grew as a consequence of its own demographic transition. While undergoing the change from high to low levels of vital rates, continuing migration aided or impeded the growth process, depending upon the nature of the net flow.

Estimates of net migration are shown in Table 3, along with estimated increase for the 120-year period between 1851 and 1971. While the estimates do indicate significant emigration to create net out-flows for the period immediately following Confederation, natural increase appeared to be sufficient to produce continuing growth in the total population. Note also the effects of heavy immigration during the early 1900s, as well as the diminished immigration of the 1930s and the resultant net emigration. Following the Second World War and during the period of continuing economic development, the balance swung again to a net immigration. In fact, net immigration during the 1951–61 decade exceeded that of the 1901–11 decade of record immigration to Canada.

Often overlooked is the fact that migration streams are two-way streets, and periods of heavy immigration are also generally periods of heavy emigration. Since there is no necessary correlation between the sizes of the opposing streams, it is difficult to determine net migration from the size of immigration alone. By way of illustration, the decades of peak immigration were 1901–11 and 1911–21, yet the largest net immigration occurred during the 1951–61 decade because of significantly lower emigration.

While the contribution of immigration has on occasion outstripped that

Table 3   Estimates of natural increase, immigration, and net migration, Canada: 1851–1971.

Period	Natural Increase	Immigration	Net Migration
		(in 1000s)	
1851–61	670	209–486	+(123–180)
1861–71	651	187–266	−(150–191)
1871–81	723	253–353	−(40–85)
1881–91	714	448–903	−(150–205)
1891–1901	670–718	250–326	−(130–180)
1901–11	1030–1120	1550–1759	+(810–716)
1911–21	1230–1270	1400–1612	+(310–351)
1921–31	1360	1203	+229
1931–41	1222	150	−92
1941–51	1972	548	+169
1951–61	3148	1543	+1081
1961–71	2606[a]	1429	+724

[a] Dominion Bureau of Statistics, and Statistics Canada, *Vital Statistics*, 1961 to 1971 annual reports.

Sources: Estimates of immigration and net immigration for the decades between 1851 and 1881 are taken from the following studies: N. Keyfitz, 1950: 47–63; McDougall, 1961: 162–75; Ryder, 1954: 71–80; Camu *et al.*, 1964: 56–64. Estimates for the decades between 1891 and 1921 include corrected estimates by Sametz in Camu, 1964: Table 3. Estimates for decades subsequent to 1891 from Department of Manpower and Immigration, 1972: Table 1.

of natural increase, its effective or net contribution to population growth relative to the latter has been considerably less during the years since Confederation. During the years of peak immigration following the Second World War, net immigration contributed 26 per cent of the 1951–61 decade's increment of growth. During the 1961–71 period, it contributed 22 per cent, and during 1941–51, just 8 per cent of the decade's growth.

POPULATION GROWTH AND PATTERNS OF CHANGE

Canada's growth following the Second World War provides an interesting example of the rapid expansion which can be experienced by countries which have supposedly completed their demographic transitions. It was originally feared that as a population approached the end stage of the transition, fertility would continue to decline below mortality levels, result-ing in a negative growth situation. While certainly possible, such a situa-tion is not inevitable, as the Canadian postwar experience has shown. During the end stage, growth is primarily dependent upon fluctuations in fertility, and the postwar "baby boom" showed very clearly just how resilient fertility rates can be.

Since Confederation, Canada's growth rate has fluctuated considerably. During the last decade of the nineteenth century, the estimated average annual rate of growth reached a low of 1.1 per cent. The picture changed rapidly during the early years of the twentieth century, however: the growth rate reached a peak of 3.0 per cent during the first decade. Subse-quently, it declined to a new low of 1.0 per cent during the depression decade of the 1930s. The rate again recovered during the period of Canada's postwar economic development. Under the influence of high fertility and heavy immigration, the average annual rate reached 2.7 per cent during the 1951–61 decade, then responding to lower immigration and rapidly declining fertility, dropped to 1.7 per cent for the 1961–71 period.

Canada's recent experience has been somewhat exceptional for a highly urbanized and industrialized country. In a comparison with thirty other nations, *circa* 1964, Canada ranked fifth in terms of its rate of natural increase, behind such countries as Venezuela, Mexico, Chile, and Peru. Canada owed its relatively high ranking to a very low death rate of 7.6 in conjunction with a high birth rate of 23.5, thus placing its fertility level close to that of Ireland, Italy, Portugal, and the birth registration area of India (DBS, 1964: Table s1, 42).

In general, the patterns of change in Canada's vital rates have followed those of the United States very closely. More specifically, however, its mortality trends have been consistently lower, while fertility trends—although following the general decline into the depression years and the rise of the postwar "baby boom"—have maintained a consistently higher level. Thus, Canada has tended to experience a higher rate of natural increase, and despite the fact that its immigration stream was smaller than that of the United States, the size relative to the total population was more significant. All factors considered, Canada's rate of growth should con-tinue to exceed that of its neighbour. The most recent estimates of growth rates for the two countries, made in 1973, were 0.8 and 1.2 per cent for the United States and Canada respectively (Population Reference Bureau, 1973). Fertility continued to decline in both countries during the 1960s, and the trends suggest that their rates of natural increase will converge. In 1971 the rate of natural increase was 9.5 per cent for Canada, and 8.0 for the United States (Statistics Canada, 1971; U.S. Bureau of the Census, 1973: Table 65).

Variations in the volume of immigration to these two countries have also been quite similar over the long term, reflecting the similarity in their immigration policies and the close links between their respective economies. There is nothing to suggest at the present time that the patterns of vital rates and immigration will not continue to converge. Given the similarity and the contrast between the North American economy and that of the Third World countries, there is every reason to expect that both countries will continue to exert a strong positive attraction for the world's potential emigrants. As fertility continues to move toward the zero-growth levels, immigration will become increasingly important for future growth, as will the policies and methods of implementing those controls in a world facing mounting population pressures and diminishing natural resources.

STRUCTURAL TRANSFORMATION

Age and Sex

The shift in a population's age distribution by sex, between pre- and post-transition periods is clearly visible in the contrasting structures of developing and industrialized countries. Somewhat the same contrast should be visible in a comparison of the early and predominately rural Canadian population with the present urbanized one. Displaying population distributions in the form of population pyramids is useful in this respect, since their distinctive shapes provide clues to their previous and current demographic experiences. For example, prolonged periods of high vital rates tend to produce high proportions of the population under fifteen years of age, and such populations, closed to migration and unaffected by abnormal mortality fluctuations, will tend to have symmetrically tapered age-sex pyramids with broad bases. On the other hand, periods of declining fertility will produce a shrinkage effect at the base, and subsequent revivals of fertility will produce a "pinched-waist" effect as successive birth cohorts are introduced at the bottom of the age pyramid and travel upward through the age ladder. Figure 2:1 presents two such pyramids, superimposed to illustrate the net effects of Canada's fertility, mortality, and immigration experience between 1901 and 1971.

Fertility is by far the most crucial factor in determining the distributional character of the population. A reduction in mortality will not have as much effect in slowing the rate of aging, for example, as an increase in fertility will. The significant reductions which have occurred in mortality have generally occured in the first years of life, so that the effect is much the same as that created by slight increases in the size of successive birth cohorts. The aging of industrialized populations is less a function of their low mortality levels than of declining fertility and the smaller birth cohorts, which more rapidly alter the shape of their population pyramids as they age and steadily progress through the age structure.

With relatively smaller numbers in the younger age groupings, the proportion of the population in the older age groups will naturally be

Figure 2:1 Age-sex distributions in Canada 1901 and 1971

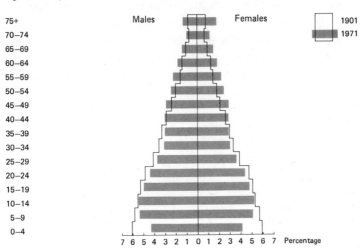

Source: Population Research Lab, Sociology, Erindale
       University of Toronto

larger. This is shown to be the case for Canada during its transition experience, both in Table 4 and in Figure 2:1; note the shift in distribution between 1901 and 1931, evident in Table 4. The proportion under fifteen years of age declined from 34 to 32 per cent, while the proportions in the population over forty-five years of age increased. It is interesting to note that while the postwar "baby boom" reversed the overall aging process by again increasing the proportion under fifteen years it did not alter the long-term trend of increasing proportions in the age groups over forty-five. By 1971 the effects of the recent and significant declines in fertility can be seen, plus the movement of those large postwar birth cohorts into the young adult age groups—fifteen to forty-four years of age.

The effects of the postwar "baby boom" are not totally hidden in the comparison of the two population pyramids in Figure 1. Had the high levels of fertility not prevailed as they did during the 1950s, the two five-year age cohorts between ten and twenty years of age would have been considerably smaller. The 1971 pyramid has the classic shape of an aging population. The sharp decline in fertility during the 1960s is clearly visible in the two youngest age groups, as is the increasing proportion in the older age groups, especially beyond forty-five years of age.

The effects of transition on the sex composition of a population are less clear cut. The ratio of males to females is basically affected by the consistent excess of males at birth, and the nature of differentials in mortality related to sex with increasing age. With industrialization and modernization, life expectancies tend to increase, but improvements in mortality

Table 4 Percentage distribution of the population by broad age groups, Canada: 1901, 1931, 1961, and 1971.

Age Group	1901	1931	1961	1971
0–14	34.4	31.6	34.0	29.6
15–44	46.6	46.1	41.1	43.7
45–64	14.0	16.7	17.4	18.7
65+	5.0	5.6	7.6	8.1
Total: % =	100.0	100.0	100.0	100.0
N =	5,371,315	10,376,786	18,238,247	21,568,310

Source: Statistics Canada, *1971 Census of Canada.*

have favoured the female; the long-range effect has been to reduce the number of males relative to females in the older age groups and in the total population as well. Trends in the sex ratio for the native-born population in Canada bear this out. From a sex ratio of 103 males per 100 females in 1911, the excess of native-born males has declined almost to the point of parity in 1971.

Age and Sex Effects of Immigration

The structural effects of migration may vary considerably from one population to another, depending upon the direction of net-flows, and the character of the migrant streams. As far as the European experience is concerned, an excess of males among emigrants would tend to reduce their sex ratios, and the relative proportions in the young adult ages would also show declines. Canada, on the other hand, being on the receiving end of the migrant stream, would experience a surfeit of males, and would show larger proportions of young adults than would have been expected on the basis of prior fertility levels. Any decline from high levels of immigration would contribute to a rapid aging of the foreign-born population, for much the same reason that a sharp decline in fertility would age the native-born population.

To illustrate: the sex ratio for the foreign-born population of Canada was as high as 158 in 1911. The sex ratio for the total population, however, was only 113 males per 100 females, and this surplus of males has been gradually depleted. By 1971 the male and female populations had essentially achieved a balance in the population as a whole. In addition to the aging and dying out of older immigrants from the period of heavy immigration in the early 1900s, and the changing sex composition of postwar immigrants, the effects of higher sex ratios at birth among native born have been increasingly counteracted by the relatively greater gains in female survival with increasing age. Thus, for Canada, the long-term net effect has been a reduction in the proportion of males. The effects of transition on a population closed to immigration would be those which have in fact occurred to Canada's native-born population: declining proportions of males with increasing age.

By comparison, the contribution of immigration to the age distribution of a population remains unique, because of the relatively stable age characteristics of arriving immigrants: they are, and continue to be, young adults whose average age since the early 1930s has hovered close to twenty-five years. They have provided significant inputs to the labour force, especially following periods of declining fertility or during periods of rapid economic expansion, both of which tend to result in manpower shortages. On the other hand, fifteen to twenty years following a period of rising fertility, such as 1946–51, new cohorts entering the labour force may face increasing competition from immigrants, especially if the economy is not expanding rapidly enough to absorb all new workers. The potential threat is always there, however, even during periods of labour shortages, and the resident Canadian worker is usually among the first to perceive the potential threat posed by large-scale immigration, particularly if it might be followed by increasing unemployment.[6]

Changes in the Labour Force

Labour-force growth, the shift to non-agricultural occupations, and increasing female participation are the significant changes which occurred during industrialization and urbanization. In Canada, between 1871 and 1971, the labour force grew from 1,201,000 to 8,859,000—an increase of 638 per cent, compared to an increase of close to 500 per cent for the total population during the same period (Denton and Ostry, 1967: Table II; DBS, June 1971).

More important than sheer growth of the labour force, which can occur at any point in a population's transition, is the change in the character of its occupational structure. The major situs of employment shifts from the rural areas, where mechanization makes the large farm-labour force increasingly redundant, to urban centres where industrial development is occurring. In Canada 55 per cent of the labour force were involved in agricultural occupations in 1871, compared to just 6 per cent in 1971 (Statistics Canada, July 1974: Table 6:1; *1873 Census*: Table XIII). In addition, there was a shift within the non-agriculture sector as the white-collar occupations expanded at a relatively more rapid rate. This significant increase in white-collar occupations relative to blue-collar ones, and

6. The government's concern with this same problem was front page news in the Toronto *Globe and Mail*: "Andras plans stiff rules to cut back immigration," September 30, 1974.

the decline in agriculture, can be readily seen in the data for both sexes presented in Table 5, in 1901 and 1961.

The changes in occupational structure during this period are reflective of the wide range of jobs which open up for members of the labour force in an industrializing society. The expansion has been particularly significant for males in professional occupations and for women in clerical and commercial occupations. It is interesting to observe that in Canada the expansion of professional employment opportunities for women appear to have barely kept up with the natural growth of the labour force during this period.

Also reflected in these data, but not directly evident, is the increasing

Table 5 Percentage distribution of the labour force[a] by occupation division as of 1951, and by sex, for Canada,[b] 1901 and 1961.

Occupational Division	Males		Females	
(as of 1951)	1901	1961	1901	1961
All occupations	100.0	100.0	100.0	100.0
White-collar occupations	14.0	30.6	23.6	57.3
Proprietary & managerial	4.8	9.6	1.2	2.9
Professional	3.1	7.7	14.7	15.5
Clerical	2.9	6.7	5.3	28.6
Commercial		5.6		10.0
Financial	3.2	1.0	2.4	0.2
Blue-collar occupations	27.5	32.4	30.1	11.1
Manufacturing & mechanical	13.8	18.4	29.6	9.9
Construction & Labourers	13.6	14.0	0.5	1.2
Primary occupations	50.5	16.1	3.8	4.3
Agriculture	45.9	12.2	3.8	4.3
All others	4.6	3.9	—	—
Transportation & communication	5.0	9.7	0.5	2.2
Service occupations	2.9	8.5	42.0	22.6
Personal	2.6	4.2	42.0	22.1

[a] 10 years and over in 1901, 15 years and over in 1961.
[b] Excludes Yukon and Northwest Territories; Newfoundland included in 1961.

Source: Ostry, 1967: Table 2.

variety of jobs and greater specialization as new industries emerge and existing ones adapt in response to changing technologies and consumer markets. Yet in spite of the rapid growth and change in the character of the labour force, many of the old occupations persist, for example clergymen, postmen, hawkers, and peddlers, in addition to rather new and exotic ones, such as computer programmers, radar operators, and nuclear engineers. While the 1961 Census provided tabulations for over 300 occupational categories—in contrast to the 131 listed in the 1871 Census —the full extent of occupational specialization in business and industry today is more clearly revealed in the occupational classification manual, published for use with the 1971 Census of Canada. This alphabetical listing gives over 21,000 occupational titles (DBS, 1971).

Female participation in the Canadian labour force during the period of economic development following Confederation has been a gradually increasing one. From 1951 to 1973, however, their participation increased from 23.5 to 38.7 per cent, while comparable estimates for males showed a decline from 83.9 to 76.8 per cent (Statistics Canada, July 1974: Table 6.1).

Significant concomitants of urbanization for women have been increasing levels of educational attainment and vocational skills. Greater participation in the labour force has been facilitated by the trend toward smaller families through earlier termination of child-bearing, and increasing acceptability of family planning and employment of birth-control techniques. Increasing numbers of labour-saving devices for use in the home, as well as greater efficiency achieved in food preparation through recent developments in the food processing and packaging industries have also been significant factors. The overall consequence of these developments and others has been a significant rise in the size of the female labour force. Earlier studies of the labour force have shown how participation rates have increased from approximately 16 per cent in 1901 to approximately 37 per cent at the time of the 1971 Census. Why this should be accompanied by a decline in male participation rates is not altogether clear. But for whatever reasons, rates for males have declined significantly from their high of 91 in 1911 to 76 per cent in 1971. Estimates for more recent years show little change (Denton and Ostry, 1967: Tables 3–7 and 10; DBS, June 1971; Statistics Canada, June 1974: Table 6.1).

The highest participation rates for women are found in the younger age group—under twenty-five years—among single women and those recently married. Participation rates for married women are inversely related to their husband's income; but they are also directly related to their own educational attainment. Ostry's analysis also showed the effect on participation rates produced by the presence of young children in the home (Ostry, 1968: Table 12).

The interrelationships of casual factors and trends are such that increasingly high proportions of young women twenty to twenty-four years of age are entering the work force, and fewer are dropping out after marriage or for the bearing and rearing of children. Sixty per cent of these women were in the labour force in 1972. For women between twenty-five and fifty-five years of age, the proportion stayed just above 40 per cent, before dropping off sharply for the older age groups (Statistics Canada, July 1974: Chart 6.3). If this trend continues, there will be a significant change from the participation profiles of recent years, which have been characterized by two peaks, the major peak caused by the traditionally higher rate for young women, and a secondary peak for women in the age group forty-five to fifty-four, representing the re-entry of older married women into the labour force (Kalbach and McVey, 1971: 223–35).

Demographic Dimensions of Biculturalism

The unique historical events during the early settlement of the New World, and subsequent demographic transition, provided Canada with the basis of its present-day population and its bicultural foundation. The mechanisms by which the populations of British and French origins have been subsequently maintained, and present-day contrasts between the two founding groups, are examined in the following sections.

FACTORS IN THE MAINTENANCE OF BICULTURALISM

British Migration

The pattern established during the early British regime—the more rapid growth of the British and other non-French-origins populations through immigration—has persisted to the present time. This is not meant to suggest that the foreign-born population ever outnumbered the native born for any significant period beyond the early years of settlement. By 1861, just prior to Confederation, approximately one-fifth of the 3,230,000 inhabitants of Canada were foreign born, and this proportion represented a high point not exceeded again until the large numbers of immigrants flooded into Canada during the early years of the twentieth century. At that time, the proportion of foreign born reached 22 per cent in 1911, and remained near that level for twenty years.

The composition of each ethnic-origin population, by nativity, provides some indication of the relative significance of contributions made by fertility and net immigration in the past. In 1971, for example, only 1.8 per cent of the French-origin population was foreign born, compared to 12.4 per cent of British origin. Fifty years earlier, the percentages were 3.0 and 25.9 per cent respectively. Data on annual immigrant arrivals also reflect the greater significance of immigration for the maintenance of the British population in contrast to the situation for the French. During the first year of the twentieth century, 24.0 per cent of the 49,149 immigrants were of British origin, compared to only 0.7 per cent French. During 1913, when a record 400,870 immigrants arrived, 39.5 per cent were British, and still only 0.7 per cent were French (Royal Commission on Bilingualism and Biculturalism, 1970: Table A-1). Thus, except during the early period of settlement under French political control, immigration has not been of any assistance in maintaining the position of the French in Canada. The British, on the other hand, because of their historical dependence on immigration for the growth of their population, have become vulnerable to the effects of fluctuations in volume, as well as to shifts in the character of the immigration streams.

French Fertility

One of the unique aspects of the French-Canadian population has been its relative stability over the years with respect to its proportionate share of the total population. That it could sustain a rate of growth equal to that of the nation as a whole without continuing assistance from immigration attests to the significance of its reproductive behaviour. On the other hand, the population of British origin, in spite of its traditionally heavy immigration input, is losing ground to other ethnic populations, which are experiencing heavier immigration and appear to have a fertility rate as high as or higher than that of the British (Henripin, 1972: 170–79).

Estimates of fertility among the French in the New World for the early eighteenth century indicate that the average number of children for women whose marriage was not interrupted before their fiftieth birthday was 8.4 children (Henripin, 1972: 10). Even "200 years later, French speaking rural Canadian Catholic women, born on a farm, and with less than eight years' schooling, had had about the same number of children" (Henripin, 1972: 10). It is also true, however, that analysis of early data shows that the general fertility rates were also very high, and sometimes higher, in other areas of Canada undergoing settlement. The major difference was that the level of general fertility in Ontario appeared to drop below that in Quebec as early as 1881, while other areas of extremely high fertility experienced very rapid declines after their initial period of settlement—British Columbia, Manitoba, and Saskatchewan, for example (Henripin, 1972: Graph 2.3 and Table 2.1).

It is important to understand that it was the high fertility of *married* women that accounted for Quebec's eminence. Declining proportions of married women in the child-bearing age groups was not a significant factor in reducing total fertility rates in Quebec relative to those in Canada as a whole until after 1941 (Henripin, 1972: 74–75). Thus, it would appear that, while the general decline in fertility since 1961 is of some concern to Quebec, the province's decline relative to the rest of Canada reflects a more unfavourable nuptiality situation. If the province wants to maintain its relative size, perhaps it would be well advised to direct its efforts toward the encouragement of couples to marry rather than worrying about ways to increase the fertility of married women. Even Ontario, however, which has had a more favourable nuptiality, has not been able to overcome the effects of its low levels of marital fertility, which are lower than for Canada as a whole.

Significant differences in the levels of completed fertility of British- and French-origin women for the older age cohorts at the time of the 1961 Census may be seen in Table 6 below. Note that the differences persist for each age cohort and for each type of urban and rural place of residence shown. It is worth remembering, however, that if fewer women of French origin are getting married, or are marrying later than those of other origins, this fertility advantage, evident in the past, will tend to be minimized in the future. Given the numerical dominance of French- and British-origin populations in Quebec and Ontario respectively, the data in

Table 6   Number of children born, per 1000 women ever married, by age, for French and British origin women, by type of residence in Canada, 1961.

Ethnic Origin and Type of Residence	Age Group			
	50–54	55–59	60–64	65+
Total				
British[a]	2519	2626	2817	3130
French	4524	4979	5483	6242
All origins	3154	3385	3650	4038
Urban: 10,000+				
British[a]	2056	2155	2359	2730
French	3319	3829	4254	5276
All origins	2473	2700	2959	3436
Rural Farm				
British[a]	3317	3301	3426	3933
French	7212	7481	7874	7891
All origins	4630	4775	4910	5202

[a] Does not include Irish.

Source: *1961 Census of Canada*, Bulletin 4.1–8, Tables H1, H4.

Table 7 clearly reflect this ethnic differential in proportions married.

Bilingualism as Official Policy

Bilingualism was officially established before Confederation in 1867, but the present legal foundation for bilingualism was established in Section 133 of the British North America Act of 1867 (Royal Commission on Bilingualism and Biculturalism, 1967: 46–47). Such legal guarantees would seem sufficient to ensure the preservation of any language, especially when almost one-third of the population was culturally predisposed to its use, and in addition were mostly concentrated in one province.

Data presented in Table 8 show the division of the population in terms of Canada's official languages. Since 1931 the numbers able to speak French only and those reporting themselves to be bilingual increased more rapidly than both the numbers speaking English only and the total population. In addition, the proportion speaking English only showed little

Table 7 Percentage married of the population 15 years of age and over, Canada, Quebec, and Ontario, 1921–71.

Year	Canada	Quebec	Ontario
1921	57.9	55.3	58.5
1931	56.1	52.6	58.1
1941	57.0	52.4	59.7
1951	64.2	59.6	66.7
1961	66.6	62.2	69.6
1971	64.4	61.1	66.4

Source: Censuses of Canada.

change during this period. Those speaking French only increased slightly from 17 to 18 per cent.

On the surface, at least, it would appear that the French language is not likely to disappear. What may be disconcerting, at least to French Canada, is the fact that 67 per cent of the population speak only English, while just 45 per cent are British in origin. In contrast, 31 per cent of the population can speak French, while the French-origin population constitutes a slightly smaller proportion of the total, or just 29 per cent. These differences obviously reflect more than the language preferences of the other ethnic groups in Canada. The heavy settlement of immigrants in English-speaking areas, for example, would tend to eliminate French as a viable option in those areas.

Table 8 Distribution of Canada's population by official language and percentage change, Canada: 1931, 1971.

Official Language	1931	1971	Per Cent Increase 1931–71
English only	6,999,913	14,469,540	107
French only	1,779,338	3,879,255	118
Both	1,322,370	2,900,155	119
Neither	275,165	319,360	116
Total:	10,376,786	21,568,315	108

Source: *1971 Census of Canada*, Bulletin 1.3–5, Table 25.

Threats to bilingualism and biculturalism appear to be posed by the inability of the French either to keep pace with total national growth or to attract their share of converts from among immigrants with non-English mother tongues. The French have, in fact, had some difficulty in retaining their own language in Canada. During the postwar period, the French population has grown more rapidly than the population of those reporting French as their mother tongue. The net result is that the latter declined from 29 to 27 per cent of the total population, while total French origins declined from 30 to just 29 per cent. At the same time, those reporting English as their mother tongue increased from 56 to 60 per cent.

Another illustration of the problem is possible with new language data from the 1971 Census. There were 6,180,120 persons of French ethnic origin; at the same time, 5,793,650 reported French as their mother tongue, and 5,546,025 reported French as the language most often spoken in the home. As very rough measures of retention, that is, assuming that these totals refer to the same population, the data on mother tongue would indicate a retention rate of 94 per cent, while data on language spoken in the home would suggest a somewhat lower retention rate of around 90 per cent. Notwithstanding this decline, the general retention level is still high.

The language problem is partly one of unequal geographical distribution. Since a relatively small number of the French-origin population reside outside Quebec, the need for bilingualism diminishes the farther one moves from that province. Thus, it is not surprising to find over half of all bilinguals residing in Quebec, with an additional 29 per cent in the adjacent provinces of Ontario and New Brunswick. As a specific example, only 3 per cent of those of Scandinavian origin in Canada were bilingual; one-third of those of Scandinavian origin resident in Quebec were bilingual, however.

Language data for Quebec itself provide some insight into the current concerns of the French-origin population, and their attempts to make the French language the required language of schooling for children with non-English mother tongues. Note in Table 9 that there is only one instance where the proportion using French most often in the home exceeded the proportion using English. Of the native born who claimed Italian as their mother tongue, 20 per cent reported using French most often in the home, compared to 18 per cent that reported English. Although the data are not shown here, this was also true of their foreign-born counterparts. In only one case did the proportion using French in the home exceed the proportions using their own mother tongue. This distinction goes to the native born who reported German as their mother tongue.

The data clearly reveal the decided preference for English in the home, as opposed to French, on the part of both native-born and foreign-born persons with non-English and non-French mother tongues living in Quebec. The effect of assimilation through changing language patterns is clearly evident in the reductions in proportions of the native-born population whose mother tongues are the languages most commonly used in the home. Yet the language of the dominant culture in Quebec does not show the gains that might be expected. Perhaps it is in recognition of this problem that the government of Quebec is taking steps to ensure that the children of immigrants with non-English mother tongues who take up residence in Quebec send their children to French-language schools. Since in most cases immigrants have exhibited a preference for English-language schools, this seems to be one of the few ways in which the provincial government can strengthen the position of the French language in the face

Table 9   Percentage distributions for selected mother tongue groups of native-born populations in Quebec, showing language most often spoken at home, 1971.

Mother Tongue	Total	Language Most Often Spoken at Home			
		Same as Mother Tongue	English	French	Other
English	100.0	92.5	—	6.8	0.6
French	100.0	98.5	1.4	—	0.1
German	100.0	28.8	41.1	29.0	1.1
Italian	100.0	61.2	18.4	20.1	0.2
Netherlands	100.0	26.8	60.6	12.0	1.4
Polish	100.0	35.0	51.2	10.5	3.4
Scandinavian	100.0	20.0	55.0	15.0	8.8
Ukrainian	100.0	42.3	50.4	6.7	0.6
Yiddish	100.0	22.1	74.3	2.0	1.5

Source: *1971 Census of Canada*, Bulletin 1.4–11, Table 32.

of declining fertility, nuptiality, and increasing non-French immigration. The Francophiles might, however, take some solace from the fact that, in spite of these unfavourable trends and the recognized dominance of the English language in the North American economy, the percentage of bilingual persons in Canada managed to increase between 1961 and 1971, following a decline of heavy immigration during the immediate postwar years.

Ethnic Endogamy

Both the preference for marital endogamy by members of the two founding ethnic groups, and any tendency toward exogamous unions between the other ethnic populations would tend to strengthen and perpetuate the bicultural nature of Canadian society. (For more on this point, see Chapter 8 in this book.) Since the French and British are numerically dominant and geographically segregated, the statistical probabilities are also weighted in favour of ethnic endogamy. On the other hand, members of the smaller minority ethnic groups can theoretically achieve higher levels of intermarriage than the dominant groups, provided that they are not highly segregated within the social system.

Tendencies for some ethnic populations to settle in specific areas, to the near exclusion of others, affect the patterns of marital choice and contribute to the maintenance of the group's cultural and ethnic identity. From time to time, the government has aided and encouraged group settlement as a means of facilitating the adjustment process which all immigrants must make. The prairie provinces are dotted with a variety of easily identifiable ethnic communities, the Hutterite colonies being, perhaps, one of the more extreme examples. Furthermore, the special consideration traditionally given by the government to immigrants whose close relatives are already established in Canada has also contributed to the establishment of ethnic communities in urban areas.

Burton Hurd has shown that rates of ethnic intermarriage vary significantly from one group to another, with the British and French exhibiting relatively high proportions of endogamous marriages (Hurd, 1929; 1942; n.d.). While other ethnic groups occasionally achieved similarly high levels, only the Jewish have consistently surpassed them during the fifty-year period between 1921 and 1971. With respect to ethnic intermarriage,

Hurd's analysis showed that persons of northwestern European origins were more likely to marry someone of British origin than someone of south, central, or eastern European origins (Hurd, 1929; 1942; n.d.). As far as the two dominant ethnic groups were concerned, a higher proportion of those of French origin would marry persons of British origin than vice-versa. This pattern would reflect, of course, the numerical minority status of the French throughout most of Canada, as well as differences in general social-status levels and personal ethnic preferences. Even in Quebec, however, the data tend to show much the same results (Kalbach, 1974). In general, the propensities for intermarriage tend to be weaker in those areas where ethnic-origin groups are strongly entrenched both numerically and culturally. For example, the propensity for ethnic intermarriage on the part of the native-born French is a low 0.31 in Quebec compared to an index of 0.84 in British Columbia in 1971.[7] In contrast, but still illustrating the same principle, is the variation in propensities for Jewish intermarriage. In Quebec and British Columbia, the indexes for native-born persons of Jewish origin were 0.09 and 0.43 respectively.

Contrary to Hurd's research, which he felt suggested a trend toward increasing ethnic mixing through intermarriage, data from the 1961 and 1971 censuses of Canada suggest that the mixing is not occurring uniformly, nor has it shown any consistent increase during the last intercensal decade. Certainly, as may be seen in Table 10, a high propensity for intermarriage is not a characteristic of either of the two founding ethnic groups when examined either at the national level or in regions where they have high relative concentrations, for example, Ontario and British Columbia for the British, and Quebec for the French. In general, endogamy seems to be the rule (Kalbach, 1974: Table 2). The analysis of twelve major ethnic populations in Canada has shown that 76 per cent of all native-born family heads in 1971 were married to wives of the same ethnic origin. In 1961 the figure was 77 per cent.[8]

7. Propensity indexes were calculated as ratios of "actual" to "possible" proportions of ethnic intermarriage for native-born heads of husband-wife families. This index, unlike that based on the ratio "actual" to "expected", has the advantage of varying between the limits of 0 and 1, with the higher values indicating higher propensities for inter-marriage. (See Hewitt's suggestion reported in Yinger, 1968: 98.)

8. Actually the Atlantic provinces have the highest concentration of British-origin population. Propensities for intermarriage among native-born family heads of British origin in this region were 0.40 and 0.38 for 1961 and 1971 respectively.

Table 10   Propensities for intermarriage expressed as ratios of "actual" to "possible" proportions of ethnic intermarriages for native-born heads of selected origins: Canada and selected provinces.

Ethnic Origin of Family Head	Canada		Quebec		Ontario		B.C.	
	1961	1971	1961	1971	1961	1971	1961	1971
British	0.33	0.34	0.44	0.54	0.47	0.48	0.55	0.55
French	0.21	0.24	0.25	0.31	0.55	0.57	0.85	0.84
German	0.81	0.76	0.94	0.92	0.78	0.80	0.87	0.82
Netherlands	0.86	0.86	0.98	0.92	0.93	0.92	0.84	0.87
Scandinavian	0.91	0.90	0.96	0.94	0.96	0.94	0.92	0.91
Hungarian	0.88	0.86	0.91	0.75	0.89	0.85	0.93	0.90
Polish	0.86	0.86	0.85	0.82	0.83	0.84	0.95	0.93
Russian	0.71	0.74	0.74	0.92	0.83	0.93	0.58	0.61
Ukrainian	0.66	0.70	0.81	0.80	0.78	0.80	0.83	0.84
Italian	0.83	0.81	0.79	0.78	0.80	0.78	0.91	0.90
Jewish	0.18	0.16	0.14	0.09	0.18	0.17	0.38	0.43
Asiatic	0.45	0.52	0.60	0.59	0.46	0.54	0.21	0.35

Source: Statistics Canada, special census tabulations.

ENGLISH-FRENCH CONTRASTS

Population Size and Distribution

In 1971 the population of British origin constituted 45 per cent of the total population, and that of French origin 29 per cent. Both populations have continued to show growth over the years, but the proportion of the total has continued to decline for the British and to remain relatively constant for the French. Higher levels of immigration on the part of other ethnic populations have increased their rates of growth and share of the national total.

The possible disadvantage occasioned by the smaller size of the French population vis-à-vis the British has been partially compensated for by its greater geographical concentration. Note in Table 11 that over three-fourths of their national total resided in Quebec in 1971, and that 79 per cent of the province's population were French. This situation is in sharp contrast to that of persons of British origin who resided in Ontario at the same time. Less than half (48 per cent) of all the British in Canada lived in that province, where they constituted only 59 per cent of the

Table 11 Number and percentage distribution of British and French origin populations for provinces, Canada, 1971.

Province	Numerical Distribution			Percentage Distribution						
	British	French	Other	British	French	Other	Total	British	French	Other
Newfoundland	489,570	15,415	17,120	5.1	0.2	0.3	100.0	93.8	3.0	3.3
Prince Edward Island	92,285	15,320	4,040	1.0	0.2	0.1	100.0	82.7	13.7	3.6
Nova Scotia	611,310	80,215	97,435	6.4	1.3	1.7	100.0	77.5	10.2	12.3
New Brunswick	365,735	235,025	33,800	3.8	3.8	0.6	100.0	57.6	37.0	5.3
Quebec	640,040	4,759,355	628,370	6.6	77.0	10.9	100.0	10.6	79.0	10.4
Ontario	4,576,010	737,360	2,389,735	47.5	11.9	41.5	100.0	59.4	9.6	31.0
Manitoba	414,125	86,515	487,605	4.3	1.4	8.5	100.0	41.9	8.8	49.3
Saskatchewan	390,190	56,200	479,855	4.1	0.9	8.3	100.0	42.1	6.1	51.8
Alberta	761,665	94,665	771,545	7.9	1.5	13.4	100.0	46.8	5.8	47.4
British Columbia	1,265,460	96,555	822,605	13.1	1.6	14.3	100.0	57.9	4.4	37.7
Yukon	8,945	1,225	8,220	0.1	—	0.1	100.0	48.6	6.7	44.7
Northwest Territories	8,785	2,275	23,750	0.1	—	0.4	100.0	25.2	6.5	68.2
Total:	9,624,120	6,180,120	5,764,070	100.0	100.0	100.0	100.0	44.6	28.7	26.7

Source: *1971 Census of Canada*, Bulletin 1.3–2, Table 3.

population. Yet the British-origin population dominates the French in every province outside of Quebec. Only in the provinces of Nova Scotia, Prince Edward Island, and Newfoundland, however, do you find the proportion of British nearly as high as, or higher than, the concentration of French in Quebec. In other words, while French Canadians exceeded their national proportion of 29 per cent in 1971 in just two provinces, Quebec and New Brunswick, the British exceeded 45 per cent in seven of the provinces, and in one of the Territories.

While these distinctive regional distributions were evolving, the entire country was becoming increasingly concentrated in urban communities. Back in 1871 only 19 per cent of the French and 22 per cent of the population of British origin were classified as urban. During the following century, the French appear to have continued to urbanize at about the same rate as the population of Canada as a whole. Persons of British origin, on the other hand, have been consistently more urbanized; yet in 1971 the rural-urban distributions of the two populations achieved congruence: 76 per cent of their populations were classified as urban—the same figure reached by Canada as a whole.

Age-Sex Characteristics

The pattern of an excess of males, typical of the frontier societies in the New World, finally ended with the Census of 1971. The long-term decline from an excess of 129 males per 1000 females in 1911 levelled at parity by 1971. Essentially both French- and British-origin populations achieved this balance twenty years earlier in 1951. A more rapid decline in the ratio of males to females for the British, however, produced a significantly greater deficiency of males by 1971 than was the case for the French.

The absence of significant immigration by the French, plus the greater male mortality characteristic of all populations, would account for this particular pattern. The more rapid change experienced by the British in part would be a reflection of both the change in the character of immigration prior to and following the Second World War, and the excess of male mortality arising from participation in that conflict.

One of the expected distinctions between the two populations, in so far as their respective age and sex characteristics are concerned, is the younger age of the French-origin population. While trends in birth rates suggest a decline in ethnic differentials, data for broad age groups (presented in Table 12 for the period 1931–71) do show a consistently higher proportion of the French ethnic origin population in the youngest age group, 0–14 years. Such data are, of course, quite consistent with the higher French fertility rate. The narrowing difference in the proportions of both populations in this younger age group, for this period, reflects the convergence in fertility previously noted.

At the other end of the age continuum, the British-origin population exhibits the larger proportion in the age groups above forty-five years. For each year shown, this population is consistently above the national average, while the French-origin population is below. These contrasts can be seen in finer detail in Figure 2:2: here again, the differences between the relative sizes of the older age groups—those forty-five and over—have continued to diminish. Only a major reversal in the fertility trends for the French would be able to check this process. The declines in fertility for this last intercensal period, however, have been severe and relatively greater for the population of Quebec.

Figure 2:2 Age-sex distributions in Canada British-French origins 1961

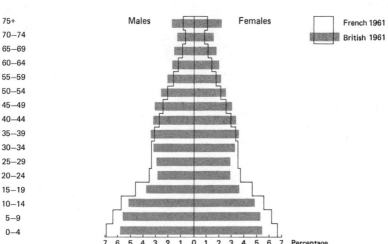

Source: Population Research Lab, Sociology, Erindale.
       University of Toronto

Table 12 Selected characteristics of British- and French-origin populations, Canada: 1931–71.

Year	Population Numbers in 1000s	Per Cent Foreign Born	Per Cent Urban	Percentage Age Distribution[a]					Per Cent Married 15 yrs.+	Sex Ratio
				Total	0–14	15–44	45–64	65+		
French Origin Population										
1971	6180	—	75.9	100.0	31.0	46.0	(23.0)[b]		—	99.1
1961	5540	1.6	68.2	100.0	37.4	42.1	15.1	5.4	61.9	100.1
1951	4319	1.6	59.9	100.0	35.7	44.8	14.2	5.3	59.4	100.1
1941	3483	2.2	54.9	100.0	34.0	47.0	14.0	5.0	51.4	101.1
1931	2928	2.6	54.0	100.0	37.9	44.3	13.0	4.8	52.5	101.3
British Origin Population										
1971	9624	—	75.9	100.0	28.0	42.0	(30.0)[b]		—	98.0
1961	7997	14.4	71.2	100.0	32.1	38.9	19.0	10.0	67.8	99.8
1951	6710	16.1	65.7	100.0	27.7	42.8	19.5	10.0	66.3	100.1
1941	5716	20.2	58.3	100.0	23.5	46.2	21.8	8.5	57.6	103.6
1931	5381	25.1	57.5	100.0	27.7	45.8	19.8	6.7	56.9	104.8

[a] 1971 age data from Statistics Canada, July 1974; Table 13.22.

[b] 45 years of age and over.

— data not published as of December 1974.

Source: Censuses of Canada.

Marital Status

Other things being equal, an older population tends to have a higher proportion of married persons than a younger one does. Thus, it is not unexpected that the proportion of the British population fifteen years of age and over who are married has tended to be larger than the proportion of the same age group in the French population. For the thirty-year period for which comparable data are available, the British proportions married tend to be consistently higher than that for Canada as a whole, while the proportions of the French tend to be lower. Since this differential can be observed for each age group in the population over the age of fifteen, during the post-Second World War period, however, one can be sure that it reflects a significant difference in the propensity to marry, rather than differences in age structures alone. As noted earlier, Henripin has pointed out the negative contribution of nuptiality to the fertility of the French-origin population in Canada since 1941 (Henripin, 1972: 75–77).

Socio-economic Characteristics: Education

Cultural and social-class differences in the attitudes toward education, access to educational facilities, and incentives to capitalize on educational opportunities are reflected in a society's educational statistics.[9] Data in Table 13 for the population five years of age and over attending school full time in 1971 show that the population of French origin still tends to be under-represented beyond secondary levels. It is possible that in this case the differences may reflect the larger proportions of those of French origin in the younger age groups, rather than educational inequalities alone.

Data from the 1961 Census allow a more precise assessment of the actual differences in educational attainment between these two groups, through utilizing data giving the highest level of schooling attained for the population twenty-five years of age and over, as shown in Table 14. Note that in 1961 almost two-thirds of the native-born French-origin population

9. Few tabulations of detailed characteristics of ethnic populations in 1971 were available in late 1974. For the most part, detailed educational characteristics, and occupational and income data, were taken from special tabulations of the 1961 Census to illustrate ethnic origin differences. While the magnitude of these differences has undoubtedly changed, the general pattern of ethnic differentials is probably still valid.

Table 13   Percentage distributions of the population 5 years of age and over for British and French origins, attending school full time, by level of schooling, Canada, 1971.

Ethnic Origin	Total		Elementary	Secondary[a]	University[a]
	Number	*Per Cent*			
British	2,663,360	100.0	64.5	28.9	6.6
French	1,763,935	100.0	66.5	29.6	3.9
Other	1,511,020	100.0	65.9	26.9	7.2
Total:	5,938,315	100.0	65.4	28.6	5.9

[a] Includes other post-secondary types of education.

Source: 1971 Census of Canada, Bulletin 1.5–2, Table 3.

had some elementary education, or none, compared to just slightly more than one-third of the native-born British, a relatively larger number of whom had achieved more than an elementary level of schooling by the time they had reached twenty-five years of age. For both intermediate levels and university, the British figures exceeded the French as well as the total national averages.

It is interesting that the positions are reversed for postwar immigrants with some university background or degree. The French immigrant not only had a decided advantage over his native-born counterpart, but also over postwar immigrants of British origin. The percentages of French and British postwar immigrants with some university background or degree

Table 14   Percentage distributions for native-born English and French origin populations, 25 years of age and over, showing highest level of schooling attained, Canada, 1961.

Ethnic Origin	Total		Highest Level of Schooling		
	Number	*Per Cent*	*Elementary or None*	*1–5+ yrs. Secondary*	*Some or University Degree*
British	3,380,596	100.0	36.4	55.2	8.4
French	2,486,881	100.0	62.1	33.6	4.3
All Origins	7,105,373	100.0	47.2	46.2	6.6

Source: Kalbach, 1970: Table 4.15.

were 19 and 14 respectively. Because of their relatively small numbers, the effect of the superior educational qualifications of the French postwar immigrant on the average attainment levels for the total population of French origin is slight.

Socio-economic Characteristics: Occupations

Because educational attainment and occupational skills are interrelated, some of the consequences of educational differences may be seen in the relative concentrations of French and British origins in the various major occupational groupings of the Canadian labour force. The indexes in Table 15 show the relatively greater concentration of native-born British in the managerial, professional, clerical, and sales occupations, and the contrasting pattern for the French in logging and mining, craftsman, and labouring occupations. In addition, there are slightly greater concentrations of French in service and recreation, and transportation and communication occupations.

Socio-economic Characteristics: Income

The pay-off for these ethnic differences in educational characteristics has been in higher incomes for those of British origin in the labour force. Table 15 shows the consistently higher income for the British in all the major occupational categories, with the exception of fishermen, miners, and labourers. Median total earnings[10] for native-born British in the labour force in 1961 was $3,471 compared to $2,940 for native-born French, while median earnings for all origins combined was $3,249 (Kalbach, 1970: Table 5:23).

While the contrast has been made between native-born French and British in the labour force because of their greater numerical importance, some additional comment is needed with respect to the foreign born, especially the postwar immigrants. It has already been pointed out that the average French immigrant has tended to be more educated than his native-born counterpart. With a much higher degree of concentration in the professional occupations in 1961, his total earnings were higher than the average for all postwar immigrants, although they still fell short of the

10. Total earnings included wages and salaries, plus any income from self-   employment.

Table 15   Indexes of relative concentration[a] for selected occupational groupings, and median total earnings[b] for native-born British and French origin population in the labour force, Canada, 1961.

Occupational Group	Indexes of Relative Concentration		Median Total Earnings	
	British	French	British	French
(Base proportion)[a] ... %	(36.7)	(26.9)		
Managerial	114	76	$5,778	$4,786
Professional & technical	118	90	4,714	3,747
Clerical	122	83	2,876	2,746
Sales	118	90	2,813	2,649
Service & recreation	92	98	2,267	1,766
Transport & communication	113	118	3,594	3,138
Farmers	95	84	2,324	1,964
Farm workers	81	98	1,357	1,194
Loggers	69	199	1,870	1,671
Fishermen	137	68	1,339	1,505
Miners	93	110	4,070	4,102
Craftsmen	82	113	3,817	3,202
Labourers	77	122	2,041	2,051

[a] The base proportions indicate that 36.7 per cent of the native-born experienced labour force was of British origin, and 26.9 per cent French. The indexes show the amount of variation about these base proportions. For example, the British actually comprised 41.8 per cent of the managerial workers, hence the index of relative concentration in this case is:

$$\text{IRC} = \frac{41.8}{36.7} \times 100 = 114$$

[b] For workers reporting income only.

Source: Kalbach, 1970: Tables 5.11 and 5.25.

average for the British, for all occupations combined. The French postwar immigrants did, however, exceed the median total earnings of their British counterparts in managerial, sales, logging, and mining occupations (Kalbach, 1970: Table 5.26).

Socio-economic Contrasts: An Overview

In terms of socio-economic position, the French-origin population in Canada clearly occupies a position below that of the British. More detailed analyses, conducted by the Royal Commission on Bilingualism and Biculturalism, has shown that much of this difference in relative position can be attributed to factors other than ethnicity *per se* (Royal Commission on Bilingualism and Biculturalism, 1969: 61–86). Specifically, the Royal Commission showed in its report that the largest part of the income disparity between those of French and of British origins could be accounted for in terms of differences in education and occupation. In combination with such additional factors as age, distribution of the labour force by industry, and unemployment, between 62 and 90 per cent of the disparities observed in the Montreal, Ottawa, and Toronto metropolitan areas could be accounted for. Ironically, these factors were least successful as explanatory variables in Montreal. Thus, ethnicity, and specifically British ethnicity, had the strongest influence on the distribution of income in the second largest French-speaking city in the world (Royal Commission on Bilingualism and Biculturalism, 1969: 45–47, 61–86).

In attempting to explain the relatively disadvantaged position of the French in Quebec, the Commission pointed out the rather obvious fact that the British, or Anglophones, simply had had a head start. Their earlier urban orientation, higher levels of education, a more democratic philosophy of public education, and their position in the occupational structure of an industrializing society simply put them in a more strategic position to participate in the economic development of Quebec and of Canada as a whole. Not only that, but "once these socio-economic patterns have been established, they tend to be self perpetuating; the momentum favouring the Anglophones was never matched in the Francophone community" (Royal Commission, 1969: 80–86). The Commission concluded that the combination of low-paying jobs and large families, coupled with little opportunity or incentive to obtain more education or skills to qualify for better employment, tends to perpetuate a pattern of poverty from which successive generations have little chance for escape.

Cultural Diversity and Change

Circumstances of history and acts of government have made Canada bicultural and bilingual. The general numerical and cultural dominance of the British and French is evidence of this fact. But the vagaries of subsequent migrant streams have contributed increasing numbers of immigrants from a variety of cultures. Thus, both the actual and the potential cultural diversity in Canada has increased with the passage of time and under the impact of successive waves of immigration.

Government policies through the years have encouraged group settlement as a means of populating the Prairies and expanding the agricultural sector of the economy. Immigration policy has also given preferential treatment to close relatives of those already established in Canada, as a means of facilitating the adjustment of new arrivals. Both policies have significantly contributed to the build-up of ethnic communities in both rural areas and urban centres, and in so doing have established a firmer basis for the maintenance and persistence of cultural diversity in Canada. The extent of this diversity may be seen through a more detailed examination of selected characteristics of the population with special references to the "other" ethnic-origin groups.

ETHNIC DIVERSITY

The 1971 Census lists forty distinct ethnic groups varying in size from the very smallest, the Byelorussians, to the British, who composed the largest group in 1971.[11] Maximum ethnic diversity would occur only if all the identifiable ethnic groups were to achieve equality in numbers—theoretically by the opposite of complete ethnic homogeneity, where the total population is of a single ethnic type. Cultural reality in Canada is obviously somewhere between these two extremes, although the possible maximum degree of homogeneity is limited by the fact of biculturalism. In other words, the lower practical limit of any measure of ethnic and cultural diversity applied to Canadian society subsequent to the demise of New France would be greater than zero.

To show the present extent of cultural diversity (as a proportion of the maximum possible at the present time), indexes of diversity have been calculated for Canada and its provinces, using the forty-one ethnic groups

11. The 1971 *Census Bulletin*, 1.3–2, "Ethnic Groups", gives information on the combined British Isles ethnic group only. Data for the major component groups show that the English with 6,246,000 were in fact the single largest ethnic group in Canada, being slightly more numerous than the 6,180,120 of French origin. In addition, there were 1,720,000 Scottish and 1,581,000 Irish. (See Kubat and Thornton, 1974: Table P-10.)

for which data were provided in the 1971 Census.[12] These are presented in Table 16. Considering the ethnic composition of Canada as a whole, the amount of diversity is shown to be approximately 75 per cent of the possible maximum.[13]

The variation in ethnic diversity by province appears more significant. The greatest degree of homogeneity is exhibited by the population of Newfoundland, where 94 per cent of the population is British in origin. Quebec and Nova Scotia have similarly low indexes of diversity because of the relative dominance of a single ethnic population. In Nova Scotia the British compose 78 per cent of the population, while in Quebec the French compose 79 per cent. The greatest degree of heterogeneity is found in the prairie provinces, where many of the other ethnic groups are concentrated and relatively few British and French are to be found. In no prairie province does the proportion of British exceed 47 per cent. While the index of diversity for Canada provides an interesting summary measure, the indexes for the provinces provide a truer indication of the range of ethnic diversity which constitutes the cultural fabric of the society as a whole.

Variations in Ethnic Distributions

The index of diversity used in the previous section does not indicate which groups are contributing to the relative heterogeneity or homogeneity of the population. For this purpose, the indexes of relative concentration are more suitable.

The changing character of immigrants to Canada and their destinations have obviously contributed to the cultural diversity of the nation. Many of those arriving before the First World War were land-hungry peasants from eastern Europe heading for the Prairies; relatively high concentra-

---

12. These are the adjusted Indexes of Diversity A'_w, where p_i represents the proportion of the "*i*th" ethnic population, and $N = 41$.

$$A_w = 1 - \sum_{i=1}^{N} (p_i)^2 \qquad A'_w = \frac{A_w}{1 - \dfrac{1}{N}}$$

(For the derivation of the index, see Lieberson, 1969: 850–62.)

13. It is interesting to note that if the total population were in fact distributed between the French and the British, in terms of their present relative size, the index of diversity would be 0.488, and 0.513 if equally divided between these two "founding" groups, assuming that only numerically insignificant numbers were present in the remaining thirty-nine ethnic categories.

Table 16   Indexes of ethnic diversity for Canada and provinces, 1971.

Province	Index of Diversity
Newfoundland	0.123
Prince Edward Island	0.305
Nova Scotia	0.395
New Brunswick	0.543
Quebec	0.373
Ontario	0.643
Manitoba	0.801
Saskatchewan	0.785
Alberta	0.764
British Columbia	0.664
Canada	0.729

Source: Based on data from the *1971 Census of Canada*, Bulletin 1.3–2, Table 2.

tions of Ukrainians and Russians, in addition to Germans, Poles, and Scandinavians, settled in this region. When immigration revived after the Second World War, both the character and destination of immigrants had shifted. Canada was predominately urban, and its expanding economy had drawn increasing numbers of professional and technical workers to the rapidly expanding metropolitan areas. At the same time, internal migration was redistributing the population within Canada, in response to the same economic developments.

The net consequences of these shifting patterns for the distribution of ethnic populations can be seen in Table 17. The indexes of relative concentration presented here show the extent to which any particular ethnic population in any province exceeds or falls short of its national average, which is represented by an index equal to 100.[14] Indexes are presented for French origin, British origin, and several other groups which represent the "old" and "new" immigrations.

14. The index of 210 for Newfoundland simply means that the proportion of British origins in that province is 2.1 times as large as its proportion in the Canadian population at large. It is calculated as follows:

$$IRC = \frac{.938}{.446} \times 100 = 210$$

The British pattern is characterized by disproportionately larger numbers in the Atlantic provinces, Ontario, and British Columbia. The French are solidly entrenched in Quebec and New Brunswick. The German ethnic population is over-represented in all the western provinces, while the Ukrainians are still heavily concentrated in just the prairie provinces. Relative concentrations of Jewish peoples are greatest in Manitoba, Quebec, and Ontario, and it is clear that Ontario has been the favourite destination of the large number of postwar Italian immigrants. The recent increase in Chinese immigrants has not disturbed their traditional settlement pattern favouring the West Coast.

Several of the "newer" groups, for which data are not shown, are also developing concentrations in current high-growth areas. Most of the East Indians, for example, are located primarily in Ontario and secondly in British Columbia; but, in terms of numbers relative to provincial totals, they show relatively greater concentration in British Columbia than in Ontario. One additional group of newcomers, West Indians, have tended to concentrate in Ontario and Quebec.

As the provinces differ in the extent of their urbanization, some of the interprovincial differences in relative concentrations can be attributed to

Table 17   Indexes of relative concentration for selected ethnic origin populations by province, 1971.

Province	Selected Ethnic Origins						
	British	French	German	Ukrainian	Italian	Jewish	Chinese
(base prop.)	(.446)	(.287)	(.061)	(.027)	(.034)	(.014)	(.006)
Newfoundland	210	10	7	12	3	5	19
P.E.I.	185	48	14	3	3	4	4
Nova Scotia	174	35	85	14	11	23	20
New Brunswick	129	129	22	3	6	12	15
Quebec	24	275	15	12	83	137	33
Ontario	133	33	101	77	177	125	85
Manitoba	94	30	204	429	31	145	58
Saskatchewan	94	21	319	344	9	17	83
Alberta	105	20	233	308	45	32	132
B.C.	130	15	149	102	72	40	338

Source: Based on data from the *1971 Census of Canada*, Bulletin 1.3–2, Table 3.

Table 18   Indexes of relative concentration for selected ethnic origin populations by rural-urban type and size groups, Canada, 1971.

Area Type and Size Group	Selected Ethnic Origins						
	British	French	German	Ukrainian	Italian	Jewish	Chinese
(base prop.)	(.446)	(.287)	(.061)	(.027)	(.034)	(.014)	(.006)
Urban							
500,000 & over	88	100	68	91	203	269	187
100,000–499,999	109	69	143	162	100	46	102
30,000– 99,999	110	115	60	56	102	22	50
10,000– 29,999	108	110	101	74	45	13	52
5,000– 9,999	115	105	94	80	28	14	42
2,500– 4,999	100	125	107	86	31	7	47
1,000– 2,499	100	129	90	74	18	7	41
Rural							
Rural non-farm	106	105	100	69	15	6	12
Rural farm	89	90	213	198	12	3	7

Source: Based on data from the *1971 Census of Canada*, Bulletin 1.3–2, Table 3.

rural-urban preferences among immigrants, reflecting earlier settlement patterns. This is illustrated by the indexes of relative concentration presented in Table 18, for the same ethnic groups as before, by rural type and urban size groups.

Of the "founding" groups, the British tend to show relatively greater concentrations in urban places of population between 5000 and 500,000 and proportionately fewer in the largest urban centres and in rural farm areas than would be expected on the basis of their national average. The French differ most from the British by their under-representation in cities of 100,000 to 500,000 inhabitants and proportionately greater numbers in small urban places of between 1000 and 5000. Their "representativeness" in urban centres of over 500,000 is an added contrast to the British patterns.

The Germans and the Ukrainians reflect both pre- and post-Second World War migration patterns with their relative concentrations in the rural farm population and in cities of 100,000 to 500,000 in size. The Italians show their clear preference for the Canadian metropolis, and the traditional preference of those of Jewish origin for the big city is even more sharply revealed. Obviously, the high indexes of relative concentration for Manitoba, Quebec, and Ontario represent concentrations in the metropolitan centres of these provinces. Like the Italians and Jews, the pattern of regional centralization of the Chinese reflects their relatively high concentrations in the regional urban centres. With urbanization reaching the high levels it has in Canada, it would be surprising to find recent immigrants who didn't settle in the urban centres, where the greatest number and range of economic opportunities are to be found.

The Religious Component of Ethnic and Cultural Diversity

Variation in the religious composition of the population adds another dimension to the cultural variations reflected in ethnic origins. Yet there is a certain congruence between the distribution of religious identification in a population such as Canada's and its ethnic origins. In this case, it is primarily due to the fact that most French Canadians are Roman Catholic, and a great majority of those of British origin are identified with either the Anglican or the United Church. As far back as 1871, 43 per cent of the population was reported as Catholic, and by 1971 this proportion had increased to 49 per cent. The various major Protestant denominations and numerous sects made up the balance of the Christian religions, accounting for approximately 44 per cent of the total. The remainder was divided among Jews (1.3 per cent), Buddhists and Confucians (0.1 per cent), other unspecified religions (1.4 per cent), and those who stated that they had no religion (4.3 per cent).[15]

The large variety of Protestant denominations adds additional facets to the basic Catholic-Protestant dualism. Like the minority ethnic groups, the smaller Catholic and Protestant denominations tend to gain in visibility through segregation and concentration. As in the case of ethnicity, the tendency toward regional segregation varies widely. Among the larger denominations, the Roman Catholics are highly concentrated in Quebec and, to a lesser extent, in New Brunswick. For the Anglicans, the areas of

---

15. In previous censuses, the proportion reporting no religion hardly ever exceeded 0.5 per cent. However, in the 1971 Census, it was made easier for the respondent to indicate "no religion", and the number showed a dramatic increase from 95,000 in 1961 to 930,000 in 1971. Certainly the greatest part of this increase would reflect procedural changes, rather than a sudden upsurge in the population disclaiming any religious affiliation or identification.

highest relative concentrations are at the opposite ends of the country, in Newfoundland and British Columbia. The smaller Protestant denominations and sects are often highly localized. The Hutterites are a classic example, since they represent a more extreme form of rural communal groups who must live together in their own prescribed way to achieve salvation. Almost their total population, 96 per cent, live in the three prairie provinces. Of all the Protestant sects, only the Baptists and the Salvation Army have tended to be under-represented in all the western provinces. On the other hand, in the Atlantic provinces, a number of Protestant groups are generally conspicuous by their relative absence. Among the most conspicuous in this sense have been the Mormons, Mennonites, Doukhobors, Hutterites, Christian Scientists, and the Evangelical United Brethren.

Among non-Christian religions, the degree of relative concentration tends to diminish for the Confucians and Buddhists as one travels from the Pacific Ocean to Toronto. The Jews, on the other hand, who are also highly urbanized as a group, have already been shown to have their highest relative concentrations in the largest urban centres of Manitoba, Quebec, and Ontario.

In sum, it appears to be as impossible to define the religious character of the average Canadian as it is to determine his ethnicity. Variations in religious identities appear to be more subtle and infinitely greater than for ethnic identity, and both seem inexorably intertwined. The Protestant Reformation contributed not only to the evolution of Canada's vertical mosaic but also to a purely horizontal pattern which gives the country a degree of cultural diversity which would be hard to match anyplace else.

Cultural Diversity Reflected in Ethnic Fertility Patterns

Attitudes toward family, fertility, and child-rearing are influenced by one's religious beliefs, social customs, values, traditions, and socio-economic position. These are all reflected in the fertility behaviour of any population. To the extent that cultural differences among ethnic and religious groups are socially significant, differences in their fertility behaviour should be readily observable.

An examination of completed fertility—the number of children ever born to women ever married, who were forty-five years of age and older

Table 19 Number of children ever born to women ever married, 45 years of age and over by ethnic origin, Canada, 1971.

Ethnic-Origin Group	Children Born Per 1000 Women
British Isles	2,846
French	4,387
Other major NW European	3,117
All other European[a]	3,124
Jewish	2,283
Asian	3,263
Native Indians	6,149
Eskimo	6,267
Other and unknown	3,060

[a] Includes German, Scandinavian, Belgian, Austrian, Czech, Slovak, and Finnish.

Source: *1971 Census of Canada*, Bulletin 1.5–11.

at the time of the 1971 Census—reveals significant differences among the major ethnic groups presented in Table 19. Among the non-native population, women of French origin who had essentially completed their child-bearing by 1971 had experienced the highest levels of fertility in Canada. At the other extreme, Jewish women had had only 2.3 children on the average.

Regional variations, reflecting in part the same rural-urban differences mentioned earlier, are visible in the completed fertility data for all ethnic groups combined. They also appear in the data for three of the four major ethnic-origin groupings shown in Table 20. Only the "other major northwestern Europeans" deviate significantly, because their lowest levels are in Quebec, rather than in British Columbia, and because their highest levels occur in the Prairies, rather than in the Atlantic provinces. The latter exception is undoubtedly due to their heavy concentration in the Prairies, while the former suggests that they are more urbanized in Quebec than in British Columbia. The relatively small numbers of Asian and Jewish women in the five regions make regional estimates of their levels of completed fertility somewhat less reliable, and for that reason they have not been included.

Table 20 Number of children ever born to women ever married, 45 years of age and over, for selected ethnic origins, by region, 1971.

Region	Total Ethnic Origins	French Ethnic Origin	British Ethnic Origin	Other Major Northwestern European	All Other European Origins
Atlantic	4,132	5,484	3,903	3,213	3,713
Quebec	3,962	4,369	2,766	2,472	2,821
Ontario	2,793	4,054	2,633	2,671	2,913
Prairies	3,401	4,552	2,979	3,676	3,593
British Columbia	2,645	3,279	2,447	2,864	2,919

Source: *1971 Census of Canada*, Bulletin 1.5–11.

Religion and Fertility

As Table 21 indicates, religious identification of the population is still very much alive in its influence over the fertility behaviour of women in Canada who completed their child-bearing period in the years prior to 1971. The significance of fertility for religious groups as an indicator of cultural diversity is revealed in the fact that the completed fertility of Roman and Ukrainian Catholic women, forty-five years of age and older, was almost 50 per cent higher than that of women who identified with the principal Protestant religions. When compared with the fertility of Jewish women, their completed fertility was 77 per cent higher. Evidence of considerable variation within major denominations, especially the Protestants, is found in the high fertility of the Mennonite and Hutterite women. However, considering the relatively small size of this group, the fertility of Catholic women would be more significant with respect to the overall growth potential of the nation.

Regional variations in fertility by religious denomination are much like those for ethnic groupings of the population. Similarly, where the effects of low urbanization and religious values reinforce each other, fertility levels tend to be higher than the national average. Thus, Catholic women in the Atlantic provinces with 5151 children per 1000 ever-married women, forty-five years of age and over—in contrast to the national norm of 4052—exhibit considerably higher fertility. On the other hand, in British Columbia, which is more urbanized and industrialized, completed fertility for the same age group is only 3183 or an average of 3.2 children per woman.

Again, cultural diversity is heightened through residential dispersion and regional concentrations of a variety of ethnic and religious populations. Ethnic groups show not only important intergroup differences but also significant internal differences, depending upon the extent of regional and rural-urban variation in their living and working environments.

Change in Ethnic Diversity

Ethnic groups, like any population, are subject to the effects of demographic processes. Consequently, they tend to experience changes in size, in geographic distribution, and in many of their structural features and population attributes. Their characteristics have significance for the analysis of ethnic differentials to the extent that their particular combination of socio-economic and psychological attributes reflect their unique historical experiences and sharing of a common culture.

The point is often made that much of what appears to be uniquely ethnic is, in fact, due only to differences in the group's demographic characteristics. While it is almost a truism that the various ethnic populations would be much more alike if they had shared the same demographic experiences, the fact remains that much of what distinguishes one ethnic

Table 21   Number of children ever born to women ever married, 45 years of age and over, by major religious denominations, Canada, 1971.

Religious Denomination	Children Born Per 1000 Women
Roman and Ukrainian Catholic	4,052
Greek Orthodox	3,077
Principal Protestant Denominations[a]	2,720
Mennonites and Hutterites	4,890
Jewish	2,286
Other	3,190

[a] Includes Anglican, Baptist, Lutheran, Presbyterian, and United Church.

Sources: *1971 Census of Canada*, Bulletin 1.5–11.

group from another is deeply rooted in their particular demographic experience and character.

For example, how can the Jewish population be abstracted completely from its low fertility, high urban concentrations, and high educational achievement? Give any other group of people this same combination of characteristics, and the two will be less ethnically distinctive from one another. Similarly, break the Ukrainian's ties with the rural Prairies, and he is perhaps, not the same Ukranian. Of course, such experiences and their resultant characteristics cannot be readily changed, or acquired, as many minority groups have discovered.

If the significance of ethnicity lies, at least in part, in the existence of observable differences in demographic, as well as psychological, attributes, then a diminishing of these differences will reflect a diminishing of the significance of ethnicity. With this fact in mind, the fertility, mortality, and migration patterns of ethnic groups are now examined for evidence that would suggest the possibility of reduction in ethnic differences in the future. (For a detailed discussion of ethnicity in Canada, see Chapter 6.)

Changes in Fertility

The pattern of changing fertility during the postwar period is well known. Only somewhat less familiar are the ethnic variations from the general trend, which saw a postwar reversal of the long-term decline in fertility, and then a subsequent and significant decline following 1957 (Henripin, 1972: 170–80). In 1971 completed fertility for all women ever married who were born before 1911 showed significant declines with successively older cohorts of women, the lowest levels being associated with urban residence and the highest with rural farm residence. While regional differences in rural farm populations have altered little during this period, there was a visible trend toward convergence among regions with respect to their urban fertility (Henripin, 1972: Graphs 4.13 and 4.14). In other words, it has been well established not only that completed fertility of urban women was declining in general, but that differences between regions were becoming less.

Similar data on fertility from the 1971 Census permit additional comparisons to determine the validity of the general trends for Canada's

Table 22   Number of children born per 1000 women ever married by ethnic origin, and for age groups who have completed child-bearing in 1971.

Ethnic-Origin Groups	Age Groups					
	45+	*45–49*	*50–54*	*55–59*	*60–64*	*65–69*
British Isles	2,846	3,093	2,874	2,640	2,533	2,589
French	4,387	4,093	4,098	3,998	4,177	4,579
Other NW European	3,117	2,943	2,875	2,836	2,920	3,115
Other European	3,124	2,834	2,775	2,846	3,105	3,390
Jewish	2,283	2,360	2,070	1,964	1,876	1,969
Asian	3,263	3,011	3,050	3,144	3,121	3,299
Native Indian	6,149	6,419	6,304	6,143	5,951	5,889
Eskimo	6,267	6,837	6,193	5,520	6,463	6,574
Other	3,060	2,924	2,971	2,937	2,931	3,088

Source: *1971 Census of Canada*, Bulletin 1.5–11, Table 31.

ethnic populations. These are presented in Table 22 for older cohorts of women who had completed their families.

It should be kept in mind that the recent and dramatic decline in fertility since 1957 in Canada's crude birth rates will not be fully reflected in these data, since other factors in addition to changes in the actual fertility of married women have contributed to this decline. In addition, most of these women were in the latter stages of their child-bearing years and would not have had much effect on the birth rates during this period. The cohorts of women born after 1916 had actually experienced higher completed fertility rates than the older women who had immediately preceded them. Thus, the long-term decline in completed fertility had come to an end with the cohort of women born between 1911 and 1916. For subsequent cohorts, completed fertility rose, but at the time of the 1971 Census it was still too early to determine which particular cohort of women still in their child-bearing ages would actually mark the beginning of the next down-turn in completed fertility.

Since changes in fertility have a marked effect on population age-sex structures, it is worth noting to what extent the general trend is reflected in the fertility experience of the individual ethnic groups. It is interesting to note that the reversals in trends for completed family size occurred at different times for different ethnic groups. The upward trend for women of British and Jewish origins began with the cohorts born during the 1911–16 period. The completed fertility for French, other northwestern European, and Eskimo women did not start to increase until the next younger five-year age cohort had completed its child-bearing. The increase for women of "other European" origins was delayed even longer, and did not occur until the cohorts born during the 1921–25 period had completed their families.

Exceptions to the more general pattern were the native-born Indians, whose completed fertility showed consistent increases from the oldest to the youngest cohort, and the Asian women, who experienced an overall decrease. With the exception of these two groups, the major ethnic groupings of women appear to have responded to changing economic and social conditions in much the same way. Considering all but the native Indians and Eskimos, the differences between the highest and lowest fertility levels reflected in these data have declined from 2610 children per 1000 women ever married for the older cohort, to 1733 for the youngest cohort of women, that is, those who were forty-five to forty-nine years of age in 1971. The extent of convergence is reduced when the two small but highly fertile native populations are included. Changes in the North have had a very positive effect on their rate of population growth. Like many other underdeveloped populations in the world, they are just entering the first stages of their demographic transition: their first response to improving living conditions and declining mortality has been an increase in fertility. High rates of natural increase among Canada's native peoples, and the possibility of increasing migration to southern population centres, will make their culture more visible and their demands for greater participation in a multicultural society more pressing.

Declining Mortality

The Canadian experience has been characterized by improving standards of living, declining mortality, and increasing life expectancy at birth and later ages. Mortality conditions have been more favourable in Canada than in the countries which have sent immigrants, and this factor, combined with generally higher fertility rates, has contributed to relatively

Table 23 Standardized male death rates[a] for selected ethnic origins, Canada, 1941, 1951, and 1961.

Ethnic Origin	1941	1951	1961
British Isles	12.6	11.3	10.8
French	14.6	12.6	11.1
German	11.2	9.5	8.2
Dutch	9.8	10.4	9.1
Scandinavian	11.7	10.5	8.8
Ukrainian	11.3	10.2	9.5
Polish	14.0	11.5	8.8
Italian	12.9	10.3	8.5
Native Indian	25.4	18.9	14.3

[a] Standardized on the 1961 British origin male population.

Source: Unpublished tabulations, Vital Statistics Section, Statistics Canada.

high rates of natural increase and population growth. Ethnic differences can be examined on the basis of age-specific rates calculated for the census years between 1941 and 1961.[16] Male death rates standardized in the British-origin male population and presented in Table 23 show considerable variation by ethnicity, as well as evidence of convergence during this period. In 1941 standardized male death rates ranged from a maximum of 25.4 for native Indians to a low of 9.8 for the Dutch. By 1961 the range had dropped to a maximum of 14.3 for native Indians and a low of 8.2 deaths per 1000 population for males of German origin. During this period, male mortality rates in the various ethnic populations tended both to decrease and to converge.

Regional variations in life expectancy at birth also show trends toward convergence, which will tend to reduce ethnic differentials in mortality to the extent that ethnic populations continue to exhibit different patterns of regional concentrations. For example, in 1931 male life expectancy in

16. Mortality data are no longer available by ethnicity but were collected by most provinces up until 1961. Ontario and British Columbia actually stopped in 1959, but the distribution of deaths by ethnic origins during the last year was used to estimate mortality rates for ethnic populations during the 1961 census year.

Quebec was just 56.2 years at birth, compared to a maximum of 63.5 years in the Prairies. By 1966 their relative positions still remained the same, but the difference in life expectancy had decreased from 7.3 years to just over 2 years. In 1966 life expectancy in Quebec had increased to 67.9, and in Saskatchewan to 70.5 years at birth (Statistics Canada, 1974: Table 6). Thus, it may be inferred that life expectancies for the French (in Quebec), and those ethnic groups concentrated in the prairie provinces, for example, Ukrainians and Germans, would also reflect this regional convergence.

Changes in the Character of the "Other" Ethnic Groups

The shift from the old to the new immigration has brought increasing ethnic heterogeneity to Canada's population. One hundred years ago, 61 per cent of Canada's residents were British and 31 per cent French. Of the remaining population, almost 80 per cent were either German (69 per cent) or Dutch (10 per cent). The only other group having numerical significance appeared to be the native Indian and Eskimo population. Only three other ethnic populations were sufficiently numerous to mention—the Italians, Russians, and Scandinavians. While the northwestern Europeans and their descendents still dominate the ethnic mosaic in 1971, main shifts have occurred with respect to the origins of the immigrant streams. The so-called "new" immigration since the beginning of the twentieth century has produced increasing numbers from central, eastern, and southern Europe. By 1971 immigrants from these areas accounted for almost half of all the "other" ethnics, and Ukrainians and Italians constituted the bulk of these.

Because of highly restrictive immigration policies in the past aimed at non-European cultures, few immigrants came to Canada from the Middle East, Africa, or Asia, prior to the Second World War. In 1871 the census reported 11 Hindus and 21,000 Africans, but no Chinese or Japanese. By 1901 the number of Asians, mostly Chinese, had increased to 23,371, while African Negroes had declined to 17,437. From these shaky and uncertain beginnings, numbers of Asiatics and others of non-European origins have gradually increased but have not consistently increased their relative proportions of the total population. In 1941, during the Second World War, there were only 74,000 Asians, 22,000 Negroes, and 42,000 other non-Europeans and "not-stated" origins. All told, they composed less than 2 per cent of Canada's population at that time.

Following the war and the lifting of wartime restrictions, the scale of immigration increased. This response to the rapid postwar economic growth was made not only by immigrants from both traditional and "new" immigrant sources, but also by immigrants from non-European countries which had been experiencing mounting population pressures. Immigrants from these countries began to increase noticeably during the 1951–61 decade, but when ethnic and racial restrictions were eliminated from the immigration regulations in 1962, the increase during the following decade was dramatic. This development is shown in Table 24.

Immigration statistics on annual arrivals are much more sensitive to shifts in the character of immigrant streams and to trends which may have future significance for both national and local ethnic composition. Since 1971, when immigration began to climb again, these data have registered extremely rapid increases in the number of immigrants coming from certain areas (see Table 25). Partly because of the small numbers, the percentage increase appears astronomical, and because of their concentration in urban centres like Toronto, their visibility perhaps creates an im-

Table 24 Population of Asian and other non-European ethnic origins, Canada, 1901–71.

Ethnic Group	1901	1911	1921	1931	1941	1951	1961	1971
Asian	23,731	43,213	65,914	84,548	74,064	72,827	121,753	285,540
Chinese	17,312	27,831	39,587	46,519	34,627	32,528	58,197	118,815
Japanese	4,738	9,067	15,868	23,342	23,149	21,663	29,157	37,260
Other	1,681	6,315	10,459	14,687	16,288	18,636	34,399	129,460
East Indian					1,465	2,148	6,774	67,925
Syrian-Lebanese					11,857	12,301	19,374	26,665
Other						4,187	8,251	34,870
Other								
Negro	17,437	16,994	18,291	19,456	22,174	18,020	32,127	34,445
Other[a]	31,684	35,242	21,436	9,579	42,028	170,401	210,382	171,645

[a] Includes "unknown".

Source: Censuses of Canada.

Table 25   Immigration to Canada for selected countries of last permanent residence, 1967–1973.

Year	Total Immigration	China[a]	India-Pakistan	West Indies
		Country of Last Permanent Residence		
1967	222,876	6,409	4,614	8,403
1968	183,974	8,382	3,856	7,563
1969	161,531	8,272	6,400	13,093
1970	147,713	5,377	6,680	12,456
1971	121,900	5,817	6,281	10,843
1972	122,006	7,181	6,239	8,233
1973	184,200	16,094	11,488	19,114

[a] 1967–70 figures given for China only, and 1971–73, includes China, Hong Kong, and Taiwan.

Source: Department of Manpower and Immigration, 1974 and 1973.

pression of greater diversity than is, in fact, the case for the population at large. Attempts to reduce the flow of immigrants at such times—purportedly through concern for future unemployment levels—may mask a more fundamental concern over the future ethnic make-up of Canadian society (*Toronto Star*, October 26, 1974: A14).

Regional Changes in Ethnic Concentrations, 1931–71

The unique patterns of regional concentrations for the different ethnic populations in Canada have already been illustrated. If these groups have contributed to the maintenance of cultural diversity in Canada, then their dispersion should be associated with increasing cultural homogeneity. Is there, in fact, any evidence to suggest that these patterns of regional concentrations have been affected by the changes in natural increase and migration noted in the previous section? A comparison of the indexes of relative concentration for selected ethnic groups in 1931 and 1971, shown in Table 26, provides little evidence of any consistent trend toward greater uniformity in their regional distribution. While the French changed very little in this respect during this period, the British concentrations increased in Saskatchewan and Alberta and to an even greater extent in the Atlantic provinces.

Table 26 Indexes of relative concentration for selected origins by province,[a] 1931 and 1971.

Province	Selected Origins						
	British	French	German	Italian	Ukrainian	Jewish	Chinese
1931							
(Base prop.)	(.519)	(.282)	(.046)	(.009)	(.022)	(.015)	(.004)
P. E. Island	161	52	7	4	0	2	9
Nova Scotia	147	39	115	41	8	27	17
New Brunswick	121	119	14	11	0	21	14
Quebec	29	280	8	96	7	139	24
Ontario	143	31	110	164	32	121	50
Manitoba	101	24	118	38	478	184	62
Saskatchewan	92	20	305	13	313	37	95
Alberta	103	19	221	72	347	34	132
British Columbia	136	8	53	196	17	26	977
1971							
(Base prop.)	(.434)	(.293)	(.062)	(.035)	(.028)	(.014)	(.006)
P. E. Island	190	47	14	3	4	4	4
Nova Scotia	179	35	84	14	10	23	20
New Brunswick	133	126	21	6	3	12	15
Quebec	24	269	14	80	12	137	33
Ontario	137	33	100	172	74	125	85
Manitoba	97	30	201	30	413	145	58
Saskatchewan	97	21	314	9	331	17	83
Alberta	108	20	229	44	297	32	132
British Columbia	133	15	146	70	98	40	338

[a] Exclude Newfoundland.

Source: Indexes based on frequency distributions for ethnic populations presented in *1931 Census of Canada*, Vol. 2, Table 31, and *1971 Census of Canada*, Bulletin 1.3–2, Table 2.

The heavy immigrations of the post-Second World War period served to increase the relative concentration of Germans in the Prairies, especially in Manitoba. Since 1931 the existing concentration of Italians in Ontario also increased, while in British Columbia it dropped significantly. The Ukrainians, on the other hand, received little reinforcement of their numbers in the Prairies; hence, their concentration declined in several of the prairie provinces, while increasing in British Columbia and Ontario, and to a lesser extent in the remaining eastern provinces.

Among the smaller minority groups, those of Jewish origin maintained their heavy concentrations in Winnipeg, Montreal, and Toronto, but at slightly lower levels than existed thirty years earlier. Similarly, the Chinese were still heavily concentrated in British Columbia, but to a much lesser extent than before because of a notable shift to eastern Canada. The historical antecedents of Chinese immigration to Canada, responsible for their initial concentration on the West Coast, have become less important since 1931, more especially during the period of economic development and urbanization following the Second World War. Thus, two groups similar in their urban orientation differed significantly from each other in terms of their patterns of settlement, and degree of relative concentration.

Clearly, no consistent trend toward a decline in the regional concentrations of ethnic populations can be detected on the basis of the indexes employed in this analysis. The degree of ethnic concentration decreased in only two of the five largest ethnic groups between 1931 and 1971. One of these, the Ukrainians, showed the greatest decline, but because of their very heavy concentration in the Prairies, they are still the most heavily concentrated of the major ethnic groups in that region. Recent arrivals of those of other ethnic origins can be expected (like the Italians) to concentrate in the rapidly growing urban centres.

The answer then to the earlier question is not a simple one. There is some evidence of convergence in the fertility and mortality of ethnic groups, and therefore in their rates of natural increase. This situation has apparently not affected regional concentrations for the major ethnic populations, however, since they have not shown any uniform tendency to disperse their numbers more evenly, that is, to eliminate unique regional concentrations. On the other hand, recent immigrants, while contributing to greater ethnic diversity, are concentrating in the large urban centres. The differences in distributions for these groups will be found less on the regional level than within the larger metropolitan areas.

Language and the Retention of Culture

Conditions which serve to alter an ethnic group's distinctive character, whether its unique regional or local pattern of residential concentration or its specific demographic character, can also serve to strengthen or weaken a group's commitment to its own culture. One indicator of a culture's viability, and a group's commitment to it, is language retention. The Royal Commission on Bilingualism and Biculturalism emphasized this point by stating that, while it is not the sole condition, "language is a necessary condition for the complete preservation of a culture. . . . The life of two cultures implies in principal the life of two languages" (Royal Commission on Bilingualism and Biculturalism, 1967: xxxvii–xxxviii).

Needless to say, whatever significance language retention has for the maintenance of the French culture and community, it must be equally important for other cultures with distinctive languages and interests in preserving their cultural heritage in Canada. The forces which operate to reduce language retention for the French must pose the same problem for other ethnic language groups in Canada. For example, bilingualism— which is more often a necessity for minority language groups than for dominant ones—appears to be a potentially significant factor in the deterioration of the status and retention of minority mother tongues (Lieberson, 1970: 236–48; Reitz, 1974).

It is not surprising, then, to find that while both the size of the French-speaking population and the number of bilinguals are increasing, the

Table 27 Per cent of French ethnic origin population with French mother tongue, 1931, 1961, and 1971.

Province	1931	1961	1971
Newfoundland	—	—	19.5
Prince Edward Island	77.3	44.5	45.0
Nova Scotia	67.7	42.8	46.0
New Brunswick	94.9	87.6	87.6
Quebec	99.4	98.2	98.0
Ontario	77.4	61.4	60.1
Manitoba	86.0	67.2	63.4
Saskatchewan	78.5	54.4	51.1
Alberta	70.4	46.8	44.2
British Columbia	48.5	33.7	33.3

Source: For 1931 and 1961, see S. Lieberson, 1970: Table 3.
1971 data from special tabulations provided by Statistics Canada.

Table 28 Percentage (1) foreign born, (2) of provincial population, and (3) with mother tongue consistent with ethnicity, for selected ethnic groups, by province and Canada, 1971.

Province	French Origin			German Origin		
	Per Cent Provincial Total	Per Cent Foreign Born	% With French Mother Tongue	Per Cent Provincial Total	Per Cent Foreign Born	% With German Mother Tongue
Newfoundland	3.0	1.8	19.5	0.5	22.7	18.1
Prince Edward Island	13.7	1.2	45.0	0.9	13.0	10.9
Nova Scotia	10.2	2.1	46.0	5.2	5.0	3.5
New Brunswick	37.0	1.1	87.6	1.3	12.5	9.6
Quebec	79.0	1.5	98.0	0.9	41.6	40.8
Ontario	9.6	2.5	60.1	6.2	29.1	33.0
Manitoba	8.8	3.3	63.4	12.5	20.7	55.2
Saskatchewan	6.1	4.5	51.1	19.4	13.0	36.9
Alberta	5.8	5.1	44.2	14.2	21.4	35.2
British Columbia	4.4	6.8	33.3	9.1	30.4	37.7

Province	Italian Origin			Ukrainian Origin		
	Per Cent Provincial Total	Per Cent Foreign Born	% With Italian Mother Tongue	Per Cent Provincial Total	Per Cent Foreign Born	% With Ukrainian Mother Tongue
Newfoundland	0.1	19.2	15.2	—	5.7	17.1
Prince Edward Island	0.1	14.3	4.8	0.1	16.0	12.0
Nova Scotia	0.5	28.0	32.1	0.3	11.7	16.4
New Brunswick	0.2	30.4	28.6	0.1	13.3	18.3
Quebec	2.8	54.4	76.3	0.3	36.6	53.6
Ontario	6.0	56.1	71.7	2.1	28.0	46.4
Manitoba	1.1	51.8	67.0	11.6	14.9	57.4
Saskatchewan	0.3	38.6	41.4	9.3	12.9	57.4
Alberta	1.5	47.6	59.0	8.3	13.5	48.1
British Columbia	2.5	44.4	53.5	2.8	12.2	29.2

Source: Special tabulations, *1971 Census of Canada.*

proportion of the French ethnic population retaining French as a mother tongue is declining. As may be seen in Table 28, this is true for each province as well as for Canada as a whole.

Following 1931, and during the postwar period, rapid economic development and continuing urbanization characterized the Canadian population. Increasing numbers of immigrants with neither English nor French mother tongues flocked to the metropolitan centres to capitalize on the opportunities offered by a rapidly expanding labour market. In addition, the postwar "baby boom" was in full swing during the 1951–61 decade, and the annual population growth rate was a high 2.7 per cent.

Between 1931 and 1951 the proportion of those of French ethnic origin in the population increased from 28 to 31 per cent, then declined slightly during the 1930s and further during the 1960s, reaching 29 per cent in 1971. While the proportion of French in Canada has remained relatively stable, the proportion with French mother tongue dropped significantly everywhere outside Quebec and New Brunswick. Between 1961 and 1971, however, the overall rate of decline slowed. New Brunswick actually remained unchanged while Prince Edward Island and Nova Scotia showed increases, albeit small ones.

Data for the three largest ethnic groups after the French are presented in Table 28. As in the case of the French, the size of these ethnic groups relative to the provincial populations appears to be significant in explaining variations in the proportions of groups reporting mother tongues consistent with their ethnic origin. Its importance varies considerably, however, from one ethnic group to another (Lieberson, 1970: 36–37).

In addition to relative size, the proportion of foreign born is also a factor, but for the French its effect appears to be opposite of that for the other groups. The obvious weakness of using the proportion of an ethnic group with a specified mother tongue as a measure of language retention is that it is unduly affected by large proportions of foreign born. Their presence alone would create a higher rate of language retention, without necessarily revealing the language-retention tendencies of later generations of native born. The high retention rates for the relatively small non-French ethnic groups in Quebec may be due to a higher proportion of foreign born in their ranks. Yet the presence of relatively large numbers of foreign born could still exert its own independent affect on the language retention of second and later generations. As is shown in the following section, language retention for the corresponding mother tongue groups of native born is also highest in these two provinces.

Learning a language as a child, and still understanding it in later years, is a necessary part of language retention. Yet unless a language is also used in the home, it is very unlikely that it will be passed along to following generations. Because the language behaviour of the second and later generations of native born is perhaps more critical in the retention link, data on language most often used in the home, in relation to one's mother tongue, are presented in Table 29 for the five major mother-tongue groups in Canada, by region.

Language retention is greatest, or language transfer least, for those with English mother tongue everywhere except in Quebec, where 8 per cent of those with English mother tongue used another language in the home. By contrast, only 2 per cent of those with French mother tongue used another language.

After the native born who had learned French as a child, the next highest retention rate for Canada as a whole is found among those with Italian mother tongues. Regional exceptions are found in the Atlantic provinces, where its retention rate is the lowest, and in British Columbia, where it is second highest among the five largest linguistic groups. Of additional interest is the fact that the Italian mother-tongue population in Quebec is the only group in Quebec, besides the French, which has a larger proportion using French in the home than English.

Table 29 Language most often spoken at home, when same as mother tongue, as a percentage of selected mother tongue groups of native born, by region, 1971.

Mother-Tongue Group	Language Most Often Spoken at Home Same as Mother Tongue					
	Total	Atlantic Provinces	Quebec	Ontario	Prairie Provinces	British Columbia
English	99.0	99.7	92.5	99.3	99.4	99.5
French	94.2	86.2	98.5	70.5	53.6	25.3
German	27.4	12.0	28.8	32.3	27.9	17.2
Italian	57.9	10.0	61.2	60.5	41.6	35.3
Ukrainian	28.5	11.6	42.3	28.7	29.8	9.4

Source: *1971 Census of Canada*, Bulletin 1.4–11.

Language retention among the native born with German and Ukrainian mother tongues is generally low, but it is unusually high for the Ukrainians in Quebec; for Germans it is highest in Ontario. Language retention, in general, tends to be highest for the native born in the two central provinces of Ontario and Quebec, and lower as one travels either east or west of these two provinces.

The circumstances which tend to strengthen or weaken language facility and usage are obviously complex. While regional variations in ethnic distributions, the presence of foreign born, and their size relative to the dominant language group are necessary parts of any explanation, they are clearly not sufficient in themselves. In terms of overall language patterns, the situation in Canada has remained quite stable. This is undoubtedly a reflection, in part, of the relatively large size of the two major language groups and their unique distributions relative to each other. Even so, as Lieberson has pointed out, it would be a mistake to assume that the situation is a static one, rather than one resulting from a state of equilibrium based on counterbalancing forces (Lieberson, 1970: 35). Nowhere is this more apparent at the present time than in Quebec, where the government continues to act on the assumption that the ever-present forces of language erosion must be continuously fought. Like any other ethnic group, the position of the French in Canada can be enhanced or weakened by changes in fertility and immigration. With these factors currently working against Quebec and its French-speaking population, the government must seek other measures to ensure the survival of its language.[17]

Concluding Note

Canada has experienced its own demographic transition and is approaching what appears to be the upper limits of its urbanization. Talk of zero population growth, though currently fashionable, is mainly an academic pastime. It will be difficult for Canada to stabilize its population at the relatively low and ideal level that would be necessary to maintain an

17. Bill 22 is the latest and one of the more controversial attempts being made by Quebec to ensure the survival of the French language in Canada. By requiring the children of non-English mother tongue immigrants to attend schools giving instruction in French, they hope to reinforce the status of French as the working language in that province as well as one of the two official languages.

optimal balance between numbers and resources, especially at a time when population pressures in the underdeveloped areas of the world are increasing rapidly.

Even if Canada's population growth is stabilized at some future point, it would not mean that its structure and character would be forever fixed. Fluctuating fertility, in response to changing socio-economic conditions and individual preferences, will continue to produce its characteristic structural waves, and the input through immigration will vary in response to changes in conditions throughout the world relative to those in Canada.

While the French and English have provided the basic structures for demographic comparisons in this analysis, it is quite possible for either or both to be supplanted by some other more idealized structural model. For simplicity, comparison with the United States was minimized, but this was not intended to imply that its political and economic position has no relevance for Canada's demographic character or experience. Increasingly, changes external to Canada are affecting internal events and shaping its future. Social and political developments, as well as technological change in other countries, will continue to have direct repercussions on the character of Canadian society.

Changes in Canada's two founding groups have reflected some of the consequences of urbanization and industrialization. The British and French ethnic populations will continue to change, as they must, in response to new conditions. If they fall behind or fail to adapt, however, they may cease to serve as appropriate models for the integration of the other ethnic populations into Canadian society. At one point in time the British were able to capitalize on the political and economic opportunities which prevailed, and in so doing, set the pattern for British-French relations to this day. There is nothing to suggest that the present mix and pattern of ethnic relationships in Canada is inviolate. That things will change is perhaps the most certain of the future's uncertainties.

Select Bibliography

BESHERS, J. M. *Population Processes in Social Systems*. New York: The Free Press, 1967.

BLADEN, V. W., ed. *Canadian Population and Northern Colonization*. Toronto: University of Toronto Press, 1962.

CORBETT, D. C. *Canada's Immigration Policy*. Toronto: University of Toronto Press, 1957.

DENTON, F. T., and OSTRY, S. *Historical Estimates of the Canadian Labour Force.* 1961 Census Monograph. Ottawa: The Queen's Printer, 1967.

ELLIOTT, JEAN LEONARD, ed. *Minority Canadians: Immigrant Groups.* Scarborough: Prentice-Hall, 1971.

GEORGE, M. V. *Internal Migration in Canada.* 1961 Census Monograph. Ottawa: The Queen's Printer, 1970.

GRINDSTAFF, C. F.; BOYDELL, C.; and WHITEHEAD, P. C. *Population Issues in Canada.* Toronto: Holt, Rinehart and Winston, 1971.

HAWKINS, F. *Canada and Immigration.* Montreal: McGill-Queen's University Press, 1972.

HENRIPIN, JACQUES. *Trends and Factors of Fertility in Canada.* 1961 Census Monograph. Ottawa: The Queen's Printer, 1972.

KALBACH, W. E. *The Impact of Immigration on Canada's Population.* Ottawa: The Queen's Printer, 1970.

———, and MCVEY, W. W. *The Demographic Bases of Canadian Society.* Toronto: McGraw-Hill, 1971.

LIEBERSON, STANLEY. *Language and Ethnic Relations in Canada.* New York: John Wiley, 1970.

MARSDEN, L. R. *Population Probe.* Toronto: Copp Clark, 1972.

OSTRY, SYLVIA. *The Occupational Composition of the Canadian Labour Force.* 1961 Census Monograph. Ottawa: The Queen's Printer, 1967.

———. *The Female Worker in Canada.* 1961 Census Monograph. Ottawa: The Queen's Printer, 1968.

PODOLUK, JENNY R. *Incomes of Canadians.* 1961 Census Monograph. Ottawa: The Queen's Printer, 1968.

PORTER, JOHN. *The Vertical Mosaic: An Analysis of Social Class and Power in Canada.* Toronto: University of Toronto Press, 1965.

RICHMOND, ANTHONY H. *Post-War Immigrants in Canada.* Toronto: University of Toronto Press, 1967.

Statistics Canada. *Perspective Canada.* Ottawa: Information Canada, 1974.

STONE, L. O. *Urban Development in Canada.* 1961 Census Monograph. Ottawa: The Queen's Printer, 1967.

———. *Migration in Canada: Regional Aspects.* 1961 Census Monograph.

WRIGLEY, E. A. *Population and History.* Toronto: McGraw-Hill, 1969.

WRONG, DENNIS. *Population and Society.* 3rd ed. New York: Random House, 1967.

The Sociology of Communication

THELMA McCORMACK

All human behaviour is communicative. From the simplest act of knocking on a neighbour's door to an elaborate investiture ceremony, from breast feeding a hungry infant to signing the Magna Carta, from a "consciousness raising" discussion group to a picket line of striking workers around a factory, from a prayer meeting to a guerrilla raid on a peasant village—there is no form of social interaction that does not carry within it a structure and content which together constitute its social meaning. When social interactions cease to have any meaning to their participants they are no longer relationships in any real sense of the word. Instead they become chance encounters, just as on a larger scale when institutional relationships have no meaning, communities and larger social collectivities become loose, drifting aggregates. Thus, to study human behaviour at all is to study communication.

But it is in the twentieth century that scholars and thoughtful people have defined communication as a critical problem. Many believe that the crisis of modern societies is one of communication, a breakdown of interpersonal communication and a failure of the great communication institutions—the press and broadcasting. Poverty, racial conflict, international tension, crime, and other indicators of social dislocation are all seen as measures of alienation or the erosion of commitment, which in turn are both cause and effect of an inability to communicate. So it is not surprising that many persons look to communication for answers to these and other problems.

Different critics offer different ways, but all come round sooner or later to the mass media of communication. Are they the great hope? Can they provide unity where there is discord? Or are they the most destructive force in our cultural life, undermining traditional values and weakening the will or the capacity to participate actively in social life? It is not necessary to agree with either of these extreme positions to recognize that social policy in the remaining years of the century will have to deal more forthrightly with the media than has been done in the past, and that the tendency among many Canadians to regard the media as mere entertainment will be an immense obstacle to overcome.

In this chapter we shall examine primarily the mass media of communication in Canada, but before doing so we must look at the more general problem of communication and society.

The Study of Communication

Because communication is ubiquitous and because every act we engage in is communicative, it is difficult to define communication as a subject of study. In theory it has no boundaries; it is a process, like breathing, which energizes all relationships. Any effort, therefore, to delimit communication is bound to seem arbitrary and to do injustice to so pervasive a phenomenon. Yet, here as elsewhere in the social sciences, a working definition must by the rules of logic—themselves the object of study— exclude as well as include. Bearing in mind, then, the problematic and provisional nature of the definition, we can restrict ourselves to those forms of social interaction which have as their most prominent component a form of symbolic expression. In other words, although all forms of human behaviour are communicative, not all forms of human behaviour are *acts* of communication. The study of communication, then, is the study of how symbolic systems—art, knowledge, religion, science, journalism, popular culture—mediate human relations.

Research in communications typically focuses on three areas: content, the initiating agents or institutions, and audiences. Content analysis may examine the themes, images, or deeper structure of novels, songs, speeches, news bulletins, films, myths, and plays, while research on the institutions may look at the organization, economics, and control of publishing, broadcasting, schools, and museums. Audience research includes investigations of the size, social composition, habits, and, of course, the most intriguing problem of all, the impact of the media on the attitudes and behaviour of audiences.

Questions concerning the historical emergence, social function, and situational use differentiate the sociological perspective on communications from the engineering one, which is primarily concerned with patterns of sound frequencies, or from the physiologist's, which examines how the brain sends and receives signals. Some scholars, like the late Norbert Wiener, the father of cybernetics, believe that there are basic laws common to all forms of communication, and that a knowledge of these laws could unify all of the sciences (Wiener, 1954; 1961). But this vision has yet to be realized; meanwhile each discipline goes its own way.

One reason so little progress has been made toward the unification of all the sciences under the rubric of communication is that for sociologists the term communication has a different connotation than it has for the engineer or physiologist. For the latter two, communication is the transmission of information between two points, between parties, or from one part of the system to another. It is a rational process distorted by "noise" rather than sentiment, by impaired switching rather than values. As a consequence of these disturbances, the system (individuals or organizations) may be misguided in the same way that an aircraft may go off course when its radar system fails.

For the sociologist, however, communication is a cultural phenomenon. Our social norms, values, traditions, and knowledge constitute social reality, which is the prism through which we experience ourselves and others. Although we treat social reality as if it were something outside of ourselves and external to us, it is internalized, sensitizing us to certain types of information and not to others and screening new experience through our values and past experience. Facts that come to our attention may be disregarded as irrelevant, but they are rarely neutral; each fact or cluster of facts is valued in some way. For example, if a scalding liquid is spilled accidentally on the arm, the brain reacts the same way whether the liquid is water, tea, or coffee. But in social life or in a culture where tea and coffee are forbidden or water is scarce and highly valued, the distinction between the three liquids is of enormous importance for our own reactions. The logic of this distinction will escape the physiologist, for whom all the liquids are the same, but it is all too evident to the sociologist that water and coffee evoke different sentiments and social sanctions. In other words, social logic follows different rules; it serves normative integration before truth, strengthening social bonds, preserving and developing a sense of community. Pure reason, as the logician understands it, is secondary to social reason.

Communication, then, involves the social meaning of information. The process of communicating, moreover, is not transmission along wires or paths of the nervous system which are open to external stimuli. When we communicate we are acting upon the world, persuading others to accept reality as we perceive it, and being persuaded, in turn, by others to accept their views. Out of this process of consensual validation we develop a stronger sense of shared experience, of social order, of our ability to control our own lives and events which may impinge upon us.

Communicating effectively is a social strategy. All of us have had the experience of hearing two people tell the same joke; one can ruin it, while the other can convulse us with laughter. It is a question of *style*, and also of *structure*. Poetry moves us differently from a scientific report, although both may be describing the moon; a funeral elegy moves us differently from a political oration, since one touches our grief, the other our political preferences. *Sequence* is important too. A misplaced pause in a speech may tell us that the speaker has forgotten his words and we begin to feel embarrassed for him, while a pause properly placed will heighten a sense of dramatic suspense.

The fascination with mediating strategies of communication, however, should not obscure the larger fact that meaning is always related to *culture* and *context*. The wartime speeches of Winston Churchill were greatly enhanced by the mood of the free world in 1940 and by his ability to reassure his listeners that the values they cherished would be preserved. The same speeches today sound "corny", excessively rhetorical and bathetic, while Hitler's orations sound ludicrous.

Verbal and Nonverbal Communication

In face-to-face or interpersonal relationships, a great deal can be said by gesture, posture, or facial expression. A shrug, scowl, salute, pat on the rump, wink, clenched fist, or tears may speak louder than words. In recent years, anthropologists have broadened our knowledge of "body language" and other forms of nonverbal communication. Thanks to their research, we are aware that rich and subtle vocabularies are possible without speech. Yet all human societies develop spoken languages, and in some, speaking may be the most highly developed form, praised and admired by those who are inarticulate or who have less verbal virtuosity. Our impatience with the "blabbermouth" who talks too much and too indiscriminately or our irritation with the person who "loves the sound of his own voice" testifies to the fact that in our society speaking can be so intrinsically pleasurable that the speaker may lose sight of his goals and risk the relationship by boring or antagonizing the listener.

Although all societies develop a spoken language, not all of them develop a written language. The reasons are not clear, but a written language and literacy have many advantages. Documents and sacred texts can be preserved so that future generations do not have to depend upon the selective memories of their immediate predecessors to reconstruct their history. Through a written language, too, social ties may be maintained without the persons being physically present. It is interesting to speculate on why in our society the written word carries more authority than the spoken. Why do we demand that agreements be put in writing, that written records of transactions be kept, that after the sacred vows of marriage a contract must be signed?

When our written language can be translated into another language or when we can understand, read, and write a foreign language our community is extended. A Canadian farmer who lives in a rural village and has never travelled much beyond may be able to empathize with a Japanese worker in Tokyo; a Soviet engineer can compare his or her life with a British peer; twentieth-century business executives can relate to fourteenth-century priests; high-school teachers in Athens, Ontario, can re-create the Athens of Plato for students. A written language multiplies the possibilities of communication, widening and deepening our social imagination so that we are less dependent on our immediate and indigenous experience.

Stretching ourselves as social and historical persons we exercise a talent no other species has. But it is not an infinite talent, for all of us have blinders, a point beyond which we are unable to go: we can translate the words but fail to understand them. The schizophrenic patient, for example, has a logic that is impenetrable by the untrained lay person who hears only a jumble of words. Similarly, we may dismiss as illogical or prelogical an ancient civilization because the thought patterns reflected in its language are beyond our comprehension.

Communication and Social Structure

Whether the system of communication is verbal, nonverbal, written, or a combination of these, all societies, including the most reticent, develop sublanguages. There are formal languages for rituals and ceremonial occasions and informal languages for everyday life; sacred languages for relationships with authorities and profane languages for peers; a proper language and a tabooed language; an in-group or "we" language for friends who are trusted and an out-group or "thou" language for strangers who are not. What these sublanguages do is establish social boundaries. When the boundaries are trespassed, when private languages are used in public places, family languages with outsiders, discourteous language with officials, and formal language with peers, the offender may elicit ridicule, ostracism, and even more serious penalties. The Anglophone visitor to Quebec who uses the "tu" form where the "vous" form is called for may be surprised by the reaction. Accents and abuses of grammar can be forgiven as long as language decorum is observed.

A complex division of labour adds more sublanguages to our repertoire. Professional athletes, doctors, construction workers, x-ray technicians, entertainers, social workers, accountants, farmers, telephone repairmen, secretaries, bank tellers, and printers all use a glossary of terms unfamiliar to persons in occupations other than their own. Role differentiation adds further sublanguages which every child must learn early in life if he is to get along in school, on the playground, at his grandparents, in the hospital, etc.

Most of these sublanguages are accessible to all of us. But certain languages are accessible to some and not to others, and it is this differential inaccessibility that suggests that language, like money, can be a form of power. Three forms of inaccessibility are worth noting. The first is the oldest and best known: the secret code. Diplomats, criminals, and adolescents, among others, develop clandestine languages intended to exclude or deceive. They are privileged languages for members who qualify, and they are meant to distance those who do not. As soon as the enemy breaks the diplomatic code, the police figure out the argot of the underworld, or adults break through the barrier of teenage idioms, each of the invaded groups re-invents a new private language. It is a measure of our linguistic ingenuity that we can do this so easily and so well.

The second type of exclusion is the technical language of scientists, which is unintentionally inaccessible. The purposes of scientific language are to state relationships with exactness and to develop a system of communication which scientists, regardless of their cultural background and mother tongue, can all understand. In that way the scientific community is extended. But in doing so, the rest of the community may be excluded to such a degree that the scientific community possesses enormous power without being accountable to anyone but themselves. If they can then control recruitment into their small community through the educational system, they can perpetuate themselves as an élite despite the controls of a democratic society.

A third type of inaccessibility is a technological one. Increasingly, government agencies, credit organizations, the police, and social agencies collect information and data without our knowledge—records which are then stored in computers. The information may be inaccurate or unfair, but how would we know? Yet, even if we were able to find out, there is a question of who else has access to this information through the data bank. Canadians are increasingly concerned, for example, about information concerning Canadian citizens and Canadian resources now stored in data banks outside of the country. How can we be sure that the information is kept confidential and could not be used against us (*Instant World*, 1971)?

At the other end of the spectrum is a sublanguage of maximum accessibility, a public language which is seldom spoken in casual conversation yet is familiar to all. It is the language of democratic governments, of elected officials, of advertising, and of the mass media of communication. What all of these bodies have in common is that they address us, the public, as members of an abstract entity, as if we had no class, regional, ethnic, religious, or other social attributes. To governments as well as merchandisers we are all alike as citizens and as consumers. Since that is hardly the case, the public language has an artificial quality about it which gives the impression of being meant for everyone but no one.

Communication and Social Inequality

The proliferation of sublanguages in modern societies means that each person must learn several languages. Consider that in a period of two hours a university student can communicate in one genre with professors, another with fellow students, still another with parents, not to mention a fourth with university administrators, a fifth with the clerk in a store, a sixth with the police officer who has stopped the student for speeding, a seventh with immigrant grandparents, an eighth with a new baby in the household, and a ninth with an employer.

This remarkable skill for learning and using so many languages is only minimally related to intelligence or IQ. It is a capacity of the brain all human beings share. Is this argument not oversimplified? Forms of retardation or brain damage are the only constraints on this natural gift. Whether and how this capacity is developed depend largely on our social structure. If we have developed this language skill to a high degree it is not because we are endowed with superior intelligence compared to people living in less complex societies, but because the world we inhabit could not be negotiated otherwise.

Within our own society, however, the opportunity to practise this skill is not equally available to all people. As a result there are people who are communications poor while others are communications rich. The former may communicate extremely well within a narrow, homogeneous social sector, but are handicapped when they venture beyond that sector or aspire to a wider world; they can "rap" but they cannot write a legal brief or a letter to their MP. Thus, one of the functions of education in a modern society is to teach communication skills to people who might conceivably get through life very well without them on the condition that they remain within their own primary groups.

Education itself, however, is part of our social structure. Class differences, for example, are often reinforced by our educational system. A cockney Liza Doolittle could, after extensive coaching by Professor Higgins, move out of her working-class milieu and into high society by learning to speak not better, but different English, the English of the upper classes. But she is the exception which proves the rule, for language is an immensely powerful tool in creating and emphasizing the lines of social inequality.

Privileged groups who enjoy more of the rewards than others do can control the language, defining what is acceptable and what is not, what is preferred and what is vulgar. Consider, for example, the following words: "subsidies", "welfare", and "allowances". To an economist and to a tax-payer they are all variants of the same thing, public monies given to persons not engaged in productive activity. But farmers, the backbone of society, receive "subsidies"; mothers, always to be honoured, receive "allowances"; and the poor receive "welfare". Of the three terms, welfare is pejorative, and it is only of the poor that we say they are "receiving something for nothing". How different the unemployed would look to us if they were described as receiving "subsidies", and farmers were described as receiving "welfare", while the respectable middle-class housewife, cashing her family allowance check, her unearned income, would be aggrieved if she were described as receiving a "hand-out".

By controlling the language, groups in power can shape their own self-image and thereby justify their position. Others—the poor, ethnic minorities, native peoples, women—are portrayed in the media of communication as being less equal: less intelligent if intelligence is valued, less decisive if decisiveness is valued, less brave if bravery is valued. Believing this to be a true reflection of themselves, the disadvantaged groups accept the rightness of others to rule or decide for them without a shot being fired. Language is not the basis of class structure, but no class structure could last for long without the yardstick of language.

Examples of groups who control language depreciate other, less powerful groups might include a white middle-class teacher who makes invidious comments regarding the speech patterns of a working-class child, or a missionary teacher who prohibits her charges from speaking their native Indian language or expressing their Indian culture. In each example, the child may fail to meet the cultural and linguistic standards of the middle-class teacher and, in the process of repeatedly falling short of expected behaviour, may develop very low aspirations and a poor self-concept. This in turn could lead to further failures, and the child would become involved in a self-fulfilling prophecy of failure. An additional example would include women, who have only just begun to discover the way in which their subordinate status has been sustained by inane stereotypes of them in school texts and in the media. But whether we are talking about women or native peoples, the principle is the same: one way a power structure is maintained and perpetuated is through language.

Once this principle is understood it is easy to see why every radical, insurgent, protest, or liberation movement in history gives high priority to restoring to itself the right to define itself. The current struggle in Quebec on the part of French Canadians to make French the official language of the province is but one in a long series of similar efforts by have-nots to rid themselves of a sense of inferiority, to develop a sense of self-worth through the use of its own language.

Communication Content, Technology, and Social Causation

Generally speaking, what disaffected groups object to is the content, the images of themselves in communication systems. Militant women, for example, complain of being constantly portrayed as moronic sex kittens in advertising, as emotionally unstable neurotics in TV soap operas, as incapable of thinking about anything other than child-rearing, food, and housekeeping in women's magazines. Similarly, the politically conscious poor protest at being described as lazy, self-indulgent, gullible welfare chisellers who are endowed with more brawn than brain. But for one group of thinkers, social change is influenced not by the content of communication, but by its technology; in Marshall McLuhan's words, "the medium is the message."

Harold Innis (1950), a distinguished Canadian economic historian and a mentor of McLuhan, was among the earliest to discuss the importance of communications technology. At the University of Chicago Innis had been a student of William Ogburn, a sociologist who had a particular interest in how new and changing forms of technology—the automobile, telephone, new weapons—altered our social life. Unfortunately, according to Ogburn, our thinking patterns were slower to change than our technology, resulting in a discrepancy which he called "cultural lag" (Ogburn, 1966).

Innis drew a distinction between economic and social technology, or between economic resources such as rivers, railroads, and trade routes, and social resources, language, and writing. Economic technology can produce wealth, but only social technology could link disparate social groups and weld a society together. Pursuing this further, he examined how different communication technologies shaped history.

Starting from the assumption that the two co-ordinates of empire were time and space, Innis contrasted societies which kept their records on heavy, untransportable stone with those who used light, transportable, but perishable parchment. The former endured by transcending time, the latter by transcending space. Accordingly, civilizations could be classified on the basis of their communications technology, whether it favoured overcoming the time or the space dimension. Emphasis on one at the expense of the other, however, made for vulnerability and easy conquest by an outside group stronger in the other direction. In turn, this group had its own fatal flaw, its own internal instability, so that history became the rise and fall of empires through their own communications technology imbalance.

McLuhan, like Innis, is a technological determinist, but McLuhan is more interested in how technologies of communication change our mind sets rather than our social systems. Specifically, McLuhan (1964) has argued that the new electronic media—radio and television—are displacing the pre-eminence of the older print media, and in so doing are replacing sequential or linear thinking with circuitry. Linear thinking, the product of print media, is divisive, separating and isolating people from each other, but the new type of thinking would restore the communal sense typical of preliterate oral cultures. The key difference between the two forms of media is that the print media are "hot" or informational and analytic; they could not, therefore, involve us. The electronic media were "cool" or unstructured, and must involve us just as an unstructured Rorschach card maximizes personal projections; whatever you see in it, you have put there. The future, according to McLuhan, would be a global village, macro in scale but micro in style.

Modern sociologists have been critical of single-factor theories of social causation and of technological determinism. Social change is a complex phenomenon, and it is doubtful if we can account for all the variations by reducing everything to one factor, material or non-material. As for technological determinism, it is easy to assert but difficult to prove that a given form of technology, whether it is the cotton gin or the supersonic jet, has determinate social consequences.

The best-known critique of technological determinism is Max Weber's study of *The Protestant Ethic and the Spirit of Capitalism* (1958). Weber notes that the technological development of many countries in Europe was about at the same level in the fifteenth century, but capitalism developed first and most prominently in countries where the Protestant Reformation had occurred. Ostensibly a religious movement, the new doctrines provided people with a new set of motives and values which he called the Protestant Ethic. They were the motives and values of an entrepreneurial outlook; hence, capitalism. The thrust of Weber's argument was that values were more decisive than material factors, although the latter may be a necessary condition and precede the former in time. Critics of Weber have claimed that the Protestant Ethic merely rationalized what was already a *fait accompli*; others have maintained that the crucial variable in the development of capitalism was neither technology nor values but the managerial knowledge of how to organize.

While this debate about capitalism may seem remote from our inquiry here, the terms of the debate can be found in discussions of the impact of new communications technology, in particular, the "wired city". Every home would have its own computer terminal; we could shop, bank, vote, and send and receive messages at home. Statements are made about the social and political impact of home terminals, on the assumption that once a technology exists or can be created by engineers it constitutes a given or a fixed variable to which we adapt, and on the further assumption that the range of social adaptations, for better or for worse, are determined by the technology itself. But who created the technology and why? Was it a priority of the business community or was it one of our priorities? Does the 25 per cent of Canadians who live below the poverty line constitute a "demand" for home terminals that would permit us to do our banking at home? Or is the "demand" created by the big telecommunications industries for business but anxious to sell this hardware as a social convenience? In other words, technological innovation and technological development are not mysterious processes which take place without any human intervention; someone makes the decisions, and the questions are who makes them and to whom are these people accountable? Throughout most of our history it has been the business community that has made our technology without consulting the people who live with its results. Only now have we begun to question the mystique of uncontrolled development; yet many people continue to believe that technology is something we must adapt to, rather than the other way round.

Communications as a Social Institution

Communications technology is a special case of technology; for as Innis correctly perceived, it is a social technology. We can examine it, therefore, as we might any other social institution such as the family, church, or school. The first question one asks about a social institution is what are its functions? The second, how well does the particular form operate? And the third, what alternatives are available? But before we can answer any of these questions we need to state more clearly what is meant by the term the "mass media of communication".

CHARACTERISTICS OF THE MASS MEDIA

Newspapers, magazines, paperback books, radio broadcasting, television, motion pictures, and popular music are what are generally referred to as the mass media of communication. It is sometimes helpful to distinguish between the news media, such as newspapers, and the entertainment media, such as motion pictures. But in many countries this distinction would not hold since all the media are news media. In any event, the common characteristic of these forms of communication is that they are mediated by a technology. Unlike face-to-face communication or primary group communication, the sender and receiver do not encounter each other directly and usually do not know each other personally.

The technology itself is special, designed for uninterrupted mass production and mass distribution. Large investments of capital and a large, stable labour force are required to keep it operational. On both counts, the mass media of communication are dissimilar to the smoke signals or drum beats used to send messages in preliterate societies—communication systems which are neither capital- nor labour-intensive. They are also unlike person-to-person or point-to-point communication, which is a private, individual service on demand.

The second thing to note about the mass media of communication is that they typically have large, heterogeneous mass audiences. The mass audience is a twentieth-century phenomenon, the result of technology, mass education, and increasing leisure. A market was created for cheaply produced and cheaply distributed periodicals and newspapers which developed a new kind of culture, popular culture. The élite culture of earlier times lost its monopoly but kept its prestige. In volume, however, it was the new, classless popular culture which became dominant in the press; sound broadcasting gave it its final thrust forward and television completed the process. Popular culture, by definition, caters to the tastes and interests of young and old, skilled and unskilled, native born and immigrant, university graduates and persons with grade-school education. Every effort is made to broaden coverage, to avoid alienating any single or sizable group by sticking to the familiar, to clichés and stereotypes, to bland rather than controversial material, with the result that the quality of the media's content ranges from low-brow to middle-brow, from tabloid sensationalism to "kitsch".

Critics who regard mass taste as uncultivated and banal are offended by media content as are those who think the mass media should be used to raise cultural levels rather than acquiesce in them; still others regard the concept of "mass" itself as antithetical to a genuine local grass-roots culture (McCormack, 1969: 220–37). Be that as it may, the mass media are differentiated from other forms of communication by being directed toward total coverage of the public.

A third characteristic of the mass media of communication is that exposure to it is voluntary. No one is legally required to read a daily newspaper or to watch television; no penalties are invoked against those who seldom attend movies or listen to the radio. Broadcasters and publishers often envy teachers who have captive audiences, while educators sometimes say that teachers might do a better job of communication if school or class attendance were voluntary. The media must attract the public, convincing them to give up competing demands for leisure time. Despite complaints from publishers and broadcasters about the public's willingness to be distracted by other activities, the media are more often competing with one another than they are with other types of leisure attractions.

Although the media must court their audiences, the public is, in general, favourably disposed. Almost everyone in modern societies engages in some form of media activity, and with few exceptions the habit develops early in life and continues into old age. In some cases, the media habit is so strong that we can speak of media addiction. Strangely enough, people want several media: AM and FM radio, daily and weekly newspapers, magazines, motion pictures, television, paperbacks, LP records, and whatever else might be available. McLuhan notwithstanding, the electronic media have not displaced the print media as the automobile did the horse and buggy. Instead, as new media are introduced, the older media accommodate them, and most people are multi-media users. To the extent that older media face extinction or hardship, such as some magazines have experienced with the flight of advertising from the print to the electronic media, the cause is economics rather than public apathy.

Finally, the media employ large numbers of persons for whom media work is a career and a life-style. As with most forms of work, legends, stories of heroic feats, inside jokes, and traditions develop which are passed on to young persons who enter the field. The novices soon learn the norms of the work, the rules of the organization, and become conscious of themselves as media people. Although most persons in the media in Canada are unionized, strikes are relatively infrequent, and among editorial workers they may be over policies related to their freedom to do their job rather than to wages and hours.

As in most jobs, people with like interests form social bonds so that relationships established at work carry over into social life. These relationships may cut across media lines. Sports writers and sports broadcasters, for example, may know one another better than they know other people in their own medium; they tend to form a media culture, and are regarded as distinctive by others outside of the sports field.

Although there are many subgroups within the media, they all share a common political culture, which, in democratic societies, is built around a belief in freedom of expression. Secrecy and censorship are abhorrent to most of us, but much more so to journalists and public-affairs broadcasters. Typically, journalists resist efforts to censor their work, whether the limitations are imposed by editors, publishers, advertisers, church groups, or other community pressure groups. To the extent that audiences and readers do not share this credo with the same enthusiasm or awe, there is a latent tension between the media culture and the larger society.

The more liberal a community is, the less tension there will be. Even so, a conflict of norms periodically surfaces. Ardent civil libertarians, for example, who defend freedom of expression against the would-be censors may still question whether justice and the citizen's right to a fair trial are served when journalists who have been given confidential information refuse a court subpoena to turn over their notes and tapes. Why should journalists be different from other citizens? And do not justice and the citizen's right to a fair trial represent higher values than freedom of expression? Not to the working journalists, who vigorously maintain that it would be impossible to function if they could not give informants a guarantee that the information they give will not be used against them.

Thus, there is an irreconcilable conflict between the duties of the profession and those of the citizen, between the culture of the media and the
public interest which defines each.

THE INTEGRATIVE FUNCTION OF THE MEDIA*

The characteristics of the mass media of communication listed here apply
to the contemporary scene in North America. They are the culmination
of a long process going back in time to that watershed of modern history,
the transition from feudal to bourgeois society in the sixteenth century.
Most of the trends which we today regard as indicators of modernization
were present at the time of Martin Luther. Rapid population growth,
increasing urbanization, increasing division of labour, and massive
migration were among the major changes and were responsible for up-
rooting large populations from their settled lives, dislodging them from
established, traditional values. People were pouring into cities where
cities had never before existed, and into villages and towns that soon
became cities. The new urban populations often lacked urban skills; many
had no knowledge of how to use a new currency or no experience in
purchasing goods and services. Older forms of authority and systems of
social control appropriate to an agricultural economy and rural social
life were strained in the new environments, where people with widely
different backgrounds encountered one another as strangers. At the same
time the new scientific ethos of the seventeenth century further undermined the authority and prestige of tradition and traditional leaders. In
the eighteenth and nineteenth centuries, industrialization took the process
an additional step by breaking up the old craft skills and the guild
organizations that had developed around them.

In Canada, and in North America generally, these trends took place at
a faster pace than they had in Europe. In North America, the European
feudal social structure had never been as deeply entrenched, so the New
World had fewer resistances to modernization. But the problems were in
many ways the same. People found themselves in an environment characterized by change, confusion, frequent crises, and the absence of firm
guides for behaviour. They were struggling to make sense of their world
without a social map and without map makers in whom they had confi-

*See McCormack, 1961: 479–87.

dence. Formerly, they had understood their environment through direct experience; all necessary knowledge could be gained first-hand and had been familiar to preceding generations. But the modern world was too fragmented, too differentiated, and too diffuse to be completely understood by any one person. Furthermore, yesterday's wisdom was often today's doubtful proposition. In this situation, the most worldly and best-educated persons were as helpless as the least, for no matter how hard they tried to understand their world totally, their views of reality based on first-hand experience would always be incomplete. They could not, therefore, always anticipate the consequences of their own actions or understand how the actions of others would impinge on them. In short, the processes of modernization created an acute problem of communication, and the more modernized a society is, the more endemic is the problem.

Against this background, the communication media structure the world for people uncertain of their directions and of the future. This situation is as true today as it was when the processes of modernization began, for the more we sense that our social universe is changing in ways which could alter our lives, the more we experience anxiety and seek information to help orient ourselves.

But what is "information"? An event like an election? A condition like pollution? A trend like inflation? A development like a new approach to cancer? A causal connection between cholesterol and heart trouble? A proof like showing that the "facts" a politician told his constituents were lies? A judgment like knowing which facts are important and which trivial? All of these are forms of information which help us to order and demystify a strange environment where the unexpected must be expected.

Information is only part of the integrative function of the media of communication. Equally important are conceptions and images of social behaviour. What is right and wrong, ethical and unethical, legal and illegal, proper and improper? And what are the rules in making these and similar judgments? Whose lives can serve as models for us? To whom are we accountable and who is accountable to us? These and similar questions lie along a normative axis rather than a cognitive one. Together they set the stage for social integration.

Historically, the problems of integration were most serious in the crowded urban industrial centres, where neighbours were strangers with different values, different habits, and different life-styles. It was here that the media first developed. This fact casts doubt on the Innis thesis that the function of communication is to reduce the social isolation of physical space and physical time, since it was precisely in the areas of dense population where there was too little space and too much time that the media became important. In these environments the obstacles to co-operation and common understanding were social ambiguity and social conflict, and it was to these that the media were a response. Problems of physical space and physical time may beset military and political élites; they may frustrate traders, financiers, and business entrepreneurs in competitive markets, but the problems of social integration originate in the social structure.

Adapting to urban industrial life is at best demanding and exhausting. From time to time all of us wish for more closure, for a simpler and more serene life among friends and relatives with whom we have the kind of trust which develops out of a common life experience, perceiving the world in the same way—a closed world of stable values and moral certitude. We should not, therefore, be surprised that the media feed these fantasies. That in an age of nuclear power the media provide us with simple "westerns". That in a society where every act we engage in must be co-ordinated with others the media furnish us with stories of individual self-sufficiency. That at a time when the greatest issues of public policy concern the morality of business corporations, the media hold up for approval examples of interpersonal morality.

Nostalgia and escapism in small doses are harmless and inevitable. But if—as the commercial media frequently do—the mass media provide only fantasy at the expense of the real world, they perform a disservice to social integration, however much people may enjoy the experience.

COLLECTIVE AND NATIONAL IDENTITY*

In saying that the mass media of communication have an integrative function in a fragmented society, we are, in effect, saying that the media provide us with our collective identity. They can also provide us with our national identity. Both are precarious in individualistic societies, but although no one doubts the importance of collective identity, many people

*See Elkin, 1972: 216–30.

contend that, in a world community, national identity is obsolete; or worse, that it is a source of conflict, pitting nations against one another, creating bitterness and chauvinistic intolerance.

If all nations were equal this might be a more compelling argument. But they are not: as long as powerful nations can dominate weak ones and imperialist nations can colonize and exploit dependent ones, the small, weak, and dependent nations have alien or impoverished identities. The first step toward a genuine international community, therefore, is equality and the independence of dependent nations.

The media may abort this attempt by discouraging mobilization or failing to provide concepts of national identity. Struggling young nations in the Third World may receive information about themselves and the world at large from the big wire services of France, Britain, and the United States. Few of them can afford the technology and personnel to tell their own story in their own words to their own people and to others outside.

Canada has been more fortunate. Although historically its culture has been more British and French than Canadian, and although currently in danger of becoming Americanized, it has responded by developing a system of media to provide news and cultural features from a Canadian perspective. The Aird Report of 1929, which recommended a public broadcasting corporation, was in this spirit, as was the National Film Board Act passed on the eve of the Second World War. During the war Canadians became still more conscious of having a distinctive identity, helped in part by a Canadian wire service, the CBC, and the NFB—organizations which had come of age and proved themselves. The wave of national pride that followed the war led to the Massey Report, a document which summarized with great elegance a commitment to cultural autonomy, which has since been reiterated by subsequent Royal Commissions and inquiries on magazines and publications, broadcasting, and the media generally. Over the years, however, the tone of these reports has become less idealistic and more defensive, as exemplified by the rulings of the Canadian Radio and Television Commission (CRTC) requiring broadcasting networks to carry a certain percentage of Canadian content.

Beneath the defensiveness there is a conflict, for although Canadians are committed to cultural autonomy they are also committed to *laissez-*

faire and free enterprise. Cultural autonomy requires large subsidies from governments, while *laissez-faire* assumes a free market. Balancing these two allegiances accounts, in part, for the difficulty in implementing the first. Consider broadcasting and the growth of privately owned cable companies. Cable companies make their money from subscribers; like telephone companies they do not produce but only carry the messages. Should they be compelled by law to provide Canadian programming? or should they be permitted to pursue their profit margins freely by providing Canadians who are prepared to pay for the service with American broadcasting? Another example of our ambivalence is the Canadian Film Development Corporation, which provides loans to private film-makers who wish to create feature films. Since these loans must be repaid, the film-makers must keep a close eye on commercial values and profitability.

The intellectual community for the most part has supported the communication agencies that contribute to our national identity by acknowledging that a public subsidy must be provided and free enterprise regulated. But it is less prepared to sacrifice a commitment to a broader international culture. It wants the best of both worlds—a thriving Canadian culture, but one that does not shut out the rest of Western civilization: Canadian opera and the Metropolitan opera, Canadian drama and Shakespeare, French-Canadian literature as well as Proust, Canadian films but Charlie Chaplin and Ingmar Bergman as well.

NATIONAL IDENTITY OR CLASS IDENTITY?

What troubles many people about national identity is that it assumes that somewhere beneath the layers of varied Canadian experience there lies a common core of shared values that can be articulated by the mass media. But suppose the existence of a consensus is a myth, that the cleavages in Canadian society along class lines run too deep for any genuine sharing of values? If that is the case then a commitment to a national identity and national integration may be regressive. Under these circumstances the proper role of the media should be to question the desirability of integration. Integration at whose expense?

A conflict model of society means that no one can be neutral or objective, no one can escape taking sides. Any illusion that journalists may have of remaining above the battle or that journalism can mediate the conflict by acting as an independent third party is false; for whether intended or not, all journalism is advocacy. Advocacy, however, should not be confused with partisanship. Male editors, for example, may support certain goals of the feminist movement, but are unable to express the deeper aspirations of women's liberation. White broadcasters may be sympathetic to particular objectives of the black civil-rights movement, but are less capable of communicating to blacks or whites the inner experience of blacks which motivates the movement. Middle-class writers can tell their middle-class audience some of the facts about poverty, but they do not perceive the world with the same sense of despair and indignation felt by the poor. With the best intentions in the world, the outsider lacks the subjective knowledge to report in depth.

The underprivileged need and want their own media in order to speak more effectively to their own groups and for them. At a certain point in the development of a social movement, the former may be more important in recruiting support, but in the more advanced stages the latter may be essential for social action. Speaking of the experience the black civil-rights movement had with the white media, one writer put it this way: "What had become clear was that while the media may inform, they cannot convert a society which is racist out of self-interest and not out of ignorance of the facts" (Hamilton, 1971: 152). The same principle applies generally: if the situation is defined as conflict based on group interest, then class identity and social change have priority over national identity and social equilibrium.

In summary, the media have a dual function: to foster social integration and social change, and to create national identity and class identity. The first leads in the direction of neutral, unbiased, objective, and creative reporting; the second, in the direction of partisan, interpretive, and polemical commentary.

Because these two modes are diametrically opposed, most people in the media, particularly those at the policy levels, believe a firm and lasting choice must be made between them. An alternative is to regard them as shifting priorities. That being the case, the function of policy-making then would be to evaluate and to re-examine periodically which one should be given the higher place. Toward this end, the media must monitor themselves, the social environment, and the relationship between them. While the media are often highly self-critical, they are so fixated on a distinction between democratic media (neutral and unbiased, representing all of the people) and totalitarian media (partisan, sectarian, representing particular groups) that they are unable to carry out the monitoring process which would allow both modes of communication.

SOURCES OF DYSFUNCTION

It is one thing to know what the media ought to be doing, another to judge how well they are doing it. What are the signs to look for, and what factors interfere with the proper performance of the media's function?

The critical intervening variable between the media and the public is credibility. When people no longer trust or believe what they read, watch, or hear, any of the three functions we have discussed here—integration, social change, evaluation—is impaired.

Censorship, whether voluntary or imposed, is one of the most serious threats to credibility. The knowledge that the media are being used to withhold information or to disseminate propaganda creates a climate of disbelief. Credibility is difficult to measure, however, because behavioural indexes may be deceptive. For example, according to a Gallup Poll (1970), two out of three Canadians feel that the media are biased, yet this does not deter them from purchasing newspapers, listening to radio stations, and watching TV channels which they feel cannot be trusted. When the Toronto *Telegram* ceased to publish in 1971, it was not for lack of loyal readers, who numbered over 200,000. To take another example, every Royal Commission on broadcasting has found strong public support for the Canadian Broadcasting Corporation, yet Canadians who can receive American signals are heavy consumers of American broadcasting. This discrepancy between behavioural and attitudinal indexes indicates the difficulty of arriving at true measures of the degree to which the public believes and trusts the media.

The appearance of an alternative or underground press is a more distinct indication that the established media no longer enjoy the confidence of some audiences. In general, however, people show their disrespect for the media by cynicism, by pressure to use the media as a vehicle for the promotion of their own sectarian interests, or by using the media as a whipping boy.

Although the difficulties in measuring credibility are great, they are not insurmountable. The construction and application of such indexes should be the primary objective of media research. Program ratings, measures of circulation, and attempts to ascertain levels of audience enjoyment could not be further from the mark. They are a form of market research aimed at selling space and time to potential advertisers; they describe what "is" and not what "could be"—what is available in the media and not what could be available.

In the absence of good research, we may examine factors that influence the people who work in the media; that is, the media culture discussed earlier. One important trend is the increasing bureaucratization of media organizations. One out of five persons in private TV in Canada is an administrator; the figure for radio is one out of four. The small daily newspaper owned and published by its editor is becoming a suburban weekly about to be absorbed by the Thompson chain of weeklies or by nearby metropolitan dailies. The cozy atmosphere of the TV newsroom which appears on the Mary Tyler Moore show is either non-existent or north of the DEW line. In the newspaper business 53 per cent of all employees are employed by 4 per cent of the industry, who are the giants of the industry and receive 63 per cent of the revenue (Special Senate Committee, 1971: 223). In Canada, as elsewhere, the modern newspaper is typically part of a chain, and the modern radio station and TV channel are members of networks whose head offices are located away from the communities the media serve.

Large size, absentee ownership, and bureaucratic organization are not fatal but they are detrimental to a media culture. If the media become depersonalized places of work, if participation is truncated, and if executives and administrators become unresponsive to their creative staffs, the results are boredom, indifference, perfunctory performance alternating with sporadic and irrational protests—the classic symptoms of a work culture which has become anomic. It may be some comfort to journalists to know that they are not state functionaries as their counterparts in the Soviet Union might be, or public relations flacks for cigarette companies as their journalism school classmates are. But a vital media culture which has gone sour and is living off such comparisons has lost its initiative.

Competition from foreign sources may also erode the media culture by depriving Canadian writers, actors, musicians, and other creative people of the opportunities to develop their talents. Canadian writers cannot sustain themselves without Canadian publications and publishers, as well as distributors and middlemen who will put their work on newstands and in bookstores. Actors, directors, and designers require Canadian theatres and film industries; Canadian musicians must have Canadian recording companies. Unless these outlets are present and stable, the creative people who define the style of the media must either direct their work to an international market or leave the country. Either way, Canadian culture suffers, but more tragically, the potential talent among a younger generation may never be developed. In its brief to the O'Leary Commission on publications, the *Reader's Digest* observed that it had purchased nearly four thousand tons of Canadian paper in 1960, that it is a major customer of the Canadian post office, that it employs Canadian printers, envelope makers, and engravers, and that it depends on Canadian news dealers (*Marketing*, 1960). In short, the *Reader's Digest* provides employment for everyone except those who matter most, Canadian writers.

Claims made by *Time* and the *Reader's Digest* that they provide employment for Canadians are indeed hollow, for it takes no great or profound knowledge of economics to know that Canadian publishers, with few exceptions, are unable to afford the economies of scale which give the imports an unfair advantage in Canadian markets. The exception is Maclean-Hunter with its trade publications. Otherwise, Canadian magazines are not financially viable, a fact which can only discourage and demoralize Canadian writers who wish to remain at home. Nor is their outlook on the future improved by the sale, in 1969, of two old and established Canadian publishers, Ryerson Press and W. J. Gage, to foreign groups. Canada's creative and famous film-maker Norman McLaren was able to develop his talent thanks to the National Film Board. But what good are the films of the NFB if film distributors and exhibitors are unwilling to book or publicize them, or if film critics fail to review them? Nor does it help Canadian journalists when Canadian newspapers take their news from abroad from American, British, and French wire services instead of developing their own corps of foreign correspondents.

A Canadian media culture surrounded by examples of imports that enjoy high visibility and prestige is in the position of a minority group. Unsure of itself, it takes on the attitudes, values, mannerisms, and thought patterns of the dominant group at great cost to its own identity. Imperceptibly, the Canadian media—their *persona* Canadian-born and Canadian-bred—begin to resemble American or other non-Canadian media. In the extreme, there is a danger that Canadian journalists will look at events in China, Africa, or Latin America through the eyes of American, British, or French foreign policies.

Less obvious but no less dangerous, Canadian reporters may begin to see Canadian society through the lens of a non-Canadian reference group: a prison riot in Kingston becomes Attica; an occupation by Canadian Indians becomes Wounded Knee; French-Canadian separatists become the Panthers. Are these parallels real or are they the perceptions of minds too accustomed to American headlines? And if it is true that Canadian protest movements have borrowed strategies successful in the United States, should the media not be evaluating such strategies in Canada? If they are not conscious of their own presuppositions, however, they are hardly able to stand apart to make such judgments.

Finally, one must question whether indigenous Canadian problems are being ignored because they are not on the American agenda and are therefore not sufficiently appreciated. Accustomed to outsiders' definitions of "newsworthiness", a Canadian journalist is apt to judge something as being without news value if it does not have an analogue elsewhere.

For every critic who complains about Canadian media becoming Americanized, there are at least two who wish they would become more so, that Canadian newspapers and magazines and Canadian broadcasting would take the best rather than the worst features of the American media, that instead of sleazy weekend supplements Canadians could enjoy something comparable to the *New York Times Book Review* section or its *Sunday Magazine*, that instead of showing the big American TV specials, Canadian television would take some of the controversial programming found in the American public broadcasting system. In other words, the primary issue is quality not national origin.

Quality, like credibility, is difficult to operationalize, for both are more than the sum of their respective parts. One measure of quality, however, is the absence of petty bias and the availability of diverse interpretations. Conventional wisdom tells us that the necessary condition for the first is freedom from control by vested-interest groups; the necessary condition for the second is competition. Does either of these conditions exist?

In Canada, as in Western democracies generally, the media have developed in such a way that they are independent of any form of political or governmental control. The reason for this was simple enough: to engage in criticism of governments without fear of reprisal the press had to be free of any obligations to groups in power. This philosophy has persisted right down to the present, despite the intervention of government in licensing radio stations and television channels, and despite the parliamentary support for the CBC and the NFB.

What the philosophers did not anticipate is that the media would become forms of business enterprise subsidized by profits from advertising. They did not foresee that the publishers of newspapers and magazines and the owners of private TV and radio stations would become entrepreneurs, seeking to maximize profits for themselves and their shareholders. Although vigorous in their criticisms of politicians and governments in power, the media are less critical of big business, of which they are themselves a part. The media may lament the excesses of the system, the practices of a particularly avaricious corporation, or the behaviour of a cunning land speculator; they may crusade against dishonest used-car dealers or run a sympathetic feature story on substandard housing, but they rarely question capitalism itself and very seldom question the morality of advertising.

There is, then, a bias in the media for capitalism and against any other kind of economic arrangement at home or abroad. But apart from this prejudice, there is another problem when the media are forms of business enterprise. They are themselves subject to the vicissitudes of the economy. During periods of economic recession or more serious crisis when the public more than ever needs to understand what is happening, the media are less able to provide the service the community requires. They must cut back, rather than expand; they must avoid controversy which could antagonize readers and advertisers; they must compete more fiercely for the vanishing advertising dollar. Thus it is no accident that the highest-paid employees in private broadcasting are in sales and promotion, and that their wage increase between 1964 and 1968 was the greatest of any other group of employees in the media (Special Senate Committee, 1971: 304). Paradoxically, then, the media are least able to serve the public when the service is most needed, and best able to do so when it is least needed.

Still, even in good times there are problems of distribution, for as long as the media are dependent on advertising revenue, they cluster and concentrate in the richest market areas—Toronto, Montreal, and Vancouver—neglecting the poor, small, and more remote areas of the country. The Davey Commission found that there were fifty-six communities in Canada with populations exceeding 10,000 which had no daily newspaper, and four with populations between 30,000 and 100,000 with no daily newspaper (Special Senate Committee, 1971: 57–58). Large and rich cities are over-serviced, while the rural and less affluent ones are under-serviced. Since the latter pay for the advertising in the price of consumer goods, they are twice cursed by supporting the over-servicing of the wealthy urban populations.

Theoretically, the cities that can choose among newspapers, radio stations, and TV channels should enjoy great diversity in programming. Experience has shown this not to be the case. One newspaper copies the successful features of the other; one radio station lures a popular disc jockey away from another; a game show on one TV channel is matched by a game show on all of the others at the same time; if one horror film produces a big box office, other studios soon copy it. All of this is not an argument against competition among the media, but suggests rather that economic competition is no assurance of maintaining high quality or diversity.

Dissent and diversity, however, are not the same thing. It may not matter if the comic strips are all much the same as long as journalists have the opportunity to speak out. In practical terms what this means is that a journalist who is fired for holding unpopular views can go elsewhere and find employment. Journalists, therefore, are very concerned that competition exists. Increasingly, however, the competition is more apparent than real, for the same corporation or same person may own both of the newspapers, or the newspapers and radio station, or some other combination. Under these circumstances, the person who is discharged or whose contract is not renewed because he was outspoken on some delicate community issue such as police abuse has nowhere else to go in the community. With luck, he or she may find work in another city, but the story about police abuse or about a local company polluting the atmosphere is lost. In the last analysis the local community suffers. The most conspicuous example of this phenomenon in Canada can be seen in New Brunswick, where the five English-language papers are owned by K. C. Irving, as well as the major radio station in Saint John and a TV channel which has over 90 per cent coverage in the province. It would be un-reasonable to suppose that these media would engage in active criticism of the Irving corporation's policies in shipping, oil, or pulp and paper. People living outside of New Brunswick may know more about factors which control the quality of life in New Brunswick than its own residents do.

What competition exists has been slowly disappearing. In 1900 Toronto had three morning and four afternoon papers; today, there are two morning papers and one afternoon paper. Canadian communities, like American and British communities, are becoming one-newspaper communities. Prior to the First World War, the Davey Commission noted, there were 138 daily newspapers in Canada and 138 publishers. By 1953 there were 89 newspapers and 57 publishers. The decline in competition has become such an accepted fact that the Davey Commission suggested that it would be interesting to know the reasons for any community in Canada having more than one newspaper. The following table presents some idea of how the number of newspapers has declined while the population has increased.

Opinion is divided about why newspapers have not increased with population growth. Some claim that the newspaper business is a "sick industry" and point to the high costs. Unionized printers are among the best-paid workers in the labour force, and in addition they have resisted

Table 1   Canadian daily newspapers by circulation and population for the years 1899 through 1961.

	No. of daily papers	Combined circulation[a]	Population
1899	119	567,892	5,371,315
1911	143	1,324,909	7,206,643
1921	113	1,609,317	8,787,949
1931	103	2,119,908	10,376,786
1938	97	2,126,244	11,120,000
1955	97	3,087,919	14,009,000
1961	108	4,064,461	18,238,000

[a] 12 newspapers have circulation of over 100,000
more than half of all papers sold

Sources: McNaught, 1940; *1951 Census*; Canada Year Books

the introduction of labour-saving technology. Poor management is also cited as a factor. On the other hand, the *Toronto Star* is said to have paid ten million dollars to the defunct Toronto *Telegram*, its former rival as an afternoon paper, for its subscription list. The preponderant evidence suggests that although newspapers are not, as Roy Thompson once said of TV, a licence to print money, they are profitable enterprises. In our capitalist system, however, other forms of investment may be more attractive, and there is nothing to prevent a newspaper publisher from disregarding the public, closing down or selling his newspaper, and investing his money elsewhere. It is sometimes said that too much concern is shown about the decline in the number of daily newspapers; the newer media—radio and television—offset the trend. But as we have already indicated, the pattern of multi-media ownership and conglomerates cancels the advantages.

To summarize, several trends in the organization and control of the media contribute to dysfunction. The media culture is weakened by bureaucratization, large size, and foreign competition; the quality of the media is eroded by absentee ownership and commercialism; dependency on advertising contributes to maldistribution of the media; competition has failed to safeguard diversity, and what competition remains is slowly disappearing, eliminating opportunities for dissent and the full expression of unorthodoxies which are crucial to a democratic society.

Countervailing Trends

Thoughtful critics of the mass media of communication have long been aware of the media's shortcomings, but are haunted by the fear that the cure might be worse than the disease. Governmental control or regulation in any form conjures up images of *Pravda*, of the media in totalitarian countries where they are instruments of government policy. The reality of economic bias in the media seems to many to be the lesser of two evils. Canadians would no doubt be incensed if the government in power disseminated wall posters denouncing a former Minister of Defence, as is currently happening in Peking and throughout the People's Republic of China. But it is also reasonable to say that Chinese citizens would be equally distressed by nationally distributed wall posters using them to buy consumer goods, procure loans from banks, and generally spend to make a capitalistic economy work. The question, then, is not control or no control, but who controls the media.

Ideological considerations aside, public ownership or some form of regulation of the media has always been a possibility in Canada, especially with growing nationalist sentiment. Older Canadians remember with pride the NFB documentaries produced during the Second World War. Rural Canadians can recall that without the CBC it is unlikely that they would have had any broadcasting, while French Canadians in Quebec are aware that only a publicly owned broadcasting system could afford to provide an extensive French-language network and organization.

Today, since more Canadians are living in cities and French Canadians can afford extensive private broadcasting, these arguments do not carry as much weight as they did twenty-five years ago. To the extent that public ownership in the past was based on scarcity and poor distribution, the newer technologies of communication—satellites, cable systems— offer the public throughout Canada the possibilities of broad service and multiple choice. Indeed, since cable can potentially offer city dwellers sixty channels, we are rapidly approaching a position of too much rather than too little choice. But, if the argument for public ownership in the past was based on scarcity, the argument for it in the present is based on national unity.

At the other end of the spectrum it is proposed that the long-range solution to media dysfunction is not public ownership but professionalization. What is meant by professionalization is more formal education combined with a strong sense of public service—in other words, a code of ethics similar to that which governs the behaviour of other professionals. The law of the business world, *caveat emptor*, buyer beware, would be subordinate to a higher loyalty which envisions the media as a public trust. Judgment of the media would be on the basis of performance rather than profit, and the judges would be other professionals using professional rather than economic criteria.

Professionalism has grown in the media as schools of journalism have developed, many of them within universities. Canada has no graduate schools of journalism yet, but it has several distinguished undergraduate programs. In the United States there are not only graduate schools of journalism, but also a number of professional journals and research centres. The older pattern of training through apprenticeship seems to be fading.

It is too soon to say whether journalism as a whole has been upgraded, or whether the standards have been raised high enough to keep up with the growing complexity of social and economic affairs. But a new type of newspaper has emerged, the élite papers which do not always have or want the largest circulations, or are prepared to sacrifice popularity on a mass scale for respectability on a small scale.

What the new élite media have and want is influence. They are regularly read or heard by heads of government, opinion leaders in the arts, business executives, and professional groups. In addition, they enjoy solvency. A British Royal Commission found in 1961 that the "quality" newspapers doubled their circulation between 1937 and 1961, a period during which the "populars" increased their circulation by only 50 per cent. The success of the "qualities" attracted advertising so that the élite media eat their cake and have it too; they enjoy respect and a reputation for being independent while carrying more advertising proportionately than many of the other media accused of being captives of their advertisers. The gamble seems to have paid off. Public ownership could be avoided by more self-discipline, a view which fits well with our individualism, our distrust of bureaucratic structures, and our fears of government control.

The gamble would not have worked, however, without the support of a better-educated public, a population of university graduates who expect and want a better quality in the media. Whether it is a column on sports or gourmet cooking, on world affairs or local government, this audience wants excellence and is dissatisfied with the mediocrity of the run-of-the-mill press and broadcasting. It is from this sector of the population that the new élites of our modern societies are recruited. Whether it is correct to describe these people as a "class" is debatable; they are not a class in the older sense of an economic class that enjoyed power because of wealth or property. The power of the new élites resides in their education, their expertise, and their positions in a bureaucratic society.

When the trend toward professionalization of the media is placed in the context of our stratification system, the question of whether professionalization is the solution or the problem arises. How independent are the élite media? Have they liberated themselves from the grip of commercialism only to become the pawns of a new group who are unaccountable to the public at large? On whose behalf do they attack government policies? In other words, the new élite media may be serving the established élites and those who aspire to élite positions, but are they serving society?

An alternative would be the people's media. Although the underground media are not the only example, they illustrate a new type of media organization, non-profit newspapers owned and run by co-operatives or collectives. The underground media started as an outgrowth of a new technique of communication, the teach-in—a group-marathon discussion of some controversial issue. In the underground papers, emphasis was on participation rather than on expertise. Indeed, expert knowledge was suspect, for to have acquired it meant that one had been through the system and had satisfied requirements created by the establishment to further its own ends. Professional education, whether in journalism or other areas, was the product of a dehumanized technological society which denied or dismissed the reality of moral conflicts by treating them as technological. Anyone who survived the system was desensitized to moral issues, and was in addition cut off from any genuine communication with people in the real world. It was assumed, and not wholly without foundation, that the professional and the expert always talk down to others; at best, they are patronizing, at worst, manipulative. The underground media reversed this pattern, encouraging spontaneity, decentralization, use of the language of everyday life, and a sense of moral commitment.

Last Post and *Guerrilla* in Toronto, *Georgia Strait* in Vancouver, and *Mysterious East* in New Brunswick were among the best-known Canadian underground papers. Some have disappeared; in some the radicalism has settled down into more traditional muckraking journalism; and some of the journalists have been co-opted by the "straight" media. Nevertheless, they have left a legacy of a new form of media control (non-profit), a new form of media organization (the collective), and a new form of communication (participatory).

Many people think that these elements are at the heart of community TV systems that, by using cable, can hook up two-way dialogues between citizen groups (CRTC, 1974). In this way groups—the poor and native peoples for instance—that have no voice and have become passive and fatalistic, groups that have been ignored by all of the media, can be encouraged to participate. The results may be very small in terms of concrete achievements, but the psychological effects could be enormous for persons who through neglect have come to believe that they do not matter. And the skills gained in participation might well have a long-run pay-off in terms of future social action.

Community TV systems and the underground media are, as we have indicated, a reaction to the professionalization and élite orientation of the established media. According to the proponents of community TV and the underground media, the élite media are doomed to failure in meeting the needs of the people. They do not speak the language of the people, and they are too centralized for the grass-roots participation required. The fact that they are also profit oriented is another minus. Thus, community TV has a battle on two fronts: the private commercial television networks, and the public system which is highly centralized, committed above all to national unity, and professional. Just how this conflict will be resolved remains to be seen.

COMMUNICATIONS AND SOCIAL POLICY

How much time is left to Canadians to work out the media dilemma? We have suggested here that the mass media of communication can be regarded as a social institution with three functions: integration, social change, and monitoring the society and themselves. That they do not perform these functions well is a matter of record. The problems are largely structural, but the various solutions proposed—public ownership, professionalization, decentralization—touch only aspects of it. Canada does not have, but needs, a social policy with respect to communications.

One reason we lack a social policy is that we persist in thinking of the mass media of communication as entertainment, a leisure-time diversion to amuse us and take our minds off the problems of the world. A second reason is that we continue to believe that we are faced with only two choices: a system based on free enterprise and a system based on government control. The first is the democratic way, the second, totalitarian. We have tried to suggest here that if we look at function, a more flexible perspective is available. Third, our Canadian tradition stemming from Innis confuses the economic functions of the media with the social.

These intellectual preconceptions leave us unprepared to deal with the new innovations in communication. Who will decide whether we will have "wired cities", the big telecommunications industries or the public? And will the criteria be advantageous to the economy or to the society? If to the society, which sectors? To the middle class looking for a new toy or a new set of appliances, or to the victims of our class structure— the poor—who will pay for it just as they now pay for a communication system which serves them badly?

Selected Bibliography

REPORTS

Instant World, A Report on Telecommunications in Canada, 1971
Royal Commission on Radio Broadcasting, 1929 (Aird)
Royal Commission on National Development in the Arts, Letters and Sciences, 1951 (Massey)
Royal Commission on Broadcasting, 1957 (Fowler)
Royal Commission on Publications, 1961 (O'Leary)
Special Senate Committee on the Mass Media, 1971 (Davey)

BOOKS

COOK, RAMSEY. *The Politics of John W. Dafoe and the "Winnipeg Free Press"*. Toronto: University of Toronto Press, 1963.
KESTERTON, W. H. *A History of Journalism in Canada*. Toronto: McClelland and Stewart, 1967.
MCNAUGHT, C. *Canada Gets the News*. Toronto: Ryerson Press, 1940.
NICHOLS, M. E. *The Story of the Canadian Press*. Toronto: Ryerson Press, 1948.
PEERS, FRANK W. *The Politics of Canadian Broadcasting 1920–1951*. Toronto: University of Toronto Press, 1969.
SINGER, B. D. *Communications in Canadian Society*. Toronto: Copp Clark, 1972.

BIBLIOGRAPHIES

HANSEN, DONALD, and PARSONS, J. HERSCHEL. *Mass Communication: A Research Bibliography*. Santa Barbara, California: Glendessary, 1968.
SILBERMANN, A. *La Sociologie des Communications de Masse*. Paris: Mouton, 1970.

Class and Status in Canada   4

ALFRED A. HUNTER*

Introduction

Wherever one lives or even visits for a brief period in Canada, some thoughtful observation will show that people differ from one another in the admiration, respect, or *prestige* they are accorded by those who know them or who know about them. Some are well thought of—a local physician, perhaps, winner of last year's Good Citizen's Award, who owns an elegant old mansion on a hill overlooking the city, with a Colville painting over the fireplace and a Mercedes-Benz in the garage. Others, such as a notorious drunkard, chronically unemployed, whose family must depend upon welfare for food, clothing, and rent, suffer as the objects of ridicule, scorn, and sometimes pity. But most live somewhere between these conspicuous extremes. Neither paragons nor pariahs, they are likely to see themselves and to be seen by others as "just hard-working, honest people".

Often it takes a more careful and patient scrutiny to discover that people also differ in the *power* they are able to exercise when decisions important to the community, the province, or the nation are made. Some, far more than others, are able to influence these decisions in the directions they desire. One of these might be a businessman—chairman of the board of a giant forest-products corporation, for instance, who decides to suspend a local pulp mill's operations pending a rise in international prices. Another might be an elected official, such as a member of Parliament, who votes in favour of a bill authorizing subsidies for petroleum exploration. Yet another might be a municipal building inspector whose interpretation of the building code delays occupancy of a new townhouse

*The author would like to thank Rita Bienvenue, Carl Cuneo, Jane Synge, Sharon Thompson, the editors, and two anonymous reviewers for their useful comments and suggestions.

complex. Whether its impact is local, provincial, or even national in scope, a decision is made by some, and it affects others.

A feature of life in all contemporary societies, inequalities in prestige and power, constitute much of what is known in sociology as *social stratification*, and it is a major task for sociologists to describe them and to identify their causes and consequences.[1] The present chapter begins with an abbreviated summary and analysis of certain basic concepts and theories in social stratification, followed by a selective review of stratification in Canada.[2]

Some Basic Concepts in Social Stratification

Inequalities in power and prestige define, respectively, hierarchies of *class* and *status*. While these terms are often used interchangeably, they will not be so here. As two major dimensions of stratification systems, power and prestige are analytically distinct, although theoretically and empirically related. A failure to distinguish clearly between class and status would be to confound whatever separate importance power and prestige might have for social relations.

In studies of stratification, sociologists concern themselves with inequalities in two distinct but related ways. The first arises out of the fact that inequalities are attached to positions in a society (including, most importantly, positions in the economic division of labour, or occupations) and, through them, to their incumbents. Here there is an interest in how positions differ from one another in power and prestige, and what the origins and consequences of these differences are. It is vital to appreciate that the power a person is able to exercise, or the prestige he or she enjoys, derives fundamentally from positions occupied, and only incidentally from force of personality or other such idiosyncratic characteristics. The second involves the processes by which people are recruited to position. In this case, sociologists want to know the extent to which recruitment occurs on the basis of performance, according to the physical or social attributes of prospective candidates (sex, race, age, religion, and kinship),

1. This is intended as a useful way to organize the materials to be presented, not as a sectarian statement of how the field must necessarily be viewed.

2. For further reading in theory, see Bendix and Lipset (1966); for further reading in social stratification in Canada, see Curtis and Scott (1973).

or in terms of some other principle, such as random selection. They are also concerned to discover the consequences of different recruitment patterns for individuals, groups, and total societies.

In some societies, recruitment hinges on *ascribed* characteristics (typically acquired at birth and difficult or impossible to mask or change). In such situations, inequalities among families in one generation are reproduced and even strengthened in succeeding ones. Where class and status are more inclined to be *achieved* in competition with others on the basis of ability and effort, there will probably be less historical continuity in class and status hierarchies. Even so, many abilities, along with the tendency to work hard, are to a degree heritable (genetically or socially) from one generation to the next, and well-placed parents often assist their children in competition, so that inter-generational rigidities in the stratification system will still arise. Finally, if recruitment occurs on a purely *random* basis, the probability of such rigidities developing is very small.

If the young in a society tend to inherit the status of their parents, clearly defined *social strata* may develop, with clusters of people at some prestige levels and none at others. Such a development would facilitate the development of *status groups*, that is, aggregates of persons similar in prestige who are capable of acting in concert to achieve shared goals. There is nothing in the concept of a status hierarchy, however, which implies the existence of identifiable social strata, and the existence of such strata need not mean that there are status groups. People might be distributed in continuous array up and down the status hierarchy. And members of a social stratum might be unaware of their commonalities or, even if aware of them, they might be socially divided by competing ethnic, religious, or other loyalties, or physically separated from one another.

With class hierarchies, the issues are somewhat different, since the class structure within any domain of power (for example, a business firm, a labour union, or a nation state) in its most basic form consists of those who control the resources that permit them to make decisions, and those who do not (Dahrendorf, 1959: 169–71). Power, then, is discontinuous in a way that prestige is not, and the potential exists for only two classes: a *dominant class* and a *subordinate class*. In the economic division of labour in a society such as Canada, this distinction corresponds to those who own (or at least control) the means of production, as opposed to those who exchange their labour for a wage or salary (Marx and Engels,

1932; Miliband, 1969). As in the case of social strata, the existence of social classes need not imply that they are organized.

To the extent that the status and class positions of members of a society are fixed by their status and class origins, that society has an *impermeable* stratification system (Svalastoga, 1965). Typically this means that individuals tend to inherit positions similar to those previously occupied by their parents. In so far as class and status inheritance do not occur, a society is said to have a degree of *vertical mobility*.

Often, a distinction is made between power exercised as a recognized right, termed *authority* or *legitimate power*, and other varieties of power (Weber, 1947). Thus, for example, one way in which the relationship between major and private can be distinguished from that between armed robber and victim is that the former is based on legitimate power, while the latter is not. In general, legitimate power in one domain loses legitimacy when exercised in another.

Two Major Theories of Social Stratification

According to the *functional theory* of social stratification (Davis and Moore, 1945), all societies are stratified, since all societies, if they are to survive, must have essential positions occupied, and the occupants must perform their duties adequately. Consequently, members of a society must be motivated to occupy these positions and, once in them, to discharge their obligations faithfully. No special problem would exist if social positions did not differ from one another in inherent pleasantness, importance to society (functional importance), and skill requirements. Since some are more pleasant, important, and demanding in skills than others, it matters who occupies them. In order to ensure that the duties of each position are performed with a diligence appropriate to its importance, rewards must be available as inducements, and these rewards must be distributed unequally according to the pleasantness, importance, and skill requirements of each position. Thus, it is argued, the position of medical doctor carries with it substantial economic rewards and considerable prestige because of the necessarily lengthy, difficult, and expensive training, while that of waitress, an unskilled position of little importance, brings few material or symbolic benefits.

In functional theory, then, stratification arises out of the social division of labour, and is both necessary and inevitable if group life is to be maintained. Unfortunately, there seem to be no convincing examples of societies that have ceased to survive as a clear consequence of the failure of the stratification system to maintain an effective division of labour.[3] Also, the idea that positions are rewarded according to their importance to society would be much more persuasive if it could be demonstrated that some positions are functionally more important than others. A further criticism of the functional theory is that it more convincingly explains stratification as it applies to societies where location in the system is *achieved* largely through open competition with others on the basis of merit, than as it applies to societies where location tends to be fixed or *ascribed* at birth. Indeed, in the latter system, stratification would seem, if anything, to threaten the survival of group life by placing restrictions on the recruitment of persons of talent and training. Finally, functional theory seems best adapted to an analysis of inequalities in prestige and material benefits. It provides no consistent treatment of the phenomenon of power, or of its role in social stratification, even though it can be argued that inequalities in power are the very essence of stratification, and that inequalities in prestige and material rewards are at once derivative and secondary in importance (Dahrendorf, 1959; Lenski, 1966).

In the Marxian tradition (Marx, 1935, 1965; Marx and Engels, 1932) social stratification is regarded as neither necessary nor inevitable. In fact, it is viewed as the major source of social conflict and human suffering. According to Marx,[4] each period in history can be described in terms of its characteristic form of economic production, which constitutes the supporting infrastructure for the legal, religious, political, and other superstructures of society. The form of production—of which modern, bourgeois capitalism is one example and feudalism another—provides the basis for a class structure, consisting ultimately of a dominant and a subordinate class, although a variety of other classes may appear and disappear from time to time before the characteristic mode of production reaches full development. For Marx, a social class is an aggregate of persons who perform a similar function in the organization of production. The crucial element in this function is not income or prestige, or even

3. See Bendix and Lipset (1966) for critical commentary on functional theory.

4. Referring to Marx alone is for ease of exposition only.

occupation as such, but whether one owns and controls the means of production, or exchanges labour for an income with someone who does. Even though two men might be engineers by occupation, if one owns a business firm and employs the other in it, the employer is a member of the dominant class, and his employee a member of the subordinate one.

Modern capitalism is distinguished by a form of production involving machines, materials, labour, and money paid in exchange for labour. In this era, there are those who own only capital, those who own only land, and those who own only their labour power. The first two combined constitute the dominant class, or *bourgeoisie*, and the third the subordinate class, or *proletariat*. If commodities produced under a capitalist system are sold at cost, no surplus value would remain for the capitalist (Marx, 1935). Since workers must provide for themselves by exchanging their labour for a wage or salary, capitalists can demand that they work extra hours for no extra pay or the same number of hours for less. By such means, the capitalist system creates surplus value and a source of profit. This profit can be consumed by members of the capitalist or bourgeois class, or it can be reinvested in equipment and materials in order to remain competitive.[5] As profits are accumulated and reinvested, wealth gathers in the hands of fewer and fewer capitalists who are able to take over the businesses of poorer capitalists, thereby increasing efficiency and eliminating competition. As a result, wages fall, unemployment rises, and business cycles become increasingly severe. At the same time, members of the working class or proletariat become more and more dissatisfied with their inability to acquire an equitable share of the available economic rewards, and are increasingly aware that together they form an oppressed, exploited class. Their dissatisfaction and class consciousness promote organization for political action, culminating in the overthrow of the bourgeoisie and the creation of a communist society devoid of private property, class, inequality, and conflict. Devoid also of any division of labour:

In communist society where nobody has one exclusive sphere of activity but each can become accomplished in any branch he wishes, society regulates the general production and thus makes it possible for me to do one thing today

5. This analysis is based on what was known to nineteenth-century economists as the *labour theory of value*.

and another tomorrow, to hunt in the morning, fish in the afternoon, rear cattle in the evening, criticize after dinner . . . without ever becoming hunter, fisherman, shepherd or critic (Marx, 1965: 45).

Marx identified the locus of social stratification primarily in class structures generated by the existence of private property, and only secondarily in such factors as the occupational structure. Class, defined in relation to the means of production, was the central issue. While he scarcely denied the existence of inequalities in material rewards and prestige, he saw them as ultimately the consequence of property relations.

Marxian analysis has been the object of much debate (Bottomore, 1966; Dahrendorf, 1959: Part One). One potentially major difficulty lies in its characterization of the relationship between ownership and control, which Marx originally viewed as inseparable in capitalism. The emergence of the joint stock corporation in more recent times, however, has created the possibility of the separation of ownership and control and, thus, the possibility of eliminating the very basis of class and class conflict. If ownership is widely diffused among the population in the form of stock ownership, and if control resides in a group of managers who run the affairs of corporations for the stockholders' benefit, then Marx's analysis could be an historical anachronism, or at least in need of fundamental revision. The evidence does suggest that relatively little separation of ownership and control has occurred in Canada (Porter, 1965: 242). At the same time, the possibility of separation has prompted a re-analysis of the entire issue, with the result that some theorists now hold the position that it is control, not ownership, which provides the basis for class formation (Dahrendorf, 1959: 136–41; Miliband, 1969: 23–45).

Canadian Class Structure

In Canada, a substantial and increasing proportion of women and the overwhelming majority of men are employed or self-employed outside the home. Table 1 shows labour-force participation rates for males and females, 1911–71. If only those between twenty-five and fifty-four years of age are considered, since many of those younger still attend educational institutions of various kinds, and large numbers of those who are older have retired, virtually all men in Canada are gainfully employed, temporarily laid off, or in search of employment. While almost 40 per cent of all women fifteen years of age and over were in the labour force in 1971, single women have higher participation rates than the widowed and divorced who, in turn, have higher rates than married women. In fact, most single women are gainfully employed, along with a majority of widowed and divorced women. An increasing minority of married women are in the labour force. During the child-bearing years, labour-force participation among married women is lower than it is either before or after (Allingham, 1967).

What kinds of occupations do the more than nine million Canadians in the labour force pursue? They are occupations in which income is earned through employment, rather than self-employment. Fully 86 per cent of the work force in 1971 received a wage or salary through employment, while the remaining 14 per cent received income from self-employment (Department of National Revenue, 1973: 13). In that same year, about 63 per cent of all Canadians reporting an income received a wage or salary through employment in a business firm, about 12 per cent

Table 1   Percentages of males and females, 15 years and over, in the labour force,[a] Canada,[b] 1911–71.

Year	Percentage	
	Males	Females
1911	89.6	16.2
1921	88.7	17.6
1931	87.5	19.6
1941[c]	85.8	20.7
1941[d]	78.4	
1951	83.8	24.1
1961	77.7	29.5
1971	75.7	39.2

[a] Prior to 1951, the concept "gainfully employed" was used, rather than "in the labour force". These figures have been adjusted to take such definitional differences into account.
[b] Excludes Yukon and Northwest Territories.
[c] Includes men in the armed forces.
[d] Excludes men in the armed forces.

Source: *1971 Census of Canada*, Cat. 94-702.

through direct employment in federal, provincial, or municipal government, and most of the remainder through indirect governmental employment (hospitals, prisons, schools, and universities). Approximately 4 per cent were self-employed as business proprietors, and 8 per cent as investors, property owners, farmers, and fishermen.

Perhaps the most significant factor is that, in the brief period of Canadian history, the nation has been transformed from one in which the majority were self-employed to one in which they are now in the employ of others. Where once small businessmen, independent craftsmen, and farmers—the Marxian petite bourgeoisie—were numerically dominant, the labour force has been, in Marxian terms, proletarianized, and the class structure greatly simplified (Johnson, 1972). Beginning in the late nineteenth century the development of modern capitalism, with its large-scale, centralized production and distribution facilities, placed small businessman and independent commodity producer alike at a competitive disadvantage from which they were unable to recover. As a result, a numerically large class of small businessmen, independent craftsmen, and farmers were replaced by a small class of owners and managers presiding over large corporate enterprises, often employing many thousands of workers, and with assets in the millions of dollars. As Johnson observes, "With the decline of the petite bourgeoisie and the consolidation and maturation of capitalism, a new situation—one more closely resembling Marx's delineation of a capitalist economy—has emerged" (1972: 178).

WORKING-CLASS STRUCTURE AND ORGANIZATION[6]

Table 2 provides the occupational composition of the labour force in Canada for twenty-year intervals between 1901 and 1961. While the overall size of the labour force has grown enormously since the turn of the century, this growth has not touched all occupational categories equally. Some categories have actually experienced large, numerical declines. During this period there has been a substantial increase in the proportion of persons employed in white-collar occupations, while by contrast the proportion involved in primary occupations has declined

6. The terms "subordinate class", "working class", and "proletariat" are used interchangeably throughout, as are "dominant class", "economic élite", and "bourgeoisie", except where they take on a very precise meaning within the context of a particular theory.

Table 2 Percentage distribution of labour force, 15 years and over, by occupation division, for Canada: 1901, 1921, 1941, and 1961.

Occupation Division	Percentage				Change
	1901[a]	1921	1941	1961	1901–61
White Collar	15.3	25.3	25.3	37.9	+22.6
Proprietary, managerial	4.3	7.3	5.4	7.8	+ 3.5
Professional	4.6	5.4	6.7	9.8	+ 5.2
Clerical	3.2	6.9	7.2	12.7	+ 9.5
Commercial, financial	3.1	5.7	6.0	7.6	+ 4.5
Blue Collar	27.8	25.8	27.1	26.6	− 1.2
Manufacturing, mechanical	15.9	11.4	16.1	16.1	+ 0.2
Construction	4.7	4.7	4.7	5.2	+ 0.5
Labourers[b]	7.2	9.7	6.3	5.3	− 1.9
Primary	44.3	36.2	30.5	12.8	−31.5
Agricultural	40.3	32.6	25.7	10.0	−30.3
Fishing, hunting, trapping	1.5	0.9	1.2	0.6	− 0.9
Logging	0.9	1.2	1.9	1.2	+ 0.3
Mining, quarrying	1.6	1.5	1.7	1.0	− 0.6
Transportation, communication	4.4	5.5	6.4	7.7	+ 3.3
Service	8.2	7.0	10.5	12.4	+ 4.2
Unknown	—	0.2	0.2	2.6	

[a] 10 years old and over in 1901.
[b] Except those in Primary.

Source: Derived from Ostry, 1967: 50–51.

sharply. The representation of blue-collar workers has remained quite stable during this sixty-year span, while that of transportation and communication workers, as well as those in service occupations, has increased.

Among white-collar occupations, all four categories listed in Table 2 have experienced some proportional growth, with clerical occupations, especially in the 1941–61 period, leading the way. The proprietary and managerial category as a whole has grown least rapidly, but growth patterns for occupations within this category have been far from uniform. In general, independent proprietors have declined as a proportion of the labour force, while managers have increased (Ostry, 1967: 11). The professional category increased fairly steadily in the period 1901–41, and rather more rapidly since that time. Commercial-financial occupations have continued to grow steadily, if not rapidly. Among blue-collar occupations, the construction category has varied little since the turn of the century in its proportion of the labour force, while the other two categories have been more volatile. The proportion of the labour force in the labourer category increased quite sharply in the early years of the twentieth century in Canada, only to begin a decline which has continued to the present. Except for a sharp decline between 1901 and 1921, the manufacturing-mechanical category has more or less maintained its proportional share of the labour force. The greatest change which has occurred in the occupational structure since the turn of the century has been the decline in the agricultural sector. In 1901 fully 40.3 per cent of the labour force were engaged in agricultural pursuits. By 1961 this figure had dropped to 10.0 per cent. In fact, the actual number of persons engaged in agricultural occupations increased in the period 1901–31. Since 1941 the representation of the agricultural sector has decreased both proportionally and in absolute numbers to the point that, as of 1951, the manufacturing-mechanical category replaced the agricultural as the largest in the occupational structure. The remaining occupational categories—transportation-communication and service—have displayed slow and generally steady growth since 1901.

Table 3 shows the percentage distribution of the labour force by broad occupational categories for 1971. The introduction of a new occupational classification scheme for the 1971 Census of Canada precludes any precise comparisons between 1971 and earlier years at the present time.

While there has been a great increase in the proportion of the labour force employed (as opposed to self-employed), only a minority of paid workers belong to labour unions, and the labour movement in Canada is dominated by a small number of large, politically conservative, international unions with headquarters in the United States (Lipton, 1972). About one-third of all non-agricultural, paid workers in Canada are members of labour unions, up from less than one-sixth in 1921. Very few agricultural workers belong to unions. Unionization is most advanced in transportation, storage, and communication (53.0 per cent in 1961), logging (51.4 per cent), public utilities (50.2 per cent), and mining (49.1 per cent), and least advanced in service (15.2 per cent), fishing (12.7

Table 3   Percentage distribution of labour force, 15 years and over, by occupation division, for Canada, 1971.

Occupation Division	Percentage
Managerial, administrative, and related	4.3
Natural sciences, engineering, and mathematics	2.7
Social sciences and related	0.9
Religion	0.3
Teaching and related	4.1
Medicine and health	3.8
Artistic, literary, recreational, and related	0.9
Clerical and related	15.9
Sales	9.5
Service	11.2
Farming, horticultural, and animal husbandry	5.9
Fishing, hunting, trapping, and related	0.3
Forestry and logging	0.8
Mining and quarrying	0.7
Processing	3.9
Machining and related	2.8
Product fabricating, assembling, and repairing	7.4
Construction trades	6.6
Transport equipment operating	3.9
Materials handling, not elsewhere classified	2.4
Other crafts and equipment operating	1.3
Not elsewhere classified	1.9
Not stated	8.6
Total	100.0

Source: Derived from *1971 Census of Canada*, Cat. 94-717.

per cent), and trade (4.8 per cent). The manufacturing and construction sectors were 39.7 per cent and 35.7 per cent unionized in 1961 (Porter, 1969: 99). In general, blue-collar workers are more highly unionized than are white-collar workers, although union membership has grown more rapidly among the latter than among the former in recent years.

As Johnson (1972) points out, labour unions have been most successful in organizing workers and exacting relatively high wages from employers in monopolistic industries with expensive production facilities, such as automobile manufacturing, steel, and chemicals. This has happened partly because of the considerable expense that would be involved were these industries to relocate in a low-wage area, and partly because increased labour costs can generally be passed on to the consumer in the form of higher prices. Competitive industries requiring relatively little in the way of capital investment are more likely to relocate or to cease operations when faced with rising labour costs, making a union's task much more difficult. Consequently, workers in such industries (textiles, furniture manufacturing, and garment manufacturing) receive much lower wages and are much less likely to be organized. The result has been a major division between two large classes of paid workers, which, combined with the conservative politics and international structure of most large labour unions, makes it unlikely that the Canadian labour movement in its present form will provide a vehicle for organized class action. Nor is it likely that organized labour's voice in Parliament or the New Democratic Party will provide that vehicle. As Teeple has argued, "The reason why the Canadian Labour Congress—in essence, the coalition of American-based unions in Canada—has affiliated with the NDP is to win political concessions in the form of 'better' labour legislation" (1972: 246).

ELITE STRUCTURE AND ORGANIZATION

If access to power in Canadian society is gained through positions that provide effective control of productive private property, then it is clear from the data presented above that only a tiny minority of Canadians could possibly be described as members of the dominant class or economic élite. Who, then, constitute this minority? And to what extent, if any, might they be described as taking on the character of an organized group?

To date, there have been three major studies of the Canadian economic élite: a little-known one by Libbie and Frank Park (1962, 1973), a celebrated one by Porter (1965), and a partial replication and extension of Porter's work by Clement (1975).

The Parks address themselves to the question of "who owns Canada", and analyse in detail what they see as "the structure of Canadian monopoly and the alliance of Canadian and U.S. capital that is bringing about U.S. domination of Canada" (p. xv). Beginning with the premise that "control is based on ownership and that without ownership control vanishes" (p. 11), they attempt to identify the members of Canada's dominant class "that owns and controls the mines and mills and factories of Canada" (p. 10). These persons, they argue, form a tightly knit group, who, on the basis of an ideology of corporate internationalism, are selling the country out to United States financiers (see Levitt, 1970). They note that "at the centre of this financial and industrial corporate structure lie the chartered banks, the members of whose boards of directors make up the 'Who's Who' of the dominant financial groups" (p. 71), and then try to show how the same group of financiers dominates both industry and the banks through the mechanism of overlapping board memberships. While the Parks agree in retrospect that their analysis was too narrowly economic (p. ix), their work provides an effective theoretical counter-balance to Porter's and, especially in its focus on the extensive and increasing penetration of United States-based multinational corporations into the Canadian economy, a useful supplement as well.

Porter identified the "economic elite of Canada . . . as the 985 Canadian residents holding directorships in the 170 dominant corporations, the banks, insurance companies, and numerous other corporations" (p. 274). The 760 of these persons for whom relevant additional information was available held 82 per cent of the directorships in the dominant corporations held by Canadian residents. Porter points out two striking aspects of the careers of these persons: a very high proportion had fathers who were members of the élite before them, and almost all achieved their positions of dominance within established corporations. Only a tiny minority came from non-élite families and went on to establish business firms which prospered and grew to dominance.

The homogeneity of background among members of the economic élite was quite remarkable. Not only did many come from élite backgrounds, but the majority were university-educated, Protestant, Anglophone males, and better than one-third had attended private schools, such as Upper Canada College. Virtually absent were Jews and Francophones. Totally absent were women. Among those élite members whose political preferences could be determined, approximately one-half supported the Progressive Conservatives, and the other half the Liberals. No New Democratic Party supporters were found.

As Porter showed, "Economic power belongs almost exclusively to those of British origin" (p. 286). Even though over 30 per cent of the Canadian population are Francophone, they made up only 6.7 per cent of the economic élite. Jews made up 0.78 per cent of the élite and 1.4 per cent of the population as a whole. Given the over-representation of Jews in upper-level, white-collar occupations (to be discussed below), their virtual absence among the élite is all the more notable.

The Royal Commission on Bilingualism and Biculturalism (1969: 53–60.) found that, even within Quebec, Francophone entrepreneurs do not operate on a scale comparable to that of Anglophone Canadians in that province. Francophone business firms are concentrated in the agricultural and service fields, whereas those owned by Anglophones are more evenly distributed across industrial sectors of the economy. Moreover, Francophone manufacturing firms employ fewer persons, yield less added value, are less productive, pay lower wages, and are more localized in the distribution of their products than are Anglophone manufacturing firms.

The high degree of homogeneity in social background among élite members, Porter argues, has produced a group of persons very similar in belief and attitude. It is a similarity reinforced through informal social contact, kinship, and membership in certain exclusive clubs. Porter observes that "the elite world appears as a complex network of small groupings interlocked by a high degree of cross-membership" (p. 304). This cross-membership is important in the degree that it permits and facilitates co-operation and internal co-ordination among members of the economic élite, particularly in the conduct of business. As unrelated individuals, each controls enormous economic resources. Were they able to operate as a group, their pooled resources would, of course, be many times larger. In fact, "the boards of the dominant corporations . . . are . . . woven by the interlocking directorship into a fabric not unlike the web of kinship and lineage which provides cohesion to primitive life" (p. 304). Of the 907 élite members for whom the relevant data could be obtained, about 22 per cent held directorships in more than one dominant corporation, and most sat on the boards of other corporations not classified as dominant. One person held ten directorships. The majority of those sitting on the boards of the nine chartered banks were also directors of dominant corporations. Likewise, there was considerable overlap in membership among the boards of directors of dominant corporations and the major life insurance companies. In aggregate, this evidence suggests a high degree of potential co-ordination among members of the economic élite (pp. 578–80).

From a Marxian point of view, the economic élite *is* the dominant class. For Porter, the economic élite happened to be the first among several, including élites from politics, the federal bureaucracy, the ideological system (mass media, higher learning, and the clergy), and labour. He found that in general the social backgrounds of members of the various élites were very similar, with the exception of the labour élite. Many friendship and kinship ties also bound members of different élites together, and there was even considerable movement in membership among élites—all of which is conducive to a degree of inter-élite co-ordination, although Porter is careful to point out that conflict does occur. Among the several élites, in Porter's judgment, labour was probably the least powerful, the most isolated from other élites, and the most distinctive in the relatively modest social origins of its members.[7]

Following Porter's lead, Clement located the economic élite in those who through a "corporate mirage . . . preside over the corporate world, using as their means of power, the central institutions of the Canadian economy—113 dominant corporations, their subsidiaries, affiliates, investments, interlocking directorships with smaller corporations, family ties and shared class origins" (p. 125). These 113 corporations had 1,454 directorships held by Canadian residents, and an additional 306 held by persons living outside the country—mainly in the United States and the United Kingdom (p. 167). Those holding multiple directorships, his data revealed, held among them 54 per cent of the total number of directorships, with 29 per cent of the 946 members of the élite holding more than one directorship, and one member holding a total of eight. In comparing these findings with Porter's, Clement concludes that "there has been . . . an increasing centralization and concentration of capital into fewer and larger firms" (p. 168), and that there has been "a further concentration of power at the top of the economic elite over the past twenty years" (p. 168). It should be pointed out, however, that differences in the manner in which Porter and Clement define such critical terms as "dominant corporation" and consequently "economic elite" render *any* comparisons between the two studies problematic. Clement's conclusions may be true, but they do not follow directly from the data he presents.

7. For critical commentary on Porter's work, see Heap (1974).

Like Porter's, Clement's élite is disproportionately upper class in background. Indeed, "three-fifths of the present elite came from upper class origins. This was an increase of almost 10 per cent from . . . twenty years ago" (p. 219), an apparent change which he attributes partly to the decline of banking as a mobility route for the middle and working classes and the emergence of new financial sectors with exclusive recruitment patterns (p. 220). Persons of modest backgrounds who have made their way into the inner circles of the corporate world, he suggests, have done so largely through "Canadian controlled corporations in the finance sectors. . . . The only notable exceptions were 15 per cent who made it through U.S.-controlled resource and manufacturing corporations" (p. 220). Not only were a majority of the economic élite of upper-class origin, but those holding multiple directorships were much more likely to be upper class in background than holders of single directorships were. And "more than one-quarter of the present elite . . . inherited important positions from previous generations" (p. 220).

Consistent with what one would expect from the historical development of the Canadian economy, persons born in central Canada are over-represented among the élite by about 8 per cent, while those born in the Atlantic provinces are under-represented by approximately 3 per cent, and those from the West by some 5 per cent (pp. 224–30). Furthermore, élite members from the West were found to be more often from middle- and working-class backgrounds than those from other parts of the country were, and more likely to be United States *comprador* élites (residents of Canada on the boards of United States-based dominant corporations who serve the interests of an external, "parasitic" élite). As in the earlier period, Anglophones were found to be vastly over-represented among the élite, with Francophones and members of most "third" ethnic groups grossly under-represented. In the interim, the Anglophone hold on élite positions may have relaxed somewhat, with Francophones and Jews gaining slightly.[8] But changes have generally been small, and in the case of the

8. Disregard Table 35, p. 234, since Clement has used a statistical technique which leads him to make inaccurate inferences from the data. As a result, his discussion of ethnic representation in the élite is either misleading or wrong. Obviously, if the relative representation of one group increases, then the relative representation of one or more others must decrease by a corresponding amount. Table 35 implies that Anglophones have maintained their relative representation, while that of Francophones and "others" has increased. This could not have occurred and, as pointed out in the text, did not occur.

Jews, those gains which have been made occurred not as the result of upward mobility within established enterprises, but rather within family firms which have prospered and grown to dominance in a single generation.

In 1972 the economic élite was still almost exclusively a male preserve (99.4 per cent), but much more the preserve of persons with university degrees and post-baccalaureate training than it was earlier (p. 241). The vast majority of élite members received their training in Canadian institutions, with fully 42.8 per cent having obtained their undergraduate education at the University of Toronto or at McGill.

As did Porter before him, Clement attempts to unravel the tangled network of associations among this small, select, and socially homogeneous group of people. It is a network that really begins with the previous generation, for, as we have seen, most members of the economic élite are drawn from Canada's tiny, already interconnected upper class, and many were born into élite families. Associations first developed in childhood are often reinforced and multiplied through attendance at one of Canada's few and "finer" fee-paying private schools. "After attending private school and typically going on to the University of Toronto, or possibly McGill, the sons of the upper class are ready for the corporate board rooms. Like their fathers, they then enter another private world— the exclusive men's clubs" (p. 247). And they enter other private worlds as well, many of which contribute directly to internal co-ordination and co-ordination with other élites in Canada and elsewhere (pp. 243–69). It is a familiar picture.

Canadian Status Structure

According to the functional theory of stratification, "a man qualifies himself for occupational life by obtaining an education; as a consequence of pursuing his occupation he obtains income" (Duncan, 1961: 116). In addition to material benefits, he or she also receives symbolic rewards in the form of prestige. The next section is devoted to an analysis of how material and symbolic benefits are distributed among Canadians, and in particular how they are tied to positions in the occupational structure. A discussion of recruitment patterns will follow and finally some comments will be offered on inter-generational mobility in Canada.

POSITIONAL STRATIFICATION

In 1971, 82 per cent of all income reported in tax returns came from employment (wages, salaries, and commissions), 6 per cent was business and professional income, and an additional 6 per cent came from investments (Department of National Revenue, 1973). Only those with very low incomes depend heavily upon transfer payments for their income, while investment income forms a significant part of the total incomes of the very poor and the very well-to-do, but not of the majority of people. Only those in the very highest income brackets receive large amounts of money from investments (Podoluk, 1968: 146).

In 1970, 24 per cent of the population fifteen years of age and over reported no money income from any source, and 12 per cent of those reporting at least some income received less than $1,000. The average individual income for that year was $5,033, and slightly more than 8 per cent of the population reported an income of $10,000 or more. Information on individual incomes does not provide a complete picture of the financial resources to which most persons have access, however, since most belong to family units in which more than one person receives income. Indeed, about nine out of ten persons in Canada belong to a family unit, and the approximately five million families in the country reported an average income of $9,600 for 1970. About 3 per cent of these families reported less than $1,000 in income for the year, and 39 per cent reported $10,000 or more. Of those persons not attached to families, some one million in all, 19 per cent received less than $1,000, and 5 per cent received $10,000 or more. The average income in 1970 for unattached persons was $3,261.

Between one-quarter and one-third of all non-farm families with both a husband and a wife present have both in the labour force. In 1961 the labour-force participation of wives had the overall effect of increasing family income by about 13 per cent. As Podoluk notes, "Obviously, the presence of the wife in the labour force is, for many families, the means by which families can move into middle-income brackets" (1968: 132–33).

In analysing incomes, the concept of poverty is frequently used and variously defined. A Special Senate Committee, organized to study poverty in Canada, established a series of poverty lines for family units of different sizes, then estimated the number of units falling below the poverty line, as shown in Table 4. In 1969 it was estimated that

the overall poverty rate for that year was approximately 25.1 per cent; that is, one Canadian in four was a member of a family unit whose income was below the poverty line. . . . the incidence of poverty . . . was highest among unattached individuals, two-person families, and families with five or more members. The lowest incidence was among families with three and four members (Special Senate Committee, 1971: 11).

These estimates are based on the incomes of Canadians *including* government transfer payments.

In a variation on the poverty line theme, Porter considered the proportion of families able to achieve a "middle class life-style" (1965: 129–32). He estimated that, in the mid- to late 1950s, this life-style (which included, at the time, an automobile, some equity in a suburban home, a television set, central heating, regular dental checkups, and children bound for university—all paid for by a single wage-earner) was certainly beyond the means of 50 per cent, and perhaps available to no more than 10 per cent, of all Canadian families.

Of course, poverty lines are always arbitrary, however carefully they might be chosen. For this reason, and because it is more consistent with the general approach taken in this chapter, it is probably more useful to

Table 4 Poverty rates by family size, Canada, 1969.

Family Unit Size	Poverty Line (dollars)	Number of Family Units below Poverty Line (thousands)	Poverty Rate (per cent)
1	2,140	629	38.7
2	3,570	408	28.4
3	4,290	161	16.8
4	5,000	157	15.6
5 or more[a]	6,570	416	28.5

[a] Figures based on average unit size of 6.2.

Source: Table adapted from Special Senate Committee, 1971: 12.

consider how equally or unequally the available income is distributed within the population. It is difficult to summarize inequalities in the overall distribution of incomes simply or neatly, but some measure of them can be gained from knowing, for example, that approximately 40 per cent of all non-farm-family income after transfer payments goes to the top 20 per cent of all non-farm families, whereas the bottom 20 per cent of these families receive less than 7 per cent of all income (Adams *et al.*, 1971: 21). Postwar changes in the income distribution, especially in very recent years, seem generally to have been to the benefit of the top one-third of income earners in Canada, and to the detriment of the rest (Johnson, 1973).

It is important to note that these income inequalities seem to persist and increase partly as a result of the income-tax structure, rather than in spite of it. Drawing on the work of Maslove (1972), Clement argues that "in Canada the overall tax structure is regressive at the under-$6,000 level (that is, the lower the income the higher the taxation rate) and only proportional above $6,000 (the same rate over a range of incomes)" (1975: 122). Not only does Canada apparently have a regressive income-tax structure, but federal and provincial income-tax revenues have been drawn increasingly from individuals, and less and less from corporations (Deaton, 1972).

Income is important to people not only in terms of the purchasing power it represents, but also in terms of the prestige it carries. One aspect of this is the value attached to one's *source* of income. Warner *et al.* (1960) ranked the prestige of different income sources in the following manner:

1. Inherited wealth (highest)
2. Earned wealth
3. Profits and fees
4. Salary
5. Wages
6. Private relief
7. Public relief and non-respectable income (lowest).

In other words, persons receiving their income from inherited wealth were, by that fact, accorded more prestige than persons who received theirs from earned wealth, and so on.

People also attach a prestige value to the *amount* of income a person receives. In general, the greater the income, the greater the prestige it carries, except that each additional dollar seems to add a smaller increment of prestige than the one before it (Schmitt, 1965). For example, a person earning $10,000 per year does not receive twice as much prestige than another earning $5,000 per year, as illustrated in Figure 4:1.[9]

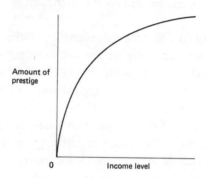

Figure 4:1
Relationship between income level and amount of prestige

The amount of income received is a function of whether or not one is in the labour force to begin with and just what occupations those who are pursue. Table 5 gives the average incomes of males and females in different occupations for 1970. As these data reveal, even when very broad categories of occupations are considered, the economic rewards attached to different categories vary enormously.

When specific occupations are considered, the contrasts in income from occupation to occupation are often far greater than those reported above, as can be seen from Table 6.

The relative income levels for different occupational categories have varied a good deal over time. Between 1931 and 1951, the incomes of professionals and managers declined relative to those of occupational groups generally (Meltz, 1968: 17), while this trend was reversed in the

9. When appropriate measurement procedures are employed, the amount of prestige is approximately equal to the square root of the amount of income.

Table 5   Average incomes for males and females, 15 years and over, who worked in 1970, by occupational division, for Canada, 1971.

Occupation Division	Average Income	
	Males	Females
Managerial, administrative, and related	$13,407	$6,135
Natural sciences, engineering, and mathematics	8,905	4,750
Social sciences and related	10,971	4,441
Religion	4,738	3,065
Teaching and related	9,014	5,401
Medicine and health	14,175	4,135
Artistic, literary, recreational, and related	6,545	3,274
Clerical and related	5,823	3,391
Sales	7,120	2,285
Service	5,276	1,954
Farming, horticultural, and animal husbandry	3,321	1,541
Fishing, hunting, trapping, and related	3,340	1,669
Forestry and logging	4,544	1,668
Mining and quarrying	6,966	4,577
Processing	5,957	2,563
Machining and related	6,695	3,263
Product fabricating, assembling, and repairing	6,402	2,828
Construction trades	6,175	3,708
Transport equipment operating	6,190	2,722
Materials handling, not elsewhere classified	5,141	2,551
Other crafts and equipment operating	7,528	3,122
Not elsewhere classified	4,496	2,603
Not stated	5,418	2,794
Total	6,574	3,199

Source: *1971 Census of Canada*, Cat. 94-768.

decade 1951–61. The relative earnings of manufacturing and construction occupations, as well as of labourers, increased in the period 1931–51, and then decreased between 1951 and 1961. In the years between 1931 and 1941, the relative incomes of those employed in agricultural and service occupations decreased, and then increased in the years 1941–61. The relative incomes of clerical, communications, and transportation occupations have declined continuously since 1931.

Occupations are not only the source of most people's incomes, they

Table 6   Average incomes for males and females, 15 years and over, who worked in 1970, twelve selected occupations, for Canada, 1971.

Occupation	Average Income	
	Males	Females
Physicians and surgeons	$26,900	$11,054
Veterinarians	14,912	6,731
Architects	14,405	5,391
University professors	13,667	7,608
Civil engineers	11,417	7,481
Commercial travellers	8,935	4,030
Insurance agents	8,680	4,485
Funeral directors	8,155	3,392
Bartenders	4,213	2,388
Cooks	4,000	2,299
Fishermen	3,141	1,992
Newsvendors	901	1,142

Source: *1971 Census of Canada*, Cat. 94-768.

are also a source of prestige (Pineo and Porter, 1967). A variety of empirical studies conducted in Canada and elsewhere show that people can rank occupations in terms of their "social standing" or prestige, and that there is a certain amount of agreement in their rankings. Table 7 shows the prestige scores accorded a selected set of occupations in Canada by a representative sample of the population. A comparison between this table and Table 6 illustrates quite well the match between prestige and income. The five occupations highest in income are also highest in prestige, while the four occupations lowest in income are also lowest in prestige.[10]

Interestingly, the prestige scores accorded different occupations in Canada and the United States are, with few exceptions, virtually identical (Pineo and Porter, 1967). An analysis of Anglophone-Francophone differences in occupational prestige evaluations in Canada conducted by the author revealed few substantial differences, and those which were found did not generally follow any obvious pattern.

10. This correspondence is to some unknown degree a function of the fact that the raters were aware of the general income levels of different occupations.

Table 7 Prestige scores, twelve selected occupations.

Occupation	Prestige Score
Physician	87.2
University professor	84.6
Architect	78.1
Civil engineer	73.1
Veterinarian	66.7
Funeral director	54.9
Insurance agent	47.3
Commercial traveller	40.2
Cook	29.7
Fishermen	23.4
Bartender	20.2
Newsvendor	14.8

Source: Pineo and Porter, 1967.

Since all persons are not equally rewarded, and since the material and symbolic rewards most people receive are in large measure determined by their occupations, it is reasonable to inquire why some occupations are more highly rewarded than others. According to the functional theory of stratification, the two major factors in the stratification of positions are their functional importance and their skill requirements. If the idea of functional importance can be set aside on the grounds that it is too imprecise to be immediately useful, we are left with the notion that some occupations are more highly rewarded than others largely because powerful incentives must be made available before people will be willing to undergo the demanding period of training which they require.

Consistent with what one would expect from the functional theory, it is generally true that those occupations whose incumbents have high levels of educational attainment tend to bring with them substantial economic and prestige rewards. At the same time, the correspondence between educational levels and rewards is far from perfect. Some occupations, for instance, are grossly overpaid relative to their educational levels, while others are grossly underpaid. Physicians and surgeons, dentists, lawyers, and airline pilots all receive much higher incomes than one would expect on the basis of their education, as do proprietors and managers of businesses generally. University professors, architects, school teachers, and professional social workers, to name but a few, have traditionally received less income than their educational levels would seem to warrant.[11] What is the reason for such discrepancies?

One possibility is that members of some occupations whose educational requirements could entitle them to higher incomes, might accept lower remuneration in exchange for other benefits, such as an added occupational prestige. Conversely, members of other occupations might forgo a degree of prestige in exchange for extra income. Still, this compensatory-reward hypothesis does not adequately account for the lack of correspondence between educational levels and economic rewards. University professors, for example, on the average have as much education and occupational prestige as physicians and surgeons, but only about half the income.

Another possibility lies in the fact that many of the relatively overpaid occupations have organized their memberships into groups which actively seek to maintain a monopoly over the services they offer, and which attempt to restrict access to group membership in order to keep their numbers small. This combination of monopolistic control and restricted access can ensure that there will be limited competition for clients and fees: competition would mean reduced income levels. Medicine, dentistry, and law all afford good illustrations of this approach. The medical profession, for example, has done battle to restrict the activities of chiropractors, optometrists, naturopaths, and acupuncturists—all of whom have posed some threat to the profession's organized monopoly on what it defines as "medical practice". Indeed, to practise medicine without a licence is a legal offence, and the profession carefully supervises the processes by which licences are obtained.[12] Many of the relatively underpaid occupations, however, are conspicuous by their lack of monopolistic control and ability to restrict access to membership. University professors, for instance, are often reluctant to organize in their collective self-interest, preferring to regard the university as a benevolent community of scholars, each in pursuit of his or her own intellectual goals. In so far as these

11. The situation for at least some of these occupations has undoubtedly changed in very recent years.
12. Note that members of these occu-

pational groups are generally forbidden by their professional associations to advertise their services or be competitive in their fees.

processes operate in the fashion described, it is difficult to see how they could be explained in terms of the functional theory of stratification.

While occupations are generally rewarded according to their educational requirements, it seems clear that the bulk of the labour force are over-educated in relation to the skill demands of their occupations. And the degree to which they are over-educated continues to increase. Table 8 provides information on the rising levels of educational attainment of persons in different occupational categories. As Collins (1971) argues, competition for a small number of desired occupational positions has led to an increase in the general educational level of the population. This development has not been accompanied by a proportional increase in the

Table 8   Percentage of labour force 15 years and over with nine years or more formal education, by occupation division, for Canada: 1941, 1951, and 1961.

Occupation Division	Percentage			Change
	1941	1951	1961	1941–61
White Collar	75.8	79.8	83.8	+ 8.0
Proprietary, managerial	56.9	66.5	73.6	+16.7
Professional	92.7	96.6	95.5	+ 2.8
Clerical	82.4	84.3	87.1	+ 4.7
Commercial, financial	65.8	69.0	73.6	+ 7.8
Blue Collar	36.7	39.3	45.6	+ 8.9
Manufacturing, mechanical	41.7	41.9	47.2	+ 5.5
Construction	33.5	38.0	43.8	+10.3
Labourers[a]	24.3	26.3	33.8	+ 9.5
Primary	19.0	23.2	31.1	+12.1
Agricultural	19.4	24.0	31.9	+12.5
Fishing, hunting, trapping	12.1	15.8	22.0	+ 9.9
Logging	11.9	15.9	22.7	+10.8
Mining, quarrying	26.3	30.0	38.5	+12.2
Transportation, communication	36.3	41.6	48.4	+12.1
Service	37.3	40.4	47.2	+ 9.9

[a] Except those in Primary.

Source: Derived from Meltz, 1968: 221.

number of élite jobs available, with the result that there has been a progressive increase in the educational requirements for jobs generally, independent of any changes in skill requirements. There seems to be no obvious way to explain the phenomenon of over-education in strictly functional terms.

In the functional theory of stratification, it is generally assumed that extended formal training is necessary to provide the skills that persons in most high-status occupations must have. Serious questions can often be raised, however, about the value of such training for the acquisition of job-related skills (Berg, 1970). Graduate engineers, for example, often find that their first job begins with a lengthy and intensive company-sponsored training program. Newly minted lawyers who join established law firms typically find that they spend their early years performing routine, almost clerical, duties. And Doctor X (Doctor X, 1965) did not feel that medical school equipped physicians adequately for the practice of medicine. It would not stretch the point too far to mention the many instances in which persons with little or no formal training have successfully masqueraded as physicians, dentists, engineers, and university professors, often to have their very success lead to their discovery (for example, Crichton, 1959). While it would be misleading to infer from these examples that the educational requirements of occupations are wholly arbitrary, some of the reasons behind them should be explored further.

One reason would seem to be that employers find educational requirements useful in selecting employees who are likely to share their general values, attitudes, and life-style preferences (Collins, 1974). Employers are often willing to pay more for well-educated workers—even though the less well educated might be just as capable of doing the work—because they are more likely to be socially acceptable persons in the employer's terms of reference.

Another reason is probably that occupational groups strive to increase their social standing by raising the educational requirements for membership as high as they can. University departments in the humanities and social sciences, for example, often try to raise their prestige by hiring only persons with the PHD degree. Figure 4:2 illustrates the relationship between levels of educational attainment and prestige as reported by Hamblin (1971), and subsequently replicated on a small scale by the

Figure 4:2
Relationship between educational level and
amount of prestige

Amount of
prestige

0   Educational level

author. Notice that, unlike income, each additional unit of education brings with it an increasingly larger increment of prestige.[13]

RECRUITMENT

Recruitment to positions in the division of labour in Canada takes place in a complex process of ascription, achievement, and random selection, only the outlines of which are presently understood.

Sex and Stratification

Perhaps the most fundamental and pervasive ascriptive criterion used in the assignment of persons to positions is sex. Generally, women are less likely to be employed outside the home than men, and those women who are employed are less likely to be employed full time. Podoluk notes that "the principal explanation given for not working a full year was staying home and keeping house" (1968: 37). When one member of a family withdraws from the labour force to manage a household, it is generally the wife who does so.[14]

13. When appropriate measurement procedures are employed, the amount of prestige is approximately equal to the square of the level of education.

14. For a more detailed analysis of women in the labour force, see Ostry (1968).

Those women who are employed are highly concentrated in a relatively small number of occupations traditionally regarded as appropriate for women, many of which are extensions into the labour market of traditional household tasks (for example, maid, waitress, nurse, nursing assistant or aide, janitor or cleaner, hairdresser, and school teacher). In addition, women have increasingly moved into white-collar occupations, most notably stenographer and sales clerk, which accounted for about 17 per cent of all women working outside the home in 1961 (Ostry, 1967: 27). Between 1901 and 1961, women's share of clerical occupations trebled, increasing from 20 to 60 per cent, and their share of commercial occupations quadrupled, growing from about 10 to approximately 40 per cent.

The considerable increase in labour-force participation among women, which was noted earlier, has not led to growth in all areas of the occupational structure. As Ostry points out, "The female share of the professional work force in 1961 was lower than at any period in this century except 1901" (1967: 28), and certain of the better-paid occupations dominated by women, such as school teaching, are increasingly being selected by men. Most women in blue-collar occupations are found in manufacturing and mechanical jobs, although their share of these has declined from 25 per cent in 1901 to 17 per cent in 1961. Since 1931 there has been a large increase in the representation of women in the agricultural sector, from about 2 per cent in 1931 to over 10 per cent in 1961. In the period 1901–61, the representation of women in transportation and communication occupations has increased from about 1 per cent to nearly 8 per cent. Nearly 70 per cent of the service occupations were held by women in 1901, but their representation had fallen to less than 50 per cent by 1961. If personal service occupations alone are considered, however, the drop has not been quite so large. Table 9 shows the percentage distribution of the labour force across occupational categories by sex.

In general, the occupations in which women are concentrated are lower in both prestige and income than the occupations of men. In 1970 women in the labour force earned on the average less than half of what their male counterparts earned (see Tables 5 and 6). This discrepancy is partly due to differences in their occupations. Part of it is also due to the fact that men are more likely to be employed full time throughout the year. If we compare men and women employed full time in the same occupations, however, substantial income differences remain. Podoluk

Table 9 Percentages of males and females, 11 years and over, in the labour force, by occupation division, for Canada, 1971.

Occupation Division	Percentage	
	Males	*Females*
Managerial, administrative, and related	5.5	2.0
Natural sciences, engineering, and mathematics	3.8	0.6
Social sciences and related	0.9	1.0
Religion	0.4	0.1
Teaching and related	2.4	7.1
Medicine and health	1.5	8.2
Artistic, literary, recreational, and related	1.0	0.7
Clerical and related	7.7	31.7
Sales	10.0	8.4
Service	9.2	15.1
Farming, horticultural, and animal husbandry	7.2	3.6
Fishing, hunting, trapping, and related	0.5	0.0[a]
Forestry and logging	1.2	0.0[a]
Mining and quarrying	1.0	0.0[a]
Processing	4.9	2.0
Machining and related	4.0	0.5
Product fabricating, assembling, and repairing	8.5	5.1
Construction trades	9.9	0.2
Transport equipment operating	5.8	0.3
Materials handling, not elsewhere classified	2.9	1.4
Other crafts and equipment operating	1.7	0.5
Not elsewhere classified	2.6	0.7
Not stated	7.4	10.8
Total	100.0	100.0

[a] Less than 0.0 per cent, but not empty category.

Source: Derived from *1971 Census of Canada*, Cat. 94-717.

argues that continuity of employment and occupation "are likely to explain away less than half of the gap that exists" (1968: 69).

In their study of Canadian university teachers, Robson and Lapointe found that "at the same type of university . . . , in the same field, with the same rank and with the same competence (measured by the highest earned degree) women earn, on the average, $1,199 less than men" (1971: 4). When this difference is projected over an entire career, and when we consider that many fringe benefits are based on earnings, the gap between males and females of apparently equivalent experience, competence, and occupational standing is very large indeed.

The gap is even larger when it is considered that men and women of equivalent competence or training do not generally work at the same jobs. Although women are concentrated in relatively low-paying, low-prestige occupations, on average, women in the Canadian labour force are not

Table 10 Percentages of males and females, 15 years and over, in the labour force, with 9 years or more schooling, by occupation division, for Canada, 1971.

Occupation Division	Percentage	
	Males	Females
Managerial, administrative, and related	93.7	94.3
Natural sciences, engineering, and mathematics	95.9	96.0
Social sciences and related	97.3	96.1
Religion	93.4	79.9
Teaching and related	98.8	98.7
Medicine and health	92.0	92.0
Artistic, literary, recreational, and related	89.2	93.4
Clerical and related	85.4	94.1
Sales	82.4	80.1
Service	65.2	61.7
Farming, horticultural, and animal husbandry	51.7	55.2
Fishing, hunting, trapping, and related	32.2	46.7
Forestry and logging	43.3	57.4
Mining and quarrying	55.4	61.8
Processing	56.8	46.7
Machining and related	62.4	57.3
Product fabricating, assembling, and repairing	63.7	44.7
Construction trades	55.0	61.6
Transport equipment operating	56.0	70.1
Materials handling, not elsewhere classified	60.1	56.6
Other crafts and equipment operating	75.1	71.8
Not elsewhere classified	59.3	58.6
Not stated	64.4	67.2
Total	69.2	79.3

Source: Derived from *1971 Census of Canada*, Cat. 94-729.

obviously less well educated than men as can be seen from Table 10.[15] Thus, equivalent educations do not yield equivalent jobs, and equivalent jobs do not yield equivalent incomes and related economic benefits.

If many women do not work outside the home at all, or if those who do find they are unable to compete on equal ground with men, it is neither an accident nor a law of nature which makes it so. It is a social fact. It can be seen most clearly, perhaps, in male-female occupational differences as these vary over time and from society to society. Films and stories of Soviet women working on road construction strike many as highly humorous, but what is revealed is a society where such a role is not at all unnatural. Lane notes that "by 1967 women . . . accounted for 52 per cent of all professional employees in the USSR, including 72 per cent of the doctors, 68 per cent of the teachers, and 63 per cent of the economists" (1971: 88). This situation, too, is in sharp contrast to the position of women in Canada. But few are likely to see these facts as whimsical, because they indicate that not only are women fully capable of working at physically demanding jobs that are generally regarded as undesirable, but they are also fully capable of working at very desirable jobs, many of which are more or less reserved for men in Canada.

Occupations are, of course, sex-typed, and even employment itself is viewed in Canada as more appropriate for men than for women. If women do not work outside the home, if they have discontinuous careers, or if they tend disproportionately to work at certain kinds of jobs, it is because of the social role assigned to them in our society. It is a social role defined in beliefs and values, learned in a process of childhood socialization, and buttressed by legal, economic, religious, and other institutional arrangements.

Ethnicity and Stratification

Ethnicity is another important ascriptive criterion used in recruitment. Table 11 shows the degree to which the occupations pursued by members of different ethnic groups vary. In general, Jews are over-represented in high-prestige, high-paying occupations, along with those of British origin

15. Proportionally more males than females have university degrees and other forms of advanced, post-secondary education. See *1971 Census of Canada*, Cat. 92-743.

(see Table 9 for comparison with the general population), while members of the other ethnic groups are under-represented in varying degrees. With some exceptions, differences in the occupational structures of these groups are constant from one province to another, but they have varied significantly over time. The overall thrust of these temporal changes has been in the direction of increasing inter-group differences, with those of Jewish and British origins strengthening their hold on occupations at the top of the hierarchy, at the expense of members of other ethnic groups.[16]

The relative positions of the British and the French in the occupational structures of the ten provinces are very similar—despite the fact that large numbers of French outside Quebec report English as their mother tongue. Another apparent anomaly occurs within Quebec, where the British enjoy an even larger advantage over the French through their grip on professional and managerial occupations than they do in the country as a whole. Moreover, within the city of Montreal itself, their advantage is greater yet. The evidence suggests that these varying disparities between the British and French occur more as a result of differences in the relative positions of the British in the occupational structures of Montreal and the Province of Quebec, than of the French (Royal Commission, 1969: 45; see also the sections on biculturalism and bilingualism in Chapter 2 of this book).

Differences among Canada's ethnic groups in levels of educational attainment closely parallel differences among them in their occupational structures. Table 12 shows the relationship between ethnicity and educational attainment for seven ethnic groups. Jews clearly stand out above the rest, followed at some distance by the British. Lowest of all are Indians and Eskimos. These differences are such that, "if the labour force of French origin had a level of education equivalent to the British, the observed differences in the occupational distribution of the two groups would be reduced by about 60 per cent" (Royal Commission, 1969: 47).

No single factor seems sufficient to account for this pattern of educational disparities. In the case of the French, Porter notes that "the educational system was inappropriate for the kind of society that by 1950 Quebec was becoming. It was an outstanding example of institutional failure" (1965: 92). To be sure, there has long been a Francophone

16. Mobility-permeability is the least well understood sub-area of social stratification in Canada at the present time.

Table 11 Percentage of labour force, 15 years and over, by ethnic group and occupation division, for Canada, 1971.

Occupation Division	British	French	German	Italian	Jewish	Ukrainian	Indian and Eskimo
				Ethnic Group			
Managerial, administrative, and related	6.9	4.6	4.5	2.3	14.2	3.8	1.6
Natural sciences, engineering, and mathematics	4.4	2.5	3.7	1.7	3.5	3.6	1.4
Social sciences and related	1.0	0.8	0.5	0.3	3.6	0.6	1.3
Religion	0.4	0.4	0.5	0.1	0.3	0.2	0.1
Teaching and related	2.5	2.5	2.3	1.1	3.5	2.4	0.7
Medicine and health	1.4	1.5	1.1	0.5	5.1	1.2	0.5
Artistic, literary, recreational, and related	1.1	1.0	0.8	0.7	2.2	0.8	1.1
Clerical and related	8.6	8.1	5.6	4.8	8.8	6.7	3.0
Sales	11.2	9.3	9.0	6.9	27.6	8.3	2.3
Service	9.1	9.1	7.3	11.2	4.9	9.0	7.3
Farming, horticultural, and animal husbandry	6.7	5.3	14.3	2.1	0.5	13.2	7.5
Fishing, hunting, trapping, and related	0.6	0.4	0.2	0.0[a]	0.0[a]	0.1	3.0
Forestry and logging	0.9	1.9	0.7	0.3	0.0[a]	0.6	8.9
Mining and quarrying	0.9	1.3	1.0	0.6	0.0[a]	1.3	1.5
Processing	4.1	6.1	4.7	6.7	1.8	4.8	4.8
Machining and related	3.4	4.0	4.9	6.9	0.8	4.0	2.6
Product fabricating, assembling, and repairing	7.7	9.0	9.4	12.0	7.8	8.7	4.1
Construction trades	8.6	10.1	11.8	22.2	2.6	10.0	13.7
Transport equipment operating	6.3	6.6	5.2	3.7	2.6	5.7	4.7
Materials handling, not elsewhere classified	3.1	2.6	2.9	3.2	0.9	3.6	3.9
Other crafts and equipment operating	2.0	1.7	1.4	0.9	0.8	1.4	0.9
Not elsewhere classified	2.3	3.0	2.1	4.4	1.3	2.7	4.4
Not stated	6.8	8.2	6.1	7.4	7.2	7.3	20.7
Total	100.0	100.0	100.0	100.0	100.0	100.0	100.0

Source: Derived from *1971 Census of Canada*, Cat. 94-734.

[a] Less than 0.0 per cent, but not empty category.

Table 12 Percentage of the population, 15 years of age and over and not attending school, by highest level of schooling and ethnic group, Canada, 1971.

Level of Educational Attainment	Ethnic Group						
	British	French	German	Italian	Jewish	Ukrainian	Indian and Eskimo
Less than 9 Years	27.0	48.4	37.0	66.0	25.6	44.1	69.1
9–13 Years	61.9	44.5	53.8	29.4	49.5	47.8	29.0
Some University	5.9	3.7	5.0	2.9	11.1	4.4	1.4
University Degree	5.2	3.4	4.2	1.7	13.8	3.7	0.5
Total	100.0	100.0	100.0	100.0	100.0	100.0	100.0

Source: Derived from *1971 Census of Canada*, Cat. 92-743.

class of lawyers, physicians, and clergymen whose educational preparation is beyond criticism, but the educational system in Quebec until recent years was not equipped to turn out large numbers of persons capable of competing on equal grounds with the British for occupations in business and industry. Partly for this reason, those of French origin in Quebec are located disproportionately in unskilled and semi-skilled blue-collar jobs. Italian immigrants generally have entered the country with relatively low levels of educational attainment. Jews have a long tradition of faith in education, and their very high levels of educational attainment in Canada reflect a pattern found among Jews in the United States and elsewhere. Unfortunately, a detailed analysis of ethnic differences in educational attainment would require more data than are currently available and more space than the present chapter provides. (The reader may refer to Chapters 2 and 6 in this book for more on ethnicity.)

Although differences in levels of educational attainment seem in large measure to explain differences in occupational distributions among ethnic groups in Canada, they do not explain them entirely. Here again, equivalence in education does not seem to yield equivalence in occupation. One reason might lie in differences in educational quality which are obscured in a simple examination of educational attainment levels, but quality is a very difficult matter to assess (Beattie, 1975: 120–25). Occupational preferences might also play a role, although, as was noted earlier, there do not seem to be any strong and consistent differences between Anglophones and Francophones in the occupations they regard as prestigious (which is not the same, however, as occupations viewed as desirable). Another possibility is that lack of fluency in English places certain groups at a competitive disadvantage (Beattie, 1975: 134–38), although Armstrong (1970) argues that this is no longer the case for Francophone professionals, at least. Finally, all questions of educational quality and language aside, it seems that the failure of equivalency in education to yield equivalency in occupation is the result of ethnic discrimination rooted in stereotype and prejudice. Here too, Armstrong argues that in the case of young, well-educated Francophones ethnicity actually operates to their advantage—an argument which finds little support in Beattie's study of the federal public service. How these processes operate for other ethnic groups in Canada remains largely unknown.

The ethnic groups considered in this analysis differ considerably in their income levels. While ethnic income disparities vary somewhat from province to province, the general pattern remains more or less the same, with Jews having the highest income levels, followed at some distance by those of British origin. When levels of educational attainment, occupational distributions, under-employment (number of weeks worked in a year), age, region of residence, and industry are all taken into account as factors influencing relative ethnic income levels, persons of English-Scottish, Irish, and Northern European origins still seem to earn more than one would otherwise expect. Persons of French, Italian, and Eastern European origins earn less. And Jews and Germans earn just about what one would expect. Table 13 shows these ethnic income disparities before and after the extra explanatory variables have been introduced. Those disparities which remain have been described as "the expression of a complex phenomenon composed of many elements which are impossible to separate: among these are the quality of schooling; work attitudes; occupational choice; motivations and values; the quality, orientation, and effectiveness of institutions; obstacles to mobility; discrimination; and the weight of the past" (Royal Commission, 1969: 35).

Since the collection and analysis of the above data, Lanphier and Morris (1974) and Beattie (1975) have studied Anglophone-Franco-

Table 13 Deviation of income above (+) or below (−) average for all groups, and deviation remaining for all groups after education, occupation, under-employment, region, age, and industry effects removed, by ethnic origin, Montreal, 1961.

Ethnic Group	Deviation from Average	Deviation Remaining
English-Scottish	+ $1,319	+ $606
Irish	+ 1,012	+ 468
French	− 360	− 267
Northern European	+ 1,201	+ 303
Italian	− 961	− 370
Jewish	+ 878	+ 9
Eastern European	− 100	− 480
German	+ 387	+ 65

Source: Royal Commission on Bilingualism and Biculturalism, 1969: 77.

phone income differentials using more recent information. Lanphier and Morris found evidence to suggest that the overall differential has probably diminished somewhat over time, although the income disparities for workers in some occupations, most notably the lesser skilled, seem actually to have increased. In commenting on the effects of the Quiet Revolution, the authors conclude that,

although it is now a commonplace that the middle class, and perhaps the skilled workers, are the main beneficiaries in terms of fresh employment opportunities, our data support the further argument that reductions in income inequality have been restricted to these same groups (p. 65).

Beattie, on the other hand, found that the Anglophone-Francophone salary differential for his sample of middle-level bureaucrats in the federal public service during this same period had actually increased (p. 188).

Social Mobility

In analyses of social mobility, the primary concern is with estimating the degree to which, and explicating the processes by which, individuals in a society inherit their class and status positions from their parents. A society in which there was complete inheritance of position (in which everyone ended up occupying positions identical to those occupied by his or her parents at an earlier time) would have no vertical mobility whatever and no permeability. One in which there was total anti-inheritance (in which everyone ended up occupying positions maximally different from those earlier occupied by his or her parents) would have the greatest possible vertical mobility, but still no permeability. Finally, a society in which the positions occupied by the parents bore no relation to those occupied by their children would have intermediate levels of mobility and maximal permeability. Each of these examples is, of course, hypothetical, useful for purposes of clarifying the concepts employed in mobility analyses, but corresponding to no known societies.

In his work, Porter found levels of internal recruitment among members of the economic élite which were far higher than one would expect on the basis of chance alone: "Of the 611 Canadian-born, 135 (22 per cent) directly inherited their positions from near kin, principally the father" (1965: 291). If those with fathers from other élites, along with those whose wives were born into élite families are considered as well, this figure increases from 22 to 31 per cent. And if still others from very wealthy, but non-élite, families are added to the total, it increases still further to 37.8 per cent. Quite clearly, the Canadian class structure is considerably less than maximally permeable, but its permeability relative to the class structures of other countries is something which porter does not analyse. Clearly, too, mobility into and out of the economic élite is severely constricted, although there is no way of knowing whether it is more or less so now than in the past, or more so in Canada compared to other countries. As noted above, Clement (1975) reports similar findings with regard to class permeability and mobility for a later point in time, but no strong inferences can be made about temporal trends, owing to differences in the methodologies he and Porter employed.

The Canadian status structure seems also to be characterized by less than maximal permeability and mobility, although the available evidence is remarkably sparse. Using data gathered on samples of Anglophone and Francophone males and females living in Toronto and Montreal, Cuneo and Curtis (1975) examined aspects of inter-generational status inheritance. For both samples of males, the higher his father's level of educational attainment and occupational prestige, the better educated a person was likely to be, and as a consequence of his education, the higher the prestige of both his first and current occupations. The same pattern of relationships held for Anglophone females. For Francophone females, the influence of father's occupation on their education was negligible, but father's occupation directly influenced both their first and their current job.

Perhaps the most frequently expressed view is that Canada stands somewhere between the United States and Great Britain in its tolerance of positional inequalities and social ascription—more tolerant than the former, and less so than the latter (Naegele, 1961; Lipset, 1963). It is a view which has not gone without serious challenge (Davis, 1971; Truman, 1971); for the data are limited and often open to alternative interpretation. Truman mounts a devastating attack on Lipset's analysis, pointing out methodological problems in his sources of information, documenting the arbitrary nature of many of his conclusions, and supplying additional information casting doubt on his rank ordering of the three nations. The debate on these issues is interesting, if inconclusive, but it suffers from a confusion between values relating to social stratification on the one hand and actual patterns of stratification on the other. It is entirely possible that the values people hold concerning inequality are only tenuously related, if related at all, to the presence or absence in a society of positional inequalities, permeability, and mobility.

In comparing their results with those reported in a major study conducted in the United States, Cuneo and Curtis were not able to conclude that the level of status inheritance in Canada was significantly different from that in the United States. The nature of the data, however, and the very difficult problems involved in making precise comparisons of this kind, prevented a more definitive statement.

At least prior to the Quiet Revolution, it was generally assumed that French Canada was a more traditional society than English Canada—late to industrialize, slow in rationalizing its system of education, less secular generally, and less mobility-oriented (Dofny and Rioux, 1964). In their study of Anglophone-Francophone mobility in Quebec, de Jocas and Rocher report evidence consistent with this characterization. They conclude that "the channels and barriers of mobility that we have observed for the French Canadians are not the same as for the English-speaking Canadians. The former go up the scale step by step, while the latter seem to move more rapidly to the top occupational levels" (1957: 66). It seems obvious that in the two decades since these data were gathered this situation has changed both within Quebec and in Canada generally, but the research necessary to demonstrate the changes remains to be done. Cuneo and Curtis's (1975) data on Montreal Francophones and Toronto Anglophones, for example, do not suggest any marked or consistent differences between the two groups in status inheritance, although it would be a mistake to generalize their findings beyond the confines of their samples.

Finally, important features of Canada's stratification system arise out of the interaction over time among migration, mobility, and the structure of class and status (Porter, 1965: 29–59). This century has seen high, if periodic, levels of immigration and emigration, largely confined to English Canada. Immigration has served as a source of recruits for occupations at all levels within the status hierarchy, although the bulk of immigrants have moved into lesser-skilled jobs (Department of Manpower and Immigration, 1974). At the same time, as Porter notes, "Canada . . . has had to rely heavily on skilled and professional immigration to upgrade its labour force in periods of industrial growth" (1965: 43). We know rather less about the characteristics of emigrants from Canada, but they seem disproportionately to have been professionals—a loss which has been more than compensated for by the influx of the professionally trained from other countries. In the 1960s, immigration reached its lowest point in 1961 and its highest point in 1967 (higher than in any other postwar year except for 1957). New immigration regulations instituted in 1962 changed the bases of selection from ethnic origin (previously, immigrants from Great Britain and northern European countries had been favoured) to education and occupation, with the result that the proportion of immigrants with high levels of educational attainment and high status occupations has apparently increased (Kalbach and McVey, 1971: 337). In this period, too, there have been rising numbers of highly qualified immigrants from the United States, while emigration from Canada to that country has declined, levels of unemployment are high, and unprecedented numbers of Canadians are enrolled in institutions of higher education. One can only guess at the long-term implications of these trends for the Canadian stratification system.

Concluding Remarks

This chapter has presented a highly selective description and analysis of social stratification in Canada. It has been selective not only because it would have been impossible to use more than a very small proportion of the available literature, but because theoretical judgments and personal preferences have led to the omission of entire topics and large bodies of material. In particular, I have deliberately not discussed many of the cultural and social psychological aspects of stratification in Canada in order to concentrate on matters of social structure and organization, with an emphasis, wherever possible, on temporal changes. Also, I have not dealt at any length with such topics as religion, the family, government, deviance, or crime and delinquency, although they are relevant to social stratification, since they are treated at some length elsewhere in this volume. Despite the separate chapters by Bienvenue and Synge, it has been necessary to devote considerable attention to education and ethnicity, as these are central to an understanding of the topic. Hopefully, this chapter will be read only as an introductory statement to be supplemented by further reading on social stratification in Canada.

Select Bibliography

ADAMS, I.; CAMERON, W.; HILL, B.; and PENZ, P. *The Real Poverty Report*. Edmonton: Hurtig, 1971.

ALLINGHAM, JOHN D. *Women Who Work: Part I*. Special Labour Force Studies, No. 5. Ottawa: Dominion Bureau of Statistics, 1967.

ARMSTRONG, DONALD E. *Education and Economic Achievement*. Documents of the Royal Commission on Bilingualism and Biculturalism, No. 7. Ottawa: Information Canada, 1970.

BEATTIE, CHRISTOPHER. *Minority Men in a Majority Setting*. Toronto: McClelland and Stewart, 1975.

BENDIX, R., and LIPSET, S. M., eds. *Class, Status, and Power*. New York: The Free Press, 1966.

BERG, IVAR. *Education and Jobs: The Great Training Robbery*. Boston: Beacon Press, 1971.

BOTTOMORE, T. B. *Classes in Modern Society*. London: Allen and Unwin, 1965.

Canada. Department of Manpower and Immigration. *Immigration and Population Statistics*. Ottawa: Information Canada, 1974.

———. Department of National Revenue. *Taxation Statistics, 1971*. Ottawa, 1973.

———. Special Senate Committee on Poverty. *Poverty in Canada: Report of the Special Senate Committee*. Ottawa: Information Canada, 1971.

CLEMENT, WALLACE. *The Canadian Corporate Elite: An Analysis of Economic Power*. Toronto: McClelland and Stewart, 1975.

COLLINS, RANDALL. "Functional and Conflict Theories of Educational Stratification", *American Sociological Review* 36 (1971): 1002–19.

————. "Where Are Educational Requirements for Employment Highest?" *Sociology of Education* 47 (1974): 419–42.

CRICHTON, ROBERT. *The Great Imposter.* New York: Random House, 1959.

CUNEO, C. J., and CURTIS, J. E. "Social Ascription in the Educational and Occupational Status Attainment of Urban Canadians", *Canadian Review of Sociology and Anthropology*, 1975, in press.

CURTIS, J. E., and SCOTT, W. G. *Social Stratification in Canada.* Scarborough: Prentice-Hall, 1973.

DAHRENDORF, RALF. *Class and Class Conflict in Industrial Society.* Stanford: Stanford University Press, 1959.

DAVIS, ARTHUR K. "Canadian Society and History as Hinterland Versus Metropolis", in Richard J. Ossenberg, ed., *Canadian Society: Pluralism, Change, and Conflict.* Scarborough: Prentice-Hall, 1971.

DAVIS, K., and MOORE, W. E. "Some Principles of Stratification", *American Sociological Review* 10 (1945): 242–49.

DEATON, RICK. "The Fiscal Crisis of the State", *Our Generation*, Vol. 8, No. 4 (1972).

DOCTOR X. *The Intern.* New York: Harper and Row, 1965.

DOFNY, J., and RIOUX, M. "Social Class in French Canada", in M. Rioux and Y. Martin, eds., *French-Canadian Society*, Vol. I. Toronto/Montreal: McClelland and Stewart, 1964.

DUNCAN, OTIS D. "A Socio-Economic Index for All Occupations", in Albert J. Reiss, ed., *Occupations and Social Status.* New York: The Free Press, 1961.

HAMBLIN, ROBERT L. "Mathematical Experimentation and Sociological Theory: A Critical Analysis", *Sociometry* 34 (1971): 423–52.

HEAP, JAMES L., ed. *Everybody's Canada: The Vertical Mosaic Reviewed and Re-Examined.* Toronto: Burns and MacEachern, 1974.

DE JOCAS, Y., and ROCHER, G. "Inter-Generation Occupational Mobility in the Province of Quebec", *Canadian Journal of Economics and Political Science* 4 (September 1971): 346–66.

JOHNSON, LEO A. "The Development of Class in Canada in the Twentieth Century", in G. Teeple, ed., *Capitalism and the National Question in Canada.* Toronto: University of Toronto Press, 1972.

————. *Incomes, Disparity and Impoverishment in Canada Since World War II.* Toronto: New Bytown Press, 1973.

KALBACH, W. E., and MCVEY, W. W. *The Demographic Bases of Canadian Society.* Toronto: McGraw-Hill, 1971.

KUBAT, D., and THORNTON, D. *A Statistical Profile of Canadian Society.* Toronto: McGraw-Hill Ryerson, 1974.

LANE, DAVID. *The End of Inequality.* Harmondsworth: Penguin, 1971.

LANPHIER, C. M., and MORRIS, R. N. "Structural Aspects of Differences in Income Between Anglophones and Francophones", *Canadian Review of Sociology and Anthropology* 11 (February 1974): 53–66.

LENSKI, GERHARD E. *Power and Privilege: A Theory of Social Stratification.* New York: McGraw-Hill, 1966.

LEVITT, KARI. *Silent Surrender: The Multinational Corporation in Canada.* Toronto: Macmillan, 1970.

LIPSET, SEYMOUR M. *The First New Nation: The United States in Historical and Comparative Perspective.* New York: Basic Books, 1963.

LIPTON, CHARLES. "Canadian Unionism", in G. Teeple, ed., *Capitalism and the National Question in Canada.* Toronto: University of Toronto Press, 1972.

MARX, KARL. *Value, Price and Profit.* New York: International Publishers, 1935.

————. *The German Ideology.* London: Lawrence and Wishart, 1965.

————, and ENGELS, F. *Manifesto of the Communist Party.* New York: International Publishers, 1932.

MASLOVE, ALLAN M. *The Pattern of Taxation in Canada.* Ottawa: Information Canada, 1972.

MELTZ, NOAH M. *Manpower in Canada, 1931 to 1961.* Ottawa: Department of Manpower and Immigration, 1968.

MILIBAND, RALPH. *The State in Capitalist Society.* London: Quartet, 1969.

NAEGELE, KASPAR D. "Canadian Society: Some Reflections", in B. Blishen *et al.*, eds., *Canadian Society.* Toronto: Macmillan, 1961.

OSTRY, SYLVIA. *The Occupational Composition of the Canadian Labour Force.* 1961 Census Monograph. Ottawa: The Queen's Printer, 1967.

————. *The Female Worker in Canada.* 1961 Census Monograph. Ottawa: The Queen's Printer, 1968.

PARK, L. C., and PARK, F. W. *Anatomy of Big Business.* Toronto: James Lewis and Samuel, 1962, 1973.

PINEO, P. C., and PORTER, J. "Occupational Prestige in Canada", *Canadian Review of Sociology and Anthropology* 4 (1967): 24–40.

PODOLUK, JENNY R. *Incomes of Canadians.* 1961 Census Monograph. Ottawa: The Queen's Printer, 1968.

PORTER, JOHN. *The Vertical Mosaic: An Analysis of Social Class and Power in Canada.* Toronto: University of Toronto Press, 1965.

————. *Canadian Social Structure: A Statistical Profile.* Toronto: McClelland and Stewart, 1969.

ROBSON, R. A. A., and LAPOINTE, M. *A Comparison of Men's and Women's Salaries and Employment Fringe Benefits in the Academic Profession.* Studies of the Royal Commission on the Status of Women, No. 1. Ottawa: Information Canada, 1971.

Royal Commission on Bilingualism and Biculturalism. Vol. III, *The Work World.* Ottawa: Information Canada, 1969.

SCHMITT, DAVID R. "Magnitude Measures of Economic and Educational Status", *Sociological Quarterly* 6 (1965): 387–91.

SVALASTOGA, KAARE. *Social Differentiation.* New York: McKay, 1965.

TEEPLE, GARY, ed. *Capitalism and the National Question in Canada.* Toronto: University of Toronto Press, 1972.

TRUMAN, TOM. "A Critique of Seymour M. Lipset's Article, 'Value Differences, Absolute or Relative: The English-Speaking Democracies'", *Canadian Journal of Political Science* 4 (1971): 497–525.

WARNER, W. L., MEEKER, M., and EELLS, K. *Social Class in America.* New York: Harper, 1960.

WEBER, MAX. *The Theory of Social and Economic Organization.* London: Hodge, 1947.

PART II

Social Process

A central fact of social life in any society is *interaction*. Behaviour systems grow out of it, and the often noted fact that certain behaviour systems occur repeatedly is what makes behaviour predictable and provides order in the social-cultural world. For the scholarly study of society, however, the situation is much more complex; because of the innumerable kinds of situations in which interaction takes place, even a complete listing of them would be virtually impossible. To bring order out of this inter-actional chaos, sociologists have found it useful to examine interaction in terms of *social processes*, which are thought of as a series of related events leading to a predictable result (Lundberg *et al.*, 1958: 242–56). Some of the more commonly described social processes are *co-operation, conflict,* and *competition*. In addition, social scientists have frequently discussed additional processes such as *assimilation, accommodation,* and *socialization*. In the second section of this book three chapters are presented in which the social processes are used to illustrate various aspects of Canadian society.

Taking a broad sociological approach in which all aspects of the society are deemed politically relevant, Rick Ogmundson of the University of Manitoba has presented an introduction to Canadian polity through an analysis of power and politics. This approach stands in sharp contrast to the more traditional political science method, which emphasizes government, political parties, and voting behaviour. Under the sociological perspective, for example, competition between the manufacturing interests of central Canada and the primary industries and agricultural interests of the West are analysed and related to the politics of the federal government. Conflict between the British and French founding groups and other ethnic groups for status and power is explored, as well as the ongoing power struggle between the federal government and the provinces. Canada is described as having an internal problem of developing and maintaining consensus and co-operation among its many groups, while at the same time having an external problem of maintaining its independence as a nation in an atmosphere of competition and latent conflict with its neighbour to the south.

Rita Bienvenue of the University of Manitoba has used the concepts of multiculturalism and stratification, along with the social processes of assimilation and conflict to present inter-group relations and ethnicity in Canada. A basic conflict is noted to the extent that the processes of assimilation and accommodation were perceived as functioning to promote cultural uniformity in the society, while at the same time other parts of the social structure are perceived as functioning toward maintenance of cultural distinctiveness and the Canadian cultural mosaic. Factors associated with assimilation and accommodation are discussed, as well as the basis for continued conflict between some of the ethnic groups within Canadian society.

Concluding the section on social processes, Stuart Johnson of the University of Manitoba has presented a social-systems approach to the criminal-justice system of Canadian society and illustrated the manner in which a set of interrelated sub-systems function together to resocialize deviant offenders with the objective that they become productive law-abiding citizens. While co-operation toward goal attainment is characteristic of many parts of the system, conflict—always latent and sometimes overt—is present to some degree in the interaction between criminal offenders and the functionaries of the various criminal justice subsystems. Problems of assimilation and accommodation of ex-offenders into conventional society are discussed against a background of rapid and planned social change.

The Sociology of Power and Politics: 5

An Introduction to the Canadian Polity

RICK OGMUNDSON*

Introduction

Governments and political parties do not operate in isolation from the rest of the community. Consequently, it is useful to consider the nature of an entire society as one begins to study the specific operations of politics as we usually understand them. It is this insight which most clearly differentiates political sociology from political science. Political science tends to focus its attention on the specifically political aspects of a polity such as government, political parties, and voting behaviour; political sociology tends to focus on the aspects of the wider society which influence such activity.

This chapter will emphasize those aspects of the general Canadian situation which are especially important to the operation of politics and government, at the expense of giving more detailed attention to topics which are considered to be more traditionally in the realm of political science.[1] The second section of this chapter outlines some of the elements

*The author is indebted to Ken Campbell, Richard Nazarewich, Marjorie Nogiec, Mark Thiessen, and Rennie Warburton for comments on an earlier draft of this paper.

1. For some standard introductions to Canadian political science, see Van Loon and Whittington (1971), Mallory (1971), and Dawson and Ward (1970). For a review of them, see Cairns (1974). Due to space limitations, theoretical and historical perspectives are also given minimal attention. For a recent review and introduction to theoretical perspectives in political sociology, see Effrat (1973). For historical perspectives on Canadian politics, see Beck (1968), Naylor (1972), and Clement (1975: Chap. 2). Similarly, provincial and municipal politics are given very little attention. On provincial politics, see Robin (1972). On municipal politics, see Lorimer (1972), Feldman and Goldrick (1972), Masson and Anderson (1972), Axworthy and Gillies (1973), and Powell (1972).

While the student should know that this exclusion of areas of knowledge normally assigned to other disciplines or sub-disciplines reflects the usual academic division of labour, he/she should not assume that this is the best way to do things. Many argue that this approach obscures far more than it illuminates.

of Canadian society which provide the environment of political behaviour at both the mass and the élite levels. The third section examines some aspects of mass political behaviour—the popular ideology, political socialization, political participation, and voting behaviour. The fourth section discusses the general power structure of Canada at the élite level, with special attention to the "non-political" élites which form a crucial part of the environment in which civil servants and politicians operate.

Some Aspects of the Environment of Canadian Political Behaviour

GEOGRAPHY AND NATURAL RESOURCES

Canada is the second largest country in the world. It is characterized by immense geographic diversity and a number of natural barriers to east-west interaction—the sea surrounding Newfoundland, the Appalachians between the Maritimes and Quebec, the Laurentian Shield between Ontario and Manitoba, and the Rockies between Alberta and British Columbia. The resulting problems of communication and transportation have directly stimulated many of the major undertakings of the federal government, such as the Canadian Pacific Railway (CPR), Air Canada, and the Canadian Broadcasting Corporation (CBC). These geographic factors have also been conducive to the development of north-south patterns of trade and to the development of regions which differ in their economic, social, and political characteristics.

Canada's natural resources, which have so far been plentiful relative to our small population, have attracted substantial foreign investment and political intervention—in particular from France, Great Britain, and the United States in that sequence. Our economy has been structured largely to fill the needs of these countries by exporting our resources to them in return for manufactured goods. In much the same way that the native Indian economy was once based on the exchange of furs for tools and trinkets, the contemporary Canadian economy is based on the exchange of other staple resources such as grain, pulp, minerals, and oil for manufactured goods like aircraft, radios, stereos, and deodorants.[2]

2. Unfortunately, it would appear that we are not doing much better for ourselves than the Indians did. Canada's natural resources are being rapidly sold out at bargain-basement prices. For confirmation of this point, see Rohmer (1973), Laxer (1974), and Bocking (1972). Furthermore, it also appears that we may soon end up in a situation similar to that of our native peoples.

REGIONAL ECONOMIC RELATIONSHIPS

As any Canadian reader will already be aware, regional conflicts, arising from different economic interests, play an important part in our politics. The major cities of southern Ontario (plus Montreal) have traditionally been the centre of manufacturing activity in Canada, while the rest of the country has depended upon primary industry. Policies which favour manufacturing tend not to favour primary industry. Consequently, there has been much economic and political conflict between manufacturing/ commercial interests in central Canada and primary industry in the West, the Maritimes, and the outlying areas of Quebec and Ontario.

A classic instance of such conflict is found in the traditional desire of the West and the Atlantic provinces to lower the tariff in order to reduce the price of manufactured goods to primary workers such as farmers, fishermen, and loggers. This lobby has been in opposition to the desire of commercial interests in central Canada for higher tariffs to protect manufacturing jobs and profits in their area. Another example is provided by Maritime resentment of the development of the St. Lawrence Seaway because it reduced the amount of trade moving through Halifax. Yet another illustration of regional conflict is provided by the recent controversy over the availability and pricing of western Canadian oil in the rest of the country. When an apparent energy crisis arrived in the winter of 1973–74, eastern Canada suddenly demanded Albertan oil at a price considerably lower than the going international price. Previously, when the western price for oil was above the international price, Easterners had not been eager to help out their western compatriots with the generosity which was now expected from Alberta and Saskatchewan. Westerners noted that a corresponding demand that tractors, cars, and other manufactured goods from central Canada be sold below the international price would not be taken seriously. The historic depths of western Canadian alienation are such that the cry "let those eastern bastards freeze in the dark" was soon heard. A more reserved expression of the frustration felt by many Westerners is put forward by Anderson (1971: 46):

Pierre Bourgeault (1972: 126), in a report to the Science Council of Canada, finds that a continuation of present policy will have this result: "Before the children of today could reach middle age most of the resources would be gone, leaving Canada with a resource-based economy and no resources" (as cited by Watkins, 1973: 114).

Instead of fostering the growth of secondary industry and facilitating the healthy diversification and decentralization of Canadian industry, then, the tariff structure has done little more than featherbed lethargic Eastern industry and stifle initiative and healthy competition. At the same time, the tariff structure has drained Western Canada of vital economic growth and thwarted its legitimate aspirations. How long do the federal government and the Eastern commercial interests expect Western Canadians to suffer silently this gross inequality? Another hundred years?

People in the Atlantic provinces, and for that matter in outlying areas of Quebec and Ontario as well, have similar feelings. As White *et al.* (1972: 15) note regarding the attitudes of people living in the Maritimes,

They consider that Ottawa is the government of the heartland and it has milked the East through high freight rates, tariffs, and other factors which have militated against the interest of the Maritimes. There is a general feeling of alienation from the centre. Government in Ottawa is not viewed as working in their interest.

It would appear that these attitudes are well grounded in fact. Campbell (1975) convincingly demonstrates that the terms of the exchange between primary and manufacturing/commercial interests have very clearly favoured the central Canadians. A discussion of regional conflict in terms of tariff and pricing policies, however, gives it an unnecessarily abstract air. The main reason why these policies attract so much attention is that they directly affect the living standards of the people involved. As you can see in Table 1, there is substantial disparity in the economic well-being of the regions and provinces of Canada. The level of income in the Maritimes is just over 60 per cent of that of Ontario, and the level of unemployment is three times as great.

A western Canadian sociologist, Davis (1971), has argued that the outlying areas of our country may best be viewed as a "hinterland" or "colony" which exports raw materials and people to the centres of economic and political control in the "metropolis" of the major central Canadian cities. These cities process the primary products and ship the manufactured goods back to the hinterland. Since primary industry provides few jobs and usually less profit than manufacturing does, the hinter-

Table 1   Indicators of provincial and regional disparities, 1969.

Province	Annual personal income per capita		Employed as % of working age population	Unemployment rate
	$	(Canada = 100)	%	%
Newfoundland	1,613	56	38.8	10.3
P.E.I.	1,818	63	48.6	5.3
Nova Scotia	2,304	79	47.0	5.4
New Brunswick	2,080	72	45.1	8.5
Atlantic region	2,032	70	44.5	7.6
Quebec	2,626	90	50.8	6.9
Ontario	3,365	116	56.1	3.1
Manitoba	2,842	98	54.1	2.7
Saskatchewan	2,516	87	51.6	3.1
Alberta	2,913	100	58.5	2.7
Prairie region	2,784	96	55.3	2.9
B.C.	3,116	107	53.9	5.0
Territories	2,542	87	n.a.	n.a.
Canada	2,906[a]	100	53.1	4.7

[a] Excluding the personal income of Canadian non-residents.

Source: *Poverty in Canada*: 51.

land areas support a smaller population at what is usually a lower standard of living than exists in the metropole. Because the metropolitan area has more power, as measured by votes and other resources such as contributions to the political parties, it is then able to manipulate the market further by means of tools such as freight rates and tariffs to increase its original advantages. Consequently, ever greater concentrations of wealth and population develop in the major Canadian cities.[3]

Since there is an obvious conflict of interests between the metropolis and the hinterland, the outlying areas periodically challenge the *status quo* in an attempt to improve their situation. The West has given birth to

3. It should also be pointed out that similar processes take place within hinterland regions. For example, Winnipeg is a metropole for Manitoba while Vancouver is for British Columbia. By the same token, as we shall see shortly, Canada itself is a hinterland area to the United States.

several significant third parties such as the Progressives, the Social Credit Party, and the Co-operative Commonwealth Federation (CCF), which has since evolved into the New Democratic Party (NDP). Likewise, Quebec has given us a whole series of protest parties—of which the most recent are the federal Creditistes, the separatist Parti Québécois, and the terrorist Front de Libération du Québec (FLQ). Similarly the hinterland provincial governments, regardless of their party label, are constantly in conflict with the federal government, which customarily represents the manufacturing/commercial interests of central Canada.

ECONOMIC RELATIONSHIPS WITH THE UNITED STATES

The Canadian economy is to that of the United States what the economy of the hinterland regions of Canada is to that of southern Ontario. Approximately three-quarters of our exports are primary products while two-thirds of our imports are manufactured goods. This is almost exactly the reverse of the situation in other affluent countries, where, on the average, two-thirds of their exports are manufactured goods, and about three-fifths of their imports are primary products (Van Loon et al., 1971: 22). Indeed, "Canadians are by far the world's leading importers of manufacturing goods, amounting to $463 per capita per year in 1969 compared to $239 per capita per year in the European common market, $116 per capita in the United States and $31 per capita per year in Japan" (Laxer, 1973b: 130). Even more striking is the fact that Canada, a leading world's exporter of nickel, paper, aluminum, asbestos, oil, and gas, actually imports substantial amounts of manufactured goods made from these raw materials (Watkins, 1973: 114). This is the equivalent of sending flour to Saskatchewan, canned cod to Newfoundland, lumber to British Columbia, and artificial ice to the Eskimos in January.

Furthermore, Canada relies heavily on foreign trade for its survival, and especially on trade with the United States (see Table 2). No other affluent country comes close to Canada's reliance on one country for exports and imports.

Canada's position as an economic hinterland to the United States affects it in much the same way as their "sub-hinterland" status affects the Maritimes, most of Quebec, much of Ontario, and the West. It leads to a smaller population with a lower living standard. It also results in a social

Table 2 Relative size of foreign trade and most important trading partners of twelve industrialized democracies, 1968.

Nation which imports and exports	Imports and Exports as percentage of national income		Trading partner providing largest percentage of imports		Trading partner taking largest percentage of exports	
	Exports	Imports	Nation	Percentage	Nation	Percentage
Australia	16.1	14.2	United States	25.8	Japan	21.1
Austria	29.6	23.6	West Germany	41.4	West Germany	23.4
Canada	24.5	27.0	United States	73.2	United States	67.9
Denmark	34.4	28.0	West Germany	18.8	United Kingdom	20.6
France	14.4	13.1	West Germany	21.4	West Germany	18.6
Italy	16.8	16.6	West Germany	17.9	West Germany	18.7
Japan	11.5	11.4	United States	27.2	United States	31.9
Netherlands	45.1	40.5	West Germany	26.4	West Germany	27.8
Norway	39.2	28.1	Sweden	19.2	United Kingdom	19.3
United Kingdom	22.9	18.4	United States	13.5	United States	14.2
United States	4.6	4.7	Canada	27.0	Canada	23.4
West Germany	19.4	23.9	France	12.1	France	12.3

Source: Manzer, 1974: 130.

structure with a relatively small middle class and a situation of political domination by the metropole.

To illustrate, let us compare the class structure of Canada with that of the United States. Because Americans do most of the management, research, and manufacturing for many hinterland areas such as Canada, the size of their middle class is much greater than that of ours. This means that there are many more good jobs per capita available to American university students than to Canadian students. "In Canada only 9.2 per cent of the 20 to 24 year-old age group compared to 30.2 per cent in the United States were enrolled in institutions of higher learning" (Lipset, 1970: 15). Thus, the United States provides a university-level education for proportionally three times as many people as Canada does, and is still able to find jobs for almost all of them. By contrast, we in Canada have difficulty finding appropriate positions for the relatively miniscule proportion of our population which does get a university education. The reason is that our hinterland economy offers considerably fewer upper-middle-class occupational positions. (For further discussion, see Lockhart, 1975.)

Just as the hinterland areas of Canada usually fare poorly in their conflicts with central Canada, so does Canada tend to suffer in its economic negotiations with the United States (see, for example, Bocking, 1972). Similarly, a situation of economic dependence leads fairly directly to a situation of political subordination. Perhaps the most striking documentation of this is provided by this interview with one of our former prime ministers.

In an interview in the Centennial Canada Day issue of the country's leading mass circulation monthly, *Maclean's Magazine*, Mr. Pearson, then prime minister, conceded that Canada was indeed a political satellite of the United States. In discussing Canada's position on the war in Vietnam, Mr. Pearson warned that "we can't ignore the fact that the first result of any open breach with the United States over Vietnam . . . would be a more critical examination by Washington of certain special aspects of our relationship from which we, as well as they, get great benefit."

To the interviewer's comment that "this isn't really very different from satellite status, is it?" Mr. Pearson admitted as much: "it is not a very comforting thought, but, in the economic sphere, when you have 60 percent or so of your trade with one country, you are in a position of considerable economic dependence" (Levitt, 1970: 2–3).

The clash of hinterland with metropolitan interests often leads to a political revolt in the outlying regions. In Canada today, there are signs of such a movement. In the intellectual world, there has been a sudden and very substantial growth in the nationalist literature since George Grant published his famous *Lament for a Nation* in 1965. A great many books have documented Canada's position of economic and political subordination at great length (for example Levitt, 1970) and have outlined innumerable means by which this subservience could be reduced (for example, Rotstein and Lax, 1974; Adler-Karlsson, 1970; Laxer, 1973). Additionally, there have been a number of protests against the further exportation of what remains of Canada's non-renewable natural resources (for example, Bocking, 1972; Rohmer, 1973; Laxer, 1974). In the political world, influential Liberals such as Walter Gordon (1966) and Eric Kierans (1967) have joined the nationalist ranks as has Richard Rohmer (1973), a prominent Ontario Conservative. The "Waffle" movement emerged and almost captured the leadership of the NDP in 1971 (see Godfrey and Watkins, 1970; Laxer, 1973). The non-partisan Committee for an Independent Canada has also been formed (see Rotstein and Lax, 1972). The federal government has struck no less than three Royal Commissions on foreign ownership (known as the Watkins Report, 1968; the Wahn Report, 1970; and the Gray Report, 1972), and has actually enacted a few small pieces of nationalist legislation in the past few years. Furthermore, studies of public opinion polls indicate that the Canadian national identity is slowly strengthening (Schwartz, 1967). Indeed, a poll taken in March 1973 indicates that no less than 57 per cent of those with an opinion favour nationalizing the foreign-owned oil and gas companies (Laxer, 1973: 14). In spite of these expressions of public opinion, none of the political parties campaigns on the nationalist issue. Indeed, they have all recently rejected their nationalist elements—John Diefenbaker and his Conservative supporters, Walter Gordon among others of the Liberals, and the Waffle group of the New Democratic Party. We shall endeavour to explain this curious phenomenon later in the chapter.

SOCIAL CLASS

Class differentiations can provide an important basis for political conflict. Those with less generally try to use the political system to improve their lot, while those with more generally resist changes which would help others at their expense. Class issues are consequently one of the predominant bases of political cleavage in most democratic countries (Rose and Urwin, 1971). Canada, in spite of its hinterland economy, has a social structural basis for class conflict somewhat like those found in other affluent countries (see Chapters 3 and 4 in this book). Indeed, Canada is characterized by relatively unequal income distribution (Adams et al., 1971:20), one of the highest unemployment rates in the Western industrialized world (Alford, 1963: 120; Adams et al., 1971: 84–86), an unusually regressive taxation system (Adams et al., 1971: 146), and a distinctly unequal access to higher education (Porter, 1965: Chap. 6). Furthermore, recent figures clearly indicate that the rich are getting richer while the poor are getting poorer! (Johnson, 1974.)

In a situation like this, it might be expected that Canada would be characterized by the kinds of class conflict found in other democracies where ordinary people attempt to use the political system to improve their situation. Indeed, when Canadians are asked which issues are most important to them, they respond in terms of class-related economic issues (see Ogmundson, 1976a). As with the nationalist issue, however, the two major parties ignore the feelings of the people on this matter (see Ogmundson, 1976b). Only a minor third party, the NDP, explicitly campaigns on the basis of class issues. Largely as a consequence of this lack of leadership (see Ogmundson, 1975a; 1975b), Canada is internationally known for the apparent classlessness of its federal electoral politics (Alford, 1963).[4]

Those concerned with the maintenance of national unity will probably find this minimization of the class issue to be unfortunate. The absence of class as a basis of political cleavage at the national level tends to increase the importance of the divisive ethnic, regional, religious, and linguistic cleavages in Canada. Class, in the Canadian context, would be a cross-

4. On the other hand, class is important in the politics of some provinces— British Columbia, Saskatchewan, Manitoba, and Ontario (see Robin, 1972).

cutting cleavage which would tend to reduce the importance of the cleavages which threaten Canada's unity. Theoretically, the workers of Vancouver, Winnipeg, Toronto, Montreal, and Halifax all have economic interests in common, as do the middle-class groups of these regions. If class and class politics were normally developed, these interests and their concomitant political loyalties would bind groups together on a national basis. People of different languages and ethnicities would at least be aware that they have economic interests in common, and this awareness would likely tend to moderate conflict on other issues.

Instead, class may make its most important contribution to Canadian politics by reinforcing ethnic hostility in the Province of Quebec. Class divisions within Quebec coincide with ethnic divisions to a striking degree. As was shown in earlier chapters, the relative economic position of the French is below that of virtually all other ethnic groups, especially within Quebec itself. This contrast has been highly visible in Montreal, Quebec's most important city, where the juxtaposition of the usually affluent English-speaking areas and the usually poor French-speaking areas makes the association between class and ethnicity evident to the most politically apathetic citizen. This coincidence between class and ethnicity has become painfully obvious to the many Québécois who have had to learn English in order to get a job or a promotion. Not surprisingly, separatists have pointed to the relatively privileged positions of the English in Quebec to underscore their argument for separation. For example, the separatist Quebec sociologist Rioux (1971: 92) points to figures which indicate the English-speaking people in Quebec occupy over 75 per cent of the jobs making $15,000 a year or more even though they form less than 20 per cent of the population. A more passionate expression of Québécois sentiment, based on a recognition of the relationship of class to ethnicity, is that of Vallières (1971: 21), in his classic book *White Niggers of America*:

The workers of Quebec are aware of their condition as niggers, exploited men, second-class citizens. Have they not been, ever since the establishment of New France in the seventeenth century, the servants of the imperialists, the white niggers of America? Were they not *imported*, like the American blacks, to serve as cheap labor in the New World?

Thus, the class cleavage, instead of providing a unifying basis of national political conflict, has been handled in such a way as to further exacerbate the tensions surrounding Canadian unity.

DEMOGRAPHY

As one would expect of a country with a hinterland economy dependent upon fluctuating commodity markets, Canada, though physically large, has a relatively small population which has been characterized by an uneven growth rate and extremely high geographic mobility during its short history. The country has experienced massive immigration from Europe (about 7.1 million people) while people have emigrated from Canada, mainly to the United States, in almost the same numbers (about 6.6 million) (Porter, 1965: 30). As a result, about a quarter of the Canadian population has consisted of immigrants during most of this century (Marchak, 1975: 75). There have also been major internal movements from east to west and from the countryside to the city in recent times. In short, the Canadian population has been in a state of flux throughout most of its history. This fact has probably inhibited the development of a national identity and culture (Porter, 1965: Chap. 2), and consequently, the development of national politics has been retarded.

The social characteristics of these many millions of immigrants and emigrants have also had implications for our national politics. In a pattern consistent with our subordinate economic status, many of the immigrants to Canadian society, especially those from the United Kingdom and the United States, have entered the society to occupy important upper-middle-class occupations, such as those of managers, doctors, and professors (Porter, 1965: Chap. 2). For example, approximately a third of our doctors and over half of our professors are foreign born or trained. Since quite some time is needed to develop a national identity, it is again likely that this phenomenon has also had the effect of inhibiting the development of a normal culture and politics. On the other hand, many of our emigrants have been among the best trained and most talented of our people. Consequently, it seems reasonable to suggest that the quality of our national politics has suffered.[5]

5. This, too, is consistent with our hinterland status. Talent, like oil, is an important natural resource. Many of our best people are exported to the

As noted in Chapter 2, the urban proportion of our population has been increasing since Confederation. Many academics believe that a more urbanized population will become less concerned about ethnic and religious issues, and more concerned about its class interests. If so, support for the New Democratic Party will likely increase in the future. As also noted by Kalbach in Chapter 2, demographic factors have been crucial to the maintenance of a limited bilingualism and biculturalism in this country. Likewise they have been at the base of the emergence of multiculturalism and ethnic pluralism in our social and political life.

ETHNIC, RELIGIOUS, AND LINGUISTIC HETEROGENEITY

There is considerable ethnic heterogeneity in our country. Almost half the population is of British origin, almost a third is of French background, while over a quarter came from a very wide variety of other nations. Chapter 2 tells us that the degree of ethnic diversity is approximately 75 per cent of the theoretical maximum! Canadians are also religiously heterogeneous: about 49 per cent of our citizens are Catholic, and about 44 per cent Protestant. The Protestant group is dispersed among a variety of denominations of which the most important are the United Church (18 per cent) and the Anglican Church (11 per cent). The small Jewish element (1.3 per cent) is also visible because it is concentrated in the important cities of Montreal, Toronto, and Winnipeg. Furthermore, ours is a bilingual country in which a quarter of the population usually speaks French. In sum, as Kalbach notes in Chapter 2, Canada is characterized

---

"metropole" of Paris, London, or New York, where they lose their Canadian identity. In return, as in the case of football players, the "metropole" sends us its surplus talent. People in a hinterland economic situation characteristically assume that art, music, literature, and science emanating from the metropole must be superior to their own. Thus, as Mathews (1973) notes, it used to be assumed that an English BA had to be superior to a Canadian MA. Today, it tends to be assumed that Americans, American-trained Canadians, and American students are usually better than their Canadian counterparts. This is true even in our graduate schools which, like our faculties, absorb the American surplus at the expense of native Canadians. Most Canadians, having internalized a negative self-image in much the same way that Indians and women do, find it easy to believe that this process results in "progress". Consequently, it should not be surprising that Ball (1973) found patterns of discrimination against Canadian football players in Canada similar to those against blacks in American football. Parallel processes doubtless take place in other spheres.

by "a degree of cultural diversity which would be hard to match any place else".

It is important to note that these ethnic, religious, and linguistic groups are not distributed evenly across the country. French is spoken mainly in Quebec. The Maritimes, Ontario, and British Columbia are predominantly British and Protestant, while Quebec is French and Catholic and the Prairies are largely populated by "third" ethnics. Consequently, these factors tend to reinforce the geographic and economic foundations for regional conflict which were noted earlier. Of greatest importance to Canada has been the coincidence of almost all these bases of conflict in the Province of Quebec. This concentration has provided an obvious social structural basis for many of the most important aspects of Canadian politics—the perpetual concern with national unity, the drive for national bilingualism and biculturalism since the 1960s, and the traditional block vote of Quebec for the Liberals. At the present time, the likelihood that Quebec will eventually separate from Canada seems greater than ever before. The separatist vote in Quebec has grown steadily from 11 per cent in 1966 to 24 per cent in 1970 to 32 per cent in 1973. The separatist Parti Québécois now forms the official opposition party in that province. Consequently, the task of maintaining Confederation seems likely to become even more challenging in the future.[6]

Many other examples of political behaviour stimulated by our social heterogeneity could be noted. The student may find it interesting to note changes in our political life which apparently reflect changes in the social composition of the population. The growing numbers of "third" ethnics have made "multiculturalism"—the official recognition and encouragement of all ethnic cultures, not just the British and the French—a significant political issue. Similarly, the increasing proportion of French Canadians in New Brunswick (up to 37 per cent by 1971) has had the effect of making that province much more bilingual and bicultural, and has

6. It is perhaps no coincidence that problems of internal disunity seem to be characteristic of countries with a hinterland economy. As Levitt (1972: 164) notes: "Political fragmentation along regional lines serves the interests of the international corporations." According to Hechter (1975: 219), Wallerstein (1974) similarly argues that a country's position in the world economy determines much about its social organization, and that "peripheral" or "semi-peripheral" countries like Canada are likely to have pluralistic cultures. For further discussion of Quebec, see Lévesque (1968), Thomson (1973), and Milner and Milner (1973).

given rise to a degree of overt ethnic conflict. Projections (for example, Henripin, 1973) of the likely decline of the use of French within Quebec itself have stimulated that province's controversial Bill 22, which will force immigrant children to go to French schools.

Political issues in most other advanced countries focus on two social cleavages—religion and class (Rose and Urwin, 1971). The factors discussed in this section help us to understand why Canadian politics have been characterized by issues—religion, ethnicity, language, region—which differ somewhat from the international norm. Awareness of these variables also leads us to realize that explanatory models developed in France, Britain, and the United States are unlikely to be of great value here. Canadian students should look instead to the work of scholars in similarly heterogeneous countries such as the Netherlands, Belgium, Switzerland, Austria, and Lebanon for ideas which will help them to explain their internal situation. Canadians should also look to those in other hinterland areas for ideas which may help to illuminate our external relationships (for example, Frank, 1967). Although Canada is affluent, it is not an industrialized country like the United States, France, and Great Britain. On the contrary, its economy is structurally similar to those of Greece, Ireland, and Portugal, in which manufacturing sectors are also underdeveloped. (See Laxer, 1974: 117.) Our present affluence is being sustained by the sale of non-renewable natural resources and, given present policies, can't be expected to last for more than another generation. Canada is thus perhaps a unique blend: an affluent, socially heterogeneous, underdeveloped country.[7]

CULTURE

Most observers, basing their opinions on subjective evaluations of the literature, have found our national culture to be "conservative, authoritarian, oriented to tradition, hierarchy and elitism in the sense of showing deference to those of high status" (Porter, 1967: 55). Furthermore, Canada is also usually understood as a country with two cultures—one

7. The inutility of the French, British, and American models is apparent in other areas as well. For example, our geographic location between two world superpowers places us in a position similar to that of Belgium or Poland.

As far as likely policy is concerned, Canadians must look to other weak countries which have achieved prosperity and independence—e.g. Sweden and Switzerland.

Francophone and the other Anglophone. Both these cultures maintain a highly exclusive existence. Indeed, many Québécois argue that, sociologically and culturally speaking, Quebec is a separate nation. It has also been argued that Canada has recently developed a pluralistic culture. The desire to maintain the ethnic identities of Canadians is a distinctive aspect of the national value system which contrasts sharply with that of most countries, the United States in particular. Another striking characteristic of Canadian culture is the low level of nationalism and the lack of a national myth, a national ethos, and other such national symbols. For example, Canada adopted a national flag only in 1964, and this flag still lacks complete national legitimacy.[8]

Yet another distinguishing aspect of our culture is the continuing importance of foreign influence. The very fact of Canadian, as opposed to British, citizenship did not exist until after the Second World War. The symbolic tie to the British monarchy remains—stamps, coins, and bills still bear pictures of the Queen—and this institution is a highly divisive issue. Recent surveys indicate that two-thirds of the Anglophone population wishes to retain the monarchy while only one-quarter of the Francophone citizenry wishes to do so (Manzer, 1974: 153–54). None the less, the declining British influence is overshadowed by the dominant and growing presence of American culture in virtually all walks of Canadian life. The degree of assimilation into American culture is already such that national surveys of young English-speaking Canadians have indicated that they feel they have more in common with Americans than they do with French Canadians (Manzer, 1974: 174). In the opinion of Englemann and Schwartz (1975: 87), "In a very real sense, Canadian popular culture is North American culture."[9]

Here again, another trait of our social structure coincides with observ-

8. For instance, when elementary students waved the new flag on the steps of the Vancouver courthouse, in celebration of Flag Week in British Columbia, they were confronted by a group of older people parading the Red Ensign. Newspaper reports stated that there was a shouting match and that the two groups almost came to blows (*Winnipeg Free Press*, June 25, 1974: 4).
9. It is euphemistic to speak of "North American" culture. American corporations with branch plants in Canada refer to themselves as "multinationals". American unions with branches here call themselves "internationals". This is a semantic convention which gives Canadians the illusion that they play a meaningful role. The North American culture of which Englemann and Schwartz speak is American culture, not some distinctive blend of two traditions.

able political events. A dual culture supports the political conflicts between the French and the English. A supposed culture of deference may help to explain our apparent lack of class conflict and nationalism. The continuing high level of foreign influence on our culture may be a cause, or an effect, or both, of our history of economic and political subordination.

THE SYSTEM OF GOVERNMENT

As a consequence of its British origins, Canada has a parliamentary type of democracy and plurality electoral laws. Unlike the United Kingdom, Canada also has a federal system of government. Each of these characteristics of our legal structure has political implications. (For a full discussion, see Englemann and Schwartz, 1975: Chap. 3.)

The parliamentary system requires that government policy be initiated by a member of the House of Commons and that a majority vote for the policy before it becomes law. This stipulation provides a very strong impetus toward party organization and party discipline. Consequently, political parties are much more important in Canadian politics than in American politics where the division of power separates the executive from the legislative branch. The parliamentary system also gives the majority party a strong advantage, since it can determine when an election is held. Conversely, the possibility of minority governments occasionally gives small third parties a position of influence—for example, the Progressives 1921–25; the Creditistes, 1963–68; the NDP, 1972–74.

Our electoral laws also have political consequences. In many democratic countries, a system of proportional representation is used. This system assigns seats to a party in accordance with their percentage of the vote; the effect of each vote is thus equalized and presumably appeals for support on national issues are encouraged. In countries with a British political tradition, seats in the House are instead assigned to whoever wins the most votes (a plurality) in a territorially defined constituency. This system has the effect of helping the strongest party at the expense of the second strongest, and of helping the two stronger parties at the expense of the other parties. It also gives the governing party an advantage, since it can make up the constituency maps, sometimes in its own favour—for example, the "rotten boroughs" of Britain and "gerrymandering" in the United States. In Canada, boundaries have typically favoured rural areas over urban areas (see Robin, 1972; Schwartz, 1975: 214). A classic example of the distortions in the vote possible because of these two factors is provided by the 1973 Quebec provincial election in which the Parti Québécois won about 32 per cent of the vote and less than 6 per cent of the seats! Clearly then, these aspects of our electoral system help the strong (and the interests they represent) at the expense of the weak.

Canada has a federal political system combined with the British parliamentary system. Given crucial Privy Council judicial decisions, the British North America Act has been defined in such a way that the provinces have a great deal of power. As a consequence and also because of the nature of our social structure, conflict between the national and provincial governments has been a constant source of stress in the Canadian system. The federal system has also encouraged the development of strong provincial political parties which sometimes oppose their federal counterparts and which speak for regional and ethnic interests (Englemann and Schwartz, 1967: 131–32). Furthermore, the federal system has helped regionally based third parties such as Social Credit and the NDP, because although their national strength is limited they have successfully formed provincial governments.

THE EXTERNAL ENVIRONMENT

One cannot understand the politics of a country by consideration of internal factors alone; the international environment also plays a role. In the case of Canada, this factor has been of special importance. Canada was a British colony until 1867, but formal ties with the United Kingdom remained long after and formal independence was achieved only on the signing of the Statute of Westminster in 1931. Even as late as the declararation of the Second World War, it was considered momentous that Canada did not declare war as soon as the United Kingdom did. Indeed, some constitutional differences may still be referred to the British Privy Council as a court of last appeal!

Preoccupation with the British tie has clouded recognition of the growing influence of the United States on the Canadian polity: Canada has moved from the orbit of one world super power directly into the orbit of another. The pervasive American influence on the Canadian polity has been alluded to many times already in this paper and in previous chapters and will become even more evident in the following sections of this chapter.

SUMMARY

There is considerable ethnic, religious, and linguistic heterogeneity in Canada, as well as significant geographic and economic bases for regional conflict. Since ethnic, religious, and linguistic groups tend to be concentrated in particular regions, the potential for regional conflict becomes even greater. Of crucial importance is the coincidence of many of these cleavages in the Province of Quebec, and to a lesser degree in the Prairies. Consequently, in many respects our internal political life more closely resembles that of countries like the Netherlands, Belgium, Switzerland, and Austria than it does the other English-speaking countries.

The other cardinal observation to be made about the environment of Canadian politics is the omnipresence of the American fact in all aspects of Canadian life. In particular, our status as an economic hinterland has a profound influence on our entire society. In this respect, our political life more closely resembles that of countries like Poland, Chile, Guatemala, or Greece than it does that of the countries to which we usually look for intellectual leadership. Thus, just as Canada has the internal problem of maintaining its unity, it has the external problem of maintaining its independence.

Canada approaches these immense tasks with a conservative, divided, and Americanized culture which still shows strong signs of its colonial history and which is devoid of the national symbols, myths, and heroes that help other countries to meet similar challenges. This culture has been further weakened by a volatile demographic history. The issues which might unite the country—social class and national independence—are avoided by the major parties.

Mass Political Behaviour

All the factors discussed in the previous section affect the political behaviour of the ordinary citizen. Four important aspects of mass political behaviour are the popular ideology, political socialization, political participation, and voting behaviour.

POPULAR IDEOLOGY

Ideology has been defined and described by Macpherson (1973: 157–58) as: "Any more or less systematic set of ideas about man's place in nature, in society, and in history . . . which can elicit the commitment of significant numbers of people to (or against) political change. . . . Ideologies contain, in varying proportions, elements of explanation (of fact and of history), justification (of demands), and faith or belief (in the ultimate truth or rightness of their case)." Ideologies reflect the nature of socio-economic relationships in a society and dependably promote the interests of one or more groups. Ideologies can be usefully distinguished as either "dominant" or "counter". Dominant ideologies, by obvious definition, represent the interests of those who are powerful and justify their position. Counter-ideologies represent the interests of other groups and seek to change existent arrangements.

The dominant ideology in Canada, reflecting the American influence, is liberalism.[10] Liberalism analyses society in terms of individuals, placing

10. One indication of the dominance of liberal ideology is to be found in the enormous size of Anglophone American psychology departments. Another is the popularity of random sample surveys in sociology. These phenomena reflect an individualistic perspective which assumes that social events can be explained by aggregating individual attitudes and behaviour.

The dominance of liberal ideology in Anglophone American culture is given logical expression in the evolution of family arrangements to the pattern of "universal permanent accessibility" of which Ramu writes in his chapter on the family in this book. A liberal ideology, after all, emphasizes individual rights at the expense of community institutions such as the family. It is intriguing to note the way in which liberal individualism is eroding even the traditional family unit, and is making one's most intimate personal relationships a matter of "free trade" in a perpetually open marketplace where it is considered fair to cast aside any partner who does not, for the moment, provide the best deal at the best prices ("free competition"). As part of this pattern, physical/emotional relationships, especially among the unmarried, are increasingly expected to involve no more long-term commitment than the rental of a motel room or a purchase at the grocery store. Since all contracts are short term, jealousy, which is indicative of "ownership" and long-term commitment, is frowned upon. All partners involved are expected to keep their cool, as though it were indeed a business transaction.

Another indicator of the dominance of liberal individualism is to be found in the nature of our popular dances, in which partners frequently fail to touch or even look at each other. (Fortunately, most couples still manage to get over this isolationism later on in the evening.) Compare this to old-fashioned dances, especially those of the community circle type which you may still encounter at weddings of ethnic groups which have managed to retain part of their former non-liberal culture.

emphasis on the value of liberty, and it is characterized by a policy concern with equality of opportunity (see Horowitz, 1966). As Marchak (1975) notes, this ideology pictures Canada as a democracy with a free-enterprise economy, general equality of opportunity (anyone who works hard can make it), basic similarity of material conditions (classlessness), and an independent, neutral government responsive above all to the wishes of its citizens as expressed through the democratic process.[11] Liberalism asserts that democracy also exists in the economic marketplace where the sovereign consumer determines what business produces. Thus, via the mechanisms of the vote and the decision to purchase, the citizenry is believed to be essentially in control of all the important aspects of economic and political life. Consequently, any complaint about the way things are becomes an attack on the popular will and upon the foundations of democracy itself. For example, pollution caused by automobiles is attributed to the public desire to drive cars.

This ideology serves the interests of the dominant groups in our society. Clearly it is in the interests of politicians to be able to explain their action (or inaction) in terms of the popular will. Businessmen also find it convenient to justify whatever they do in terms of consumer desires. Furthermore, these ideas are particularly useful to Canadian businessmen because they defuse the kind of class conflict which might otherwise result in higher wages, inheritance taxes, and income redistribution. If people believe that there is equality of opportunity, they will blame themselves, not the nature of social arrangements, for their disappointments in life. Instead of becoming involved in political protest, they are likely instead to sublimate their sorrows in religion, television, alcohol, drugs, or sex. Likewise, this belief system is of great utility to American interests. A liberal ideology in the economic sphere suggests that there is (or should be) genuine free enterprise, equality of opportunity, and honest competition. A recommendation of a policy of free trade with the metropole (be it the United States or American plants in southern Ontario) has the practical effect of allowing that area to extract maximum benefits from its hinterland. A liberal ideology in the cultural sphere argues for the free flow of ideas and individuals (for example, professors) in such a way as

11. Perhaps it should be noted that Marchak ultimately concluded, after consideration of much empirical ma-terial, that the liberal version of our society bears little relationship to reality.

to encourage the dominance of the arts and science of the metropole. This domination leads those people in the hinterland area who believe that equality of opportunity exists to think that their own traditions must, therefore, be inferior, and that efforts to preserve them are reactionary. (For further study, see Mathews, 1973; various essays in Lumsden, 1970.)[12]

There are at least four significant counter-ideologies in Canada. These are conservatism, nationalism, democratic socialism, and Marxism. All of these points of view similarly differ from the liberal perspective in that they analyse society in terms of groups, not individuals. Conservatives are concerned with the maintenance of a traditional community conducive to the original Canadian ideal of "peace, order, and good government", rather than the liberal American ideal of "life, liberty, and the pursuit of happiness" (see Grant, 1965). Nationalists view Canada as worthy of more than a superficial legal preservation, and this belief usually leads them to recommend some kind of government intervention (see Christian and Campbell, 1974: Chap. 6). Social democrats of the NDP variety emphasize the value of equality of condition and advocate gradualistic policies aimed at improving the situation of the less-privileged citizenry. Marxists generally seek the destruction of all class distinctions based on private property; many are also concerned with complete independence from the United States.

It is not quite clear at this point whose interests these various counter-ideologies serve. All, of course, claim that their approach would be best

12. One example of the important role played by cultural workers trained by the metropole is to be found in the implications of conventional American economic theory, which generally recommends policies which benefit the metropole at the expense of the hinterland areas. Individuals trained in such a perspective find it difficult to adapt to the very different task of attempting to maximize benefits for a hinterland (see Levitt, 1970).

It is perhaps less obvious that an Americanized liberal/radical in Canada objectively supports American imperialism. A liberal/radical who begins with the liberal paradigm (see Kuhn, 1970) quite logically ends up advocating greater individual liberty and freedom. In a metropole, this is heady stuff indeed for it means a change in status for blacks, Chicanos, Indians, and women. In a hinterland like Canada, greater freedom for businesses and individuals means further absorption into a continental arrangement with the United States (see Grant, 1965). This, in turn, means the destruction of the Canadian community and a victory for American imperial interests. Thus, in an ironic twist of fate, the Americanized enemy of oppression himself becomes an oppressor in the Canadian context.

for almost everyone. Conservatism used to represent the interests of the dominant business classes in Canada but no longer seems to do so; thus it has declined markedly in its importance (see Grant, 1965). Judging by patterns of voting support, the NDP variety of democratic socialism represents the interests of skilled labour more than those of any other group. Marxism claims to represent anyone who is not an owner, but currently it is the province of fringe intellectuals and trade unionists. Nationalism in Anglophone Canada appears to represent the interests of the small businessmen who are being eliminated by foreign competition, and of professionals in the ideological system who are in danger of losing, not only their jobs, but also a country to write and talk about. Nationalism is a successful competitor with the liberal ideology only in Quebec where, as Guindon (1967) notes, it serves the interests of a newly emergent Francophone middle-class group which wishes to occupy positions currently held by Anglophones.

POLITICAL SOCIALIZATION

Political socialization is the process by which individuals or groups learn ideological interpretations of political life. By definition, the ideology most often taught and accepted will be the dominant one which legitimates the position of the most powerful groups. Consequently, Elia Zurick (1975: 7) views political socialization as a "process of system legitimation whereby individuals are assigned differential access to power resources in society."

The major agencies of political socialization are the family, the church, the political parties, the mass media, and the school system. The family provides the first orientation to authority, to class and sexual roles, to the political parties, and to society in general. Most often this orientation encourages an individual to accept the status quo, and, very often, to vote for exactly the same party as his or her parents. The churches usually advocate obedience to authority and to the law, the maintenance of the nuclear family with its traditional sex roles, and the acceptance of one's material position in the present life. In short, organized religion usually functions to support the civil authorities and the dominant groups they represent. Political parties are also an important source of opinion leadership. In Canada, virtually all have supported the present political arrangements. They have also tended to emphasize religious and ethnic issues at the expense of class and nationalist issues.

"Of the various socialization agencies, the school and mass media are central in terms of their legitimizing roles" (Zurick, 1975: 20). Unfortunately, little formal empirical study has been done on political socialization by the mass media in Canada. However, it is clear that people spend a great deal of time watching television. For example, Caron (1971) reports that Canadian children of ages three to five spend 64 per cent of their waking time watching the tube! Even in the absence of conventional research, it can be said with confidence that the image of the world presented on television must be quite influential. Not unexpectedly, the content of our daily viewing generally encourages faith in authority and the maintenance of conventional class and sexual roles. Figures such as doctors, lawyers, and policemen are routinely portrayed as paragons of virtue, strength, and wisdom, and females regularly do little but scream for help. Working-class and minority people are usually pictured as basically happy (Good Times!), even if, like Archie Bunker, they are also prejudiced and ignorant.

Advertisements successfully encourage us to buy all kinds of goods (shampoos, shaving lotions, patty-stackers) which we might otherwise live happily without. Other advertisements directly encourage the gullible to believe that any number of large corporations are out there conserving energy, fighting pollution, and selflessly serving the community. The unrealistically affluent positions of most television characters obscure our own problems and give the impression that deprivation exists only in far-away places like India and Ethiopia. The news itself, in all the media, is largely managed by the government and by important business interests (see Clements, 1975: Chap. 8). Available empirical information on literature indicates that books for pre-school children stereotype sexual roles (Pyke, 1975). It also shows that both history books (Mealing, 1965) and novels (McDougall, 1971) minimize class as a theme.

Just as these characteristics of mass-media content in Canada serve the interests of our indigenous dominant groups, so other aspects of the content affect our metropole. Ample information is available which demonstrates that a process of American assimilation into our culture via the mass media is well under way. Although it is so much a part of life in Canada that it rarely enters the conscious mind (in itself a symptom of assimilation), anyone who reads a newspaper, listens to the radio, or watches television will be exposed to a high proportion of American content. Likewise, almost 80 per cent of the magazines sold in Canada are American. Indeed, we spend as much on American comic books as we do on the seven leading Canadian-owned magazines combined (Manzer, 1974: 111–13). Similarly, less than 2 per cent of the films shown in Canada are Canadian (Manzer, 1974: 110).

A parallel situation exists in our school system. "Schools have, in some measure, taken over the earlier task of the church in actively (if sometimes unwittingly) educating each class and ethnic group to its 'rightful' position in the social and economic order" (Pike, 1975: 17). The "third" ethnic groups are encouraged to assimilate into one of the two Charter Groups (Pike and Zurick, 1975: ix). The French and the English learn to differentiate themselves and are thus "socialized into discord" (Lamy, 1975; see also Johnstone, 1969; Reilly, 1971). The schools are structured so that the most privileged, not the most talented, are the ones which graduate and continue to university (see Porter, 1965: Chap. 6; Breton, 1972); this process is legitimized by the supposedly "objective" criteria which are used in the sorting-out process (Pike, 1975: 7, 17; Zurick, 1975: 21). Other such processes are apparent in the content of history books (Hodgetts, 1965) and other texts (Pratt, 1975) which, like the mass media and the political parties, portray Canada as a land of "bland consensus" which has no important economic conflicts between classes. Another striking characteristic of the Canadian school system is the lack of explicit political socialization which it gives the citizenry. White *et al.* (1972: 93) maintain that "the attitudes of the educational bureaucracy has been that politics, like sex, should be learned in the streets rather than the classroom." As they also note, political socialization via the schools is fragmented because of the ten different provincial systems. This situation contrasts sharply to the centralized school systems of other countries which typically give their students systematic exposure to a set of nationalist political ideas about their country.

As might be expected, our schools also reflect the pervasive influence of American popular and political culture (Manzer, 1974: 151). This process is probably much more advanced at the university level, where less than half of the members of Anglophone Arts and Science faculties are Canadian, and about a quarter are of American origin (Cottam,

1974: 14).[13] Of the Canadian half, many obtained their graduate degrees in the United States or under the direction of Americans in Canada. These factors have been shown to reduce course offerings on Canadian topics, the use of Canadian books, and the amount of research done in Canada (Steele and Mathews, 1970).[14] Not surprisingly, studies have revealed that grade eight students in Kingston (Van Loon *et al.*, 1971: 27) and students in a Canadian university (Singer, 1971) know more about

13. Contrary to popular impression, the massive hiring of non-Canadians has taken place at a time when ample numbers of qualified Canadians were available. Indeed, Hugh MacLennan has calculated that in 1967–68 only 9.5 per cent of available and academically qualified Canadians were hired (Cottam, 1974: 37). More recently (1971–72), Cottam (1974: 5) has calculated that approximately 40 per cent of new Canadian PHDs were not able to obtain appropriate employment. Similarly, the Economic Council of Canada has estimated that there will be 7,000 unemployed PHDs in Canada by 1977. The same study indicates that while unemployment among Canadians has been steadily increasing, so has the hiring of foreigners which increased from 36 per cent of available jobs in 1962–63 to 75 per cent in 1970–71 (Zur-Muehlen, 1972: 112–13). A similar pattern exists in our graduate schools where approximately half of the doctoral students are not Canadians (Cottam, 1974: 32). In sum, there exists a pattern of *de facto* discrimination against Canadians in their own country.

It is apparent that a curious situation exists here. Canadian taxpayers massively subsidize the American educational system by training their excess students. They also provide employment for surplus American scholars who are unable to find jobs in their own country. They also educate, at great expense, native Canadian PHDs and then refuse to allow them to work. One can say only that the generosity of Canadians certainly sets a fine example for the rest of the world to follow.

This otherwise amazing phenomenon is quite consistent with our hinterland status. At the same time as Canadian professors began to experience unemployment, so did those in the United States. Consequently, we were gracious enough to give up a valued resource—university positions—to the surplus talent of the metropole, while consigning our own people to unemployment or underemployment. We also send our natural resources to the metropole even when innumerable studies have indicated that it is not in our best interests. Similarly, our leaders have also agreed to send about half of whatever surplus cash we may accumulate to the States (see Levitt, 1970: Chap. 1). Our generosity with university positions is only part of the same pattern. Likewise our willingness, at least on the Anglophone side, to be assimilated reflects our pattern of acquiescence to the needs of the metropole.

14. Steele and Mathews (1970: 172) cite one classic instance of this process:

At Winnipeg University, for example, the only Canadian on the Political Science Department there resolved to use two US and three Canadian texts instead of four out of five US texts for an introductory Political Science course in 1969–70. . . . In the fall some one hundred and twenty students unanimously approved of the change for their course. Professor Rodgers received a letter from the chairman of his department on September 15, "insisting I use the four out of five American texts or else face 'disciplinary steps' ".

American news and politics than they do about Canadian news and politics. Thus, in the schools as in the mass media, a process of assimilation into the culture of the metropole is taking place—especially so in Anglophone Canada.

Clearly, however, it would be mistaken to give the impression that processes of political socialization in Canada are such that only the dominant ideology has a chance to survive. Change can and does take place. The very presence of counter-ideologies indicates that some sources of socialization encourage alternate interpretations of reality. Furthermore, there is another socialization agency—personal experience—which often forces people to consider alternative perspectives. When the reality of personal experience changes for large numbers of people, the dominance of an ideology may be threatened. For example, it has been argued that a deteriorating economic situation will soon rally the populace to the nationalist cause (Laxer, 1973).

POLITICAL PARTICIPATION

Studies of electoral political participation indicate a pattern of intensive activity by a very few and relatively little input by the bulk of the population (except for the vote itself). For example, a study of the 1965 federal campaign found that only 14 per cent of the citizenry had attended a political meeting, and only 5 per cent had helped in the election campaign (Manzer, 1974: 304). Those who do take part tend disproportionately to be males of high status. Women and males with ordinary occupations tend not to be active. In fact, Van Loon (1974: 303) has concluded that a full 30 to 40 per cent of our citizens (the poor ones) are virtually excluded from the electoral process. This pattern of apparent exclusion is even more striking at the level of elected politicians where "third" ethnics, as well as women and men of ordinary status, are rarely to be found (Manzer, 1974: 256). For instance, less than 1 per cent of the people elected to the provincial and federal legislatures have been female (Manzer, 1974: 253).

One plausible explanation for this pattern is that past patterns of legal exclusion of women, the poor, and third ethnics continue to inhibit participation today. As Manzer (1974: 276) notes: "At various times in Canadian history, Roman Catholics, Quakers, Jews, Mennonites, Doukobors, Eskimos, Indians, Chinese, Japanese, women, and people without property have been by law ineligible to vote." The first election with something resembling universal manhood suffrage took place in 1900. "Third ethnic" males were largely deprived of the vote in the conscription election of 1917. The first election with almost universal male and female suffrage took place in 1921. The gradual extension of the franchise to remaining minority groups has continued until recent times. For example, Indians were given the right to vote in federal elections only in 1960 and they still cannot vote in Quebec provincial elections! (Schwartz, 1975: 214.) Consequently, Canada's history as a democracy is relatively short —especially if we compare ourselves to the United States.

Another variable which may help to explain this pattern is the simple fact that people of ordinary status lack many of the resources—money, time off work, access to information—which those of higher status enjoy. It is possible too that genuine discrimination against women, "third ethnics", and males of ordinary status still does exist among those who control party nominations. Yet another factor may be the attitudes which our citizenry has toward the political process. Surveys indicate that Canadians are characterized by high levels of alienation (Presthus, 1973: 291), and by low levels of political interest, trust, knowledge, and efficacy (see Presthus, 1973: 38; Manzer, 1974: 306); these attitudes may be a reflection of historical experience. Hinterland areas have often supported movements of populist protest, but they have rarely had any significant impact at the federal level. It has been persuasively argued that the democratic process lacks legitimacy in Quebec where many feel it has only served as a tool by which the English subordinated the French (Trudeau, 1968: 103–23). The lack of participation by working-class people may reflect the fact that neither major party appeals to their economic interests (see Ogmundson, 1976b).[15] Finally, there may be increasing recognition of the fact that the locus of power has been shifting from Ottawa to the provinces and to Washington.

Non-electoral activities such as writing letters, demonstrating, and

15. It may be relevant to note that Canadian politics have been characterized by a number of third parties since universal suffrage appeared in 1921. This is extraordinary because our electoral laws strongly favour a two-party system (see Rae, 1967). This pattern may indeed reflect hinterland/working class/Québécois alienation from the major parties.

striking are also a form of political participation. As Van Loon *et al.* (1971: 81) point out, these activities are probably more influential than electoral participation. Canadians have traditionally been quite active in non-electoral political activities. During the nineteenth century, there were rebellions led by Papineau and Mackenzie in 1837, and by Riel in 1870 and 1885. Early in the twentieth century, farmers' movements were extremely active in the Prairies and Ontario. There has also been a long history of bitter class conflict. Some notable examples of such conflict are the Winnipeg General Strike of 1919, the "trek to Ottawa" of 1935, the Oshawa General Motors strike in 1937, the co-ordinated national strikes of 1946, the Asbestos strike of 1949, the Murdochville strike in 1957, the Newfoundland logger's strike in 1961, and the Quebec Common Front general strike in 1972.[16]

VOTING BEHAVIOUR

Liberal ideology holds that the citizen chooses in the political marketplace after giving careful consideration to alternative party platforms and making a rational decision about which party would best serve his interests. Given the dominance of this viewpoint, early American students of the vote designed their studies to ascertain the process by which the voter decides (for example, Lazarsfeld *et al.*, 1944). Much to their surprise, they found that little rational calculation goes into the typical vote, and that partisan identification (loyalty to a given political party) is the best predictor of the vote in most countries. Very often these loyalties are formed because of some important historical event such as the Depression and are then passed on from generation to generation in much the same way that religious affiliations are (see Campbell *et al.*, 1960). Voting patterns thus often reflect events which have long since passed out of the consciousness of the citizenry. The direction of aggregate partisan identification is, of course, very important to the electoral fortunes of the various parties. At the federal level in Canada, the Liberals usually enjoy

16. Many of these strikes were put down by the army, the RCMP, or the local police (see Brown, 1973). As noted earlier, their memory has been suppressed by Canadian journalists, novel- ists, historians, and social scientists who, until recently, ignored the role of social class in Canadian life (see Mealing, 1965; McDougall, 1971; Meisel, 1965).

the allegiance of just over 40 per cent of the population, the Progressive Conservatives just over 30 per cent, and the New Democrats just over 15 per cent.

Meisel (1972: Chap. 1; see also Schwartz, 1974) has outlined other recent patterns of the federal vote in Canada. Of all the characteristics of Canadian life, religion relates most strongly to the vote; overall, Catholics display a strong tendency to support the Liberals, while Protestants, in turn, display a weaker tendency to support the Conservatives. As far as ethnicity is concerned, French Canadians show a strong tendency to vote Liberal, and the British a much weaker tendency to vote Conservative. In terms of region, Quebec votes solidly Liberal with a few Creditiste and Conservative seats while the Prairies vote solidly Conservative with a few NDP and Liberal seats. Except for the occasional NDP member from Cape Breton, the Maritimes split their allegiance between the Liberals and Conservatives, with the latter holding the edge in recent times because of the electoral appeal of John Diefenbaker and Nova Scotian Robert Stanfield. British Columbia always elects some NDP members while the remainder of the seats alternate between the Liberals and the Conservatives. All three Anglophone parties consistently win seats in Ontario with the bulk of the seats shifting between the two major ones (for historical figures, see Beck, 1960). Most other characteristics display a minimal or variable relationship to balloting. In sum, Canadian voting patterns are strongly related to religion, ethnicity, and region, while showing a minimal relationship to other characteristics—in particular, social class (see Alford, 1963).

Consideration of these patterns immediately reveals that some of the social cleavages discussed in the previous section are clearly related to the vote, while others are not. Liberal ideology leads one to expect that political party behaviour will faithfully reflect the wishes of the voters, and it is tempting to conclude that Canadians apparently care a lot about religious, ethnic, and regional issues and simply do not give a whit about other issues such as social class or nationalism. This conclusion, in turn, could be attributed to Canada's unusual socio-economic situation and history.

A growing body of research conclusively indicates, however, that the voting public is only a small part of the environment in which political parties behave and that the opinions of the citizens often do not coincide at all with what the decision-makers actually do. There are many instances on record when the voters clearly want one policy while the government follows another. For example, Butler and Stokes (1969) found in the United Kingdom that the two main political parties failed to provide a choice on the issue most important to the British population at the time of their study. Similarly, Hamilton (1972) found that majority desires in the sphere of domestic economic welfare in the United States have been largely ignored by the major political parties, and in Canada, research has indicated that working-class interests have not been given viable outlets in Quebec (Pinard, 1970). As has already been pointed out, similar findings apply to Canada as a whole on the class and nationalist issues. Furthermore, a great deal of evidence suggests that the propagandizing of civil servants and politicians has a stronger influence on the attitudes and actions of the voters than vice-versa. (For a survey, see Ogmundson, 1972: Chap. 3.) In short, it has been found that in politics, as in the economy, the existence of an oligarchy creates a situation of restricted competition in which the major parties (like the major firms) are able to determine the kind of policy (or product) which they offer the voter (or consumer) (see Ogmundson, 1976a). Thus, in order to understand voting patterns, we must consider the environment in which the voter behaves, and look to the history of the behaviour of the major political parties in Canada in order to understand our patterns of voting behaviour.

As one might expect, the religious cleavage has historically been a major source of conflict between the two major parties. As Porter (1965: 512) notes: "In Canada, religion has been one of the major bases of political conflict." Many instances of such conflict, even in this century, can be found. For example, a violently anti-Catholic Ku Klux Klan group in Saskatchewan actively supported the Conservative Party during the 1920s (Englemann and Schwartz, 1967: 230). Similarly, ethnic conflicts have been exacerbated by both major parties: in particular, Conservative decisions to hang Louis Riel and to enforce conscription during the First World War have alienated the French; Liberal campaigns also have kept such divisive issues alive in French areas, especially in Quebec (Cairns, 1968). Likewise, differences in regional economic interests have often been at the root of the competition between the two main parties (see Campbell, 1975), while class differences have been minimized. In sum, religious, ethnic, and regional issues have been emphasized while other issues have not provided a consistent basis for electoral competition—as reflected in voting patterns.

In order to understand why the voters behave as they do, it has been necessary to consider the environment in which they have operated—the historical patterns of competition among the parties, especially those with a chance of forming the government. Similarly, to understand the behaviour of the political parties, and why they choose to emphasize some issues and not others, it has been necessary to understand the environment in which they behave, that is, the pressures from other élite groups.

SUMMARY

Reflecting the American influence, liberalism is the dominant ideology in Canada. Significant counter-ideologies are conservatism, democratic socialism, Marxism, and nationalism. Political socialization via the families, the churches, the political parties, the schools, and the mass media predominately tends to support existing social arrangements and trends. Electoral political participation is largely confined to Charter Group males of high status. An important history of non-electoral participation, very likely by those groups which tend not to be represented in the electoral process, is also notable. Voting patterns reflect the fact that the two major political parties have historically competed on religious, ethnic, and regional issues.

Elites and the Structure of Power[17]

Political party leaders function in an environment which is strongly conditioned by influences from other élite groups: power does not reside with politicians alone. In any modern country, there is a considerable division of labour. Institutions develop to fill the major needs of society—government, politics, business, labour, religion, academia, and so forth. At the head of these institutions, there are small groups of people who have the

17. There has been an outstanding study of the overall power structure of Canada in The Vertical Mosaic (1965) by John Porter. The next section of this chapter will depend heavily upon his analysis. His findings, when supplemented by more recent work (most notably that of his student Wallace Clement in The Canadian Corporate Elite, 1975) provide the best generally available picture of the operation of power in Canadian society. (For critiques of Porter, see Heap, 1974.)

power to make the major decisions in that area, for example, generals, bishops, deans, and cabinet ministers. Consequently, one of the major tasks of political sociology is to study the factors which systematically affect the decisions which these small groups make.

ELITE COMPOSITION, RECRUITMENT, AND ACCOUNTABILITY

Two factors which influence such decisions are the type of people who occupy these positions and how they attain them. On this question the evidence is clear: Canadians of élite status tend very disproportionately to be Anglophone, British, Protestant (especially Anglican) males of highly privileged background. Females, people of ordinary status origins, and members of "third" ethnic groups appear to be virtually excluded. The French, Catholics, and Jews are also minimally represented except in the political and civil service élites where their participation has recently become somewhat more proportionate. The only other exception to this generalization is provided by the labour élite, which has a representative ethnic and religious composition, as well as the expected working-class participation. Trend studies indicate that recruitment to the civil service and political élites has begun to open up (Manzer, 1974: 257; Clement, 1975: 234), but that it is becoming even more difficult for ordinary people to advance to the economic and mass-media élites (Clement, 1975). In sum, present information indicates that our society is controlled by a highly atypical group of people who cannot be expected to be sympathetic to the needs of most Canadians. It also indicates that positions of power in our polity are more usually inherited than earned and that very few in our society have a reasonable potential, at birth, of ultimately enjoying the privileges of power. As Clement (1975: 206) notes: "The idea that Canada is a free society with everyone competing on some great marketplace for the positions and prerogatives of power is a good ideology for the elite and the privileged but it is *not* good sociology."

These patterns of composition and recruitment reflect another factor which influences élite behaviour—accountability to the general population. Contrary to democratic values, most élites in Canada are minimally accountable to the citizenry. Exceptions occur with the same élites noted earlier. The labour élite is elected by a constituency which forms a significant portion of the overall public. The political élite is elected and the civil service is also subject to some popular pressure from the public which pays the bills. The continued apparent exclusion of females and "third ethnics" may reflect the fact that, while the electorate is democratic, the "selectorate", those who nominate and finance the candidates, is not. The other élites tend to be self-selecting. It can be expected that such élites will not be representative of the population in their composition, and that their policies will reflect the desires of a select few rather than the interests of the general community. For example, the business élite is responsive to, at the very most, the 2 per cent of the population which possesses about a third of our total wealth. As John Porter (1965: 370) notes:

The political system is the only system in which all members of the society participate. Not all have ownership rights in the economic system and there are great inequalities among those that do, because votes in the economic system are not one per person but one per share.[18]

Furthermore, many of our élites are under great foreign influence. Clearly, these interests are not at all accountable to our citizens and have no reason to be concerned about the welfare of Canadians.

Since there is substantial variability as far as other factors which influence élite behaviour are concerned, the élites will now be discussed separately. It is convenient to group élites, according to their major functions, into the economic subsystem consisting of the business and labour élites; the ideological subsystem which consists of the mass media, educational, and church élites; the state subsystem consisting of the public service, judicial and political élites; and the defensive subsystem consisting of the military and police élites.

18. Until the turn of the century, a person in Canada usually had to own property to be able to vote on the composition of the political élite (this is still the case in many cities). If the process of democratization continues, we may all eventually have an equal vote on who runs Eaton's and Massey-Ferguson. Similarly, democratic control of the mass media can be achieved by the use of a co-operative form of organization (see Robertson, 1973). Similar techniques could be developed regarding other élites. This would seem preferable to further concentration of power in a government controlled by well-meaning individuals who think they know what's best for us all—the apparent practical implication of fascist and communist proposals.

THE ECONOMIC SYSTEM

The function of the economic system is to provide goods and services to the general society. In our country, it also has the function of making a profit for private owners. There are two major kinds of organizations in this subsystem—business corporations and labour unions. Consequently, "those who occupy the major decision-making positions in the corporate institutions" (Porter, 1965: 264) may be defined as the business élite. "Along with the corporate elite, there is in the economic system another elite group whose decision-making has important consequences for the society. This second elite group is made up of trade union leaders. Their power in economic decision-making stems from the control which in varying measure they have over the supply of labour" (Porter, 1965: 309).

The Business Elite

Porter (1965: Chap. 8) found that relatively few corporations controlled the better part of the Canadian economy, in other words, there was a great concentration of economic power. To illustrate, a conservative estimate suggested that forty-four firms controlled 44 per cent of the private economy (Porter, 1965: 237). Porter also found that this high concentration of power was controlled by a small, homogeneous group: 907 individuals controlled 81 per cent of the directorships of the major corporations, 58 per cent of the directorships of the banks, and 58 per cent of the directorships of the insurance companies (1965: 234). This select group consisted almost entirely of Anglophone, British, Protestant males of privileged background (Chap. 9). Contrary to popular impression, Jews were found to be substantially under-represented. Porter also found that the business élite had a great deal of influence over other élites. It owned most of the indigenous mass media (Chap. 15) and had great influence over the two major political parties. Many members of this élite also held other influential social positions such as memberships on the boards of governors of universities. Consequently, Porter was led to conclude that the business élite was by far the most powerful one in Canada.

Clement (1975), in a replication of Porter's research, found that economic power had become even more concentrated, that a very similar small group still controlled this strengthened base of power, that entrance to the élite was becoming even more difficult, and that relationships with other élites had increased. In particular, he found that the business and mass media élites, though analytically distinct, had become empirically fused into a single élite, which he called the "corporate" élite. In sum, the indications are that the business élite is becoming even more powerful and even more dominant, relative to other native élites, than before.

Once again, however, the Canadian situation cannot be understood without reference to external, that is, American, influence. Porter found that 27 per cent of the positions in the business élite were foreign controlled, while Clement (1975: 155) found that the proportion was up to 46 per cent by the time he did his study. As Table 3 indicates, non-residents control most of the manufacturing and mining while Canadians control most of the remainder. In sum, as Reynaud (1967: 413), chairman of the Economic Council of Canada, notes: "With the exception of the chartered banks and the railroads, the major decision making centres within the Canadian economy are for all practical purposes foreign centres."

As the figures on directorships indicate, the degree of foreign control in Canada has been increasing rapidly. Curiously enough, Canada has more than enough money to finance its own development, and most of this continuing takeover of our economy is being financed with our own money. In 1964, for example, only about 5 per cent of American investment in Canada originated in the United States. The rest came from Canadian banks and from the profits of Canadian subsidiaries (see Levitt, 1970: 11). As with so many aspects of our behaviour, this situation is probably unprecedented.

Since the business élite is the dominant one in our country, and since American influence on the business élite is so great, it follows that American business has a strong influence over almost all aspects of the Canadian economy and society. As Englemann and Schwartz note: "The economic impact of the United States is at the time so extensive, it bears comparison with a situation of true political colonialism" (1975: 83).

Naylor has an explanation for this extraordinary situation. Our business élite was founded on commercial or financial capital derived from

Table 3   Percentage majority of non-resident ownership as measured by assets.

Industrial Sector	Per Cent
Manufacturing	58.1
Food and beverages	31.3
Tobacco	84.5
Rubber products	93.1
Leather products	22.0
Textiles and clothing	39.2
Wood	30.8
Furniture	18.8
Printing, publishing, and allied	21.0
Paper and allied	38.9
Primary metals	55.2
Metal fabricating	46.7
Machinery	72.2
Transport equipment	87.0
Electrical products	64.0
Non-metallic mineral products	51.6
Petroleum and coal products	99.7
Chemicals and chemical products	81.3
Miscellaneous manufacturing	53.9
Mining	63.0
Construction	14.5
Transportation	8.9
Communications	1.0
Public Utilities	2.7
Wholesale Trade	27.9
Retail Trade	20.5
Financial Industries	12.8

Source: Marchak, 1975: 40.

performance of a merchant's "middleman" function in Canada's trade with the various metropoles which have alternately dominated Canada. Thus, our indigenous élite continues to control those sectors of the economy essential to performance of their traditional function: banks, insurance, transportation, communication. Moreover, they are quick to have the government enact legislation to protect them from foreign competition in these areas (see Clement, 1975). Businessmen who derive their fortunes from commerce, however, are characteristically different from those who derive their fortunes from industry. In particular, they tend to be much more cautious,[19] and as a result, they prefer not to take unnecessary risks by entering heavily into manufacturing or resource extraction ventures. Furthermore, they prefer to lend their money, not to the small native entrepreneurs who are ready to take such risks, but to large foreign corporations which can offer better security. This accounts for the apparent lack of Canadian entrepreneurs and for the large foreign participation in our economy. It also acounts for the remarkable lack of legislation to protect our economy. Our dominant business classes have been making a great deal of money, and have been able to invest heavily in places like the Caribbean where they can make still more. Since their primary loyalty is to their money, they have not been concerned about the plight of the small businessman, the unemployed workers, or the erosion of our political sovereignty. Those people who have been most concerned have been the small businessmen in the manufacturing and resource areas, and others whose livelihood is visibly affected by the foreign incursion (professors, for example). These groups have not had enough power to effect any significant influence on the federal government, however. Hence, our present situation.

The Labour Elite

As noted earlier, the basic source of power for the labour élite is its ability to control the supply of labour. In Canada, however, only about 27 per cent of the Canadian labour force is unionized (Manzer, 1974: 137), compared with 40 to 60 per cent in most European countries (Bell, 1973: 139). Unlike the business situation, therefore, the degree of concentration of power is quite limited. Furthermore, control of this base of power is not held by a small, socially homogeneous group: the labour élite is badly fragmented on ethnic, regional, and occupational lines. Furthermore, since this élite has few relationships with other élites, it is relatively weak. Not too surprisingly, the political party which represents the interests of

19. A more technical explanation holds that financial capital is characterized by a low ratio of fixed to circulatory capital and is, therefore, oriented to safe, quick profits rather than risky, long-term investments. (See Naylor, 1972: 21; see also the important discussion of Clement, 1975: Chaps. 1, 2, esp. p. 42.)

labour—the NDP—is not nearly as strong as the two parties financed by the business élite.

As ever, one cannot understand Canada without reference to its friendly metropole. A full 62 per cent of the membership of the unions in Canada belong to American "international" unions (Manzer, 1974: 137). This fact has a number of implications for our unions. One is that Canadian unions have adopted American-style *business unionism* rather than European-style *movement unionism*; as a result, they often do not attempt to organize workers unless the new dues can be expected to pay rapidly for the original cost of mobilization, and little or no attempt is made to organize workers in medium- and small-size firms (Watkins, 1973: 185). Therefore, the labour movement's base of power does not increase, and this élite remains weak. The division between American and Canadian unions further fragments the leadership of workers, as does an excessively complicated organizational structure suitable to a nation of 200 million, not 20 million. American unions have also often intervened directly in the management of Canadian unions (see Watkins, 1973; various essays in Teeple, 1972). In sum, the American influence has further weakened Canadian labour.

In contrast to the situation of the business élite, the labour élite in Quebec differs substantially from its counterpart in Anglophone Canada. Labour unions in Quebec are somewhat independent of external influence, and their leaders are homogeneously French and Catholic. It may be no coincidence that they have become much more militant and movement-oriented than Anglophone North American unions (see Drache, 1972). One manifestation was the Quebec Common Front strike in May 1972, in which over 200,000 participated and in which workers occupied factories, blocked roads, and took over broadcasting outlets. It does appear that the labour movement in Quebec may become quite strong.

The Ideological Elite

The function of the ideological system is to articulate and to reinforce social values. "Because values tend to be conservative and traditional, the reinforcement of old values is more general than the articulation of new ones" (Porter, 1965: 457). These activities help to maintain social cohesion and the dominance of powerful groups. The major institutions of the ideological system in a modern society are the mass media, the educational system, and the churches. The ideological élites are those at the top of these organizations.

Mass-Media Elite

Porter (1965: Chap. 15) found that the Anglophone media were highly concentrated, and that their ownership was, in turn, highly concentrated among the familiar group of upper class, British, males. Unlike the situation in European countries, labour in Canada does not control even one major newspaper. A striking illustration of this general situation is provided by K. C. Irving of New Brunswick, who controls much of that province's economy, some of the radio stations, and all of the English newspapers. Porter consequently concluded that the newspapers were, "in effect, the instruments of an established upper class" (p. 463), and that the pattern of ownership led to a conservative orientation in the media (p. 484). Porter also noted an apparent pattern of exclusion of "third ethnics" from key media positions while recent immigrants from the United Kingdom were often given strategic roles (pp. 486–87). For example, an Englishman with limited Canadian experience was appointed editor-in-chief of the Toronto *Globe and Mail*, the only Canadian newspaper which might be considered national. On the other hand, ownership of the Francophone media was not highly concentrated. Quebec has one high-quality newspaper, *Le Devoir*, staffed by a team of skilled journalists, who "as a group . . . have no counterpart among English-Canadian editors who do not seem to have the skills, or who are not in a position, to articulate for English Canada, or the whole of Canada, a national and indigenous ideology" (p. 489).

Clement found that the media themselves had become more concentrated, and that ownership had also been further centralized. Of particular interest was the fact that Power Corporation, a massive investment company, had moved in the intervening years to gain control of six of the seven leading Francophone newspapers in Quebec (p. 310). Clement (Chap. 8) also documented some of the means by which control over the content of the media is exercised by the business élite. For instance, he noted that when Power Corporation took over the largest Francophone newspaper, *La Presse*, there was a clear change in editorial policy which was achieved partly by dismissing dissident editors and reporters (p. 294). He also noted an even greater degree of overlap with the business élite, and he was led to conclude that the two élites were virtually one and the same. Like Porter, he concluded that the media could thus be expected to "reinforce the existing political and economic systems" (p. 343).

A complete report on the mass-media élite in Canada would include a discussion of the external élites which control much of the television, radio, magazine, and book content to which the typical Canadian is so often exposed. It is sufficient to reiterate here, however, that the content also reinforces existing arrangements and facilitates the American presence. See Chapter 3 for a discussion of this point.

The Church Elite

The source of power of the churches lies in their control over the behaviour of their adherents. Since Canada is a religiously heterogeneous country, this power base is more fragmented than it is in many other countries. None the less, there are three churches in Canada to which a substantial portion of the population is affiliated: the Catholic Church (49 per cent), the United Church (18 per cent), and the Anglican Church (11 per cent). Only two of these religious organizations are hierarchically organized: the Catholic Church and the Anglican Church. The Catholic Church élite consists mainly of native Canadians and has been especially important in Quebec where it directly controlled the Francophone educational system until quite recently. Porter (1965: 515–16) argues that the church in Quebec has played an important role in strengthening that society by articulating a coherent and powerful native ideology. By contrast, he notes that sixteen of twenty-six Anglican bishops were from the United Kingdom, and were thus more likely to maintain links with a former metropole than to make contributions to an indigenous ideology (p. 515). Since Anglicans form a highly disproportionate part of the British upper class, which controls both the business and mass-media élites, this is a point of some significance.[20]

20. The United Church, while it has a minimal hierarchy and hence no readily identifiable élite, merits mention because it is a unique Canadian institution. As Porter (1965: 519) notes: "In many respects it is as Canadian as the maple leaf and the beaver." This organization is one of the few in Canada which

The Educational Elite

Since all citizens are exposed to the educational system at a formative period of their life, it plays a powerful socialization role. At the higher levels, the educational system also provides trained expertise and plays an important role in the articulation of whatever ideology a society may have. In Canada, however, control over this power base is fragmented among the ten provinces and the federal government. Unlike many European countries, there is no centralized civil service which controls the content of this socialization. Furthermore, the educational system— like the mass media—is a dependent élite, since it relies on other élites for its funding (especially the government, but also the churches and business). At the elementary and high-school levels, the influence of the church has been quite significant in many provinces. At the university level, the boards of governors are normally dominated by members of the business élite. For example, thirteen of twenty-one members of the board at the University of Toronto, probably Canada's most influential university, are also members of the economic élite (Clement, 1975: 252).

Perhaps largely as a consequence, the educational élite in Canada has been remarkably conservative. Canadian intellectuals rarely write popular or critical works, and seldom become involved in political or social movements. Their most prominent activity has been working for the government on Royal Commissions. As Porter (1965: 503) notes: "It would probably be difficult to find another modern political system with such a paucity of participation from its scholars."

A definition of the educational élite which was broad enough to include all professors would force us immediately to note that Anglophone higher education is highly Americanized, while Francophone higher education is dominated by native Québécois. Again, one finds a pattern in which Quebec is favoured by an élite able and willing to articulate a native ideology, while Anglophone Canada is substantially crippled by the presence of a foreign élite. If you define the élite more exclusively as the

---

recognized that our situation demands forms of organization which differ from those in England and the United States. It amalgamated three churches—the Methodist, the Congregational, and Presbyterian. Our business firms and unions should follow this lead. It has been repeatedly demonstrated that the "miniature replica" effect has deleterious effects on our economic life. It has a similar undesirable effect on our intellectual behaviour (see Smiley, 1974).

members of the Royal Society, as Porter did (1965: Chap. 16), a similar picture emerges, except that the Anglophone élite is largely British or British trained (p. 489). Other Francophone-Anglophone differences emerge in that Québécois intellectuals take some role in the politics and general life of their community, while Anglophones are remarkable for their inactivity.

In sum, all three ideological systems in Canada are conservative in the values they espouse. As Porter (1965: 494) notes: "Neither Canadian newspapers, churches nor universities have harboured social critics in any large numbers." The Anglophone and Francophone ideological systems differ sharply, however, in that the Francophone system has developed and articulated a strong indigenous ideology, while the Anglophone system has not.

THE SYSTEM OF THE STATE[21]

The function of the state is to co-ordinate the activities of the other systems, and to pursue collective goals as set forth by those with influence over its activities. The state system consists of the public service, the judiciary, and the various elected parliaments. Those at the heads of these subsystems—deputy ministers, senior judges, and cabinet ministers—form the élite of the state.

The Federal Public Service Elite

The power base of the various civil service groups in Canada has increased very substantially in recent times with the expansion of government activity. By 1972 Canadian governments were expending 38 per cent of the gross national product and were employing 12 per cent of the total labour force (Presthus, 1973: 16). Furthermore, the civil services derive power from the fact that they are often virtually the only source of expertise on many aspects of public policy. This monopoly, in turn, gives the civil services a great deal of influence over politicians. As Max Weber (cited by Porter, 1965: 419) notes: "Generally speaking, the trained

21. The Carleton School of Canadian Macrosociology will soon update Porter's work on this system in a doctoral dissertation by another student stimulated by Porter, Dennis Olsen.

Anyone seriously interested in the study of Canadian politics should obtain a copy of this work as soon as it becomes generally available.

permanent official is more likely to get his way in the long run than his nominal superior, the cabinet minister, who is not a specialist."

On the other hand, control over this power base is decentralized among a variety of provincial and municipal organizations which function somewhat independently of the federal public service. Thus, control cannot be concentrated in the manner characteristic of the business élite. None the less, Porter (1965: 433) was able to isolate a small élite of "243 senior officials of the federal government departments, agencies, and Crown corporations." He found that about half the élite had had previous careers in other spheres, and he argued this factor probably served to reduce the independence and strength of the élite. For example, a member of the public service élite who had previously been a member of the business élite might not be independent from business influence. Since members of this group did not appear to have the multitudinous connections with other élite groups that business did their influence would be further limited. None the less, this group emerged as probably the second most powerful élite in Canada.

The continued expansion of the federal government, as well as greater internal recruitment (Porter, 1965: 451–56), has probably served to further increase the power of this élite. More recent research has tended to confirm this point (Van Loon et al., 1971: 329–31; Presthus, 1973: 211). On the other hand, studies indicate that it is becoming more heterogeneous—a development which conceivably could reduce its unity, and therefore its strength. Contrary to public belief in Anglophone Canada, however, French-Canadian participation in this élite is still not proportionate (Clement, 1975: 234). Indeed, Beattie (1975) has found that patterns of discrimination against Francophones are still quite apparent. This élite is one of the few in Canada which does not appear to be under direct external influence, and Grant (1965) has argued that it must lead any restoration of Canadian autonomy.

The Judicial Elite

The judiciary has the important function of interpreting the law. "Through their interpretations they make the law; they define rights; their role as arbitrator now extends far beyond their normal judicial duties" (Porter, 1965: 607). Control over this function is centralized in the provincial and federal higher courts, and the judges in these courts may be designated as the judicial élite. Since these positions are federal appointments, the judicial élite can be expected generally to reflect the interests of those with influence over the national government. Porter (1965: 415–16) found that approximately half were appointed without previous judicial experience, and that about half had had previous careers in politics. As he notes (1965: 416), this practice constitutes "what must be one of the most curious of occupational systems, one in which a person whose political role is marked by partiality, irrationality, and opinion-expressing assumes a judicial role marked by impartiality, rational inquiry, and attention to fact." (Females concerned with the treatment of their sex by Canadian courts may find this observation to be of some interest.)

The Political Elite

In theory, the political élite might be expected to be the most powerful, because it has the legal right to direct the civil service and the defensive system, to appoint the judiciary, to tax the population, and otherwise to regulate almost all aspects of life. In Canada, however, control over this power base is limited by a number of factors. To begin with, the power is shared between the federal government and ten relatively strong provincial governments. The fact that the federal élite itself is somewhat more heterogeneous than most others in the country, as in the case of the public service, may reduce its unity and strength.[22] Also, our federal (and provincial) political élites are characterized by an avocational career pattern such that most members have had minimal previous political experience. A classic example would be our present Prime Minister, Pierre Trudeau, who assumed the office after only three years of political experience.[23] Porter (1965: Chap. 13) argues that such inexperienced politicians are especially likely to take the advice of their civil servants, a

22. Contrary to impressions in much of English-speaking Canada, French representation in the political élite has become fully proportionate, with access to the powerful cabinet positions, only during the time of Prime Minister Trudeau. No French Canadian had been a Minister of Trade and Commerce, a Minister of Industry, a Minister of Finance, a Minister of Defence, or a Minister of Health and Welfare before Trudeau became Prime Minister in 1968 (see Van Loon *et al.*, 1971: 350).
23. Courtenay (1973: 80) finds in his study of party leaders that "the fewer the years a leadership candidate has served in parliament, the greater his chances of being elected party leader."

situation conducive to a pattern of weak administrative politics which reflect civil service characteristics: caution and inertia. Porter also argues that a pattern of heavy recruitment into this group from others, such as public service and business élites, is likely to reduce the independent strength of this élite. Similarly, kinship links with those in other élites may reduce independence. To provide but one of a multitude of possible examples, the stout defender of Canada's oil producers, Premier Lougheed of Alberta, has a brother who is vice-president and general manager of Imperial Oil (Clement, 1975: 263). The political parties, like the mass-media and educational élites, are dependent upon others for funding. The political élite is also reliant, since it periodically needs legitimation from the citizenry, and since sympathetic treatment by the mass media (controlled by the business élite) is virtually essential to such support.

The excessive dependence on the civil service for advice and on the business élite for financial support may help us to understand why Porter (1965: 373) was led to suggest that "nothing is so striking in Canada . . . as the society's incapacity to meet its internal and external problems." Similarly, the environment in which the political parties behave helps us to understand why they choose to emphasize some issues and to minimize others. As noted earlier, the two major political parties have historically competed on ethnic, regional, and religious bases while minimizing the class and nationalist issues—despite surveys which indicate substantial interest in the latter among the citizenry. If one believes in liberal ideology, this presents a considerable puzzle. No mystery exists, however, when one remembers that the influence of public opinion on the élites is minimal, and that other élites provide the crucial aspect of the environment in which the political parties operate. The business élite is the most powerful one in Canadian society: American and Canadian corporate interests dominate not only the economic, but also the ideological spheres of our society and thus profoundly influence the setting in which politicians behave. An even more direct avenue of influence is provided by party finance. The two major parties are almost entirely financed by the business élite (90 per cent), while the NDP is largely financed by the big unions (40 per cent) (Paltiel, 1970). The fact that much of big business and most of the big unions are American-controlled may help to account for the avoidance of the nationalist issue. Likewise, patterns of financing may also help to explain the failure of either of the major parties to appeal to working-class interests. As Marchak (1975: 51) notes: "While there may be more than one party seeking election, there is one interest group behind them. In effect, the alternatives are removed in advance." By contrast, it serves the interests of both our internal and external business élites to "divide and rule" by emphasizing divisive ethnic and religious issues. Competition on a regional basis may reflect genuine conflict among local élites (Campbell, 1975) while such regional division is clearly in the interests of foreign economic élites. (See Levitt, 1970.)

Other indications of this pattern of influence are provided by government policy itself. Clement (1975: 349) notes that the government subsidizes business in many different ways at the expense of the general taxpayer. For example, Ford Motor Company, hardly an ailing firm, had $75 million in taxes cancelled in 1969. Similarly, Watkins (1973) notes that taxation rates, always an indicator of where the power is, are very low for American resource extraction companies. To illustrate, those in the metal-mining industry paid taxes on only about 15 per cent of their total profits during the years 1965–70. Perhaps even more significantly, the capacity of our political élite to control the national economic life has been severely limited by the refusal of American corporations to obey our laws, and by our agreement to surrender control of important portions of our monetary policy (see Levitt, 1970). In 1968, for example, Canada agreed to convert over half of its monetary reserves to United States securities, which can only be used at American discretion. Thus, "Canada has moved towards a colonial monetary system whereby foreign exchange earnings are automatically lent to the metropolis" (Levitt, 1970: 15).

As might be expected, the general pattern of American economic dominance is also reflected in the non-economic behaviour of our political élite. For example, President Kennedy directly intervened in our domestic cultural affairs in 1961 when he asked that *Time* magazine be exempted from any legislation designed to help the Canadian magazine industry. His wish was our command. (See Levitt, 1970: 8.)

THE DEFENSIVE SYSTEM

The function of the defensive system is to protect the polity from external invasion, internal rebellion, and ordinary crime. Defensive systems tend to serve the interests of the dominant classes of a society. The military and the various police forces form the organizations of the defensive system; the individuals at the heads of these institutions—generals, police chiefs— form the defensive élite.

Since physical force is the ultimate basis of power,[24] the defensive élite has a great deal of potential to exercise its will on the rest of the community. As Porter (1965: 202) notes: "The loyalty of the police and the army to political power-holders is the acid test of power in the political system." There is some fragmentation over the indigenous control of this source of power. Many cities and provinces have their own police systems. Furthermore, a significant portion of the citizenry possesses weapons and some knowledge of how to use them. None the less, there is centralized control over the military, and Canada does have a national police force— the Royal Canadian Mounted Police (RCMP)—available for use at the behest of the authorities. Both the military and the RCMP have the highly centralized organizational control characteristic of coercive organizations. Indeed, Canada is notable for its unified military in which the army, navy, and air force are under one authority. The concentration of power here is great. Little is presently known about the characteristics of the men who occupy these strategic positions, but both Porter (1965) and Clement (1975) have reported that members of the business élite appear to have relatives in the military. In the absence of better information, it seems reasonable to assume that the people in these positions are similar to those in our other élites—Anglophone, British, Protestant males of privileged backgrounds.

Perhaps this social composition accounts in some measure for the fact that the defensive system appears to be firmly under the control of various kinds of civil authorities. It could be, indeed, that a study of the defensive élite would indicate that they are as much a part of a cohesive upper-class group as are the business and mass-media élites. The defensive élites are also directly dependent upon the government for economic support in ordinary times, and individuals in this élite are reliant upon others for promotions while in the service, and for jobs once they leave it. Norms

24. Sociologists tend to agree that there are three basic sources of power— physical force (coercive power), money (utilitarian power), and beliefs (normative power) (see Etzioni, 1961: xvi). They disagree, however, as to which of the three is most important. My position is that a man with a gun can easily get some money, and that with the money he can quickly hire a professor or a priest to legitimate his status.

concerning obedience to civil authority are strong.

In any case, the defensive system can be expected to serve the interests of those with influence over the state—in particular, the indigenous and foreign business élites. The internal system has thus played an active role in subordinating the native population, and in supporting the interests of business against those of labour in a number of confrontations (see Brown, 1973). The external system has also been highly active in the service of our metropoles during the Boer War, the First World War, and the Korean War. Thus a hinterland country gives more than just resources, jobs, and money to its metropole. It also gives its blood.

Again it is of particular interest to note the relationship of one of our élites to the United States. For all intents and purposes, our military has been integrated with, and subordinate to, that of our most recent metropole since the Second World War (see Resnick, 1970; Marchak, 1975: 43–44; Warnock, 1970).[25] One implication of this military convergence has been the integration of our defence industries resulting in a further continentalization of the economy.[26] Another has been that Canada is committed to the support of American foreign policy in whatever form it takes (see Resnick, 1970, for examples). Not too surprisingly, our "peacekeeping" forces have come to be viewed abroad as representatives of American interests, just as those of Poland or Hungary are viewed as agents of the Russians. Internally, our military and economic absorption

25. This may also be true in the sphere of internal policing as well. There are stories of FBI agents crossing the border to make arrests. Similarly, there have been reports that our intelligence is automatically forwarded to the CIA.
26. There is an interesting story here. Canada was one of the first countries to develop a viable commercial jet airplane. We gave up development of this vehicle to help build military jets during the Korean War. By the end of the war, the Americans had an insurmountable lead in the development of commercial jets. By 1958, however, we had developed one of the finest jet fighters ever built. Then the Americans told us that jet fighters were obsolete. So we shut down our plants, putting 13,000 out of work, and bought Bomarc missiles. No sooner had we done this than Secretary of Defense McNamara told the United States Congress that the Bomarcs stationed in Canada were useless, except that they might attract part of the enemy nuclear attack. So we bought some very expensive jet fighters from them. Then they told us that both the missiles and the fighters were useless without nuclear weapons. So we bought the nuclear weapons, thus ensuring that the Russians would have to attack us directly in case of a war.

Perhaps by now the student will understand why a great Canadian political economist, Harold Innis, once said that the danger of being a social scientist in Canada is that you might die laughing.

into the American empire has served to further erode whatever political independence Canada may have had.

As noted earlier, the acid test of political power lies in the loyalty of the defensive system to its authorities. When the police and the military refuse to obey the orders of the politicians, the latter's power must be in question. It is rare that social scientists are granted a "natural experiment". Such an event did take place, however, during the Cuban missile crisis of 1962. President Kennedy ordered American and Canadian armed forces to go on full alert. Prime Minister Diefenbaker refused for forty-eight hours to give the alert order. Faced with two conflicting commands, the Canadian armed forces knew what to do. They obeyed President Kennedy. (For further discussion, see Warnock, 1970.) This event likely marked the end of whatever genuine independence Canada may have been said to possess. In the words of Harold Innis, "Canada moved from colony to nation to colony."[27]

27. This is not the end of the story. In the subsequent election in 1963, there were many signs of active American intervention. Canadian reporters were given a briefing at the American embassy on how to bring about the defeat of John Diefenbaker. The United States State Department unprecedentedly came forth with a news release which accused our Prime Minister of lying. One of our own people, General Norstad, gave an "impromptu" press conference in which he soundly denounced our government. American periodicals with large circulation in this country, such as *Newsweek*, attacked our leading minister, describing his appearance as "grotesque and gargoyle-like" (Beck, 1968: 357). The American pollster who had helped Kennedy win in 1960, Lou Harris, showed up in Canada as an adviser to the Liberal Party. (For further discussion, see Grant, 1965: 27, 29.) Not unexpectedly, our business élite also joined the attack: one indication was that virtually all the newspapers in the country rejected Diefenbaker and supported Pearson.

We shall probably never know for sure if these actions were part of a program of conscious intervention as an aspect of American foreign policy. Older scholars would reject the notion of planned intervention as unlikely, unless definite proof were available. Younger scholars who came to maturity observing multiple mysterious assassinations, the Vietnamese war, the Pentagon Papers, Watergate, and revelations about the CIA, can only consider such a position to be naïve. It is by now a well-established fact that American interests have been known to intervene directly and massively in the domestic politics of other political democracies (see Agee, 1975; Marchetti and Marks, 1974). The case of Chile is particularly well documented (see Marchak, 1975: 48–49; Sampson, 1973; *Canadian Dimension*, Vol. 9, Nos. 7 and 8, 1973). The motivations of the United States to maintain control over Canada are much greater than those which exist in Chile. Thus, in the absence of definitive proof to the contrary, it seems reasonable to assume that American interests have kept an eye on events in Canada, and have intervened directly whenever it seemed necessary, as in 1963.

Relationships Among the Elites

The various institutional orders and the different élites are analytically distinct in that they perform different functions and control separate bases of power. As we have seen, however, this does not necessarily mean that they are controlled by different groups of people, and that power in our democracy is thereby diffused. At one extreme of a theoretical continuum, it is possible to imagine a situation of maximum possible concentration of power in which all the élites of all the institutional spheres are under the direct control of a small and exclusive ruling class. Stalinist Russia and Hitler Germany came close to approaching this situation. At the other extreme of such a continuum, one might picture a situation of minimum concentration of power in which all the élites are independent of each other, in which recruitment to these positions is open and democratic, in which all élites are accountable by some direct mechanism to the population they serve, and in which power-relevant resources such as wealth, knowledge, and leisure time are distributed as equally as practicable among a citizenry which has full legal rights to use them. Unfortunately, no modern state approaches this end of the theoretical continuum. While it may plausibly be argued that Western political democracies emulate this ideal more successfully than most countries with other forms of political organization, it is an obvious solecism to argue that the pluralist distribution of power of countries like the United States and Canada brings them as close as reasonably possible to the democratic ideal. Social scientists who argue this position are promulgating the dominant liberal ideology in the commonly expected manner in the ideological system. However, as Porter (1965: 556) notes: "To use the liberal theory as a basis for empirical research into the processes of power would be absurd in view of the frequency with which that theory has been empirically refuted."

The degree of concentration of power among the élites of an entire society is, as with the separate élites, ultimately an empirical question which cannot be settled by citing contrary authorities or by theoretical disputation. Much of the empirical evidence required to speak to this question in Canada has already been outlined. To summarize, Canadian élites generally consist of a highly atypical group of Anglophone, British (or American), Protestant males of privileged origin who are minimally accountable to the citizenry, and who thus cannot be expected to be sympathetic to the concerns of most of the population—especially women, "third" ethnics, and those of ordinary economic status. Furthermore, a single élite appears to have predominant influence over several of the others—that is, the business élite controls the mass media, finances the major political parties, and is in a position of influence over the educational system. The labour élite appears to be quite weak. The ideological system and the political élite are conservative, and dependent upon other élites for support. The public service emerges as an élite of some independent and growing strength. Furthermore, as other chapters have shown, power-relevant resources such as wealth and education are distributed unequally among the population—as is the opportunity at birth to gain access to these resources. Consequently, most of the Canadian population is not in a position to utilize many of the democratic rights to which they are legally entitled.

Further information, not previously outlined, on the degree of interaction among the élites also indicates a very substantial concentration of power. Porter (1965: Chap. 17) found that interaction among the élites, with the exception of labour, is quite high. This interaction is facilitated by homogeneous social and educational backgrounds, kinship ties, a normative consensus, private clubs, transfer of individuals from one élite to another, and by formal mechanisms such as boards and councils. Clement (1975: Chap. 10) found that the degree of overlap among the business, mass media, public service, and political élites had doubled since Porter did his study. Indeed, "39.4 percent of the current economic elite members either were themselves or had close kin in the state system" (Clement, 1975: 346). If this trend continues, it may soon become reasonable to argue that Canada is controlled by a small "ruling class" just as it was in the days of the Family Compact and the Chateau Clique. For the present, however, it should also be noted that the independent power of the public service and the labour unions, as well as some limited degree of independence in many of the other élites, provides a significant counterweight to the dominance of the business élite. It is at least conceivable, if not likely, that an informed citizenry may in the future be able to reverse this unwelcome trend toward greater concentration of power.

Another notable aspect of our élite structure is the substantial American influence over the military, business, labour, mass media, educational, and political élites. If this influence continues to grow, our defensive, economic, and ideological systems may be virtually absorbed by their American counterparts. Only the state system, in particular the civil service, would continue to have significant Canadian roots. Canadians would then appear to be faced with a choice between control by American businessmen or by Ottawa civil servants. (Thus, in a Canadian context, sociology, not economics, merits designation as "the dismal science".) For the present, however, considerable power continues to be controlled by Canadians, especially in Quebec. Consequently, it is again at least conceivable, if again unlikely, that an informed citizenry may in the future be able to reverse this trend toward complete subordination to American interests.

Finally, one must again differentiate between Anglophone and Francophone élite structures. As Porter (1965: 527) notes, kinship links between the two are minimal, and "with the two charter groups there are in fact two elite systems." Largely because of the language barrier, the ideological system of Quebec, as well as the labour movement, is under native control. This bifurcation in the national system was perhaps to be expected. In any case, this indicator, as with so many others, seems to bode ill for the survival of Confederation, although it does bode well for the survival of an independent Quebec.[28]

Final Summary

Canada is an affluent, socially heterogeneous, underdeveloped country with a history of sequential domination by three countries which were the superpowers of their day—France, Britain, and the United States. It is characterized by considerable ethnic, religious, and linguistic heterogeneity as well as by significant geographic and economic bases for

---

28. René Lévesque (1968), leader of the separatist Parti Québécois, argues that our "bad marriage" consumes so much of our energy, in the continuing effort to keep it alive, that it becomes impossible for either Quebec or Anglophone Canada to pursue effectively the goals of national independence and greater social justice. He predicts that present arrangements will eventuate in total American control of both nations. Consequently, he argues that the separation of Quebec is the best thing that could happen to Anglophone Canada. Like open heart surgery, this move would be risky indeed. When the patient is dying anyway, however, there would not seem to be much to lose.

regional conflict. The coincidence of several of these cleavages in the Province of Quebec places severe stress on national unity. A hinterland economic relationship with successive metropoles has placed substantial limitations on national independence. A dominant liberal ideology, today actively promulgated by the mass media and the universities, has facilitated continuation of hinterland status and legitimated present social arrangements. Since American and Canadian business interests control the mass media and finance the major political parties, the parties compete on ethnic, religious, and regional issues while minimizing class and nationalism. Mass political behaviour reflects this leadership.

Important decision-making positions are overwhelmingly dominated by an atypical group of Anglophone, British (and American), Protestant (especially Anglican) males of highly privileged backgrounds who cannot be expected to be sympathetic to the needs of most Canadians. Relationships among the élites are sufficiently extensive to indicate, contrary to democratic values, a very high concentration of power which is minimally accountable to the citizenry. The degree of external influence over the military, business, labour, mass-media, educational, and political élites is substantial enough that Canadian activity in these areas cannot be understood without constant reference to American interests. Quebec, defended by the language barrier, controls its own ideological system and maintains a much more distinctive existence than Anglophone Canada.

Select Bibliography

BECK, J. MURRAY. *Pendulum of Power*. Scarborough: Prentice-Hall, 1968.

CLEMENT, WALLACE. *The Canadian Corporate Elite: An Analysis of Economic Power*. Toronto: McClelland and Stewart, 1975.

ENGLEMANN, FREDERICK C., and SCHWARTZ, MILDRED A. *Canadian Political Parties: Origin, Character, Impact*. Scarborough: Prentice-Hall, 1975.

FOX, PAUL, ed. *Politics: Canada*. 3rd ed. Toronto: McGraw-Hill, 1970.

GRANT, GEORGE P. *Lament for a Nation: The Defeat of Canadian Nationalism*. Toronto: McClelland and Stewart, 1965.

LAXER, ROBERT, ed. *(Canada) Ltd.: The Political Economy of Dependency*. Toronto: McClelland and Stewart, 1973.

LÉVESQUE, RENÉ. *An Option for Quebec*. Toronto: McClelland and Stewart, 1968.

LEVITT, K. *Silent Surrender*. Toronto: Macmillan, 1970.

MANZER, RONALD. *Canada: A Socio-Political Report*. Toronto: McGraw-Hill, 1974.

MARCHAK, M. PATRICIA. *Ideological Perspectives on Canada*. Toronto: McGraw-Hill Ryerson, 1975.

MEISEL, JOHN. *Working Papers on Canadian Politics*. Montreal: McGill-Queen's University Press, 1972.

PINARD, MAURICE. *The Rise of a Third Party.* Englewood Cliffs, N.J.: Prentice-Hall, 1971.

PORTER, J. *The Vertical Mosaic.* Toronto: University of Toronto Press, 1965.

PRESTHUS, ROBERT. *Elite Accommodation in Canadian Politics.* Toronto: Macmillan, 1973.

ROBIN, MARTIN, ed. *Canadian Provincial Politics.* Scarborough: Prentice-Hall, 1972.

ROTSTEIN, ABRAHAM, and LAX, GARY, eds. *Independence: The Canadian Challenge.* Toronto: Committee for an Independent Canada, 1972.

TEEPLE, GARY, ed. *Capitalism and the National Question in Canada.* Toronto: University of Toronto Press, 1972.

VALLIÈRES, PIERRE. *White Niggers of America.* Toronto: McClelland and Stewart, 1971.

VAN LOON, RICHARD J., and WHITTINGTON, MICHAEL S. *The Canadian Political System.* Toronto: McGraw-Hill, 1971.

ZURICK, ELIA, and PIKE, ROBERT M., eds. *Socialization and Values in Canadian Society.* Toronto: McClelland and Stewart, 1975.

Intergroup Relations: 6

Ethnicity in Canada

RITA M. BIENVENUE*

Introduction

Social scientists recognize that most if not all societies are pluralistic in the sense that they contain a multiplicity of ethnic groups. Broadly defined, ethnic groups "consist of those who conceive of themselves as being alike by virtue of their common ancestry, real or fictitious, and are so regarded by others" (Shibutani and Kwan, 1965: 47). This common ancestry may include citizenship, national, or cultural origins, race, religion, or any combination of these. A crucial aspect of this definition is that individuals share commonly understood attributes and in turn are identified by others as being of a kind.

The term "national" or "cultural" origins refers to an individual's male ancestry. Thus, within the general Canadian context, there are peoples whose origins are British, French, Norwegian, Jamaican, Inuit, to name only a few. This definition of ethnicity does not imply degrees of commitment to the group nor does it imply participation in the activities of the group. These two attitudinal and behavioural components vary from individual to individual and from group to group.

The concept of "race" refers to physical characteristics which distinguish or are thought to distinguish one group from another. To phrase it more precisely, race is a term used to identify a group which defines itself and/or is defined by others as different by virtue of innate and immutable physical characteristics (Van den Berghe, 1967: 9–10). Thus,

*I want to thank the editors, G. N. Ramu and Stuart Johnson, for their helpful comments. I also want to thank my colleagues, Leo Driedger, Jay Goldstein, Alfred Hunter, and Richard Ogmundson. I regret I was unable to include all their suggestions, but their comments did contribute toward the final draft of this chapter.

individuals may identify or be identified as blacks, whites, Indians, Chinese, or Japanese. This identification does not deny cultural characteristics, for all races have cultural attributes. Whites, for instance, may be French Canadians or Italian Canadians and blacks may be of Jamaican or African ancestry. The Chinese may originate from Korea, China, or Hong Kong.

Religions include all major world faiths and all denominations. Thus, there are Christians (Anglicans, Roman Catholics, etc.), Jews, Buddhists, Hindus, Bahai, and many others living in Canada.

Although most societies contain a multiplicity of ethnic groups, because of historical events and political and social definitions where one country such as Northern Ireland places emphasis on religion, another, such as South Africa, is primarily concerned with race. Canadians, on the other hand, have placed most emphasis on cultural origins. This does not mean that race and religion are inconsequential. On the contrary, race is an important visible criterion which operates in the process of prejudice and discrimination. Religion, on the other hand, constitutes an important basis for group affiliation and a salient characteristic for groups such as the French Canadians, Ukrainians, and Jews. For purposes of this chapter, however, ethnic groups will be identified according to cultural characteristics, but race and religion will be considered in terms of intergroup relations when these characteristics are important to the understanding of group processes.

The entire field of intergroup relations in Canada has received considerable attention. Four main topics will be covered here: ethnic diversity, stratification, assimilation, and conflict. Each topic is organized within a selected conceptual framework. The content is by necessity abbreviated, but references and a bibliography are meant to guide the student to further readings.

Ethnic Diversity

Multi-ethnic societies emerge as a result of diverse patterns of group contact. In Canada, these patterns include a gradual encroachment of Europeans, the displacement of native peoples, the conquest of New France, the political union between English and French Canada, involuntary migration and official immigration.

THE EMERGENCE OF ETHNIC DIVERSITY

Native Peoples

Before the European settlement of Canada, native peoples themselves were culturally diverse. Anthropological studies identify six culture areas, each containing several tribes and bands, members of which spoke at least fifty-four related languages and dialects (Jenness, 1932). Similarly, the Eskimo, or Inuit as they now prefer to be called, were identified as consisting of several culture groups, speaking several different dialects. Each of these indigenous groups had developed a culture and a political and economic system suitable to the environment in which it flourished.

Patterson (1972), who traces intergroup relations between Europeans and Indians, shows a gradual process of political and cultural disruption. The power of the European colonizers, in terms of technology, military and persuasive skills, resulted in a subordinate status for the non-Europeans which persists to this day.

The initial contact, Patterson claims, frequently led to an era of greater prosperity for the native. But as fur trading increased, the advantages of the interaction favoured the Europeans. The native population became increasingly dependent upon trade goods, thus weakening their own economic self-sufficiency and their indigenous political organizations. The creation of reservations through a succession of treaties, many of them poorly defined, established segregated, isolated communities. Surrendering valuable lands for less-favourable territories, the natives adapted to new forms of political and economic exploitation. Those Indians and Inuit not included in the treaties pursued their native customs and livelihood as long as ecological and political circumstances permitted.

In terms of cultural identities, very few empirical observations are available. There are indications, however, that original cultural identities such as Cree, Iroquois, Haida, etc., are still relevant. At the same time, there is a growing tendency for social movements to urge native peoples to see themselves as a group, historically and culturally different from others. According to such authors as Cardinal (1969), this is a crucial step in gaining equality and retaining cultural traditions.

The Charter Groups

The first settlement of Europeans consisted of Acadians who established a colony in what is now Nova Scotia. During the 1700s when Britain and France struggled for control of the territory, the Acadians were deported *en masse* to the New England coast. They were permitted to return in the early 1760s, and their descendants constitute the present French-speaking populations of New Brunswick, Nova Scotia, and Prince Edward Island (Clark, 1968). Through a concerted effort to retain identities, culture, and language, most continue to support their own ethnic institutions—particularly in New Brunswick, where approximately two-thirds of the Acadians are situated.

The colony in Quebec, settled and developed under the French in the seventeenth and eighteenth centuries, remains the main centre of French-Canadian culture. The arrival of the British and the Loyalists sparked off years of conflict and hostility. In 1867, the groups united and laid the foundation for a bilingual and multicultural society. Despite the legal union, however, sustained conflict in terms of language rights, constitutional provisions, mass media, education, and federal-provincial powers has continued to characterize the relationship between French and English Canada (Rioux, 1971). Moreover, discrepancies in terms of economic control and economic management have placed the Québécois in a disadvantaged position. Findings from the Royal Commission on Bilingualism and Biculturalism report (1969, Bk III: 53–60) show that in comparison with English Canadian and foreign-owned enterprise, the Québécois industries are fewer in number, smaller in scale, and generally lower in production. And although they are represented in power structures at the political level, they are under-represented among the corporate élite and the national unions (Porter, 1965).

In terms of ethnic identity, French Canadians have persisted in sustaining cultural, linguistic, and historical identities. It is important, however, to realize that

the French-speaking people in Quebec are developing a new "Quebecois" identity as opposed to a "French Canadian" identity. Each subgroup will develop attitudes vis a vis each other. The "Quebecois" may think of others as less "genuine" or as being assimilated, hence "lost"; the other French Canadians on the other hand are likely to resent these exclusionist attitudes and to think of the "Quebecois" as aiming for a closed society (Breton, 1972: 36).

French Canadians in other parts of the country vary considerably in size and concentration. While some are clustered in distinctive regions such as eastern Ontario and rural Manitoba, others are scattered among heterogeneous populations.

Other Ethnic Groups

Given a mandate through the British North America Act to develop the Canadian territory, Canadians were in a position to *select* immigrants. The ethnic prejudices of Canadian officials have in the past denied or restricted immigration to groups such as the Chinese, the Japanese, and blacks. Persons of northern European origin in general, and people of British origins in particular, were considered to be the most desirable immigrants. But in order to settle the West and later to satisfy the needs of an industrializing nation, diverse European peoples and some Asians and blacks were admitted (Richmond, 1967: 1–25; Kalbach, 1970; Peterson, 1955).

People entering Canada differed widely in cultural origins, but even more in terms of occupational status. Early immigrants tended to be rural people, many with relatively little educational preparation and with little or no knowledge of the English language. Later immigrants, that is, those entering since the Second World War, have tended to be more educated, more highly skilled, and, in accordance with immigration policies, to have some degree of proficiency in either English or French (Royal Commission on Bilingualism and Biculturalism, 1968, Bk. IV: 11–31; hereafter referred to as Royal Commission).

Within the last decade, changes in immigration policies have eliminated all criteria based on race, colour, or religion. New policies are primarily based on level of education, training, occupation, and employability. As a consequence, Canada has admitted increasing numbers of non-Europeans. Immigration from Jamaica, for instance, totalled 11,202 in 1971 compared to 5,169 for the period extending from 1946 to 1955 (Henry, 1973: XI).

The entry of these other ethnic groups can be traced through four distinct phases (Royal Commission, 1969, Bk. IV). The first phase extended from the seventeenth century to 1901, and included the arrival of such groups as blacks, Chinese, Jews, Germans, and Icelandics. The second, extending from 1901 to the First World War, aimed to settle the West. Among these diverse peoples were settlers from the Ukraine, Poland, Norway, Russia, Germany, Japan, Iceland, and Italy. The third phase, from the Depression to the Second World War, was characterized by small numbers who settled in various parts of the country, but particularly in Ontario and Quebec. These immigrants included Ukrainians, Germans,and Scandinavians. The final phase, extending from the Second World War to the present, included a wide variety of people from Europe, Asia, the West Indies, and Africa. Settling mostly in Toronto, Montreal, and Vancouver, these peoples have increased the ethnic diversity of Canada's major metropolitan centres.

GROUP SIZE AND DISTRIBUTION

In terms of numerical strength, the charter groups have persisted as the two major entities. Primarily as a result of natural increase, that is number of births minus deaths, the numbers of French Canadians have remained relatively stable, although they constitute somewhat less than one-third of the population. They constituted 30.7 per cent of the population in 1901, 28.2 per cent in 1931, 30.4 per cent in 1961, 28.6 per cent in 1971 (Kalbach and McVey, 1971: 148–69). Recent statistics show, however, that their birth rate is now one of the lowest in the country.[1] It has dropped in fact from 30.0 per thousand in 1960 to 16.3 per thousand at the present time. If these trends continue, the proportion of French Canadians relative to all other groups in the country may diminish (Breton, 1972; Grindstaff *et al.*, 1971). Canadians of British origin, on the other hand, have maintained a numerical plurality. They made up 57 per cent of the population in 1901, 51.9 per cent in 1931, and they accounted for 43.8 per cent in 1961, and 44.6 per cent in 1971.

If we were to summarize the 1971 Census, the charter groups account for 73 per cent of the population—French Canadians making up 28.6 per cent and English Canadians 44.6 per cent. This means that approximately 27 per cent of Canadians are of non-French, non-British origins. Of these, German Canadians are the most numerous, constituting 6.1 per cent, followed by the Italians (3.4 per cent), the Ukrainians (2.7

1. Birth rate refers to the number of   given year.
children born per 1000 population in a

per cent), the Dutch (2.0 per cent). All other groups constitute less than 2 per cent—including native Indians who now comprise approximately 1.4 per cent and the Inuit who make up approximately one-tenth of 1 per cent. Despite increasing immigration from Asia and the black nations, no one group constitutes more than 1 per cent.[2]

ETHNIC INSTITUTIONS

While multiculturalism can be traced in terms of group contact, and groups identified according to cultural origins, size, and distribution, the maintenance of culture, language, and identity rests in part on the degree to which groups are able to develop their own social institutions. In other words, a culturally pluralistic society develops a structural facet which can be identified in terms of institutions (Van den Berghe, 1967: 137): churches, voluntary organizations, schools, social services, and the mass media. Providing fundamental socialization agencies, institutions perpetuate values, norms, language, and identities.

BICULTURALISM

The situation of French and English Canadians in Quebec can best be described in terms of *dual institutions*. As Hughes and Kallen (1974: 127) point out, the strong ethnic identity of French Canadians has facilitated the development of a distinct culture. In this province both French and English Canadians have developed their own identifiable institutions: each has its own schools, mass media, churches, and voluntary organizations. Members of these two cultural identities—frequently referred to as "two solitudes"—live side by side and interact most intensely in the commercial, industrial, and political sectors of the province.

French Canadians in other parts of the country vary considerably in institutional maintenance; those located in New Brunswick have considerable ethnic differentiation, but other French Canadians located in Ontario and westward vary in numbers of kinds of institutions. French-language schools are perhaps the most variable. Historically, provincial legislation

2. For a more complete analysis of population distribution, see Warren Kalbach's chapter, "Canada: A Demo-graphic Analysis", especially pages 31–35 and 50–55.

has prohibited the development of such schools. In Manitoba, for example, when the provincial government abolished bilingual schools in 1916, all languages of instruction other than English officially disappeared (Royal Commission, 1969, Bk. II: 124–25). French communities, particularly in rural areas, continued to teach French and a private-school system enabled other areas to support an ethnic system, but it was not until 1970 that French and bilingual schools were officially supported.

While Canada's dual system maintains cultural pluralism, it has tended also to create problems of cohesion. One usually believes, for instance, that a common national history serves to integrate a society. Studies indicate, however, that the charter groups relate to different periods in the development of the country. Since French Canadians tend to place most emphasis on their own historical origins, they find the settlement period most salient. English Canadians and others tend to relate to both the settlement and the discovery of Canada, but more specifically, to the post-Confederation period. When children are asked to identify heroes, French Canadians are more likely to name early historical figures who are predominantly French Canadians while the English students are more likely to include heroes from both the settlement period and the nineteenth and twentieth century (Richert, 1974).

Similarly, French and English Canadians differ considerably on several major national issues. There are variations by regions, but in general English Canadians tend to favour the retention of the monarchy, while French Canadians tend to favour its abolition. English Canadians tend to reject ethnic identities, most preferring to be identified as simply Canadian. French Canadians, on the other hand, place considerable emphasis on the importance of retaining ethnic identities and ethnic institutions. Similarly, English Canadians tend to be critical of bilingualism policies, while French Canadians tend to support such legislation. And finally, English Canadians generally perceive the country as "one Canada", while French Canadians perceive it as an English-French partnership (Manzer, 1974: 138–82).

The value system of French Canadians, in the past at least, derived from the Catholic Church and the humanistic traditions of its educational system. English Canadians, on the other hand, tend to be socialized within the Protestant ethic, which places emphasis on competition, individualism, and achievement. Although much more research is needed in this area, particularly since there has been an increasing secularization of the French schools and a recent renovation in the commercial and scientific areas, these different value systems are seen as factors which explain the under-representation of French Canadians in prestigeful occupations (Porter, 1965).

The linguistic dualism in Quebec has also placed the French-Canadian majority in a disadvantaged position. As we shall see in later sections, the necessity to know English in order to function effectively in most business and industrial sectors of Quebec is another factor constraining the rising aspirations of the Québécois. (For an account of the demography of biculturalism and bilingualism, see Chapter 2.)

VARIATIONS IN INSTITUTIONAL COMPLETENESS[3]

The degree to which other ethnic groups sustain their own institutions varies from group to group and from time to time. Native peoples, for instance, have had very little opportunity until recently to develop their own institutions. Programs in education were left largely to the churches, both Anglican and Catholic, until the 1950s, when the federal government assumed the responsibility for education. In both situations, the use of boarding schools meant that children had to leave the family setting for new and strange environments. When Hobart and Brant (1966) assessed northern education, they concluded that a policy of cultural replacement had denied the natives an opportunity to appreciate their own peoples. Teachers introduced a new value system of individualism, competition, and success symbols, thus alienating the young from their own families as well as from their traditional cultures. The learning of new life-styles in terms of foods, consumer goods, and general sanitation resulted in many of them regarding their own people as inferiors. The use of English and in some cases French as languages of instruction contributed to a gradual erosion of native tongues. The lack of effort on the part of teachers to learn local dialects created communication barriers which in many ways inhibited the learning process. Residential segregation between teachers, administrators, and the local people increased mutual

3. Degrees of institutional completeness in a concept first introduced by Breton (1964). It essentially means that groups differ in the degree to which they associate with one another and the degree to which they establish their own institutions.

distrust and hostility. The establishment of churches and the efforts at conversion undermined indigenous religions to the point where little remains of former beliefs and rituals.

The advent of urbanization and increasing affluence are currently altering previous patterns. Native peoples are increasingly involved in school affairs and curricula are being modified to acommodate Indian and Inuit children. Furthermore, urban Indians, much like new immigrants, are developing social institutions to promote their cultures and solve their urban problems. It is reported, for instance, that there are twenty such institutions in the city of Winnipeg.

The degree to which other ethnic groups sustain institutions varies considerably. Driedger and Church (1974) in a study of Winnipeg found, for instance, that both French and Jewish Canadians were maintaining a considerable degree of institutional completeness. Scandinavians, on the other hand, were territorially dispersed and not maintaining ethnic institutions to any significant degree.

Several factors have been isolated to acount for the maintenance of ethnic institutions. When religion is important to a group, ethnic churches provide a focus for group activity (Royal Commission, 1969, Bk. IV). The Ukrainian Catholic and Orthodox churches, for instance, have had significant impact on the survival of the group. Churches not only provide a mechanism through which members may interact, but they also perpetuate cultural ideologies and group identity. Equally important, they provide an institution where language is legitimized and reinforced. For newcomers, either recent immigrants or migrants, they provide a meeting place where they feel a sense of belonging. Ethnic churches, therefore, tend to persist when new waves of immigrants enter a society. The Italian churches in Toronto, for instance, persist as long as the Italian population demands them. At the same time, however, acculturated members may move to other locations and become absorbed in non-ethnically defined congregations.

When language and cultural ideologies are important to group identity, schools are developed to socialize the younger generations. Programs may include general cultural orientations, as well as particular religions, social, and economic ideologies. Still other programs may concentrate on music, dance, and crafts. The Royal Commission (1969, Bk. IV: 150) identified over five hundred part-time schools for sixteen culture groups; of which

Table 1 Part-time ethnic schools. . . . Number of schools for selected ethnic origins—Canada and provinces, 1965.

Ethnic Origin	Total	Quebec	Ontario	Manitoba	Saskatchewan	Alberta	British Columbia
Total	507	68	254	64	21	74	20
Ukrainian	170	9	94	19	12	35	1
German	157	4	66	36	8	32	11
Polish	57	10	38	5	0	2	2
Jewish	24	15	—	—	—	—	3
Italian	22	12	9	—	—	1	—
Lithuanian	15	2	10	1	0	1	1
Hungarian	14	3	5	1	1	3	1
Latvian	14	1	12	1	0	0	0
Estonian	10	1	8	0	0	0	1
Greek	8	3	5	0	0	0	0
Slovene	5	1	3	1	—	—	—
Armenian	3	2	1	0	0	0	—
Portugese	3	3	0	0	0	0	—
Dutch	2	—	2	—	—	—	—
Japanese	2	1	1	—	—	—	—
Chinese	1	1	—	—	—	—	—

— Data were not available.
Source: Royal Commission on Bilingualism and Biculturalism, 1969, Book IV: 150.

two-thirds were German, Ukrainian, and Polish. About 65 per cent of all students enroled in the ethnic schools were German, Ukrainian, or Jewish (see Table 1 and Table 2). But relative to total numbers in corresponding ethnic-origin categories, Lithuanians, Latvians, and Estonians were the most highly represented. Members of the larger groups, numerically speaking, such as the Poles and Italians, had lower representations in ethnic schools. Similarly, the Dutch and Germans, along with the Ukrainians, had low proportions relative to their group size. In other words, while numerically large groups support ethnic schools, the interest in a culture influences the proportion of children sent to those schools.

The establishment of *full-time* schools has a dual function. It brings together youth of the same cultural group for educational as well as recreational activity. In these institutions ethnic identities are strengthened and future leaders of ethnic groups are prepared. The Mennonites, Jews, Ukrainians, and Greeks operate such schools (Royal Commission, 1969, Bk. IV).

The various types of mass media provide another institution for the maintenance of multicularlism. The ethnic press, for instance, provides a medium whereby individuals gain recognition and a group is recognized by the society at large. It transmits news of the homeland as well as news of the group's activity in Canada. It can provide information and opinion about life in Canada. It can influence members regarding issues relevant to the group, and, in this context, it can be an instrument for mobilizing public opinion.

While numbers of newspapers can be counted, their strength relative to numbers in the population is more difficult to assess. According to a 1965 assessment, however, the Lithuanian press, with five periodicals for 28,000 group members, had the highest ratio of subscriptions to population, followed by the Chinese, Hungarians, and Ukrainians (Royal Commission, 1969, Bk. IV: 172–77). The number of readers and therefore the chance for survival of these newspapers appear to fluctuate over time. Nevertheless, they continue to circulate and continue to provide some degree of group cohesion for the ethnic groups which support them.

Many types of voluntary associations are constituted to meet the needs of specific ethnic groups. There are mutual-aid associations designed to help other members secure employment; other groups provide social welfare and health services and recreation and leisure activities. Some of

Table 2 Enrolment in part-time ethnic schools. . . . Number of students in part-time schools for selected ethnic origin categories—Canada and Provinces, 1965.

Ethnic Origin	Total	Quebec	Ontario	Manitoba	Saskatchewan	Alberta	British Columbia
Total	39,833	10,397	16,224	3,529	1,054	4,084	4,545
German	12,623	250	4,752	2,166	325	1,630	3,500
Ukrainian	8,702	1,106	3,896	879	38	2,101	682
Jewish	5,038	4,443	—	—	—	—	595
Polish	4,000	760	2,400	300	0	200	310
Italian	2,887	2,040	822	0	0	25	0
Greek	1,750	850	900	0	0	0	0
Lithuanian	1,520	120	1,360	40	0	0	0
Latvian	992	40	850	45	0	20	37
Estonian	685	60	600	0	0	0	25
Hungarian	601	198	190	18	47	108	40
Slovene	335	53	231	51	—	—	—
Armenian	328	216	112	—	—	—	—
Japanese	156	45	111	—	—	—	—
Chinese	120	120	—	—	—	—	—
Portugese	96	96	0	0	0	0	0
Dutch	0	0	0	0	0	0	0

— Data were not available.
Source: Royal Commission on Bilingualism and Biculturalism, 1969, Book IV: 151.

these organizations become elaborate and long lasting, others disintegrate when members become assimilated and no longer need them. Research on the topic indicates that the Ukrainian, German, and Italian ethnic groups maintain the greatest number of associations. Membership, however, was found to be predominantly among immigrants, as opposed to Canadian born, indicating perhaps that interest in the ethnic organizations decreases with succeeding generations in the country (Royal Commission, 1969, Book IV: 110–11).

Generally, the more a group finds its origins a handicap, the more likely it is to form a strong structure of service-type associations. Jewish Canadians, for instance, who have experienced prejudice and discrimination in most Canadian cities have developed a multiplicity of voluntary organizations, ranging from social-welfare agencies and mutual-benefit associations to recreational organizations like country clubs. Such organizations promote group solidarity and, in general, sustain the religious and cultural aspects of the group (Royal Commission, 1969, Bk. IV).

In short, diverse social institutions tend to perpetuate the culture and language of several ethnic groups. In this sense degrees of institutional completeness are important to the maintenance of multiculturalism. Whether they tend to promote inequalities, however, is a matter for continuing research: there is always the possibility that degrees of cultural distinctiveness may perpetuate or even promote ethnic prejudices; members of these groups may be viewed by the majority as "clannish", "inferior", "foreign", or "eccentric".

Secondly, differential school systems may perpetuate values which are incongruent with social mobility. Schools may produce students who are not equipped to cope with the social and economic requirements of the larger system. Vallee and Shulman suggest that

the more a minority group turns in upon itself and concentrates on making its position strong, the more it costs the members in terms of their chances to make their ways as individuals in the larger system. . . .

Among ethnic minority groups which strive to maintain language and other distinctions, motivation to aspire to high-ranking social and economic positions in the larger system will be weak, unless, of course, it is characteristic of the ethnic groups to put a special stress on educational and vocational achievement (Vallee and Shulman, 1969: 95).

SUMMARY

Multiculturalism has emerged in Canada as a consequence of diverse patterns of group contact. A gradual encroachment of Europeans, the displacement of native peoples, and the imposition of educational and religious institutions has meant a gradual erosion of native culture. The charter groups through a century of accommodation have sustained dual institutions; now frequently referred to as French and English Canada, these two systems perpetuate culture, language, and identities. Other ethnic groups vary considerably in degrees of institutional completeness. While some persist in sustaining identifiable structures, others, after succeeding generations in the country, tend to abandon ethnic institutions for complete or partial absorption in the general Canadian society. But although the nature of multiculturalism sustains diverse cultures, language, and identities, at the same time it creates inequalities and problems of cohesion.

Stratification

A multi-ethnic society can be described in terms of social differentiation. As Gordon (1964) claims, when a society is stratified by social class, then logically each group will be stratified within. Thus, for any given category there will be some members who are professionals, some who are white-collar workers, some labourers and some who are unemployed. Referring to this overlap as the *ethclass*, Gordon claims that this conceptual interception serves to delineate differences in life-style, attitudes, and prestige. While this chapter does not pursue life-styles as such, some illustrations of class differences within groups will be briefly described in order to introduce the student to the complex nature of ethnicity. From these internal differences, it becomes clear that some segments of each ethnic category are more advantaged than others. But at the same time, when groups are compared to each other, inequalities become apparent.

For purposes of this essay, the analyses of social class will focus on occupational categories. Fundamental differences within and among groups can vary by rural and urban residence, but general findings suggest that ethnicity has become a criterion for recruitment into prestigeful positions. Thus, the Canadian stratification system tends to be a vertical mosaic with groups arranged in a hierarchical system of ethnicity as well as social class.

INTRA-GROUP DIFFERENCES

Native Peoples

When a society such as Canada has an indigenous population which has been geographically isolated and generally undereducated, differences within that population are less accentuated. According to a case study by Dosman (1972), internal stratification does exist. Using occupational and income criteria, he identifies four classes on the reservations and three classes in the city. Reservation categories include leading families, the self-supporting, the semi-dependent, and the dependent (see Chart 1). Each class differs in total income, source of income, occupation, and prestige. When individuals migrate to the urban areas, they fall into three categories. The leading families become the affluent, the two middle reservation categories are referred to as the *anomic*, and the dependent reserve group becomes the urban welfare category. Dosman claims that leading families emerged on reservations as a result of Indian Affairs administrative policies. White superintendents at the outset selected those families they considered to be most co-operative and the most likely to become assimilated. Through them they made contact with the bulk of the population. These selected families acquired prestige in the process, but the system served to create a deep cleavage between them and the bulk of the population. Through succeeding years of continual contact with white administrators, these families became more assimilated and more integrated into Canadian life-styles. When they migrate to urban areas, they maintain their prestige and influence. They adapt quickly to city life, have professional or semi-professional jobs, live in white neighbourhoods, and tend to associate with their ethclass.

Many become administrators of Indian and Métis associations, counsellors, and, in general, leaders. In the process they gain recognition from the white community and in large measure are able to present themselves as spokesmen for the group. Instrumental in identifying crucial areas of change (such as practices of discrimination), they have influenced legislation and public opinion.

Chart I Reservation Indians: suggested "classes"

Leading Families	Self-Supporting	Semi-Dependent	Dependent
1) farm extensively and raise cattle	1) do not farm profitably or own machines	1) intermittent welfare	1) welfare
2) have property on reserve such as house and machinery	2) do not raise cattle or farm profitably. Do part-time work	2) occasional employment	2) usually unemployed
3) have earned income over $4,000	3) less than $4,000	3) fluctuates	—
4) have important positions on reserve governments and contact with Federal Government	4) are not prestigeful	4) low prestige	4) low prestige

Source: Dosman, 1972.

In the process, however, many tend to lose touch with the realities of the urban poor. There is a tendency within all bureaucratic structures to develop formal, impersonal relationships with the clientele, which in the long run alienate those who are most in need of assistance. Remote from the bulk of the Indian population, bureaucrats tend to perpetuate themselves and to promote the interests of the organization.

In terms of ethnic identities, however, members of leading families do not suffer an identity crisis when moving to the city:

Increasingly the affluent appear to share a common consciousness of "Indianess". "Pan Indianess" as this phenomenon is now labeled, has unquestionably matured in the affluent community in Saskatoon in the last years. One of the indications of this is the wholesale collapse of Christianity among these Indians and Metis, even the Indian Churchmen in the group—once the pride of Indian Affairs and Missionaries. Not a single family or individual in the city displayed even a lingering loyalty to the most pervasive ideological movement in the reserve; many now speak with great interest about indigenous religious and cultural practices. Many have also renewed their interest in Indian languages and native art work (Dosman, 1972: 55).

At the other extreme are the dependent Indians, who, when they move to the city, remain on welfare and inhabit what is commonly known as "skid row". Constituting a large proportion of urban Indian dwellers, they share a life-style with other poverty groups who live in the same neighbourhood. This group rarely finds stable employment, and unless the men are completely unemployable, they have considerable difficulty in obtaining assistance from welfare agencies. On the other hand, women who have difficulty in finding employment can more easily obtain social assistance, particularly if they have children to support.

Based upon several indicators of what Dosman refers to as "personal disintegration", members of this group generally are seen as apathetic and alienated. Moreover, they tend to participate in the drinking subcultures which proliferate in urban areas. Many social scientists view the use of alcohol and/or drugs as a reaction to minority-group status. Dozier (1960: 72–87) and Lemert (1958), for instance, explain drinking patterns as withdrawal behaviour stemming from feelings of inadequacy and frustration. Brody (1971), who also focuses on the urban migrant, views the drinking patterns as a mode of community association. Extending beyond the native peoples to incorporate the marginal and transient white men, it involves a subculture which functions to integrate the neighbourhood and ease the transition for the newcomer.

To drink on skid row is to do more than drink. This kind of drinking, stretching as it does over a long period of time, entails residence in the neighbourhood, with the attendant need for a place to stay, for food and for ready cash. The needs of these drinkers are not the minimal needs of the clinical alcoholic; conversations and the pursuit of sexual conquest are elements in this as in other forms of life. The gratifications of life here extend beyond the pleasures of palliation of drunkenness (Brody, 1971: 12).

According to Dosman, the third category of urban Indians is composed of those reservation families who are classed as self-supporting and semi-dependent. It is these individuals who, when migrating to the city, become disillusioned. Referring to them as *anomic*, the author claims they experience "anxiety and social isolation of such magnitude that they either are forced down into the welfare group or return dejectedly to the reserve" (Dosman, 1972: 84).

There are several patterns of employment-seeking and employment stability. Most Indians, however, have relatively few occupational skills and are therefore subject to the variance in unskilled-labour opportunities. Many also experience discriminatory treatment on the part of employers and landlords alike. Continually striving to better their lot, they move from job to job, from city to city, or from city to reserve.

Charter Groups

French Canadians who have been in the country for many generations have developed a class structure which in many ways sets them apart from other ethnic groups, but at the same time separates them from one another. There have always been élitist French families consisting of those who have perpetuated a status through the professions and the business world. These families are extremely wealthy, highly educated, and tend to associate across ethnic lines with others who share prestige, university education, and wealth. The bulk of the French population, however, is predominantly at the lower end of the class system, constituting, in essence, the work force of Quebec (Porter, 1965: 91–98). Within the last two decades, however, with educational innovations and growing aspirations toward mobility, an increasing number of lower- and working-class youth are attending universities (Ossenberg, 1971: 118–21). In 1961, 13.5 per cent of French Canadians in Quebec were in professional, technical, and managerial occupations; 31.4 per cent were in blue-collar occupations; 7.5 per cent were labourers; 47.6 per cent were in other occupations such as transport, communications, primary industry, agriculture (Royal Commission, 1969, Bk. iii: 38–40).

English Canadians also have their leading families who perpetuate a professional corporate and political élite. But as Porter discusses (1965: 91–98), Canadians of British ancestry are distributed among all occupational categories. Since as a group they are more highly educated, a greater proportion of them occupy positions of authority and influence. Recent immigrants from Britain and other English-speaking countries tend also to be highly educated and highly skilled (Richmond, 1967: 40–41). According to 1961 figures, 21 per cent of all Canadians of British origin were in professional, technical, and managerial positions, 30 per cent were blue-collar workers, 5.6 per cent were labourers, and the remaining 47.5 were classified as other (Royal Commission, 1969, Bk. iii: 38–40).

Other Ethnic Groups

Other groups in Canada differ internally along several dimensions. Blacks, for instance, who arrived in Canada over a century ago, are predominantly rural and working class. Patterns of accommodation to prejudice and discrimination resulted in what is known as *marginal adaptation*. Essentially this term means that a group cultivates occupational fields where the majority offers the least resistance. One such pattern has been the streaming of many males into low-status and low-paying positions in Canada's railroad companies. Most recent immigrants are more highly educated, more highly skilled, and therefore tend to qualify for more prestigious positions (Winks, 1970).

Italian Canadians, who are predominantly urban, are concentrated in skilled and unskilled occupations: 8.4 per cent are professionals, techni-

cians, and managers, 43.7 per cent are skilled workers, and 19.2 per cent
are labourers. The Jewish Canadians, on the other hand, are more highly
educated, with 43 per cent in the professional, technical, and managerial
categories and only 15.6 per cent in skilled occupations, and 1.1 per cent
are labourers (Royal Commission, 1969, Bk. III: 38–40).

INTERGROUP DIFFERENCES

A study of ethnicity and stratification by Porter examines the differential
distribution of groups among occupational categories (see Table 3).
Comparing each ethnic group to the general Canadian distribution in
each occupational class, he was able to estimate over- or under-representation for three successive decades, 1931, 1951, and 1961. The com-
putation essentially involves calculating the total male distribution of
the labour force in Canada among six occupational groupings. In 1961,
for instance, 5.6 per cent of the total male force were in professional and
financial occupations and 6.9 per cent in clerical fields. Ethnic groups are
compared to this distribution in terms of percentages above or below this
figure. Thus a +2 means that in that occupational category a group has
2 per cent over the national figure and a −2 means that a group has 2
per cent less than the national figure.

Using this method, Porter illustrates that for three periods of time,
English Canadians are consistently over-represented in the top categories.
The French Canadians, on the other hand, are consistently under-represented in top categories. This pattern does not mean that the French
Canadians have not increased their proportions in these categories—for
indeed they have—but that relative to others, they have had a slower rate
of increase.

The explanation for this phenomenon is complex. The former educational system of the Québécois and the traditional value system may
explain a lack of preparation in scientific and business skills. Achievement
in terms of educational levels has also been lower than it has in many
other groups (Porter, 1965). Despite these factors, recent research suggests that the Québécois, even *with* educational attainment, tend to receive
a lower income than other groups with the same educational achievement,
a pattern most accentuated among the working classes (Beattie and
Spencer, 1971; Lamphier and Morris, 1974).

Other analyses of the situation suggest that language is an important factor in determining the status of the group. As indicated, English is generally required at most managerial and even technical levels. In other words, the higher the occupational status, the greater the demand to know English. As Brazeau explains, this requirement inhibits many and in the long run it can mean that an entire group's potential and diversity is curtailed. "The dominance of English language structures has resulted in the development of adaptability among the French Canadian, they are disposed to learn English, at least the English technical vocabulary, to better their lot" (Brazeau, 1958: 536). But if English is not fully developed to a high degree of proficiency, they may not benefit fully from their work experience. They may have difficulty expressing themselves to others, thus handicapping necessary communications between employer and employee and between peers. Furthermore, since the technical and work concepts are learned in English, "and not necessarily translated into French, individuals are handicapped by the fact that they depend on two languages and thus are without one with which they can express the whole range of their experience" (Brazeau, 1958: 536). There is a likelihood, therefore, that individuals in these situations may develop low self-esteem and feel a general resentment of the structures they see as inhibiting.

When the federal civil service and the military were examined by the commissioners of the Bilingualism and Biculturalism study, similar patterns of under-representation and language barriers emerged. Their study indicated that, in 1965, 22 per cent of the civil service were French speakers, but they were under-represented in such major sectors as the industrial, financial, and scientific. When they were represented at the management level, most did not participate on an equal footing with English-speaking Canadians. Many were hampered in being required to use English, whereas most English speakers were not generally required to use French. In addition, French Canadians were absorbed in an English milieu, working alongside a majority who had little awareness of the intellectual traditions developed in French-language universities and research centres.

In terms of civil service career patterns, the commissioners found that, among officers (middle-level men) in five government departments, levels of education, seniority, and age brought greater economic gain to English

Table 3 Percentage of representation in Canadian occupational classes by ethnic origin, male labour force, 1931, 1951, and 1961.

	British total	British			French	German	Italian
		English	Irish	Scottish			
1931							
Professional and financial	+1.6	+1.6	+1.0	+2.2	−0.8	− 2.2	− 3.3
Clerical	+1.5	+1.8	+1.0	+1.4	−0.8	− 2.2	− 2.5
Personal service	−0.3	0.0	−0.5	−0.7	−0.3	− 1.2	+ 2.1
Primary and unskilled	−4.6	−4.4	−4.9	−4.8	+3.3	− 5.3	+26.1
Agriculture	−3.0	−6.1	+2.7	−1.5	+0.1	+21.1	−27.6
All others	+4.8	+7.1	+0.7	−3.4	−1.5	−10.2	+ 5.2
Total	0.0	0.0	0.0	0.0	0.0	0.0	0.0
1951							
Professional and financial	+1.6	+1.6	+0.9	+2.5	−1.5	− 2.2	− 3.1
Clerical	+1.6	+1.8	+1.3	+1.4	−0.8	− 2.5	− 1.7
Personal service	−0.3	−0.2	−0.4	−0.5	−0.2	− 1.2	+ 2.0
Primary and unskilled	−2.2	−1.7	−2.2	−3.2	+3.0	− 3.7	+ 9.6
Agriculture	−3.2	−5.5	+0.5	−1.6	−0.3	+19.1	−14.7
All others	+2.5	+4.0	−0.1	+1.4	−0.2	− 9.5	+ 7.9
Total	0.0	0.0	0.0	0.0	0.0	0.0	0.0
1961							
Professional and financial	+2.0	—	—	—	−1.9	− 1.8	− 5.2
Clerical	+1.3	—	—	—	−0.2	− 1.8	− 3.2
Personal service	−0.9	—	—	—	−0.2	− 0.7	+ 2.9
Primary and unskilled	−2.3	—	—	—	+2.8	− 2.1	+11.5
Agriculture	−1.5	—	—	—	−1.4	+ 8.8	− 9.5
All others	+1.4	—	—	—	+0.9	− 2.4	+ 3.5
Total	0.0	0.0	0.0	0.0	0.0	0.0	0.0

Source: Porter, 1965: 87.

Jewish	Dutch	Scand.	East European	Other European	Asian	Indian and Eskimo	Total Male Labour Force
− 2.2	− 1.1	− 2.9	− 3.9	− 4.4	− 4.3	− 4.5	4.8
+ 0.1	− 1.9	− 2.7	− 3.4	− 3.5	− 3.2	− 3.7	3.8
− 1.2	− 1.5	− 1.5	− 1.1	− 1.7	−27.3	− 3.1	3.5
−14.5	− 4.8	+ 1.4	+12.4	+35.8	+10.2	+45.3	17.7
−32.4	+18.5	+19.8	+14.5	− 5.8	−20.9	− 4.9	34.0
+45.8	− 9.2	−14.1	−18.5	−20.4	− 9.6	−20.1	36.2
0.0	0.0	0.0	0.0	0.0	0.0	0.0	100.0
+ 4.2	− 1.7	− 2.1	− 2.9	− 2.4	− 2.8	− 5.2	5.9
0.0	− 2.4	− 2.8	− 2.8	− 2.5	− 2.9	− 5.2	5.9
− 1.4	− 1.2	− 1.0	+ 0.6	+ 2.0	+23.9	− 0.6	3.4
−11.5	− 1.7	+ 0.5	+ 2.3	+ 5.7	− 1.9	+47.0	13.3
−18.7	+17.3	+14.7	+11.2	+ 3.4	− 8.7	− 7.8	19.4
+27.4	−10.3	− 9.3	− 8.4	− 6.2	− 6.2	−28.2	52.1
0.0	0.0	0.0	0.0	0.0	0.0	0.0	100.0
+ 7.4	− 0.9	− 1.9	− 1.2	− 1.1	+ 1.7	− 7.5	8.6
− 0.1	− 1.7	− 2.4	− 1.7	− 2.0	− 1.5	− 5.9	6.9
− 2.4	− 0.5	− 1.1	+ 0.9	+ 5.1	+19.1	+ 1.3	4.3
− 8.9	− 2.0	− 0.2	0.0	− 1.8	− 3.6	+34.7	10.0
−11.7	+10.3	+10.6	+ 6.9	+ 0.6	− 6.5	+ 6.9	12.2
+15.7	− 5.2	− 5.0	− 4.9	− 4.4	− 9.1	−29.5	55.0
0.0	0.0	0.0	0.0	0.0	0.0	0.0	100.0

Canadians than to their Francophone counterparts. In other words, discriminatory processes operate in such a way that education and experience provide fewer rewards for the minority group.

The social-class analysis of other groups indicate that Jewish Canadians are consistently over-represented in the top occupational categories. Others are under-represented, but after generations in Canada, and with more educated immigrants, the discrepancy is diminishing—particularly for groups such as the Dutch, Germans, and Asians. The under-representation of the Dutch, for instance, diminished over the decades from —1.1 in 1931 to —0.9 in 1961 and that of the Germans from —2.2 to —1.8. The under-representation of Asians changed from —4.3 to an over-representation of +1.7. These figures suggest that some groups can alter their social-class status from one generation to another. More research is needed, however, to reveal systematically the degree to which education and occupation are related to the nature of intergenerational mobility. The occupational integration of an immigrant group, for instance, is dependent upon its occupational status when entering Canada. Secondly, groups differ in the degree to which they value education. And thirdly, groups differ in the degree to which they experience prejudice and discrimination. All of these factors need to be explored in order to understand more fully the dynamics of ethnicity and social class as it relates to new immigrant groups.

In terms of stratification systems, native peoples are clearly the most disadvantaged. On all other objective measures of social class they are at the bottom of the ladder. As Harding writes, 40 per cent of the Indian and Métis have incomes less than $1,000 per year, while this is the case for 13 per cent of the general population; only 25 per cent reach the sixth grade, with many receiving no education at all. Occupationally, they are concentrated in the unskilled categories and more grossly under-represented in the top occupational categories than any other ethnic group in the country.

In terms of life chances, Indian and Métis have an infant mortality of seventy per thousand as compared to twenty-six per thousand for the general population. The pre-school mortality rate is eight times the national average and that of teenagers one and a half times greater. They require hospitalization twice as often as other Canadians and are more likely to die from pulmonary and infectious diseases. The life expectancy for males and females is eight to ten years less than it is for the average Canadian (Harding, 1971).

A generally low socio-economic status is also reflected in patterns of deviant behaviour. The relationship between social class and law-breaking behaviour which has typified the situation of minorities in other countries is replicated in Canada. According to statistics compiled for the city of Winnipeg, for instance, peoples of native ancestry are over-represented in terms of arrests, incarcerations, and recidivism (Bienvenue and Latif, 1974).

In summary, when ethnicity is viewed as a variable in the Canadian stratification system, English and Jewish Canadians are over-represented in top occupational classes. Others, including the French Canadians, are to some degree under-represented. While some groups improve their distribution through the decades, native peoples clearly remain the most disadvantaged groups.

Assimilation

While institutional structures in some cases maintain cultural distinctiveness, trends toward assimilation promote uniformity. The assimilation process itself is a complex phenomenon involving changes on the part of the individual, changes in terms of groups, and ultimately changes in the nature of the Canadian society. Three aspects of the process will be discussed here: acculturation, structural integration, and linguistic assimilation.

ACCULTURATION

Very broadly defined, acculturation refers to the process of acquiring the culture of another group (Shibutani and Kwan, 1965: 140). It essentially involves learning and adopting technology, folkways, and patterns of dress. It requires accepting norms pertaining to such things as family life, law, employer-employee relationships, politics, and public behaviour. It includes the learning and internalization of value systems, the idea of success, the importance of education, and the meaning of material goods.

Although Canadians like to believe that theirs is a country of cultural equalities, the main trend has been one of Anglo-conformity. As Elliott

(1971: 3) points out, the British as a charter group have consistently enjoyed a more prestigeful position in Canadian society. Peoples of other ethnic origins, including French Canadians, have experienced pressures to alter their own folkways, norms, and values. These pressures to conform are exerted by peer groups, schools, neighbourhoods, and the mass media. Anxious to eliminate differences considered strange or even inferior, many within ethnic groups abandon traditional patterns for attitudes and behaviour considered more appropriately Canadian. Others are motivated by the realization that acculturation leads to social mobility. Most groups therefore experience some degree of change.

While the process of acculturation is experienced by most if not all groups, several factors appear to account for varying rates of change. Studies in the Canadian North, for instance, suggest that degrees of *contact* account for varying rates of modernization. While there are still isolated communities which persist in maintaining traditional ways, a trend toward settlement in small towns accelerates acculturation processes. Vallee (1971), who traces stages of white-native contact, illustrates a gradual disappearance of indigenous cultures. In those northern communities where schools, churches, and federal administrators have permanent residence, native peoples are gradually adopting modern ways. There has been considerable resistance and some lack of internalization, but succeeding generations seem to experience increasing acculturation.

There seems to be little doubt that *education* has served to break down the normative system of indigenous people and facilitated varying degrees of assimilation. The degree to which native peoples adopt a Western perspective depends in part on the type of education and the degree of exposure to the dominant society. Whether one views assimilation as negative or positive depends on the value placed on preserving native cultures as opposed to the dominant Euro-Canadian culture.

Accumulating evidence suggests that increasing levels of education reduce differences between natives and others. Honigmann (1970: 30), for instance, in his discussion of northern education, recognizes some assimilationist aspects of boarding-school experiences. These aspects helped to make English a language shared by all groups, thus facilitating communications and spreading literacy throughout the population. The curriculum introduced norms of family living, homemaking, employment patterns, and civic responsibilities. The religious emphasis gave rise to new forms of emotional expression on occasions such as Christmas and Easter, thus replacing the loss of traditional ceremonies.

Among southern Indian populations, there are variations from region to region and from generation to generation, but here too, the educational system appears to account for a gradual absorption of native peoples. Dosman (1972) suggests, for instance, that the affluent Indian has accepted norms relating to work, bureaucratization, and modern living. Zentner (1966), in a study comparing values in regard to education, found few differences between native students and others.

The acculturation of immigrants depends in part on degrees of initial *cultural similarity*. Those immigrants arriving from the western hemisphere, particularly from English-speaking countries, tend to experience fewer difficulties in adjusting to Canadian society. Immigrants from dissimilar cultural background, however, tend to adhere to their traditional patterns for longer periods of time. Lai (1971) demonstrates that Hong Kong immigrants express a preference for the extended family and for a male-dominated household. They tend to be conservative in regard to norms governing male-female relationships, particularly those relating to premarital sex and public displays of affection.

In general, acculturation accelerates with succeeding *generations of Canadian born*. There are exceptional groups, such as the Hutterites, whose social organization is designed to maintain group boundaries, but for most groups, acculturation proceeds with time. Where first and second generations may adhere to ethnic communities, younger members gradually begin to drift away. We need much more research in this area, but the Royal Commission (1969, Bk. IV) study suggests that attendance at ethnic schools tends to diminish with generations of Canadian born. Boissevain (1971), in his study of Italians in Montreal, alludes to generational differences where younger people become critical of their parents and their attachments to the Italian culture.

STRUCTURAL INTEGRATION

While acculturation refers to the learning of another culture, structural integration refers to associational patterns in which individuals develop relationships with members of other ethnic groups. These relationships may be of the formal type, that is, *secondary relationships* consisting of impersonal or sometimes utilitarian interaction. *Primary-group relation-ships*, on the other hand, consist of intimate face-to-face relationships usually found in friendship and family groupings (Gordon, 1964).

Friendship Groupings

Research suggests that once acculturation has taken place, patterns of association change. Informal networks restricted to cultural group members at the outset are gradually extended to include others. With increasing facility in the English language and increasing levels of education, friendship groups become more heterogeneous. A study of immigrants in Montreal showed that those who were fluent in French or English had a greater number of friends outside their own group. Furthermore, individuals with higher levels of education established contacts more quickly than those with lower educational achievement. Younger persons were more likely to associate with others than older individuals were (Breton and Pinard, 1960).

In a setting where prejudice and discrimination are common practices acculturation may occur, but structural integration may be prohibited. In such situations, the subjects of discrimination are, by necessity, confined to their own group for most of their primary-group relationships. Observational studies of Indian and white communities, for instance, suggest that Indian-white associations generally are restricted to secondary-type relationships in business and commercial transactions. Patterns of avoidance and withdrawal reduce the stress of intergroup contact, but at the same time they promote segregated communities (Braroe, 1965). Similar patterns have been observed in urban areas among low-income peoples. According to Brody (1971) there are more frequent, casual associations between Indians and others in this milieu, but for most Indians, the native community still provides the main source of primary-group formation.

The acculturation process and the entrance into associations with members of the dominant society frequently results in a phenomenon known as *marginality*. Marginal persons are individuals caught between "two worlds", having to make adjustments to the society at large, as well as to their own changing ethnic communities. The entire subject cannot be dealt with here, but Shibutani and Kwan (1965: 354–59) summarize certain aspects worth noting. Individuals who wish to become integrated but who are not accepted by others may experience frustrations and self-doubts. They very often develop a resentment toward their own group as well as a general critical approach to the society as a whole. Others may compartmentalize their world, playing accepted roles when in the presence of their own group, and another set of roles when in the company of others. A working person, for instance, may accept the dominant society's role patterns of colleague relationships, but adhere to traditional ethnic patterns within the family circle. Other marginal persons are able to integrate both cultures; moving easily between them, they have mixed associations and are able to develop meaningful relationships with other marginal persons. Marginality may also result in creativity, particularly in the area of music, poetry, and writing. Finally, marginal men and women have become leaders of reform and revolutionary movements.

Intermarriage

Rates of ethnic intermarriage are perhaps the most sensitive indicators of structural assimilation. Marriage across groups (exogamy) tends to reduce cultural diversity, while endogamy (marriage within the group) tends to perpetuate pluralism. As Kalbach (Chap. 2) explains, it is important to point out that exogamy/endogamy rates are related to group size and group dispersion.[4] In this context, since the French Canadians and British are numerically large, there is a greater probability that individuals will marry within their own ethnic group. Secondly, endogamy is a more likely pattern where ethnic groups are geographically concentrated. Thus, the Québécois, who are regionally concentrated and comprise 79 per cent of the provincial population, are more likely to marry within the group. Similarly, native people in isolated northern areas are more likely to marry one another. This is not to deny the importance of ethnic survival as a motivation for endogamy, nor to deny the impact of prejudice and discrimination: these are certainly important factors in explaining rates of intermarriage. What needs to be pointed out, however, is that size and distribution can promote or inhibit assimilation.

According to Kalbach's data (Chap. 2: p. 40), the British and French populations as a whole have low exogamy rates but in areas where these

4. For a more extensive analysis of endogamy, see Warren Kalbach's chapter, "Canada: A Demographic Analysis", pp. 38–40.

groups are less numerous and less concentrated, exogamy rates increase. On the other hand, Scandinavians, Hungarians, and Poles, who tend to be more evenly dispersed, have higher exogamy rates. In short, demographic characteristics play an important part in determining the possibilities for inter-ethnic marriage. More research is needed to investigate specific attitudes toward endogamous and exogamous marriages. Which groups, for instance, tend to promote endogamy as a means of cultural survival? Which groups tend to promote exogamy as a means of social mobility? When inter-ethnic marriages take place, does religion function as a common denominator?

LINGUISTIC ASSIMILATION

The dynamics of language transfer are not fully understood, but the existence of a dominant language in any area tends to reduce the feasibility and eventually the desirability of maintaining another language. Thus, despite the fact that ethnic groups in Canada have become bilingual in the sense that they speak English and another language, many among the younger generations are now unilingual. The process of assimilation results in ever-increasing numbers who speak English only.

In order to illustrate the increasing loss of mother tongues, language retention rates have been computed for Canadian-born individuals[5] (see Table 4). With the exception of French speakers in Quebec, where language loss is minimal, figures indicate a discrepancy between numbers within each ethnic group who claim the language as a mother tongue and numbers who state that they usually speak that language in the home. Mother tongue (MT) here essentially means the language first learned as a child and still understood. Home language (HL) refers to the language usually spoken in the home.

As Table 4 indicates, persons of Jewish, Dutch, Scandinavian, Polish, and German origins have experienced the greatest language loss. In all of Canada, 7.5 per cent of Jewish Canadians still have an ethnic language as a mother tongue, and only 1.9 per cent usually speak that language in the home. Among those of Scandinavian origins, 7.8 per cent have retained the original language and 0.4 per cent usually speak it at home.

5. I want to thank Jay Goldstein, Assistant Professor at the University of Manitoba, for computing these figures.

Table 4 Percentage of native-born members of ten ethnic groups whose mother tongue (MT) and home language (HL) correspond to ethnic group, Canada and provinces/territories, 1971.

Ethnic Group		Can.	Nfld.	PEI	NS	NB	Que.	Ont.	Man.	Sask.	Alta.	BC	Yuk.	NWT
British	MT	97.7%	99.9%	99.3%	99.3%	97.7%	80.6%	99.0%	98.0%	98.2%	98.6%	99.1%	98.9%	96.8%
	HL	98.3	99.9	99.7	99.7	98.2	79.9	99.6	99.5	99.7	99.7	99.8	99.9	98.7
French	MT	89.5	19.0	45.0	45.9	87.6	98.1	60.4	63.1	50.3	43.7	32.3	31.3	41.3
	HL	85.6	12.7	27.6	32.3	81.7	97.6	45.0	42.3	25.7	21.7	9.2	9.7	21.3
German	MT	21.1	2.8	2.5	1.0	1.4	11.7	12.8	46.7	30.6	23.2	19.1	12.1	13.1
	HL	6.5	1.1	1.2	0.3	0.3	5.4	5.0	20.5	6.0	5.8	4.0	2.2	1.9
Italian	MT	44.0	5.0	****	13.1	8.8	56.4	43.8	40.0	16.7	32.3	25.8	10.5	36.4
	HL	32.0	1.2	****	5.2	3.1	40.2	33.5	26.0	11.1	18.5	12.7	5.3	22.7
Jewish	MT	7.5	6.9	****	3.2	5.9	10.0	5.0	14.5	6.2	5.9	2.6	****	****
	HL	1.9	5.2	****	1.1	1.3	3.3	1.1	1.4	0.6	0.6	0.7	****	****
Netherlands	MT	7.8	3.9	8.2	1.6	1.5	7.6	5.4	16.7	12.7	10.3	7.4	1.3	6.0
	HL	2.4	****	4.4	0.2	0.2	3.9	1.3	7.0	3.8	3.7	1.4	****	****
Polish	MT	20.1	4.6	****	8.3	11.1	30.6	23.5	23.4	17.0	14.7	9.5	9.8	10.9
	HL	5.7	****	****	1.1	3.3	12.7	9.3	3.6	1.8	2.1	1.4	****	****
Scandinavian	MT	7.8	****	2.6	1.7	5.7	3.1	4.8	17.1	11.3	6.8	5.7	4.8	5.7
	HL	0.4	****	****	0.6	2.2	1.0	0.5	1.7	0.2	0.1	0.2	****	0.6
Ukrainian	MT	40.8	14.7	14.3	9.5	12.4	38.0	32.1	51.7	52.4	42.1	23.5	21.6	24.6
	HL	13.2	2.9	****	1.7	****	18.6	10.9	19.2	19.5	10.9	2.8	2.6	3.3
Canadian Indian	MT	55.7	58.3	33.3	45.8	69.2	53.4	45.7	73.3	64.2	66.8	35.2	38.5	76.4
	HL	41.4	48.3	23.3	39.0	61.5	45.4	33.3	58.6	51.9	48.9	16.9	15.1	54.2

****less than 0.1%.
Source: Data for all groups except Canadian Indians were obtained from the *1971 Census of Canada*, Cat. 92-736, Vol. 1–Part 4, Tables 22 and 23. Data for Canadian Indians were obtained from the *1971 Census of Canada*, Cat. 92-726, Vol. 1–Part 3; Cat. 92-725, Vol. 1–Part 3; Cat. 92-723, Vol. 1–Part 3.

Similar trends can be observed among the Ukrainians: the national figures indicate that 40.8 per cent have retained the original language, but only 13.2 per cent speak it at home. In other words, over half of the total population now claim English as a mother tongue, and about 87 per cent of the same total are apparently transferring to English. These rates vary across the country, with the highest retention rates associated with group concentrations; Ukrainians in the prairie provinces appear to be the least assimilated.

When Indians are analysed in these terms, assimilation processes appear to be reducing linguistic diversity. Where there are 295,000 people of native ancestry, the mother-tongue retention rate is 55.7 per cent. In other words, about 45 per cent appear to have learned English (or perhaps French) as a child. Moreover, among all Indians in Canada, 41.4 per cent claim that they usually speak the native language in the home. This figure suggests that about 60 per cent usually speak either English or French. Viewed from another perspective, of all those who learned a native language as a child, some are in the process of transferring to English; in any event, there is the possibility that children are being socialized in English. These trends are reflected in each province, but with some variation. Assimilation is least apparent in the Northwest Territories where the MT figure is 76.4 per cent and home language is 54 per cent Indian. In other areas, however, assimilation is more pronounced. In British Columbia, for instance, 35 per cent still claim a native language and 16.9 per cent speak it at home. What impact these trends will have on future generations of natives is yet to be assessed. There is a possibility that some will learn a native language on a secondary basis since these languages are being introduced in school curricula.

When the French language is examined at the national level, 89.5 per cent of all French Canadians still claim French as a mother tongue and 85.6 per cent still speak it in the home. In Quebec, the retention rate is highest, with 98.1 per cent claiming French as a mother tongue and 97.6 per cent of them usually speaking it at home. In other words, the linguistic assimilation rate of the Québécois appears to be minimal. It should be noted, however, that 80.6 per cent of English Canadians in Quebec claim English as a mother tongue and 79.9 per cent usually speak it at home. According to these figures, one must assume that a significant proportion

—apparently 20 per cent—have transferred to French. Other ethnic groups in the province show assimilation trends, but it is impossible with the available data to ascertain whether the transfer has been to English or French. Among those of Italian origin, for instance, 56.4 per cent claim Italian as a mother tongue and 40.2 per cent speak it at home. In other words, almost half of that population have transferred to either English or French. Similarly, the figures for German Canadians are 11.7 per cent and 5.4 per cent and for the Polish, 30.6 per cent and 12.7 per cent.[6]

Unlike the Québécois, the linguistic trends of French Canadians in other parts of the country show considerable assimilation trends. In accordance with Joy's (1972) and Ares's (1964) works, linguistic assimilation increases as groups become more dispersed. In New Brunswick, where the Acadians are locally concentrated, 87.6 per cent still claim French as a childhood language and 81.7 per cent still speak it at home. Among French Canadians elsewhere, however, assimilation is much more pronounced. In Ontario, the mother tongue figure is 60.4 per cent and home language, 45 per cent; in Manitoba, the figures are 63.1 per cent and 42.3 per cent. These trends increase as one moves west: 50 per cent of French Canadians in Saskatchewan and 43.7 per cent of those in Alberta claim French as a mother tongue.

In short, an analysis of linguistic trends suggests that, while French speakers in Quebec tend to retain their language, trends elsewhere suggest a gradual transfer to English. There are variations from group to group and province to province, but in general there is a gradual reduction in numbers who retain their ethnic language and numbers who claim to speak it in the home. Previous studies on this topic suggest that factors influencing the rate of acculturation and the degree of structural integration also operate to promote linguistic assimilation. Urban residents, for instance, have higher rates of assimilation than rural people. Younger people experience a more rapid language loss than older people (Royal Commission, 1969, Bk. IV; Joy, 1972; Ares, 1964; Lieberson, 1970; Maheu, 1970).

6. The reader is probably well aware that the Quebec provincial government has introduced Bill 22 to ensure the survival of the French language in Quebec. This includes making some provisions to stream non-English-speaking children into French-language schools and making French the official language of Quebec.

SUMMARY

In summary, assimilation in Canada includes acculturation processes whereby individuals learn and accept dominant norms and values. Structural integration involves primary-group formation across ethnic lines; exogamy involves marriage outside the group. Linguistic assimilation entails a gradual transfer to the English language and a possible loss of mother tongues. Each process may be viewed as an entity in itself, but the occurrence of one tends to be related to the occurrence of another. Acculturation can lead to structural assimilation, and structural assimilation can promote linguistic assimilation. Each process, however, is dependent upon several factors; among these are size and group distribution, both of which tend to affect the rate of assimilation. In other words, territorially located groups are more likely to develop their own institutions, and thus are least likely to assimilate. Dispersed groups, however, are likely to have lower degrees of institutional completeness, and therefore higher degrees of assimilation.

Social Conflict

The emergence of conflict may take many forms, some violent, others more subtle. In a broad sense, conflict includes wars, expulsions, boycotts, strikes, sit-ins, reform movements, pressure groups, and secessionist movements. A conflict situation may be initiated by a dominant group as was the case when Europeans settled the continent. On the other hand, conflict may be the manifestation of a subordinant group aiming to correct inequalities and redress past grievances (Berry, 1965).

The focus of a subordinant's discontent can be categorized in three main areas of perceived deprivation: welfare conditions, power, and interpersonal values (Gurr, 1970: 23–27). Welfare conditions are those material goods which members feel are unequally distributed—income, food, shelter—and those physical conditions they feel are denied them—health, longevity, medical care. Secondly, groups articulate discrepancies in the exercise of power—under-representation in decision-making bodies, voting rights, ability to determine one's own destiny. Interpersonal values are needs for status and recognition, for stable, supportive, community associations, for coherence and security in culture and language.

SOCIAL CHANGE AND THE EMERGENCE OF CONFLICT

When educational and economic patterns change, systems of ethnic stratification are altered. Some members of ethnic minorities acquire the culture of the dominant society more rapidly than others do, and as they advance in the social scale, they frequently find themselves in marginal positions. Experiencing prejudice and discrimination, they begin to perceive their own group in terms of a subordinate status. As increasing numbers develop new conceptions of themselves, they reinforce one another's discontent. Once this discontent is widespread, reform movements emerge and compete with one another for public support (Shibutani and Kwan, 1965: 360–70). Thus subordinated groups, such as native peoples and the Québécois, over the last two decades have developed an increasing awareness of their minority status; leaders have emerged— some reformists, some more radically oriented.

One obvious consequence of the changing patterns among native peoples has been the development of organizational structures at the local, provincial, and national levels. As stated earlier, these organizations do not necessarily represent all members of the ethnic group, nor do they necessarily represent the diversity of orientations usually found in a changing society. Nevertheless, they have been instrumental in confronting the dominant society in their concerns regarding aboriginal rights. Within the last few years, there have been several court cases aiming to clarify past treaties and claim territorial rights. The Nishgas in British Columbia, for instance, claimed their rights to 4,000 square miles of the province. They lost, but the fact that three out of seven judges dissented signalled the ambiguities in Canada's view of native rights. Natives of the Northwest Territories demanded and got a caveat, which means that 400,000 square miles of land which they ostensibly gave up may, in fact, be theirs. Natives in the James Bay area are contesting the rights of the Quebec government to alter irreparably the ecological conditions of their territories. In the black communities of Nova Scotia, Toronto, and Montreal, organizations have developed in response to discrimination in housing, employment, and social services. Many of these, including the National Black Coalition and self-help programs in low-income areas, are staffed by recent black immigrants.

When political norms permit peaceful change, the initial attempts to improve the lot of disadvantaged groups occurs within the legal framework, but when changes are slow in developing and members of the dominant society are generally non-responsive, segments of groups engage in more militant behaviour. A series of sit-ins, marches, and violent confrontations typical of such behaviour have recently involved Indians in Kenora, Acadians at Moncton University, and blacks at Sir George Williams University.

During periods of heightened ethnic consciousness, intellectuals become prominent in the rewriting of history and in political activities. Canadian Indians, for instance, are reviving past traditions, and authors such as Cardinal (1969) in *The Unjust Society* and Campbell (1973) in *Halfbreed* articulate the grievances and needs of their people. Among other groups, ethnic histories are gaining attention, and efforts are renewed to organize activities and promote cohesion. With the advent of the multiculturalism policies, such groups have been important in developing organizations to promote ancestral traditions in music, art, and dance; cultural centres and annual events have developed, attracting not only the ethnic groups themselves but local populations as well. Contributing variety to the general Canadian culture, they have become relatively permanent institutions in most cities and in many rural areas.

SECESSIONIST MOVEMENTS

When groups are treated differentially, they may develop a heightened awareness of their uniqueness. Identities develop which tend to redefine the group and permit its members to distinguish themselves from others. French Canadians, for instance, have traditionally shared identities based on religion, language, family life, and historical origins.[7] This pattern of identification continued until the event of growing urbanization and the decline in the role of the Church. At this juncture group consciousness became more diverse and some sectors of the population began to question the traditional definitions they had given themselves. A redefinition of ethnic identities occurred as segments of the population became more acutely aware of their own political and economic situation.

7. For readings on this complex topic   1969; Garigue, 1963.
see Keyfitz, 1963–64: 163–82; Moreux,

When French Canadians began to see themselves as an industrial society rather than as an ethnic community, they initiated all the difficulties which were to appear in the traditional relationships between Quebec and Canada. . . . When Quebecers began to question the old ethnic definitions they had given themselves, they also implied a criticism of the political society they had lived in since 1867 (Rioux, 1971: 178).

Leaders who become convinced that their aspirations cannot be realized under the existing system will organize to secede. The ideal becomes one of unification and political organization; the ultimate aim is the creation of a new nation where members may then be able to control their own destinies. The strategy may involve violence or it may focus on legitimized political processes. The Front de Libération du Québec, or the FLQ, was organized by men who became convinced that Quebec could not develop its potential under a capitalist system (Vallières, 1971). Founded in 1963, its espoused aim was to awaken the Québécois to their colonial status. At the outset, their bombings were aimed at British and federal symbols, such as the Wolfe monument, the Queen Victoria monument, and mail boxes. A second and third episode involved attempts to organize a revolutionary army. Throughout, robberies were committed to secure equipment and provide funds. The fourth wave of activity involved bombings of provincial as well as federal establishments. The culmination was the kidnappings of Pierre Laporte and Robert Cross[8] (Morf, 1970; Milner and Milner, 1973: 185, 203–7).

The Parti Québécois, a recognized political party, questions the adequacy and legitimacy of federalism. Under its leader, René Lévesque, it hopes to gain independence for Quebec. Most empirical studies focusing on the support for independence find supporters to be among the young, the intellectuals, professionals as well as among the underprivileged segments of the population. In other words, support derives from both the upper level and the base of the stratification system (Latouche, 1973; Cuneo and Curtis, 1974). In two elections, the party has increased its popular vote from 24 per cent to approximately 30 per cent. Still a viable

8. Pierre Laporte was a cabinet minister in the Quebec government and Robert Cross was the British Consul posted in Montreal. M. Laporte was murdered but Mr. Cross was eventually released.

force in Quebec, the party now forms the official opposition in the National Assembly.

Most democratic societies respond in some way to protests of inequalities. However, effective new legislation becomes dependent in part on the willingness of the population to co-operate in redressing social injustices. Human Rights Commissions have been established in almost all provinces; they aim to provide an avenue where discriminatory treatment can be reported and prosecuted if necessary. Other legislation includes changes in the administrative policies governing Indian Affairs. Most notable has been the establishment of band councils, enabling reservation populations to formulate policies regarding political and economic matters (Hawthorn, 1968). Also at the federal level, the Language Bill and the Multiculturalism policies were passed in response to the recommendation of the Bilingualism and Biculturalism Commission.

An overview of intergroup relations in Canada includes themes of multiculturalism, stratification, assimilation, and conflict. Pluralism includes the historical emergence of group contact and the eventual crystallization of intergroup relations. Thus, native peoples have been placed in subordinate positions, the charter groups persist in conflict and accommodation processes, immigrants continue to enter and adjust. Patterns of social pluralism involve institutions whereby groups sustain their own structures, thus perpetuating and developing their specific culture, language, and identity.

When ethnicity is viewed from a stratification perspective, patterns of inequalities within groups and patterns of social class differences between groups become apparent. Empirical findings indicate that while Canadians of British origin occupy positions of authority and influence, other groups are to some degree disadvantaged—most notably native peoples.

Patterns of assimilation highlight trends toward uniformity: patterns of acculturation, patterns of integration, and linguistic transfer. As an ongoing process, assimilation tends to reduce cultural diversity and to promote a common language. Social conflict is a complex phenomenon whereby groups or segments of groups promote cultural identities and language, and others make attempts to redress inequalities and establish a more equitable power distribution.

Select Bibliography

BOISSEVAIN, JEREMY. *The Italians of Montreal.* Ottawa: Information Canada, 1971.

BRAROE, NIELS WINTHER. "Reciprocal Exploitation in an Indian-White Community", *Southwestern Journal of Anthropology* 21 (October 1965): 80–100.

BRETON, RAYMOND. "Institutional Completeness and Ethnic Communities and Personal Relations to Immigrants", *American Journal of Sociology* 70 (September 1964): 193–205.

BRODY, HUGH. *Indians on Skid Row.* Ottawa: Northern Science Research Group, Department of Northern Development, 1971.

Canada. Royal Commission on Bilingualism and Biculturalism. Ottawa: The Queen's Printer, 1969.

CARDINAL, HAROLD. *The Unjust Society: The Tragedy of Canada's Indians.* Edmonton: Hurtig, 1969.

CLAIRMONT, DONALD H., and MAGILL, DENNIS W. *Africville.* Toronto: McClelland and Stewart, 1974.

CUNEO, CARL J., and CURTIS, JAMES E. "Quebec Separation: An Analysis of Determinants Within Social Class Levels", *The Canadian Review of Sociology and Anthropology* 11 (February 1974): 1–29.

DOSMAN, EDGAR. *Indians: The Urban Dilemma.* Toronto: McClelland and Stewart, 1972.

DRIEDGER, LEO, and CHURCH, GLENN. "Residential Segregation and Institutional Completeness: A Comparison of Ethnic Minorities", *Canadian Review of Sociology and Anthropology* 11 (February 1974): 30–52.

ELLIOTT, JEAN LEONARD. *Minority Canadians: Immigrant Groups.* Scarborough: Prentice-Hall, 1970.

FRIDERES, JAMES S. *Canada's Indians: Contemporary Conflicts.* Scarborough: Prentice-Hall, 1974.

HENRY, FRANCES. *Forgotten Canadians: The Blacks of Nova Scotia.* Don Mills: Longman Canada, 1973.

HUGHES, DAVID R., and KALLEN, EVELYN. *The Anatomy of Racism: Canadian Dimensions.* Montreal: Harvest House, 1973.

JOY, RICHARD. *Languages in Conflict.* Toronto: McClelland and Stewart, 1973.

LANPHIER, C. M., and MORRIS, R. N. "Structural Aspects of Differences in Income Between Anglophones and Francophones", *Canadian Review of Sociology and Anthropology* 11 (February 1973): 53–66.

LIEBERSON, STANLEY. *Language and Ethnic Relations in Canada.* New York: John Wiley and Sons, 1973.

NAGLER, MARC. *Perspectives on North American Indians.* Scarborough: Prentice-Hall, 1972.

VALLEE, FRANK G., and SHULMAN, NORMAN. "The Viability of French Groupings Outside Quebec", in Mason Wade, ed., *Regionalism in the Canadian Community, 1867–1967.* Toronto: University of Toronto Press, 1969.

Criminal Justice and Corrections
in Canada

STUART D. JOHNSON

Every society has a system of rules and standards designed to regulate and make predictable the behaviour of its members. These rules usually reflect the interests and values of the dominant or ruling groups within the society, changing from time to time according to evolving needs and historical developments. Rules range from simple *techniques of adjustment*, which are usually unwritten but widely shared ways of doing things, through *folkways*, which are ways of behaving that have the force of etiquette, and *mores*, which are customs that many people feel are important to the survival of the group and which are supported by a strong moral imperative, to formal *laws*, which are institutionalized behavioural requirements the violation of which results in the application of negative sanctions.

In all known societies, however, there exist variations in the amount of shared agreement which supports the rules and standards. Sociologists have called this common shared agreement *consensus*. In homogeneous societies, where social distinctions and the division of labour are minimal, support for the rules is widespread and standards of expected behaviour are observed and shared by nearly everyone. This is especially true with respect to pre-literate societies such as hunting and gathering bands, some tribal organizations, and relatively isolated agricultural villages. Here, any deviation from the rules and standards usually produces a response such as gossip, ridicule, and other forms of *informal* social control. In contrast, modern industrial societies, with their extreme division of labour and highly stratified social arrangements, tend to produce many groups and individuals who do not form a consensus on rules and standards of behaviour.

When consensus is lacking, deviance is very likely to occur and to take a number of specific directions. It may consist of deviation from the official religious or political ideology of the society, or it may be deviation from the accepted ways of perceiving the self, the external world, and the relationships between the two. On the other hand, deviation may take the form of a life-style that is in conflict with the accepted standards of the society, or even total withdrawal from the society through self-destruction. Finally, it may take the form of deviance from the law codes which set forth the actions which are required or prohibited in the society.

Whatever its form, when deviation is recognized in modern industrial society, it is apt to produce a response that is societal rather than personal, and formal rather than informal. This is especially true with respect to the criminal, whose deviation from the law codes leads to formal efforts to protect society (and the offender himself) from his dangerous actions, to deter other persons from engaging in similar deviant behaviour, and, when possible, to bring about changes within the deviant so that he will be less likely to engage in future criminal activity.

This chapter represents an attempt to acquaint the reader with how this formal societal response to criminal deviation is carried out by the adult criminal-justice and corrections system currently operating in Canada. It is not a theoretical treatise on crime causation, nor does it include a discussion of juvenile delinquency and the juvenile court. Instead, it seeks to apply a social systems approach to the adult criminal-justice system in which emphasis is placed upon the *organization* of the system, showing how it is put together; upon the tasks or *functions* which each part or subsystem is expected to perform; and upon the manner in which *social change* is affecting the operation of the whole. Bertrand's (1967: 24–25) definition of the concept of a social system will be used here. He stated:

The model is designed to help one visualize that certain human collectivities (groups) are systems whose parts are interdependent and which, as unities, are in turn interlinked with one another through mutual dependencies. The prerequisites for a social system are two or more people in interaction directed toward attaining a goal and guided by patterns of structured and shared symbols and expectations.

The definition fits the present case very well because the criminal-justice and corrections system is an apparatus through which the Canadian government seeks the objective of enforcing standards and behaviour which the crown requires of its subjects. The apparatus does have a definite form or structure made up of recognizable and interdependent parts or subsystems. Its task is the enforcement of standards of conduct, or as Mr. Justice Ouimet and the Canadian Committee on Corrections (1969: 11) expressed it, "the basic purpose of criminal justice is to protect all members of society, including the offender himself, from seriously harmful and dangerous conduct." The interaction is what goes on within and between the subsystems, and social change is illustrated by alterations going on within the system and its various parts.

What is crime? In attempting to define crime one immediately confronts the concept of relativity. Crime is relative to time, place, and circumstances. It usually reflects the needs and values of a particular society at a given point in time. What constitutes a crime in one jurisdiction may not be considered criminal in another jurisdiction, or at a different time in the same jurisdiction. Although many religious acts or omissions were considered serious crimes during the middle ages, few examples of religious crimes exist today in most Western nations. McGrath (1965: 1) has defined the term primarily in terms of existing legislation by stating, "In its generally accepted legal sense, it refers to acts or omissions that violate the provisions of criminal legislation." Criminal legislation, in turn, refers to those laws which *proscribe* particular acts, such as assaults, or *prescribe* the performance of other specific acts, such as paying taxes. It is important to note, however, that when behaviour becomes part of criminal legislation, the legislation always provides negative sanctions or penalties if the law is violated. Much behaviour may be objectionable or obnoxious to the observer, but it is not criminal unless proscribed by a law to which some penalty for non-observance is attached. As Macleod, former Commissioner of Penitentiaries, expressed it (1965: 91), "A person commits a crime when he does anything that the law says he must not do or fails to do something that the law says he must do, if by reason of his act or omission he becomes liable to punishment under the law."

In examining crime and criminal justice in the Canadian context, it is important to realize that under the British North America Act, the federal Parliament of Canada has the exclusive right and jurisdiction to legislate in the area of criminal law, although this right has been delegated to the provinces with respect to regulations of highway traffic, alcoholic beverages, hunting and fishing, and a few other areas where provincial legislation may be enacted. Accordingly, the federal Parliament has passed the Canada Criminal Code, which contains the vast majority of the criminal laws of the country. It must not be thought, however, that once enacted criminal law becomes immutable and unchanging: like a living thing it grows and changes through time, reflecting the changing needs and circumstances of society. To ensure that the changes will be orderly and systematic, the federal Parliament proclaimed an act in 1971 establishing a permanent Law Reform Commission of Canada. This Commission was established "to keep the laws of Canada under continuing and systematic review and in this way to complement the legislative and judicial processes" (Hartt, 1972: 5).

With some understanding of crime and criminal law in mind, the reader is next asked to consider the much more difficult question of who is the criminal? For present purposes the simple straightforward definition offered by Haskell and Yablonsky (1974: 239) will suffice. These authors state that "the term *criminal* should properly be limited to people who have been convicted of crimes." While it is recognized that many scholars over the years have argued for a broader social definition of criminal, ranging from any person who violates customary usage to anyone who has committed any act causing substantial harm to social interests, each of these broader definitions lack the preciseness or explicitness deemed necessary for present purposes.

The reader should be cautioned, before proceeding with a detailed examination of the criminal-justice and corrections system, that far more crimes are committed each year than ever come to the attention of the authorities. Of those crimes which do become known, many go unsolved, since they are never cleared through the arrest of any person or a charge being laid. Finally, of those charged with criminal offences, many are dismissed, acquitted, or otherwise removed from the system without being convicted of anything. When we discuss crime, therefore, we really mean crimes known to the police, and when we discuss criminals, we mean persons who have been convicted of those crimes in a court of law. The total number of violations and law violators vastly exceeds those who become involved in the criminal-justice system or who are ever dealt with under the correctional procedures about to be discussed. Nevertheless, and despite the limitations noted above, the Canadian system of criminal justice and corrections does operate in a systematic manner to protect society and the individuals who comprise it from the more dangerous acts of those who violate the laws. It is to this process that attention is now directed. The raw material to be processed in the system consists of (a) persons who are believed to have committed crimes, and (b) information linking the individual person to the crime which has allegedly been committed.

Law Enforcement

The organization, powers, and jurisdiction of Canadian law-enforcement agencies were decided at Confederation. As previously noted, Section 91 of the British North America Act confers exclusive power to the federal Parliament for making criminal law and establishing procedures in criminal matters. In Section 92 of the Act, however, the legislature of each province is made responsible for organizing and establishing both criminal and civil courts and for the administration of justice within the province. The federal government makes the criminal law, but the provinces are required to enforce it. This means that the provinces must create and maintain courts and police departments to carry out their responsibility; to this end, each province has passed a Provincial Police Act and the necessary acts to establish courts of law.

The vast majority of law enforcement in Canada is carried out at three organizational levels—federal, provincial, and municipal. In addition, there are a few small specialized agencies with enforcement powers which are not included in the foregoing. Examples include railway police, who are authorized to operate at railway terminals and within a quarter-mile of the tracks, company police who operate on the grounds of private companies, and a few other special groups such as campus police, who are authorized to perform their duties on the campuses of colleges and universities. Their jurisdiction is closely limited to the property of the company or organization which employs them. Finally, there are a few public officials, such as customs and excise officers and game-wardens, who do possess enforcement powers but are limited to one or a very few specific statutes related to their regular work. They are not usually thought of as police in the usual sense of the term.

The Royal Canadian Mounted Police enforce laws made by or under the authority of the federal government in all parts of Canada. Originally established as a constabulary force in 1873 to police the Northwest Territories, it is currently organized under the authority of the RCMP Act. An interesting and uniquely Canadian feature of the jurisdiction of the RCMP is found in the contractual relationships which the force may undertake with the provinces and with individual municipalities. Although provinces clearly have responsibility to administer justice and enforce the Criminal Code within their respective boundaries, all provinces except Ontario and Quebec have contracted the RCMP to perform policing duties for them. The details of these arrangements were illustrated by Kelly (1965: 113) who noted,

Where the R.C.M.P. acts as the provincial police force, there must be a provision in some provincial legislation appointing members of the R.C.M.P. as peace officers for the province. In Manitoba, for example, under the provisions of the Provincial Police Act, all members of the R.C.M.P. are appointed constables for the province and are thereby given authority, which they would not have otherwise, to enforce provincial statutes.

In addition, 169 communities were reported to have contracted with the RCMP for municipal policing services (Solicitor General's *Annual Report, 1972–73*: 9). In such situations the Mounties enforce municipal by-laws, and officers are usually appointed as Town Constables for this purpose.[1]

At the provincial level, peace officers are primarily concerned with enforcing the Criminal Code and the statutes of the province in which they are employed. This applies equally to the provinces that have provincial police forces and to the RCMP, when it is under contract as a provincial police force. Generally speaking, the authority of a provincial police officer is limited to the province that employs him. Officers are not required to enforce the law in municipalities which employ their own police forces. In Ontario and Quebec, many municipalities have contracted their respective provincial police forces to act as municipal police in much the same way that municipalities elsewhere in Canada have contracted the RCMP. This practice reflects the belief prevalent in many

1. For a detailed account of the organizational form and work load of the RCMP, the reader is advised to consult the *Annual Report* of the Solicitor General of Canada. The annual report of the RCMP is included as a part of that document.

cities and towns that it is more economical to contract police services than it is to recruit, train, and maintain their own municipal forces.

A large number of Canadian cities, towns, counties, and townships, however, prefer to have their own police departments. Taken together, these municipal policemen make up the largest segment of Canadian law enforcement. The quality of municipal police ranges from very high to very low, depending upon the financial resources available for the administration of justice in the respective jurisdictions. Many town constables are concerned primarily with directing traffic and enforcing municipal by-laws, duties which require markedly less training and ability than enforcement of the Criminal Code or federal statutes demands.

With respect to the role of the police in contemporary Canadian Society and the functions which they are expected to perform, the Report of the Canadian Committee on Corrections (1969: 39) asserts that the primary functions of the police are:

a) To prevent crime.
b) To detect crime and apprehend offenders. This latter function involves the gathering of evidence sufficient not only to warrant the laying of a charge against a specific individual but to establish the guilt of that individual in a court of law.
c) To maintain order in the community in accordance with the rule of law.
d) The control of highway traffic has also become an important police function in modern time.

What many people do not appreciate, however, is the wide range of discretion which the Canadian policeman employs in carrying out his functions. As Grosman (1975: 1) stated, "The decision whether to invoke the awesome machinery of the criminal justice system is often made by the policeman on the street." It is he who, in many cases, decides whether to arrest a suspect or to handle a complaint informally with a warning or cautionary statement. This single decision can profoundly affect the life of an individual and may determine whether or not he ever acquires a record of criminal conviction. At higher levels of police organization, further discretionary decisions are made regarding whether or not a formal charge will be laid or a complaint dismissed as unfounded. The significance lies in the recognition that Canadian police agencies, far from being rigid and inflexible in their operations, carry out their work with a great deal of discretion. Thus, it is particularly vital that they are staffed with mature, fair-minded, and well-educated people, in order for the ends of criminal justice to be achieved.

For present purposes, the police are viewed as the first *subsystem* within the social system of Canadian criminal justice and corrections. As a subsystem, they carry out three important functions: *investigate crimes, enforce the law,* and *keep the peace.* In addition, they process information and people for later stages in the criminal-justice system. Peace-keeping is, of course, of prime importance to law-abiding citizens: it can usually be accomplished by persuading people to want to keep the peace rather than through direct coercion. It is because of the rather considerable moral authority which most citizens accord to the police that they can use influence and persuasion rather than coercion in the peace-keeping function. When enforcing the law, however, for instance, while apprehending criminals fleeing from a robbery, influence and persuasion are virtually meaningless and powers granted by Provincial Police Acts, Canada Criminal Code, and other relevant legislation must be exercised. Information is accumulated about crimes, which, together with the suspected perpetrators, are sent forward to the next subsystem for possible prosecution. In the vast majority of cases, the criminal-justice system is set in motion by such police action, in which an alleged crime is investigated, with the result that a charge or information is laid and a suspect taken into custody, usually through an arrest.

It is around the information-gathering and people-processing activities of the police that most community relations problems and police controversies develop. Allegations of police brutality or coercive interrogation are frequently described in the press, along with stories suggesting improprieties connected with wire tapping, unauthorized searches and seizures of evidence, and undercover police investigations which seem to some persons to be unethical if not illegal. Canadians are fortunate that, outside of the Montreal area, very few police scandals have occurred. The vast majority of allegations of police malpractice prove groundless upon investigation, in large measure, because of the honesty and fair-mindedness of most people working in law enforcement, and because of the system of accountability and supervision within which they operate. In fact, with very few exceptions, one can generalize that Canadian police do not arrest people unless they are guilty of some specific law violation. This situation stands in marked contrast to other countries, such as the United States or the Republic of South Africa, where people are often arrested and held without charge, presumably for engaging in protests of one kind or another or espousing unpopular life-styles. One indication of that fact that Canadian police usually arrest the right people is seen in the high rate of convictions obtained in magistrates' courts, often on the basis of guilty pleas or overwhelming evidence of guilt beyond a reasonable doubt.

With respect to trends and development in law enforcement, several important changes are taking place at the time of writing. At the federal level, the RCMP has reversed its long-standing policy of recruiting single males and has routinely begun to accept applications from females and from married persons of both sexes. The trend toward recruitment of females into police work is occurring generally throughout Canada. This is especially noticeable at the level of municipal police, where female constables are being given the same training as males. Moreover, they are being assigned to general duty in all branches of police work, whereas in the past, the few women who obtained employment in police departments were nearly always assigned to the juvenile division, to matron jobs in detention facilities, or to clerical positions in police stations. While it is still too early to evaluate the overall effect of this change, preliminary reports seem to suggest that females do about as well as their male counterparts in most, if not all, police work.

Somewhat the same pattern of change can be observed in the ethnic basis of police recruitment. In the past recruitment was disproportionately from persons of English, Scottish, or Irish backgrounds; the trend today is to disregard ethnic variables when the potential recruit can meet set physical, mental, and moral standards. Even then, recruitment standards are sometimes challenged on a purely political basis by representatives of ethnic groups. It is necessary therefore to distinguish among applicants on the basis of *relevant variables* such as height and strength, and on the basis of *non-relevant variables* such as religion or ethnic origin. In the former case, the police seem quite properly reluctant to change their standards for recruitment, and do so only under considerable political pressure. With respect to contested discrimination based upon irrelevant criteria, the trend is toward rapid change in the direction of perceived national standards and values.

Fundamental to the performance of the police role in society is *technical training* in traditional police subjects such as law, use of fire arms, physical fitness, criminal investigation, and protection of evidence. Although excellent training has long been offered by the RCMP, the provincial police, and the larger municipal departments, it is being greatly improved through extensive use of videotapes and other media devices. This essential training in the technical skills of the job is usually provided for new police recruits in a police academy or some other training facility. Technical training is also offered periodically in the form of refresher courses in which experienced officers learn of new developments, and advanced technical skills are taught to officers who have specialized in some area of police work such as counterfeiting, arson, or fraud.

In the smaller municipalities and rural areas, town constables may lack technical training or receive it in extremely limited amounts. An area of major change and expansion is presently taking place in the form of *professional* courses designed to provide the experienced career officer with alternative ways to achieve predetermined goals: leadership courses, police administration courses, and courses in man management are offered. It is important, however, for these courses to be made available to police officers at the appropriate points in their careers. This area has perhaps received its furthest present development by the RCMP, which offers a series of graded professional courses to their men at regular points in their careers. Somewhat newer in law enforcement and greatly needed at the present time are the *social science courses* which are coming into increasing use by the larger departments. These courses are *not* designed to teach an officer how to be a policeman. They do teach a social science subject which may have great relevance for a particular kind of police work. For example, courses in race and ethnic relations, pathological behaviour, adolescent psychology, and child development ought to increase the officer's understanding so that he could make better use of his technical training skills when policing minority groups and juveniles, or when he must intervene in a family crisis situation. Without the background knowledge of the social situation, technical skills alone might prove to be of little value.

Finally, the importance of the preceding trends, especially the trend toward broadening police education with social science input, is clearly related to the growing movement toward decentralizing police decision-making and placing more emphasis on community policing and the officer in the neighbourhood. Speaking to this point, Grosman (1975: 136–37) has stated:

> The progressive movement in policing today is aimed at encouraging each individual police officer to become more aware of the community needs in those areas in which he spends his time. The transition from a predominantly closed institutional approach to a community-based system of police depends upon developing leadership, freedom to innovate and commitment to human resources which should take place at the locus of the action, rather than in a geographically remote hierarchy and within distant power sectors. It is the police officer on the street who will have prime responsibility for an effective police-community relations program.

In short, what is happening is the professionalization of an occupational group in which technical skills are being improved and augmented by management capabilities and an increased understanding of the complex society in which the essential work is to be performed.

Prosecution

In contrast to other subsystems within the criminal-justice and correctional system, not much information is available concerning the next stage in the processing of information and persons linked to alleged crimes. Here the decision must be made whether or not to prosecute an alleged offender who has been arrested and against whom a charge has been laid. In addition, other equally difficult decisions have to be made concerning the exact nature of the charge and in quite a few cases, the number of counts of the offence for which the accused will be tried. While these questions may seem simple to the casual observer, they are often complicated by intricate negotiations and a difficult decision-making process which often results in confusion and misunderstanding by some of the parties directly involved. This situation is further compounded by the fact that, while the duties of a police officer are set forth in the Criminal Code and in the Provincial Police Acts, legislation to define the duties and powers of prosecutors is noticeably absent. Certainly the role of the prosecutor during a formal criminal trial is clearly defined and easily observable; it is his role between the arrest of the suspect and his appearance in court for trial which involves many low-visibility acts of discretion. These acts are extremely important, because to a large extent they determine what will follow during the formal trial of issues which may ensue.

Although there were Crown officers who handled prosecutions in Canada in the early days, the present system of prosecution began in 1867 under the British North America Act. The Attorney General of Canada had the duty of conducting and defending all criminal proceedings for the Crown, or any part of the federal government, with respect to everything within the legislative jurisdiction of the federal government, *except for matters relating to the Criminal Code.* The provinces and their respective attorneys general were responsible for establishing criminal courts and administering criminal justice. They appointed local Crown prosecutors and magistrates and undertook to prosecute and try Criminal Code offences and offences against provincial legislation. As a result, most of the criminal prosecutions in Canada are currently conducted by regular Crown prosecutors who are civil servants appointed by, and accountable to the Attorney General of the province in which they work. As Grosman (1969: 18) stated the matter, "Every local Crown prosecutor is an agent of the provincial Attorney General for the purpose of prosecutions under the provisions of the Criminal Code and provincial statutes." In other words, at least in the larger metropolitan jurisdictions, he is a full-time public employee prohibited from engaging in his own private law practice. In rural areas, however, he may be a local lawyer engaged in his own practice, but hired to serve as an agent of the Crown for criminal prosecutions in the county or township where he resides. In that case he will likely be paid on a fee basis for his work. In isolated areas, such as the far North, police officers may act as an agent of the Attorney General for the purpose of prosecuting summary conviction offences and other legal matters of a less serious nature. Considerable controversy sometimes develops concerning the possible conflict of interest when the police officer, who may have investigated a complaint and made an arrest, is allowed to act as the Attorney General's agent in the same case.

Speaking of the work of the Crown prosecutor, Ryan (1965: 182) has stated:

The Attorney-General's Agent, by whatever name he is known, works in conjunction with the police, advising them with reference to the investigation of offences, the laying of charges, and applying for summonses and warrants. He is not an investigator and does not employ investigators. That work is for the police. He conducts the prosecution of all charges of indictable offences within his territory. . . . He conducts prosecution of summary offences on instructions from the Attorney-General or on request from local authorities.

For present purposes, perhaps the most important feature of the Crown prosecutor's office is the broad discretionary power which he is privileged to exercise with respect to criminal proceedings. Justices of the peace, magistrates, and judges regularly listen to his recommendations on applications for bail, and in some courts he seems to have a virtual veto over the granting of bail to particular defendants (Ryan, 1965: 182), or the setting of bail so high that it constitutes a *de facto* denial of bail. With respect to sentence, the Crown prosecutor supplies the court with the criminal record of the accused and expresses a view of the matter which often carries great weight with judges and magistrates. This aspect of his power has been considerably reduced in recent years by the extensive use of probation officers who also may make recommendations with respect to sentence as a part of the pre-sentence assessment which they may provide to the court.

Without a doubt, the most controversial aspect of the Crown prosecutor's role concerns the negotiations which he may conduct with the accused and/or the defence counsel *prior* to the actual trial. This often takes the form of *plea bargaining* or *plea negotiation*, which can be anything from a hurried conference in the corridor outside the courtroom before the trial begins to a series of thoughtful, considered negotiations. As Grosman has suggested (1969), pre-trial negotiations provide the prosecutor with an opportunity to evaluate the strengths and weaknesses of his case and to explore the alternatives which may be available to him. The bargain which the defence counsel seeks to negotiate is, according to Spetz (1974: 202), "that if the Crown will not insist upon a conviction for a major offence, the defendant will plead guilty to a minor offence, or to a lesser included offence." The Crown, for instance, might agree to drop the charge of burglary if the accused will plead guilty to possession of burglary tools. Such negotiations are considered important, because, in reality, a criminal-court system is a large formal organization which operates on a very closely planned and restricted timetable. Jury trials, regardless of what ideological or theoretical merit they may possess, require a great deal of time and expense. A plea of guilty, on the other hand, allows the prompt disposition of a case before the court, since it leaves little more to be done than the passing of sentence. For this reason alone it is in the interest of bureaucratic efficiency to keep the number of cases that go to trial at a minimum. In addition, if the prosecution's evidence is not too strong, or Crown witnesses are unavailable, a plea of guilty to a lesser charge may appear to the prosecutor as the best that can be accomplished under the circumstances. For the offender, reduced charges, or the promise of other considerations in exchange for a plea of guilty may seem far more desirable than risking a trial on the original charge, which could result in a long period of incarceration. Such compromises represent the exercise of considerable discretionary power carried out *without court scrutiny or control*. The exercise of discretionary power with such a low level of public visibility calls for an unusual degree of honesty and professional ethics. Canadians have been very fortunate that the position of Crown prosecutor has always been occupied by honourable and fair-minded men and women whose conduct of the office has left it singularly free from scandal.

In summary, when Canadian police have taken someone into custody on the assumption that a crime has been committed and that the suspect committed it, they forward the relevant information to the Crown prosecutor who, as an agent for the Attorney General, must decide whether or not to prosecute the alleged offender in criminal court. In addition, the Crown prosecutor may enter into negotiations with the accused or his lawyer concerning the exact nature of the charges, the number of counts of the offence for which the accused will be charged, and a variety of other considerations. With respect to admitting the accused to bail, the Crown prosecutor has considerable influence, as he does when speaking to sentence. In short, prosecution is a vital part of the system of criminal justice and corrections where discretion is exercised and low-visibility decisions are taken which directly affect what happens from that point onward throughout the system.

The Adult Criminal Court System

Before discussing the organization and operation of the criminal courts, a few words need to be said about the legal basis upon which they rest, and the historical currents which have merged to produce a truly Canadian system.

As previously indicated, the British North America Act of 1867 granted exclusive authority to the Canadian Parliament to enact criminal law. It did not, however, grant Parliament the right to constitute courts of criminal jurisdiction, although it did grant the right to establish procedures to be followed in criminal matters. The creation and operation of criminal courts, therefore, is a provincial matter, except that appointment of judges to superior, county, and district courts is done by the Governor General of Canada. Magistrates, provincial judges, and justices of the peace are appointed by each province as required, by the Lieutenant-Governors-in-Council. In practice, this means that provincial cabinet officers work with the Lieutenant Governor to make the necessary judicial appointments, with the exceptions noted above (Report of the Canadian Committee on Corrections, 1969: 165).

The origins of the Canadian criminal-court system have been discussed by Ryan (1956: 136–38), who indicated that it represents a blend of characteristics derived from the legal systems of Great Britain and the United States, with some influence from the French system which formerly existed in Quebec. As a former colony, and as a member of the Commonwealth, Canada has been much more directly affected by Britain than by the United States. With the development of modern mass communications, especially television, the influence of the United States seems to be increasing. Many Canadian students, for example, seem to have obtained a large part of their knowledge and many of their attitudes relating to crime and corrections from the content of American television programs, which are at best a source of entertainment, but which generally constitute a very poor source of factual information about the structure and functioning of the Canadian criminal-justice system. Despite the growing American influence, Ryan (1965: 136) has clearly stated that

Canadian legal tradition, the training, attitudes, and methods of judges, magistrates, and lawyers, and the atmosphere of Canadian courts resemble those of England more closely than they do those of the United States, but there are subtle blendings of English and American influences with Canadian materials that have produced a result neither English nor American, but Canadian.

Structurally, there is considerable variation in terminology and in organizational form of the criminal courts in the various parts of Canada. The generalization seems warranted, however, that they may be viewed hierarchically in terms of their jurisdiction over criminal matters, and dichotomously in terms of their composition.

Courts that have jurisdiction to conduct trials of persons charged with indictable offences—the most serious offences in Canada—are of two kinds: (a) *Superior Courts of Criminal Jurisdiction,* of which there is one in each province and territory. These are usually called Court of Queen's Bench or some variant of that title. Trials are conducted by single judges, or by judge and jury. For some offences the accused has the option of a bench trial conducted by a judge alone, or a jury trial.[2] (b) *Courts of Criminal Jurisdiction.* These are lower courts which have jurisdiction to try those indictable offences which are not within the exclusive jurisdiction of the superior criminal courts. Again, these may be presided over by a judge and jury, or by a judge sitting without jury, depending on the location and the option of the accused, when applicable; the usual practice, however, is for a judicial officer called a magistrate to preside over them. These officers are appointed by the province within which they serve and are empowered to try those indictable offences in the Criminal Code which are not reserved for Superior Courts of Criminal Jurisdiction. (c) *Trial Courts for Summary Offences.* These courts, often called Courts of Summary Jurisdiction, are not really courts at all. According to Ryan (1965: 153), it is a *person* who is given jurisdiction to try offences punishable on summary conviction. The court is in the person of a judicial officer and does not have a jury or other aspects of an institutionalized criminal court. Justices of the peace are authorized to try summary offences, although some offences must, by statute, be tried by a magistrate. The normal practice, however, is for magistrates to try such cases, but justices of the peace may act when a magistrate is not available or has requested them to do so. In the territories, certain specific RCMP officers have been sworn in as justices of the peace and may try summary offences. In any event, the summary offences which they try are usually less serious misdemeanours, punishable on conviction by relatively small fines and short periods of incarceration. Like convictions for in-

2. Preliminary hearings, when these are necessary, are usually presided over by a magistrate, or by a justice of the peace, if no magistrate is available.

dictable offences, summary convictions may be appealed if errors have been made or if correct procedures have not been followed.

In terms of *function*, the pivotal institution within the Canadian system of criminal justice and corrections is the adult criminal court. It is here that preliminary inquiries are conducted to determine whether or not sufficient evidence exists to warrant a trial for the accused. If so, a *prima facie* case is said to exist, which, on the face of it, could result in the Crown obtaining a conviction of the accused. If sufficient evidence is not available, however, the accused is entitled to a discharge at that point in the process. Thus, the preliminary hearing is in a sense a discretionary decision based upon an assessment of the prior work of the police who have investigated a complaint and arrested a suspect, and of the Crown prosecutor who has reviewed their case and decided to prosecute it in court. If the preliminary inquiry indicates that the accused ought to be tried, the next step in the process is arraignment at which the accused is brought before the court to be presented with an indictment or hear the formal charges to which he must plead. Should the accused plead guilty to the charges, little remains but to record a conviction and pass sentence.[3] If the accused pleads not guilty, however, or any of a number of other special pleas, a trial will ensue to determine the question of his guilt or innocence of the particular offence with which he is charged. If the accused is found to be guilty, the court must pass sentence, or otherwise dispose of the case before it. Should the accused or the prosecution find fault with either the verdict or the sentence, recourse may be had to the provincial court of appeals, and, ultimately, to the Supreme Court of Canada. While not all of these steps would ordinarily be found in every criminal case, especially those classified as summary conviction offences, this discussion does serve to indicate the pivotal nature of the criminal courts as an important subsystem within the Canadian system of justice and corrections.

While the adult criminal courts have been treated as a separate subsystem within the Canadian criminal-justice system, it must be kept in mind that they are closely related to the earlier subsystems and are

3. This, of course, is highly desirable from a bureaucratic point of view when time is at a premium and court calendars are crowded. It is this organizational pressure which gives rise to much of the plea bargaining and pleading guilty for considerations discussed with respect to the Crown prosecutor.

directly influenced by the discretionary decisions which have been taken before any case reaches the court. As Boydell and Connidis (1974: 303) have indicated, "The police and crown prosecutor by filtering out cases which they believe will have less of a chance of standing up in court are providing the judge with a rather selective clientele." With respect to this clientele, however, the judge must make formal decisions concerning the adjudication of guilt (in a bench trial) and, although somewhat limited by the range of legally permitted dispositions, concerning the matter of sentence. It is here that the judge brings to bear his own highly personalized views concerning the purposes of sentencing and the effectiveness of different kinds of dispositions for reaching the sentencing objectives. As Hogarth (1974: 212) has expressed it:

The model which emerges from the analysis (of sentencing as a human process) is one that sees sentencing as a dynamic process in which the facts of the cases, the constraints arising out of the law and the social system and other features of the external world are interpreted, assimilated, and made sense of in ways compatible with the attitudes of the magistrate concerned.

Hogarth's conclusion was that the results took the form of sentencing decisions consistent with the judges' definitions of the situations facing them. It seems that sentencing is not a rational, mechanical process, but rather a human process based upon the exercise of discretion leading to flexible decisions.

What happens in the court and at the trial determines, in large measure, what will happen with respect to any given case. Perhaps of greater importance, it is crucial in determining the future attitudes and subsequent behaviour of the accused as a member of society.

Adult Probation

One of the characteristics of the Canadian correctional system is that by no means all of the convicted offenders go to gaol or prison. Among the alternative methods of disposition which judges have at their disposal at the time of sentencing are: (a) suspension of sentence pending the good behaviour of the offender; (b) posting bond, where the convicted offender signs a paper stating that he owes the Crown a certain sum. He forfeits

his bond if he breaks the conditions under which the sentence was suspended; (c) incarceration in a prison; and (d) probation.

Probation comes from the Latin word *probare*, meaning "to prove".
In effect, it represents a situation where a convicted offender says to the
court that, if allowed to remain in the community rather than serving a
period of incarceration, he will prove that he can refrain from further
law violation and abide by whatever conditions the court may set. Probation may be viewed as a sentencing alternative whereby the sentence of
the offender is suspended and he is allowed to remain in the community,
subject to the control of the court (including possible recall for an
alternative sentencing disposition), and under the supervision of a probation officer. The convicted offender who is placed on probation is given
the opportunity to prove that he is worthy of his freedom. The factor that
distinguishes probation from the much older practice of suspending
sentences on the good behaviour of the offender is the presence of the
probation officer. Such supervision is necessary, because probation is
usually contingent upon a number of relevant conditions which must be
observed if the offender is to remain in the community. Whether explicitly
stated or not, the alternative disposition of confinement in an institution
is a distinct possibility which is held in suspense in every case of probation.

Provision for the use of probation in Canada is contained in Section
638 of the Criminal Code, although its use is not required, and no federal
probation service has been established up to the time of writing. Providing
probation services is basically a provincial matter. Speaking to this point,
the Canadian Committee on Corrections (1969: 298) stated:

All provinces have public adult probation services although none have a
sufficient number of probation officers to meet all requests for service from
the courts. In some provinces the public service is supplemented by private
agency service. The stage of development of probation and details of practice
vary greatly from one province to another. Some of the provinces have
probation acts setting out the conditions under which the service operates.
Other provinces do not have such legislation and operate directly under the
provisions of the Criminal Code.

To maintain a proper perspective, the reader should be aware of the
possible advantages of probation services, if they are available in sufficient

quantity, and if they are correctly administered. It must be clearly understood that probation is a substitute for a commitment to a correctional institution, and that almost all persons who are sent to correctional institutions return to the community, usually after a relatively short time. Probation, therefore, should be seen as a substitute for short-term sentences in institutions where there is usually little that can be done to rehabilitate or reform the offender, and from which he is frequently discharged into a hostile community with very little guidance or assistance. Specifically, it is argued that the advantages of probation include the fact that the probationer remains in the community where he can learn to assume the duties and responsibilities of a law-abiding citizen and, more importantly, can lead a relatively normal life. Commenting on this point, the Canadian Committee on Corrections observed that "probation provides one of the most effective means of giving expression to one of the fundamental principles of which this report is based—that, whenever possible, efforts to rehabilitate an offender should take place in the community." Also, when an offender is on probation in the community, he is not exposed to the very destructive and disorganizing penal experience which can leave him stigmatized as a convict, embittered, and far better versed in criminal attitudes and techniques than he was at the time of sentence. In effect, the institutional experience often makes it difficult, if not impossible, for the convict to re-establish a normal life in the community where he must ultimately make an adjustment.

There are further advantages, mostly of an economic nature, which should be mentioned in connection with the use of probation. A probationer has always been able to support himself and his dependants—something no prisoner could do until the recent advent of work release and day parole programs. In addition, he can "make restitution and reparation to any person aggrieved or injured for the actual loss or damage caused by the commission of the offence", as required by Section 638 of the Criminal Code. Last but not least, the cost of keeping an offender on probation is very much lower than keeping the same offender in a correctional institution.

Perhaps one of the most valuable services which a probation service can render is the provision of pre-sentence assessments or reports as an aid to judicial sentencing. When an accused has either pleaded guilty, or has been found guilty in a criminal trial, the court may ask the probation officer to prepare a report on the social circumstances of the offender and of the offence, and to make recommendations as to sentence. There is, at this point in the procedure, no question of guilt; but the judge's knowledge of the case lacks a number of significant pieces of information, which, under the rules of evidence, could not be presented during the trial. In preparing a pre-sentence report, the probation officer will, according to a brochure of the Manitoba Probation Service (1972),

inquire into the personality, character, home background, education, employment and other circumstances of the accused person, so as to provide it [the court] with a picture of the offender as a person, some of the reasons he has broken the law, and some suggestion as to what steps might serve to rehabilitate him.

Information contained in the report together with other considerations such as the seriousness of the offence, the prior criminal record of the suspect, and the evidence proven against him during the trial, hopefully will enable the court to impose a just sentence which will protect society and at the same time help with the rehabilitation of the offender.

To ask for and to receive probation, the offender must be eligible. Under Section 638 of the Criminal Code, probation was granted only to a person who had no previous conviction or who had no more than one previous conviction, if the previous conviction took place at least five years prior to the current offence or if the previous offence is not related in character to the current offence. The problem connected with this restrictive section of the law was that the term "previous conviction" is not clearly defined, thus giving rise to a variety of interpretations. Some judges interpreted it to mean any prior conviction under the Criminal Code. Others interpreted it to mean any previous conviction under the Criminal Code or any federal statute. Still others interpreted it to mean any previous conviction of any kind whatsoever. In any event, this section of the Code was widely criticized (St. John Madeley, 1965: 299; Ouimet Report, 1969: 298) and in 1969 it was changed, so that virtually all restrictions have been removed except where the minimum penalty is prescribed by law. The court now has discretion to grant probation whenever the judge feels that circumstances of a particular case warrant it.

In the event that an applicant is granted probation, he enters into a kind of a contract in which he agrees to abide by a number of provisions or conditions. Conditions of probation include such things as keeping the peace and being of good behaviour; reporting to and being under the supervision of a probation officer; and appearing when required during the period of probation so that the probation order may be modified or judgment imposed. In addition, special conditions may be deemed relevant to a particular case; they might include refraining from consumption of alcoholic beverages, making restitution to victims, making support payments to dependants, or seeking and obtaining psychiatric care. The first type is usually referred to as "mandatory", in that the conditions are required of all probationers. The second type is called "discretionary", in that the imposition of these conditions is at the discretion of the court.

One other type of probation should be examined—the Canadian custom of placing some offenders on probation for a specified time following a period of incarceration. The justification of this practice is found in the fact that some offences may not be of a serious enough nature to warrant a lengthy sentence, while the relevant program for rehabilitation of the offender may require more time than the sentence includes. The post-incarceration period of probation allows time for the treatment program the court feels is necessary. Arguing against this pactice, the Canadian Committee on Corrections (Ouimet Report, 1969: 294–95) stated, "The court cannot measure the effect of a period of imprisonment before it is served and, consequently, is not in a position to determine the length of time which should be allowed for supervised release." The Committee recommended that this practice be deleted from the law.

When an offender has been granted probation and has signed the contract, or recognizance, containing the conditions under which the probationary period will be served, he reports to a probation officer, who will have responsibility for supervising his compliance with the probation order. The probation officer is often a social worker, or at least possesses some social-work skills which he will use in his work with the cases that he supervises. He will frequently help the offender obtain employment, habitation, and the services of whatever community facilities he may require. Such practical assistance coupled with strong moral support can offer the probationer guidance toward his own rehabilitation and eventual discharge from probation, and a significant personal relationship can develop which will help him re-establish his self-respect.

Sometimes, despite the best efforts of the probation officer, a breach of the probation contract occurs, either through the commission of a new crime or failure to abide by one or more of the conditions which the court imposed. In either case the court has the power under Section 538 to order the accused brought before it to be sentenced. The actual power of the court to pass sentence, however, is contained in Section 639 of the Criminal Code. Breach of recognizance does not always require an end to probation and a sentence. If the breach is minor, the court might allow the probation to continue, but use its discretion to modify the conditions. If the breach took the form of another crime, however, probation would be terminated and sentence passed.

In the final analysis, whether or not probation will be in the public interest depends upon three things other than the good behaviour and intentions of the probationer: (a) there must be a properly prepared pre-sentence report written by a probation officer who is competent to do his work; (b) a judge or magistrate must read the report carefully and make an intelligent decision to grant probation in light of the facts of the case at his disposal; and (c) there must be a well-trained and adequately motivated probation officer, who is not overburdened with an excessive work load, and who can provide the offender with the necessary friendship, support, and supervision to make the difficult transition from convicted criminal to law-abiding citizen. If these conditions are not met, probation will not be in the public interest, and may, in fact, become a meaningless sham of little benefit to anyone, least of all to the offender himself.

Adult Correctional Institutions

Canada, among all of the nations of the Western world, is most likely to view incarceration in a correctional institution as the appropriate response to those convicted of crimes. Cousineau and Veevers have pointed out that, "in Canada during 1960, the rate of incarceration of adults over the age of 16 was 240 per 100,000. This was higher than the rate of 200 per 100,000 in the United States, and markedly higher than the rate for other countries, such as the United Kingdom, where the rate was 59 per 100,000 or Norway, where the rate was only 44 per 100,000."[4] To comprehend the meaning of these data, the reader must know what a correctional institution, or prison, as it is more honestly titled, is designed to accomplish. Within the limits of a few pages, an attempt will be made to indicate who goes to prison, how prisons are organized in Canada, and what they are supposed to do as part of the system of criminal justice and corrections. In addition, some information will be presented on how Canadian prisons are changing in philosophy and sometimes in practice.

The term "prison", as defined by the Canadian Committee on Corrections (1969: 307), is "any institution which holds adults committed by the courts for illegal behaviour for periods longer than a few days." This rather broad definition includes penitentiaries, gaols, reformatories, and detention centres, to mention but a few of the designations.

It should not be assumed that all adults guilty of criminal offences are sent to prison. In fact, there is great attrition between the large but unknown number of crimes committed and the relatively few persons who serve sentences in prison. This drastic reduction in numbers was called the "funneling effect" by the United States President's Commission on Law Enforcement and Administration of Justice (*Task Force Report: Science and Technology*, 1967: 55–64). Quite probably most crimes remain unknown to all but the criminal who committed them and in many cases the victim. Scholars who study crime and corrections (Sutherland and Cressey, 1966: 27–32; Silverman and Teevan, 1975: 67–80; Bloch and Geis, 1962: 141–50) have frequently noted that only a small portion of crimes are reported or become known to the police. Some research (Cousineau and Veevers, 1972) suggests that only about half of the crimes known to the police result in a charge being laid, or in the matter being cleared from police records in some manner. Finally, Cousineau

---

4. The figures presented by Cousineau and Veevers have been disputed by Waller and Chan (1975) who, in a study sponsored by the Solicitor General of Canada, redefined such terms as, "prison", "length of sentence", "person", and "rate of imprisonment", to reach the alternative conclusion that Canada has an incarceration rate of only 93.3 persons in prison per 100,000 population. These data would make the Canadian rate appear to be similar to other Commonwealth countries and less than half of the incarceration rate reported for the United States. Since a technical discussion of definitional practices and statistical computations is beyond the scope of the present undertaking, the reader is merely alerted to the fact that Cousineau and Veevers data is not without its critics, although in the case of the Solicitor General's Department, the critic can scarcely be viewed as detached or uninvolved.

and Veevers (1972: 10) assert that of those persons against whom charges are laid only 2.3 per cent are actually incarcerated. Many who are convicted by the courts are disposed of through fines, suspended sentences, and probation, rather than through incarceration. Of those who are sent to prison, however, a large portion are repeat offenders who have been imprisoned on previous occasions. The Solicitor General's Department (*The Criminal in Canadian Society*, 1973: 18) found that, "of offenders sent to federal penitentiaries, 74 percent have had previous commitments to provincial institutions," and that "eighty percent of offenders have been at liberty for less than 18 months after completing a previous term of imprisonment." As a result, although Canada has a very high incarceration rate compared to other Western nations, those who are sent to prison are largely repeat offenders who appear to be firmly committed to crime.[5]

There is no single Canadian correctional system. Instead, there is a federal system consisting of more than twenty-two separate institutions and ten provincial systems containing in excess of 174 institutions of various types. While all are derived from sections 91 and 92 of the British North America Act, they have little in the way of systematic integration among them. As Fornataro (1965: 302) described it, "The division of responsibility is purely arbitrary and has its explanation in historical tradition rather than in logic or in a scientifically deduced plan." What Canadians have is an arrangement by which the Government of Canada operates institutions for offenders who receive sentences of two years or longer. These are called correctional institutions, although until recently they were designated penitentiaries. The provinces and the territories, on the other hand, operate custodial institutions for offenders serving sentences of less than two years in length. They have traditionally been designated gaols (or, following the American custom, jails). In actual practice, some gaol inmates serve sentences longer than two years, and some prison inmates serve less than two years, although the arbitrary two-year distinction is undoubtedly applicable in the vast majority of cases.

5. For a lengthy evaluation of the difficulties associated with the measurement of crime and delinquency, and some suggestions regarding how present methods could be improved, the reader is referred to a recent discussion of these questions by Silverman and Teevan (1975).

The federal system is administered under the Department of the Solicitor General through a Commissioner of Penitentiaries. Historically, each of the federal institutions has been headed by a warden, who was the chief executive of his prison and who reported directly to the Commissioner. In recent years, perhaps reflecting a changing philosophy, wardens have been retitled Directors of Institutions, and three Regional Directors have been established between them and the Commissioner. An excellent source of information concerning the organization and operation of the Canadian Penitentiary Service is found in its annual report which is published as a part of the *Annual Report of the Solicitor General of Canada.*

At the provincial level, prisons are known by a variety of different labels which reflect historical circumstances, and sometimes, the sincere hopes of those who established them. These designations include terms such as reformatories, detention centres, prison farms and annexes, and of course the more popular recent term, correctional institutions. For present purposes they will be subsumed under the term gaol. Provincial gaols, whatever their label, have in common the task of confining criminals serving sentences of less than two years, and in addition, they have the somewhat more difficult task of providing secure holding facilities for persons on remand awaiting trial or awaiting sentence and possible transfer to a federal institution. Most inmates, however, are there for a variety of petty offences for which they have received short sentences of a few weeks to several months. Under such conditions, very little can be accomplished either to punish or to reform the offender. Gaols are like "warehouses" in which society's misfits are held out of sight and out of mind for short periods of time. With respect to offenders serving longer sentences—sometimes up to two years less one day—a number of provincial systems are making substantial efforts to be more than "warehouses" and to provide effective programs for their inmates. This effort is illustrated by a recent paper on corrections published in Manitoba (Government of Manitoba, Department of Health and Social Development, 1972: 21) which stated that "the correctional system is a part of the spectrum of interrelated public services designed to protect and enhance human potential in Manitoba."

When the objectives of imprisonment and the functions which the correctional institutions play within the larger Canadian system are examined, the results are far from clear or encouraging. Sutherland and Cressey (1966: 519–20) have suggested four objectives of incarceration: rehabilitation, protection, retribution, and reduction of the crime rate. Rehabilitation reflects the interest that society has in changing criminals so that they will commit no further crimes. Put bluntly, the prison is expected to rehabilitate offenders, or literally make them "again livable", from the point of view of society. Speaking to this objective, Cousineau and Veevers (1972: 25) found that

of all offenders sent to Canadian penitentiaries in 1969, more than eighty percent had been in prison before, and among the recidivists, two-thirds had three or more previous convictions. Such high rates suggest that the prison system in Canada, as it is presently structured, is not a very effective means of rehabilitating and reforming of criminals.

With respect to protection from criminals, the situation is even more ambiguous. While it is true enough that criminals who are serving sentences in prisons, whether federal or provincial, have little opportunity to commit further crimes, they are prevented from doing so only for very short periods of time. After showing that most Canadian prisoners receive very short sentences, Cousineau and Veevers (1972: 26) indicated that, "of all those who were released from penitentiaries in 1969 [3,780], sixty-eight percent had served less than two years, and over ninety percent had served less than four years." From the point of view of a criminal serving a two-, three-, or four-year sentence, the time may well seem interminably long. From the point of view of the citizen who looks to the prison system for protection, however, sentences of that nature seem very short. When, in addition to the above, it is noted that the population of Canadian prisons has been relatively stable over the last ten years (Correctional Institutions Statistics, 1961–1970) with approximately 13,000 offenders confined in provincial gaols and an additional 7,000 offenders incarcerated in federal penitentiaries, it is clear that nearly as many offenders are being released from prison back into society as are sent to the system from the criminal courts. In attempting to deal with the problem which these data represent, the Canadian Commitee on Corrections (1969: 308) stated, "A primary aim of the prison is to reeducate people to live law-abiding lives in the community. This is society's best protection against a recurring sequence of criminal acts." If protection is an objective of the correctional system, and if the results of rehabilitation efforts are as limited as has been suggested above, then the situation is indeed ambiguous.

Turning now to retribution as an objective of incarceration, it is commonly known that many members of society believe that wrong-doers, especially if their crimes have resulted in death or physical injury to their victims, should be punished and that such punishment is the prime purpose of a prison. The main difficulties with this perspective are that advocates of retribution cannot agree upon how much punishment is enough, and the evidence is by no means clear that identical amounts of punishment have the same meaning for different offenders. In any event, the probability of an offender being charged, convicted of his offence, and sent to prison is very small. This fact was demonstrated by Cousineau and Veevers who reported that, "of those persons who are both charged and subsequently convicted, only 2.3 percent are actually incarcerated."

In light of these observations it seems quite unlikely that fear of retribution and society's wrath plays a significant part in the thinking of potential criminal offenders. Indeed, this is the case when consideration is given to deterrence as an objective of the correctional system. On the basis of the high rates of recidivism (or criminal repetition) in Canadian gaols and prisons, it seems reasonable to conclude with Cousineau and Veevers (1972: 27) that "for many individuals neither the threat of imprisonment, nor the actual experience of incarceration, necessarily effect much deterrence from future crime."

Far from being a static system, full of ambiguities and depressing inefficiency, the correctional institutions of Canada reflect a growing and important realization of the need for new philosophies and new programs to enable them to perform effectively their important role in the system of criminal justice and corrections. For example, the shift in philosophy from one of static custody and confinement to one of treatment and rehabilitation of the offender can be traced in the orientation of various Royal Commissions over the last several decades. The Royal Commission to Investigate the Penal System in Canada produced a report stressing the need for a penal system which would serve the primary purpose of protecting society (Archambault Report, 1938: 355). It did add, however, as a secondary emphasis, the reformation of prisoners as a proposed objective. Development of the rehabilitation emphasis was furthered considerably by the Committee to Inquire into the Principles and Procedures Followed in the Remission Service of the Department of Justice of Canada which nearly twenty years later stressed the fact that one of the main recommendations of their Report (Fauteux Report, 1956: 37) concerned the concentration of effort upon treatment rather than custody and protection. More recently, the *Report of Canadian Committee on Corrections* (Ouimet Report, 1969) indicated an almost single-minded preoccupation with treatment, although it did, in a secondary sense, realize that there will probably be a continuing need for custodial care. What this development represents clearly is a major change in the philosophy of Canadian corrections from one of retribution and secure custody as the central concern to one of treatment and rehabilitation as the necessary major focus, if protection of the public is to be achieved and the crime problem controlled.

While it is beyond the scope of this chapter to present detailed accounts of the myriad new programs and revisions of older programs which are currently being introduced into Canadian corrections, it would be appropriate to consider three policy statements which reflect both the commitment to change and the direction which change will take. The former Commissioner of the Canadian Penitentiary Service (Faguy, 1973: 7–8) recently stated:

The principles and concepts that are now accepted by the Canadian Penitentiary Service are based on the needs of each individual inmate and aim at the return to society of the inmate as a law-abiding and productive citizen. Changes in the penitentiaries do not mean permissiveness and laissez-faire and undue tolerance, but rather a teaching of a sense of responsibility to inmates by providing inside, and indeed outside our institutions, conditions that are as close as possible to those of "normal" society, so that they will be able, hopefully, to participate in the normal activities of the same society. . . . Our main responsibility is the custody of inmates. They must remain under our control until sentence has expired. . . . If our main responsibility is custody and security, our main *objective*, however, in our programs is rehabilitation. Rehabilitation is the best protection for society.

Speaking in a similar vein, but placing more emphasis upon the integration of corrections into the network of social services in the larger community, the Department of Health and Social Development of the Government of Manitoba (Paper on Corrections, 1972: 21) stated:

The emphasis and focus of corrections from the point of view of society is protection; the emphasis and focus from the point of view of the correctional service is rehabilitation. There is no necessary contradictions between these views. That is to say, society has established the correctional sequence for the overriding purpose of protecting the majority of its members from the aberrant behaviour of minority. Having been established to achieve this societal goal, the corrections system takes as its working goal the positive reintegration of the offender into society. It is true there are some offenders whose behaviour is of such a nature that segregation must be the primary method used to ensure the protection of society. But in these, as in all cases, the focus of the correctional service will be towards rehabilitation.

Finally, in the preface to a policy paper entitled *The Criminal in Canadian Society: A Perspective on Corrections*, which he had prepared for the landmark Federal-Provincial Conference on Corrections, the Solicitor General of Canada (Allmand, 1973) stated:

The criminal justice system has one basic aim: to protect individual members of society by reducing the level and effects of crime and delinquency. This paper stresses the importance of the social and human value of the individual who comes into conflict with the laws of our society and the need to protect him, and the society as a whole, by keeping him from falling into a life of crime. What this means is essentially that the first and most important function of the criminal justice system is to prevent individuals from entering into criminal activity. Second is the diversion of offenders from criminal careers prior to sentencing, third is the reduction in the level and seriousness of recurrent criminal activity.

In summary, adult corrections in Canada are currently organized into a federal system receiving offenders with sentences of two years or longer and ten provincial systems receiving remand prisoners and prisoners serving sentences of less than two years. Federally, the system is administered under a variety of departments and ministries of government. Four major correctional objectives have been identified: retribution, protection, deterrence, and rehabilitation. Of these, the present emphasis is clearly upon rehabilitation, which is viewed as the best way for the public to achieve the protection it desires and an eventual reduction in the crime rate.

Parole

One of the distinctive features of the Canadian criminal-justice system is that almost no convict spends his full sentence in prison. Nearly all of them have returned to the community before the expiration of the full time period to which the court sentenced them. Speaking to this point, the Task Force on the Release of Inmates (Huggesen Report, 1973: 1) indicated that there are three separate ways in which an inmate can be released from prison before his sentence has been completed: remission, temporary absence, and parole. Remission, whether it is called "earned remission", "statutory remission", or the prisoner designation "good time", is simply a way of letting an offender out of prison a bit before his sentence is completed in recognition for his good behaviour and co-operation with the staff. In the absence of corporal punishment, there is little reason for prisoners to co-operate with their captors unless some rewards are offered as incentives. Implicitly, misbehaviour will result in the loss of remission time and the serving of the full sentence. In any event, remission is a widely used positive sanction within the Canadian correctional system.

Temporary absence, on the other hand, is a recent innovation by which the prison authorities may allow an offender to be out of the prison for a short period of time for compassionate or other relevant reasons. The decision whether or not to grant a request for temporary absence rests solely with the institutional authorities. (It is not to be confused with a somewhat similar program called "day parole", which is administered by the National Parole Board and which will be discussed later.)

Although many good definitions of the term "parole" exist in the literature, for present purposes the definition offered by the Canadian Committee on Corrections (Ouimet Report, 1969: 329) will be used. Parole was defined by the Committee:

As procedure whereby an inmate of a prison who is considered suitable may be released, at a time considered appropriate by a parole board, before the expiration of his sentence, at large in society but subject to stated conditions, under supervision, and subject to return to prison if he fails to comply with the conditions governing his release.

Historically, parole grew out of an ancient royal prerogative of remitting part of a prisoner's sentence as an act of clemency. Very often there were conditions attached to the remission, such as the requirement that the offender leave the country, or promise future good behaviour. Another source which is frequently cited is the ancient military custom of captured officers being released if they gave their word (the Latin term for "word" being *parole*) that they would take no further part in the hostilities. In any event, the clemency required the recipient to give his word that he would abide by conditions as set by the captor. Supervision is a more recent addition, in recognition that no agreement can be enforced or sanctions imposed without it.

In Canada, according to Miller (1965: 329–36), the first parole act, which was passed in 1898, adopted the current English term and was titled the Ticket of Leave Act. It was passed with a recognition of the problems faced by inmates who were attempting to re-enter society after discharge from a penal institution. A ticket of leave was conditional liberation in an attempt to bridge the gap between the controls of the institutional life and the freedom and responsibilities of community life. When the Ticket of Leave Act came into effect, Canada was a wide-open, unsettled country where parole supervision was next to impossible. About all that could be done was to have the parolee report regularly to the nearest police department, but that procedure proved unsatisfactory, since little help was offered to the parolee in his efforts to readjust to society.

In the early days, the Salvation Army often undertook to provide supervision and one of its officers became the first Dominion Parole Officer in 1905. Since this was not a very workable arrangement, the Department of Justice, which administered the Act, finally set up a branch which became known as the Remission Service. Slowly over the years the Service developed standards of operation whereby applications could be investigated and parolees supervised. The major change in the parole situation in Canada occurred in 1956 following a report to the Minister of Justice from a committee which he had appointed to look into the subject. This committee did its work under the chairmanship of Mr. Justice Gerald Fauteux of the Supreme Court of Canada. Among its recommendations was the establishment of a national parole board. The present authority and jurisdiction of the National Parole Board is set out in the Parole Act which was proclaimed in force on February 5, 1959.

In terms of organization, the National Parole Board consists of nineteen members (of whom one is the chairman) who are responsible to the Department of the Solicitor General. They are supported by an executive director and a staff. In addition, there is the National Parole Service, which includes thirty-four local offices throughout Canada. Each local office has a director and a staff to collect information, supervise parolees and make recommendations to the Parole Board. Total strength, as of 1973, was approximately 475 persons.

The Parole Act gives the National Parole Board exclusive jurisdiction and absolute discretion to grant, refuse, or revoke parole for any adult inmate in a federal or provincial institution who is serving a sentence under any federal statute. (The only exceptions to this rule are found in Ontario and British Columbia, where the courts use indeterminate sentences and the Parole Act provides for provincial parole boards, which have jurisdiction to grant parole with respect to the indeterminate part of the sentence.) The National Parole Board has no jurisdiction over inmates serving sentences for violation of provincial statutes. The Board does have jurisdiction, however, to revoke or suspend any order made under the Criminal Code prohibiting a person from operating a motor vehicle.

The National Parole Board has often emphasized its policy of reform and rehabilitation rather than static custody or retribution (Street, 1971; *Annual Reports*, 1968–73). In a recent undated publication entitled *An Outline of Canada's Parole System for Judges, Magistrates and Police* (National Parole Board, n.d.: 2) the Board stated:

Parole is not a question of interfering with the sentence of the court. Parole is not a matter of mercy or clemency. The national Parole Board believes that an inmate should be paroled to assist in his rehabilitation: (a) *when the maximum benefit has been gained from imprisonment;* (b) *when the offender has responded favourably to treatment and training programs;* (c) *when he shows a definite indication of his intention to reform;* (d) *when his reform and rehabilitation will be aided by parole;* (e) *and when his release would not mean an excessive risk to society.* Those who do not show an indication or do not respond to the programs should remain in custody for the protection of society, until they can be successfully treated.

On the question of eligibility, parole regulations provide that an inmate serving a sentence of two years or more in a federal penal institution must serve at least nine months before parole may be granted. If the sentence is for three or more years, one-third of the sentence, or four years, whichever comes first, must be served before the inmate becomes eligible to be granted parole. An inmate serving a life sentence must serve seven years before eligibility is reached. If it is a life sentence for non-capital murder, however, or if it is a commuted death sentence, then the inmate must serve a full ten years before becoming eligible for parole. Inmates serving sentences of less than two years in provincial institutions may apply for parole after serving one-third of their sentence. There is an exception, however: the Parole Board is not absolutely bound by the parole regulations and may release an inmate at any time in his sentence when it believes it would be in the best interests of the community and of the inmate to do so.

Shortly after an inmate is sentenced to two or more years in a federal institution, the Parole Service prepares and opens a record on that individual. It notifies him of the date when he will be eligible to apply for parole. When that time arrives, if he so desires, the Parole Service will help him prepare an application. Many inmates choose not to apply, however, and instead serve their sentence, gaining only remission time over their release date. If the inmate chooses to apply, the Parole Service prepares a report, including its recommendations in the matter, and sends it to the Board in Ottawa. At this point, the Parole Board must make a decision on the suitability of the inmate for early release on parole. Statutory eligibility has been attained, but suitability depends on a number of factors including: the nature and gravity of the offence; whether the offender is a recidivist; his adjustment in the correctional institution; whether the inmate's plans are feasible; and whether there is a job available and anyone who can help the inmate in the community where he wishes to be released. Perhaps the most important factor in any case of parole application is whether or not the Board feels that the inmate has changed his attitude toward crime, or whether he will commit further offences if released on parole. As Street, former chairman of the Parole Board (1972: 3), stated in an address to the Senate, "The decision of the Board to grant parole is not taken lightly. The Board recognizes the gravity of this decision and the serious consequences which may follow if a person released on parole turns once again to criminal activity."

If parole is granted, it may be "full parole", which means that a parolee is in the community full time, under supervision of a parole agent until his sentence expires. He may, however, be granted "day parole", which would allow him to be in the community for a period of fifteen days to three months, and to return part time to the community for purposes of continuing school or holding a job, if it was in the interest of his re-habilitation. Day parole differs from temporary absence in that it is parole granted by the Parole Board, whereas temporary absence is at the discretion of head of the institution where an offender is serving his sentence.

One of the major conditions of parole is that the parolee report to and be under the supervision of a parole officer in the community where he is released. Parole supervisors are usually, but not always, officers of the Parole Service. In Canada, as distinct from some of the other countries which have parole, supervision may be performed by members of after-care agencies such as the John Howard Society and the Elizabeth Fry Society, or by provincial probation officers, or, in some special cases, by responsible private citizens appointed by the Parole Board.

Parole supervision is difficult to perform, if it is done properly. The offender on parole is still under sentence and is subject to control until the sentence is completed. Parole is not just a way of shortening the court's sentence: it is a change in the type of control over the offender as he moves from the close security of an institution to the relatively free conditions of the outside community—but control it is, without any doubt. The National Parole Board (n d.: 8) defined it as follows:

Supervision involves both guidance and surveillance; the casework and the authoritative type of approach. It should be adequate and fair but firm. Parolees should be assisted with their problems and given friendly counsel and advice. At the same time they must learn to accept the responsibilities of being a law abiding citizen. If they misbehave, or if it is apparent they do not intend to reform, they should be returned to prison.

Parole supervisors, whether they are Parole service officers or others authorized to supervise parolees, are aware that they should promptly report any breach of the conditions of parole or any misbehaviour, so that the Parole Board may act quickly. If a parolee seems headed for trouble, or if he actually gets into trouble, the Board may suspend the parole, or it may revoke the parole and return the offender to the institution. If the parolee commits an indictable offence, the parole is automatically forfeited and he is returned to serve the remainder of his sentence plus any sentence resulting from the new offence.

One other aspect of parole should be mentioned: "mandatory supervision", which applies to inmates to whom parole was not granted, or who chose not to apply for parole. These inmates usually leave the institution before their sentences expire, because of remission time which they have earned through good behaviour or received otherwise. When they are released they are automatically under the same supervision as any parolee until the date that their sentence expires. Since they have not applied, or have been turned down for parole, they are often very hostile toward any supervision and create difficult cases for the parole supervisor.

Unless there are additional offences and convictions, or unless the parole has been suspended or revoked for some other reason, it automatically expires on the date when the inmate would have completed all of the prison time which he received at the time of sentence. He is at that point free of any official supervision and control. Frequently, however, he has not completed some program of rehabilitation, education, or training at the time the sentence expires, or perhaps he may simply feel the need for continued advice and help in adjusting to the demands of life in the community. At any rate, if he chooses to make use of them, there are a number of prisoner aid societies and after-care agencies upon which he may call for advice and help.

After-Care

Every province in Canada has at least one after-care agency. They are sometimes called prisoners' aid societies, or in some instances they constitute specialized departments within larger organizations, as with the Correctional Services Department of the Salvation Army. Whether organized separately or as part of larger organizations, they all have in common the recognition that prisons are, in the words of a former director of the John Howard Society (Kirkpatrick, 1965: 384), "places that men leave". It has long been recognized by sensitive people that former prisoners usually face a difficult and frustrating task of re-entry into society. The longer the period of confinement, especially in circumstances of static custody in a maximum security environment, the more difficult the re-entry experience. In fact, it may be said that for some prisoners release from prison marks the beginning of a second punishment, sometimes more severe and prolonged than that which the courts imposed. In any event, the after-care agencies, which constitute the last subsystem within the Canadian system of criminal justice and corrections, have been established to help with this problem.

Following the definition employed by the Government of Manitoba (1972: 40) " 'after-care' is the term applied to that assistance and service which the offender may accept on a voluntary basis after his mandatory involvement with the system is finished." The Canadian Committee on Corrections (Ouimet Report, 1969: 37) pointed out that the after-care agencies constitute an essential part of the correctional system and that treatment within the prison and treatment on after-care should be recognized as aspects of a continuing process.

Historically, the oldest after-care agency in Canada is probably the John Howard Society of Quebec, which was organized in Montreal by the Anglican Church in 1892. Prisoners' aid work, although on an unorganized basis, dates from farther back in time to 1867 when, according to Kirkpatrick (1965: 386), "a group of church workers in Toronto first began to bring spiritual consolation to inmates in jail." This work was on a rather discontinuous and casual basis, however, and certainly was not the type of service offered by the well-established after-care agencies which developed in the twentieth century. Although a number of provinces such as Ontario and British Columbia soon developed after-care agencies, it was not until 1960 that the John Howard Society of Canada was consolidated. Since that time, together with the Elizabeth Fry Society, the organization has played quite an important role in Canadian corrections.

The main task of the after-care agencies is the re-establishment of former prisoners in the community where they are to live and work. In the early days, the services offered were mostly what has been called "aid on discharge". The after-care worker, usually a volunteer without professional training, would provide the ex-prisoner with lodging, food, and friendly assistance. This support was usually limited to the first few days or weeks after release. In recent years, the trend has been to employ professionally trained case workers, who provide individualized and specialized after-care on a sustained basis. There are, however, many prisoners' aid societies which still operate with volunteers, although usually some guidance and direction is offered by professionally trained staff members. Philosophically, however, the worker in the after-care agency, whether professional or volunteer, seeks out the individual's strengths and abilities. The task is to help the inmate earn his living by these strengths and abilities rather than by his weaknesses and criminal tendencies.

In the normal course of events, an inmate in a provincial or federal institution will receive an interview from an after-care worker before release. The pre-release interview informs the inmate of the services available to him and instructs him in how to request the service, if he so desires. Often the pre-release interview yields an assessment of the prisoner, his strengths and weaknesses, the institutional programs of rehabilitation in which he has been involved, his plans for the future, and any special problems he may face in returning to the community. This procedure, in theory, makes possible the ideal of continuity in treatment from the institutional to the community setting. Some after-care agencies, such as the John Howard Societies of Manitoba and British Columbia, have instituted counselling with prisoners' wives in the community prior to the release of the imprisoned husbands. The offender must decide, however, whether or not he wishes to accept the services offered.

In recent decades, mainly since the 1950s, after-care agencies have co-operated with the National Parole Board in supervising offenders on parole. An important distinction is that, while the offender is released under the *authority* of the regional representative of the National Parole Service, he is under *supervision* of the after-care agency. With prisoners who are discharged from sentence, the contact with after-care is voluntary and is often very brief. These people may want help in getting settled, and then usually want only to break all links with their prison past. The parolee, in contrast, must maintain his agreement to accept supervision as a condition of being outside the institution. For him it is not voluntary. This is particularly true for those on mandatory supervision who may dislike the idea and may be very hostile to the after-care worker who has the responsibility for supervising them. If violations of the agreement occur, the after-care worker must report to the Parole Service all facts concerning the parolee and his circumstances, so that, if necessary, they may intervene at any point in the parole period. Establishing a sound working relationship under these conditions is at best difficult, and is often impossible. Despite such difficulties, the work of the after-care agencies in supervising parolees is well thought of by the National Parole Board, which stated in its *Outline of Canada's Parole System for Judges, Magistrates and the Police* (n.d.: 11)

The role of the private agencies is particularly vital during those difficult days immediately after release; days in which an inmate attempts to adjust to community life. It is here that the broad spectrum of services can be employed whether it be for financial assistance, shelter, counselling, or employment. . . . The Board appreciates the skill and understanding with which these problems have been attacked and it believes after-care agencies must continue to be an integral part in rehabilitation of the offender.

Perhaps the best statement summing up the work of the after-care agencies was made by Kirkpatrick (1965: 405), who stated:

But the greater justification and reward for those engaged in this work is the knowledge that human values have been conserved and that former offenders have productively re-established in our communities. There is today a new happiness in many lives that were formerly wasted and ruined by past misdeeds, and abounding evidence of increased usefulness to friends, relatives, and society as a whole.

In any event, offenders coming out of Canadian prisons are not released on the street without supervision or assistance. They may be released via parole or mandatory supervision, or, if they wish, with the assistance of an after-care worker. Supervision may be from a public agency such as the National Parole Service or a private agency such as the John Howard Society, but either way, the former inmate has help and guidance with his re-entry problem and the public is protected to the extent that the offender is supervised until his sentence expires.

SUMMARY

In this chapter the reader has been introduced to the Canadian criminal-justice and corrections system. It was described as having several parts or subsystems including: law enforcement; prosecution of criminal offenders; the adult criminal courts; probation services; prisons, including federal penitentiaries and provincial gaols; parole; and after-care. Far from being a highly integrated system with a consistent philosophy throughout, it was defined as a loosely articulated set of subsystems characterized by a very great deal of discretion and autonomous decision-making. The result is that only a very small proportion of offenders, whose crimes are known to the police, are processed completely through the system from arrest to release from prison. In addition, some information concerning the legal basis and historical development of each sub-system was presented, along with a brief description of how each is organized and what it attempts to accomplish. Some of the difficulties and ambiguities associated with the system were discussed, along with new programs and developments which are taking place. The over-riding emphasis was clearly on the process of social change, whereby the system was viewed as moving from an early stress upon *retribution*, in which attempts were made merely to punish the offender, and *protection*, in which the convict was held in static custody for his full sentence, to an emphasis upon *treatment and rehabilitation*, which is presently perceived as providing the greatest likelihood for reforming the offender and con-trolling crime.

Select Bibliography

For those who wish to read further in the literature of criminology correc-tions, the following readily available sources are recommended.

General Criminology

BLUMBERG, ABRAHAM S. *The Scales of Justice*. New York: Transaction Books, 1970.
CONQUEST, ROBERT, ed. *Justice and the Legal System in the U.S.S.R.* Toronto: The Bodley Head Publisher, 1968.

HOOD, R., and SPARKS, RICHARD. *Key Issues in Criminology*. New York: McGraw-Hill, 1970.
JOHNSTON, N., SAVITS, L., and WOLFGANG, W. E., eds. *The Sociology of Punishment and Corrections*. Second Edition. New York: John Wiley and Sons, 1970.
RECKLESS, W. C. *The Crime Problem*. New York: Appleton-Century-Crofts, 1967.
SCHAFER, S. *Theories in Criminology*. New York: Random House, 1969.
VOLD, G. B. *Theoretical Criminology*. New York: Oxford University Press, 1958.
WOLFGANG, M. E., SAVITZ, L., and JOHNSTON, NORMAN, eds. *The Sociology of Crime and Delinquency*. 2nd ed. New York: John Wiley and Sons, 1970.

Law Enforcement

BORDUA, DAVID J., ed. *The Police: Six Sociological Essays*. New York: John Wiley and Sons, 1967.
CAIN, MAUREEN E. *Society and the Policeman's Role*. London: Routledge and Kegan Paul, 1973.
CRAY, E. *The Enemy in the Streets: Police Malpractice in America*. New York: Doubleday and Company, 1972.
Great Britain. *Royal Commission on the Police, Report*. London: Her Majesty's Stationery Office, 1962.
United States of America. United States President's Commission on Law Enforcement and the Administration of Justice. *Task Force Report: The Police*. Washington, D.C.: U.S. Government Printing Office, 1967.

Criminal Courts

CECIL, H. *The English Judge*. London, U.K.: Stevens Publisher, 1971.
GROSMAN, BRIAN A. *The Prosecutor*. Toronto: University of Toronto Press, 1969.
HOGARTH, JOHN. *Sentencing as a Human Process*. Toronto: Centre of Criminology, University of Toronto, 1971.

Probation and Parole

British Journal of Criminology 13, No. 1 (January 1973). Special Issue on Parole.
CARTER, R. M., and WILKINS, L. T. *Probation and Parole: Selected Readings*. New York: John Wiley and Sons, 1970.

Prisons

CARNEY, LOUIS P. *Introduction to Correctional Science*. New York: McGraw-Hill, 1974.
CARTER, R. M., GLASER, DANIEL, and WILKINS, L. T., eds. *Correctional Institutions*. New York: J. B. Lippincott, 1974.
GIALLOMBARDO, ROSE. *Society of Women: A Study of a Woman's Prison*. New York: John Wiley and Sons, 1966.
HOWARD, D. L. *The English Prisons*. London: Methuen, 1970.
IRWIN, JOHN. *The Felon*. Englewood Cliffs, N.J.: Prentice-Hall, 1970.
THOMAS, J. E. *The English Prison Officer Since 1850: A Study in Conflict*. London: Routledge and Kegan Paul, 1972.

PART III

Social Institutions

In all societies certain relatively constant problems arise which have to be met effectively on a continuing basis if the society is to succeed and perpetuate itself through time. Around these problems emerge a set of customs and practices which become relatively permanent and therefore predictable behaviour patterns: they are ideas in the minds of people about how problems should be solved plus a set of functionaries to carry them out. Together they constitute the main referents for the term *social institution*. Speaking about this concept, Bell and Sirjamaki have stated, "Institutions and institutionalized behavior then refer to culturally and socially established ways of doing things. Institutional behavior is enforced by the authority and sanctions of society. . . . It reflects the consensus of a society relative to the behavior which is right and proper in response to a situation" (Bell and Sirjamaki, 1965: 466–67).

A set of four chapters pertaining to Canadian social institutions is presented in the final section of this book. These institutions are related to problems of continuity of the society through orderly recruitment and rearing of the young, mediating between the known empirical world and the unknown, socializing the young to become conventional members of society, and, finally, the governance of man in a complex and rapidly changing society.

G. N. Ramu of the University of Manitoba has contributed a chapter on marriage and the family in Canada. The major themes of stability and change are developed in terms of the ideal type concepts of orderly replacement of family culture, in contrast to the idea of permanent availability of individuals. This is, of course, a specific example of the more general cultural conflict between collectivity orientation where primacy is accorded to the institution and its function in society, and self-orientation where primacy is directed toward individual self-aggrandizement. The organization of family, its tasks or functions, and the changes which seem presently to be occurring with respect to it are presented and related to the culturally unique situation represented by Canadian society.

Harry Hiller of the University of Calgary has examined the religious institution and has related changes in the social context of the nation to variations and adaptations in religion. Basically, the sociology of religion is presented as an analysis of the kinds of people who hold beliefs and the religious patterns of behaviour in which they engage. The author believes that examination of the religious institution will yield a great deal of information about the kinds of people who make up the population and the tensions and conflicts that are present in the society.

The Canadian way of education and the difficult task of socializing the young into knowledgeable members of the society has been described and analysed by Jane Synge of McMaster University. The educational institution is described in terms of its parts, with particular emphasis upon what the parts do in the context of the larger society. The reader is presented with an historical perspective on change relating to the development of Canadian education and an awareness of its importance for survival of Canada as a cultural entity.

In the final chapter of this section, C. R. Santos of the University of Manitoba has presented an analysis of governmental bureaucracy in Canada. A very precise discussion is developed concerning the various parts of the federal government, what the parts do in relationship to each other and to the larger society, and the historical development of the political and administrative process for the formulation and implementation of public policy.

In each of the four chapters, the reader is provided with an understanding concerning a salient and continuing problem in society, the patterned and predictable ways which have evolved to meet it, and some understanding of what Canadian society defines as the correct and proper response to each situation.

The Family and Marriage in Canada   8

G. N. RAMU*

The major objective of this chapter is to present a review of significant literature and data on Canadian family and marriage. The chapter is divided into five broad sections. In the introductory section, the conditions which have led to the neglect of sociological studies of the family in Canada are suggested. The second section presents an argument within a conceptual framework which is helpful in interpreting both stable and changing aspects of family and marriage in Canada. The third section includes an analysis of the six major functions of the family in Canada. The next brief section shows how Canadians in general maintain close ties with their kin. In the fifth section on marriage, it is pointed out that while marriage and divorce rates continue to reflect a strong conformity to family culture, the changes occurring are conspicuous enough to indicate a move toward individualism and secularism in courtship and marriage concerns.

Research on Family Life in Canada

The study of the family is an area which has been neglected by sociologists in Canada for a long time. There appear to be three reasons for this neglect. First, Canadian social science has tended to have a pragmatic orientation, one in which research was encouraged only in those areas of social life which needed social reform. As a result of this focus, attention was given to substantive areas such as ethnic relations, deviance, and social stratification in the 1950s and 1960s. Since, in relative terms,

*I am deeply indebted to Paul D. Wiebe of the University Sains Malaysia who made many useful comments on the first draft. Among my colleagues at the University of Manitoba, I owe particular thanks to Leo Driedger, Stuart Johnson, Eric Linden, and Emily Nett for reading the final manuscript. I regret that I could not respond to all suggestions made by each of these colleagues, but in general their criticisms have definitely helped me to improve the end product.

marital and family relations did not pose a serious enough set of problems to threaten the social order, social scientists and the agencies which provide funds for research were not attracted to research in this area.

Second, the influence of American sociology has considerably reduced research efforts in the area of the Canadian family. "The prevalent assumption is that, by and large, the Canadian family can be equated with the American family," according to Ishwaran (1971: 3). This widely held assumption led to a belief that the conclusions derived from research on American marriage and family patterns were applicable to Canadian society, and therefore that there was little need for duplication. This assumption provided a context in relation to which the expansion of the United States textbook market could occur. In the last twenty years, "Canadian educational systems primarily relied on the approximately forty family text books produced in the United States" (Schlesinger, 1972: vii). This situation needs an immediate correction: given the pluralistic nature of the Canadian society, the relevance of American studies of family life is progressively declining, whatever its applicability was once.

Third, in the "hierarchy" of substantive areas within the general field of sociology, the sociology of the family has tended to occupy a relatively lowly position. A British sociologist, Anderson (1971: 8), expresses his concern for his colleagues' mistaken perception of the sociology of the family in the following words:

The reputation of the sociology of the family among professional sociologists is still rather low. Many see it as an academic deadend—which contributes little or nothing of importance to the discipline as a whole; as concentrating in trivial and value-laden problems of more concern to journalism or social work than hard sociology; as methodologically naive and conceptually underdeveloped.

In Canada, however, as late as 1969 there existed the combination of belief "(1) that family sociology is an interdisciplinary area without an independent existence, and (2) that there is no theory in this area" (Wakil, 1970: 154). Wakil, a Canadian family sociologist, expressing disbelief in such misunderstandings on the part of his colleagues, assesses the state of the sociology of the Canadian family thus: "The conclusion that followed from these premises was that therefore there was no need to develop a sociology of the family life in Canada!" (1970: 154).

Whatever the reasons, in Canada research in the area of sociology of the family is not conducted at the level and magnitude it should be. Yet it is interesting to note that the French Canadians have provided initial leadership in this direction. Garigue (1962) studied the French-Canadian family and kinship structure, and his pioneering research is by far the most comprehensive study of the family life in Canada. There are no comparable studies, in terms of detail and magnitude.

Nevertheless, there are certain mild indications that research is now increasing. The Canadian Conference of the Family which met in Ottawa in 1964 commissioned Frederick Elkin (1964) to (1) conduct a preliminary study of the family, (2) write a source book on Canadian families, and (3) provide an account of present knowledge and gaps in this area. Elkin accomplished this in his book *The Family in Canada.* The Vanier Institute of the Family, meanwhile, published a useful *Inventory of Family Research and Studies,* an inventory now being maintained on a continuing basis. In 1971 Ishwaran compiled an anthology of essays, *The Canadian Family,* which provides an analysis of variations and uniformities in family life among various Canadian ethnic groups. Ishwaran's anthology lacks, however, sociological materials on courtship processes, sexual behaviour, and divorce. The publication of such books is an indication not only of the growing interest in the study of the family in Canada but also of the determination of Canadian sociologists interested in the area of the family to move ahead, despite the kinds of restraints pointed out earlier.

A Conceptual Framework

In this section we will first examine a few definitions of the family and the household commonly found in Canadian materials. Later, we will discuss a conceptual framework used in our analysis of the family in Canada.

DEFINITIONS OF THE FAMILY AND THE HOUSEHOLD

The Canadian Census Bureau has developed definitions of the family and the household for the purpose of enumeration. An enumeration of families and households is essential for determining the growth of population, from time to time, and for planning for the development and allocation of national resources.

A *census family* is defined as a group of two or more persons living in the same dwelling and related to one another, as husband and wife, and with or without unmarried children (Census of Canada, Vol. II, Part I, Bulletin 2.1–3). Any other persons in the dwelling who might be related to the family head are not counted as members of the family. If a married son and his wife and children reside in the same dwelling, sharing food and other living facilities, for example, according to census definitions there would now be two families in one household. The census definition, therefore, includes only the nuclear family: the lineally extended three-generation family is not viewed as one family. The census definition of the family operates on the "principle of exclusion" of the married lineal kin. Discussing this aspect, Jacobson (1971: 26–30) is critical of the census definition because it assumes the structural isolation of the nuclear family (Parsons, 1943). Contending that the Canadian family is an institution enmeshed in a wider kinship system, she acknowledges that the family may be nuclear, but claims that what characterizes the family here is the nature of the kinship ties maintained by its members: she sees a modified extended family in operation in Canada.

Obviously, the census definition takes demographic as well as "limited" kinship ties into account in its definition. But it ignores the socio-cultural dimensions of family life in Canada. Elkin and Ishwaran draw the distinction between the "Canadian family" and "family in Canada". Says Elkin (1964: 31): "There is no one Canadian family. With its distinctive geography and history, Canada is much too heterogeneous to have one or ten or twenty distinctive family types. As the geographical setting, and as the social class, religious, ethnic, occupational, and other groupings vary, so too are families." Supporting Elkin, Ishwaran (1971: 3–20) claims Canada has a mosaic of family types, each kind based on differing socio-cultural traits.

In sum, there are at least three kinds of definitions. Census definitions take demographic and limited kinship ties into account. Helga Jacobson uses a definition of a modified extended family, claiming this is relevant to the Canadian situation. Finally, Elkin and Ishwaran take a pluralistic approach in their definitions. After a discussion of households, a definition of the family will be presented which will take into account the concerns expressed by Jacobson, Elkin, and Ishwaran.

The census household is not defined by blood and/or affinal ties. Thus, the household need not have a kinship group within it, being simply a residential group. Accordingly, "A household consists of a person or group of persons occupying one dwelling. It usually consists of a family group, without lodgers, employees, etc. However, it may consist of two or more families sharing a dwelling, or a group of unrelated persons, or of one person living alone. . . . Every person is a member of some household and there is a one-to-one relationship between households and occupied dwellings" (Census of Canada, Vol. ii, Part i, Bulletin 2.1–3).

What are the distinctions between the family and the household? First, all census families are households while not all census households are families. Second, a census family is a kinship and "cultural" unit whereas a household may be merely a residential and demographic unit.

Table 1 shows census data on numbers of households and families for four decades beginning 1941. The data reveal that in the last decade the number of households has doubled while the number of families has also increased, but not in the same proportion as households. The implication, is that in Canada the number of single-member households is on the increase. These single-member households represent unmarried young persons who have moved out of their parental families, separated or divorced persons, and the aged.

Table 1 Showing Census families and households for the last four decades.

Period	Families	Households + Families	Households Only
1941	2,509,664	2,706,089	196,425
1951	3,297,384	3,349,580	252,196
1961	4,147,444	4,554,736	417,292
1971	5,070,682	6,041,305	970,623

Source: *Census Canada, 1951*, Volume iii, Table 1-1.
   Census Canada, 1961, Volume ii, Part i, Bulletin 2.1, Table 1.
   Census Canada, 1971.

A DEFINITION OF THE FAMILY IN TERMS OF ITS CULTURE

Although the Canadian census definition of the family is consistent with certain sociological definitions, for our purposes its analytical utility is rather limited. For us, the family is not simply an aggregation of such role performers as wife, husband, son, and daughter. It is not merely a residential arrangement providing regularized services and food, clothing, and recreation. The family signifies a cultural and normative order which remains more or less constant over time. The traditional definition of the family as a social unit does not allow for the full understanding of the family's role in the maintenance of social differentiation of integration. Indeed, the definition of the family should transcend empirical referents represented in the unity of roles constituting the nuclear family. Therefore, we suggest a general definition of the family following Bernard Farber, who suggests that the family should be understood in terms of its culture: "The norms and values which people hold regarding courtship, marriage, divorce, kinship identity and obligation, socialization, residence, and household maintenance are the elements of family culture" (Farber, 1964: 55).

We consider that an analysis of the family in Canada in terms of its culture will be useful in that it will enable us to account for the continuing pluralistic character of the Canadian society (see Elkin's and Ishwaran's discussions). For example, it is true that socialization is an important function of the family in Canada. Yet the values and norms involved in socialization processes tend to vary from one group to another. The Hutterites of Alberta (Hostetler and Huntington, 1967: 57–90) and the upper-middle-class residents of Toronto's "Crestwood Heights" (Seely et al.) differ not only in their ways of socializing their children but also in the goals underlying their child-rearing practices. Similarly, people living in cities and villages hold different attitudes toward their relatives and vary in terms of kin solidarity and patterns of interaction. Therefore, a definition of the family in terms of its culture will help us to understand social variations. When Elkin (1964: 31) and Ishwaran (1971: 3–20) refer to variant family types or a mosaic of family types, they are, in effect, pointing to the family culture which differs from one group to another.

A CONCEPTUAL FRAMEWORK

A conceptual framework, as used here, is an analytical tool which helps us to summarize, classify, and interpret widely assorted data. The composition of a conceptual framework depends on how a social scientist wishes to analyse the data related to a given social phenomenon. Consequently, there is enough scope for an application of several conceptual frameworks to the analysis of a single social phenomenon. This is true of the study of family life. In the United States, Hill and Hansen (1960: 299–311) have identified five conceptual frameworks in the area of the sociology of the family: (1) interactional, (2) structure-functional, (3) situational, (4) institutional, and (5) developmental.

A conceptual framework often determines how we define the family or similar social institutions or processes. For example, one framework tends to view the family as a *small group* with ongoing interaction among its members, while another tends to consider the family as a perpetual social institution composed of relatively unalterable values, norms, and roles. These are called *interactional* and *structure-functional* frameworks respectively. At this stage of the development of the sociology of the family in Canada, it is rather difficult to identify major conceptual frameworks, although, in general, major research studies conform to structure-functional tradition.

One of the crucial tasks of the family is to enable long-range cultural survival. For such a survival each "family of orientation" (the family into which an individual is born and in which he is socialized) must be organized to produce in its children's families' patterns of norms and values identical or at least similar to its own. This process of replacement is conceptualized by Farber (1964) as the orderly replacement of family culture. Certain family and kinship characteristics become inevitable in those societies or social groups where the emphasis is on orderly replacement. For example, in Canada there will be rigorous normative controls over courtship processes, and endogamous or homogamous alliances will be encouraged. The reason for such a control is to restrict the blending of different family cultures. In a multi-ethnic society such as Canada, orderly replacement of family culture thus contributes directly to the maintenance of pluralism.

Furthermore, close kinship ties are maintained between lineal and affinal kin; lineal kin are reckoned with one's parents, while affinal kin are identified through one's spouse. Kinship identity and obligation are important. Then too, the nuclear-family role structure tends to be organized in a hierarchical fashion in relation to generational and sexual principles. In such a situation, patriarchy usually is the accepted form of authority structure within the family.

In essence, in order to facilitate efficient orderly replacement of family culture, the elements of family culture are scrupulously observed. The manner in which this is accomplished will be discussed below in relation to family functions. At this point, it is necessary to keep in mind that cultural continuity is at least partially accomplished through the family, given the assumption of an orderly replacement of family culture.

In fact, orderly replacement undoubtedly emphasizes cultural continuity and stability. But seldom do family groups remain unchanging today, given technological developments, specialized formal education, urbanization, and other secular factors. In the changing social context, familism as implied in the framework of orderly replacement becomes weak. The crucial change has occurred in the area of relationships between the individual and his family, and more extensively in kinship relations. From the point of view of the individual, marriage and the family lose some of their institutional significance, acquiring more of the characteristics of voluntary associations. Individual commitments to such associations can remain strong, of course, as long as they gratify needs. If they prove unsatisfactory, the individual is free to seek gratification elsewhere and may withdraw his commitment from the family and marriage to which he belongs. Ideally in such a situation, individualism in family and marriage issues is emphasized.

To conceptualize this emerging process, Farber suggests, in contrast to the concept of orderly replacement, the concept of the universal permanent availability of individuals for marriage with any one at any time, the only restraining norm being the norm of incest. The notion of universal permanent availability implies the declining importance of family and kinship organizations in the marital life of an individual, making random matings possible. It also implies that individuals tend to maintain skills and attributes which continue to make them desirable mates in the marriage market. Therefore, as opposed to the orderly replacement concept, marriage and family become much more open institutions with far fewer social controls.

What are some of the consequences of this situation of permanent availability? First, less emphasis is placed on premarital chastity and marital fidelity. Second, love and other emotional and sexual considerations, rather than the perpetuation of the family culture, become the basis for marriage arrangements. Consequently, more and more persons tend to marry without giving any attention to each other's ethnic, religious, and class backgrounds. Thus, marriage becomes a highly personal matter freed from other social concerns. Third, children are traditionally the means by which family culture was perpetuated, but in a permanent availability situation, children do not so necessarily serve the interests of the couple. Therefore, they are seldom seen as the means by which family culture is transmitted, and the number of children per couple is likely to decline. Fourth, in a situation of high rates of divorce and remarriage, an individual is expected to maintain youthfulness, glamour, and communication skills, resulting in an increased expenditure on clothing, cosmetics, beauty parlours, and physical self-maintenance. Finally, more women participate in educational activities leading to job opportunities. As a result, increasing economic independence will make them more available than when they were dependent on others (parents or husbands).

In the orderly replacement of family culture framework, the family is viewed as a relatively stable and closed institution. It is held by its members to be a sacred institution where values and roles are maintained intact. On the other hand, the universal permanent availability framework views marital and family processes as modern and open. These two conceptualizations help us to account for both stable and/or dynamic aspects of family and marital behaviour in a given social setting. It is also possible to apply these two concepts to a single family. For example, older people are more likely to emphasize principles of orderly replacement, while younger people move toward values identified in the universal permanent availability construct.

In the following analysis, the concepts of orderly replacement of family culture and universal permanent availability will be used. The ways in which available data support these concepts will be shown in the discussion of the functions of the family in Canada, kinship ties, and marriage.

On some points the discussion remains hypothetical, however, because of inadequate data.

Functions of the Family

A function of the family may be understood as a task or duty performed by the family, as a social group, in the interest of its members and the wider society. Depending on its nature and significance, a function may be classified as either primary or secondary. The primary functions of the family are reproduction, socialization, and status-conferring; the secondary functions include those that are political or educational, and the gratification of emotional needs, for example, companionship and affection. We do not suggest that all family groups in Canada perform these functions or that they are all performed in the same way. Whether a family performs any or all and the manner in which they are performed varies with (1) such social conditions as ethnicity, class, and urban and rural location, and (2) such economic conditions as wage-earning, farming, or hunting and fishing. For example, within the Eskimo family of the North nearly all of the primary and secondary functions of the family may be performed, while within the families of blue-collar workers in Toronto only the primary functions may be performed.

For analytical purposes, Canada may be viewed in terms of a geographic setting in which several social groups are located at various stages of a continuum reflecting economic development and social complexities. At one end of the continuum we may locate a few simple societies such as the Eskimo society with its economy of hunting, fishing, and trapping. At the opposite extreme we may locate complex, highly differentiated, and dense urban societies such as those exemplified in Toronto, Montreal, and other industrial centres. In between are the farming and ranching communities of the Prairies.

Although such classifications are crude, they help us perceive how family life and functions differ from one place to another. For example, from the point of view of our conceptual framework, the lower the level of economic development the greater the probabilities the family will conform to the characteristics conceptualized in the concept of orderly replacement. Conversely, the higher the level of social and economic development, the greater are the probabilities of identifying the characteristics related to the notion of universal permanent availability.

REPRODUCTIVE FUNCTION

Individuals as biological and social entities embody family culture. They inherit it from their family of orientation and transmit it to their children. There is a need to make arrangements for the continuing replacement of the deceased members, and from time immemorial, the family group has been entrusted with this task. The norms of reproduction in Canada, as elsewhere, stipulate that reproduction be carried out exclusively within the family groups. Further, the norms also prescribe that the bearing of a child should be preceded by a legal marriage of the couple. One of the major purposes in this arrangement is to assign the responsibilities of bringing up the child to its parents. Despite such an expectation, however, a considerable proportion of births do occur out of wedlock; this point will be dealt with later.

It is difficult to establish whether all families in Canada perform the reproductive function as expected. We can only determine by using general measures and here we have chosen two such measures: crude birth rate and the number of children per family. Instead of crude birth rate one may use refined birth rate but for our discussion crude birth rate will be a sufficient measure. The crude birth rate is calculated on the basis of the number of children born every year per thousand population. This measure gives a picture of basic trends in fertility behaviour. The data on both crude birth rate and the average number of children per family are presented in Table 2.

Kalbach and McVey (1971: 56) state that the estimated birth rate

Table 2   Crude birth rate 1921–71 (per 1000 population) and average number of children per family 1941–71.

Year	Birth Rate	Average number of children per family
1921	29.3	not available
1931	23.2	not available
1941	22.4	1.9
1951	27.2	1.7
1961	26.1	1.9
1971	16.8	1.7

Source: *Canada Year Book*, 1972.

around 1660 in New France was 60 per 1000. By 1870 the rate for the entire settlement stood at 40 per 1000. The continuing decline reached an unprecedented low of 16.8 per 1000, in 1971, a rate lower than the rate of 20.1 which occurred during the Depression of the 1930s. This low rate is causing some concern among the demographers and social planners, because if the trend continues there may be serious problems in replacing the deceased. This point will be discussed at the end of this section.

Regarding the average number of children per family, however, the statistics for the last forty years do not indicate a dramatic change. On an average, a Canadian family is likely to have two children. Despite this figure, Canadians tend to prefer families of more than two children. An analysis of opinions of selected samples of Canadians in different regions reveals that the preference is for three or four children. For example, Elkin (1964: 26) cited the Gallup Poll and studies in the provinces of Quebec and British Columbia in which the respondents generally preferred three or four children. In a more recent study, Hobart (1973) indicated that a sample of university students in Edmonton and Montreal considered three or less children as the ideal number for a family. Although general statements on the basis of limited sample data cannot be made, we may hazard the assumption that in the 1970s the attitudinal trends is toward an expressed preference for three or less children per family, while the demographic trend is in the direction of two or fewer children.

The discussion of birth rate and average number of children per family obviously should not imply that all those who get married or that all women who are in child-bearing age groups will bear children. According to the 1961 Census, 14 per cent of women in the cohort group of child-bearing age did not have any children (Veevers, 1973). Biological reasons may explain why some couples do not have children, but Veevers, who has studied "child-free marriages", estimated that one-half of all childless couples were childless by choice. By implication, then, some of the childless couples did not subscribe to the norms and values underlying the reproductive function of the family.

As we indicated earlier, there are instances where children are born out of wedlock. The crude birth rate presented in Table 2 includes such children. Statistically, the proportion of children born out of wedlock are presented as a percentage of all live births in a given year. Accordingly, in 1960, 4.3 per cent of all live births occurred out of wedlock; in 1971 the per cent was 9.6. In 1973, however, the per cent declined to 9.0. The reasons, circumstances, and consequences associated with children born out of wedlock are too complex to be treated here, and the interested student may refer to Roberts (1966), Vincent (1961), Guyat (1971), and a study by the Canadian Council on Social Development (1971) entitled *The One-Parent Family*.

What are the implications of the census data on fertility behaviour for analysis of the reproductive function of the family in Canada? The declining birth rate and the declining average number of children per family should not be interpreted as indicative of the decreasing significance of the reproductive function of the family. Rather, it should be seen as a control over the number of children reproduced by each family group. Indeed, judging from attitudes toward parenthood and family size, the values and norms associated with reproduction have certainly not disappeared. Socio-economic developments have made difficult the continuation of large family groups: the increase in necessary per capita expenditure on child-rearing and decrease in the value of disposable income available nowadays to a family may be suggested as major factors. In contrast to pre-industrial societies, such as India, children do not protect and care for their parents in their old age and illness, and thus large numbers of children are not desired by modern couples. Furthermore, children in many ways hinder the occupational pursuits of women, and an increasing number of women are making the decision to have fewer children. We may infer that the family is no longer performing a reproductive function only, when in Canada a significant proportion of married couples make a decision to remain childless. It is not likely such a stage will ever be reached.

If the declining birth rate does not become stabilized at the current level in the next decade or so, however, Canadian society may face serious problems of replacement. According to the chief demographer with Statistics Canada (George, 1973),

The average family size is 2.19 children—or close to the replacement level of 2.13 children, the minimum needed to replace deaths in statistics theories. This level has already been reached in Quebec. However, all other factors remaining the same Zero Population Growth—or equilibrium between births and deaths—will not be reached in Canada for about another 67 years because of the large percentage of young people moving into the child rearing age group.[1]

Therefore, in the context of such demographic predictions, we hypothesize that the fertility behaviour of the Canadian family will be maintained at about the present rate for the foreseeable future and the biological replacement of the family will continue in a relatively orderly fashion over the same period of time.[2]

SOCIALIZATION FUNCTION

Socialization is a complex and ongoing process. Throughout the life of an individual many social institutions and organizations in addition to the family participate in this process. Examples are the church, peer groups, mass media, and formal educational institutions. In our discussion of socialization we are mainly concerned with that which occurs within the context of the family.

The family is the child's first primary group and it is here that the child learns the basic skills related to routine behaviour and expected roles and family-directed values, norms, and aspirations. It is through socialization that children internalize family culture; in turn, they try to pass it on to the following generation, thus facilitating orderly replacement.

How much of what we learn in our pre-school days guides our behaviour and attitudes in our adult lives? We need longitudinal research to answer this question conclusively. Social scientists assume, however, that many of the values and aspirations internalized during one's childhood are influential later on, to the extent that resocialization during adolescence and adulthood does not replace such values and aspirations with new ones.

Although the *form* of the values and norms internalized is the same, the *content* differs from one family to another, the differences being deter-

1. The family size to which the chief demographer is referring is the number of children per woman in the child-bearing age.
2. The replacement of the population we have discussed refers to the one which occurs within the families situated in Canada. There are other mechanisms such as immigration which may help Canada to maintain its growth of stability in demographic terms.

mined by variables such as ethnicity, religion, or class. For example, the notion of the continuity of family culture is likely to have greater significance for many Jews and Roman Catholics than to certain Protestants. The discussion which follows will present a few illustrations of the content of socialization patterns in Canada.

Identity

Ethnic, religious, and linguistic identifications form an important component of family culture. In Canada, pluralism has become both a political slogan and a social ideology. Families strive to retain their identities, and socialization is one of the principle means by which this is accomplished. In certain parts of Canada, the family- and church-supported parochial schools act as insulation against acculteration into either a dominant Anglo-Saxon culture or into the secularism of urban-industrial societies. Speaking about French Canada, Elkin (1964: 32–33) points to the historical circumstances which led to the family being the cornerstone of French-Canadian social organization: "After 1760, French Canada 'withdrew' and fell back upon itself and the family, in its distinctive religious context, became the cornerstone to survival. The family came to be viewed as a central institution from which flowed the sacred values of the society" (Garigue, 1962, cited by Elkin, 1964: 32). Although many structural changes have occurred in the French-Canadian family in the last few decades, it is still the principle means by which French identity is maintained.

More recently, Ishwaran (1971: 231), who studied a Dutch-Canadian community near Toronto, points out that the family and parochial schools make efforts to ensure "Dutchness" in terms of the values, beliefs, and ethics related to Calvinism. Latowsky (1971), discussing the "child-centered" and the "future-directed" Jewish family in Canada, suggests that the close alliance between the family and the synagogue is directed toward an orderly continuity of Jewish tradition and identity. The Hutterite commune, meanwhile, is basically structured to allow for the maintenance of the Anabaptist heritage, as professed by Joseph Hutter.

For many groups, however, the maintenance of identity has not been easy. Barclay (1971), for example, indicated that the Lebanese Muslims in Alberta are facing an erosion of their religious heritage and family customs because of the influence of the secular milieu. Elkin's (1964) summary of data on the French-Canadian family similarly suggests that changes are occurring, though apparently at a slower pace.

Occupation

The family's ability to socialize its children into productive skills depends on the degree of complexity of the overall economic structure. The greater the complexity of the economic structure, the higher will be the need for specialized occupational skills. Therefore, the higher the level of occupational specialization needed, the less the ability of the family to train children specifically for an occupation. For example, among some hunting and fishing communities of the North, occupational skills are transmitted through the family. The father takes adolescent boys with him on trapping, hunting, and fishing expeditions, while the mother teaches girls how to cook, sew, or care for children. The children in this environment have minimal alternatives, as far as possible other occupations are concerned. Occupation is part of one's family inheritance.

The economic changes going on in the North of Canada have resulted in serious occupational disorganizations among some natives. Cruikshank (1971: 41), while discussing the causes for the emergence of matrifocal family life, suggests, "Men are no longer able to teach their sons the prestigious skills once known by all Indian men, since youngsters are required to attend school."

In a slightly more advanced economy, however, such as that involving farming and ranching, the number of alternatives and their accessibility are greater than in more simple communities. The child may seek an urban occupation by successfully accomplishing formal education, or he may remain on the farm or ranch. Because of such alternatives, farm and ranch families may make an extra effort to socialize children into the family's occupational tradition. For example, the ranchers in southwestern Saskatchewan studied by Kohl (1971) have created the impression (true or not) that the ranching tradition is unique and that only certain special kinds of persons can successfully undertake it. Further, the geographic setting "in terms of sparse population restricts the child's opportunities to enter into social relationships with his peers, and limits the opportunity to experiment in social situations which are not controlled by the adult world, such as school, church and family gatherings" (Kohl, 1971: 85). In essence, then, the attractions of remaining on the farm or ranch are greater than the attractions of migrating to cities for other kinds of work.

Urban families often do not have the technical competence to train their children for specialized jobs. Hence, many non-familial agencies have taken over this function. This point will be discussed when we examine the role of the family in the formal education of children.

Role

There are many sociological and psychological explanations for the manner in which basic roles are internalized by children within the context of the family. From the point of view of the orderly replacement, the main purpose of socialization is to inculcate values and ideals of parents among children so that when they grow up they will have behaviour patterns identical to their parents. Then the family as a culture is expected to continue.

One method of ensuring such continuity is to carefully categorize roles in terms of sex, generation, and duties to be performed in one's lifetime. For example, over two decades ago, Zelditch (1955) did a cross-cultural study of the roles within the family, paying special attention to husband/ wife roles. He found that in most societies in his sample the husband's major role was that of an economic provider. He was the point of articulation between the family and the world outside it. As the family became less and less an economically productive unit, the husband—the sole bread-winner, at least ideally—emerged as more powerful than the rest in the family. Therefore, his role was defined in terms of an instrumental leader. The wife, on the other hand, progressively played a diminishing economic role: her primary concerns were reproductive, emotional, sentimental, and socializing; she was in charge of the family as a domestic group and worked toward the maintenance of cohesion and solidarity. Her role was characterized as an expressive leader. Such a role-typology derived from Zelditch's study became the focus of Parsons and Bales's (1955) analysis of the family within the framework of structure-functionalism. Finally, Parsons (1955) inferred that such a role differentiation within the Western contemporary family is essential to the development of a balanced personality among children. Therefore, a natural division of roles and labour by sex and generation became imperative.

In Canada, Garigue's (1962) analysis of the French-Canadian family illustrates the manner in which the instrumental-expressive role typology influences socialization. "The family, as a structure, is primarily characterized by the attribution of authority to the husband . . . although a majority of French Canadians say that the father and mother are mutually responsible for rearing their children, it is the father who plays the main role where punishment is concerned;—the husband is usually employed outside the home . . . while the wife has full time responsibility for the maintenance of the household and the rearing of children" (p. 132). More recent studies of the Jewish family (Latowsky, 1971), the Dutch family (Ishwaran, 1971), and the Hutterite family (Peter, 1971) support the notion of the instrumental and expressive roles among some subcultural families.

It is true that a person learns a wide variety of roles other than the instrumental and expressive roles. But some scholars question the principle and the wisdom of exposing a child to rigidly dichotomized role-patterns based on sex alone (for example, Slater, 1974; Rossi, 1968). The instrumental and expressive roles imply a hierarchy of power and responsibility between the husband and wife. The husband/father is viewed as more powerful, more responsible, and more important than the wife/mother and he derives such a position from his economic role and outside contacts. The wife, in turn, becomes a submissive dependant playing a less visible domestic role and deriving her subsistence and identity from her husband. If children are socialized into such rigidly categorized role-patterns, many strains are likely to occur in their marriage and family lives, especially in the context of social changes which are taking place at a fast pace. For example, what happens when the wife leaves home to work and thus plays the instrumental role? In that case, should the husband, in turn, switch either partly or in full to the expressive role? Or should he demand that the wife play both roles?

Recent sociological literature on sex roles and socialization points out that rigid categorization of roles by sex should be abandoned. Children should be taught role flexibility and interchangeability. Modern children ought to learn role sharing and neither sex should have a monopoly on either instrumental or expressive roles (Tomeh, 1975: 4–5).

STATUS PLACEMENT FUNCTION

The family confers certain ascriptive characteristics on the individual, and these in turn determine opportunity structures. The ascriptive characteristics are language (English, French, or others), ethnicity (English, French, German, Asian, or others), race (Caucasian, Negroid, Mongoloid, or others), religion (Protestant, Catholic, Jewish, Buddhist, or others), and sex (male or female). (For a thorough discussion of these factors and their relevance for an understanding of Canadian social organization, see the chapter on social stratification by Hunter, pp. 111–52.) Once ascribed, these characteristics generally remain, influencing the life, attitudes, self-perception, emotional and intellectual resources, and motivations toward goal attainment of the individual. Technically, except for race and sex, the characteristics can be changed. Language, religion, and class, for example, can be changed relatively easily and, in fact, sometimes are. For example, in a study of membership additions to conservative congregations in a western Canadian city, Bibby and Brinkerhoff (1973: 277) found that in 1,532 membership additions reported by twenty churches 132 (9 per cent) came through direct conversion. (For more information on changes in religion, see Hiller's discussion in Chapter 9 on religion, pp. 384–96.) Similarly, shifts from one's native language to English lead to linguistic assimilation. In terms of class, ideally upward mobility is possible in Canada. The changes which occur within a lifetime or across generations, however, are not substantive enough to suggest that the ascribed status can be easily altered. This point is substantiated in the chapters on social stratification and ethnicity.

It is a matter of common sense that birth into a wealthy family puts individuals into a different set of "life chances" than would be the case if they were born into the set of life chances of persons in a family on welfare rolls. Elaborating on this theme, Adams *et al.* (1971: 24, 68), in their critique of the Senate Committee's Report, *Poverty in Canada*, observed:

To be born in Canada is not necessarily to be born equal to all other Canadians. And to be born in the wrong place in Canada, to wrong parents, into the wrong race, is almost certainly to be introduced into a life of endless humiliation and mindless drudgery. . . . If you have the misfortune to be a woman, an Indian, an Eskimo, or a French Canadian your chances of being poor are greater—much greater—than if you were young, white, male and English-speaking.

At the other end of the spectrum, John Porter, in a study of economic élites in Canada, shows that a person's social class is largely determined by his family's socio-economic background. Most of the economic élites of Canada which he studied were recruited from the middle and upper classes. Discussing this point, Porter (1957: 69) states, "In most social systems certain biological and social characteristics stand out as putting an individual in a preferred group for recruitment to positions of power. . . . Religion, ethnic affiliation, educational experiences, social class and other social characteristics form the basis of preference." What is evident here is that the status-maintenance function of the family perpetuates social differentiations in terms of class and cultural pluralism.

GRATIFICATION OF EMOTIONAL NEEDS

The exchange of a certain degree of love, affection, and companionship among members is essential for the family to remain as a stable group. Such an exchange may occur between parents and children, wife and husband, and among other kin. The continued absence of an exchange of love and affection may result in emotional maladjustment eventually leading to the disorganization of the family. In our discussion of the function of emotional gratification, we will focus mainly on emotional bonds between parents and children.

Gratification of emotional needs is crucial to the personality development of children. Bettelheim (1967), who studied children receiving inadequate emotional supports from their parents, found that such children try to remove themselves from the real world and often develop schizoid tendencies. They often identify with inanimate objects (like electric appliances or plastic robots), establishing emotion-free patterns of relationships. Says Bettelheim (1967: 25) "It is an extremely debilitating experience if our emotions fail to meet with fitting reply . . . if we consistently and from an early age fail to meet the appropriate response to our expression of emotions, we stop communicating with others and eventually lose interest in the world."

An extreme example of lack of affection and concern for the emotions of children can be seen in the abuse and violence many suffer. Stolk (1972) estimated that at least 4,180 incidents of child-battery occur in Canada per year, and of these cases between 96 and 140 result in death. Many parents who abuse their offspring simply don't care enough for children. Others assume that children are capable of adult responses to their social environment; because of this unrealistic expectation, they may punish the child severely when he misbehaves or makes a mistake.

The role of the mother remains significant in emotional development of the child. One possible reason is the father's absence from the home for long periods of time and to the social distance between father and children which is a result of his authoritarian-disciplinarian image. Another reason may be the child's strong dependence on the mother during its pre-school years. For example, as Garigue (1962) points out, the French-Canadian child tends to develop greater emotional rapport with the mother, and in later years she becomes the focal point of the family of orientation. Some French-Canadian youths in Garigue's study considered the "mother" to be synonymous with the "family".

If the children are to serve as a medium for transmitting family culture, affection and love on the part of the parents can definitely act as a positive force, because such an attachment increases the commitment of children to their family culture and enhances their degree of conformity, at least in their early years. When children are emotionally well integrated into their families at an early age, it becomes difficult for them to withdraw in later years. Furthermore, such a withdrawal becomes all the more difficult if parents continuously support and recognize the status passage of their children to adolescence by recruiting the children into the family decision-making processes. Moreover, the expression of interest by parents in their children's school work and other extracurricular activities tends to enhance the children's commitment to the family values.

There is evidence supporting the conclusion that Canadian parents generally express an interest in the scholastic achievements of their children. In a study of parent-adolescent relationships regarding authority, support, and aspirations among a national sample of Canadian secondary-school students, Breton and MacDonald (1971: 167–68) found that "approximately 75 percent of the boys and girls in both white and blue-collar families are praised for their accomplishments by at least one of their parents. . . . In comparison with English-speaking parents, French-speaking parents are less likely to allow adolescent participation in family decision-making; on the other hand they are more likely to show interest in the school work of their sons and daughters and give praise for their accomplishments." The family can be the nexus of emotional gratification: when a person's emotional needs are met here, his commitment to the family remains intact.

POLITICAL FUNCTION

The political function of the family can be interpreted in relation to four dimensions. First, the family can be seen as a seat of political power and authority. Second, the family can be understood as an influential force in general political processes. Third, the family is the agent of political socialization. And fourth, the family is a political unit and of itself, given its role structure and decision-making power, distributed according to age and sex criteria. A brief discussion of each of these dimensions follows.

The Family as a Seat of Political Power

Among simple social groups with a hunting and trapping economy, a given family or clan (for example, the chief's family of a band among the natives) often embodies political authority and power. Political functions may involve the decision to develop strategies of defence against hostile and invading tribes. Such a family may have the final say in decisions regarding hunting or fishing programs. In more complex economic settings, however, such as those found in urban Canada, the "average" family wields little political authority or power, and its ability to perform political functions is minimal.

The Family as an Organizing Force in Political Action

Some families control an unusual amount of political power and influence. For example, the Kennedy, Taft, and Rockefeller families in the United States have consolidated power among themselves for generations. In Canada, the families Bourassa (Quebec), Meighen (Ontario), Lewis (Ontario), Woodsworth (Manitoba and British Columbia), Roblin (Manitoba), King (Ontario), and Bennett (British Columbia) have been prominent in provincial and federal political life.

Porter's (1965) analysis of social class and power in Canada revealed that a large proportion of the economic élite did not enter politics, choosing rather to exercise influence on political processes in other ways (recent conspicuous exceptions are the Stanfield, [James] Richardson, and Trudeau families). At the same time, Porter's analysis does indicate that 16 per cent (N = 157) of the political élite come from families in which previous generations had occupied élite roles in various other institutional systems. In some cases families demonstrate a political heritage in that they are able to pass on their élite status to members of their succeeding generations. Observes Porter (1965: 394), "In fact there is the beginnings, at least, of a political class in that one quarter of the entire elite came from families in which some member of an earlier generation had occupied roles, though not all of these roles were at the level of the elite. Considered separately, the French members of the elite had a higher proportion with inherited political status: two fifths of them came from political families." At least some families in Canada transmit political culture in terms of leadership, attitudes, and values to their succeeding generation.

Political Socialization

Political attitudes and values, like other attitudes and values, are learned and related learning generally begins early in life in the context of the family. That is, political socialization is part of general socialization and should be understood as the way in which the family transmits its political culture to its offspring (Langton, 1969; see also a brief discussion of this point in Ogmundson's chapter on power and politics in Canada). In later years, various secondary socializing agencies often inculcate values different from those which children earlier learned. Yet it is generally true that the values and attitudes learned initially continue over time despite the numerous modifications necessitated by secondary socializing agencies.

In Canada, Zurick (1971) has studied political socialization within the family context. His sample included children drawn from primary schools on the outskirts of Vancouver, British Columbia. The object was to study children's attitudes toward the national political community, to assess their reaction to various public authority figures, and to examine the variations between parental and children's political attitudes. His evidence shows that the home environment acts as a reinforcing element in fostering a favourable image of politics among the offspring. A sense of national identification and awareness and a sense of integrated political community were felt by children as young as eight years of age. Furthermore, there were no significant differences between parent's and children's attitudes toward and conceptions of national, regional, and local political realities. Whether or not such children will maintain such attitudes when they grow up can be assessed only after a longitudinal study. In brief, however, Zurick's study illustrates the political socialization function of the family.

The Family as a Decision-Making Unit

Either on an everyday or on a long-range basis, the family makes decisions which affects each of its members. Such decisions may range from what to cook for dinner to what kind of car should be bought. The decision-making, though often appearing superficially simple, involves a complex set of factors. Traditionally, it was assumed that the husband/father, by virtue of his instrumental leadership, made all critical decisions. Although he sought input from his wife and grown-up children, he alone assumed the final responsibility. Thus in the context of decision-making the husband/father roles are endowed with more power and authority than the wife/mother roles.

Although Canadian data on the distribution of power and authority are sparse and in some cases dated, what little are available do support the above description. For example, Garigue's (1962) and Ishwaran's (1971) analyses of French-Canadian and Dutch-Canadian families, respectively, illustrate the presence of a hierarchy in which the eldest male tends to occupy the apex. Even though in practice the decision-making power and authority are diffused and democratic, the male assumes symbolically and ritualistically an authoritarian role. Even in a more egalitarian family system, such as the one prevalent in Toronto's Crestwood Heights, the husband enjoys a "superior" position in some economic activities (Seely *et al.*).

Recent indicators tend to suggest that the process of decision-making is becoming increasingly democratic because of the changes in the redistribution of power and authority between the husband and wife. For example, in relation to studies conducted in the United States, Blood Wolfe (1960, 1963) and Heer (1963) have shown that the basis for the distribution of power within the family is the comparative contribution of resources by the husband and the wife. The distribution of power and authority occurs in relation to economic contributions, significance of the roles played outside their marriage and family, and each other's personal skills and appearance. This is contrary to the notion of instrumental and expressive leadership where institutionalized power is not based on husband's and wife's resources but on normative expectations. Canadian data supporting such a position are not yet available. But on the basis of other evidence, such as the increasing role of women in the labour force, it may be inferred that certain changes are occurring in the decision-making process within the family.

EDUCATIONAL FUNCTION

The concept of education has divergent meanings and definitions. In this section, it is used in a narrow sense. Education is a process of socialization by means of which an individual is introduced to a body of knowledge and skills relevant to an occupation. Such an introduction starts very early in life and continues for a decade or two, depending on the nature of the occupation for which the individual is trained. The family's role in this endeavour is contingent upon its culture, its social identity and the economic resources available to it, as well as the nature and complexity of the knowledge and skills sought. We shall consider the role of families situated in different phases of economy in Canada.

Families located in isolated areas of northern Canada undertake the responsibility of training children in hunting and trapping skills. Children start learning about hunting and trapping through their play activities, and are gradually recruited by parents and other kin into expedition teams. Through their continuing association with elders, individuals learn the music, art, and folklore of their clan or band. In turn, they pass this on to their children. Often there is no formal schooling among extremely isolated groups.

For families situated in the agricultural setting, a dichotomous educational process occurs. The education provided among farming and ranching families and that provided among the Hutterite colonies of midwestern

Canada are examples. Although formal statutory education on a universal basis is often simultaneously sought, the familial expectation often is that fathers will train their sons in ranching and farming skills while mothers will pass on culinary and child-rearing skills to their daughters. Among the Hutterites, instead of the mother and the father independently passing on sex-bound occupational and cultural skills, the entire commune assumes the responsibility.

The educational function of the family is much more complex in advanced phases of economic development; for occupational specialization is relatively complex. Over 85 per cent of the families in Canada are involved in the advanced economic pursuits. The family does not formally educate children in the same way as the Eskimo family does. Its contribution toward the educational development of the children is important, however, since the family provides a milieu in which levels of academic and occupational aspirations are developed. The family also provides the economic resources and direction necessary for children to accomplish their educational and occupational aspirations.

The ability of the family to provide monetary and intellectual resources is derived from its status within the system of ethnic and occupational stratification. In relative terms, upper- and middle-class families obviously are endowed with more of these resources than are lower-class families. Such an imbalance prevents lower-class individuals from acquiring educational qualifications required for élite occupational positions. Thus, education and prestigious jobs become the prerogatives of the privileged class. (For a more detailed discussion on this point, see the chapter on social stratification.) To offset such imbalances, the Canadian educational system is moving from an élitist to a liberal and open educational philosophy. This means that educational opportunities are becoming increasingly available to all Canadians, regardless of their family status. Yet a number of sociological studies (for example, Hall and McFarland, 1962; Pike, 1970; Crysdale, 1971) have demonstrated beyond a doubt that the educational opportunities available for contemporary Canadians are still, in many ways, determined by the socio-economic status of their families.

In conclusion (and this has been shown in detail in the chapters on social stratification, education, and ethnic relations), the family's ability to perform effectively the task of educating its children for prestigious occupations depends upon its socio-economic status. At present, at least, the family remains a custodian of social differentials.

SUMMARY

Our discussion of the major functions of the family in Canada was within the context of the concept of orderly replacement of the family culture. The main implication of our discussion was that these functions encourage not only social stability but also social differentiation consistent with the ideology of pluralism. Changes leading toward more personal freedom in courtship and marriage decisions are appearing, but no patterns can yet be delineated. These changes will be discussed later. First, however, a brief analysis of kinship structure in Canada would be useful.

Kinship Structure

Our definition of family culture involved values and norms related to kinship identity and obligation, and rules of residence. Kinship identity is important because it is an indicator of a person's membership in a kinship group. A person at any given time can be a member either of father's kinship (patrilineal), of mother's kinship (matrilineal), or of the kinship groups of both parents (bilateral). Expectations are that a person should have membership in one or another of these groups in order to be defined as legitimate. Besides, privileges are often conferred on a person in relation to whether or not he has legitimate membership—for example, rights pertaining to the inheritance of wealth and succession to titles, other symbolic assets, such as the family name; and other hereditary honorific positions. The principle by which a person traces his membership is known as descent.

Rules of residence refer to the ways in which residential arrangements are followed by newly married couples. Three alternatives are found: the couple can live with the groom's parents (patrilocal residence), with the bride's parents (matrilocal), or it can establish its own new home (neo-local). From the point of view of the couple, residential norms in many ways define the nature of their marriage relationships.

The nature of any grouping's kinship structure (understood here in terms of descent and residence) is directly related to the phases of economic development. In simple hunting and fishing societies, kinship is a localized system: all relatives are situated in a specific geographic territory and a close interaction and participation in socio-economic activities is possible. A unilineal (either matrilineal or patrilineal) descent and unilocal residence is practical.

In an agricultural setting, similar practices may prevail, but agricultural communities are more exposed to the provincial and federal marriage and family laws which support bilateral and neolocal kinship practices. For example, among Hutterites, the newly married couple will move into their own private quarters although these quarters are an extension of the groom's parents' home. Similarly, among the ranchers and the farmers, the newly married couple will, in many cases, establish a separate residence on the farm or ranch. Therefore, these situations cannot be called patrilocal residence despite the residential propinquity.

In urban Canada, the kinship structure remains bilateral and neolocal in character. The legal stipulations and economic conditions do not encourage other patterns. Besides, few married adults desire to live with their parents, although they tend to retain their affection toward them.

The nature of a society's kinship structure has implications for the orderly replacement of family culture. A social group which conforms to unilineal descent and unilocal residence can better facilitate an orderly replacement of the family culture than the social group which follows bilateral descent and neolocal residence. In the former residence, the new couple spends its life under the direct supervision of parents and is often forced to conform to family culture. On the other hand, in a situation where bilateral descent and neolocal residence occur, the couple do not have as direct a supervision and kinship norms are less intricately defined.

A neolocal-residence situation allows a greater degree of personal freedom to experiment with new life-styles and the following of new marital and family practices. Farber (1964) hypothesizes that while the orderly replacement of the family culture is most likely to occur in those kinship orders which have unilineality and unilocality, universal permanent availability is most likely to occur in kinship systems which are bilateral and neolocal in character. Since a large proportion of Canadian society follows bilateralism and neolocalism, we can identify a greater degree of freedom in courtship and marital processes than would otherwise be possible. This point will be elaborated in the next section.

Another dimension of kinship structure involves interaction among relatives. In hunting and fishing settlements of the Canadian North or on Indian reservations, most important relatives live in close proximity, although they maintain separate households encompassing specific nuclear families. Residential propinquity in such settings usually necessitates interaction and mutual help on a regular basis. In the more complex urban setting, however, all close kin are not likely to live in the same town or city because of the mobility necessitated by educational and occupational pursuits and the emphasis on establishing neolocal residences away from kin. This emerging situation has led some sociologists (for instance, Parsons, 1942, 1955) to develop the hypothesis that in modern industrial societies the nuclear family tends to be "structurally isolated"—an isolation reinforced in the tendency among newly married couples to move away from parental families, to maintain restricted relations, and to be increasingly independent.

In Canada, we do not yet have enough data to allow for general observations, and some of the available data are contradictory in nature. For example, in their study of life in a Toronto suburb called Crestwood Heights, Seeley *et al.* (1956: 160) report,

The family unit is not embedded in any kind of kinship system. The newly formed family is frequently isolated geographically and often socially from the parental families. . . . In a period of social change, parents and children may no longer share attitudes and beliefs. *The isolation of each family acts to decrease the ability of the family to transmit traditional patterns of behavior, which might otherwise be absorbed from close contact* with, for instance, grandparents [our italics].

Thus, in Crestwood Heights, structural isolation of the nuclear family restricts an orderly replacement of family culture.

Data from other relevant studies contradict what Seeley *et al.* found in Crestwood Heights. For example, Garigue (1956) and Piddington (1971), in their studies of kinship structure among the French Canadians in Montreal and the residents of St. Jean Baptiste (a township forty miles away from Winnipeg), and Pineo (1971), in his study of kinship among lower-class groups in Hamilton, point out that the structural-isolation hypothesis is inapplicable in these particular settings. They found that in these communities family life is very much enmeshed in wider kinship structures. Despite physical isolation, emotional linkages still develop, and modified kinship relationships are represented in the emergence of a pattern of obligations which encourage the maintenance of kinship solidarity. Letters, long-distance telephone calls, visits, and the giving of mutual aid in terms of money, gifts, or personal services when needed (for example, during childbirth and illness) all contribute to this maintenance.

In essence, in Canada, bilateral descent and neolocal residence patterns are common. It is impossible to generalize about kinship solidarity and interaction, because of a lack of data. On the one hand, in an extremely industrialized and urban setting such as the Crestwood Heights, an attenuated kinship system is apparent, but on the other hand, in a comparable milieu (Hamilton and Montreal), we find indications of strong kinship solidarity. As Pineo (1971) suggests, the factors involved here are complex and need further exploration.

Nevertheless, at the risk of being simplistic, the evidence, though dated and contradictory in nature, tends to affirm the characteristics envisaged in the distinction between orderly replacement of family culture and universal permanent availability of individuals. In some social groups, like Crestwood Heights, neolocal residence and structural isolation may imply minimum kin interference and restraints on courtship and marital processes. Individuals then enjoy greater freedom with regard to their marriage and family affairs. In others, such as the respondents in Garigue's and Piddington's studies, since kinship is influential enough to compel conformity to the traditional expectations, the degree of personal freedom available is minimal.

Courtship and Marriage

Marriage is a legal union of cross-sex adults, involving rights and obligations pertaining to economic, social, sexual, and psychological matters. It is expected that a normal person enters such a legal union at least once in his/her lifetime—although there are some exceptions to this expectation. Marriage is generally considered to be a phase in one's developmental cycle and is generally thought to precede a family phase. As mentioned above, in the discussion of the reproductive function of the family, not all women bear children. Therefore, marriage does not necessarily ensure the emergence of a family including children.

Marriage plays an important role, both in the continuity of family culture and in the life of an individual. Reproduction and socialization are crucial to the maintenance of family culture, and marriage provides an enduring human social network for the performance of these tasks. It might be argued that nothing prevents an unmarried couple from raising a child. Although this argument is practical, social customs in most, if not all, societies generally stipulate that a child should be born within wedlock to be a legitimate member of society. Therefore, besides the task of reproduction and socialization, marriage accords legitimate social status to children born of the union.

From the point of view of the individuals involved, the functions of marriage are mainly psychological (emotional gratification, love, affection) and sexual. Marriage is a context within which sexual needs are expressed and met regularly. The sexual regulation function of contemporary marriage is more important today than ever before, since contemporary social norms about premarital sex are rather permissive. The implicit purpose beneath such a permissive attitude may be that premarital experimentation with sex may enhance later marital compatibility and stability. Premarital permissiveness should help persons find mates who not only meet various other social criteria but also meet sexual needs. Once a marriage is legalized, the couple are expected to maintain mutual conjugal fidelity. Thus, marriage becomes an effective element in the regulation of the sexual behaviour of the couple: any violation of conjugal fidelity could dissolve the marriage.

The following discussion raises the hypothesis that marriage in Canada is a process characterized by conformity to both stability and change. While general trends still seem to conform to the maintenance of family stability, certain specific indications suggest changes. Such changes are conspicuous in the courtship process, which is becoming more and more person-centred, pleasure-oriented, and permissive. Also important are considerations of an increased proportion of mixed marriages, increasing divorce and remarriage rates, and experiments with alternate marriage and family patterns. Such manifestations are directed toward universal permanent availability patterns.

DEMOGRAPHIC PROFILES OF MARRIAGE

Marriage Rate

Marriage rate is calculated on the basis of number of marriages contracted each year per thousand population. Marriage rates for selected years are presented in Table 3. As Elkin (1964: 25), Kalbach and McVey (1971: 265–66), and Wakil (1971: 319–20) have observed, the fluctuation in marriage rates between 1921 and 1951 was due to economic conditions and the Second World War. For example, during the 1930s, the marriage rate and the birth rate reached their lowest ebb. But during the postwar years, the marriage rate reached an all-time peak of 10.9. The 1960s witnessed a declining rate roughly comparable to the rate during the pre-Depression years.

Table 3 Marriage rates per 1000 population in Canada for selected years.

Year	1921	1929	1932	1942	1944	1946	1951	1961	1966	1971	1972	1973
Rate	7.9	7.7	5.9	10.9	8.5	10.9	9.2	7.0	7.8	8.9	9.1	8.8

Source: *Canada Year Book*, 1972.
News releases by Statistics Canada.

The data for the years 1971, 1972, and 1973 suggest a slight increase in marriage rates. One of the attributed reasons for the increase is that the postwar baby-boom has now come of age. Between 1966 and 1971 there was an increase of 1.5 per cent in the total married population in Canada. Census data showed that in the year 1966 the population of Canada was 20,014,880, of which 8,723,217 (or 43.6 per cent) was made up of married persons. But in 1971 the population rose to 21,568,310 of which 9,777,605 (or 45.3 per cent) were married persons. Considering the youth movements of the 1960s and the search for alternate marriage and family patterns, illustrated by conspicuous "living together arrangements" and communal and group marriages, one might have expected a decline in the marriage rate. But the evidence is to the contrary. Marriage seems to be more popular now than ever, with the exception of the war years.

Age at Marriage

Over the last fifty years, there has been a clear decrease and convergence in the ages of marriage. A comparison of data for 1921 and 1970 reveals a decrease of 6.2 years for the average age of bridegrooms at marriage, and a decrease of 2.9 years for brides. The 1970 data suggest an upward revision although there is a decline in the age differential between ages at marriage for bridegrooms and brides. In a study of a sample of University of Saskatchewan students, Wakil (1971: 321) found that there is a correspondence between the age differential desired by the students and the actual age differential as indicated by census data.

How do we interpret the statistics presented in Table 4? We offer the following discussion as a hypothesis to be verified by actual field investigations. First, the courtship process starts very early nowadays. Although few would consider high-school dating to be the beginning of the serious mate-selection process, we consider it to be so because individuals at this time develop their skills in heterosexual relations. With an earlier start, individuals are also likely to make decisions to marry earlier. Nevertheless, it should be realized that the duration of "playing the field" and/or the "filtering process" lasts as long as, if not longer, than it did a generation ago.

Second, in the past, marriage generally occurred after an individual achieved his educational and occupational goals, and the educational and occupational spheres of life were relatively isolated from the courtship process. In modern days, the courtship and educational processes seem

Table 4   Average age and age differentials of first marriage for bridegrooms and brides in Canada for selected years.

Year	Bridegrooms	Bride	Average age differential
1921	29.9	25.5	4.4
1931	29.2	24.9	4.3
1940	27.7	24.4	3.3
1950	26.6	23.8	2.9
1960	25.8	23.0	2.8
1965	25.3	22.6	2.7
1970	23.7	20.8	2.9
1971	24.9	22.6	2.3
1972	24.8	22.6	2.2

Source: Vital Statistics *Annual Reports*, 1941.
DBS *Occasional Report, Nuptuality 1950–1964*, Catalogue 84-523.
Vital Statistics, *Preliminary Annual Report*, 1971, 1972.

to be very much intertwined, thus increasingly providing individuals with earlier opportunities to start their mate-selection procedures.

Third, evidence related to the United States shows that earlier marriages also represent a greater probability of divorce. In the absence of sufficient data in this respect, one tends to assume that this conclusion is also applicable for Canada; from the perspective of permanent availability, however, early marriages are not dysfunctional. Considering the stability of marriage as an institution in the context of changing life expectancy, a male born in 1931 had a life expectancy of sixty years, and, according to the average age at marriage of his cohorts, he then married when he was around the age of twenty-five (or in 1956). He then had nearly thirty-five years of married life, according to average life expectancy. A male born twenty years later, in 1951, had a life expectancy of sixty-seven years and was likely to marry at an earlier age, twenty-three, for instance. He then would have the expectation of nearly forty-four years of married life—an increase of eight years. A decreasing age at marriage and an increasing life expectancy expands the possible duration of the marital union. Such a duration is expected to increase by about five years in the coming decades, provided the current trends related to age at marriage and life expectancy remain stable.

Generally, considering the coverage of demographic trends in the mass media, individuals who now marry young are well aware of the expanding potential duration of their marital union. But nowadays, a potential relief is derived from the notion that one need not stay married to the same person for the entire period. Liberal divorce laws and acceptance of divorce both as a corrective measure for errors committed in judgment during courtship and also as a solution for marital disharmony have enabled some couples to follow the path of serial monogamy. Therefore, early marriage may not be viewed as dysfunctional.

An analysis of the data presented in Table 4 suggests that the age differential is declining over the years, although even in 1971 the groom tended to be more than two years older than the bride. Traditionally, such differences have been explained in many ways. First, the male physiologically matures slower than the female. Second, the male, consistent with the normative expectations that he be the breadwinner, takes a longer time to prepare himself for this role (Eshleman, 1974: 288). Third, older age contributes to the maintenance of authority within the matrimonial contexts. The greater the age of the husband, the greater will be the potential to exercise authority over his wife. The increasing "age-homogamy" (Eshleman, 1974: 288) suggests that modern marriages are gradually moving toward a more open, democratic, and egalitarian framework. A large proportion of women now work before marriage and the remaining have the skills to be employed if they so wish after marriage. Therefore, the male can no longer be viewed as the sole breadwinner. The implication is that both partners often possess enough economic skills to maintain economic independence within marriage. Furthermore, consistent with the permanent availability notion, each one now often attempts to maintain personal skills on an equal basis, and, therefore, age at marriage has little influence on the authoritarian structure of the marrige. Marriage in such a context becomes not a venerated institution but a voluntary association, lasting as long as the couple maintains a mutually acceptable level of commitment. Because the partners are always potential candidates in a marriage-market situation, they can withdraw their commitment to each other if and when they find a person more suitable as a mate than the one to whom they are currently married. Therefore, the declining age at marriage can be considered as an indication of the increasing egalitarian orientation implied in the permanent availability model.

FACTORS IN MATE SELECTION

It is widely assumed that the courtship process in Canada and in other Western societies is based on personal choice and mutual romantic love. This assumption is further reinforced by the dating process among teenagers who apparently have freedom to choose their dating partners, hoping that they will be able similarly to select their spouses eventually. It is true that in Canada, unlike in most non-Western societies, marriage is a personal, not a family, matter, and individuals are responsible for their choices. Dating is a socially acceptable and approved practice in which two persons of the opposite sex come together with an expectation of scrutinizing each other's eligibility to be partners. Romantic love is considered an important factor in not only bringing together two relative strangers but leading them to make a decision about getting married (Goode, 1959; Greenfield, 1965).

Research in the United States, however, has established that the court-ship process is not as open as it is commonly believed. It has been shown that besides romantic love, other factors such as socio-economic status, ethnicity, race, religion, and residential propinquity also play a decisive role. There are some Canadian studies which suggest that the same factors influence the choice of marital partner. In the following discussion, two of these factors—endogamy and premarital sex—will be discussed.

Endogamy

Earlier we observed that the marital process in Canada includes trends supporting stability (in terms of orderly replacement) and change (toward permanent availability). Of the many ways by which stability can be accomplished two may be considered here: (1) careful socialization, and (2) endogamy. In socialization, essential cultural elements are internal-ized so that they become part of one's personality. In turn, endogamy (defined as the custom requiring marriage within one's own social group) can reinforce stability, since both spouses often hold similar values and norms with reference to family culture.

Intermarriages can introduce disorder, because the husband and wife are not as likely to have similar backgrounds, and therefore may find it more difficult to try to maintain a particular kind of family culture. The socialization of children magnifies the problem. Whose cultural values should be transmitted? Mother's? Father's? Often, given the question, children are socialized into more cosmopolitan and secular values, rather than into any of those related to a particular orientation.

Table 5 Percentages of inter-religious marriages for major religious groups for selected years.

Religious Groups	*Years*			
	1961	*1965*	*1966*	*1968*
Total intermarriages for Canada	29	30	33	35.3
Jews	8	10	9	14.0
Catholics	12	13	15	17.0
United Church	39	41	45	47.0

Source: *Canada Year Book*, 1972.

We suggest that endogamy should be viewed as an indication of stability and structural differentiation, while intermarriage should be interpreted as moves toward individual freedom and secularism in marital choice.

Table 5 presents the percentages of intermarriages in three major religious groups at four points in time in the 1960s. The data suggest that there is a continuing decline in the amount of religious endogamy among the Jewish, Catholic, and United Church groups, especially in the United Church. In Table 6, we have presented data on the percentages of intermarriages for major religious groups in Canada for a three-year period (1959–61). The Jewish, Roman Catholic, and Mennonite groups demonstrate a higher degree of endogamy than the rest.

Latowsky (1971: 100–101), who carried out a study of Toronto Jewish

Table 6   Average percentage of brides having same religious affiliation as grooms, Canada, 1959–61.

Denomination of Groom	Number of Marriages	Per Cent of Brides
Jewish	1,533	89.0
Roman Catholic	60,564	88.2
Mennonite	1,149	75.9
Greek Orthodox	2,607	63.8
United Church	23,996	61.6
Adventist	171	59.6
Pentecostal	1,102	58.5
Mormon	342	53.5
Greek Catholic	1,549	50.8
Anglican	14,851	49.6
Salvation Army	578	47.8
Baptist	4,533	45.8
Evangelical United Brethren	207	44.9
Lutheran	5,590	44.5
Churches of Christ, Disciples	155	41.3
Presbyterian	4,843	36.7
Christian Science	74	28.4

Source: Dominion Bureau of Statistics, *1961 Census of Canada*, Bulletin, 7:1–11 (Ottawa, The Queen's Printer, 1965), Table XII, cited in W. E. Kalbach and W. M. McVey (1971:190).

families, points out that "Jewish intermarriages tend to occur in higher
frequencies in smaller Jewish communities with 10 to 20 families. More
concentrated communities of over 100 families with well developed
Jewish institutional facilities have a lesser number of intermarriages." In
an analysis of inter-religious marriages in Protestant, Catholic, and
Jewish groups, Heer (1962: 245–50) found an increase in the proportion
of intermarriage. In 1927 the percentage for Canada as a whole was 5.5;
by 1957 the proportion had doubled. Heer observes (1962: 247), "The
trend toward increased proportion of persons marrying outside their own
faith is thus seen to be quite general in Canada, extending in varying
degrees to all provinces and to all groups." (For a discussion of attitudes
toward interreligious marriages, see the Hiller's chapter on the sociology
of religion.)

Ethnicity is also an important criterion associated with endogamy.
Persons belonging to the same ethnic origin tend to marry each other; this

Table 7 Percentage of family heads with wives of same ethnic origin for
selected origins of total and native-born family heads, Canada: 1961,
and 1971.

Ethnic Origin of Family Head	Total Family Heads		Native-born Family Heads	
	1961	1971	1961	1971
British Isles	81.2	80.9	79.9	79.7
French	88.3	86.2	88.6	86.5
German	52.0	49.2	37.9	38.3
Netherlands	54.9	52.5	29.5	26.9
Scandinavian	31.2	26.9	18.0	19.1
Hungarian	62.8	53.3	22.8	25.8
Polish	49.0	43.2	25.5	24.1
Russian	47.7	43.1	44.7	41.0
Ukrainian	61.8	54.0	50.5	45.0
Italian	76.6	76.5	27.2	30.1
Jewish	91.1	91.2	87.5	89.8
Asiatic	79.9	80.5	67.7	63.8
Total[a]	77.7	76.4	76.9	75.6

[a] Total for the twelve combined groups only.
Source: Statistics Canada special census tabulations.

tendency is indicated in the data presented in Table 7. The native and the Jewish groups tend to rank high while the Scandinavian and the Russian groups tend to rank low.

Peter D. Chimbos (1971) studied the attitudes of a sample of Dutch, Greek, and Slovaks in an Ontario city toward inter-ethnic and inter-religious marriages for their children. The Dutch responses were more favourable than the Greek and the Slovak. The strongest objection came from the Greeks. Their main objection was their desire to maintain immigrant culture and religion. The Dutch appear to be moving along the acculturation path in the Anglo-Saxon direction. While they were willing to accept inter-ethnic alliances, they seem to be closed as far as inter-religious marriages are concerned. Ishwaran (1971: 307), in his study of a Dutch-Canadian community, found that 78 per cent of those interviewed objected to marrying outside their church. The reasons given for this centred around potential incompatibility, socialization difficulties, and the disruption of the Christian way of life.

In sum, our discussion of endogamy suggests that it is still the modal form for mate-selection in Canada. Nevertheless, attitudinal and behavioural changes strongly suggest a drift toward a more open system of mate selection where individuals transcend the limits of ethnicity and religion. This inference is more applicable to some religious and ethnic groups than others (see Tables 6 and 7). The universe from which mates are chosen is likely to become increasingly open, cosmopolitan, and secular in future years.

Premarital Sex

Consistent with the Judeo-Christian heritage, our marital values still reflect an emphasis on premarital chastity. But the publication in 1948 of Kinsey's report on human sexual behaviour brought home the fact that the practice of premarital chastity is not nearly universal. Kinsey also found that the traditional male double standard in sexual behaviour and attitudes continued to flourish. In the decade following Kinsey's study several cross-sectional and longitudinal studies have been conducted, most of which have affirmed Kinsey's findings. The recent study by Reiss (1967), in the United States, has been the most definitive work on the subject.

The studies conducted in the 1960s allow us to compare the proportion of individuals who had premarital sexual experience in the 1940s (Kinsey's study) and in the 1960s (for example, studies by R. Bell, 1966; Reiss, 1967). The general conclusion is that there has been little, if any, increase in the proportion of persons having premarital intercourse since the Kinsey study in 1948: at both times, over 50 per cent of the women and over 75 per cent of the men in the United States had had coitus at least once before marriage.

Studies of premarital sexual behaviour in Canada have been carried out by Mann (1970), Packard (1968), Hobart (1972), Perlman (1972), and Ramu (1972). Most of these studies analysed the sexual behaviour of university students. While these studies cover a broad range of sexual attitudes and behaviour, we will present in Table 8 only the findings related to one aspect of the premarital sexual behaviour: coitus.

The studies of premarital sexual behaviour in Canada and the United States allow us to infer that sex is becoming independent from the traditional courtship path leading to marriage. Not too long ago, sexual relationships between engaged couples were often viewed as normal. Now it appears that marriage plans are no longer as important. Instead, it seems that what determines whether a couple has sexual intercourse or not is the emotional attachment between them at the time. Such an attachment need not be enduring. This situation has been conceptualized as "permissiveness with affection" (Reiss, 1967) or "situation ethics" (Kirkendal, 1961).

In sum, while family mores in Canada still adhere to the ideal of premarital chastity, in practice Canadian youth seem to be moving in the opposite direction. Although sexual freedom is not as widely prevalent as the media would have us believe, there is an undeniable decline in family control over the sexual behaviour of its unmarried members. Conversely, individuals now enjoy a greater freedom in matters of ego-gratification, and marriage is increasingly viewed as a means of personal gratification rather than as an institutional requirement. Individuals now seem more concerned about entering an alliance with a person who serves his or her needs best rather than conforming to the ideal of premarital chastity. The "permissiveness with affection" approach to sex and the practice of exogamy permit a search for such a person.

Table 8 The incidence of premarital coitus among samples of Canadian post-secondary level students.

Researcher	Year in which the study was conducted	Sample Area	Nature of the Sample	Male		Female	
				N	%	N	%
W. E. Mann[a]	1965–69	York University	Random	93	50.0	60	36.0
W. E. Mann	1965–69	Western Ontario	Random	80	35.0	40	15.0
V. Packard	1966	"Eastern University"[b]	Non-Random	88	56.8	85	35.2
C. Hobart	1968	University of Montreal and Trade School in Montreal	Random	194	63.0	177	30.0
C. Hobart	1968	University of Alberta and Trade School in Alberta	Random	336	56.0	363	44.0
D. Perlman	1970	University of Manitoba	Non-Random	69	54.0	87	30.0
G. N. Ramu	1973	University of Manitoba	Random	116	71.6	57	56.1

[a] The reference may be found at the end of the book.
[b] The name of the University has been kept anonymous.

DIVORCE

The Christian tradition upholds the view that marriage is a permanent bond. Marital expectations concerning the duration of marriage are derived from this premise and violations are defined negatively. Divorce —the major form of marital dissolution—is viewed in terms of the personal miseries and the deprivations that the children (if any) and couple undergo. Implicitly, divorce is seen as an obstacle to the orderly replacement of family culture. Consequently, Canadian society, like many other industrial societies, has developed measures to prevent divorces.

One of the measures used in the past was the maintenance of conservative divorce laws. Legally, marriage was seen as a contract between the spouses, involving conjugal rights and obligations. A divorce could be granted only upon proof of the violation of such rights and obligations. Thus, the divorce process tended to become an adversary situation in which one spouse tried to establish the fault of the other. Laws established the kinds of faults which served as grounds for divorce, and these included adultery (violation of monogamy and conjugal fidelity norms) and such offences as rape, sodomy, and bestiality. Strict enforcement of the laws encouraged the use of devious means to secure divorce, such as the staging of a simulated act of adultery. Also, many marriages remained "empty-shell", meaning they "appeared" to be normal marriages but actually involved little interaction of any kind.

In Canada, in the 1960s, an increasing number of people started questioning the appropriateness of the divorce laws which stipulated that *fault*, in terms of violation of the conjugal rights at least on the part of one spouse, must be established before a final dissolution of the marriage would be granted. It was clear that such a rule encouraged deceptions such as mocked-up evidence. Also, there emerged a consensus that, despite the need to maintain marital stability, "empty-shell" marriages served no useful purpose to the couple involved or to their children. Furthermore, divorce came to be seen as a means of correcting the errors in judgment committed during the courtship process. After a long public debate, and an examination of a report prepared by a special joint committee of the Senate and the House of Commons (1967), new divorce laws were introduced in 1968. Without excluding such marital offences as adultery and sodomy, they established a new criterion for the dissolution of a marriage—"marital breakdown". If a couple could establish that their marriage was not working, they could now get a divorce. One method was to go through a three-year separation.

We can understand the changes occurring in this aspect of marriage in Canada by examining two sets of data: the absolute numbers of divorces granted every year or the statistics demographers call the divorce rate. The divorce rate in Canada is understood as the number of marriages legally dissolved each year per 100,000 population. Although, as shown in Table 9, the Canadian divorce rate has been the lowest among the Western industrial societies, there has been a steady increase in the number and rate of divorce. The increase seems to be higher after the 1968 reform of the divorce laws: it is generally assumed that the introduction of new divorce laws has enabled many couples whose marriages were "empty-shell" to seek divorce under the new provisions.

Using current divorce rates demographers have attempted to predict the probability rate of divorce in Canada. The probability rate refers to the proportion of marriages contracted annually which is likely to be dissolved eventually. It is calculated by

relating the divorces of a given year to the cohorts of marriage from which they originated. This permits calculation, for a given year, of the proportion

Table 9   Number of divorces and divorce rate for selected years.

Number of Divorces		Divorce Rate per 100,000	
Year	Number	Year	Rate
1921–25	About 500		
1931–35	About 1,000	1941	21.4
1941	About 2,500	1947	64.0
1951	5,270	1951	37.6
1962	6,270	1961	36.0
1968	11,343	1968	54.8
1969	26,093	1969	124.2
1970	29,775	1970	139.8
1971	29,626	1971	137.4

Source: Vital Statistics, *Preliminary Annual Reports*, 1972.
Canada Year Book, 1973.

of marriages which would eventually end in divorce if the conditions existing during that year were to remain constant indefinitely. . . . About one marriage in 100 would have been dissolved by divorce if the conditions of 1921 had remained constant. This probability rose to between 1 and 2 in 1931, to between 3 and 4 in 1941 and 5 in 1951, staying at that level until 1962. The advance since that time has been sharp and figures for 1968 indicate a divorce probability of about 8 per 100 marriages or about one marriage in 12 that will eventually end in divorce. This last increase is probably related to the high proportion of early marriages during the postwar period. In other words, the probability of divorce would in all likelihood have been lower in 1968 had the average age at that time of marriage not gone down during that period. . . . On the basis of the number of the divorce decrees handed down, the probability rate of divorce in 1968 would be 20%, and that of 1971, 23% or nearly one marriage in four that would eventually be dissolved by divorce. These figures very likely over estimate the long-term trend since a disproportionate number of divorces granted to couples married for more than 20 or even 30 years and who were probably unable to obtain a divorce under previously existing legislation (*Canada Year Book*, 1973: 202).

Such a statistical prediction can be interpreted in at least two ways. First, from the point of view of orderly replacement of the family culture, increasing divorce rates suggest a disorganization of marital and family stability. And this trend inhibits a stable maintenance of family culture. Second, divorce is a direct function of conformity to the values inherent in permanent availiability notion: marriage is viewed as a personal matter with minimum social constraints. Individuals dissolve their present marriages when these do not serve their personal pleasures. Thus, marriage and divorce are directly related to personal happiness and welfare, rather than social expectations in terms of stability of culture.

In brief, rates of divorce are indicative of changes in marital values. If, in a marriage, one's personal welfare and emotional needs are not met, divorce becomes a means to withdraw from such a union. In this context, marriage ceases to be a sacred bond and remains a source of personal pleasure.

The foregoing interpretations remain hypothetical till we have more sociological data on factors associated with divorce in Canada. Currently there is some information on the grounds on which divorces are decreed by federal courts. There seems to be a modification in the grounds on which divorce is sought. Before 1968 it was common for individuals to seek divorce on the grounds of adultery. Only in exceptional cases did they use other grounds such as insanity or incurable disease. After 1968 new legislation permitted sixteen justifiable grounds, including a three-year separation. Data on the grounds on which divorces were decreed after the new legislation, however, show that adultery still remains one of the major grounds on which divorce is petitioned. Table 10 provides data for a three-year period. The petitioner can cite many grounds and the listing here refers to the most frequently cited grounds. "Most frequently stated grounds in a descending order are: separation, adultery and desertion. . . . The relative frequency of grounds for divorce varies with the petitioner. Adultery or separation are listed more frequently when the husband is the petitioner. On the other hand, women more frequently petition for divorce on grounds of cruelty or alcoholism" (*Canada Year Book*, 1973: 202–3).

A significant proportion of divorced persons remarry (Schlesinger, 1971; Kuzel and Krishnan, 1973). Such a trend tends to confirm the belief that divorce may be functional to marriage if marriage is understood as a voluntary association aimed at meeting the personal needs of the individuals. To the extent that this is true, divorce no longer constitutes a social stigma reducing the chances of remarriage. It should be remembered, however, that despite the increase in divorces, Canada still has one

Table 10   Grounds for divorces granted under the new legislation for years 1969, 1970, and 1971.

Grounds	1969	1970	1971
Number of divorces:	21,964	29,168	29,605
Adultery	28.9	34.3	38.0
Physical cruelty	15.5	16.1	17.2
Mental cruelty	16.4	17.9	19.1
Separation	57.0	51.1	46.7
Desertion	10.9	8.6	6.7
Other grounds	8.1	6.0	5.5
Total	100.0	100.0	100.0

Source: *Canada Year Book*, 1973.

of the lowest rates among the industrial societies. This may mean that marriage, in general, is still a relatively stable union of partners conforming to the values of and norms inherent in their family culture.

RESPONSES TO MARITAL INSTABILITY

An efficient performance of functions by the family depends upon a number of factors, including a stable marital arrangement. An increasing divorce rate is seen as an indicator of marital instability. Therefore, many individuals tend to develop attitudes and behavioural patterns which according to them are aimed at providing for marital stability later. These attitudinal and behavioural responses are numerous, but only three will be dealt with here. First is the emergence of a critical approach to marriage. Second is an extension of the courtship process from "engagement" to a "living together" arrangement, as a trial run for a better marriage in the future. Third is the emergence of "mate-swapping" behaviour as a means of maintaining marital stability. A brief discussion of each of these points follows.

Critical Attitude Toward Marriage

Many contemporary youths are generally disappointed that family culture and its supporting legal norms are so rigid, especially in the context of the liberal and secular changes that are occurring in the wider society. Their disappointment has led them to resort to at least two actions—a more critical analysis of marriage and behaviour contrary to established marital and family norms (group marriage, homosexual unions). In Canada evidence on such topics is available, although much of it is neither systematic nor conclusive.

For example, Whitehurst and Plant (1971) studied the attitudes of samples of Canadian and American students toward marriage. They found that Canadian students were more critical of traditional marriage philosophy and supporting legal norms than were their American counterparts. One of their criticisms was directed mainly at the rigidities of the legal structure, especially in the context of the couple's immaturity and ignorance of marital responsibilities at the time of marriage. The students held that a more liberal law would offset any mistakes in their courtship.

Such a re-evaluation of courtship and marital processes may be seen in terms of their desire to maintain marital stability.

Living Together

An awareness of individual shortcomings in relation to mutual evaluations in courtship led many students in Whitehurst and Plant's study to advocate living together as a final step before a marriage contract was signed. The following quotation exemplifies the attitudes of those who were critical of marriage: "Before marriage, a couple should be able to live together in a type of common law or communal arrangement to see whether or not they really will be able to spend their lives together" (Whitehurst and Plant, 1971: 86).

The data on such arrangements are scarce and what is available tends to be confined to college populations. Robert Whitehurst (n.d.) has summarized the relevant literature in a review article, estimating that over 25 per cent of the student sample from the universities in the United States have had some living-together experience. In Canada, Hobart (1972) found about 5 per cent of a sample drawn at two universities cohabited without marriage. Ramu, in his study of sexual behaviour among a sample of students at the University of Manitoba, found 10 per cent of his 173 respondents living together at the time of the study. Research to date on this aspect (see Whitehurst, n.d.; and Arafat and Yorburg, 1973) suggests that living together does not necessarily serve as the final step toward marriage in many cases. While females often consider such an arrangement a final step toward marriage, males tend to view living together as a matter of personal convenience.

Data regarding the "drop-out" rates for such unions have not yet been determined. Even assuming that more and more "disappointed" persons drop out of living-together unions, we would still hold living together to be functional, for "drop outs" discover their mutual incompatibility before marriage and save themselves from the psychological and financial costs involved in marriage and divorce.

Mate-Swapping

Mate-swapping generally occurs among persons who are married, conform to traditional marital mores, and who, in general, maintain a rather conservative posture toward marriage. In fact, motivations for mate-sharing are often said to be the desire to preserve the institution of marriage, an institution which would otherwise disintegrate in the face of sexual boredom (Bartell, 1970). Mate-swapping is not as common as the popular literature suggests, however (Hunt, 1974).

In Canada, Henshel (1972) studied a group of Toronto wives who participated in mate-swapping activities, and her findings supported earlier research in this respect. She found that most couples in her sample belonged to the middle class and were financially successful in life. The husband persuaded the wife to participate in mate-swapping; the wife was usually reluctant, but eventually went along with the wishes of the husband. The wife generally did not enjoy these activities as much as her husband did, and in most instances, took part despite her unwillingness and lack of enjoyment in the belief that swapping was a way of saving her marriage.

Responses toward divorce, and other aspects of marital instability (which we have not considered here), have resulted in various innovative behaviours. These tend to suggest a growing individualism in the areas of marriage and the family.

Sex Roles and Family Structure

In the earlier discussion of the functions of the family allusion was made to the nature of sex roles and to certain changes that are taking place. In this section, this point will be elaborated. First, we will present a traditional picture as it emerges from the available literature, and relate it to the notion of orderly replacement of family culture. A discussion of the changing participation of women in the labour force will follow. Finally, the impact of changing sex roles on marital and family patterns will be examined.

TRADITIONAL PATTERNS

In discussing the traditional pattern of sex roles we are compelled to make distinctions between the French- and English-Canadian families because each developed in different historical and religious circumstances. Initially, the policies related to the French-Canadian family were developed in France, for example, when there was a shortage of marriageable women, brides were sent from France to ensure the firm establishment of French-Canadian males. Marriage also was made compulsory and motherhood was encouraged; bonuses were offered to those women who bore ten or more children.

When France halted the outmigration of its citizens to Canada, however, the French-Canadian family became independent, but it was directly subjected to the supervision by the Roman Catholic Church. The Church encouraged family solidarity, procreation, sanctions on divorce, and for political reasons, the superiority of French-Canadians over others. Consequent to such religious and political influence, the French-Canadian family, which was predominantly rural and patriarchal, became an insulated group perceiving itself in sharp contrast to the English-Canadian family. In short, the French-Canadian family developed ethnically and culturally as a homogeneous group and its dependence on agriculture and church accentuated its traditional character.

The English and other Canadians lacked such systematic and homogeneous beginnings. The arrival of Loyalists and waves of immigrants and their dispersed settlement contributed to the emergence of multiple family systems in various ethnic enclaves all over Canada. There was a degree of ambivalence as far as their family culture and life-styles were concerned. For example, they were not certain about whether they should give up their old ways; assuming that they were willing to do so, there was no single all-Canadian family pattern which they could follow. As a result, we assume, some sort of compartmentalization might have occurred in relation to their familial and economic activities. While they demonstrated entrepreneurship and adaptability in the economic sphere, they maintained, at least initially, traditional features in marriage and family spheres. (For more on historical development, see Elkin, 1964, and references cited in Tomeh, 1975: 75–78.)

In short, the traditional family pattern in Canada supported a system of roles which encouraged family solidarity and continuity. The family was seen as a means by which a group's cultural heritage was stored and transmitted over generations. Toward this end, the division of labour was developed in terms of sex and age criteria. As discussed earlier, the husband/father and the wife/mother roles became crucial, but nevertheless these two role configurations were ranked in terms of their attributed significance. Thus, the roles played by the male were deemed more significant than the roles played by the females simply because of the economic and biological differences.

Sociological investigations conducted in both French and English Canada support the presence of a traditional sex role pattern during a period as recent as the 1960s. For example, Garigue (1956, 1968) points out that the French-Canadian husband has a superior position in the family; he sees family life as involving the exercise of power over other members of the family. The main authority in decision-making belongs to the husband, even in spheres that are specifically defined as the wife's. In a study of upper-middle-class family life, Seeley *et al.* found that men had superior power and authority in the family life primarily because of their instrumental functions. There was a clear division of functions along the sex lines and those chores performed by men were perceived to be more important than those performed by women.

Crucial to such a belief were the assumed biological and psychological differences between male and female. For example, male was seen as aggressive, competitive, entrepreneurial, and outgoing, characteristics necessary for success in contemporary society. Female, however, was supposed to be shy, withdrawing, and equipped with all the necessary characteristics to fulfil her impending affective functions. Given that through socialization the family shapes a person's attitudes, values, and norms, a rigid sex-role pattern became part of an orderly replacement of family culture in Canada, as it was in most other societies.

Increasing urbanization and industrialization, two world wars, and inflation compelled a gradual entrance of women into the labour force. Although they were not defined as breadwinners, they gradually assumed significant economic roles, thus diminishing the significance of the traditional role patterns. In the next section, some details on the role of women in the labour force will be presented.

WOMEN IN THE LABOUR FORCE

In order for women to participate productively in the labour force, certain educational qualifications are necessary. At the turn of the century, although women attended school, few of them had occupational pursuits in mind. Education gradually became more important for women as a means by which they could enter the labour force. For example, the proportion of female school-age population (five to twenty-four years) attending school increased from 41.4 per cent in 1911 to 64.1 per cent in 1961. The percentage of bachelor degrees earned by women also increased from 18.3 in 1920–21 to 38.1 in 1970–71. In general, however, the percentage of MA and PHD degrees earned by women showed no definite trends (Kubat and Thornton, 1974: 116–24).

An increasing proportion of women are giving up what are traditionally known as female fields (for example, home economics, family studies), preferring to graduate in certain professions considered to be male domains (for example, architecture, law, medicine, dentistry). Of all bachelor's and first professional degrees, 27.4 per cent were awarded to women in 1960–61; by 1970–71 the per cent increased to 38.1. Such a conspicuous accomplishment in the field of education indicates, in the words of Nett (1975), "a new psychological syndrome for women— confidence, self-assurance, and assertiveness."

The consequences of such a psychological syndrome are clearly seen in the accomplishment of women in the occupational sphere. The labour-force membership of women rose from 14 per cent in 1901 to 33.2 per cent in 1972. For example, the female labour force in 1972 showed a percentage increase of 64.3 compared with the 1962 participation level. The bulk of the female labour force is composed of married women, and there has been an increasing trend in this direction. In 1962, 21.6 per cent of all married women in Canada were in the labour force, and in 1972 the percentage rose to 33.9. Married women constituted 56.9 per cent of the female labour force in 1972; in 1962, the percentage was 48.4. Finally, there is also an increase in the number of working mothers: in 1967, almost one-quarter of the female labour force included women with one or more children.

It is quite possible to infer that such a change in the participation of women in the labour force is a result of militant feminism. But Nett (1975) argues that, "even before the [feminist] movement, the proportion of women participating in work outside the home and contributing to family finances had soared." The increasing role of women as co-providers precedes the emergence of the neo-feminism of the late 1960s. For example, the participation rate of married women in the labour force in 1961 was 50 per cent of all married women, and in 1971 it was 57 per cent. "That is, by 1961 . . . in only 44 percent of all families was there a sole income recipient; yet the myth of the husband-father as the bread-winner persisted. By 1971 the figure had fallen to about 37 percent of all families having only one income, yet many still view the husband as the family provider" (Nett, 1975).

It is not our purpose to undermine the liberating role of feminism. Although feminism provided an ideological orientation to the changing status of women, women in Canada were heading toward liberation even before the movement gained ground in the social conscience. Such a fundamental change was mainly due to the economic pressures on the family and also increasing desire on the part of women to work toward their independence and self-fulfilment.

IMPACT ON MARITAL AND FAMILY ROLES

The increasing economic independence of women has contributed to a progressive decline of women's dependent and secondary roles within marriage and family contexts. Once the wife assumes the role of a co-provider, it is a matter of course for the husband to redefine his role and functions consistent with her position. Nett (1975) describes the changing situation as follows:

In this kind of arrangement wives and husbands are considered *equal* in all respects: sexually, emotionally, intellectually, and personally (and eventually legally). The most drastic consequences of this standard for the marriage relationship have been two fold: first, it requires the same degree of commit-ment from both partners, not her 90 percent and his 10 percent or her 50 percent and his 50 percent, but her 100 percent and his 100 percent. Secondly, it requires that both spouses have equal opportuiities to achieve self-actualization both in and out of the marriage relationship, either in the home or out in the so-called real world. . . . The real issues in the new marriage are *commitment* and *self-definition*.

To what extent the Canadian dual-career families conform to Nett's description is unknown. It is quite possible that some working wives may not claim equal partnership and instead prefer to remain as "junior partners". In other cases resistance to a demand for equal partnership by the authoritarian husbands may lead to marital strain and conflict. Nevertheless, the demand for equality based on economic independence will not only blur the distinction between instrumental and expressive roles but also necessitate a redefinition of marriage.

Accordingly, a wife's status will not be that of a dependant (see Eichler, 1973). Her contacts outside home enhance the degree of her permanent availability. Therefore, she is not bound into a marriage for economic and/or biological reasons. A marriage—defined in institutional terms, which normatively binds her to a male in an unequal partnership— will have neither appeal nor significance to the female. Instead, a marriage defined as an association of two partners, who contractually express their commitment to each other becomes more acceptable to her. Such a marriage will be seen as an open arena with unrestricted opportunities for both partners to actualize their full potentials. Yet it is not construed as detrimental to the overall welfare, because genuine interpersonal ties can exist only in the context of sincere commitment and affection. In short, changing sex roles brings about purified but intense marital and family relations.

In essence, the changing sex roles demand a reorganization of the division of labour and distribution of power and responsibilities within the family. As far as women are concerned, participation in activities outside home will provide them with new opportunities in terms of interaction and gaining of personal skills, which, in turn, enhance their permanent availability status.

Conclusions

Our main objective in this chapter was to present the student with a brief review of significant materials on the family and marriage in Canada. In our effort to bring together a divergent body of materials, we used a conceptual framework involving two ideal-type core concepts: the concept of the orderly replacement of family culture and the concept of the permanent availability of individuals. Given the space restrictions and the scarcity of data on various aspects of marriage and the family in Canada, a full application and delineation of these concepts was impossible. Therefore, wherever the data was unavailable, our discussion tended to be hypothetical.

Select Bibliography

ELKIN, FREDERICK. *The Family in Canada.* Ottawa: The Vanier Institute of the Family, 1964.

FARBER, BERNARD. *Family: Organization and Interaction.* San Francisco: Chandler, 1964.

ISHWARAN, K., ed. *The Canadian Family.** Toronto: Holt, Rinehart and Winston, 1971.

LARSON, L. E., ed. *The Canadian Family in Comparative Perspective.*† Toronto: Prentice-Hall, 1975.

SCHLESINGER, B. *Families.* Toronto: McGraw-Hill Ryerson Ltd., 1972.

*Recently this Reader has been revised with many additional chapters.

†This Reader was not available at the time of preparation of this chapter.

The Sociology of Religion
in the Canadian Context

HARRY H. HILLER

One of the earliest concerns of sociologists was the analysis of religious phenomena. It was readily apparent that religion consisted not only of supernatural and supra-empirical entities but of human beings who individually and collectively were responding to what they conceived to be "ultimately significant". Sociologists then could study religion because they focused on the *people* who were religious; and by noting the existence of relationships between beliefs and social behaviour patterns, it became quite clear that religion was sociologically relevant.

Every society has possessed some form of religion and therefore it was inevitable that sociologists would have to become involved in its study and analysis. Religion has usually reflected and contributed to the formulation of basic values, norms, and customs in a society, and has created institutions and roles which have societal significance. Because of this integral social role, the study of religion is in a unique sense an important key to the analysis of a society; for it tells us how men understand their world and their actions in it. Even if a religion does not span an entire society, the fact that it is embraced by only a segment of the population is significant: religions establish their own norms for behaviour which in turn reflect the view of the world of the people involved. It was this type of observation that led all of the early sociological analysts, such as August Comte, Emile Durkheim, Max Weber, and Karl Marx, to construct theories about the role of religion in a society.

Although the sociology of religion *per se* is a developing discipline, the sociology of Canadian religion is still in embryonic form. Our knowledge of religion and society in Canada is largely dependent on the work of historians. Research by sociologists is beginning to increase, however. It is interesting to note that French Canadians have provided most of the leadership, particularly through the Centre de Recherches en Sociologie Religieuse at Laval University.[1]

CAN SOCIOLOGY LEGITIMATELY STUDY RELIGION?

Admittedly, sociology does not have the tools to evaluate the ultimate truth claims of any religion. Whether the Presbyterian or the Buddhist is right is immaterial to the scientific study of religious behaviour. The methodology employed by a sociologist insists that he only analyse that which is empirical and observable. To say that something is not observable does not mean that it does not exist—merely that it is beyond the bounds of sociological analysis. Sociologists thus avoid the metaphysical debate by bracketing the transcendental and by becoming "methodological atheists" (Berger, 1969: 100) for the purpose of their study. Science demands that methodology not be coloured by any theistic stance so that the analysis will be as objective as possible. Thus a sociologist is interested not in making any value judgments about any religion but in observing the differences among the participants of numerous religions. From a scientific perspective, all that can be said is that religious beliefs and practices exist, and because they exist, they tell us something about the nature of that society and in turn have consequences for the society.

Whereas theology is concerned with religious beliefs, sociology is concerned with those who hold religious beliefs (Demerath and Hammond, 1969: 4). It is clear that the starting points of the two disciplines are entirely different: theologies begin with the supra-empirical while sociology begins with man. It could be argued, however, that religion is essentially a personal thing, and, as a result, sociology can make little claim to examine it.

Few people are religious, or for that matter irreligious, in a vacuum. Moreover, few people claim private revelations and then maintain their religion as a private personal activity. The point is that whatever else it is religion is most frequently a social phenomenon; it is a collective activity or a shared pattern of belief and behaviour. It is socially transmitted from

1. Most of the publications of this institute are available only in French. One study in English is Paul Stryckman and Robert Gaudet, *Priests in Canada*, 1971. For summary histories of the Christian religion in the Canadian setting, see Wilson (1966) and Walsh (1956). Clifford (1969) presents an excellent review and critique of all work done on religion in Canadian society.

parent to child, from friend to friend, and taught by social institutions such as the family or churches. Religion is socially conditioned by the form and nature of childhood training, the influence of friends, or the conformity pressures and expectations within a religious group. Religion also had social consequences, since beliefs are seldom aloof from human behaviour. If you believe that the end of the world is at hand, you may debunk any efforts to improve society, as the Jehovah's Witnesses have done. On the other hand, if you believe that the world is essentially evil, you will withdraw from society, as the Hutterites have done. Finally, religion is sociologically appropriate. It flourishes best when it relates to specific needs that have emerged from man's socio-economic milieu. Religion explains poverty to the poor, wealth to the rich, and sickness to the invalid. Beliefs and practices are embraced by persons as they are appropriate to their social world. The form and shape of religious expression in times of depression will certainly be different in a time of affluence. Similarly, the religious style in a slum area will contrast sharply with that in a suburban community because individual needs vary with social position.

It is clear then that there are many aspects of religion that are sociologically observable and open to analysis: to insist that this is the extent of religion would be foolhardy. For instance, there are many psychological and doctrinal aspects of religion which will not be elaborated. A sociologist will interpret religion only from his own scientific perspective and does not claim to give the final word on religion itself.

WHAT IS RELIGION?

Religion is man's response to his own humanity. It is his attempt to create meaning and order out of his existence. The elements of his existence which precipitate the need for meaning and order are contingency, powerlessness, and scarcity (O'Dea, 1966: 5). Contingency means that life and its events are uncertain; powerlessness refers to man's inability to control his world so that his needs go unmet; and scarcity suggests that inequalities persist unresolved in the society. These three factors summarize the apparent need for religious activity as an effort by man to adjust to his human world.

Sociologists stress the fact that religion is a human activity, meaning that it is man's attempt to come to grips with his finite existence. Just as man seeks to order the affairs of the state in political activity, and just as he aims to prepare the young for participation in the world through educational activities, so he establishes religion as an activity by which he adjusts to the basic facts of human existence. Since the social world that man has created from this finite reality is itself actually quite precarious or tenuous, religion represents man's attempt to give stability or permanence to what Berger (1969: Chap. 1) calls the "world building" process.

It has been quite a popular tendency within sociology to define or explain religion in terms of its functions (for example, Yinger, 1970: Chap. 1). Obviously definitions with this emphasis avoid stating exactly what religion is, and clearly provide difficulties in distinguishing religion from science, nationalism, or even philosophies, because each may attempt to fulfil similar functions.

Durkheim (1965: 37–63), on the other hand, stresses the emotional character of religion as that of fear or awe. He distinguishes between those objects that are set apart or forbidden—which he calls the "sacred" and the rest of reality which he identifies as the "profane". Things which are sacred are not so because they inherently possess that quality, but because of the attitude which exists in the mind of the observer. Religion, according to Durkheim, refers to beliefs about those things identified as sacred, which consequently form the basis for uniting all members of a society into a moral unit. Again the question emerges whether the flag, a political hero, or a sacred text could be equally designated as the object of religion.

Must the concept of religion necessarily have a supernatural referent? Traditionally, within the context of the Western world, religion has been identified as any activity that focuses on a Being or Beings which lie above empirical reality. The growth of non-supernaturalist religion has been a recent phenomenon. At the same time, numerous movements of the non-supernaturalist variety have arisen, which reject the label of religion, yet structurally appear to have similar characteristics to what is commonly accepted as religion. Therefore, we are caught between acknowledging as religion only that which has a supernatural referent (the narrow view), or accepting as religion anything which is merely structurally or functionally similar to what we previously accepted as religion (the broad view).

For the purposes of this paper, the use of religion will be restricted to that which has a supernatural referent of some sort, because it is most relevant to the Canadian setting. The student of sociology ought to be aware of the controversy on this point, however. The broader conception of religion will be examined again when the notion of secularization is discussed later in the chapter.

The sociologist can study religion because he focuses on the people who believe and practise religion in all of its manifestations. Differences in belief tell us about differences in people, and religion becomes interwoven with many events of the life process. Because it is a human activity, the sociologists cannot neglect religion without neglecting an important means by which significant numbers of people organize their lives.

Religious Organization

Religion is most sociologically observable in its organized form. It is often quite difficult to understand individual religious experiences, but it is relatively easy to locate the institutions and organizations which have been created to foster and develop these experiences. We readily identify religious activity by observing a person participating with others in a group which has specific religious ideas as its focus.

Because religions compel commitment in their devotees, religious beliefs are not sterile philosophical doctrines. They are convictions which must be deepened, beliefs which must be shared, and ideas which must be preserved. Therefore religion is seldom merely the fleeting experience of a moment but is encapsulated and solidified in an institution and organization with the express purpose of protecting and fostering the development of the perceived truths. Organization is the form and character a group of adherents give to their ideas about religion. If the religious beliefs give the follower a particular view of the world, then it is clear that the religious group will be organized in such a way as to reflect that view to the world. As a result, there is considerable variation in the organization of groups such as Roman Catholics, the Salvation Army, and Spiritualists. The particular manner in which a religious group organizes and orients its adherents tells us something about that group's perception of society and the world in general.

CHURCH-SECT HYPOTHESIS

An early distinction among religious groups was made by Ernst Troeltsch (1960: 461ff.). Troeltsch argued for an inherent tension in the Christian religion between spontaneity and institutionalism on one hand and conformity and protest on the other. Some groups appeared to be quite conservative and institutionalized while other groups were more radical and loosely organized. This distinction was expressed in two opposing types of organizations known as the "church-sect dichotomy". The church type accepted the secular order, attempted to dominate society, and was usually accepted by the upper class. In contrast, the sect type was indifferent, hostile, or detached from the society and was largely a product of the lower classes. The church type stressed compromise in order to widen its base of support and was given stability by an elaborate hierarchy and bureaucracy. On the other hand, the sect type demanded rigorous discipline and equality, lay participation, and fellowship, which together were accepted patterns for interaction. The sect was entered voluntarily— usually as the result of some individual decision or conversion—whereas the church was entered by birth.

As the sect-church dichotomy was developed and applied in the ensuing years, it was clear that the dichotomy was far too simplistic, and instead of there being two types, it was more likely that a modern complex society would show evidence of organizations at varying mid-points between these two poles. Other problems with the classification arose, such as the observation that sects were not necessarily only a lower-class phenomenon, as they were at the time of Troeltsch's writing.

Niebuhr (1957) refined the typology from a dichotomy into a continuum with the category of "denomination" as the mid-point. The denomination was the product of specific historical conditions including a plurality of religious groups from which individuals could choose and none of which claimed a monopoly on the truth, and the possibility of considerable upward social mobility among the adherents. In surveying the American scene, Niebuhr noted that many groups which were denominations had been sects at one time. The concern to transmit the faith through the adequate socialization of the next generation, in addition to new recruits, led to a greater institutionalization of the sect which made it somewhat less radical and more conservative, and thus denominational.

Since Niebuhr's analysis, it has become obvious that some sects institutionalize but only partially lose their protest, while other sects remain very small, uncoordinated minorities, displaying considerable hostility to the world. In other words, not all sects become denominations. It is also clear that while the church type conforms to the social order, it is seldom embraced by all members of a society. In other words, the pure church type seldom exists. What we find then is a multiplicity of types of religious groups whose characteristics vary in being more sect-like or more church-like.

When a sociologist uses these terms "church" and "sect", he uses them in a non-judgmental sense to describe the degree to which a religious group approximates the sociological traits of the pure church or sect type. Because the sect is by nature a multi-pronged protest in which the beliefs support behaviour which deviates from that which is common within the society, sects are of special interest to sociologists. It is because sects are self-conscious attempts by men to construct their own societies that they teach us something about the pressure and tensions present within the host society (Wilson, 1970).

The church-sect hypothesis and all of its revisions obviously emerged from a Christian context, as the concepts themselves indicate. Therefore the typology has significance for Canada. Attempts have been made, however, to apply the concepts to non-Christian societies (Bhatt, 1968) and even to observe the sectarian character of non-religious organizations, such as political protest groups, who also set themselves off in hostility from the rest of the society (O'Toole, 1971).

CHURCH-SECT TYPOLOGY IN CANADIAN CONTEXT

In Canada's short history, the closest that we come to the pure church-type situation has been on a regional basis in Quebec (Falardeau, 1949; 1964: 343–57). French residents were automatically considered to be loyal Catholics merely because of their nationality and the fact of their residence in that society. This was particularly the case in the years prior to the First World War (Walsh, 1966). In the church-oriented agricultural society, the *habitant* family was organized around the parish and the priest emerged as leader. As Quebec began to urbanize and industrialize, however, the monopoly of the Roman Catholic Church began to weaken.

Just as the French brought Catholicism with them in their settlement of Canadian territory, so the British brought their national church—Anglicanism—with them. Both the French Catholic and the Anglican churches were transplanted versions of what Yinger (1970: 262-64) calls an "ecclesia" in which there is a close interrelationship between the state and the dominant classes. Therefore, along with its political, economic, and administrative interests, the religious interests of the colonizing country were also transplanted. Canada was initially settled by religious organizations whose characteristics were more church-like than sect-like. This pattern stands in sharp contrast to the experience of the colonists of New England. In that location, population settlement took place under the auspices of religious sects searching for religious freedom, whereas in Canada settlement was led by individuals under allegiance to national churches (Clark, 1948: 3).

The only sociologist who has done a consistent and comprehensive study of religion in Canadian society is S. D. Clark. In a pioneering work entitled *Church and Sect in Canada*, Clark takes as his starting point the basic church-sect distinction which we have already outlined. He ties the existence of each particular type of religious organization to the social conditions present within the society. Clark argues that the sect type of religion is a product of the unstable conditions of the frontier and that the church type is the result of a socially stable and mature society. Following this argument, it is therefore to be expected that Clark's interpretation would lead to the discovery of numerous sectarian religious movements and organizations in each newly settled area of Canada.

Using historical data, Clark first looks at the revival movement of the Maritime provinces (1783–1832) and notes how closely related this area was with the New England colonies, where sect forms of religious or-ganizations were quite influential. The Church of England was unable to extend its influence beyond the migrated Loyalists, because its close identification with the state had alienated large segments of the rural population. Because traditional loyalties were weakened by recent settle-ment, the churches were unable to provide the right type of leadership. As a result, the sect-like evangelical New Light Movement was an import-ant mechanism in the social reorganization of the pioneer society through development of local preachers who could more easily adapt to the needs and style of the local population. The sect was a response to the need for more intimate social relationships in a frontier society whose new milieu put severe strains on traditional culture and required a new basis for social solidarity.

In writing of the Great Revival in Upper Canada, Clark concludes again that the fact that people were cut off from traditional ties made them susceptible to the sectarian appeal of the evangelical movements. Since most of the migrants from the United States were second-generation Europeans, they had been separated from the heritage of the first generation, with insufficient time to have developed a heritage of their own. Sectarian religion with its emphasis on frequent meetings and free expression and participation by all was an important agent in the unification of the population. Churches such as the Church of England or the Presbyterian Church became very much an upper-class phenomenon, leaving the organization of the masses to the sects.

As towns grew and agricultural areas were no longer backwoods settlements of culturally isolated and economically deprived people, sectarian religion became more respectable and denominational in character according to Clark. As Baptists and Methodists began to improve their economic position and attain higher social standing through upward mobility, these groups became denominational and successfully accommodated themselves to the secular world, even becoming involved in politics. As social conditions changed, however, Clark argued that new sects emerged in response to the depopulation of rural areas and the growth of towns and cities. He asserts that the commercial growth of the Canadian community after 1860 meant that it would be the marginal elements of the growing urban population which would be attracted to the new sects, as well as the new population in the new frontier—the expanding Prairies.

Clark's basic thesis is that as the societal maturation process continued sectarianism would weaken and denominationalism would grow. Sects would disappear or change and become more church-like.[2] In addition, denominational ties in England or elsewhere outside the country would weaken and national bodies would form in what he calls the rise of the "territorial church". For example, he points to the fact that the numerous

2. The same theme is explored as it relates to the role of religion in economic development, politics, and national development in Clark (1962: 115–84).

Methodist bodies in Canada united, devoid of their British sponsorships, five years after the inauguration of the National Policy. In retrospect, it is evident that the religious sect was an important mechanism of adjustment and reorganization where traditional social institutions such as the church had alienated the population.

Clark's work merits careful attention; he has uncovered important historical information and provided a significant framework of interpretation for the appearance of different forms of religious organizations at varying points in the development of Canadian society. Several problems do need to be pointed out, however. If sects are the products of the unstable and disorganized frontier possessing a newly migrated population, how can the perpetual birth of sects in urban areas or older communities of Canada be explained? What explanation is there for the recent rise of sects among the middle and upper classes if sects appeal only to the marginal elements of a society? In other words, sects have continued to rise and grow in areas long since past the frontier stage, and perhaps additional explanations are needed to update the analysis. The assumption that sects are the product of backward people in backward areas is a historically dated assertion which needs qualification in the light of our present knowledge of sects.

RELIGION AS A DEMOGRAPHIC VARIABLE

Canadian society contains numerous religious organizations which individually seek the voluntary allegiance of the population. Religious organizations give people labels by which they can identify others as well as themselves. People are frequently asked or given the option to respond to the question "What is your religion?" And we learn to use the label we prefer.

The Canadian census asked such a question about religious preference. Respondents were urged to answer according to which group they prefer or favour rather than according to which group they have been affiliated or are presently a member of. A response is usually a learned response given by rote to the variety of labels known to be available. What is being suggested here is that census statistics are by no means a measure of depth of commitment and tell us nothing of levels of participation in that religious group. Without passing judgment on the propriety of individuals using these labels and their "real" significance,[3] such census figures are valuable in indicating with which religious group Canadians identify. To claim to be "United" could mean everything from being an active member to having attended only a few times in one's youth. Nevertheless, the identification with the United Church is likely to be indicative of the importance of that religious organization for "rites of passage" such as those involving birth, marriage, or death.[4] Being cognizant of the limitations of such data, let us examine the Canadian statistics more closely.

Figure 9:1 Distribution of major religious organizations among the Canadian population 1971

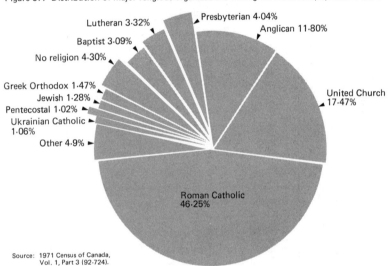

Presbyterian 4·04%
Anglican 11·80%
Lutheran 3·32%
Baptist 3·09%
No religion 4·30%
Greek Orthodox 1·47%
Jewish 1·28%
Pentecostal 1·02%
Ukrainian Catholic 1·06%
Other 4·9%
United Church 17·47%
Roman Catholic 46·25%

Source: 1971 Census of Canada, Vol. 1, Part 3 (92-724).

Figure 9:1 illustrates the religious composition of the Canadian population in 1971. The overwhelming strength of Roman Catholicism over any other single religious group is striking. When those indicating "No Religion", "Other", or a non-Christian religious preference are removed from the remaining respondents, it is clear that all Protestants combined barely compose one-half of the total population of Canada. No single Protestant group approximates the size of the Catholic population of 46.25 per cent. The United Church's 17.47 per cent and the Anglican

3. For a discussion on religion as a social label, see Budd (1973: 96–103).
4. Bryan Wilson (1966: 18) argues that in spite of increasing secularization,

religion still appears to be vital for large segments of the population on these occasions.

Table 1 Population by religious group, for Canada 1921–71.

	1921 (%)	1941 (%)	1961 (%)	1971 (%)
Adventist	14,200 (0.16)	18,485 (0.16)	24,999 (0.14)	28,590 (0.13)
Anglican	1,410,632 (16.05)	1,754,368 (15.24)	2,409,068 (13.21)	2,543,180 (11.80)
Baptist	422,312 (4.80)	484,465 (4.21)	593,553 (3.25)	667,245 (3.09)
Buddhist	11,316 (0.13)	15,676 (0.13)	11,611 (0.06)	16,175 (0.075)
Christian Reformed	—	—	62,257 (0.34)	83,390 (0.39)
Christian & Missionary Alliance	283 (0.003)	4,214 (0.036)	18,006 (0.09)	23,390 (0.11)
Church of Christ Disciples	13,125 (0.15)	21,260 (0.18)	19,512 (0.11)	16,405 (0.08)
Confucian	27,185 (0.30)	22,282 (0.19)	5,089 (0.027)	2,165 (0.01)
Congregationalist	30,788 (0.35)	(1)	(1)	(1)
Doukhobor	12,674 (0.14)	16,878 (0.15)	13,234 (0.073)	9,170 (0.04)
Free Methodist	—	8,805 (0.08)	14,245 (0.078)	19,125 (0.09)
Greek Orthodox	170,069 (1.93)	139,845 (1.21)	239,766 (1.31)	316,605 (1.47)
Hutterite	(4)	(4)	(4)	13,650 (0.06)
Jehovah's Witnesses	6,689 (0.08)	7,007 (0.06)	68,018 (0.37)	174,810 (0.81)
Jewish	125,445 (1.42)	168,585 (1.46)	254,368 (1.39)	276,025 (1.28)
Lutheran	286,891 (3.26)	401,836 (3.49)	662,744 (3.63)	715,740 (3.32)
Mennonite	58,874 (0.67)	111,554 (0.97)	152,452 (0.84)	168,150 (0.78)

	(1)	(1)	(1)	(1)
Methodist	1,161,165 (13.21)			
Mormon	19,657 (0.22)	25,328 (0.22)	50,016 (0.27)	66,635 (0.31)
Pentecostal	7,012 (0.80)	57,742 (0.50)	143,877 (0.79)	220,390 (1.02)
Presbyterian	1,411,794 (16.07)	830,597 (7.22)	818,558 (4.49)	872,335 (4.04)
Roman Catholic	3,399,011 (38.69)	4,806,431 (41.77)	8,342,826 (45.74)	9,974,895 (46.25)
Salvation Army	24,771 (0.28)	33,609 (0.29)	92,054 (0.50)	119,655 (0.55)
Ukrainian Catholic	(2)	185,948 (1.61)(3)	189,653 (1.04)(3)	227,730 (1.06)(3)
Unitarian	4,943 (0.06)	5,584 (0.05)	15,062 (0.08)	20,995 (0.09)
United Church	8,739 (0.10)	2,208,658 (19.19)	3,664,008 (20.09)	3,768,800 (17.47)
Other	138,555 (1.58)	158,337 (1.38)	277,508 (1.52)	293,240 (1.36)
No Religion	21,819 (0.25)	19,161 (0.17)	94,763 (0.52)	929,575 (4.30)

(1) Included with the United Church.
(2) Greek Catholic and Greek Orthodox combined under "Greek Church".
(3) Includes other Greek Catholic.
(4) Included with "Mennonite".

Source: Computed from *1971 Census of Canada*, Vol. I, Part 3 (92–724).

Church's 11.80 per cent of the total population come closest and are the largest Protestant bodies. The diversity of other groups, only one of which retains slightly more than 4 per cent of the population, and the lack of a co-ordinating body to unite these diverse elements, indicates that Catholicism has by far the greatest potential influence in the society.

The growth of these religious bodies in absolute numbers and their percentage of the total population for 1921, 1941, 1961, and 1971 is indicated in Table 1. Many groups have shown a growth in absolute numbers over the fifty-year time period but their growth has not kept pace with the total population growth. Anglicans, for example, grew from 1,410,632 in 1921 to 2,543,180 in 1971. That is a growth rate of almost 60 per cent. But this growth rate is considerably short of the rate of growth of the Canadian population as a whole, so that although Anglicans made up 16.05 per cent of the total population in 1921, they had decreased to 11.80 per cent by 1971. Many of the mainline denominations—including Presbyterians, United, Baptist, Lutheran, and Jewish—display the same trend. Some groups, such as the Doukhobors and Confucians, display a marked decrease in number of adherents over this time period. Groups which were originally quite small, such as Pentecostals, Salvation Army, Buddhist, and Jehovah's Witnesses, have demonstrated appreciable growth in terms of absolute numbers although their percentage of the total population is still relatively small. The largest numerical gain and percentage gain is evidenced by Roman Catholics, who demonstrated a gain of 8 percentage points over the time period. Again this growth indicates the relative strength of Catholicism as at least part of the heritage and background of almost one-half of the population of Canada. Significantly, those indicating "Other" have increased numerically but have not kept pace with population growth.

One of the interesting facts shown in Table 1 is the sharp increase from 1961 to 1971 in those registering "No Religion". In absolute numbers, the increase was radical and the percentage increase moved from 0.52 to 4.30 per cent. This category has become the fourth largest single group in the population with a sudden jump in a ten-year time span. What is the significance of this fact? Numerous interpretations might be advanced but the most likely appears to be that the social climate is such that individuals now feel more secure using no organizational labels, whereas previously they answered with a label they felt was expected. The point is that individuals who were quite marginal to a religious group before no longer feel any social pressures to answer in a conventional manner. This is not to say that all of those who still use the label are committed to the group they have named. They might be quite marginal as well, but the fact that the label is still utilized in spite of secularization still has some significance.

REGIONAL DISPERSION OF RELIGIOUS GROUPS

Table 2 illustrates the religious composition of each provincial unit or territory in Canada. No single group dominates in any area to such a great extent as Catholicism. Roman Catholics compose 86.7 per cent of the population of Quebec, 52.2 per cent in New Brunswick, and 45.9 per cent in Prince Edward Island. From Ontario eastward Roman Catholics make up at least one-third of the population of each province. From

Table 2 Percentage composition of population by religious denomination for each province, 1971.

	Roman Catholic	United	Anglican	Presbyterian	Lutheran	Baptist	Others
Canada	46.2	17.5	11.8	4.0	3.3	3.1	14.0
Newfoundland	36.6	19.5	27.7	0.6	0.1	0.2	15.4
Prince Edward Island	45.9	24.9	6.2	11.7	0.1	5.7	5.5
Nova Scotia	36.3	20.6	17.2	5.1	1.5	12.7	6.6
New Brunswick	52.2	13.4	10.9	2.1	0.3	14.0	7.1
Quebec	86.7	2.9	3.0	0.9	0.4	0.6	5.5
Ontario	33.3	21.8	15.8	7.0	3.5	3.7	14.8
Manitoba	24.6	26.0	12.4	3.1	6.6	1.9	25.5
Saskatchewan	27.9	29.6	9.4	2.2	9.8	1.6	19.4
Alberta	24.0	28.1	10.5	3.5	8.2	3.1	22.7
British Columbia	18.7	24.6	17.7	4.6	5.5	3.0	25.9
Yukon	25.4	16.9	25.3	3.8	5.0	4.7	18.9
Northwest Territories	41.3	8.6	36.4	1.3	2.1	1.1	9.1

Source: Adapted from *1971 Census of Canada*, Statistics Canada *Advance Bulletin* (92–763).

Table 3   Percentage regional dispersion of each religious group by province.

	Total	Nfld.	P.E.I.	Nova Scotia	New Bruns.	Que.
Adventist	100.00	1.84	0.33	4.57	3.09	2.62
Anglican	100.00	5.68	0.27	5.34	2.72	7.15
Baptist	100.00	0.16	0.95	15.04	13.34	5.67
Brethren in Christ	100.00	1.94	1.05	1.22	1.43	3.46
Buddhist	100.00	0.12	—	0.34	0.22	6.98
Christian Reformed	100.00	0.005	0.25	1.09	0.08	0.52
Church of Christ, Disciples	100.00	0.27	5.61	7.10	5.24	0.82
Church of Nazarene	100.00	0.33	4.08	5.26	3.42	1.80
Confucian	100.00	0.23	—	1.15	0.23	16.82
Doukhobor	100.00	—	—	0.05	0.22	2.40
Free Methodist	100.00	0.13	—	0.99	1.28	2.98
Greek Orthodox	100.00	0.03	0.01	0.49	0.12	18.92
Hutterite	100.00	—	—	0.22	—	1.28
Jehovah's Witnesses	100.00	1.06	0.24	2.84	1.63	9.80
Jewish	100.00	0.08	0.01	0.79	0.30	40.17
Lutheran	100.00	0.07	0.01	1.62	0.26	3.33
Mennonite	100.00	0.03	0.009	0.05	0.05	0.39
Mormon	100.00	0.04	0.11	1.16	0.47	1.33
Pentecostal	100.00	13.06	0.46	3.11	7.67	3.87
Plymouth Brethren	100.00	0.09	0.18	1.69	0.28	1.79
Presbyterian	100.00	0.35	1.50	4.63	1.50	5.94
Roman Catholic	100.00	1.91	0.51	2.87	3.32	52.39
Salvation Army	100.00	34.50	0.24	3.97	1.83	3.37
Ukrainian Catholic	100.00	0.02	0.01	0.33	0.31	10.95
Unitarian	100.00	0.30	0.10	1.62	1.79	12.93
United Church	100.00	2.70	0.74	4.32	2.26	4.69
Other	100.00	1.74	0.44	2.11	2.08	7.12
No Religion	100.00	0.25	0.12	2.06	1.28	8.24

Source: Computed from *1971 Census of Canada*, Vol. I, Part 3 (92–724).

Manitoba westward the United Church usurps Catholic dominance although not to the same extent. It is interesting that Catholics and Anglicans rival each other most closely in the areas susceptible to colonialism either presently or in the past (Newfoundland, Yukon, Northwest Territories, and British Columbia). Except for British Columbia, it is also

Ont.	Man.	Sask.	Alta.	B.C.	Yukon	N.W.T.
32.24	3.87	7.99	18.23	25.15	0.07	0.05
47.99	4.84	3.43	6.70	15.20	0.18	0.50
42.50	2.76	2.25	7.45	9.72	0.13	0.06
68.22	2.25	2.69	4.05	13.66	—	0.05
34.68	4.57	0.87	14.09	37.89	0.12	0.03
65.55	2.19	0.43	16.09	13.74	0.02	0.03
43.04	5.58	9.08	14.63	8.35	0.06	0.12
33.44	1.36	6.88	28.92	13.87	0.26	0.33
17.05	3.68	10.13	5.99	43.78	0.46	—
1.91	1.42	18.28	2.18	73.32	—	0.11
68.97	3.16	6.30	6.27	9.73	0.13	0.05
42.47	8.03	8.43	14.90	6.48	0.05	0.05
1.90	35.09	16.20	44.69	0.55	—	—
38.73	4.94	5.65	10.25	24.20	0.33	0.30
45.40	6.80	0.64	2.27	3.52	0.005	0.009
37.34	9.04	12.69	18.59	16.81	0.13	0.10
23.86	35.42	15.65	8.70	15.77	0.03	0.03
25.23	2.05	3.68	46.65	19.01	0.11	0.15
34.77	4.57	5.62	10.48	15.98	0.09	0.32
50.00	3.96	3.96	5.66	32.45	—	—
61.90	3.53	2.38	6.55	11.57	0.08	0.05
25.75	2.43	2.59	3.92	4.09	0.05	0.14
36.64	2.84	2.75	3.88	9.93	0.03	0.025
24.91	25.38	15.00	18.03	4.96	0.04	0.04
43.90	5.45	2.76	8.24	22.64	0.14	0.09
44.65	6.80	7.27	12.12	14.26	0.08	0.08
42.27	4.38	4.85	12.56	22.13	0.18	0.11
36.97	4.57	3.66	11.66	30.88	0.17	0.11

these areas where Anglicans are stronger than the United Church. Presbyterians, in contrast to Lutherans, are distributed throughout Canada with their heaviest concentrations, historically explainable, in Prince Edward Island and Ontario. Lutheranism is almost exclusively a western phenomenon and most of their adherents live west of Ontario. While Baptists show some strength in western provinces, their largest percentage compositions are in the Maritimes where again historical immigration reasons provide an explanation. The Maritimes and Quebec demonstrate the least religious diversity in the "Other" category and from Ontario west the diversity is greatest. This no doubt is at least partly explainable by the fact that these regions have been the recipients of most of Canada's immigration, which contributes to the plurality of religious groups.

The regional locations of strength for each religious organization are indicated in Table 3. The large general population in Ontario plus the existence of much religious pluralism is revealed in large percentages for almost every group. The large urban concentrations in Ontario and British Columbia have resulted the strongest concentrations of most Protestant religious groups in these two provinces. Asian religions such as Buddhism and Confucianism are strongest in British Columbia port communities and are seldom found outside of the large metropolitan centres. Some groups like Nazarenes and Greek Orthodox are stronger in Alberta, with British Columbia as their second area of strength, while the Hutterites are almost exclusively a prairie phenomenon. Sects like Jehovah's Witnesses and Mormons appear to be located principally in the three largest Protestant provinces—Ontario, British Columbia, and Alberta. In striking contrast, Judaism is concentrated in two provinces—Ontario and Quebec (over 85 per cent). The distribution of Roman Catholics throughout Canada is significant because Quebec contains only 52.3 per cent of all Canada's Catholics in spite of the fact that 86.7 per cent of Quebec's population is Catholic. Catholics make a strong showing in Ontario, but the United Church, Protestantism's largest body in Canada, makes a poor showing in Quebec. Notice also that it is the Protestant provinces of Ontario and British Columbia which register more persons with "No Religion" than the populous province of Quebec.

Table 4 demonstrates the extent to which each religious group is rural or urban. Most Jews, for example, are found in cities 500,000 and over but Buddhist, Confucian, Greek Orthodox, and "No Religion" also reveal their largest concentrations in these locales. Surprisingly, the Salvation Army is weakest in large urban centres but shows a strong small-town adherence. Only the Hutterites and Mennonites are dominantly rural. Small denominations like the Alliance, Reformed, and Church of Christ reveal greater strength in cities 100,000–499,999 than in larger cities.

Table 4 Percentage distribution of each religious group by urban size groups, and rural farm and non-farm, 1971.

	Total	500,000 & Over	100,000 to 499,999	30,000 to 99,999	1,000 to 29,999	Rural Non-Farm	Rural Farm
Adventist	100.00	24.31	16.09	6.87	13.96	24.99	13.76
Anglican	100.00	31.94	17.51	8.76	19.68	18.54	3.58
Baptist	100.00	20.83	15.80	10.99	20.88	24.99	6.50
Buddhist & Confucian	100.00	61.46	10.85	8.48	8.23	7.00	3.95
Christian & Missionary Alliance	100.00	13.12	26.43	7.83	25.88	14.38	12.38
Christian Reformed	100.00	11.74	18.62	8.66	18.40	18.67	23.90
Churches of Christ, Disciples	100.00	11.80	19.45	7.95	23.99	26.64	10.18
Greek Orthodox	100.00	53.90	19.95	3.54	8.52	6.32	7.78
Hutterite	100.00	3.00	0.51	0.37	1.03	4.65	90.48
Jehovah's Witnesses	100.00	34.62	15.26	6.85	17.58	19.30	6.39
Jewish	100.00	88.83	6.90	1.74	1.74	0.63	0.16
Lutheran	100.00	25.73	22.92	5.40	18.33	15.87	11.75
Mennonite	100.00	15.54	10.95	1.60	19.16	22.91	29.85
Mormon	100.00	12.91	24.98	11.32	24.54	16.00	10.25
Pentecostal	100.00	17.56	13.47	8.33	24.10	29.16	7.37
Presbyterian	100.00	31.97	17.59	9.29	20.70	14.32	6.12
Roman Catholic	100.00	33.78	13.43	10.27	20.43	16.56	5.54
Salvation Army	100.00	20.57	10.82	11.14	31.17	24.56	1.74
Ukrainian Catholic	100.00	34.00	21.16	4.80	13.04	11.87	15.13
United Church	100.00	24.19	17.53	8.43	21.51	19.29	9.05
Other	100.00	33.94	17.83	6.76	16.41	17.06	8.00
No Religion	100.00	42.25	17.63	6.13	14.68	14.88	4.43

Source: Computed from *1971 Census of Canada*, Vol. I, Part 3 (92–724).

RELIGION AND ETHNICITY

It has frequently been observed that religion is a far more viable societal activity in the United States than in Europe (Wilson, 1966: 86–102). Church attendance and church participation tends to involve much greater numbers of people in the New World. In religious activity, Canada comes close to approximating the United States (although how close we have not yet adequately determined) in the relative strength of its religious

Table 5   Percentage distribution of ethnic origins by religious denominations.

	Total	British Isles	French	German	Italian	Jewish
Anglican	100.0	85.0	2.3	2.8	0.3	0.1
Baptist	100.0	74.1	5.7	8.6	0.3	0.1
Greek Orthodox	100.0	3.1	0.5	0.5	0.1	0.1
Jewish	100.0	—	—	—	—	100.0
Lutheran	100.0	17.8	1.3	45.0	0.3	0.1
Mennonite & Hutterite	100.0	5.9	1.1	69.7	0.3	—
Pentecostal	100.0	66.8	3.4	10.0	1.6	—
Presbyterian	100.0	84.6	1.9	3.4	0.3	—
Roman Catholic	100.0	19.9	58.3	3.4	6.8	—
Salvation Army	100.0	85.7	3.6	2.4	0.5	0.1
Ukrainian Catholic	100.0	3.5	7.2	0.6	0.4	—
United Church	100.0	78.6	3.0	5.5	0.4	0.1
Other	100.0	46.7	4.0	8.3	0.8	0.3
No Religion	100.0	56.0	7.5	7.9	1.0	1.1

Source: *1971 Census of Canada*, Vol. I, Part 4 (92–735).

institutions. Among the explanations given for the European-North American contrast is the assertion that religion in North America is an integral element in ethnicity. The heavy dependence of Canada on immigration meant that each ethnic group would probably bring with it its own religious heritage, and if religious activity increased on coming to this continent, it was probably the result of ethnicity and religion having become closely aligned.

Table 5 illustrates to some degree the relationship between religion and ethnicity in the general population. The correlation between being Anglican and of British descent is very close. Fully 85 per cent of the Anglicans in Canada are of British descent. Presbyterian, Salvation Army, United, and Baptist populations also show a heavy constituency of British origin. Other than a small French and German contingency within Baptist and United Church bodies, other ethnic groups make only a small contribution to their total size. In contrast, few people of British descent are affiliated with Greek Orthodox bodies, Mennonites, Ukrainian Catholic, or Roman

Dutch	Polish	Scandin-avian	Ukrainian	Asian	Indian & Eskimo	Other & Unknown
1.0	0.5	1.3	1.1	0.6	2.7	2.4
2.3	0.6	1.6	1.2	0.8	0.7	4.2
0.1	1.8	0.2	36.9	4.1	—	52.6
—	—	—	—	—	—	—
1.1	1.3	17.9	1.4	0.3	0.1	13.2
17.8	0.3	0.4	0.7	0.3	0.6	3.1
2.4	0.8	3.6	2.5	0.9	3.0	4.8
2.3	0.4	1.1	0.9	1.3	0.4	3.2
1.0	2.3	0.3	0.9	0.6	1.7	4.8
1.2	0.4	1.2	0.8	0.3	1.3	2.6
0.1	3.2	0.3	81.9	0.2	0.1	2.6
2.1	0.7	2.7	2.1	1.0	0.9	2.8
14.0	1.0	3.3	2.3	10.2	1.3	7.8
3.7	1.5	3.5	3.2	6.9	0.9	6.8

Catholic. Greek Orthodox tend to be Ukrainian, Russian, or southeast European; Mennonites are Dutch or German; Ukrainian Catholic are Ukrainian; and Roman Catholic are French, Italian, German, or British. Lutherans on the other hand, are strongly German or Scandinavian.

Viewing this data in terms of the entire society, however, obfuscates small-scale but significant information. For example, a Danish Lutheran group meeting in a large city may have a numerically small membership of 150, yet serve as a viable organization for the Danish participants involved because the language and customs of the old country are maintained in such a way. The same might be said for a Ukrainian Pentecostal church or an Italian Catholic church. Large numbers do minimize small, but meaningful organizations which serve relatively few people and the numerous religio-ethnic groups in Canada must not be overlooked even when numbers are small.[5]

5. See, for example, a study of the Jewish community in Canada by   Rosenberg (1939).

Table 6 Percentage distribution of religious denominations by ethnic groups 1971.

	Total	Anglican	Baptist	Greek Orthodox	Jewish	Lutheran	Mennonite & Hutterite
British Isles	100.0	22.5	5.1	0.1	—	1.3	0.1
French	100.0	0.9	0.6	—	—	0.2	—
German	100.0	5.4	4.3	0.1	—	24.5	9.6
Italian	100.0	1.2	0.3	0.1	—	0.3	0.1
Jewish	100.0	0.6	0.1	0.1	93.0	0.2	—
Dutch	100.0	5.8	3.6	0.1	—	1.9	7.6
Polish	100.0	3.9	1.2	1.8	—	3.0	0.2
Scandinavian	100.0	8.4	2.7	0.1	—	33.4	0.2
Ukrainian	100.0	4.6	1.4	20.1	—	1.8	0.2
Asian	100.0	5.1	1.8	4.6	—	0.8	0.2
Indian & Eskimo	100.0	22.3	1.4	—	—	0.3	0.3
Other & Unknown	100.0	5.5	2.5	15.0	—	8.5	0.5

Source: Statistics obtained from *1971 Census of Canada*, Vol. I, Part 4 (92–735).

It is clear from Table 5 that many religious groups have one or perhaps two main ethnic contingencies. It ought to be pointed out, however, that the term "British Isles" encompasses a host of other significant differences. British Isles includes the English, the Irish, the Scottish, and the Welsh: the English may be strongly Anglican but the Scottish usually are Presbyterian, and the Irish frequently Catholic. Again ethnicity and religion demonstrate a high correlation. This becomes clearer in Table 6, where those of British descent show a variable distribution among religious groups named. French, Polish, and Italians, on the other hand, are overwhelmingly Catholic, while Scandinavians tend to be either Lutheran or United Church.

The fact that there is a correlation between religion and ethnicity is merely interesting information, unless it can be shown that one reinforces the other. If religion strengthens an ethnic identity and if ethnicity has religion as one of its component parts, then an apparent interest in religion may mean more than is readily observable.

The relationship between religion and ethnicity was first most clearly

Pente-costal	Presby-terian	Roman Catholic	Salvation Army	Ukrainian Catholic	United Church	Other	No Religion
1.5	7.7	20.7	1.1	0.1	30.8	3.7	5.4
0.1	0.3	94.0	0.1	0.3	1.9	0.5	1.1
1.7	2.3	25.7	0.2	0.1	15.8	4.8	5.6
0.5	0.4	93.0	0.1	0.1	1.9	0.8	1.3
—	0.1	1.1	—	—	0.7	0.8	3.3
1.3	4.8	23.0	0.3	0.1	18.7	24.7	8.2
0.6	1.1	70.9	0.1	2.3	8.4	2.4	4.3
2.1	2.6	8.2	0.4	0.2	26.9	6.5	8.5
1.0	1.3	15.3	0.2	32.1	13.9	3.0	5.1
0.7	4.1	19.4	0.1	0.1	13.7	26.9	22.5
2.1	1.2	55.6	0.5	0.1	10.4	3.0	2.7
1.0	2.5	43.3	0.3	0.5	9.4	5.3	5.7

pointed out in the American context by Herberg (1955) and later by Greeley (1972: 108ff.). Herberg argues that when immigrants first arrived in North America, there existed the hope that they would be able to establish the old world in the new society. The pressures to conform to dominant cultural patterns, to seek employment away from one's compatriots, and to become part of the social processes of the new society, however, reduced any possibility of remaining separate and distinct. Assimilationist pressures, as subtle or as forceful as they might be, were experienced as part of daily interaction. Yet there was one sphere in society where differences were more likely to be tolerated and that was in the area of religion. The ethnic church then became the institution where the immigrant deposited his ethnicity. It was here that not only his language and customs could be expressed but his ethnic culture could be propagated.

While we must selectively interpret Herberg to fit the Canadian scene, it is clear that immigrant churches were vital mechanisms in giving immigrants an ethnic anchor in an alien society. This was particularly true in the early settlement of agrarian lands when ethnic churches were often the first permanent buildings to be constructed. Even in later years, the ethnic church provided urban immigrants with a gathering place and an organization with which they were familiar. Here persons with similar backgrounds could gather, communicate in their native language, and celebrate the same festivals as in the country of origin. It is not uncommon in Canada to hear of persons who displayed little religious interest in their native country but suddenly become actively involved in ethnic religion in the new world. Ethnic religion provides a continual source of identity, as well as having served as an important mechanism in the adjustment of immigrants by providing the old and the familiar within the strange society (Mol, 1961).

Ethnic churches begin as transplanted churches but they too must adapt to the forces of the new environment. The major problem always appears to be the securing of religious professionals from the same ethnic group. Without a leader who speaks the language and propagates the customs, the ethnic church is ripe for assimilation. For example, numerous efforts were made by the Presbyterians and Methodists to train Ukrainian converts in their own schools as a means of ensuring speedier assimilation of the Ukrainians to Anglo-Canadian life. The Ukrainians resisted, however, by seeking to import religious leadership from home (Marunchak, 1970: 99). More recently, a Lebanese community in northern Alberta experienced the foundering of their ethnic identity when their native religious leader, or "imam", left the area (Barclay, 1971: 77).

To remain Presbyterian is a way that Scottish people can remain loyal without being unpatriotic to their new country. To attend a Greek Catholic church is a way of retaining Greek customs and traditions. To support a German Lutheran church may be a way of ensuring that your children will learn the native language, its songs, and customs in the minister-taught Saturday language school. And to participate in a Dutch Reformed church is a way to support actively the cultural tradition while still assimilating in other spheres of Canadian life.

Millett (1971: 58–60) has observed that many immigrants came to Canada adhering to a national church in their country of origin. Upon experiencing poverty and isolation in the new land, there was a tendency for these groups to exhibit sect-like behaviour as a protective mechanism. These small struggling groups which emerged from a church-like background yet acted in a sect-like manner he calls a "minority church". Its ties in the home country give it life and hope beyond itself for the time being. But as the ties with the mother country weaken, the group may Canadianize and become an "indigenous church", such as the Ukrainian Greek Orthodox Church, with services in English. Survival as an independent unit in the long run requires sufficient accommodation to the new society to make it authentically Canadian.

Thus, religious organizations are important in providing the framework for religious activity in Canadian society. Most Canadians identify with some religious body, although the extent of their participation in that organization may be another matter. Religion may be a more vital force in Canadian society for more people, however, because it is frequently part of an ethnic culture. This is not to suggest that ethnic religion is the only means of expressing ethnic distinctions but it may be one of the important ways in which traditional ties are maintained.[6] The plurality of religious denominations which are found in Canadian society are largely the result of the diversity of ethnic backgrounds present. The growth of sectarian bodies and their random recruitment from residents in the society is another matter, which is related to secularization and social change.

ECUMENISM

A study of religious organization in Canada would not be complete without a discussion of the merging of organizations in what is referred to as ecumenism. From a sociological perspective, ecumenism is the reduction of barriers between groups in order to facilitate interaction between individuals and organizations which were formerly distinctly separate and at least relatively exclusive. Ecumenism can mean tolerance between groups in terms of attitudes or it can mean the complete merger of organizations to form one body. Attitudinal ecumenism is much more difficult for a sociologist to analyse than organizational ecumenism, which involves considerable structural change and membership reaction. Therefore, organizational ecumenism has attracted greatest attention among

6. Secular ethnic associations have been and continue to be quite prominent in Canadian society and we do not wish to minimize their importance.

sociologists in Canada. This focus has not been entirely unwarranted, however, since the organizational merger of some religious groups in Canada made ecumenism an issue at the beginning of this century—considerably before it became currently fashionable.

Two principles regarding organizational ecumenism can be extracted from the Canadian experience. First, religious organizations amalgamate when insufficient population makes the duplication of facilities among two or more groups with a similar doctrine and from a similar culture uneconomical. Second, religious organizations amalgamate when ethnic traditions become less important in groups carrying the same denominational label. Both principles can be illustrated.

There is no question that the formation of the United Church of Canada in 1925 from the Congregational, Presbyterian, and Methodist churches in Canada was a result of conditions stated in the first principle. It was primarily the lack of sufficient population in the prairies and parts of Ontario which led to co-operative efforts, particularly between Presbyterians and Methodists. Often by mutual agreement, they would divide up an area and each place their churches in alternate towns along a railroad line, in order to reduce the direct competition. Competition between two English-speaking churches with only small doctrinal differences in a small town was economic suicide—if nothing else. It was virtually impossible to remain organizationally viable and difficult to find enough clergymen. Therefore, even before organic union became official, it was commonplace for groups to federate in one town while remaining dually or triply aligned.

From these sorts of pressures, the impetus for union developed. There was little culturally to keep the three groups apart. All three emerged from the British Isles. Interestingly enough, the greatest dissent was expressed in the Presbyterian Church, where the Scottish tradition was still alive. But this slight cultural distinction prevented a merger only where adequate numbers enabled the Presbyterian group to remain as a viable organization. This is not to minimize doctrinal reasons either for or against merger, because they were certainly part of the controversy (Morrow, 1923). But Mann (1963: 174) has pointed out the significant role of non-theological factors in either predisposing merger or defending against it. For instance, Anglicans were generally of a higher social status than Methodist, and because its clergy were largely recruited from England, they were more anxious to maintain traditional ties. Another sociological reason for merger which occasioned response from other parts of Canada where competition had been longstanding was the desire for a religious basis for national unity (Silcox, 1933). What was happening automatically in the West was hoped would be a beginning for uniting all Canadians in one Christian church. Needless to say, the fact that the residents of the new nation were so ethnically diverse meant that such a goal would necessarily be postponed for at least a couple of generations, if indeed it would ever be attained. Recent talks of further merger with other groups has evidenced flagging interest, since there is nothing to make it a pressing issue.

The second type of organizational ecumenism that we have experienced in Canada has occurred when numerous groups with the same denominational label unite. This is particularly the case when each of the separate organizations were originally established as the result of differences in ethnic background. We have shown how much of the religious diversity in Canada was the result of ethnic diversity. When immigrants arrived from Norway, Denmark, or Germany, they did not get together because they were all Lutherans. It was their differences in language, customs, and nationalities which kept them apart (Freitag, 1963: 94–101).[7] The Lutherans are a good example of this phenomenon, since they form the state church in a number of European countries from which Canada has recruited immigrants. The variety of Lutheran churches present in Canada at one time included groups such as the United Danish Church, Finnish National Church, Danish Lutheran Church, Missouri Synod, Slovag Synod, Norwegian Lutheran Church, American Lutheran Church, and Augustana Synod among others (Eylands, 1945). As ethnicity and language declined in importance, merger developed naturally. At present, there are three Lutheran bodies in Canada. The largest is the Lutheran Church in America, which united the Danish Lutherans, Augustana Synod, and numerous other fragmented bodies. Running a close second in size is the Missouri Synod, which contains mostly persons of German descent, and the smallest body is the Evangelical Lutheran Church in Canada, which primarily consists of the Hauge Norwegians. The difference between these three bodies is less ethnic compared to the earlier diversity and more doctrinal, although ethnicity is still a factor. Talks of

7. Freitag's article is part of a series in J. W. Grant (1963) on all of the major religious bodies in Canada. It provides good summary reading.

further merger and co-operation to form one Lutheran Church in Canada recur from time to time. While we have illustrated this type of ecumenism with Lutherans, a similar analysis of such groups as Baptists or Catholics would reveal a similar pattern of the lowering of barriers between groups of similar denominational label but of different ethnic tradition.

One consequence of the trend toward ecumenism and its large bureaucratic religious organizations might be the re-emergence of numerous small religious groups with a sect-like character. Sociologists have observed that many people find a sense of community through their religious group which counteracts the impersonal world in which they live. The continued existence of numerous small religious groups then may fill important sociological functions for their adherents.

CONCLUSION

In this section, we have seen how man organizes his religious activity into numerous groups within Canadian society. These groups may form as a result of factors such as social class, ethnicity, and societal tensions, and each reflects the social diversity within that society. Clearly not everyone embracing a religious world view chooses to participate in or identify with religious organizations, but it is these organizations which serve as the primary vehicles for overt religious expression.

Religion and Social Stratification

Religious organizations are essentially associations of like-minded people. We have become accustomed to viewing the basis for these associations as a similarity of beliefs and practices shared by a group of people. Members of the group are therefore perceived to be compatible because of allegiances to the same doctrinal position. Sociologists have frequently observed, however, that religious associations are also dependent on the social and economic compatibility of their members.

Without making this principle into a law which demonstrates no exceptions, we can speak of the tendency of religious groups to represent a particular social class level in a society. Persons who are compatible socially and economically are more likely to be compatible doctrinally. This does not mean that all persons of similar status will hold the same religious beliefs, but that those who choose a religious association will likely choose one that is relevant to their class position. A steelworker is more likely to engage in religious activity with other blue-collar workers than with professional persons. People who are of similar educational and income levels are more likely to possess similar world views than persons of divergent levels. Since world view includes the explanation one's religion gives to the world, it is clear that in Canada the diversity of religious groups which have emerged from the Christian tradition is in a real sense at least partly the result of the desire of people of different socio-economic levels to develop more adequate meaning systems and forms of religious expression appropriate to their world.

Several examples can make this point clearer. The doctrinal world view of Jehovah's Witnesses with their negation of this world and their present anticipation of the end of the world gives us some indication why Kingdom Halls are seldom constructed in upper-class neighbourhoods. Their beliefs are incompatible with business executives who require a belief system which affirms the world as a legitimate sphere for business activity. As a result, Kingdom Halls are placed in working-class neighbourhoods where their ideology is more likely to find persons who find their specific beliefs appropriate. Similarly, persons whose education includes a university degree and who have developed a very rational mind-set tend to congregate with persons who possess similar characteristics. They will usually prefer a learned sermon, orderly worship, and more stately hymns. Persons with little education, on the other hand, are more likely to prefer a religious association which stresses a more emotionally demonstrative and personal participatory style of religion.

In our society it is common for people to drive to another part of the city merely to gather with those who share this compatibility on the socio-economic as well as doctrinal level. Few make such decisions consciously, but repeated sociological analyses demonstrates that this type of correlation exists (Demerath, 1965). Thus it is clear that suburban churches tend to represent the middle-class world view of the local residents. The content and style of religious activity found there can be set off quite sharply from the appeal that groups like the Salvation Army or storefront Pentecostal churches make to residents in the inner city.

Empirical studies of the social-class composition of churches in Canada have been few. However, Crysdale's (1965) study of the membership of the United Church of Canada demonstrated that that church tended to appeal to people of higher occupational status, such as professionals and technical people, and fared relatively poorly among blue-collar workers. Crysdale points out that the orientation of the United Church must apparently be more relevant to this particular class. For several generations United Church members have tended to attain a higher level of education than the population as a whole and Crysdale implies that religious associations based on theological consensus requires a similarity of social lifestyle.

This does not mean that representatives of other social classes are absent; rather that particular religious groups tend to recruit more from one particular class. There may be greater variation in denominations as a whole than in local churches where the class appeal may be more obvious. Even in Roman Catholicism, Falardeau (1949: 361) indicates that parishes are socially ranked, often by the class area in which they are located. He argues that when attendance moves out of the territorial boundaries of the local parish, as is frequent in urban areas, choice of church will reflect the social world view of the attender, since all churches actually offer the same basic services. The point of this discussion is that similarity of social characteristics is likely to be a major component in the formation of religious groupings.

Religion is adaptable to the needs of people and the needs vary with the socio-economic milieu in which people find themselves. Religion helps people interpret their own life pattern and role in the world and therefore can be referred to as a legitimating agent. A "legitimation" is an explanation or justification for the ways things are. It is an answer to "why" society is ordered as it is and explains "my" role in it. A legitimation need not necessarily be religious, but Berger (1969: 32) points out that religion is the most powerful legitimating agent because it relates the precarious social constructions of man with ultimate reality. Religion explains, for example, both poverty and wealth or illness and health to the persons involved.

Karl Marx (1963: 27–43) acknowledged this legitimating function of religion but criticized religion precisely because it conservatively justified man's place in society whatever it was. Religion, said Marx, gave people an illusory sense of happiness when what they really needed to do was change the societal conditions which produced the need for such illusions.

The existence of religion was evidence of the fact of man's alienation from ownership of the means of production. Religion comfortably legitimated the ruling class and acted as "opiate" by mesmerizing the proletariat into accepting their subjection. Because religion pacified the masses into accepting the status quo, Marx argued that it prevented them from participating in the anticipated proletarian revolution as the inaugural for the socialist society.

It is clear that Marx related religion primarily to man's economic position in society. He underscores the fact that religion is always made meaningful to socio-economic position even if he does become impatient with the ill-advised nature of that meaning system. Marx correctly asserted that religious preoccupations usually turn men's attentions away from social revolutions. What Marx failed to see is that to correct the economic injustices in a society is not to remove other elements of the human condition which may also prompt the need for religion.

The process by which individuals select their belief systems and their "brothers" in the faith is a very subtle process. People are seldom conscious of all the factors operating in their choices and preferences. A sociologist is bound to point out, however, that beliefs, practices, and comrades embraced are frequently a response to similarity in social position among believers. As people's social position changes, it is common to expect a change in religious affiliation from one church to another within a denomination or even from one denomination to another (Glock and Stark, 1968: 183–203).

RELIGION, ETHNICITY, AND SOCIAL CLASS

The rural orientation of French-Canadian society easily lent itself to domination by the British after the Conquest (Jones, 1972: 40–42). The departure of French administrators and entrepreneurs left a void which English-speaking Canadians came to fill with greater frequency, particularly as French Canada began to industrialize around the time of the First World War. It was the British ethnic group who provided the capital, expertise, and personnel and who actually were the leaders of industrialization in all of Canada, including Quebec. Since agricultural parish communities did not lend themselves to capitalist expansion, English-speaking Canadians took over as the directors, financiers, and managers of Canadian development. As a result there emerged a substantial gap between British and French in levels of income, occupation, and education. The gap was not only of ethnicity, however, but also of religion; for the British were the financiers and entrepreneurs with higher incomes and were also strongly Protestant. In contrast, the French were typically agrarian, lower class, and considerably poorer, as well as being Catholic (Porter, 1965: 100–3).

One of the classic studies of Protestant-Catholic differences in participation in rational worldly pursuits was written by Max Weber and entitled *The Protestant Ethic and the Spirit of Capitalism*. Weber observed that it was the Protestant countries which proceeded most rapidly in the industrialization process. Catholic countries, on the other hand, remained much more traditional and failed to develop a full-blown capitalist enterprise. Weber attempts to find the answer within the religious belief system of the Calvinist strain of Protestantism. He notes how the doctrine of "predestination" (predetermined salvation) and the concept of a "calling" turned anxious men (those who did not know if they were one of the elect) loose to engage in worldly activity "for the glory of God". The Calvinist saint wanted to prove to others and to himself through his this-worldly ascetic life that he was one of the elect. The end result of teaching the denial of pleasure, the absence of leisure, and the dominance of values such as thrift and disciplined hard work was the accumulation of large amounts of capital as well as the assured existence of a docile work force. Weber observes that these doctrines were seldom found in Catholic countries such as Spain and Italy, and that they were little involved in industrial and capitalist activity and much more tied to the traditional society. Protestantism then contained within itself the mechanisms to encourage social change and release the acquisitive and creative spirit while Catholism encouraged the perpetuation of the old order.

For many years Quebec clearly represented this type of traditional society quite at odds with the English Protestant communities surrounding it.[8] The leaders of French Canada in the frontier rural society were the priests, doctors, and lawyers, as opposed to the entrepreneurs, financiers, and corporation executives in leadership positions in English Can-

8. For a good analysis of the disparities between French and English in terms of income, occupation, and education, see Report of the Royal Commission on Bilingualism and Biculturalism (1969: 12–86).

ada (Rossides, 1968: 173–75). The maintenance of the rural French society was to the advantage of the old élite in Quebec and the Anglo-élite as well. The Anglo-Canadians agreed not to disturb the traditional society and its élite as long as they had full control over the capitalist development of Quebec. It is clear now why the Quiet Revolution has been not only an attempt to bring Quebec under French economic and industrial control but also in some sense to spurn Catholic control and influence as a drag or brake in the changes required for modernization. Classical colleges in Quebec could not adequately prepare a labour force for participation in industrialization as long as education focused on the humanities in such courses as Latin and philosophy under religious auspices. Furthermore, the level of school attendance was much lower among Roman Catholics than among Protestants (Royal Commission on Bilingualism and Biculturalism, Bk. iii, 1969: 25–34) thus relegating French Catholics to subordinate positions. As French educational institutions broke the bonds of traditionalism and moved away from religious tutelage, a technologically equipped labour force clamoured for equality with their Anglo-Canadian Protestant fellow citizens in what is known as the Quiet Revolution (Milner, 1973: 52–68).

Because religion and ethnicity are so intertwined and because ethnicity shows a high correlation with social-class level in Canada, particularly among the British and French, the important function of religion in explaining class positions within the society cannot be overestimated. Porter (1965: 516) has pointed out that persons of British descent and of Anglican affiliation are over-represented among all élites in Canada. Thus it is clear that the Protestant orientation in the country is not because Protestant numbers are so overwhelming, but because the class and power positions of Protestants have been much higher and have given them control.

Porter has argued that the only élite in Canada in which the French have been over-represented has been in the Catholic clergy (1965: 516) and their dominance has been felt in that area. The Catholic hierarchy has tended to recruit their members among Canadian-born rather than to rely heavily on external recruitment as the Anglicans have done. In general, however, the absence of French-Catholic élites in power positions in Canadian society has produced an imbalance of control by English Protestants in higher status positions.

RELIGION AND COLONIALISM

The spirit of adventure and commerce inherent in the exploration and colonization of the New World by major European countries was paralleled by a religious zeal and missionary spirit. New colonies were not merely trading outposts but were the vanguards of religious civilization to be brought to the new land. Along with the trader, explorer, and colonial administrator went religious personnel who together represented all aspects of the state and mother country: the land was claimed for both the state and the church. Missionaries were emissaries not only of religion but of religion as established in the mother country. Therefore the creation and propagation of the colonial church was an additional measure to ensure the maintenance of ties with the sponsoring state.

Walsh (1966: 34) argues that French-Canadian society actually emerged as a response to Catholic missionary zeal among the native Indians of North America. These converts could serve as a basis for the extension of the Catholic world and provided religious impetus for the colonization of the New World. Although not all early French settlers in Canada were Catholic, Quebec consisted of thoroughly Catholic colonies. Louis XIV had intended that New France would become a replica of France itself, with the same set of focal institutions, although it was clear that certain adaptations of the parish system would be necessary (Falardeau, 1964: 20). From the beginning, religion played an integral role in stimulating both the exploration and the colonization of Canada among the French. No doubt this stimulation was the foundation of a long-standing messianic doctrine in French-Canadian society whereby remaining French and Catholic was important in fulfilling a unique role in civilizing the continent.

In terms of Canadian society as a whole, the growth of the British presence introduced a new element of religious competition. The fact that the British then conquered the French placed the British in a position of dominance, which they were quite eager to retain. In that type of milieu, Protestantism became not merely a religious allegiance but a "political badge" of loyalty to the ruling power (Elgee, 1964: 2). Catholicism, on the other hand, became a badge of opposition or at least a threat to British control. Nevertheless, it was the divisions among English-speaking Canadians which ultimately gave French Catholics new hope for their independent existence in Canada (Walsh, 1956: 2).

In representing the mother country, the Church of England attempted to reconstruct its superior position by becoming the established church as it was at home. Government support for the Anglican Church would not only ensure its existence but also ultimately ought to strengthen British ties and loyalties. Land set aside for the support of the church was known as Clergy Reserves (Moir, 1959: 27–81). It was thought that the semi-established position of the Catholic Church in Quebec needed to be countered by a strong unified culture of church and state among English Canadians. However, as Elgee (1964: 10–47) points out, the Baptists, Methodists, and Presbyterians objected to this aristocratic idea, and by 1854 the notion of establishment of a particular religion in Canada crumbled. The separation of church and state meant equality before the law of all religious groups with no special favours or support given to any religious body by the government. Such a situation was the result of the existence of a plurality of religious bodies of English descent, however, and it was this fact that prevented the establishment of the Church of England in Canada. On the other hand, the unity of French Canadians in just one religious body and in one area location left the door open for Catholic insistence on state participation and support of education.

In this competitive setting, it is not surprising to find that in the opening of the West, Anglican missionaries participated right behind Catholic missionaries in outreach among the Indians. The gospel message notwithstanding, frontier evangelism appeared to have a bit of an imperial connotation, at least for the Anglican Church (Dawson and Younge, 1940: 209). The battle was not merely Anglicanism or Protestantism versus Catholicism (a religious conflict) but the English versus the French (a linguistic and cultural conflict). The later settlement of the West by Protestant groups such as Scandinavian and German Lutherans, Scottish Presbyterians, British and German Baptists, and numerous sectarian bodies ensured the English-Protestant dominance in that part of the country in spite of French-Catholic settlements and Catholic success among Indians and Métis.

The colonial ventures of two major European powers made an indelible mark on religion in Canadian society. The fact that religion was a significant factor in the colonization process of both France and England ensured that the society would perpetuate ethnic divisions easily reinforcible by religion.

CONCLUSION

Sociology has made it clear that a tendency persists for various forms of religion to be more appropriate to persons of similar rank on the stratification ladder. We have pointed out that the highest positions of power and control of the commercial sphere of Canadian society are mainly held by those who are not only English but also Protestant. Religious identifications are thus useful indexes of relative power roles in a society.

Religion and Social Change

Because religious activity takes place in a social context and social milieu, any change in that context or milieu will inevitably have some effect on the religious activity. Certainly there is a big difference between depression, war, societal revolution, and times of affluence. As the social environmental conditions change, new forms of religion may emerge or new emphases in a religion become appropriate to people searching for more adequate meaning systems. For example, Methodism as a new form of religious expression arose in England during a period when the agrarian society was being displaced by the Industrial Revolution and its requirements for urbanization. Similarly, the current emergence of the Jesus People movement is a response to a secular, technological, and impersonal society and its formal institutional religion (Enroth et al., 1972: 223–44). Changes within a society evoke changes within religion as well. We are therefore rejecting the notion that religion is impervious to social change. In spite of the fact that religion is concerned with non-empirical matters, religion is not immune to change, because those who practise that religion must constantly adapt to change.

The relationship between religion and social change displays two basic possibilities. Religion may be either a conservative force which thwarts social change or a potentially disruptive force which instigates change. Before we deal with either of these possibilities, let us prematurely resolve the dilemma by noting that both alternatives are likely to be present at least latently in a society. Furthermore, a religion which may once have been radical and conducive to social change may later become very staid and conservative.

THE CONSERVATIVE FUNCTION OF RELIGION

Earlier it was pointed out that religion assists people in interpreting their social position, and as a result it legitimates things the way they are and preserves the status quo. This suggests that there is a conservativeness inherent in religion because it reinforces the existing arrangement of society.

There is a school of thought within sociology known as "functionalism", in which emphasis is placed on how the parts of a social system function in order to maintain the equilibrium of a society. It is presumed that the presence of religion as a part of society indicates that it must have an important function in sustaining the social system or it would cease to exist. In carrying this argument to its conclusion, religion begins to take on an aura of indispensability for it is assumed to play some role in maintaining social cohesion in every society. While these presuppositions are clearly debatable, analysing religion through functionalist eyes does have the advantage of helping us determine the effect of religious behaviour on the society as a whole.

The repeated quest for the functions of religion has produced the persistent predisposition to identify the conservative or integrative aspects of religion. How does religion help to keep a society functioning efficiently and keep it together? It was Durkheim (1965) who first discussed this matter theoretically after his study of Australian aborigines. Durkheim concluded that religious behaviour was primarily a means by which individuals indicated their commitment to the life of the group and therefore religious activity was really the worship of the norms, values, and symbols of society. The basic norms of the group were contained in the religious beliefs, and religious ritual acted out the values which held the group together and reaffirmed its solidarity. Religion functioned to preserve the society by sacralizing the social tradition and conserving the society as it exists.

It is obviously much easier to see the integrative function of religion in a simple society than in a complex, highly differentiated society. The type of tribal society which Durkheim analysed is seldom found in the modern world. Since contemporary societies are characterized by a plurality of religions, it is virtually impossible to speak of one common religion which gives cohesion to the society. Attempts have been made, however, to speak of national religions in the United States in what have been referred to as the "American Way of Life" (Herberg, 1955: 75) or "civil religion" (Bellah, 1967: 1–21). The notion of a common religion or value system which pervades Canadian society is difficult to determine. Generally, our legal system and moral codes reflect Christian themes but that is all that can be said.

It is within particular regions or communities in Canada that we find that religion has harnessed human energies to the socio-religious group. In French Canada, there is no doubt that the Catholic Church was a unifying influence in the creation of a single culture and in the creation of community (Garigue, 1965: 129; Moreux, 1973: 324–35). While the traditional French Catholic community was appropriate to the rural agricultural era of Quebec, it was not necessarily accepted that way later. Rioux (1973: 260–78) notes that the desire to preserve French culture against Anglicization produced an ideology of conservation in which the Catholic Church and its leaders were the chief bulwark. Following the First World War, the desire to update Quebec society began to be voiced as industrialization and urbanization accelerated. It was here that social change took place so rapidly that the Church began to lose its centripetal position. Hence the Church was more likely to defend the traditional society because control for the building of the new Quebec was wrested from their hands and assumed by the new middle class. It is this new group of educated professionals who blame the Church for maintaining the old parish society into the new age and failing to stimulate the industrial development of Quebec. It has also been pointed out by Lacoste (1973: 167) that the Catholic Church in Quebec was facing social change on two fronts—that of the Quiet Revolution and that of the pressures of secular society through Vatican II.

Several other examples can be given of how religion often acts as a conservative force in a society. At one extreme are groups like the Old Order Amish-Mennonites whose religious association forbids contact with the secular world except on a regulated basis (Gingerich, 1972). The resistance to change and modernization is acute and the solidarity of the group is threatened when compliance to the religious prescriptions is questioned. As a result, there are strong conformity pressures and means of discipline to ensure the adherence of the Amish to traditional values in spite of social change surrounding them. Religion clearly reinforces and preserves the traditional society.

On the other hand, we find that among those who participate more freely in Canadian society, there appears to be some link between religious participation and conservatism. A preoccupation with religious concerns frequently has the effect of reducing interest in innovation and social change. Proselytization and institutional activity have priority over political crusading. In addition, the establishment nature of many religious institutions with their bureaucratic élites ensures that they will champion tradition more frequently than change. Schindeler and Hoffman (1968) found a correlation between political conservatism, anti-communism, and theological conservatism among Baptist ministers in Ontario and Quebec. Meisel (1956) made the surprising discovery in Kingston, Ontario, that Catholics who were closer to the Church tended to vote strongly for the Conservative Party in contrast to the usual tendency of Catholics in general to vote Liberal. McDonald (1969) has also suggested that degree of involvement in a religious community is directly related to voting habits. The point to be taken is that religious institutions and participation in them appears to be more conducive to strengthening societal institutions than to reorganizing them.

A study of religion in Alberta during the 1940s (Mann, 1955) has demonstrated that the inability of traditional religious institutions to adapt to the needs of a different environment was the effect of the institutional conservativeness of the churches. The traditional liturgy, formal style of worship, centralization of control in an ecclesiastical bureaucracy, and more sophisticated social background of the leadership meant that the transplanted mainline churches lost ground to the new non-denominational groups which emerged from within the prairie society. The new groups were much more adaptable to the changes required by the frontier than the staid churches with their built-in resistance to change. As a result, the more "radical" and "non-conformist" religious groups experienced significant success at the expense of the more institutionalized and thus conservative forms of religion.

The possibility of some forms of religion throwing off the mantle of conservativeness and actively responding to change leads us to a discussion of the potential conflict role of religion. The fact that some left-wing priests and Archbishop Charbonneau of Montreal supported strikers in the Asbestos Strike of 1949, and received opposition from within the Church for doing so, demonstrates the conservative cast of religious bodies from a social change perspective (Garry, 1970: 252–60). Nevertheless, because religions are leaders and motivaters of men, the potential for religion serving in the vanguard of social change and in opposition to the status quo remains.

RELIGION AS A DISRUPTIVE FORCE

Even though religion usually assumes a conservative role in a society, there are notable instances of religion proving a significant source of divisiveness, threatening the integration of a society. For example, Whitaker points to the denominational system of education operating in Newfoundland, which is guaranteed by its constitution. Five distinct educational administrations are set up to provide schools under the guidance of Roman Catholics, Anglicans, United Free Church, Salvation Army, and Pentecostals. Denominational differences which are an integral part of residents' childhood socialization even become a basis for sociality later in life (for instance, longshoremen in St. John's are divided by denominational differences). These differences have also produced a procedure whereby public offices are allocated to persons on the basis of their denominational affiliation.

Religion has also contributed to divisions along political lines in Canada. In fact, there is a high correlation between religious affiliation and voting habits (Anderson, 1966; McDonald, 1969; Meisel, 1956; Regenstreif, 1964). Catholics show a strong disposition to vote Liberal, regardless of whether they reside in Quebec, while Protestants display a strong tendency to vote Conservative. On the popular level there has been the feeling in some quarters that the Liberal Party is the political arm of the Catholic Church because of the co-operation between the two units, and perhaps conversely that the Conservative Party is the political weapon of the Protestant industrial establishment. While such an assumption overstates the case, it reveals something of the nature of the conflict and makes it clear that religious organizations have a political tradition to which its affiliators unofficially adhere. This type of polarization on linguistic, ethnic, religious, and now political lines reinforces the divisions in Canadian society. All four factors reinforce one another but it is religious differences which makes the conflict all the more intense.

In a deeper sense, religion has not only legitimated opposition between groups in the society; it has also been an important generator of conflict and change. Religion may provide new goals or ideals and inspire people to attain them even when it requires a break from traditional social patterns. There is no doubt that since the turn of the century, Canadian Protestantism has contained within it a strong stream of response to and leadership in social change (Allen, 1971). The impact of industrialization, immigration, and urbanization awakened the social consciences of the leadership of Methodist, Presbyterian, and Anglican churches by the First World War, and they frequently passed resolutions of concern and action. It was particularly the Methodist Church, however, which produced the leaders to carry this crusade in a public way. For example, during the Winnipeg General Strike in 1919 the leadership included several Methodist ministers such as William Ivens, J. S. Woodsworth, and A. E. Smith. As a body, the Methodist Church had called for a radical reconstruction of Canadian society in order that co-operation might be substituted for the competitive system then in operation (Crysdale, 1961: 41). All Methodists did not necessarily agree with such a course of action, but sufficient feelings were present among both the leadership and the rank-and-file to evoke a call for change. In opposition to industrial competitive capitalism, they advocated a Christian socialism, and clergymen like Woodsworth, Baptist clergyman Tommy Douglas, and United Church minister Stanley Knowles became active in the founding of the Co-operative Commonwealth Federation (CCF). The pressure for social change under religious inspiration encouraged the formation of a group called The Fellowship for a Christian Social Order in 1931 and it sponsored the publication of a book entitled *Toward the Christian Revolution* (Scott and Vlastos, 1936).

Similarly, William Aberhart, a high-school principal and religious radio broadcaster brought religion directly into politics in an attempt to re-arrange the social system—though on the basis of free enterprise. He found biblical parallels and religious motivations for his attacks on establishment politicians, financiers ("Bay Street Barons"), industrialists, and establishment denominations in the name of social justice (Irving, 1959). The success at the polls of the Social Credit movement in Alberta in 1935 was evidence that the religious legitimations for the changes that were advocated had persuaded and convinced many persons who ordinarily might not have become involved in this type of activity.

There are times then when religion can be a vital force in social change. It is seldom, however, that entire religious institutions or organizations give themselves to such usage. Institutions are conservative by definition. This does not preclude the possibility that individual religious leaders will not utilize their influence and ideology to promote social change. For example, in their attitudes to specific issues requiring considerable change in Canada, United Church ministers have demonstrated a distinct desire to reform the status quo rather than adopt an accommodative and pietistic stance (Crysdale, 1965: 57). But as a general principle, we can say that in Canada organized religion has generally been a conservative force, supporting the solidarity of the society (or one of its constituent parts). Nevertheless, individual leaders have arisen, particularly Protestantism, whose influence for change has been considerable.

SECULARIZATION

In a world experiencing rapid social change, it is inconceivable that religion would not also be a party to such changes. The question raised in this section is how have changes in the social context in which religious beliefs are held and religious practices take place affected the form and content of religious expression through time. Certainly the role and style of religion in a feudal manor was considerably different from the religion we find in an industrial metropolis.

It is very difficult blatantly to claim people were more religious or less religious in comparative periods of history. Our standards of measurement of what is considered to be religiosity may be different, and it is always difficult to determine what people really mean by engaging in a particular activity. For example, in the modern era, sociologists entered into considerable debate to determine the significance of the marked increase in church attendance in North America in the 1950s and early 1960s (Glock and Stark, 1965: 68–85). Particularly in the light of the recent decrease in church attendance, does this mean that we were less religious prior to the 1950s and now, but more religious in the period of so-called religious revival? Such rapid shifts cause us to look much deeper at whether there is any significant relationship between external religious activity and inward conviction, and we are always left to speculate about the "real" import of our data.

In spite of this caution, it is possible to conclude that in earlier periods of history, men were more likely to view the world through religious eyes than they are today. They were much more aware of the supernatural and participated in religious activity without question. Religion was part of the taken-for-granted social world which the individual inhabited.

The world in which we presently live, however, is anything but taken for granted. "Criticism", "invention", "improvement", and "creativity" are all lauded and contain within themselves the seeds of change. In addition, it is rationality that predominates in the modern world (Weber, 1958: 24) and which has made our technological development possible. Education is a matter of analysis, criticism, and reflection, and all of these features combine to produce differences in individual evaluations of the world. Thus, it is clear that a uniform religious world view held by all members in a society is a phenomenon of the past, in addition to the fact that it is science which encourages man to control his own world rather than depend on other forces. As a result, religious world views have become less important, and when they do appear they exhibit considerable diversity from person to person.

Obviously this shift did not take place over night. The change in the role of religion in society was a gradual process that we refer to as "secularization". Considerable controversy exists, however, over the meaning of the term secularization and what precisely it signifies. One approach to secularization emphasizes the retreat or withdrawal of religion from involvement in the secular sphere of society. Secularization in this case means the removal of religious institutions, leaders, and symbols from influential participation in any other sphere of society but religion itself. Parsons (1963) argues that religion has been structurally differentiated from the rest of society, from involvement in politics, education, industry, etc., and that as a result religion has become purer because it is no longer being meddled with or is meddling in secular societal activity. Religion has a more powerful and central role in society, he argues, because it operates more directly through personal values. While this statement is difficult to substantiate, it is clear that religion has been separated from other social institutions and relegated to its own sphere of activity.

Berger (1969: 109–25) asserts that secularization as the social differentiation of religion was inherent in Christianity itself but only blossomed fully with the advent of Protestantism and industrial capitalism. The institutional specialization of religion in the church, for example, removed religion into one sphere of society so that other spheres of the society were identified as the profane and secular world. Protestantism went further and placed the essence of religion in the biblical text and thus minimized the role of the institution. When the authority of the text was questioned, Berger argues, and the believer no longer had the social support of the institution, the secularization of individual consciousness could take place, leaving large numbers of individuals without any religious world view. While both Parsons and Berger begin with the structural differentiation of religion in modern society, as evidence of secularization, Berger disagrees with Parsons's conclusion and notes that it has left religion on the sidelines as a peripheral endeavour for many people.

Another approach to secularization stresses the generally decreasing importance of religion in a society, rather than merely its compartmentalization. From this perspective, secularization is "the process whereby religious thinking, practice, and institutions lose social significance" (Wilson, 1966: xiv). Religion has become a private venture for many and as a result has lost its societal impact. Wilson argues from British data that institutional religion as we know it has seen its day, although he warns of the social costs of this event.

The third approach to secularization is the functionalist approach and is best represented by M. J. Yinger (1970: 5–16). Religion existed in the first place, according to Yinger, because it served certain human needs. Since the problems of the human condition are the same so that these needs still remain, the decline of one form of religion ought to cause us to determine in what new form of religion these needs are being met. Secularization then means religious change, not the gradual disappearance of religion as in the second approach. New forms of religion might mean that the traditional religion re-emerges but dressed in different garb, such as the Jesus People movement; or it could mean the development of new religions. Functionalism insists that every society will possess something which functions like religion even if it is not what we have customarily called religion. Attention then is focused on religious substitutes or "surrogates", which may take the place of traditional religion.

The reader may want to take his choice regarding which view of secularization is most accurate. Probably elements of all three are present. While the functionalist theory presents many theoretical problems, it is more likely that religious change describes the situation in Canada better than religious decline. While the decline of institutional religion may be obvious, the rise of such diverse groups as Transcendental Meditationists, Hare Krishna, Worldwide Church of God, Universal Truth, Marxists, and Jesus People indicate that man's "ultimate concerns" have not disappeared. A Toronto study of Roman Catholics indicated that even those who have ceased to attend church generally do not reject Catholic doctrine, although they may tend to interpret it symbolically (Northover, 1974: 450–51).

In a survey, taken in July 1973, the Canadian Institute of Public Opinion discovered that 50 per cent of all Canadians claimed that organized religion was a relevant part of their life. An interesting point is that on a regional basis, a continuum of positive responses ran from east to west. The Atlantic region was highest with 63 per cent, Quebec 58 per cent, Ontario 46 per cent, and the West 40 per cent. More women (55 per cent) than men (44 per cent) found organized religion an important part of their life and almost two-thirds of those over fifty years of age as opposed to just over one-third of those eighteen to twenty-nine years of age agreed that organized religion was a part of their life. This indicates that organized religion is more attractive to the older generation and that younger persons are perhaps the participants in the new forms of religion.[9]

It has been argued elsewhere (Hiller, 1969: 179–87) that several sociological factors have produced this religious change. The reification of the institution of religion as a formidable, unchangeable, bureaucratic force, the compartmentalization and therefore irrelevance of religion, and a socialization crisis in which weak socialization into traditional patterns fosters shallow rootage in a religious faith has resulted in a predisposition toward religious creativity and change.

9. For a report of attitudes toward   Sévigny (1974: 462–76).
religion by youth in Quebec, see

Evidence for our thesis of religious change rather than mere decline in Canada is further substantiated by a September 1971 survey of belief in God by the Canadian Institute of Public Opinion. The poll revealed that nine out of ten Canadians believe in God as a personal being or some kind of spirit or force. Among Catholics, the percentage was 96 per cent while Protestants registered 89 per cent. Canadians may be less religious in the traditional or sociologically observable sense, but they are far from being irreligious. We can speak of this trend as the "privatization" of religion. Whether it will eventually reverse itself, however, remains to be seen.

Two other interesting side issues to secularization emerge from the Canadian Institute of Public Opinion. Canadians have always tended to guard Sundays as a day distinct from the rest of the week, with the closure of retail stores and offices. Support for this practice still continues: 54 per cent of all Canadians reject Sunday retailing (April 3, 1974). People of French descent (63 per cent) and other ethnic groups (55 per cent) felt more strongly about this issue than those of English descent, only 50 per cent of whom rejected Sunday opening. Only one-third of those opposed to Sunday retailing, however, cited religious reasons for their objection. Concern for the worker was the primary motive that was stated. Therefore, blue laws regulating Sunday retailing are perhaps more of a vestige of a religious tradition which the society as a whole still prefers, although the reasons for maintaining the tradition may be based on different grounds.

The tendency toward less parochialism and greater tolerance is reflected in an August 1973 survey of Canadian attitudes toward religious inter-marriages. Sixty-seven per cent approved of marriages between Catholics and Protestants whereas only 61 per cent approved in 1968. Approval for marriages between Jews and Gentiles showed a smaller jump from 52 per cent to 56 per cent. But when the data are analysed by age group, approval of intermarriages in both categories is considerably higher in the eighteen to twenty-nine years age group than it is for older persons. Tolerance and social change is also reflected in Crysdale's (1965: 19) study, which pointed out that whereas dancing would have been frowned upon in the United Church prior to the Second World War, it was over-whelmingly accepted by laymen and ministers alike in 1963.

Secularization has produced an interesting mixture of tendencies in Canada from which it is difficult to project the future of religion. It is clear, however, that just as we are in the throes of social change, we are also facing the dilemmas and paradoxes of religious change.

RELIGION AND URBANIZATION

One of the most revolutionizing social changes which Canada has experienced has been the rapid urbanization of the population. Urbanization changes not only the physical environment but also the social environment of individuals. The rural dweller's dependence on nature, his relative occupational isolation, and his residence among a sparse but stable population stands in marked contrast to the artificial, man-made environment of the city and its high occupational specialization and interdependencies among a population of high mobility and density. Traditions die much harder in rural environments because there are not the perpetual pressures for change that are present to the same extent in urban areas. Obviously, rural areas are no longer the cozy traditional areas which they were often journalistically described to be, for urbanization has been a process of change that has not only affected cities. What we wish to specify is in what ways urbanization has effected changes in religious behaviour.

Crysdale's (1965) study of the United Church of Canada was essentially an attempt to determine how urbanization has affected the religiosity of members of that body. In terms of membership, urbanization generally meant the growth of suburban congregations and the decline of membership in inner city or downtown churches. In matters of belief, urbanization meant the tendency toward a more liberal theology. The more highly urbanized a people were, the more doctrinal liberalism was pronounced regardless of age, marital status, or ethnic origin. As income and education increased, liberalism was also found to increase. Crysdale's use of the term urbanism is not necessarily related to place of residence but refers to openness to new ideas, high personal interaction, and high social mobility, among other things. His data therefore leave us with some confusion as to the effect that rural or urban community residence has on religious beliefs. What does emerge, however, is the existence of a definite correlation between theological liberalism and urbanization.

Urbanization has also had an effect on religion in rural areas (Whyte, 1966). The dwindling population and the lack of qualified clergy has made rural religion less organizationally viable, often forcing churches to close their doors or seek new mergers or coalitions at the local level. In addition, rural churches in Canada usually possess older and less well educated clergymen than are found in urban areas. Rural churches may thus appear more conservative or orthodox than their urban counterparts. Whyte argues that technology has changed rural man considerably, while at the same time, rural religion has remained much more static than urban religion. This lag on the part of the rural church in adapting to the secular world has made it a conservative institution often quite at odds with the form and style of religion found in urban locales. Urbanization in the long run has reduced the vitality (and perhaps even the need for vitality) or rural religious institutions.

Urbanization has also meant the development of huge sprawling suburbs at the periphery of metropolitan areas. It is here that denominations have had some of their greatest success, most frequently among middle-class people. It is here, too, that the family orientation is strongest, and it has frequently been observed that the suburban church is an important mechanism in fostering family integration and reinforcing and socializing desired values among the children. In contrast to the central city, it is here that perpetual religious activity and modern facilities are readily visible. The flourishing of religious activity in the suburbs is often accounted for by the greater orientation of its residents to the local area as a place for community. Carlos (1970) tested this thesis among Catholics in Montreal and determined that suburban residents view their local territory more as the basis of a quasi-community than do people in other locations. This community orientation precipitated a higher level of public religious activity (attendance) as one moved toward the periphery of the city. The proportion of those attending who took communion (as an index of individual religiosity), however, was much lower in suburban areas. It is clear that the higher participation rate in the suburbs has a sociological explanation rooted in the role of the church as a vehicle for family and community integration.

CONCLUSION

The social context contributes greatly to variations in religious behaviour. Any change in that social context will produce further variations and adaptations in religion. Parallel to our discussion of secularization ought to have been a discussion of the sociology of irreligion or of those who claim no religious interests or affiliations at all. Unfortunately, our knowledge of this segment of the population is woefully inadequate, and sociologists are just beginning an analysis of this phenomenon, which, since it is not organized, is very difficult to locate. Nevertheless, as long as social change is a major theme in our society, the adaptations made by religions, or the reluctance to make adaptations, will provide interesting data on the interrelationship between religion and society.

A Final Note

We began with the assumption that in so far as religion was available to sociological investigation, an analysis of people who believe and practise religion would tell us something about the social diversity and tensions experienced in any society. It has become clear that religion has been far from an insignificant factor in Canadian society and that it has been caught up in everything from the settlement of Canada to the industrial development of Canada. Whatever shape and form the religion of the future will take, we can be guaranteed that it will reflect the needs which emerge from the social contexts in which man finds himself.

Select Bibliography

ALLEN, R. *The Social Passion: Religion and Social Reform in Canada 1914–28.* Toronto: University of Toronto Press, 1971.

ANDERSON, G. M. "Voting Behavior and the Ethnic-Religious Variable: A Study of a Federal Election in Hamilton, Ontario", *Canadian Journal of Economics and Political Science* 32 (1966): 27–37.

BARCLAY, HAROLD B. "A Lebanese Community in Lac La Biche, Alberta", in J. L. Elliott, ed., *Minority Canadians 2, Immigrant Groups.* Scarborough: Prentice-Hall, 1971.

BELLAH, ROBERT N. "Civil Religion in America", *Daedalus,* Winter 1967, pp. 1–21.

BERGER, P. L. *The Sacred Canopy: Elements of a Sociological Theory of Religion.* New York: Doubleday, 1967.

BHATT, G. S. "Brahmo Samaj, Arya Samaj, and the Church-Sect Typology", *Review of Religious Research* 10 (Fall 1968): 23–32.

CARLOS, S. "Religious Participation and the Urban-Suburban Continuum", *American Journal of Sociology* 75 (1970): 242–59.

CLARK, S. D. *Church and Sect in Canada.* Toronto: University of Toronto Press, 1948.

———. *The Developing Canadian Community.* Toronto: University of Toronto Press, 1962.

CLIFFORD, N. K. "Religion and the Development of Canadian Society: An Historiographical Analysis", *Church History* 38 (December 1969): 506–23.

CRYSDALE, STEWART. *The Industrial Struggle and Protestant Ethics in Canada.* Toronto: Ryerson, 1961.

———. *The Changing Church in Canada.* Toronto: The Board of Evangelism and Social Service, 1965.

DAWSON, C. A., and YOUNGE, E. R. *Pioneering in the Prairie Provinces: The Social Side of the Settlement Process.* Toronto: Macmillan, 1940.

DEMERATH, N. J. *Social Class in American Protestantism.* Chicago: Rand McNally, 1965.

DEMERATH, N. J. III, and HAMMOND, P. E. *Religion in Social Context.* New York: Random House, 1969.

DURKHEIM, E. *The Elementary Forms of the Religious Life.* New York: The Free Press, 1915.

ELGEE, W. H. *The Social Teachings of the Canadian Churches.* Toronto: Ryerson, 1964.

ENROTH, R.; ERICSON, E. E.; and PETERS, C. B. *The Jesus People: Old-Time Religion in the Age of Aquarius.* Grand Rapids: Eerdmans, 1972.

EYLANDS, V. J. *Lutherans in Canada.* Winnipeg: Columbia Press, 1945.

FALARDEAU, J. C. "The Parish as an Institutional Type", *The Canadian Journal of Economics and Political Science* 15 (1949): 354–67.

———. "The Seventeenth-Century Parish in French Canada", in M. Rioux and Y. Martin, eds., *French-Canadian Society.* Toronto/Montreal: McClelland and Stewart, 1964.

FREITAG, W. "Lutheran Tradition in Canada", in J. W. Grant, ed., *The Churches and the Canadian Experience.* Toronto: Ryerson, 1963.

GARIGUE, PHILIPPE. "Change and Continuity in Rural French Canada", in M. Rioux and Y. Martin, eds., *French-Canadian Society.* Toronto/Montreal: McClelland and Stewart, 1964.

GARRY, CARL. "The Asbestos Strike and Social Change in Quebec", in W. E. Mann, ed., *Social and Cultural Change in Canada,* Vol. I. Toronto: Copp Clark, 1970.

GINGERICH, O. *The Amish of Canada.* Waterloo, Ont.: Conrad Press, 1972.

GLOCK, C. Y., and STARK, R. *Religion and Society in Tension.* Chicago: Rand McNally, 1965.

GRANT, J. W., ed. *The Churches and the Canadian Experience.* Toronto: Ryerson, 1963.

GREELEY, A. M. *The Denominational Society.* London: Scott, Forseman, 1972.

HEER, DAVID M. "The Trend of Interfaith Marriages in Canada: 1922–1957", *American Sociological Review* 27 (1962): 245–50.

HERBERG, W. *Protestant-Catholic-Jew.* New York: Doubleday, 1960.

HILLER, H. H. "The New Theology and the Sociology of Religion", *The Canadian Review of Sociology and Anthropology* 6 (August 1969): 179–87.

IRVING, J. A. *The Social Credit Movement in Alberta.* Toronto: University of Toronto Press, 1959.

JONES, RICHARD. *Community in Crisis: French-Canadian Nationalism in Perspective.* Toronto: McClelland and Stewart, 1972.

LACOSTE, NORBERT. "The Catholic Church in Quebec: Adapting to Change", in D. C. Thomson, ed., *Quebec Society and Politics: Views from the Inside.* Toronto: McClelland and Stewart, 1973.

MANN, W. E. *Sect, Cult and Church in Manitoba.* Toronto: University of Toronto Press, 1955.

———. "The Canadian Church Union, 1925", in N. Ehrenstrom and W. G.

Muelder, eds., *Institutionalism and Church Unity*. New York: Association Press, 1963.

MARUNCHAK, MICHAEL H. *The Ukrainian Canadians: A History*. Winnipeg: Winnipeg Ukrainian Free Academy of Sciences, 1970.

MARX, K., and ENGELS, F. *Manifesto of the Communist Party*. New York: International Publishers, 1932.

MCDONALD, L. "Religion and Voting: A Study of the 1968 Canadian Federal Election in Ontario", *Canadian Review of Sociology and Anthropology* 6 (1969): 429–41.

MEISEL, JOHN. "Religious Affiliation and Electoral Behaviour: A Case Study", *Canadian Journal of Economics and Political Science* 22 (November 1956): 481–96.

MILLETT, D. "The Orthodox Church: Ukrainian, Greek and Syrian", in J. L. Elliott, ed., *Minority Canadians 2: Immigrant Groups*. Scarborough: Prentice-Hall, 1971.

MILNER, H., and MILNER, S. H. *The Decolonization of Quebec: An Analysis of Left-Wing Nationalism*. Toronto: McClelland and Stewart, 1973.

MOIR, J. S. *Church and State in Canada West*. Toronto: University of Toronto Press, 1959.

MOL, J. J. "Churches and Immigrants Research Group for European Migration Problems", *Bulletin* 9 (May 1961): 1–80.

MOREUX, COLETTE. "The End of a Religion", in G. A. Gold and M. A. Tremblay, eds., *Communities and Culture in French Canada*. Toronto/Montreal: Holt, Rinehart and Winston, 1973.

MORROW, E. L. *Church Union in Canada*. Toronto: Thomas Allen, 1923.

NIEBUHR, R. *The Social Sources of Denominationalism*. New York: The World Publishing Company, 1957.

NORTHOVER, W. E. "Variations in Belief Among Roman Catholics", in C. Beattie and S. Crysdale, eds., *Sociology Canada*. Scarborough: Butterworth, 1974.

O'DEA, T. F. *The Sociology of Religion*. Englewood Cliffs, N.J.: Prentice-Hall, 1966.

O'TOOLE, ROGER. "A Consideration of 'Sect' as an Exclusively Religious Concept: Notes on Underground Traditions in the Study of Sectarianism". Unpublished paper, University of Toronto, 1971.

PARSONS, TALCOTT. "Christianity and Modern Industrial Society", in E. A. Tiryakian, ed., *Sociological Theory, Values, and Sociocultural Change*. New York: The Free Press, 1963.

PORTER, JOHN. *The Vertical Mosaic: An Analysis of Social Class and Power in Canada*. Toronto: University of Toronto Press, 1965.

REGENSTREIF, S. P. "Group Perceptions and the Vote: Some Avenues of Opinion Formation in the 1962 Campaign", in J. Meisel, ed., *Papers on the 1962 Election*. Toronto: University of Toronto Press, 1974.

RIOUX, MARCEL. "The Development of Ideologies in Quebec", G. A. Gold and M. A. Tremblay, eds., *Communities and Culture in French Canada*. Toronto/Montreal: Holt, Rinehart and Winston, 1973.

ROSENBERG, L. *Canada's Jews: A Social and Economic Study of the Jews in Canada*. Montreal: Bureau of Social and Economic Research, Canadian Jewish Congress, 1939.

ROSSIDES, D. W. *Society as a Functional Process: An Introduction to Sociology*. Toronto: McGraw-Hill, 1968.

Royal Commission on Bilingualism and Biculturalism. Book III, *The Work World*. Ottawa: Information Canada.

SCHINDELER, F., and HOFFMAN, D. "Theological and Political Conservatism: Variations in Attitudes Among Clergymen of One Denomination", *Canadian Journal of Political Science*, Vol. I (December 1968).

SCOTT, R. B. Y., and VLASTOS, G., eds. *Toward the Christian Revolution*. Chicago: Willett Clarke, 1936.

SÉVIGNY, R. "Religious Experience Among Quebec Youth", in C. Beattie and S. Crysdale, eds., *Sociology Canada*. Scarborough: Butterworth, 1974.

SILCOX, C. E. *Church Union in Canada: Its Causes and Consequences*. New York: Institute of Social and Religious Research, 1933.

STARK, R., and GLOCK, C. Y. *American Piety: The Nature of Religious Commitment*. Los Angeles: University of California Press, 1968.

TROELTSCH, E. *The Social Teachings of the Christian Churches*. New York: Harper and Row, 1960.

WALSH, H. H. *The Christian Church in Canada*. Toronto: Ryerson, 1956.

———. *The Church in the French Era*. Toronto: Ryerson, 1966.

WEBER, MAX. *The Protestant Ethic and the Spirit of Capitalism*. New York: Scribner's, 1958.

WHYTE, D. R. "Religion and the Rural Church", in M. A. Tremblay and W. J. Anderson, eds., *Rural Canada in Transition*. Ottawa: Agricultural Economics Research Council of Canada, 1966.

WILSON, B. R. *Religion in Secular Society*. London: C. A. Watts, 1966.

———. *Religious Sects*. Toronto/New York: McGraw-Hill, 1970.

WILSON, D. J. *The Church Grows in Canada*. Toronto: Ryerson, 1966.

YINGER, M. J. *The Scientific Study of Religion*. New York: Macmillan, 1970.

The Sociology of Canadian Education 10

JANE SYNGE

Introduction

Every human society faces the lengthy, difficult, and absolutely essential task of converting its new-born infants into smoothly functioning members of the group. Children arrive without the habits, beliefs, attitudes, and characteristic ways of behaving which constitute a human *personality*. They also lack any knowledge regarding the patterned, shared ways of behaving and interacting which are called *culture*. The manner in which the neonate acquires a human personality and learns how to behave as a member of a society is designated by the term *socialization*. Throughout most of the vast sweep of human experience, and currently in some tribal and folk societies, socialization has consisted chiefly of learning during face-to-face interaction with parents, kinsmen, and other members of the primary group. In modern industrial societies, however, socialization has increasingly been transferred from the primary group to formal organizations called schools, and in this way the process of socialization has been rationalized to meet the demands of rapidly changing social and economic conditions. This chapter will examine this formal educational institution as it has developed in Canadian society.

From the Canadian perspective, the sociology of education is a largely underdeveloped branch of the discipline. In contrast to other aspects of the society, there is a definite paucity of published material on the topic. What is available consists mainly of government reports concerning schools, studies of socialization with respect to native peoples, immigrants and specific ethnic groups, and, more recently, a growing body of protest literature about schools and the socialization process in general. These materials, while important in and of themselves for the purposes for which they were intended, require a great deal of work and effort before they can be integrated into a systematic and scholarly body of knowledge about the educational institution comparable to the work already accomplished in other areas of Canadian society.

Given the importance of educating the young and the limited amount of published research on the subject, this chapter must depend on available works. First, material on the historical development of educational institutions and practices in Canada is presented. A discussion of educational controversies and policies with respect to language and ethnicity is next, followed by information concerning the structure of the school system in Canada, with special emphasis upon the concept *social class* and its relationship to the vital question of access to education. Finally, the chapter relates information about the school system and formal education to the broader and more inclusive concept of socialization as a basic and fundamental social process.

The Historical Development

Early nineteenth-century Canada was an agricultural society, and few ordinary people received extensive schooling. Children were sometimes taught in church schools, sometimes in community schools, and often their own parents taught them to read and write and understand the elements of their religious faith. Advanced education was for the small minority who attended grammar schools, the classical colleges, and the universities. Research in Hamilton, Ontario, in the 1850s and 1860s showed that school attendance was often seasonal and that substantial numbers of children did not attend school at all or left early; only the children of professionals and small-business people stayed in school in any numbers once they had reached their teens (Katz, 1971). Colonial governments did provide grants in aid to some schools but much of the cost was met directly by parents.

By the mid nineteenth century, education was starting to be considered of public importance. The general education of the populace was viewed by the established groups as one means of achieving national unity and political stability. Similar ideas were also being aired in many parts of Europe and North America.

There was considerable contact between educationists in English-speaking Canada and those abroad. Egerton Ryerson, who became superintendent of education in Upper Canada in 1846, was largely responsible for implementing the plans for public education in Ontario, and many features of the Ontario system were adopted later in the western provinces. Ryerson had studied the public educational systems being introduced in countries such as Ireland, Prussia, and the United States (McNeill, 1974). Public education was to bring basic education to the masses. Its introduction also involved elements of social control. Ryerson was among those who complained that subversive ideas were being introduced by American teachers and through the use of American school books (Ryerson, 1847).

Public education would be available to all, and its content could be determined by the state. Increased attendance and the maintenance of certain standards in content and teaching were seen as important goals. To increase attendance, school taxes were eventually levied. School fees, which might prevent some from attending, could then be lowered or abolished. To achieve control of standards and content centralized administrative bodies were set up with power to appoint inspectors, certify teachers, and specify the texts to be used. Such a system was being developed in Ontario in the 1850s and 1860s, and by the 1870s the western provinces were adopting systems based on this model. In Quebec, on the other hand, the school system remained, until recently, under the control of the Catholic Church.

New public school systems, centrally administered, were not acceptable to all, of course. There were instances of opposition in the mid and late nineteenth century, sometimes involving the burning down of schools (Phillips, 1957). A major source of difficulty was the changed role of the church in education. Protestants in early nineteenth-century Ontario had sometimes attempted de-emphasizing their religious differences, and most Protestant parents were amenable to sending their children to public schools emphasizing common Christian and essentially Protestant values. Roman Catholics, on the other hand, were strongly opposed to state control of education. The Catholic Church opposed both the secular nature of the new public schools and the central control of education by the state. The church wanted to continue its own school system. Depending on the political power of Catholics within the provinces, a variety of compromises were worked out; only in British Columbia and Manitoba was there no provision made for separate Catholic schools within the public school system. In Manitoba, over the period 1890 to 1896, Roman

Catholics fought and were overpowered in a political battle for the establishment of separate schools under the provisions of the British North America Act.

Thus, two themes had come to dominate late nineteenth-century educational change—expansion in provision of schooling and the lessening of the power of both the church and the local community in education. During the same period the secondary stages of education moved from private into public hands. Because of the heavy expense to the upper social groups of maintaining these institutions, they offered little resistance to that particular change. There was probably less enthusiasm for tax-supported education among members of the working classes but their views are generally unrecorded. The endowed classical colleges of Quebec, however, which were run by the Catholic Church, elected to remain independent of the state.

In the early twentieth century, it was generally accepted that the function of the high school was to provide a liberal, or sometimes a commercial, education to a small segment of the population. Only the children of the affluent groups uniformly attended high school. Until the 1860s girls were often excluded from state-supported high schools, and upper-middle-class girls commonly attended private girls' schools. Of course, only a few families could afford to pay fees and forgo the earnings of their children; very few rural children went on to high school. Not only was the teaching in the small country schools often of a lower standard than that in town schools, but high schools were located in the towns, and before the days of automobiles, rural high-school students would have had the expense of boarding in town. Thus, high schools in the early years of the twentieth century catered largely to the upper social groups and to the town dwellers.

By the turn of the century and with the growth of industrial cities in Canada, new ideas about the social functions of education emerged. Interest developed in providing practical training in public schools, and new technical secondary schools were established. Education was also seen as having new social purposes over and above the training of industrial workers. The middle classes believed that schools might play some part in alleviating social problems of the time—in stemming the drift from the land and curbing juvenile delinquency. There were also moves to change the nature of the curriculum and the general approach of teachers to their pupils. Educators discussed how the school should be more responsive to the child's interests. The abstract, academic, and impersonal approach to schooling was to be replaced by a more personal approach. By the early twentieth century greater emphasis was being placed on the social-control function of education, and on the training of an industrial working class.

From this period on, a philosophy emphasizing democratic goals and the value of relevance in the curriculum has been prevalent among educators. Because of the economic instability of the 1920s and the Depression of the 1930s many desired changes were not introduced until after the Second World War. In the 1950s the increased resources were devoted to the provision of elementary education for the increased numbers of children. Secondary and post-secondary institutions, previously attended by a small and select group, have been the last institutions to adapt themselves to progressive ideals.

The proportions attending high school rose somewhat in the 1940s and 1950s, and high schools in the western provinces in particular were beginning to offer a greater variety of programs as alternatives to the traditional academic courses. In the 1960s there were sharp changes in rates of high-school attendance within a period of a few years. Not only did rates of participation in secondary and post-secondary education rise, but the actual numbers enrolled rose even more steeply as those born in the postwar baby boom came into their teens. Table 1 shows that the numbers of young people aged eighteen to twenty-four rose from 1.7 million in 1960–61 to 2.6 million in 1970–71. The numbers involved in full-time post-secondary education more than doubled in ten years, rising from 163,000 in 1960–61 to 475,000 in 1970–71. In 1960–61, 9.7 per cent of the age group were enrolled while ten years later 28.9 per cent of the age group were enrolled. Colleges and universities have expanded not simply because of the increased number of young people in the population but also because far higher proportions of young people are now enrolled. Particularly significant has been the increase in numbers of women at university. In 1960–61 male undergraduate enrolment was 16.2 per cent of the eighteen to twenty-one year-old age group, three times the female undergraduate enrolment rate of 5.4 per cent. Over the decade male enrolment did not double, reaching 25.8 per cent in 1970–71, while female enrolment nearly tripled, rising to 15.5 per cent of the age group

Table 1   Full-time undergraduate university and non-university enrolment, 1960–61 and 1970–71. Numbers are shown as proportions of those aged 18–21.

	Undergraduate University Level		Non-University Level	
	Male	Female	Male	Female
1960–61	16.2%	5.4%	2.9%	7.1%
1970–71	15.5%	15.5%	7.6%	7.5%

Source: Statistics Canada 1973: 150–51.

(Statistics Canada, 1973: 150–51). There is clearly some relationship between this increase and the recent resurgence of the women's movement.

Various factors have been responsible for these broad changes. Increased financial resources were important. Another impetus was the desire of governments to promote economic growth through education (Economic Council of Canada, 1965). Canada had been experiencing a shortage of educated and skilled labour. The country's needs for skilled craftsmen and technical and professional workers were being met partly by immigration rather than by the development of facilities for the education and the training of the Canadian-born (Blishen, 1970).

The 1950s and 1960s also saw a call for the democratization of the educational system. Porter's *The Vertical Mosaic* documented the extent to which the upper social groups dominated the secondary schools and universities. In Quebec the Parent Commission had recommended the widening of access to advanced secondary and university education. During the 1960s there was also a substantial rise in personal and national wealth (Hunter, 1975). Parents could keep children in school. With more women working, there may have been more emphasis on the education and training of daughters. The service sector, in which women are traditionally employed, was growing. Thus, many factors, such as increased wealth, changing social philosophies, and the needs of industry, all contributed to educational change.

The high-school curriculum had to change as more and more young people stayed in secondary school until their late teens. The traditional academic curriculum had been developed for the middle and upper-middle-class groups which had in the past dominated Canadian high schools. In the last decades more technical courses and more new subjects have been introduced, and less rigid streaming of students into academic and non-academic courses has occurred.

With the extension of secondary education has come an important ideological shift in Canadian education from an *élitist* to what might be called a *populist* or liberal approach. Evidence comes from the fact that with the increase in secondary education there has developed the official goal of making university and college education available to all who wish to attend, provided that they can meet the minimum entrance requirements and pay the fees. Whether this policy shift results in university and college education remaining limited, as it does in Britain, to a relatively small proportion of the age-group, or whether the system expands as it has in the United States, remains to be seen. Either way, however, it has important implications for the internal organization of Canadian education and for the society as a whole. Government policy and the practical returns of various types of education and training will, of course, be important factors.

Turner's analysis (1960) of the modes of social ascent through education provides a good framework for discussing this change in Canada. Turner described two models or modes of upward social mobility through education: *sponsored* and *contest mobility*, which he thought represented the patterns found in Britain and the United States respectively. He compared *sponsored mobility* with the British system of entry through sponsorship into a private club. Those who are selected for eventual entry to the élite of the society are chosen early and educated separately; during this time they not only learn skills, but also internalize the value system and standards of the élite group. Turner contrasted this process to the system of selection called *contest mobility*, which he felt was characteristic of the United States. Here he described a lengthy competition with no clear stages at which some are accepted and others barred. Comparison is made with a sporting event where all may compete and the prize is earned rather than bestowed by the established élite as under the sponsorship model.

Canada has moved from a system which had some elements of the sponsorship model to a system which has some elements of the contest model, which is neither British nor American, but Canadian. Some implications of this move from a highly élitist to a less élitist post-secondary system are already apparent, as illustrated by the changing relationship between university education and occupational status. Those who graduated in the early 1960s found occupations of higher status, with higher pay and more prospect for promotion than did those who graduated in the later 1960s. The numbers of professional, technical, and managerial openings of high status had simply not risen as fast as the numbers of qualified university graduates (Harvey, 1974).

The secondary and post-secondary education sectors are, of course, closely connected with the labour market. Unemployment rates can be readily manipulated by changes in school attendance rates. Mass unemployment, especially of the young, is a threat to any established order. One means of dealing with unemployment is to ensure a decrease in the numbers of young people entering the labour market. Had not rates of participation of young people in secondary and post-secondary education increased, unemployment problems of the 1960s would have been greatly exacerbated. Introduction of compulsory public education and the raising of school leaving age are often coincident with a period when fewer young people are needed in the work force (Musgrove, 1963; Friedenberg, 1970).

All aspects of educational systems are closely interrelated. While curriculum changes, changes in ideas about social mobility through education, and changes in the labour-market situation of schooling can be analytically separated and individually discussed, they are interrelated and their effects upon the population are not fully understood. For example, the extent to which the upgrading of the educational level of the populace will stimulate the economy is not known. It is known, however, that the poorly educated are greatly affected, because a generation ago those without a full high-school education were in the majority, while today the high-school dropout faces very restricted job opportunities. (Note that the word "dropout" is itself pejorative.) Likewise, university graduates, in the past an élite group, now find themselves less privileged in the labour market.

Language and Ethnicity in Canadian Education

The fact that Canada was originally settled by Europeans representing two distinctly different cultural traditions is, perhaps, the most obvious characteristic of the society. Language and culture are not synonymous, but the vitality of the language is a necessary condition for the complete preservation of a culture (Royal Commission on Bilingualism and Biculturalism, 1968: 8).

Emphasis on bilingualism as a national policy cannot be regarded as a solution, as it is in a country such as Switzerland with several official languages. Not only are there political tensions between Anglophones and Francophones, but bilingualism is by no means common among Canadians. Many Francophones know both French and English. Relatively few Anglophones are fluent in French. In 1961 only 12 per cent of the population were bilingual, and the majority of the bilingual group were Francophones (Joy, 1972: 13). In the Anglophone cities of Toronto and Vancouver, the Census of 1961 showed that over 90 per cent of the population spoke only English, with less than 6 per cent of the working male population in both cities claiming fluency in both French and English. In Montreal, on the other hand, more than half of the employed men could speak French and English. Meanwhile, many universities no longer require proficiency in a second language as a condition for entry or graduation perhaps partly because of the current system of financing universities according to student enrolment. Thus many Anglophones in high school have not thought it worth their while to learn French.

The recent passage of the Official Languages Act, giving English and French equal status, rights, and privileges in all federal departments and agencies, may provide a practical incentive for Anglophones to learn French. A national survey of high-school students taken prior to the Languages Act showed that students had sharply differing views on the benefits of being bilingual (Johnstone, 1969). Francophones felt that a better knowledge of English would be helpful in finding a job and getting ahead in a career. They also saw benefits in reading, watching television, and talking with friends. Anglophone students, on the other hand, were far less likely to think that knowledge of French would be important in their careers or social life.

Over the last century isolated pockets of English speakers in Quebec have been disappearing, as have pockets of French speakers in what is now primarily English-speaking Canada. This pattern of solidification of Canada into two language blocks, Anglophone Canada and Francophone Canada—consisting of Quebec and some adjoining areas of northern

Ontario and northeastern New Brunswick—has been a predictable process. Anglophones in the cities of Quebec have been able to maintain a cultural nucleus, use English as a working language, and send their children to English schools. Francophones who left Quebec have tended over a generation or so to become English speakers. Without the support of a French church, school, or newspaper, children soon forget the French language (Joy, 1972).

The Royal Commission on Bilingualism and Biculturalism has emphasized that the educational system could have an important role in the development of a more balanced partnership between French-speaking and English-speaking Canadians. In the past, Francophones have had few French facilities in English-speaking provinces. What facilities that did exist had been granted by provincial governments in grudging response to political pressures. French-Canadian minorities were well aware that provision made for them outside Quebec compared very unfavourably with that made for the privileged English-speaking minority in Quebec. The Commission, however, recommended that all institutions should reflect and foster equality for both groups.

In recent years there has been a move to provide more French schools in English-speaking areas and to establish more bilingual high schools. Whatever the practical difficulties, which are legion, these French schools constitute a recognition of the rights of Francophones outside Quebec and provide a centre around which a French community can organize itself (Havel, 1972). Bilingual high schools developed in northern Ontario because the higher grades had not previously been taught in the French language. In many areas French Catholics had suffered difficulties; for example, in Ontario the teaching of higher grades in Catholic secondary schools has not been publicly financed as it is in public secondary schools.

In New Brunswick, as in northern Ontario, there are counties in which Francophones form a substantial group, and sometimes a majority. The Francophones, mostly Acadians, comprise one-third of the population. Steps have been taken to provide education in French for Francophones. An important development was the establishment of the University of Moncton as a French-speaking institution, as recommended by the Deutsch Commission in 1962.

The western provinces have also begun to make limited provision for Francophones. School boards in British Columbia were permitted in 1967 to offer classes given in French, if the demand was sufficient. Before that time the province had made no allowances for Francophone education. In the same year legislation was passed in Saskatchewan which allowed French to be taught or used as the language of instruction for one hour per day. Manitoba accepted French as a language of instruction for as much as half the school day, provided that the school board submitted an acceptable proposal to the Minister of Education.

In Quebec, as more business becomes conducted in French, Anglophones may find themselves forced to become truly bilingual. Whether any region will, in the future, be bilingual is an open question. It is unlikely that the traditional North American disregard for languages other than English will be overcome, although in several European countries— Switzerland, Holland, and Scandinavia—fluency in several languages is expected of the ordinary citizen.

Certain ethnic and religious groups are not comfortable with existing curricula, whether designed for Francophones or Anglophones in the public school system. As an extreme solution such groups send their children to private schools. Many of the private schools in Canada are run by non-Catholic religious groups—such as Calvinists and Lutherans —who desire greater religious orientation in their children's schooling. Jewish groups have a number of schools, and in Toronto there are negotiations under way in an attempt to secure some public funds for Jewish schools. The private schools of religious groups actually outnumber the élite schools, yet these élite schools are usually what people are thinking of when they discuss private education.

The requirement of certain basic educational standards is viewed by some groups as a threat to their way of life. For example, the Hutterites on the Prairies, a German-speaking religious group valuing the simple agricultural life, have feared that high-school education of their children alongside non-Hutterite Canadians would lead them to reject their parents' way of life and develop a taste for what the parents regard as frivolities. Hutterite communities in Manitoba and Alberta have worked out compromises with the provincial education departments. Schools within the Hutterite community itself provide a basic education, and young Hutterites are not exposed to conflicting views and values (Davis and Krauter, 1971: 97).

The commitment of the state to some uniform socialization is shown by the strong and perhaps brutal reaction of provincial authorities to the keeping of children out of school. Doukhobors, who reject on principle all demands and constraints imposed by the state, have long regarded state education as a threat. Children have often been kept out of school, with the result that provincial authorities have sometimes taken the children from their parents. As recently as 1963 there were over a hundred Doukhobor children who were wards of the state (Davis and Krauter, 1971: 79).

In Quebec there arises the politically important question of whether non-English-speaking immigrants are to be assimilated to the Anglophone or the Francophone cultural group. In recent years immigrants have increasingly chosen to educate their children in English schools, feeling that there was greater opportunity for the English speaker in North America (Boissevain, 1971). With changes in legislation any non-English-speaking immigrants may well be assimilated within the Francophone group regardless of their personal desires.

The question of which language and which cultural values are to be transmitted comes clearly to the fore in the case of Indian and Eskimo education. Until the 1950s the federal government remained largely aloof from the education of native peoples, which was conducted mainly by missions of various churches. Many of these schools had a clear evangelical purpose—to gain converts to their particular brand of Christianity. Less obvious were the cultural and political purposes. These schools encouraged rejection of native culture and adoption of the white man's ways. Along with this thrust was the implied acceptance of white man's encroachment into northern lands.

Government policy has largely been one of cultural replacement, the substitution of white men's habits for traditional ways of life and thought (McElroy, 1975; Hobart and Brant, 1966). In federal schools in the Far North, teachers, even at the elementary school level, have been southern Canadians rather than local people. Southern curricula have been used, and teachers have generally stayed no longer than a few years, hardly long enough to learn the nuances of local ways. The teachers have usually lived in separate quarters and have relied on supplies airlifted from the South. They have not engaged in extensive contact with local people in the course of day-to-day life or in hunting and fishing parties.

Until recently the practice of sending native children off to boarding schools also served to separate children from their parents and from their accustomed traditions and way of life. The resulting academic performance was poor; children and parents did not communicate; children did not learn craft and survival skills of their parents; children living in relative luxury learned to despise their own traditions and their parents, who could not support them in such a manner.

Modifications are being introduced. In some places native teachers are being accepted without full university and college degrees (Hobart, 1960). Curricula previously imported intact from the South are now being adapted. Native languages are increasingly being used, and stories and legends once passed by word of mouth are being collected and incorporated into school books for native children. Where possible, the children are being encouraged to attend local schools rather than residential schools. The federal and provincial governments are seeking some middle ground in the area of native education.

The situation of native peoples raises the question of whether the state has any right to impose an alien way of life and thought, even if adhered to by a national majority, through compulsory education. Native children have often been unhappy and unsuccessful in schools. Retention rates are low: in 1967 the retention rate in the Arctic for Eskimo children in grade five was only 30.1 per cent (Hobart, 1970). By remaining in school some children become unable to take their place either in white man's society or in the traditional hunting and fishing society of their parents. Many young men in the North cease to belong in the traditional culture, yet cannot assume wage-earning jobs. Some simply drift, relying on the sharing traditions of the community for their livelihood (Clairmont, 1963). But no institution can alleviate the conflicts arising from the intrusion of North American technological society into traditional economies and cultures. Perhaps the best that schools can do is to meld some features of the traditional and the white men's cultures and to make possible some bridge between the two worlds.

When discussing ethnicity and education one must consider not only the language in which a person should be educated but also to a large extent the contents of curricula of certain subjects in elementary and secondary school levels. In this section attention has been focused particularly on language and culture, and on the policies of the federal and provincial governments. In the next section the organization of the Canadian educational system will be considered.

The Structure of the Education System

A distinguishing feature of the education system is a high degree of central control. In fact, education has been a deliberate instrument of nation building and social control at least since Confederation (Lawr and Gidney, 1973). The highly centralized structure which has persisted from the introduction of public education in the mid nineteenth century reflects the view that local communities are not competent to administer their own affairs. As pointed out earlier, one impetus for the introduction of standardized public school education in Upper Canada was the establishment's fears of the consequences of the introduction of republican ideals by American teachers and literature. In the early twentieth century, schools played a part in the "Canadianization" of non-English-speaking immigrants in the West.

The traditional role of education in Canada as an instrument of assimilation has undergone significant change in the last decade. The rise of French nationalist movements in Quebec and the threat of separatism stimulated a reassessment of the relationships of different cultural groups in Canada. Once a policy giving limited recognition to French language and culture in English-speaking Canada was instituted, the next logical step was the recognition that non-British, non-French cultural groups should also have opportunities to maintain their own languages and cultures within the educational system, if they indicate sufficient interest in doing so.

There is no one system of education in Canada. The British North America Act designates the administration of education as the responsibility of the provinces. This provision has led to the development of ten different systems in the ten provinces. In some parts of Canada, the changes of the 1950s and 1960s have been so great that the organization of education is still undergoing transition. Educational expansion has not simply been the response to demographic fluctuations, but is also the result of increased rates of participation in secondary and post-secondary institutions. It has involved increased rates of attendance among the young and changed ideas about the content and social goals of education. These changes in participation and ideology were outlined in an earlier section; here the present structure of the educational systems of the various provinces is the primary concern.

The great majority of elementary and secondary schools are operated at public expense. They are established and run by local education authorities. Under the terms of the public school acts of the various provinces these education authorities are responsible to the provincial government and the resident rate-payers. Thus, public education is the joint responsibility of provincial and local bodies. Both elementary and secondary schools are under school-board control. In the past, in rural areas, schools often served small areas, and there were numerous rural school boards. Recent amendments to provincial legislation, however, have brought about the consolidation of school units in many areas. The one-room rural school is an institution of the past, and recent consolidation has led to the building of larger, better-equipped, but perhaps more impersonal, schools. In fact, over the decade beginning in 1960–61, the average size of Canadian public schools more than doubled, rising from an average size of 160 pupils to one of 350 pupils per school (Statistics Canada, 1973: 22).

In each province, a department of education under a cabinet minister has authority over the school boards. The authority of the provincial education department is defined by the public school act of that province. The role of the department of education varies somewhat from province to province, but in general its responsibility is the development of educational policies and curricula, the supervision of teacher training and certification, and the provision of guidance and financial help to local educational authorities in the operation and building of schools (Munro, 1974).

Public schools are financed from payments made by local taxpayers and payments made to the local educational authority by the provincial government. The trend has been for provincial governments to take increasingly greater responsibilitiy for local school-board finances. In 1970, 55 per cent of Canadian school-board expenditures were financed by provincial governments (Statistics Canada, 1973: 65). This sharing of educational costs between the local taxpayers and the province has meant that there has been some uniformity within provinces in the quality of teaching and in the facilities provided. This situation is in marked contrast with that prevalent in the United States: there, curriculum and financial support are largely the responsibility of the local school district. The result is marked differences in expenditure and the quality of schooling provided in the central parts of cities as compared with suburbs, and in rural as compared with urban areas. In Canada, of course, there are still substantial provincial differences in support of education.

A few thousand children attend federal schools—mainly schools abroad for children of armed forces personnel. Federal schools also include a few Indian schools, run by the Department of Indian Affairs and Northern Development. Indian schools are, however, becoming integrated within provincial systems.

There also exist private schools of various kinds, often run under the auspices of religious groups. These schools are administered not by school boards or provincial education departments, but by their own boards of trustees and governing bodies, and are financed largely from school fees, endowments, contributions from religious groups, and donations. In

Table 2   For 1970–71. Enrolment in grade 9 and higher expressed as percentage of the 14–17 age group in the population by province.

Province	Enrolment in Grade 9 and higher as a percentage of the 14–17 age group Percentage	
	Male	Female
Newfoundland	62.5	66.1
Prince Edward Island	76.9	94.8
Nova Scotia	76.8	85.8
New Brunswick	81.6	85.7
Quebec	98.7	98.1
Ontario	107.5	103.2
Manitoba	93.5	91.8
Saskatchewan	90.2	93.2
Alberta	99.0	96.6
British Columbia	99.0	96.4
Yukon & Northwest Territories	66.2	54.7
Canada	98.5	97.1

Source: Statistics Canada, 1973: 338–39.

1970–71, 2.5 per cent of those in elementary and secondary schools attended private schools.

Turning now to enrolment rates in secondary education, throughout Canada the proportions of young people staying on in secondary school until their middle or late teens have risen sharply in recent years. In 1960–61 the numbers enrolled in grade nine and higher amounted to 66 per cent of the fourteen to seventeen age group (Statistics Canada, 1973: 388). Table 2 shows that in 1970–71 the numbers enrolled in grade nine or higher amounted to 98 per cent of the fourteen to seventeen age group. Young people in Quebec, Ontario, and the western provinces were considerably more likely to remain in school than were those from the Atlantic provinces.

The Atlantic provinces have for a long time lagged behind the rest of Canada in resources devoted to education. It is quite understandable that provinces with less demand for skilled manpower and more limited resources have not found it worth while or possible to invest as much in education as have the wealthier central and western provinces.

Table 3 presents educational expenditure per full-time student in the various provinces. Provinces even vary in the highest grade provided in high school. In most provinces the highest grade is twelve; in Ontario it

Table 3 Total expenditures on education at all levels in relation to total full-time enrolment in 1970 by province.

Province	Expenditure Per Full-Time Student Dollars
Newfoundland	646
Prince Edward Island	805
Nova Scotia	1,162
New Brunswick	896
Quebec	1,089
Ontario	1,307
Manitoba	1,073
Saskatchewan	1,055
Alberta	1,267
British Columbia	1,041
Canada	1,165

Source: Statistics Canada, 1973: 216–21.

is grade thirteen; and in Newfoundland it is grade eleven. If regional differences in provision are to be eliminated, federal subsidies to some of the poorer regions may well be necessary.

With the exceptions of British Columbia and Manitoba, all provinces make some allowances for denominationalism, but the degree to which Roman Catholic separate schools and some Protestant denominational schools have been accommodated within the public school system has depended on local circumstances and on the political power of the groups involved. In Newfoundland, however, financial support is still granted directly to churches or church bodies which are running schools, as it was in nineteenth-century England. Both Protestant and Catholic groups run schools supported by the province.

In Quebec the entire structure of the educational system was overhauled with the adoption and implementation of the Parent Report. The Parent Commission, established in 1963, recommended a democratization of the Quebec educational system and the placing of greater emphasis on technical and scientific subjects as more in keeping with the industrial society Quebec had become. The changes which took place involved the upgrading of the Francophone educational system, the development of greater secular control, and the closer linkage of elementary, secondary, and post-secondary education in the Francophone sector.

Until the early 1960s the Anglophone population of Quebec, a substantially middle-class group, attended separate schools. Secondary education was free, and a larger proportion of English-speaking than French-speaking youth attended secondary schools. The situation facing the French-speaking population provided a sharp contrast. Academic secondary education leading to university was generally available only in classical colleges and was expensive. Classical colleges, some of which had substantial endowments, were run by the Catholic Church and emphasized the humanities rather than scientific and technical subjects. Attendance rates were low. Few could afford the fees, which in the early 1950s were between $450 and $600 per year (Porter, 1965: 190). The academic secondary course available in classical colleges was longer than elsewhere in Canada, lasting eight years and overlapping with the first years of university. The relatively few French universities emphasized traditional rather than modern curricula.

The Liberal government elected in 1960 and headed by Premier Jean LeSage committed itself to the reform of the Quebec social structure and the educational system. Important changes came following the investigation of the educational system by the Parent Commission, and the structure was modified within a few years. A college level was introduced, between the upper levels of secondary education and the lower levels of university. These colleges, the CEGEPS (collèges d'enseignement générale et professionelle), were created under an act of 1967, often being built on existing institutions such as classical colleges or teachers colleges. The CEGEPS offered both academic courses leading to university study and courses which prepared the students for employment. Technical and scientific subjects were emphasized in the new curriculum. A wider group of young Québécois now had access not only to university but also to previously neglected technical studies. These colleges provided bridges to occupations and courses previously closed to the majority of Francophones. These changes in the structure of secondary and post-secondary education in Quebec have had special political significance, since a greater balance between the more developed Anglophone sector and the less developed Francophone sector has been achieved (Denis, 1975).

Canada has long had universities. Many of the older institutions were founded under the auspices of particular churches and their important functions were the training of clergy and the education of the élite. They depended mainly on endowments, church funds, and students' fees. As universities have come to play a more important role in society and in the economy, their financial dependence on governments has increased. In 1970 fees constituted only 10 per cent of universities' current income and most costs were being met from government sources. As the costs of supporting post-secondary education have increased, so have the contributions and hence the control of the government (Statistics Canada, 1973: 178).

Until recently there were few non-university post-secondary institutions other than teachers colleges and schools of nursing. In response to the desire for more technical education, various community colleges and junior colleges were established in the 1960s. Alberta established public junior colleges; Ontario established Colleges of Applied Arts and Technology. Growth was most marked in Quebec and the western provinces.

By 1970–71 there were 134,000 students attending these community colleges, nearly half as many as were attending university in that year (Statistics Canada, 1973: 41).

Many provinces have established independent departments within their administrative structures to plan and administer post-secondary education. Universities and colleges can no longer be regarded as autonomous bodies: they now constitute another sector in a government-financed and provincially controlled public education system. The increased expense of colleges and universities and their importance in a technological society have led to changes in their relationships with government (Porter, 1970).

Social Class and Access

For as long as scholars have studied human social life, they have noted that in most societies not all people have the same life-style nor do they participate in the ongoing affairs of the society in the same way. Groups of people having roughly similar prestige, wealth, and influence have been designated by the term *social class*. The importance of social class, for present purposes, lies in the fact that despite the formulation of educational policy to accommodate all and a shift from an élitist to a populist model, various classes of Canadians have differential access to the educational system, and this, in turn, has a profound and demonstrable effect upon their respective life chances.

In an industrial society such as Canada the educational system does not merely train people for particular types of occupations and adult roles, it also allocates them to particular social classes. The development of an industrial economy has resulted in changes in the relationships between the family, the economy, and the educational system. In a largely agricultural society few occupations required educational qualifications; the use of the educational system for economic or social ascent was rare. Education was for doctors, priests, and teachers, and, perhaps, for gentlemen of leisure. Now many occupational skills are taught through the school and college systems, at public expense, while the age-old system of apprenticeship is in decline.

The importance of educational qualifications to employers has become such that for men, but not so much for women, educational level is closely associated with type of occupation and with level of remuneration. Advanced education is not necessarily associated with higher productivity, however, and some employers may perhaps place too much emphasis on education when choosing employees (Berg, 1971). Education is, of course, only one mechanism for the maintenance or achievement of high income or status. For example, in the Toronto Italian community there is much upward mobility through small business. Because Anglo-Canadians are favoured as employees in certain bureaucracies and large corporations, small business is at present a more productive activity for many Italian-Canadians (Kelner, 1970).

Educational philosophies involve important ideological principles. Since the Second World War the goal of equal educational opportunity for all children has been made explicit. The ideal is that schools are to provide all children, regardless of social background, family income, religion, race, or region of origin, with equivalent opportunities for self development and educational and occupational advancement. This official educational philosophy implies that greater efforts are to be made to provide advanced education for those who desire or merit it, and that talented children from the lower socio-economic groups should have greatly increased chances for post-secondary education and entry to professional, technical and managerial occupations.

Despite this ideology, class background has been and remains a major factor in educational allocation. For example, the children of professionals and managers comprise at least half of those in professional schools, while the children of labourers are scarcely represented; yet professionals and managers comprise one-sixth of the working population and labourers one-tenth (Marchak, 1975: 21). If no children of working-class parents ever went to university a class system would be recognizable, but, because some do, class lines are obscured.

The prevailing ideology emphasizes equality of opportunity in education. In fact, one of the major arguments put forward in defence of the existence of an open-class system is the existence of free public education for all. The ideology of equality of opportunity places the onus of non-achievement on the individual, rather than on the social structure. Those who do succeed are encouraged to think that they have done so by their own efforts, rather than because of their position in the class structure. Acceptance of such an ideology discourages any questioning of the existing system. As the following tables show, however, factors such as class, ethnicity, and sex are very important in determining the extent of the educational opportunity open to a particular group.

Prior to the 1960s many students left school after only a few years of high school. Those who completed high school were drawn disproportionately from the upper social groups and were generally bound for white-collar occupations or university study. Table 4 shows the disproportionate representation of the children of professional, executive or managerial workers in grade twelve in Ontario high schools in 1956.

Over a period of a few years the rates of retention in high schools have risen sharply. But class differences in patterns of allocation to high-school programs and in access to post-secondary education still exist. In most provinces students are placed in a particular program of study by the end of the first year of high school. Different programs correspond very roughly to different levels in the occupational structure. For example, academic programs often prepare the student for entry to post-secondary education which in turn often leads to professional, managerial, or technical work.

Some of the most gifted from the lower socio-economic groups do follow academic programs. Results of a Canada-wide survey conducted in 1966 showed that high measured ability is just as closely associated with entry to a non-terminal academic program as is social-class back-

Table 4   Occupational level of fathers of Ontario grade 13 students in 1956.

Father's Occupational Level	Students %	Ontario Males 35 Years & Over %
Professional, managerial, executive	39	16
Sub-professional, minor supervisory, proprietors	11	7
Skilled manual	28	29
Semi-skilled manual	10	19
Unskilled	4	12
Unknown, disabled, etc.	8	17
	100%	100%

Source: Porter, 1965: 181.

Table 5 Percentage of students in non-terminal academic program by mental ability rank and occupational status of father.

	Boys	Girls
1. Mental Ability Rank		
High	82.6	85.0
Medium	60.3	66.3
Low	40.9	48.6
2. Occupational Status of Father		
High	70.7	71.3
Medium	59.3	62.2
Low	63.9	69.4

Source: R. Breton, 1972: Table 1–5.2.

ground. This survey also indicated the value of a comprehensive rather than a single-program high school. When measured intelligence, social class, ethnicity, and school program were held constant, students from comprehensive high schools showed higher retention rates and levels of performance than did students from single program high schools (Breton, 1970 and 1972). The provision of varied programs in schools serving various neighbourhoods and social groups is likely to encourage a higher level of performance than exists in schools devoted to a single program and serving only one social group (Bélanger and Duval, 1968). The internal organization of the school appears to affect the level of performance among students.

The structuring of secondary education varies somewhat from province to province. In 1969 Ontario introduced a credit system. Other eastern provinces are adopting this pattern. Instead of rigidly dividing students into four- and five-year programs, between which transfer was difficult, students and their parents are now responsible for selecting courses. Even under this system, children of middle-class parents will likely be at a distinct advantage. They will probably receive better grades, and in many cases their parents will ensure that their own children will take the right sequence of courses to ensure an honours graduation diploma.

The lower-class student generally enters high school with more modest aspirations than his or her middle-class counterpart, and will often opt for the four-year course or its equivalent long before financial considerations become important (Clark *et al.*, 1975). Thus any plans to pay salaries to post-secondary students from the lower socio-economic groups would, in the first year, have relatively little effect, as these students have often made irrevocable decisions at a very early stage. Any policy of rigid separation of children into different classes and courses at an early age may well mean the perpetuation of low educational achievement and occupational status among certain groups, such as the ill-educated and the non-English-speaking immigrant. The school may become, not as the official ideology has it, a means of ensuring that each child has a reasonable opportunity to develop his or her abilities on a roughly equal footing with others, but a means of perpetuating the status quo.

Examination of how students are placed in particular programs raises interesting questions. In 1965–66, a sample of secondary-school teachers drawn from across Canada were asked to rank the importance of criteria used in placing the students in various courses of study (Breton, 1970). Teachers rated school grades and the judgments of teachers and counsellors as by far the most important factors. They considered students' interests and preferences and students' scores on intelligence and achievement tests as far less important. The wishes of the parents seemed to be of very little importance to teachers.

We do not know exactly what factors teachers and counsellors take into account in making their decisions, only that they think their own judgments are crucial. Research in one high school in Chicago showed that counsellors deliberately placed the children from poor families, obviously unable to afford to send their children to universities, in the vocational rather than the academic programs (Cicourel and Kitsuse, 1963). Certain factors—classroom behaviour, language, dress—may influence teachers' and counsellors' judgments as to which program is most suitable for which student (Lacey, 1970; Hargreaves, 1968). Teachers and counsellors are themselves uncertain about this allocation process (Breton, 1970).

The importance of socio-economic background, level of measured ability, sex, and region of origin in determining students' chances of entering post-secondary education have been well documented (Porter, 1965: 165–200; Pike, 1970; Porter *et al.*, 1973). As more public funds are devoted to post-secondary education questions relating to class and other differentials in access become important political issues. For example, the

Canada Student Loan Program, instituted in 1964, with, as one of its aims, the stimulation of lower-class attendance, does, in fact, function as an important subsidy to middle-class families. Similarly, a policy of keeping university fees at only a fraction of the real cost means that all social groups are subsidizing the attendance of middle- and upper-middle-class groups.

The results of a survey carried out in 1971 among high-school students in Ontario showed that students from the higher socio-economic groups were considerably more likely to expect to graduate from university than were those from the lower socio-economic groups. Table 6 shows that 60 per cent of the children of professional workers planned to graduate as compared with only 24 per cent of the children of unskilled workers. Of course, many who expect to graduate may never do so, but the class differences in the expectations of grade twelve students are striking.

Even among students of very high mental ability there were marked differences in the proportions planning to go to university, depending on social-class origins (Porter *et al.*, 1973: 42–107). Also, children from small families were more likely to plan to attend university than were those from large families. Finances are an important factor. Many highly intelligent students from the lower socio-economic groups planned to go to community colleges where fees are relatively low and where the period of training is short. It appears that the new community colleges are extremely

Table 6   Percentages of grade 12 students, in spring 1971, expecting to graduate from university by socio-economic status of father.

Socio-Economic Status of Father (Blishen scale)	Percentage of grade 12 students expecting to graduate from university
Class I (mainly professional)	60%
Class II (mainly managerial)	53%
Class III (lower managerial and lower professional)	43%
Class IV (skilled)	38%
Class V (farmers)	25%
Class VI (unskilled)	24%
Total	37%

Source: Porter *et al.*, 1973: adapted from Table 2.4.

important in providing opportunities for those from the lower socio-economic groups.

A student's sex also has an important bearing on his or her chances of attending university. About one-third of the university students are women. The lower proportion of women at university is no reflection on their high-school grades. In fact, at the high-school level, girls often do better than boys (Maccoby and Jacklin, 1974: 63–133). There are clear class differences in the proportion of men in relation to women attending universities. The sons and daughters of the highest occupational groups attend in equal proportions. But in the lower socio-economic groups, men are far more likely to attend than are women (Porter *et al.*, 1973: 121). Where a family can afford to educate only one child, the son is usually given preference over the daughter. Some families may even feel that it is simply not right that girls should be educated.

Males see themselves as working and assume that work will be of central importance in their lives. The prevailing norms governing family and occupational life are such that women are expected to modify educational and occupational pursuits and goals to suit the convenience of their husbands and families. The educational system plays an important part in channelling women into certain types of courses, clerical and liberal arts, rather than technical and scientific. Eventually many of them are led to certain "female" occupations, and as a result, their earning power is likely to be limited. In 1972 one-third of the men with secondary-school education made $10,000 or more, as compared with only 1.9 per cent of the employed women with that level of education (Marchak, 1975: 24). Even though most women now expect to work for a major portion of their lives (Breton, 1972)—one-third of the labour force is now female—the school system still streams them, by means of their courses and the advice of guidance counsellors, to sex-segregated occupations in clerical work and the "helping" professions, and away from challenging accepted notions about sex roles.

Many other factors, some of which are not directly associated with social class, have been found to affect performance in school. In Ontario, for example, there are marked differences in patterns of achievement among children of different ethnic groups. Some groups, for example, the Jewish, outperform the English Canadians (King, 1968). For Jews, the long tradition of religious study may be of importance in shaping family values and attitudes toward education. Certain other groups, for example, the Chinese and the Ukrainians, also appear to place an especially high value on education (Ramsey and Wright, 1969). Ontario French-Canadian students were among those with the lowest levels of performance. Not only were these students coping with an English-language school system, but the influence of the Anglophone school constituted a threat to their continued existence as a cultural group.

Verbal abilities are of particular importance in the kinds of tasks required of children in school. Research by Bernstein (1971) in England suggests that the advantages of middle-class children may stem in part from their learning from their parents the complex sentence structures and modes of thought required for dealing with abstract concepts at an early age. This research suggests that children exposed to the more limited vocabularies and sentence structures characteristic of parents in the lower socio-economic groups are not as well prepared to cope with verbal tasks, abstract thinking, or the day-to-day interaction with a middle-class teacher.

Discussion of performance in school raises the issue of the role of the environment and of the role of genetic factors in determining intelligence and achievement. The extent to which a person's abilities are determined by environmental factors and the extent to which they are inherited from parents is not known. Even the existence of some relationship between the measured intelligence of children and the socio-economic status of their parents, however, would not explain the very wide differences in achievement and attendance rates among the children of different social classes.

Region of origin also affects educational level. For example, rates of university attendance are higher in western and central Canada. Among males in particular, rates of attendance are lower among those who grew up in small towns or in rural areas (Porter *et al.*, 1973: 66). Because of lack of other opportunities, rural women are often oriented toward teaching and nursing (Kohl and Bennett, 1971). Very few Indians or Eskimos enter post-secondary education.

Even this brief discussion of the interrelationship of the educational system and the stratification system is not complete without some consideration of the role of the few élite private schools. These schools play an important but little noticed role in national life in that they cater to a politically powerful group. Research on those holding directorships of major corporations showed that one-third of the members of the English-speaking economic élite had attended private schools (Porter, 1965: 284).

These schools go against the North American democratic tradition of the neighbourhood high school. They are associated with the aristocratic traditions of Europe, particularly with the so-called "public" schools in England. Yet, as Porter points out, from the point of view of the élite groups, they fulfil important functions. They teach the next generation of the élite the values and attitudes appropriate to their future roles. These schools appear to emphasize getting along with people and training for leadership and special character-building more than public schools do. In addition, and of great importance, these schools offer opportunities for making contacts which may be useful in later business and social life. For example, the social gatherings to which boys and girls from private schools are invited provide opportunities for the sons and daughters of the élite to meet and eventually marry one another (Maxwell and Maxwell, 1971). The very fact that these schools are boarding schools contributes to the success of this socialization process. Contacts with past friends and schoolmates are cut off, and because all social life takes place within the school, the influence of peers and teachers is at a maximum.

In essence, despite the philosophy of egalitarianism and equal opportunity in education in Canada, there is a strong relationship between a person's parents' class status and his or her educational accomplishment. Research has focused on class differentials in access to various types of secondary and post-secondary education, and we know little about the experiences of the majority, who begin to work in their late teens. Further, the educational institution itself becomes an agent of socialization for certain other values which will be the theme of the next section.

The Socialization Function of Education

The school, through formal and informal means, is one of the institutions which teaches children some of the main values and norms of society and the implications of certain roles. As such, it constitutes one of the most important agencies of socialization. It is partly through experiences in school that children in Canada learn that they are living in a society which is achievement-oriented and universalistic rather than ascriptive and particularistic. Leaving the family for the school, the child enters a new social world. In the family each member can be treated with special consideration, and affection can be shown freely. In the school new norms of behaviour apply. All pupils are treated in a similar manner. When distinctions are made, they are often made on the basis of performance (Dreeben, 1968; Davis, 1975). In our society it is acceptable to make distinctions on the basis of achievement, but less acceptable to make distinctions on the basis of ascriptive features such as religion or family background.

The school also socializes children to study and work in large-scale organizations characterized by rigid hierarchies of power and regulated through established rules and procedures. Many of the activities that take place in school—sitting still, obeying teachers, waiting in line, and arriving on time—certainly provide early socialization for coping with and working in large-scale organizations. Literature on the sociology of education in general focuses attention on the implications of classroom interaction for the teaching of competitive rather than co-operative behaviour and on the concern with grades, performance, and deference to teacher, rather than with the subject or the activity itself (Henry, 1955).

The school plays an important part in shaping children's views about the behaviour appropriate to their sex. Various aspects of school life have implications for the learning of sex roles. Sports programs often provide more for boys, the implication being that girls are less active. Children's books often present stereotyped images of male and female behaviour (Weitzman, 1972). The Royal Commission on the Status of Women (1970) investigated sex typing in Canadian textbooks.

In the Young Canada reading series, used in Ontario and Alberta, the more versatile characters were almost invariably males. Pirates, Eskimos, Bible figures—interesting figures in general—are seldom women. Boys in the stories are typically active and adventurous but the girls are not. In another series, the Language Patterns Program, used in Ontario, the father is often shown as an understanding and kind person who takes children on interesting expeditions. The mother, on the other hand, stays at home to prepare the meals and tells the chidren what is best for them. We found the reprimanding function of mothers in a variety of Canadian school books (174).

These are values expressed in school books and thus carry some official sanction.

The school system plays some part in socializing males to desire occupational status, power, and financial rewards, and females to value love, children, and domestic life. It is women, rather than men, who are socialized to be nurturant and to dissociate themselves from issues relating to power and money (Breton, 1972). Children's books often show men in occupational roles, while women are usually shown as mothers, and where they are shown in occupations, they are usually depicted in helping and glamour roles—as teachers, nuns, nurses, and dancers (Pike, 1975: 68).

If there were greater class awareness in Canada, there might be more conflict over the kinds of values emphasized in school, and over more subtle aspects of streaming school program. The many issues that arise relating to ethnicity, religion, and language should not obscure the fact that we know little about this important issue. Many studies of schools in Britain and the United States attest to the importance of social class in streaming, in the relationships between students, in their dealings with teachers, and in the making of decisions about schooling and occupations (Hargreaves, 1968; Lacey, 1970).

The political socialization which takes place in school is important. Canadians are not so given to the singing of patriotic songs or the making of political pledges in school as are Americans. Yet it is through school classes that aspects of history, political values, and cultural heritage are transmitted to the next generation.

Anglophone and Francophone students have tended to identify with historical symbols of their own culture and there are few reconciliation symbols in Canadian history (Richert, 1974). The Canadian National History Project (Hodgetts, 1968) attempted to gain a picture of the teaching of Canadian history and civics in the schools. Several hundred classes were observed, numerous textbooks were read, and 4,000 students from coast to coast were asked about their history and civics classes and their reactions to them. It became apparent that Anglophones and Francophones were exposed to quite different versions of Canadian history. History in French Canada has tended to deal with the period before 1760. Less interest has been accorded later national developments. Canadian history, as Francophone students have learned it, has a strong emotional appeal and has given children "a picture history peopled with saintly heroic figures motivated by Christian ideals" (Hodgetts, 1968: 31). Children have been encouraged to develop an attachment to their cultural and religious heritage. One school book expressed this sentiment as follows:

> To all those who belong to the French Canadian race, their ancestors bequeath the language and the faith of the discoverers, founders, and missionaries. . . . You know about the struggles these ancestors had to keep their customs, their rights, their laws, and their religion. . . . All French Canadians have a right to be proud of their lineage of heroes and patriots and to state boldly for everyone to hear: "We are French Canadian Catholics" (Hodgetts, 1968: 32).

The English version of Canadian history has not had this emotional appeal.

Furthermore, research in Ontario showed high-school students identifying with the national, rather than with the provincial, level of government, while French-speaking students in Quebec had strong separatist leanings and regional rather than national identifications (Harvey *et al.*, 1975). Alberta students, on the other hand, also showed strong regional identification (Skogstad, 1975).

The *consensus* view of history implicit in many of the materials used in Anglophone schools also leads to a certain type of political socialization. The phenomena of class and class conflict are de-emphasized. Inequality, while recognized, is attributed to individual differences, to particular cultural heritages, or to historical circumstances. Canadian history deals, not with class issues, but with the struggle to tame the environment and build the national railroad. The development of urban working classes, as cities came into being, and the exploitation of certain groups of immigrant labour have been largely ignored. Similarly, Canadian novelists have not set their works in class settings, but have tended to deal with individual struggles, and with the implications of ethnicity. In *Survival* (1972), a discussion of Canadian literature, Margaret Atwood finds coping with the environment the dominant theme.

Within Canada there is the important issue of maintaining a definite cultural and historical identity in the face of dominant American influence.

Porter (1970) and Milburn and Herbert (1975) maintain that the further development of the education system may be crucial to the continuance of a separate cultural and political existence. (For further discussion on this issue, see Ogmundson's chapter on the sociology of power and politics.)

Problems associated with the transmission of the country's historical and cultural heritage have also arisen in the universities. These problems themselves have implications for school curricula. Canada has traditionally imported large numbers of teachers and academic professionals, but during the period of rapid expansion of universities in the late 1960s, the proportion of non-Canadians teaching in Canadian universities rose sharply (Matthews and Steele, 1969; also see Chapter 12 in this book). This trend has important implications for particular subjects such as the social sciences, literature, and history. It is often through research and teaching in the universities that new interpretations of Canadian history and society are developed. In fact, one common criticism of Canadian history classes and texts has been that too much reliance has been placed on out-of-date material, which reflects the concerns of the previous rather than the present generation. Some of the liveliest classes observed in the National History Project were those conducted by young teachers who simply discarded their texts and used their university notes.

Power and Control

It is clear that the education system, as it is now structured, embodies many features of a bureaucracy. There is a hierarchy of power. The duties of teachers and educational authorities are defined in contracts and legislation. There is a definite career structure for administrators, teachers, and students. Administrators and teachers have power by virtue of their positions in the bureaucracy.

The bureaucratic structure of education has important implications for teachers. Teaching, at least in the case of men, is not viewed as a long-term vocation, but rather as a stage in a career. Research has shown that ability to get along with colleagues and a pleasant personality is viewed by many teachers as more important than an ability to teach well en route to promotion to administration (King and Ripton, 1970). As the career is now structured, many male teachers do not wish to remain "just a teacher", and even during their student years aspire to promotion to administration. Only 14 per cent of a sample of male student teachers expected that they would be classroom teachers fifteen years after graduation.

Women are less oriented toward administration, perhaps partly because of discrimination against them. The majority of teachers are women, but in 1972, only 1 per cent of the educational administrators in Ontario were women, and of the nine hundred principals of secondary schools, only nine were women, and these were mostly in girls' schools (University of Toronto, Faculty of Education, Student Handbook, 1972).

Thus, classroom teaching is not the main concern of the male teachers, and women teachers, who form the majority, do not hold the positions of power in the educational system in Canada.

Power is, of course, concentrated at the upper levels, and groups such as working-class people or small religious sects often have little control over the education of their children. Governments pass legislation, allocate money, and set up commissions. At the local level, educational administrators are responsible to local school boards. Research in Alberta showed that matters relating to curriculum and students were rarely discussed in board meetings and that matters relating to general administration and staffing received most attention (Holdaway, 1970).

The issue of the relative power of the different social classes is important. School-board members and others who influence the system tend to be drawn from the upper social groups. Elected bodies and voluntary associations tend to be drawn from the upper socio-economic groups in the population and probably reflect the concerns of this group (Head, 1971).

The same middle-class dominance is apparent in the social origins of teachers. For example, research among Hamilton teachers in the early 1960s showed that nearly one-half were from professional and managerial backgrounds. Less than one in three were from homes where the father had been a manual worker (Jones, 1963). Relative to other professions, however, teachers are drawn from a wide range of backgrounds, and teaching has long been an important avenue for upward mobility. None the less, the fact that elected officials, administrators, and teachers are drawn predominantly from particular social groups suggests that certain class interests may be advanced through the educational system. The reasons for the general neglect of popular culture in school curricula is a topic worthy of research (Goblot, 1925).

In Canada many aspects of education are controlled by provincial departments of education—curricula, policy-making, and certification of teachers generally being the responsibility of these bodies. In Ontario, for example, teachers choose texts from lists compiled by the department of education. In the past, the grade thirteen examinations functioned as a means of central control of curriculum. In fact, one of the arguments for abolition of these examinations was that teachers and students often concentrated so heavily on preparation for them that courses in the upper levels of high school tended to become narrow and rigid. Provincial departments of education may also exert considerable indirect influence simply through publicity. Ontario's Hall-Dennis Report, *Living and Learning* (1968), was produced as an attractive and profusely illustrated volume, clearly designed for a wide range of readers, and as suitable for the coffee table as for the bookshelf.

Any dissatisfaction with public schools as they presently exist raises the issue of the desirability of schools controlled in other ways. Tax-supported schools run by teachers and community groups have been one suggestion (Mackinnon, 1966). The issue of educational vouchers to be redeemable at the institution of one's choice has been another suggestion (Coleman, 1974: 169–70). Such a system would be to the particular advantage of religious and ethnic groups presently seeking special provision for their children. If one function of the Canadian school system is the development of understanding between children of different backgrounds through close association in childhood, however, then the institution of more schools for separate groups might increase divisions within society. Sociologists have not yet investigated the consequences for Canadian society of the existence of separate or of private schools for different religious groups.

Private schools do provide some alternative for groups and individuals dissatisfied with various aspects of the public school system. They can act only as a slight counterbalance to what is, in effect, a monopoly situation in the public sector. One function of the private sector is the preservation of social and cultural groups. Another is that of experimentation. For example, a school such as Summerhill in England, run by the late A. S. Neill (1960), could not conceivably exist within the state system.

State support and control of education are likely to continue. The cost of the provision of the range of educational services now regarded as necessary is so high that it can rarely be met by groups of families. Moreover, the fact that schools serve relatively homogeneous areas means that the upper socio-economic groups, the group most able to afford private ventures, can still send their children to socially exclusive schools. The numbers of privately financed and controlled schools is likely to remain low and responses to any expression of dissatisfaction are likely to involve greater flexibility within the public system.

In contrast with the tradition of community control of educational finance and curriculum in the United States, there is, in Canada, great power lying with the educational bureaucracies. One advantage of a centrally financed system is, as indicated, that within each province there exists some uniformity in educational expenditure and in standards. In the United States there are great disparities, even within particular cities, a pattern which exacerbates racial tensions and perpetuates economic differences.

Within the Canadian educational system there is strong male and middle-class dominance. Positions of power within the teaching profession are almost exclusively held by males. And both the teachers and the local groups which influence educational policy—parents' associations, school boards, and pressure groups—tend to be dominated by the middle classes. In the discussion of education in relation to stratification it was pointed out that one of the reasons posited for the relatively poor performance of children from the lower socio-economic groups was the strong middle-class ethos of the educational system.

SUMMARY AND CONCLUSIONS

The educational system is the formal aspect of the socialization process which has as its main task converting the young into smoothly functioning members of society with a shared core of values and basic knowledge based upon a common educational experience. In all but one of the Canadian provinces this process is accomplished by means of a centralized and highly institutionalized school system. A salient feature of this system is that it is overwhelmingly a *public* school system, although in some provinces provision is made for some groups to have their own separate schools, if they so desire. Closely related is the fact that education has been a deliberate instrument of nation building and social control at least since Confederation.

A major task of the educational system is to prepare people for particular types of tasks and occupations. In practice this has meant differential allocation based on social class, race, and ethnicity. An élitist orientation has given way in recent times to a more populist approach, although social-class factors are still evident in access to various types of secondary and post-secondary education. The entire situation is further complicated by a wide range of issues focusing on ethnicity and religion.

Perhaps the major characteristic concerning the literature on Canadian education is the lack of empirical research on all but the most basic aspects of class differentials in access, and socialization. Issues relating to control and power within educational institutions and to the relationship between government and education have so far scarcely been considered. This chapter has, of necessity, presented only a general outline of Canadian education; for the most part, any detailed analysis must await further research.

Selected Bibliography

BANKS, O. *The Sociology of Education*. London: Batsford, 1968.

BELL, R. R., and STUB, H. R. *The Sociology of Education: A Sourcebook*. Homewood: Dorsey, 1962 and 1968.

BERG, I. *Education and Jobs: The Great Training Robbery*. Boston: Beacon Press, 1971.

BRETON, R. *Social and Academic Factors in the Career Decisions of Canadian Youth*. Ottawa: Department of Manpower and Immigration, 1972.

Canada. *Report of the Royal Commission on the Status of Women in Canada*. Chapter 3, "Education". Ottawa: Information Canada, 1970.

———. Statistics Canada. *Education in Canada: A Statistical Review for the Period 1960–61 to 1970–71*. Ottawa: Information Canada, 1973.

Canadian Review of Sociology and Anthropology 7, No. 1 (February 1970). Special issue on education. Contains articles by E. Z. Friedenberg, and R. Breton, and A. J. C. King, and R. A. Ripton.

CICOUREL, A., and KITSUSE, J. I. *The Educational Decisionmakers*. Indianapolis: Bobbs-Merrill, 1963.

CLARK, B. R. *The Open Door College*. New York: McGraw-Hill, 1960.

COLEMAN, J. S. *Youth: Transition to Adulthood*. Report of the Panel on Youth of the Presidential Advisory Commission. Chicago: University of Chicago Press, 1974.

HARVEY, E. *Educational Systems and the Labour Market*. Don Mills: Longman, 1974.

HOBART, C. W., and BRANT, C. S. "Eskimo Education, Danish and Canadian: A Comparison", *Canadian Review of Sociology and Anthropology* 3, No. 2 (May

1966): 47–66. Reprinted in Malik, A., ed. *The Social Foundations of Canadian Education.* Scarborough: Prentice-Hall, 1969.

HODGETTS, A. B. *What Culture? What Heritage? A Study of Civic Education in Canada.* Curriculum Series Number Five. Toronto: Ontario Institute for Studies in Education, 1968.

KING, R. A. *The School at Mopass: A Problem of Identity.* New York: Holt, Rinehart and Winston, 1967.

LAWR, D., and GIDNEY, R., eds. *Educating Canadians: A Documentary History of Public Education.* Toronto: Van Nostrand Reinhold, 1973.

MCDARIMID, G., and PRAT, D. *Teaching Prejudice: A Content Analysis of Social Studies Textbooks Authorized for Use in Ontario.* Toronto: Ontario Institute for Studies in Education, 1971.

PORTER, J. *The Vertical Mosaic: An Analysis of Social Class and Power in Canada.* Chapter 6, "Social Class and Educational Opportunity". Toronto: University of Toronto Press, 1965.

PORTER, M. P., PORTER, J., and BLISHEN, B. R. *Does Money Matter? Prospects for Higher Education.* Toronto: Institute for Behavioural Research, York University, 1973.

ROSENTHAL, R., and JACOBSEN, L. *Pygmalion in the Classroom: Teacher Expectation and Pupils' Intellectual Development.* New York: Holt, Rinehart and Winston, 1968.

STEVENSON, H. A., et al., eds. *The Best of Times, The Worst of Times: Contemporary Issues in Canadian Education.* Toronto: Holt, Rinehart and Winston, 1972.

WILSON, J. DONALD, STAMP, ROBERT M., and AUDET, LOIS PHILIP. *Canadian Education: A History.* Scarborough: Prentice-Hall, 1970.

ZURICK, E., and PIKE, R. M., eds. *Socialization and Values in Canadian Society: Volume I: Political Socialization.* Toronto: McClelland and Stewart, 1975.

———. *Socialization and Values in Canadian Society: Volume II: Socialization, Social Stratification and Ethnicity.* Toronto: McClelland and Stewart, 1975.

Bureaucracy in Canada

C. R. SANTOS

The governmental bureaucratic administrative system has emerged as a societal response to various social, economic, political, and other related problems. Among the conditioning factors which have contributed to the emergence of bureaucracies within or outside the government are the size of organizations, the complexity of the tasks to be performed, the technological advances made, the capitalist money economy, and the structural differentiation of social life.

Introduction

Initially, we shall attempt to develop a theoretical framework for analysing bureaucratic organizations based on the Weberian model of bureaucracy. Given such a theoretical framework, the political setting, the structure, and functions of the various components of the Canadian governmental bureaucracy, in relation to the basic political task of formulating and implementing public policies, will be described. In so doing, it will be necessary to inquire into the nature of the Queen's Privy Council for Canada, focusing particularly on its active political segment known as the cabinet; the composition and functions of the Prime Minister's Office and the structure and functions of the Privy Council Office in relation to the cabinet committee system. The various roles being performed by the Treasury Board of Canada and the changing role and diminishing functions of the Public Service Commission will also be closely investigated. In the course of our discussion of the various departments and agencies of the federal government, the growth and geographical dispersion of the federal public bureaucracy, including the systems of personnel administration under the Civil Service Employment Act of 1967 will be examined. Of particular concern will be the types and manner of appointments which could be made under the Public Service Employment Act, the various personnel placement processes and the several modes of separation of personnel from the Canadian public service. Also described will be the comprehensive system of collective bargaining in the public sector established by the Public Service Staff Relations Act of 1967 and the alternative settlement of disputes by binding arbitration or by conciliation. Finally, what we consider to be the more significant developmental changes taking place in the Canadian federal bureaucracy and the issue of bureaucratic power and responsibility will be identified and defined.

Bureaucracy as an Organizational Construct

Bureaucracy may be defined as a form of organization consisting of a systematic distribution of formalized statuses, offices, or positions into a hierarchical pattern of three or more levels, governed by a consistent set of norms, possessing a number of characteristics rationally calculated to promote efficiency, and requiring specialized knowledge on the part of those who are to become its members. Bureaucracy, as a theoretical organizational construct, is capable of comprehension separable from the bureaucratic organization as a concrete entity found in the practical world (Wolff, 1962: 178). Considered as a totality, however, bureaucracy is more than a set of interrelated concepts and propositions about organizations. It is a system involving a complex of mutually related parts which act and interact to create and maintain the whole, which patterns the operations of each part; the functioning of these parts, in turn, influences the operations of the whole. Bureaucracy is a form of organizing which is peculiarly adapted to maintaining efficiency and stability in large and complex undertakings. Nevertheless, bureaucracy is not the only form of organization or system of administration which is rationally productive of efficiency. Craft administration found in the construction industry (which depends on specialized division of labour interconnected by a system of contracts and sub-contracts) while not a bureaucracy, is found to be equally rational and efficient (Stinchcombe, 1959: 168–87).

As a form of organization, the distinguishing mark of a bureaucracy is the existence of three or more levels of authority. One supposedly important reason for the existence of several levels of authority in the bureaucratic organization is the inherent limitation on the number of items to which a person can give his attention at any one moment of time.

This sphere of attention fixes the span of control, which determines the maximum number of subordinates whom the bureaucratic superior can effectively supervise. Precisely what this magic number is has been the topic of considerable discussion and debate in the literature on organization and management.

The structural characteristics possessed by bureaucratic organizations, which vary from organization to organization, have dimensions which exist as continua rather than as dichotomies, and they may not even be intercorrelated. Therefore, organizations that are highly bureaucratized in any one dimension or characteristic are not necessarily so in other dimensions or characteristics (Hall, 1963: 34).

Characteristic Features of Bureaucratic Organizations

From the formulated definition of bureaucracy as a form of organization rationally calculated to promote efficiency, it is possible to deduce the following characteristics (Weber, 1947: 331–40), one or more of which may be present in any bureaucratic organization:

1. Formal Positions, that is, that there is an integrated series of formalized statuses, positions, or offices;

2. Jurisdiction, that is, that each position has its own sphere of competence, its rights and obligations as well as privileges and responsibilities resulting from the division of labour.

3. Hierarchy, that is, that these positions are arranged in a pyramidal stratification pattern, involving superior-subordinate relationship, each lower position or set of positions being under the supervision, direction, or control of a higher one;

4. Office Rules and Work Procedures, that is, that there exists a body of generalized rules, more or less stable, governing the management of each of the positions and the relationships existing among them, in addition to a set of procedure dealing with work situations;

5. Qualification Requirements, that is, that individuals who are to occupy the positions in the hierarchical structure of authority of the organization are selected on the bases of specialized qualifications and training.

The bureaucratic organization is composed of a number of formalized positions. Each official position carries with it a bundle of rights and privileges, duties and responsibilities, calling for the time and attention of the individual occupying the position. While it is true that the rights and privileges, duties and responsibiilties are exercised by the occupant of the formalized position, they are attached to the position and not to the individual. Thus, when the individual occupying the position has resigned or has been dismissed or removed therefrom, he can no longer exercise the rights and privileges nor be bound by the duties and responsibilities attached to his previously occupied position.

Each position in the bureaucratic structure of the organization has its own jurisdiction or sphere of competence imputed to it. The official action of the incumbent is valid only if performed within the sphere of his assigned functions, that is, within the area of activities properly appertaining to his position. The idea of limited jurisdiction is the direct result of the functional division of labour designed to promote task specialization.

The hierarchical nature of the bureaucracy implies definite gradations of positions in a firmly ordered system of superior-subordinate relationship in the shape of a pyramidal structure. The pyramidal shape of the bureaucratic structure enables a core of élite personnel to co-ordinate and integrate from a central vantage point the activities of the members of the organization. Although action is not always initiated from the top, all actions are potentially controllable from the apex of the bureaucratic hierarchy. The bureaucratic form makes for the speed, economy, and convenience in communication which is essential to secure co-ordination in the organization. The hierarchical pattern of the organization means that any position at any rank between the very top and the very bottom of the pyramidal structure of the organization stands in a relation of authority to the position below but in a relation of responsibility to the position above it.

The bureaucracy is governed by a body of rules which prescribe the boundaries or limits to official actions. The presence of these rules removes the warmth and directness in the human interactions so that human relations become more or less official relations. Such a formality makes possible the interactions of the occupants of the various positions despite their private or personal attitude toward one another. Since the actions of both the superior and the subordinate are constrained by a mutually recognized set of rules, the subordinate is protected from the arbitrary or capricious exercise of authority by his superior.

Special qualification requirements for the various positions in the bureaucratic structure of the organization necessitates training and, most often, examination of the individuals seeking to become members of the bureaucratic organization. Personnel, therefore, are normally selected and distributed to the different positions according to their most relevant specialized abilities. In most instances, these special qualification requirements give rise to professionalization of the class of bureaucrats. Professionalization normally implies that there is now developed among the bureaucrats a common spirit of consolidation manifested by a single bureaucratic philosophy more or less shared by all the members of the bureaucracy.

Informal Structure of Bureaucratic Organizations

When the bureaucratic organization is studied as a concrete social institution rather than as a theoretical model, the scholar is confronted with the reality of the informal structure of the organization. The informal structure may either facilitate or hinder purposive co-operation and communication within the bureaucratic organization. The growth of the informal structure of the organization is brought about by the necessity of adjusting to the changing environmental conditions.

Basically, "informal structure" of the organization means the aggregate of personal contacts and interactions—not specifically prescribed by the official rules of the organization—of associated groups, or of individuals who, having no common or deliberately planned purpose, nevertheless accomplish common or joint results and who are essentially oriented toward the techniques of control. The informal structure of the concrete organization is based on personal and social relations involving prestige, acceptance within the group, personality traits, friendship ties, and other emotional and non-rational factors. It serves to control the behaviour of the worker group, acts as a mechanism of expression of personal relationships, serves as a communication network, establishes control of the conditions of work in a particular working group, and, lastly, maintains a feeling of personal integrity, self-respect, and independent choice. The informal structure of the organization may be viewed as the synthesis of the incongruency between the organizational needs and the individual interests of the organization members. Individuals who work in large formal organizations, experiencing the accompanying conditions of dependency, subordination, and passivity, seek group sanctions and informal work groupings in the process of adaptation. Thus, informal social groups are spontaneously formed within the framework of the formal structure of the organization. For instance, an informal working relationship among some office workers may replace the formal superior-subordinate pattern of work distribution.

Governmental and Non-Governmental Bureaucracy

Governmental bureaucracy is the machinery through which the state, which is the reification of the political community, exercises political authority over all the members of the community. The enormous and multifarious tasks of government require large numbers of men and women to put the political decisions and major policies of the government into effect. These men and women are brought together and are organized into bureaus, departments, agencies, commissions, government corporations, and other organizational units, each of which, if it possesses the minimum characteristics of a bureaucratic organization, is a bureaucracy. Thus, the great governmental bureaucracy of the federal government is, in reality, a conglomerate of many bureaucracies. Whether it was deliberately organized at any one moment of time in history or whether it is the result of an evolutionary process, the primary function of the governmental bureaucracy is to act as the agent of the state and thus vicariously exercise political authority. Apart from its role as the agent of the state, the governmental bureaucracy also has inherent authority to preserve, maintain, and enhance the bureaucratic order. The governmental bureaucracy possesses authority of a dual nature: it is bureaucratic and with few exceptions it is also the sovereign political authority of the state.

Government officials occupying formal positions in the governmental bureaucracy are bound, not only by the body of rules peculiar to it as a governmental bureaucratic organization, such as, for instance, its manual of departmental rules, but also by a body of normative principles governing the entire political order, such as the relevant provisions of the British North America Act of 1867. Because the scope of the activities of government is so vast, its subject-matter so complex, and its problems so interrelated, however, it is not practicable to write down in advance or formulate in any detailed manner all the rules that may be applied in specific cases. Consequently, governmental bureaucrats are invested with tremendous discretionary power both executive, as well as quasi-legislative and quasi-judicial, in deciding many important matters subject to governmental regulation or control.

Non-governmental bureaucracy refers to a system of consciously coordinated activities of two or more persons within an organizational structure, hierarchical in nature, designed to accomplish specific ends by rationally efficient means. It has its own system of authority lesser than, and subject to, the political authority of the state.

Outside the governmental organizations, large aggregates confronted by huge and complex administrative tasks tend to become bureaucratically organized. The features of the Weberian model of bureaucracy, although abstracted primarily from extensive studies of government bureaus, are applicable to any complex formal organization. Thus, business corporations, political parties, labour unions, industrial organizations, universities, hospitals, churches, prisons, and other large institutions are most likely to become bureaucratized in order to cope rationally with complex tasks requiring much manpower. A proposition referred to as the "iron law of oligarchy" asserts that political parties and labour or trade unions, regardless of how democratic their respective ideologies might be, invariably tend to become bureaucratically organized and centrally controlled by their officials, with the help of their administrative staffs. The proposition also asserts that in the course of its existence any organization will incline toward the rule of the few by gradually reducing decision-making powers and meaningful participation from the membership at large in favour of the dominant élite within the organization. Even the most egalitarian organizations are likely to be transformed in time into centralized bureaucracies dominated by self-perpetuating oligarchies, unless some intermediate semi-autonomous sub-units are created. They must be viable enough to arrest the process of centralization of power and thus achieve the preservation of democratic processes as shown in a study of the International Typographical Union (see Lipset et al., 1956).

Non-governmental bureaucracies may be one of the outcomes of the capitalist money economy. The economic dependence on his job of the salaried employee and his independent ability to advance himself in his career has stimulated the societal orientation toward administratively disciplined conduct and bureaucratically responsible behaviour. Moreover, with the separation of management from the ownership of private property and the consequent rise of the managerial class, the modern corporate business structure has gradually emerged, promoting both the industrial concentration of economic power and the bureaucratization of the private sector of society. The giant corporations, in turn, threatened the industrial workers. Being unable to bargain individually with their respective corporate employers, they began to organize themselves into large labour unions with complex administrative structures. Thus, the free capitalist economy has fostered bureaucratization among both the private companies and the labour unions. The development of large industrial amalgamations and big labour organizations has necessitated an increasing number of governmental regulations leading to increased bureaucratization in the public sector.

Governmental bureaucracies may be distinguished from the non-governmental ones. While governmental bureaucracies are inextricably linked with public policy implementation, non-governmental bureaucracies are primarily concerned with property relations and private wealth. Governmental bureaucracies strive to render public service, whereas non-governmental bureaucracies are basically concerned with the making of monetary profits. Finally, governmental bureaucracies are exposed to a greater degree of public scrutiny than non-governmental or industrial bureaucracies.

The majority of non-governmental or industrial bureaucracies are highly centralized, and therefore all direction and authority tend to flow from the top to the bottom of the pyramidal structure of the organization. A few of the formal structures of certain industrial organizations, however, consist of several independent and autonomous centres of authority. A good example of this organizational pattern is the case of the divisional plan like that employed in the General Motors Company.

Monocratic and Polycratic Organizations

On the basis of the mode of structuring the channels of authority, organizations, whether bureaucratic or non-bureaucratic, governmental or non-governmental, may be classified into either a monocratic or a polycratic organization (Mayer, 1957: 172). This classification is illustrated in Figure 11:1. *formal structure (hierarchy)*

A monocratic organization possesses a hierarchy of positions where all authority cascades from the top by progressive delegation, and responsibility rises from the bottom of the pyramid structure of the organization and is owed to the next superior and so on up to the vertex. A polycratic organization, on the other hand, implies a collegiate decision-making entity where several individuals, rather than a single person, are responsible for the making of authoritative decisions. While monocratic organizations exercise the executive type of authority, polycratic organizations exercise the collegial type of authority. The executive type of authority refers to a system of controls in which a superior official in a hierarchical organization exercises ultimate authority over his subordinates and usually makes decisions without significant consideration of their views. While he may delegate certain aspects of his decision-making functions to those persons occupying middle-management positions, ultimate authority and control actually resides in his executive position. In contrast, the collegial type of authority refers to a system of controls shared by all the members

Figure 11:1 Types of organizations

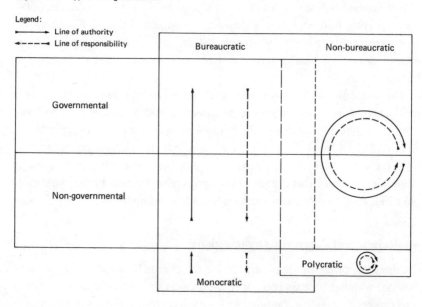

Legend:
▶──────▶ Line of authority
◀────◀ Line of responsibility

of the polycratic organization. While decision-making authority may be delegated to and exercised by specific individuals, the members of the organization view such delegation as involving authority emanating from the collegial membership as a whole. This type of authority is best exemplified by the federal cabinet. In general, a cabinet in a parliamentary system of government is normally a collegial company of equals who bear a great deal of corporate authority to determine the direction of public policies in the governance of the political community.

Most bureaucratic organizations tend to be monocratic in nature. They tend to possess one centre of authority usually located in the position at the top of the chain of command in the organization. Even in the so-called "decentralized" organizations, there is normally one centre of authority where the final decisions on fundamental questions are made and where conflicts among officials in the lower levels of the organizational hierarchy are ultimately resolved. This monocratic character explains the high degree of effectiveness of this mode of organizing; for it enables the top central management group, which is usually committed to the organizational goals, to retain control of many of the activities of the other segments of the organization. Thus, the so-called "principle of latent control" (Sykes, 1953: 147–49) is secured; that is to say, the structure of authority, either explicitly or implicitly, recognizes higher positions as controlling all lower positions in the organization, according to the chain of command.

The bureaucratic model and the typology outlined in this chapter, necessarily tentative in nature, may be serviceable as a guide to scholarly activities in the study of bureaucratic organizations, particularly of governmental bureaucracy as an aspect of society. The discussion will now be focused specifically on the Canadian governmental bureaucracy, which may be better understood using the Weberian model as a theoretical framework of analysis.

The Political Setting of the Canadian Governmental Bureaucracy

The Canadian governmental bureaucracy is located within a sociopolitical system characterized by several factors: the enormous size and physical diversity of the country; the existence of a number of linguistic, religious, and cultural groups, led by the two founding groups of English-speaking and French-speaking Canadians; a parliamentary system of government; a federal division of governmental powers; and the undisputed primacy of the federal cabinet in the basic task of political governance.

The most striking feature of the Canadian society is the large size and geographic diversity of the country, which extends from the Pacific coast in the west to the Atlantic coast in the east; from the Arctic region in the north to the United States-Canadian border in the south.

Another salient feature of the Canadian society is the existence of the two founding linguistic, cultural, and religious groups of people. The Anglo-Canadians speak the English language, are the bearers of a predominantly British culture, and, in the great majority, are Protestants. The French-Canadians speak the French language, are the bearers of the French-Canadian culture, and almost all are Catholic. Each founding group has its own philosophical outlook on life, attitudes, systems of personal and communal values, and modes of expressing those values in the manifold activities of social and political life.

The Canadian society has a parliamentary form of government based on the constitutional doctrine of the supremacy of Parliament. Thus, Section 17 of the British North America Act declared that "there shall be One Parliament for Canada, consisting of the Queen, an Upper House styled the Senate and the House of Commons." In a parliamentary system of government, there is a fusion of the legislative and executive powers in the cabinet, which governs as long as its policies are being supported by a majority of the members of Parliament.

Federalism is a method of dividing governmental powers, resulting in a system in which, in a legal and constitutional sense, the central and the regional (that is, provincial) government each has an independent legal existence. Each has its own share of the functions of government (exclusively, competitively, or co-operatively), but in a political sense, as a result of the political process, the central and regional governments are "in a mutually interdependent political relationship" such that "neither level of government becomes dominant to the extent that it dictates the decisions of the other but can influence, bargain with, and persuade the other" (Vile, 1961: 199). The federal division of governmental powers was laid down in the British North America Act of 1867. The federal structure guarantees diversity with unity, a pluralistic weaving of divergent interests, and a successful balancing of multiple centres of political power.

The primacy of the Canadian federal cabinet has been assured by its legislative leadership role and its collective executive dominance. The cabinet is usually constituted by the prime minister in such a way that its representative character is maximized to reflect the regional, industrial, cultural, religious, and other interests in the country.

The Collective Executive of the Canadian Governmental Bureaucracy

Although the executive authority over Canada is declared by the British North America Act to continue and be vested in the Queen, acting through her representative, the Governor General, the BNA Act also created "a Council to aid and advise in the Government of Canada, to be styled the Queen's Privy Council for Canada." Constitutionally speaking, it follows that the Governor General cannot legitimately act alone to exercise executive power; he must act as the "Governor-General-in-Council", which shall be construed as referring to the "Governor-General acting by and with the Advice of the Queen's Privy Council for Canada." While there are many members of the Canadian Privy Council, only a few constitute the politically active segment known as the Committee of the Privy Council. It is composed of the ministers of the Crown, chosen by the prime minister from among the members of the House of Commons or the Senate, who belong to the ruling political party in Parliament. Although the cabinet has no explicit constitutional or legal basis, as the executive committee of the Canadian Privy Council, it is the ultimate source of executive and administrative power in the Canadian governmental bureaucracy. Thus, although we may hear in constitutional terms about a given decision of "the Governor-in-Council", what is actually meant is a decision of the Canadian cabinet under the leadership of the prime minister.

The prime minister is the most important member of the cabinet. As the chief minister of the Crown, the political power of the prime minister derives from the political reality that, as the chosen leader of the ruling parliamentary party, he is the directing force both in the cabinet and in Parliament. He selects his colleagues in the cabinet and prescribes their respective duties; he is the official spokesman of the government with respect to the administration's goals and policies; and, as the national leader, he has to be consulted by every cabinet minister on all important policy decisions affecting their respective departments (Dawson and Ward, 1970: 188–89). As the chairman of the cabinet, the prime minister controls the agenda and is principally responsible for the total activity of the governmental administrative machinery. He oversees the operation of the other ministers' departments in his capacity as the chief co-ordinator of governmental policies, programs, and activities. The prime minister's personal staff, which constitutes an organizational unit known as the Prime Minister's Office, assists him so that he can effectively exercise his powers and discharge his responsibilities. The principal functions of the Prime Minister's Office are, among others, to allocate the prime minister's time for all his official duties; to brief him in advance of the question period in the House of Commons; to process his correspondence; and to order for him the cabinet documents, papers, reports, and memoranda to be studied, read, and digested prior to actual decision-making in the cabinet and in the committees of the cabinet. Without a personal staff the prime minister obviously could not perform effectively his manifold duties and responsibilities as the national leader of his country, the ruling party, and the administrative governmental bureaucracy.

The Privy Council-Cabinet Committee System

When the Queen's Privy Council was established on July 1, 1867, its first members were sworn in as privy councillors by the first Governor General, Viscount Monck. The administrative base of the Queen's Privy Council— the politically active segment of the Privy Council otherwise known as the cabinet—is the Privy Council Office. It is directed by a high-ranking officer known as the clerk of the Privy Council, whose principal function is to assist the president of the Privy Council in the council business relating to the recommendations of the various ministers of the Crown in the areas of concern where decisions have to be made by the cabinet. From 1867 to 1939 the cabinet had operated in what can be described as an unbelievably haphazard way, without any agenda and without minutes in its meetings. The prime minister alone had any idea of the order of business and could always alter the items to take up first what he considered important or urgent matters. The other attending ministers could not tell in advance what would be discussed in any given meeting, and most of them were frequently surprised by proposals suddenly and unexpectedly introduced by their colleagues for decision (Heeney, 1967: 366–75).

When Arnold D. P. Heeney was appointed both the Clerk of the Privy Council and the Secretary to the Cabinet, he was able gradually to persuade the then Prime Minister, Mackenzie King, to accept the orderly introduction of items for the agenda of cabinet meetings, the giving of adequate notice of proposals requiring decisions, the circulation of relevant documents and papers, the systematic recording of decisions, and the arrangements for a follow-up review of action by the responsible ministers and their departments charged with administrative implementation of cabinet decisions. This particular historical experience illustrates the process of bureaucratization of organizations, manifested in the crystallization of office rules and work procedures and the increasing rationality of decision-making. Mr. L. B. Pearson reorganized the cabinet committee system in 1964 by having matters discussed first by the appropriate standing committee chaired by the minister concerned before its consideration by the cabinet as a whole for decision, under the doctrine of collective cabinet responsibility. The cabinet committee system initiated by Mr. Pearson survives to the present day, with the addition in 1968 by Mr. P. E. Trudeau of a Cabinet Committee on Priorities and Planning. Prime Minister Trudeau further modified the cabinet committee system by providing for regular committee meetings and, most significantly, by permitting the committees themselves to make specific decisions. Cabinet committee decisions, however, only become operative as part of government policy when listed in the annex of the cabinet agenda and when no particular minister has given notice to the deputy secretary to the cabinet that he wishes to have any particular decisions discussed in the full cabinet meeting. There are presently four co-ordinating committees of the cabinet: the Cabinet Committee on Priorities and Planning, the Cabinet Management Committee which is the Treasury Board, the Cabinet Committee on Federal-Provincial Relations, and the Cabinet Committee on Legislation and House Planning. In addition, there are also a number of standing functional subject-matter committees on External Policy and Defence; Economic Policy; Social Policy; Science, Culture and Information; Government Operations; the Public Service; and Security and Intelligence.

The Privy Council Office provides the respective secretariats assisting each one of the standing committees of the cabinet in their decision-making processes to cover all the major fields of governmental activities. Each secretariat is responsible for moving forward to the particular committee and to the full cabinet itself policy proposals that must be considered and decided. Any policy decision, arrived at by any of the cabinet committees and approved by the full cabinet explicitly or implicitly, is passed on by the Privy Council Office directly to the particular minister and his relevant department for administrative implementation. The Privy Council Office is, therefore, the direct link between the policy-makers in the cabinet and the ministers, and the deputy heads and directors of the various departments and agencies of the governmental bureaucracy responsible for implementing those policy decisions through programs of activities.

The Treasury Board

No description of the Canadian federal bureaucracy is complete without an understanding of the Treasury Board, its multiple roles and basic functions.

Section 5 of the Financial Administration Act, as amended, declared that

. . . the Treasury Board may act for the Queen's Privy Council for Canada on all matters relating to: (a) general administrative policy of the public service; (b) the organization of the public service or any portion thereof, and the determination and control of establishments therein; (c) financial management; (d) the review of expenditure plans and programs of the various departments of government, and the determination of priorities; (e) personnel management in the public service, including the determination of terms and conditions of employment; and (f) such other matters as may be referred to it by the Governor-in-Council.

The Treasury Board, as presently constituted, consists of the President of the Treasury Board, a position which is a cabinet portfolio, the Minister of Finance, and four other members of the Queen's Privy Council for Canada who are ministers of the Crown. The Treasury Board secretariat, the administrative arm of the Board, is charged with the examination of spending programs of all government departments and agencies; the making of recommendations to the Treasury Board on proposed expenditures; the review of the development of approved programs; and the recommendation of personnel management policy in the public service to the Treasury Board in the areas of manpower utilization, salary administration, pensions, staff relations, and the negotiation of collective bargaining agreements with the various certified bargaining agents of organized public service employees (Information Canada, 1973: 9000–99).

The Treasury Board, assisted by its secretariat, performs a number of roles in relation to the political policy-makers in the cabinet and also in relation to the administrative departments, agencies, and other organizational units of the government: (1) the role of the cabinet committee on the expenditure budget; (2) the role of the cabinet committee on public service management; and, (3) the role of the central control and co-ordinating agency of the entire federal governmental bureaucracy. As the cabinet committee on the expenditure budget, the Treasury Board, assisted by its secretariat, is intricately involved in the budgetary planning process, working closely with the appropriate units of the Department of Finance, the co-ordinating and substantive committees of the cabinet within given particular areas of policy concern, the full cabinet and, of course, Parliament.

The Treasury Board, within the limits of the overall governmental objectives, policies, and priorities, would group all departmental claims for expenditures into three budgetary categories (Johnson, 1971: 346–66): (1) those departmental programs which are already being implemented as part of the present expenditure budget (the so-called "A" budget); (2) those departmental programs which are new or additional and which are yet to be approved (the so-called "B" budget); and (3) those departmental programs or parts thereof which are of low priority and therefore might be expected to be discontinued. Within the broad outlines of the priorities and policy directions of the government, the Treasury Board and its secretariats would formulate a total expenditure plan for the coming fiscal year taking into account the budgetary submissions of the various departments and agencies but ultimately deciding on the precise amounts to be allocated to the programs and projects of the various governmental departments and agencies.

454 INTRODUCTION TO CANADIAN SOCIETY

Briefly, the primary task of the Treasury Board, assisted by its secretariat, in its role as the cabinet committee on the expenditure budget, is to help carry out the framework of governmental objectives, policies, and sets of priorities in the form of allocation of precise dollar amounts to the programs, projects, and activities budgets of the various departments, agencies, and other organizational units of the federal governmental bureaucracy constituting the Canadian public administration system.

In its role as the cabinet committee on public administrative management, the Treasury Board, assisted by its secretariat, is actually performing its statutory grant of discretionary authority to act for the Queen's Privy Council for Canada on all matters relating to the general administrative policy and personnel management. Moreover, the Treasury Board, acting as the Cabinet Committee on Management, performs the unavoidable role of being the public employer which bargains on behalf of all the departments and agencies of the government with the certified agents of the employee organizations. It also formulates and implements guidelines and regulations relating to the quantity and quality of administrative inputs such as personnel, equipment, supplies, and services.

As the Cabinet Committee on Administrative Management, the Treasury Board is empowered to delegate certain managerial functions to the departments under section 7 (2) of the Financial Administration Act which, as amended, provides that

the Treasury Board may authorize the deputy head of a department or the executive officer of the public service to exercise and perform, in such manner and subject to such terms and conditions as the Treasury Board directs, any of the powers and functions of the Treasury Board in relation to personnel management in the public service and may, from time to time as it sees fit, revise or rescind or restate the authority so granted.

The Treasury Board also acts as the cabinet committee for central control and co-ordination of the entire federal governmental bureaucracy. Section 6 of the Financial Administration Act states that "the Treasury Board may make regulations for the purpose of ensuring effective co-ordination of administrative functions and services among and within departments" and also to provide "for the establishment of general administrative standards of performance" and to make regulations "for any other purpose necessary for the efficient administration of the public service."

In the actual day-to-day operations of the various organizational units of the Canadian federal bureaucracy, there are certain personnel functions which, of necessity, must be centrally co-ordinated if the entire public service is to operate as a single total system of public administration. The establishment of a position-classification system and of salary plans for the entire governmental bureaucracy can hardly be done on the basis of diversified and different rules from department to department or agency to agency. It would be both chaotic and unjust if basically the same position consisting of the same bundle of administrative duties and responsibilities are located in different levels of hierarchy, and are assigned different salary scales in the various departments and agencies of the government. Hence, the need for centralized authority to establish and administer position-classification systems and compensation plans in the public service. Standardized rules and procedures as a feature of the Weberian model of bureaucracy can be applied to the centralized administration of the position-classification and compensation systems of the Canadian federal bureaucracy.

In addition, there are certain other administrative functions of an auxiliary or housekeeping nature, which, for reasons of economy and efficiency, must be centrally provided, such as the procurement of supplies and services provided for by the Department of Supplies and Services. As the central directing and co-ordinating agency with respect to the personnel and housekeeping functions of the governmental federal bureaucracy, the Treasury Board is uniquely situated to act also as the central control agency. Co-ordination cannot be achieved without central control, and control is undesirable unless it is intended to secure co-ordination. Perhaps the primary tool being used by the Treasury Board in trying to secure co-ordination of all departmental programs and activities of the various departments and agencies of the government is its fiscal control of expenditures. The Treasury Board also uses its regulatory power over personnel functions of determining manpower requirements to promote the co-ordination of the many programs and activities of the various departments and agencies.

The Public Service Commission

Imbued by the social sentiment to eliminate political patronage in the public service, the Civil Service Amendment Act of 1908 created a Civil Service Commission to replace the then existing Board of Civil Service Examiners. The 1908 Civil Service Commission, which consisted of two commissioners, was authorized to set up open competitive examination for entrance into what was known as the Inside Civil Service, that is, those positions in the Canadian federal bureaucracy located in and around Ottawa; all other federal positions in the provinces or areas outside the national capital were called the Outside Civil Service.

The original composition of the 1908 Civil Service Commission was structurally defective. As stated by one of the first two commissioners, Dr. Adam Shortt (Shortt and Malcolm, 1972: 35):

It was rather an unusual experiment to provide for a Civil Service Commission of two members with equal authority, yet without any provision for possible differences of opinion between them. . . . A difference of judgment involves the paralysis of appointments or promotion without any provision for solving the difficulty.

Accordingly, the Civil Service Amendment Act of 1912 was passed, providing for three Commissioners: two members of the Civil Service Commission and a chairman to act as the senior member and official spokesman to Parliament and to the public. From its inception in 1908 to 1917, the Civil Service Commission slowly established itself as the central recruitment agency for the then virtually autonomous governmental departments.

The Civil Service Act of 1918 placed both the Inside and the Outside Civil Service under the jurisdiction of the Civil Service Commission. It also increased the powers of the Civil Service Commission by including not only appointments, promotions, and transfers, but also position-classification and salary determination. In addition, the Civil Service Commission was required to "prepare plans for the organization of the Inside and the Outside Service of each department and of each branch or portion of the civil service, such organization as far as possible to follow the same general principles in all branches of the civil service. . . ." Again, this is an example of the emergence of the Weberian bureaucratic feature of generalized rules indicative of increasing rationality in organizations.

Following the recommendations of the Glassco Royal Commission on Government Organization, which reported in 1962, the central direction of personnel policy for the entire public service was removed from the Civil Service Commission and transferred to the Treasury Board by an act to amend the Financial Administration Act, vesting in the Treasury Board "personnel management in the public service, including the determination of terms and conditions of employment." The Civil Service Commission was mercilessly stripped of its power over position-classification, salary determination, and the primary responsibility for training and development of personnel. Two important powers left with the Civil Service Commission, now renamed by the Public Service Employment Act of 1967 as the Public Service Commission, are: the authority to (1) "appoint or provide for the appointment of qualified persons to or from within the public service" and (2) "operate and assist deputy heads in the operation of the staff training and development programs in the public service."

With the passage of the Public Service Staff Relations Act of 1967, a collective bargaining system in the public service was inaugurated and the Treasury Board became the undisputed "employer" for the public service, with authority to enter into collective agreements with organized public service employees on behalf of the government. The Public Service Commission, however, remained as the central staffing agency of the governmental bureaucracy, enjoying the exclusive right and authority to make appointments to or from within the public service. Such appointments are to be based on selection according to merit, as determined by the Public Service Commission, which may prescribe selection standards it considers necessary or desirable, in its assessment of merit. Thus, the Public Service Commission may define merit in a flexible and changing manner.

The Public Service Commission may delegate any or all of its personnel functions to the deputy heads of departments. The Public Service Commission proceeded to delegate recruitment, selection, and appointing authority to the departments in a manner opposite to that suggested by the Glassco Commission by starting with the lower salaried classes of position. Simultaneously with delegation of staffing authority, the Public Service Commission has begun to develop its monitoring system and its periodic reviews of departmental actions to ensure that the merit principle is being upheld by the departments.

The Federal Departments and Agencies

The organizational form of the federal departments and agencies was initially established by the Civil Service Act of 1882, which set up a five-tiered hierarchy with the deputy minister at the top (immediately under the political executive who was the cabinet minister). Under the then prevailing doctrine of almost absolute departmental autonomy, there were no uniform principles of organization adhered to. The 1912 Murray Report on the Organization of the Public Service of Canada noted the fact that:

Men will be found in one Department with high salaries doing work which is performed by a much lower class in others; and the numbers of the various classes have been increased from time to time to meet the supposed claims of individuals without any special reference to the nature of the duties to be performed. It would be easy to quote numerous cases in which an officer has been allowed to proceed from one class to another without any change of work whatever, merely because it was desired to improve his position (Hodgetts *et al.*, 1972: 34).

The Civil Service Act of 1918 recognized and extended the principle of appointment by open competitive examination for all positions. The Civil Service Commission was called upon to reorganize and classify the public service, such reorganization to follow as far as possible the same general principles in all branches of the public service. Again, this procedure is an application of the notion of rationality which lies at the heart of the Weberian model of bureaucracy. The merit principle was assumed by the Civil Service Act of 1918 without explicitly defining it, and an elaborate merit system of rules, regulations, policies, and procedures was set up to implement the merit principle. The merit principle may be defined as the fundamental rule under which persons are selected and promoted on the basis of achievements measured in a standard way by means of open competition. In contrast, the merit system is the body of rules and procedures which establish, enforce, and uphold the merit principle.

Thus, the existence of generalized rules governing the management of the positions, and their interrelationships, as a distinctive feature of Weberian bureaucracy, is once more confirmed in the Canadian governmental administrative system. The Civil Service Commission, in the exercise of its position-classification function, was to prepare a plan of organization for each department, including the number of employees required, for submission to the governor-in-council before any such organization could be approved. Similarly, in the exercise of its salary determination function, the recommendation on salaries and allowances for the various classes and grades of position in the public service made by the Civil Service Commission could be accepted or rejected *in toto* only by the governor-in-council, which could not modify them. In brief, the Civil Service Act of 1918, in its ardent desire to create a unified public service, effectively deprived the departments and agencies of formal power to control the selection, organization, classification, salary determination, and career development of public service employees, vesting such powers to a central personnel agency which had also enjoyed since 1908 the traditional authority, formerly vested in the ministers of the Crown, to appoint or to promote personnel within their respective departments.

The Growth of Federal Bureaucracy

Despite the lack of adequate historical statistical data and the changing statistical categories used, the growth of the federal departmental employment can be discerned by a perusal of available information on the number of employees in the public service in some selected years as shown in Table 1. A visual portrayal of the pattern of growth of federal employment is presented in Figure 11:2.

The growth of public employment in Canada, or more specifically, the increase in the number of federal employees, is due to a certain set of interdependent factors. First, the increase in population (for example, from 5.3 million in 1901 to 20 million as early as 1966) has brought about increasing demands for services provided by the government, such as mail, health and welfare, housing, and other essential public functions. Second, war and similar international events tend to stimulate government employment. During the First World War, federal employment

Table 1   Federal employment in Canada.

Selected Years	Estimated Number of Employers (including those not subject to Civil Service Act)
1914	25,107
1920	47,133
1924	40,068
1930	44,175
1934	40,469
1939	46,106
1941	66,926
1943	104,055
1950	127,196
1955	143,150
1960	198,162
1965	211,077
1969	212,941
1971	216,488
1972	230,756
1973	269,927
1974	284,376

Sources: Royal Commission on Government Organization, 1962: 305.
Civil Service Commission, 1950–72.
Canadian Tax Foundation, 1973–74: 86.

doubled and during the Second World War, federal employment expanded almost three times. Third, industrialization has drawn the government more and more to assume the roles of planner, regulator, and in some areas entrepreneur, with a consequent growth in the responsibilities largely devolving upon the numerous Crown corporations designed to administer governmental commercial and quasi-commercial activities. Fourth, urbanization was brought about by the concentration of population in few large major centres of 100,000 population and over. In 1871 only 18.3 per cent of the total Canadian population lived in urban communities of relatively small size; by 1901 the urban population had reached 34 per cent of the total; and by 1966, the percentage of urban population climbed to 74 (Plunkett, 1973: 40–51; for a more extended discussion, see Kalbach's chapter on Canadian demography).

Figure 11:2 Growth of federal employment

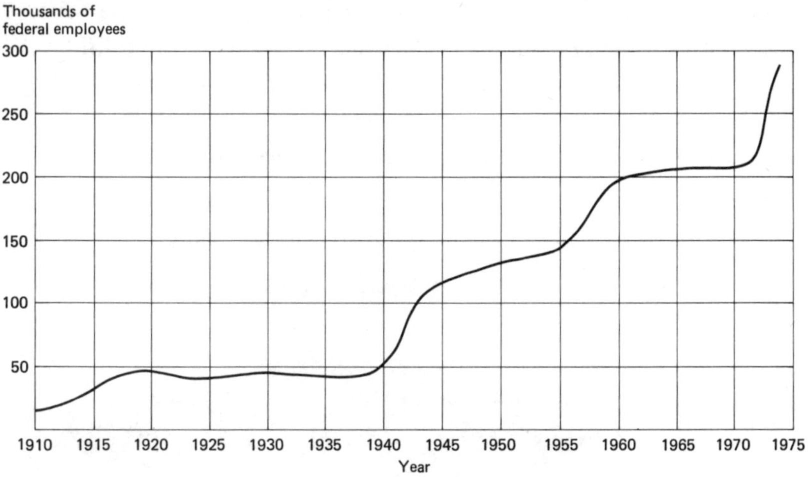

Thousands of
federal employees

Year

Sources: Royal Commission on Government Organization, 1962 : 305
Civil Service Commission 1950–1972

Finally, the changing posture of the state from the passive to the active positive role in attempting to rectify social and economic inequalities through social welfare programs has brought about the establishment of new agencies such as the Unemployment Insurance Commission, as well as the consolidation and expansion of existing departments and agencies into some new organizational form, as exemplified by the Department of Environment.

Geographical Dispersion of the Canadian Federal Bureaucracy

Geographical decentralization of the Canadian federal bureaucracy refers to the administrative arrangement and placement of several types of offices whose locations are dispersed in various areas outside the central headquarters. In discussing geographical decentralization, it is useful to focus on the relationship between the type of office involved and the level of organization of the total governmental bureaucratic hierarchy. For the sake of clarity, the political segment consisting of Parliament, the cabinet, and the minister of the Crown is equated with the first level, and the deputy minister and directors with the second level of bureaucratic hierarchy, and both the first and second levels constitute what is designated the central headquarter. Interposed between the field offices and subfield offices located respectively at the fourth and fifth level of the bureaucratic hierarchy are the regional or district offices located at the third level of the federal bureaucratic hierarchy. These points are illustrated in Figure 11:3.

Figure 11:3 Geographical distribution of federal departmental bureaucracy by levels of organization and types of offices involved

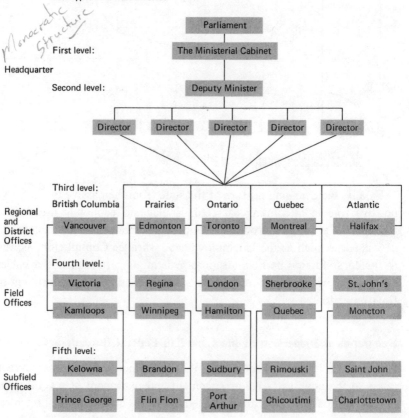

Source: Bowland, 1967:327.

Two competing principles of organization are relevant to any consideration of bureaucratic hierarchy. The principle of span of control asserts that administrative efficiency is enhanced at any given level if any superior official has under him only a limited number of subordinates whom he can effectively supervise. Wide span of control, implying too many subordinates to be supervised, weakens administrative control, since in the task of supervising any given number of individuals, the supervisor is actually dealing with that number of individuals plus all possible combinations in twos, threes, and so forth of the subordinates, each combination being an additional separate social unit in itself (Graicunas, 1937: 9).

Observance of the principle of span of control, however, normally results in an increase in the number of organizational levels through which problems must pass before a final decision is reached, thus creating more opportunities for error or delay. Herbert A. Simon pointed out a counter-vailing organizational principal of keeping at a minimum the number of organizational levels through which a matter must pass before it is acted upon, in order to increase overall administrative efficiency (Simon, 1957: 26). Since in geographical decentralization the main lines of communication are the single direct relationships linking headquarters, regional or district offices and field offices, possible cross-relationships between groups of two, three, or more offices are minimal or nil. Therefore, regional and field supervisory offices are in a favourable position to widen the span of control, without weakening administrative control itself; and the two competing organizational principles of limited span of control and limited number of levels of organization are reconciled in the Canadian system of geographically decentralized federal public administration. In a 1965 survey of the field-office organizations of some twenty agencies (Bowland, 1967: 323–61), one scholar found that given the dispersal of the clientele population to be served, the desirability of equalization of work load, the field office locations of co-operating provincial or municipal agencies, transportation convenience and other factors influencing the choice of location of the field offices of a federal agency, most regional and district boundaries follow the boundary lines of a province or a set of provinces.

The field offices within the regional and district boundaries are situated below the regional and district offices and are located at the fourth level of the bureaucratic hierarchy. Since a great majority of federal field offices divide the provincial boundaries into four or fewer parts, centres of dominance tend to emerge within each province. Geographical de-centralization as a distinctive characteristic pattern of the Canadian federal bureaucracy seems to be inevitable in a country as wide and large as Canada, if governmental programs are to be implemented according to the felt needs and wants of the Canadian people.

Personnel Processes in the Canadian Federal Bureaucracy

The Civil Service Act of 1961 provided for at least three kinds of competitive examinations for appointment to civil service positions: open competition; closed competition; and promotional competition, which is a type of closed competition restricted to employees of one particular department (intradepartmental) or an even more restricted portion of a single department. Appointments to the civil service were to be made only after competitive examination, except in the following instances: (1) where an appointment to a position was urgently required; (2) where the availability of suitable candidates for a position was limited; and (3) where a person having a special skill or knowledge was required for a position involving duties of an exceptional nature.

The Public Service Employment Act of 1967 reaffirmed the merit principle as the cornerstone of the federal public service bureaucracy since 1918. Appointments to or from the public service will be based on selection according to merit as determined by the Public Service Commission having the authority to prescribe selection standards as to education, knowledge, experience, language, age, residence, or any other matter the Commission thought to be necessary or desirable. Necessary or essential qualifications refer to the minimum factors or circumstances having regard to the nature of the duties of the position or class of positions. Desirable qualifications refer to those factors or circumstances which are to be taken into account in addition to the essential qualifications—having regard to the nature of the duties to be performed when assessing the relative merits of the candidates for the position or class of positions (Regulations, 1967: 4).

According to the essential nature of the appointment itself, the kinds of appointments which could be made under the Public Service Employment Act of 1967 are the following: (1) probationary appointment; (2) provisional appointment; (3) term appointment; (4) temporary appointment; (5) permanent appointment; and (6) acting appointment.

A probationary appointment is one made for a period of trial under which the employee is subject to observation to determine whether or not he is capable of performing satisfactorily the full range of his duties and responsibilities and, if not rejected while on probation, is entitled to a permanent appointment. An employee is considered on probation from the date of his appointment until the end of such period as the Public Service Commission may establish for any position or class of positions. For example, the probationary period of twelve months has been established for the position of messenger.

A provisional appointment is one which is issued to a person who has not qualified in an appropriate examination but who otherwise meets the qualification requirements for appointment to a regular position in the competitive public service because the interest of the service requires that a position be filled immediately and there is no appropriate eligible list from which appointment may be made.

A term appointment is one which is issued to a person for a specified period at the expiration of which he automatically ceases to be an employee.

A temporary appointment is one made for a position needed for only a limited period, usually not exceeding six months; the employee has no chance with respect to permanency of appointment and does not enjoy the normal opportunities for promotion, salary increments, or superannuation benefits.

A permanent appointment is one whose tenure is for an indeterminate period and is without term. A probationary appointment automatically becomes a permanent appointment when the probationary period has expired and the employee is not rejected, or when the probationary period has been waived.

Finally, an acting appointment is one offered by a deputy head to an employee to perform for a temporary period the duties of a position which normally has a higher maximum rate of pay than the pay of the position held by such an employee.

During the tenure of federal employment, there are a number of personnel placement processes other than the initial appointment which could take place such as promotion, transfer, detail, demotion, and reinstatement.

Promotion is the upward movement of an employee from his present position to a progressively higher position involving new duties and greater responsibilities. If there is no change in the position but there is an increase in salary, there is what is known as an "advancement" only, as distinguished from a promotion.

Transfer is a horizontal personnel action moving one employee from one position to another position within the same class, involving substantially the same duties and responsibilities at substantially the same salary.

Detail is the temporary reassignment of an employee to another comparable position to meet transitory needs. Detail could work harmoniously with a well-organized promotion policy. For example, since 1967, the Public Service Commission has implemented a Career Assignment Program (CAP) which involves special assignments to potential executives to work for a period of two years in policy or staff areas in the several departments, task forces, Royal Commissions, or any of the external agencies, such as the United Nations.

Demotion is the appointment of an employee to a position in a lower class, which entails a diminution in duties and a decrease in the salary appropriate to the lower level of the class of position to which the employee has been demoted.

Finally, reinstatement refers to the reappointment to the same or equivalent position in the same class of an individual who, for personal reasons, has previously resigned voluntarily from his position. Reinstatement should be distinguished from re-employment, which is the reappointment to the same or equivalent position in the same class of an individual who has been involuntarily laid off.

In the Canadian federal bureaucracy, the various modes of separation from the public service are: (1) layoff, (2) voluntary resignation, (3) abandonment of position, (4) rejection for cause by the deputy head at the end of the probationary period, (5) dismissal, (6) retirement, and (7) death.

The Public Service Staff Relations Act of 1967 has established a comprehensive system of collective bargaining, dispute settlement, and grievance adjudication within the Canadian federal bureaucracy. It includes, with some exceptions, the several positions in or under any department or other portions of the public service of Canada in respect of which the Queen of Canada is represented by the Treasury Board as the employer. One feature peculiar to the Public Service Staff Relations

Act, which distinguishes it from other labour relations statutes of Canada, is the inclusion of public employees within the classical professions such as law or medicine in the operation of the Act. These professionals are, therefore, eligible for inclusion in collective bargaining units. Another feature which differentiates it from ordinary labour relations statutes is the right of choice accorded the bargaining agent to specify which of the two alternative methods for resolution of a dispute should apply to the bargaining unit in respect of which it has been certified: either (1) the method of referral to a binding arbitration by the Public Service Arbitration Tribunal, or (2) the referral thereof to a tripartite *ad hoc* conciliation board for report and recommendation. Finally, a third feature in which the Public Service Staff Relations Act differs from other labour relations legislation is the statutory right to present grievance.

The Public Service Staff Relations Act created a Public Service Staff Relations Board consisting of a chairman and a vice-chairman and eight other members representing in equal numbers the interests of the employer and the interests of the employees respectively. The Public Service Staff Relations Board, acting as a single body, or any division thereof (either the chairman or the vice-chairman and at least two other members equally representing the respective interests of the employer and the employees) has major responsibilities including, among others, the determination of units of employees appropriate for collective bargaining, the certification of bargaining agents for bargaining units, and the investigation of complaints alleging violations of statutory law.

Where the establishment of a conciliation board has been requested by one of the parties and the chairman of the Public Service Staff Relations Board has decided not to establish any such conciliation board, a lawful strike may take place immediately upon receipt by the parties of such decision. In general, employees in the public service of Canada are expressly forbidden to engage in a strike in the following circumstances: (1) if such employees are not included in a bargaining unit for which a bargaining agent has been certified by the Public Service Staff Relations Board; (2) if such employees are included in a bargaining unit for which the dispute settlement process chosen is the method of referral to arbitration; and (3) if such employees are included in a bargaining unit for which a collective agreement is still in force.

Where the certified bargaining agent has selected the method of referral of matters in dispute to a binding arbitration, the parties, if they are unable to reach any agreement despite the help of individual conciliators, may invoke the assistance of the Public Service Arbitration Tribunal. In any particular dispute, the Public Service Arbitration Tribunal is to consist of the chairman of the Arbitration Tribunal and two other members selected by the chairman from each panel representing the interest of the employer and the employees, respectively. The Public Service Arbitration Tribunal has the statutory authority to render binding awards.

The Public Service Staff Relations Board has the statutory authority to regulate: (1) the certification of bargaining agents for collective bargaining units of employees; (2) the presentation of employee grievances and grievance adjudication; (3) complaints alleging violations of the Public Service Staff Relations Act; (4) the specification of the dispute settlement process, either by referral to a conciliation board or referral to the arbitration tribunal; and (5) references of questions of law or jurisdiction.

Developmental Changes in the Canadian Federal Bureaucracy

There are a number of developmental changes which have been taking place in the Canadian federal bureaucracy. The more important ones include: (1) administrative bilingualism, (2) Planning-Programming-Budgeting System, (3) collective bargaining in the public service, and (4) the emancipation of public employees from the prohibition against partisan political activities.

ADMINISTRATIVE BILINGUALISM

Administrative bilingualism means the attainment of linguistic and cultural equality between the English-speaking and the French-speaking Canadians in the Canadian public administration system, under the basic postulate of equal partnership between the two founding races ("le principe de l'égalité entre les deux peuples fondateurs"). It implies that members of the two historically significant cultural and linguistic groups of Canadians of British and French origin have the same opportunities in the Canadian federal bureaucracy. To implement the bilingual and bi-cultural policy of the federal government, a Commissioner of Official

Languages with the rank and power of a deputy head of a department has been charged with the responsibility of ensuring the recognition of the equal status of the official languages of English and French in the affairs of Parliament and the Canadian government.

Administrative bilingualism, which has been firmly established at the present time as a policy in the Canadian federal bureaucracy, is perhaps the most significant development relating to meeting the problem of French-speaking Canadians' historical disenchantment with the federal public service. Political leaders have come to realize that a bilingual and bicultural policy in the public service is not only conducive to more effective public administration but has perhaps become a political necessity in preserving national unity, advancing French-English Canadian harmony and ensuring the continued existence of Canada.

PLANNING-PROGRAMMING-BUDGETING SYSTEM

The Planning-Programming-Budgeting System is the integration of long-range planning of governmental objectives and various programs to meet these objectives using the tool of budgeting as an allocative process among competing claims to limited resources. While planning is the identification and formulation of a range of meaningful options for the selection of courses of action through a systematic consideration of alternatives, programming is the more specific determination of the requirements of administrative inputs, such as manpower, material, and facilities necessary to carry out a given program. Basically, the Planning-Programming-Budgeting System entails the following ingredients: (1) on the basis of concrete data, the formulation of an objective-oriented structure of program categories (groupings of agency programs which serve the same or similar objectives), program sub-categories (combinations of agency programs on the basis of narrower objectives contributing directly to the broad objectives of the program category as a whole), and program elements (the specific products in terms of concrete goods and services which contribute to the department's or agency's objectives); (2) analysis of possible alternative objectives and of the alternative programs for meeting these objectives, primarily using the technique of systems analysis in which alternative programs are compared with respect to costs and benefits; (3) the measurement of the total cost estimates of programs, not just for one year but for at least several years in the future, adhering to a time cycle within which information and recommendations will be produced at the times needed for executive decisions on the budget; (4) the review of objectives and the conduct of program analysis on a continuing year-round basis in order to translate specified departmental or agency objectives into concrete activities and operations designed to meet those objectives in each of the stated time periods; and (5) the analysis—through systems analysis, operations research, and other pertinent techniques—of the effectiveness and the cost of alternative objectives, programs, and levels within any given category, seeking effectiveness, efficiency, and economy in carrying out existing and proposed programs (Lyden and Miller, 1968: 405–18).

The adoption by the Canadian federal government of the Planning-Programming-Budgeting System is necessitated by the difficult task of converting the broad policy objectives in their order of priorities as formulated by the Planning and Priorities Committee and approved by the full cabinet into specific programs of operations. In April 1969 the president of the Treasury Board formally announced the adoption of the Planning-Programming-Budgeting System by the Canadian federal government. In February 1970 the expenditure estimates were categorized in terms of programs and activities, instead of objects of expenditures. The House of Commons has started to alter the method of reviewing budgetary estimates submitted by the cabinet by referring them to the several functional subject-matter committees, rather than to the Committee of Supply which is a committee of the Whole House. Finally, the Treasury Board, in co-operation with several departments, has introduced measures of operational efficiency, such as ratios of cost per unit output, for evaluating program performance. There have been a number of completed efficiency evaluation studies of the programs of such agencies like the Unemployment Insurance Commission and the Department of Veterans' Affairs. Several other departments, including Manpower and Immigration, National Health and Welfare, National Revenue, and the Post Office, have been collaborating with the Treasury Board in developing multiple cost-effectiveness indicators of performance of their respective programs (Johnson, 1973: 23–31).

Despite some difficulties, the Planning-Programming-Budgeting System, as a developmental pattern of change in the Canadian federal bureaucracy, has been firmly established as a useful management tool in converting the broad policy objectives of the government into specific programs of operations and activities.

COLLECTIVE BARGAINING

Another significant developmental change taking place in the Canadian federal bureaucracy is collective bargaining in the public sector. Collective bargaining is essentially a process of periodic negotiations between the public employer or management and the representative of organized employees resulting in some written agreement on a basic rule system to govern the employer-employee work relationships, tending toward some orderly resolution of disagreements. Collective bargaining implies the performance of the mutual obligation of the employer and the representative of the organized employees to meet at reasonable times and confer in good faith with respect to wages, hours, and other terms and conditions of employment. The transition in Canada from paternalistic unilateralism to participative bilateralism in the employer-employee relationship in the public sector has been a slow and arduous process. Larger membership in employee organizations, the postwar growth of the public service whereby thousands of employees with trade-union backgrounds from private industry had joined the government service, and the occasional strikes of letter carriers and mail sorters, however, have hastened the recognition by the Canadian government of collective bargaining.

One of the basic issues relating to collective bargaining is the determination of the proper scope of bargaining. While the actual scope of collective bargaining can be derived ultimately as a result of experience between the parties in the negotiations, there are certain areas of concern or items which are beyond the proper scope of collective bargaining and therefore are not negotiable. They include: (1) the preservation of the merit principle, (2) position-classifications in the public service, (3) the so-called rights or prerogatives of management, (4) the nation-wide retirement system, and (5) pension rights. It is possible, however, that in the foreseeable future some subjects such as retirement or pension rights may be included as within the proper scope of collective bargaining.

The usual legal framework for collective bargaining involves the following ingredients: (1) designation both of the employer and the exclusive representative of the organized employees; (2) meeting, conferring, and negotiating in good faith; (3) bargaining on wages, hours, terms, and other negotiable conditions of employment; (4) the collective agreement to be embodied in a written document; and (5) the bilateral administration, interpretation, and enforcement of the collective agreement (Newland, 1968: 117–26).

POLITICAL EMANCIPATION OF PUBLIC EMPLOYEES

The doctrine of the political neutrality of the public service employees has been one of the cornerstones of the institutionalization of the merit system. It prohibits any deputy head and, except as authorized, any government employee of the Canadian federal bureaucracy from engaging in work for, on behalf of, or against any candidate or any political party, or be a candidate for an elective federal or provincial or territorial legislative seat. Under the Public Service Employment Act of 1967, a government employee may apply to the Public Service Commission for a leave of absence without pay if he wishes to seek a political nomination as a candidate for an elective office in the federal, provincial, or territorial legislature. If the Public Service Commission is of the opinion that the usefulness of the employee in the public service would not be impaired, the Commission may grant such leave of absence. If granted, the leave of absence ends on the day on which the results of the election are officially announced or on such an earlier day as may be requested by the public employee. If elected to a legislative office, the person who is on leave of absence automatically ceases to be a public service employee.

Circumstances and conditions in modern Canadian society have changed immensely toward favouring the political emancipation of career public service employees. The triumph of the merit principle in the selection process, the professionalization of the public service, the high degree of administrative and technical competence of government officials, the increasing level of the educational attainment of public employees— all have contributed to the continuing growth and development of a new breed of politically conscious and administratively responsible public administrators today.

Under the doctrine of the political neutrality of public employees, public servants are expected to administer policies and carry out programs which are contrary to their personal ideological convictions or beliefs. Career public service employees cannot effectively execute a specific public policy they abhor and it is not realistic to expect them to do so. If, as a consequence of change in the party in power, certain commitments make it truly embarrassing or awkward for top career public administrators to shift to new policies, it might become necessary and prudent to transfer or reassign them to equivalent positions elsewhere, without loss of rank, salary, or other perquisites of office. This would give the necessary flexibility to facilitate administrative and bureaucratic adaptability to political changes resulting from change of ruling parties, ideologies, or political directions.

Bureaucratic Power and Responsibility

There is little doubt that bureaucrats, although theoretically working under the political leadership of the elected officials, exercise tremendous influence on public policy both before and during administrative implementation. A political superior, such as a minister of the Crown, often finds himself at the mercy of his administrative subordinates, like the deputy minister, assistant deputy ministers, and other high-ranking administrators who have the relevant knowledge, skills, and information about a given subject matter. When bureaucratic civil servants as a group do not agree with proposed changes in certain areas of governmental activities, which originated in the political arena, they are usually able to modify public policy at the administrative level without much fear of detection. The bureaucratic class, through its administrative discretion, expertise, experience, knowledge, and information, undoubtedly has adequate power and opportunity not only to initiate public policies it likes but also to modify public policies it does not like.

If government bureaucrats are capable of using the administrative process against, or without reference to, the wishes of their elective political superiors, then there is a need to search for some means of achieving greater administrative responsibility in appointive public officials. In democratic theory, elective public officials are deemed to be responsible and accountable to the voting public during election. In turn, the permanent government bureaucrats are supposed to be responsible and accountable for their decisions and actions to their political superiors.

Most of the time, however, the elected and politically responsible heads are partly or wholly dependent upon the career civil servants for the formulation and implementation of administrative programs to pursue certain politically determined objectives. In view of this fact, democratic processes in the political society are in particular danger of being undermined by the consequences of bureaucratization in government: non-elective officials are in actuality participating in the formulation of public policies and, thereafter, are carrying them out, yet they are not politically accountable to the public through election.

The problem is more acute in parliamentary democracies, including Canada, than it is in republican polities with their built-in systems of checks and balances as exemplified by the United States. While in theory Canada adheres to the doctrine of the supremacy of Parliament, in actuality Parliament has become an ineffective appendage to the cabinet, which has become the source of real political decisions. The authority of Parliament to govern has been diluted primarily by the continuing trend toward delegation of governmental powers to the individual departments and agencies. The average member of Parliament cannot possibly compete with the administrative expertise, experience, knowledge, and familiarity of career senior public servants with the details of their work. Thus, the government bureaucrats, who are supposed to be merely servants of the public policies made into law by Parliament, are in reality active participants both in the formulation of policies and in their administrative implementation.

Perhaps greater bureaucratic responsibility could be achieved by a more effective communication between the minister as political superior and his high-ranking departmental officials. The minister needs to familiarize himself with all existing departmental programs so that he may be made fully aware of all the operations of his own department. This means that the bureaucrats must be more willing to discuss policy objectives and strategies for implementation to attain political objectives. The minister, with the help of his personal assistants, must be able to evaluate programs in terms of costs and in terms of their impact on policies, so that he can judge which program to expand, which one to modify, or discontinue, as the case may be.

Another method by which greater bureaucratic responsibility could be achieved is by a collective and conscious attempt on the part of the Public

Service Commission and the agency heads to develop a socially representative bureaucracy which would reflect a reasonable cross-section of the population in terms of social classes, occupations, ethnic groupings, economic interests, and other demographic characteristics. If the members of the bureaucratic class basically share the values and the attitudes of the members of the society at large, there is more probability that the bureaucracy would exercise its power with a view of pursuing and promoting the public interest.

Finally, some mechanism for the effective review of administrative decisions and actions is needed to ensure administrative accountability. The reviewing entity, whether in the form of a standing committee of Parliament, an administrative ombudsman, or a system of administrative courts patterned after the French model, must be able to initiate investigations and inquiries, with or without complaints from private citizens, not only to assess past administrative performance but also to suggest new approaches or new directions in the various areas of administration demanded by the post-industrial society. The reviewing entity must be given the authority not only to publicize official administrative decisions and actions of the bureaucrats but also to prosecute administrative officials where evidence seems to lead to some gross negligence, wilful misconduct or other serious irregularities. The reviewing body, if it is to be effective, must have its own permanent staff of experts enjoying security of tenure for a reasonably long period of time. It will be acting under the authority of Parliament, with powers to require documents, summon persons, and publish its reports. The irony of the present practice of effectively insulating administrative departments and agencies from judicial review, under the doctrine of the supremacy of Parliament, lies in the fact that at present Parliament is itself largely ineffective to perform political governance.

Conclusions

Bureaucracy is a form of organization which consists of a systematic arrangement of formal positions into a hierarchical pattern of three or more levels, governed by a consistent set of norms, possessing structural characteristics rationally calculated to promote efficiency, and requiring special qualifications for those individuals who are to become its members. The bureaucratization of organizations is a universal process at work in both the public and the private sectors of society. The growth of public and private bureaucracies reinforces the existing social and political order in the community by rationalizing human interactions. Rationality is the faculty which seeks an objective, intelligent, and efficient course of action in every situation. In a bureaucratic organization, rationality is sought by directing the component parts of the enterprise so that each part contributes to the attainment of the organizational goals in the most effective, economical, and efficient manner possible. The outstanding features of a bureaucracy include, among others, an area of jurisdiction for each position, a hierarchical arrangement involving superior-subordinate relationship between or among stratified positions, a body of internal rules and work procedures, and a set of special qualification and training requirements.

In general, organizations in society may either be bureaucratic or non-bureaucratic. If bureaucratic in form, a given organization may either be governmental or non-governmental. And regardless of whether an organization is bureaucratic or not, it may be of either the monocratic or the polycratic type. A governmental bureaucracy is the machinery through which the state, which is the reification of the political community possessed with a political order, exercises political authority over the members of the community. Non-governmental bureaucracy refers to any system of co-ordinated activities of two or more persons within a hierarchical structure of three or more levels, designed to accomplish specific ends by rationally efficient means, having its own system of authority lesser than and subject to the political authority of the state.

This chapter has focused solely on the Canadian governmental bureaucracy at the federal level. Within the framework of the Weberian model of bureaucracy, but within the matrix of a parliamentary democratic society, we have described, sometimes with considerable detail, the historical development, the structure, characteristics, and functions of the Canadian federal bureaucracy in relation to the political and administrative process of formulating and implementing public policies.

In brief, the federal governmental bureaucracy in Canada is the most salient feature of the political aspect of the Canadian society. It is a significant part of the Canadian social system, through which public and social policies are formulated and by means of which they are implemented for the general welfare of the citizens and residents of Canada.

Select Bibliography

BOWLAND, JAMES G. "Geographical Decentralization in the Canadian Federal Public Service", *Canadian Public Administration* 10 (September 1967): 323–61.

CARSON, JOHN J. "The Changing Scope of the Public Servant", *Canadian Public Administration* 11 (Winter 1968): 407–13.

COLE, TAYLOR. "Wartime Trends in the Dominion Civil Service in Canada", *Public Administration Review* 6 (Spring 1946): 157–67.

CRISPO, JOHN. "Collective Bargaining in the Public Service", *Canadian Public Administration* 16 (Spring 1973)): 1–13.

DEUTSCH, JOHN J. "The Public Service in a Changing Society", *Canadian Public Administration* 11 (Spring 1968): 1–8.

GOW, DONALD. "The Setting of Canadian Public Administration", *Public Administration Review* 33 (January–February 1973): 5–13.

HEENEY, ARNOLD D. P. "Mackenzie King and the Cabinet Secretariat", *Canadian Public Administration* 10 (September 1967): 366–75.

HICKS, MICHAEL. "The Treasury Board of Canada and Its Clients: Five Years of Change and Administrative Reform", *Canadian Public Administration* 16 (Summer 1973): 182–205.

HODGETTS, J. E.; MCCLOSKEY, W.; WHITAKER, R.; and WILSON, V. S. *The Biography of an Institution: The Civil Service Commission of Canada, 1908–1967*. Montreal and London: McGill-Queen's University Press, 1972.

HODGETTS, J. E., and DIVIVEDI, O. P. "The Growth of Government Employment in Canada", *Canadian Public Administration* 12 (Summer 1969): 224–38.

Information Canada. *Organization of the Government of Canada*. Ottawa: Crown Copyright Information Canada, 1973.

JOHNSON, A. W. "The Treasury Board of Canada and the Machinery of Government in the 1970's", *Canadian Journal of Political Science* 4 (September 1971): 346–66.

KWANVNICK, DAVID. "French Canadians and the Civil Service of Canada", *Canadian Public Administration* 11 (Spring 1968): 97–112.

LALOND, MARC. "The Changing Role of the Prime Minister's Office", *Canadian Public Administration* 14 (Winter 1971): 509–37.

PRIVES, M. Z. "Career and Promotion in the Federal Civil Service of Canada", *Canadian Public Administration* 3 (June 1960): 179–90.

ROBERTSON, R. G. "The Changing Role of the Privy Council Office", *Canadian Public Administration* 14 (Winter 1971): 487–508.

Royal Commission on Government Organization. *Report: Management of the Public Service*. Vol. I. Ottawa: The Queen's Printer, 1962.

SMILEY, DONALD V. "Equipping the Functional Specialist for Administrative Responsibilities in the Public Service", *Canadian Public Administration* 3 (June 1960): 171–78.

VAISON, ROBERT A. "Collective Bargaining in the Federal Public Service: The Achievement of a Milestone in Personnel Relations", *Canadian Public Administration* 12 (Spring 1969): 108–22.

WHITE, WALTER L., and STRICK, JOHN C. "The Treasury Board and Parliament", *Canadian Public Administration* 10 (June 1967): 209–22.

PART IV

Discipline

Toward a Canadian Sociology 12

G. N. RAMU AND

STUART D. JOHNSON

In the last five years, the past, the present, and the future of sociological enterprise in Canada has been subjected to serious discussion and critical evaluation by concerned academics. The issues are much too complex to be presented in this brief chapter. In an effort to sensitize an introductory student to the problems underlying the emergence and development of Canadian sociology, however, we will indulge here in a direct presentation of the main issues. Our position (to be developed below) is that sociology as a discipline emerges in specific national contexts and in response to critical problems facing a national society. We argue that a truly Canadian sociology did emerge several decades ago, but for reasons to be specified below, its growth was stifled. Recent developments in the profession, however, enable us to infer that a re-emergence of a strong Canadian sociology is likely before long.

Origins and Development of Sociology in Canada

SOCIOLOGY IN NATIONAL CONTEXTS

Social sciences are to a large extent shaped by the processes and forces they study (Macpherson, 1957). This is true of sociology in general and Canadian sociology in particular. There is still a widespread belief among sociologists that sociology, being a positive science, searches for universal principles of human behaviour and of social organization. Accordingly, it is held that sociology being a true science (or attempting to be one) should address itself mainly to a study of social behaviour, transcending national and cultural boundaries. Evidence drawn from particular national societies should be used only to enhance the generalizability of sociological conclusions beyond particular and national confines.

Despite its overall goal toward a general science, sociology emerged in specific national contexts and in response to the immediate and pressing problems. For example, although Auguste Comte, a mathematician and natural scientist, was the first to argue for and develop a science to study the general principles of human behaviour and to christen it "sociology", what initially motivated him were the consequences of the French Revolution. Karl Marx, Emile Durkheim, Max Weber, and George Simmel, to name other early contributors, were undoubtedly dedicated to the notion of scientific sociology, but their immediate concern was to analyse stresses and strains which societies in western Europe were experiencing as an aftermath of the industrial revolution. In the words of Clark (1973), "What the sociologists of Europe were looking for were questions about their society which troubled them, how capitalist forms of social organization developed out of feudal forms, how the nation state came into being, how revolution became legitimated when an older order gave way to a new, what were the bases and limits of individual liberty where the survival of society called for the maintenance of a state of order."

In short, most early sociologists focused on the problems which confronted their societies in everyday life. Yet, in terms of their theoretical and methodological strategies they maintained universalistic postures. The burden of establishing the relevance or irrelevance of their findings to other national or cultural settings fell on the sociologists operating in those settings. But when European sociology was applied to national societies such as India and the United States, native sociologists soon found that imported theories and conceptual frameworks had limited validity in their own national contexts. For example, Max Weber's explanation of why capitalism did not emerge in India was found to be inadequate (Singer, 1956, 1961, and 1966). In turn, calls for explanations based on conceptual frameworks developed through local research gained momentum.

Similar processes occurred in the United States. Many pioneering American sociologists—for example, Franklin Giddings, Lester Ward, Albian Small, and Edward Ross—were trained in and influenced by European sociological traditions. But as Clark notes (1973), imported traditions had little meaning within the American context, because the nature of American society and its problems were different. Here, it was not the consequences of the industrial revolution but the problems of immigration and urbanization which early became the focus of American sociology (Mauss, 1966; Rossides, 1968: 1–50; Clark, 1973; Forcese and Richer, 1975: Chap. 12). The "Chicago School" of sociology, under the leadership of Robert Park, Ernest Burgess, William Ogburn, and Louis Wirth and others emerged in response to the needs of a developing society and its attendant problems.

In essence, although it is true that sociology as a scientific discipline attempts to explain human social behaviour in general terms, thus transcending national boundaries, its development and emphases have always been in relation to specific national contexts. What we have in general, then, are French, British, German, American, and other traditions in sociology. To be sure, these traditions deal with general principles in social organization. But such principles were derived in the study of particular societies. Sociological theories, conceptual frameworks, hypotheses, propositions, and concepts were developed from contexts with national and cultural boundaries. Yet they maintain cross-cultural and cross-national relevance.

SOCIOLOGY IN CANADA

Although sociology in Canada began with concerns for national problems, as did sociology in Europe and the United States, somewhere along the line it lost its "Canadian character". What were the factors which contributed to this loss?

In an excellent discussion of the origin and development of the social sciences in Canada, Macpherson (1957: 181) identifies two factors as being especially important in this country as they emerged: expansion and survival.

Expansion of population, of settlement, and of production were essential from the beginning, at first for political survival, and always for cultural survival, in face of the older and more powerful United States. And within the broad problem of survival of the nation as such, there has been constantly the inner problem of the survival of the culture of French Canada in the face of superior wealth and numbers of the English-speaking Canadians. The patterns of social and historical thought in Canada, their rates and directions of growth, have been shaped by the two impulsions of expansion and survival, which in a sense, contain each other.

Initially sociology in Canada began with concerns for problems of an expanding society, as did sociology in the United States.

As massive immigration and the rapid opening up of the west are both twentieth century phenomena in Canada, problems of assimilation and of the adjustment of social institutions to new environments have naturally attracted much attention. Ethnic groups, pioneering communities and the development of social institutions in relation to successive advances of settlement and changes of economic organization have been the main themes of Canadian sociology (Macpherson, 1957: 215).

The early Canadian sociological enterprise was mainly descriptive—analytic and socio-historical in character. No identifiable efforts were made toward systematic theory-building. This does not mean that early sociological works were atheoretical: clearly, there were propositions and concepts which would have served as stepping stones in this direction, for example, the writings of S. D. Clark and W. E. Mann on Church and Sect. More importantly, pioneering sociologists in Canada did not seriously attempt to import alien conceptual frameworks and theories and validate them in relation to Canadian data. Had the trend set by early sociologists continued, perhaps a truly Canadian tradition in sociology would have emerged eventually.

But several things happened which prevented the continued growth of Canadian sociology. First, sociology as a discipline was not well institutionalized in the Canadian educational system until very recently. Second, what little growth sociology had sustained had occurred in relation to two primary linguistic and cultural groups: the Anglophones and the Francophones. Thus two kinds of sociologies took shape in terms of varying orientations and directions. Finally, in general, the dominant growth of American sociology stifled in many ways the development of a Canadian sociology. Of the two kinds of sociology, the Anglophone sociology became much more American-directed.

Although Canadian sociology started with correct orientations, it suffered a retarded growth in course of time. Compared to universities in the United States, Canadian universities did not attempt to accommodate and nourish the development of sociology until recently. Forcese and Richer (1975: 453) offer this explanation:

The American university system, in its youth less fettered than European universities by traditional and rigid disciplinary boundaries and by budget restraints, was able to accommodate a new and quite unproven social science. This flexibility in the university structure was relatively absent in Canada: the universities and colleges of Anglophone Canada were bounded by traditional British definitions of appropriate university-based subjects, while in Quebec the concept of classical education and involvement of the Roman Catholic Church in education discouraged the development of secular sociology.

While sociology flourished in the United States as a full-fledged academic enterprise, it had to establish itself in Canada under the shadow of traditional disciplines such as economics and history.

The position becomes obvious when one scrutinizes the history of sociology in both English and French Canada. In discussing the nature of sociology in English Canada, Forcese and Richer (1975: Chap. 12) delineate three principal influences which shaped the course of Anglophone sociology: 1) the influence of Protestant religions, 2) the influence of established academic history, and 3) the influence of American sociology.

Forcese and Richer (1975: 454–55) clearly document the point that the initial efforts in English Canada to establish sociology were clearly based on religious and humanistic concerns emphasizing the overall welfare of society and its members. Besides, as sociology was part of either history or economics departments, it was clearly influenced by them and this point, too, is well illustrated in the works of S. D. Clark and others. The growing American influence, however, to a large extent emancipated sociology in Anglophone Canada from its theological and socio-historical framework. The influence of American research techniques, data, theories, and sociologists teaching in Canadian universities, although considered useful and attractive in early days, came with a price and the price was a loss of opportunity to develop a Canadian sociology.

Francophone sociology also went through a similar process of development, although it subjected itself less to the influence of American sociology. Early French-Canadian sociology was principally influenced by a French tradition as illustrated in Le Play's work on the relationship between the household and the worker. The emphasis was on the family life in rural Quebec (Forcese and Richer, 1975: 458). Later, however, "The major input into the formal sociology which developed within Francophone universities was the Catholic social action movement which addressed itself to the social problems caused by a changing society, and to providing an alternative to socialist political action" (Forcese and Richer, 1975: 459).

In later years, however, as the influence of the Roman Catholic Church on the educational system declined, the development of French-Canadian sociology progressed in secular directions. French-Canadian sociologists began to draw from various traditions of sociological thought, including several American forms, thus avoiding the dominance of any single sociological tradition.

What we have outlined thus far is an encapsulated history of early Canadian sociology and the problems associated with its restricted development. We now turn to more recent developments. During the 1960s, a series of unprecedented social changes occurred in Canada. These changes were brought about, among many other things, by the cumulative forces of demographic growth, increasing industrialization, urbanization, the influence of internal problems (such as ethnic and regional conflict), and the growing and threatening influence of the United States over the national identity and autonomy. Policy-makers in Canada needed more information than they had, and explanations of the social processes which emerged, complex as they were, could not be obtained from routine statistical and governmental reports. The role of social scientists in general, and sociologists in particular, became increasingly important in the development of various national policies. Impetus was thus provided for the expansion of sociological research, such expansion, in turn, established the need for more sociologists in Canada.

The increasing numbers of students in colleges and universities contributed in many ways to the growth of the sociological enterprise within Canada. In the 1960s, many students looked to those disciplines which were issue-oriented and which dealt with contemporary problems when looking for fields to study. Sociology gained in popularity. As a result, enrolments increased in many sociology courses. Although this development was welcomed in many ways, it also resulted in numerous problems. First, with the pressure to expand university sociology programs with specialized courses, more information on Canada in textbooks and other forms of teaching aids were required. The quality and quantity of sociological materials in the early 1960s, however, was not nearly adequate to meet the demand. Second, the need to increase the teaching staff in response to the expanding student body became obvious. But Canadian universities came nowhere near producing enough doctors of philosophy to fill the country's needs. Between 1956 and 1969, for example, only seven PHDs were awarded in sociology in all of Canada (Coburn, 1970: 43–44).

Given such a situation, Canadian society and its universities had a limited number of alternatives. One alternative was to limit enrolments. But such a move would have run contrary to prevailing educational philosophy of the times, a philosophy encouraging a move from an élitist to an egalitarian approach. Consequently, universities responded to the situation they confronted by importing teachers from abroad, principally from the United States and Europe. They also drew up plans to train Canadians in the social sciences so they themselves would eventually be able to meet expanding requirements. One such plan was for the Canada Council to liberally fund postgraduate students. (For a discussion of the problems and prospects of such a funding scheme, see Clark, 1973.) In addition, efforts were made to improve existing graduate programs and introduce new programs.

Meanwhile, the importation of teachers from abroad continued. In retrospect, this practice had obvious advantages. Most importantly it helped sociology departments enlarge sufficiently to cater to the needs of an increasing number of students. Furthermore, importation proved to be an inexpensive way of finding professional help on short notice, because, in most cases, practically no Canadian resources were spent in the training of these professionals. Finally, it reduced the burden, at least temporarily, of producing professional sociologists in Canadian universities.

In the long run, however, disadvantages have come to offset to a great extent whatever immediate advantages the importation policy involved. They have been the subject of profound discussion among concerned sociologists in contemporary Canada (see for example, Macpherson, 1957; Coburn, 1970; Rocher, 1970; Davis, 1970; and Clark, 1973).

Macpherson (1957: 185), while comparing the expansion of the Canadian economy and Canadian social science, points out the basic problem, as follows:

In all the stages of its expansion the Canadian economy has grown by importing, and applying to the abundant natural resources, techniques, capital, and labour from more mature countries, especially from Britain and the United States. In this process, the imported labour became Canadianized, and the Canadian capital grew up alongside the imported capital though the techniques did not require much alteration. As with the economy itself, so with the understanding of it; Canadian scholarship in the social sciences began by importation of economic, political science and sociology as mature and well-established techniques from Britain and the United States. Initially the practitioners of these techniques were also largely imported. But here the parallel ends. For whereas the economy could be developed with imported methods and equipment which needed little adaptation, the economy and society could not be fully understood or mastered by the use of only imported social science and scientists.

Macpherson argues that when it became evident that a distinctive Canadian social science could not emerge solely through the contribution of "imported scholars" and "imported scholarship", disciplines such as economics and political science tried with success to modify their perspectives to suit Canadian contexts and problems. But sociology lagged behind. Imported scholarship and scholars, to a large extent, inhibited Canadian sociology from growing out of its infancy. No one ever deliberately planned to reduce the pace of growth, but various factors contributed to such an outcome. First, many imported scholars were trained in sociological traditions specific to schools of thought and countries.[1] Their researches were thus mainly applicable to data and theories specific to these traditions and countries. Second, many of those Canadians who graduated from non-Canadian universities were generally exposed to data and theories relevant particularly only to non-Canadian contexts. Third, upon placement in Canadian universities many of these scholars found that, in most instances, no specific Canadian sociological tradition was in

1. As examples one could mention the general sociological orientations manifest in sociological training at Harvard, Michigan, and Chicago.

operation. Very few appropriate textbooks were available either for their own information or for class adaptation. Besides, only a few sociology departments had ever had any kind of institutionalized program for the orientation of immigrant scholars to national issues and problems. The immediate result was that most immigrant scholars presented sociologies more relevant to the societies of their origins than to Canada. The justification was that after all "sociology deals with universal principles of human behaviour."

Addressing this problem, in particular reference to influence from the United States, Clark (1973) observes:

As sociology became carried over from the United States to Canada, however, it was the universality of its ends that secured emphasis. Initially, of course, there was good reason for this. The sociologist in Canada had to teach out of American text books, refer his students to readings relating to American society. In thus being forced into this position, however, he sought justification for it by the vigorous assertion of the principle that sociology knew no national boundaries. . . . The consequence had been a studied effort on the part of many sociologists in Canada to avoid types of study that do not fit into the framework of American sociology. What is studied in Canada must be on such a level as to make its results comparable to studies carried out in the United States.

It is obviously incorrect to infer that all immigrant scholars have designed their research and teaching activities in conformity with American, European, or other "outside" traditions. In fact, there is much evidence to show that a good many immigrant scholars have been very much dedicated to the cause of Canadian sociology. Yet a large proportion of immigrant scholars maintain, at least implicitly, that sociology knows no national boundaries and hence that sociological analyses may deal with any content as long as the general concepts are clearly stated. These same scholars would argue that, even if one wanted to use Canadian materials, adequate sociological information and conceptual frameworks are not yet available.

While English Canada's discipline and profession of sociology was experiencing intense American influence, Francophone sociology was being shaped more or less independently of either American or European influence. Faced with the problem of maintaining their cultural and political identity, Francophone sociologists turned inward and undertook problem-oriented research. Their motivations were comparable to the motivations of early American sociologists, who discovered the limited relevance of imported sociology. What followed was systematic research on community organization, social institutions, political and economic behaviour, and implications of demographic trends to the future of Quebec. We do not maintain or believe that Francophone sociological research occurred in a theoretical and methodological vacuum. To be sure, certain researches, for instance, family studies by Philippe Garigue, did use outside theoretical perspectives. But unlike English-Canadian sociology, French-Canadian sociology did not develop under the monolithic influence of American sociology. Such an accomplishment encouraged Fortin to argue that there is no *Canadian* sociology outside French Canada. According to him, only in French Canada did sociologists concern themselves with the fate of their society, and only with such a concern could there be a truly Canadian sociology (cited in Clark, 1973).

On the one hand, Canadian sociology departments outside Quebec continued to expand and recruit non-Canadians in direct proportion to their expansion. On the other, there has emerged a growing concern among some academics and numerous decision-makers regarding the influence of non-Canadians in the development (or underdevelopment) of Canadian sociology. Such concerns were not especially clear or well articulated in the early part of the 1960s. It was about the latter part of the 1960s that the concern became a movement within the profession and some sociologists began demanding change.

Several methods of remedying the situation have been attempted in various university sociology departments. First, as already indicated, additional graduate programs in sociology were introduced in universities across the land, and existing programs were revitalized in the general expectation of producing Canadian scholars who could later be recruited to teaching and research jobs. Second, many sociology departments started to give preference to Canadians, or to persons with Canadian experience and training, in recruitment. As the policy was informal and lacked any sanctions (either positive or negative) by which it could be enforced, many institutions did not observe it as meticulously as had been expected. Furthermore, at least in the 1960s, the demand for well-qualified sociologists continued to exceed the supply, so the policy was not practical. Third, an informal pressure was applied to faculty members to focus on issues and problems related to Canadian society in their lectures and research activities. Research-granting agencies and research contracted by government bodies directly or indirectly encouraged immigrant as well as native scholars to undertake research on various aspects of Canadian society. These and other factors gradually led to the accumulation of some information on Canada, in the later part of the 1960s. Finally, a growing number of Canadian university sociology departments began to introduce courses on Canadian society. This development created an increasing interest among the student body in Canadian issues. As Hedley and Warburton (1973) suggest, the main reasons for the introduction of such courses were growing nationalism, the need to understand one's own society, and the belief that sociology as a discipline should develop in national contexts. Sufficient materials are now available to implement such course offerings on a solid academic basis.

The concern over the development of sociology in Canada became quite acute in the beginning of the present decade. The Canadian Sociology and Anthropology Association held a symposium in 1970 on the future of sociology in Canada. Five concerned sociologists (Claude Gouse, Guy Rocher, Arthur Davis, David Coburn, and J. J. Mangalam) presented what they understood to be the problems and prospects underlying the development of Canadian sociology. The generalized thinking was that a distinctive Canadian sociology would not emerge as long as the influence of American sociology and American sociologists continued. Coburn (1970: 37) summarizes the generalized concern as follows:

The basic assumption here is that Canada should exist as a country independent of the United States. I argue that if it is to exist independently, Canadian policy makers and Canadians generally require much more information, in the broadest sense, about their society, that it is one of the duties of sociologists to provide this knowledge, and that sociologists in Canada have been remiss in this duty.

In the following years various professional pressure groups and committees came into existence with the sole purpose of "Canadianizing" not only the discipline of sociology but also the profession in general.

In essence, the development of sociology in Canada has occurred in three distinctive phases. The first phase is the emergence of *a Canadian sociology* in response to the needs of a growing nation (Macpherson, 1957). The second phase refers to the *internationalization of Canadian sociology*, a process which occurred in response to the unexpected and unprecedented expansion of sociology programs in numerous colleges and universities and also in response to the increasing demands from non-academic agencies for sociologists. In the third and current phase, we are witnessing an emerging demand for a new *nationalization of the discipline and profession* because of a belief among some sociologists that sociology in Canada should contribute more toward maintaining a Canadian identity and national interests.

On the one hand, it is possible to argue that the process of nationalizing sociology in Canada is contrary to the spirit of sociology. After all, the primary objective of sociology is to provide a highly generalized discipline to account for social behaviour. But on the other hand, it is possible to maintain that the nationalization of sociology in Canada will not in itself contradict the primary objective of sociology. The reason is that in order to find out whether Canadian social organization and institutions conform to the general principles of sociology developed elsewhere, one should conduct extensive research in and on Canadian society. As a society Canada has its own geographic and social boundaries, its own ethnic composition, history of migration, and economic and political institutions, which make it unique. It would be unscientific to maintain that conclusions drawn from studies outside Canada are relevant to Canada. Therefore, the nationalization of sociology requires both immigrant and native scholars to devote their attention to the problems of Canadian society. We hypothesize that this situation is gradually leading to two kinds of sociologies in Canada: (1) sociology of Canada and (2) Canadian sociology.

SOCIOLOGY OF CANADA AND CANADIAN SOCIOLOGY

Sociological research involves at least two objectives. The first has to do with the development of concepts, conceptual frameworks and theories in the light of empirical materials collected in a given cultural and/or national contexts. Thus, Ernest Burgess's study of residential distribution in Chicago resulted in the formultaion of his "concentric-zone hypothesis". Similarly, Warner's study of Jonesville helped him to develop his assumptions about a class system based on various socio-economic criteria. Second, sociological research may also involve the verification of a theory or conceptual framework developed in another research context. Consequently, it is possible to investigate whether or not Burgess's concentric-zone hypothesis is applicable, for example, to Toronto.

In our view, sociological research in Canada has occurred and *is* occurring in both directions just specified. There is a concerted effort on the part of many immigrant and native sociologists in English Canada to use Canadian social settings to test some of the well-known hypotheses or theories developed in non-Canadian contexts. Thus Mills's notion of power élite, Duncan and Blau's study of occupational structure in the United States, and Frank's notion of hinterland versus metropolis are used either in their entirety or with modifications in the analysis of various aspects of Canadian society. Furthermore, certain sociology departments in Canadian universities tend to maintain sociological traditions developed elsewhere. In this respect, as an illustration, an observation by Forcese and Richer (1975: 457–58) is relevant:

Given the preeminent status and influence of McGill University and the University of Toronto in English Canada, at least up to the late 1950's, it is fair to conclude that the dominant styles of professional sociology which crystallized in Anglophone Canada were modelled on the two dominant American styles: the Chicago school, and the structure functionalist theory.

By this discussion we do not imply that there should be an intellectual compartmentalization restricting our exposure to various sociological traditions and innovations. But what we want to establish is how, in the absence of a significant sociological tradition, Canada became one of the many human laboratories in which assumptions developed elsewhere are applied with an ultimate belief in the general and abstract character of sociology. The role of a sociologist, according to this perspective, is to look for evidence relevant to his theoretical orientations. Some might characterize this process as a form of "intellectual colonialism" others as "sociologically unimaginative". But given the tradition in which many of these researchers are trained and the conspicuous absence of an influential Canadian sociological tradition, this form of research has become inevi-

492 INTRODUCTION TO CANADIAN SOCIETY

table. One of the useful results of such efforts has been the accumulation of a relatively systematic body of knowledge about Canadian society. It is this body of knowledge we conceptualize as belonging to *a sociology of Canada*.

The development of a sociology of Canada in the recent past is comparable to the economics of Canada prior to the contributions of H. A. Innis toward the emergence of a Canadian economics and the institution of the Rowell-Sirois Royal Commission. The discipline of economics before the 1920s was primarily an "economics of Canada", based on imported theories and models. It was mainly due to the later contributions of Innis and his contemporaries that this economics became distinctively Canadian and that a distinct intellectual tradition began to emerge.

Stolzman and Gamberg (1975: 103) argue that "the mere accumulation of Canadian data channelled into unexamined theoretical boxes may bring about an increase in the volume of sociological literature on discrete Canadian topics, but it cannot be the basis for the creation of a genuine Canadian sociology." True. But given the historical conditions which shaped the development of sociology in Canada, internationalization (or more specifically Americanization) of Canadian sociology was a matter of course, especially in the absence of an organized resistance. Yet one conspicuous advantage of the emergence of sociology of Canada was the availability of Canadian materials for instructional purposes, thus limiting the role of American textbooks, at least in some areas.

A Canadian sociology, like any other national sociology, should emerge within the context of national experiences. It is a result of research efforts aimed at developing concepts and theories explaining social phenomena characteristic of Canada as a national society. As a national society, Canada is composed not only of the dominant English- and French-speaking groups, but also groups like Ukrainians, Italians, Poles, East Indians, Natives, and Middle-Easterners. Each of these groups claims inheritance from a distinct social, linguistic, national, cultural, and religious tradition. Such a unique but complex setting blended with the ideology of pluralism provides an unlimited scope for the local development of concepts and theories. Earlier works in sociology fit this mould (for example, Clark, 1942, 1948; Mann, 1955; Dawson, 1936; Hughes, 1936). A more recent example is Breton's (1971) work on ethnic relations.

Recent arguments against the influence of American sociology on the development of a genuine Canadian sociology are emotionally intense (eg: Davis, 1970; Coburn, 1970; Clark, 1973; Stolzman and Gamberg, 1975; O'Neill, 1975). The major premise of these arguments can be summed up in two words, using Macpherson's terminology (1957): *expansion* and *survival*. Internally, Canada is growing into a complex urban-industrial society with all the attendant benefits and problems of an industrial society. Expanding externally is Canada's image, not as an hinterland to the United States but as an independent political and economic entity.

Furthermore, Canada is faced both internally and externally with the problem of survival. Externally, the presence of well-entrenched American economic controls poses a serious problem to Canada's expanding political and economic freedom. Inherent in this problem is the question of Canada's sovereignty. No nation worthy of its national integrity and character would let its economic ties with others dictate its future. The problem becomes acute in the case of Canada, an economically stable and self-reliant country. Also, as already sufficiently documented by Ogmundson in this book, there is the threat of cultural assimilation of Canada by the United States.

Internally, the problems of survival are enhanced by the growing dissension based on language, allocation of natural resources, and federal-provincial strife for power. This dissension has gained such enormous proportion and significance that doubt has been cast on the future of Confederation.

Obviously it is inappropriate to hold the American influence *totally* responsible for the absence of a Canadian sociology. To a large extent there seems a clear voluntary acceptance of American models in the early stages of development of sociology in Canadian universities. Until very recently there was no visible resistance to either American scholarship or scholars. Besides, as indicated earlier, Canadian universities in the early 1940s failed to institutionalize secular sociology, and that failure later forced an open-door policy regarding scholars and scholarship. This, in turn, led to the current underdeveloped or undeveloped state of Canadian sociology.

It is quite possible to consider that the problems underlying *expansion* and *survival* of Canadian society could themselves become fertile grounds

494 INTRODUCTION TO CANADIAN SOCIETY

for creating a national sociology and a sociology responsive to the critical problems and issues of its constituents. (This view is well articulated in Stolzman and Gamberg, 1975.) It would be a disservice to the society (to which sociologists in Canada claim membership and about which they express concern), if sociologists seek refuge behind the "cosmopolitan and respectability" themes (Berger), and continue to propagate the position that sociology is a general, abstract, and value-free science. Such a position would unduly promote various forms of macro-sociology which in turn compels an application of grand theories to an analysis of Canadian society. Instead, we maintain, that micro-sociology dealing with specific problems of a national society could (and would) pave the way for the re-emergence of the Canadian sociology.

References

ADAMS, I.; CAMERON, W.; HILL, B.; and PENZ, P. *The Real Poverty Report*. Edmonton: Hurtig, 1971.

ADLER-KARLSSON, G. *Reclaiming the Canadian Economy: A Swedish Approach Through Functional Socialism*. Toronto: Anansi, 1970.

AGEE, PHILIP. *Inside the Company: CIA Diary*. Markham, Ont.: Penguin, 1975.

ALFORD, ROBERT. *Party and Society*. Chicago: Rand McNally, 1963.

ALLEN, R. *The Social Passion: Religion and Social Reform in Canada 1914–28*. Toronto: University of Toronto Press, 1971.

ALLINGHAM, JOHN D. *Women Who Work: Part I*. Special Labour Force Studies, No. 5. Ottawa: Dominion Bureau of Statistics, 1967.

ANDERSON, G. M. "Voting Behavior and the Ethnic-Religious Variable: A Study of a Federal Election in Hamilton, Ontario", *Canadian Journal of Economics and Political Science* 32 (1966): 27–37.

ANDERSON, MICHAEL, ed. *Sociology of the Family*. Baltimore: Penguin, 1971.

ANDERSON, OWEN. "The Unfinished Revolt", in J. Barr and O. Anderson, eds., *The Unfinished Revolt: Some Views on Western Independence*. Toronto: McClelland and Stewart, 1971.

ARAFAT, IBITHAJ, and YORBURG, B. "On Living Together Without Marriage", *The Journal of Sex Research* 9, No. 2 (1973).

ARÈS, RICHARD. "Comportement Linguistic des Minorités Françaises au Canada", *Relations*, April 1964, pp. 108–10.

ARMSTRONG, DONALD E. *Education and Economic Achievement*. Documents of the Royal Commission on Bilingualism and Biculturalism, No. 7. Ottawa: Information Canada, 1970.

ASTRACHAN, A. "People Are the Most Precious", *Saturday Review-World*, October 19, 1974.

ATWOOD, M. *Survival: A Thematic Guide to Canadian Literature*. Toronto: Anansi, 1972.

AXWORTHY, LLOYD, and GILLIES, JAMES M. *The City: Canada's Prospects Canada's Problems*. Toronto: Butterworth, 1973.

BALL, DONALD W. "Ascription and Position: A Comparative Analysis of 'Stacking' in Professional Football", *Canadian Review of Sociology and Anthropology* 10 (1973): 97–113.

BARBAGLI, M. *Disoccupazione intelletuale e sistema scolastico in Italia (1859–1973)*. Bologna: Il Mulino, 1974.

BARCLAY, HAROLD B. "A Lebanese Community in Lac La Biche, Alberta", in J. L. Elliott, ed., *Minority Canadians 2, Immigrant Groups*. Scarborough: Prentice-Hall, 1971.

———. "The Lebanese Muslim Family" in K. Ishwaran, ed., *The Canadian Family*. Toronto: Holt, Rinehart and Winston, 1971a.

BARTELL, GILBERT. *Group-Sex*. New York: Peter Wyden, 1971.

BEATTIE, CHRISTOPHER. *Minority Men in a Majority Setting*. Toronto: McClelland and Stewart, 1975.

———, and SPENCER, B. G. "Career Attainment in Canadian Bureaucracies: Unscrambling the Effects of Age, Seniority, Education, and Ethnolinguistic

Factors on Salary", *American Journal of Sociology* 77 (November 1971): 472–91.

BECK, J. M. *Pendulum of Power*. Scarborough: Prentice-Hall, 1968.

BÉLANGER, P. W., and DUVAL, R., eds. *L'École Pour Tous: Études Critiques de la Réforme Scolaire*. Québec City: Université Laval, 1968.

BELL, DANIEL. *The Coming of Post-Industrial Society*. New York: Basic Books, 1973.

BELL, E. H., and SIRJAMAKI, J. *Social Foundations of Human Behavior*. New York: Harper and Row, 1965.

BELL, ROBERT R. *Premarital Sex in a Changing Society*. Englewood Cliffs, N.J.: Prentice-Hall, 1966.

BELLAH, ROBERT N. "Civil Religion in America", *Daedalus*, Winter 1967, pp. 1–21.

BENDIX, R., and LIPSET, S., eds. *Class, Status, and Power*. New York: The Free Press, 1966.

BERG, IVAR. *Education and Jobs: The Great Training Robbery*. Boston: Beacon Press, 1971.

BERGER, P. L. *The Sacred Canopy: Elements of a Sociological Theory of Religion*. New York: Doubleday, 1967.

BERNSTEIN, B. "On the Classification and Framing of Educational Knowledge", in M. F. D. Young, ed., *Knowledge and Control: New Directions for the Sociology of Education*.

BERRY, BREWTON. *Race and Ethnic Relations*. Boston: Houghton Mifflin, 1965.

BERTRAND, A. L. *Basic Sociology: An Introduction to Theory and Method*. New York: Appleton-Century-Crofts, 1967.

BESHERS, J. M. *Population Processes in Social Systems*. New York: The Free Press, 1967.

BETTELHEIM, BRUNO. *The Empty Fortress*. New York: The Free Press, 1967.

BHATT, G. S. "Brahmo Samaj, Arya Samaj, and the Church-Sect Typology", *Review of Religious Research* 10 (Fall 1968): 23–32.

BIBBY, R. W., and BRINKERHOFF, M. "The Circulation of the Saints: A Study of People Who Join Conservative Churches", *Journal for the Scientific Study of Religion* 12, No. 3 (1973).

BIENVENUE, R., and LATIF, A. H. "Arrests, Dispositions and Recidivism: A Comparison of Indians and Whites", *Canadian Journal of Criminology and Corrections* 16 (1974): 1–11.

BLADEN, V. W., ed. *Canadian Population and Northern Colonization*. Toronto: University of Toronto Press, 1962.

BLISHEN, B. R. "Social Class and Opportunity in Canada", *Canadian Review of Sociology and Anthropology* 7, No. 2 (1970): 110–27.

BLOCH, H. A., and GEIS, G. *Man, Crime and Society*. New York: Random House, 1962.

BLOOD, R. O. "The Measurement and Bases of Family Power", *Marriage and Family Living* 25 (1963).

———, and WOLFE, D. M. *Husbands and Wives: The Dynamics of Married Living*. Glencoe, Ill.: The Free Press, 1960.

BOCKING, RICHARD C. *Canada's Water: For Sale?* Toronto: James Lewis and Samuel, 1972.

BOISSEVAIN, JEREMY. *The Italians of Montreal: Social Adjustment in a Plural Society*. Studies of the Royal Commission on Bilingualism and Biculturalism, No. 7. Ottawa: Information Canada, 1971.

BOTTOMORE, T. B. *Classes in Modern Society*. London: Allen and Unwin, 1965.

BOURGEAULT, PIERRE L. *Innovation and the Structure of Canadian Industry*. Special Study No. 23. Ottawa: Science Council of Canada, 1972.

BOWLAND, JAMES G. "Geographical Decentralization in the Canadian Federal Public

Service", *Canadian Public Administration* 10 (September 1967): 323–61.
BOYDELL, C. L., and CONNIDIS, I. A. "The Administration of Criminal Justice: Continuity Versus Conflict", in C. L. Boydell, P. C. Whitehead, and C. F. Grindstaff, eds., *The Administration of Criminal Justice in Canada*. Toronto: Holt, Rinehart and Winston, 1974.
BRAROE, NIELS WINTHER. "Reciprocal Exploitation in an Indian-White Community", *Southwestern Journal of Anthropology* 21 (October 1965): 80–100.
BRAZEAU, JACQUES. "Language Differences and Occupational Experiences", *Canadian Journal of Economics and Political Science* 49 (1958): 536.
BRETON, RAYMOND. "Institutional Completeness and Ethnic Communities and Personal Relations to Immigrants", *American Journal of Sociology* 70, No. 2 (September 1964): 193–205. Also in B. Blishen *et al.*, eds., *Canadian Society*. Toronto: Macmillan, 1968.
———. "Academic Stratification in Secondary Schools and the Educational Plans of Students", *Canadian Review of Sociology and Anthropology* 7, No. 1 (February 1970): 17–34.
———. "The Socio-Political Dynamics of the October Events", *Canadian Review of Sociology and Anthropology* 91 (February 1972): 33–56.
BRETON, R., and MCDONALD, J. C. *Career Decisions of Canadian Youth*. Vol. I. Ottawa: Department of Manpower and Immigration, 1967.
———. "Aspects of Parent-Adolescent Relationships: The Perceptions of Secondary School Students", in K. Ishwaran, ed., *The Canadian Family*. Toronto: Holt, Rinehart and Winston, 1971.
BRETON, R., and PINARD, M. "Group Formation Among Immigrants: Criteria and Processes", *Canadian Journal of Economics and Political Science* 26 (August 1960): 465–77.
BRETON, R., *et al. Social and Academic Factors in the Career Decisions of Canadian Youth*. Ottawa: Department of Manpower and Immigration, 1972.
BRODY, HUGH. *Indians on Skid Row*. Ottawa: Northern Science Research Group, Department of Northern Development, 1971.
BROWN, LORNE. "Breaking Down Myths of Peace and Harmony in Canadian Labour History", *Canadian Dimension* 9, No. 5 (1973): 11–35.
BUTLER, D., and STOKES, D. *Political Change in Britain*. New York: St. Martin's Press, 1969.

CAIRNS, ALAN C. "The Electoral System and the Party System in Canada, 1921–1965", *Canadian Journal of Political Science* 1 (March 1968): 55–80.
———. "Alternative Styles in the Study of Canadian Politics", *Canadian Journal of Political Science* 7 (1974): 101–27.
CAMPBELL, A., *et al. The American Voter*. New York: Wiley, 1960.
CAMPBELL, KENNETH G. "Regional Conflict in Canadian Development". Master's Thesis, Sociology Department, University of Manitoba, Winnipeg, 1975.
CAMPBELL, MARIA. *Halfbreed*. Toronto: McClelland and Stewart, 1973.
CAMU, P.; WEEKS, E. P.; and SAMETZ, Z. W. *Economic Geography of Canada*. Toronto: Macmillan, 1964.
Canada. *British North America Act, 1867–1951*. Ottawa: The Queen's Printer, 1951.
———. *1871 Census of Canada*. Ottawa: Taylor, 1873.
———. Canadian Committee on Corrections. *Report: Toward Unity: Criminal Justice and Corrections*. Ottawa: The Queen's Printer, 1969.
———. Civil Service Commission. *Annual Reports, 1950–1972*.
———. Committee Appointed to Inquire into the Principles and Procedures Followed in the Remission Service of the Department of Justice of Canada. *Report*. Ottawa: The Queen's Printer, 1956.

————. Department of Manpower and Immigration. *Immigration and Population Statistics.* Ottawa: Information Canada, 1974.

————. Department of National Revenue. *Taxation Statistics, 1971.* Ottawa, 1973.

————. Department of the Solicitor General. *Annual Report, 1972–1973.* Ottawa: Information Canada, 1973.

————. Department of the Solicitor General. *The Criminal in Canadian Society: A Perspective on Corrections.* Ottawa: Information Canada, 1973.

————. Dominion Bureau of Statistics. *Canada Year Book.* Ottawa, 1972, 1973.

————. Dominion Bureau of Statistics. *1964 Vital Statistics.* Ottawa, 1965.

————. Dominion Bureau of Statistics. *Labour Force* 27, No. 6 (June 1971).

————. Dominion Bureau of Statistics. *Occupational Classification Manual*, Census of Canada, 1971. Vol. II. Ottawa: Information Canada, 1971.

————. Glassco Royal Commission on Government Organization. *Report.* Vol. I. Ottawa: The Queen's Printer, 1962.

————. Information Canada. *Organization of the Government of Canada.* Ottawa: Crown Copyright, 1973.

————. Law Reform Commission of Canada. *First Research Program.* Ottawa: Information Canada, 1972.

————. National Parole Board. *An Outline of Canada's Parole System for Judges, Magistrates and the Police.* Ottawa, n.d.

————. Public Service Commission. "Regulations Made by the Public Service Commission Pursuant to the Public Services Employment Act", Sec. 2(1) a, b, c, *Canada Gazette* 101 (March 17, 1967): 4.

————. Royal Commission on Bilingualism and Biculturalism. Ottawa: Information Canada. Vol. I, *The Official Languages*, 1967. Vol. II, *Education*, 1968. Vol. III, *The Work World*, 1969. Vol. IV, *The Cultural Contribution of the Other Ethnic Groups*, 1970.

————. Royal Commission of Inquiry on Education in the Province of Quebec. *Report (Parent Report)*, 5 vols. Ottawa: The Queen's Printer, 1963–66.

————. Royal Commission to Investigate the Penal System of Canada. *Report.* Ottawa: The King's Printer, 1938.

————. Royal Commission on the Status of Women in Canada. *Report.* Ottawa: Information Canada, 1970.

————. Special Joint Committee. *Report on Divorce.* Ottawa: Information Canada, 1967.

————. Special Senate Committee on the Mass Media. *Report.* Vol. II. Ottawa: Information Canada, 1971.

————. Special Senate Committee on Poverty. *Poverty in Canada: Report of the Special Senate Committee.* Ottawa: Information Canada, 1971.

————. Senate Committee. *Report on Poverty.* Ottawa: Information Canada, 1972.

————. Statistics Canada. *1971 Vital Statistics.* Vol. I, Births. Vol. III, Deaths. Ottawa: The Queen's Printer, 1973.

————. Statistics Canada. *Education in Canada: A Statistical Review for the Period 1960–61 to 1970–71.* Ottawa: Information Canada, 1973.

————. Statistics Canada. *1973 Vital Statistics.* Vol. III. Ottawa: Information Canada, 1974.

————. Statistics Canada. *Perspective Canada.* Ottawa: The Queen's Printer, 1974.

————. Task Force on Release of Inmates. *Report.* Ottawa: Information Canada, 1973.

Canadian Radio-Television Commission, *A Resource for the Active Community.* Ottawa, 1974.

Canadian Tax Foundation. *The National Finances*, 1973–74.

CARDINAL, HAROLD. *The Unjust Society: The Tragedy of Canada's Indians.* Edmonton: Hurtig, 1969.

CARLOS, S. "Religious Participation and the Urban-Suburban Continuum", *American Journal of Sociology* 75 (1970): 242–59.

CARON, ANDRÉ. *The Effects of Advertising on Children.* Montreal: Le Publicité-Club, 1971.

CHIMBOS, PETER D. "Immigrants' Attitudes Toward Their Children's Inter-Ethnic Marriages in a Canadian Community", *International Migration Review* 1 (1971).

CHRISTIAN, W., and CAMPBELL, C. *Political Parties and Ideologies in Canada.* Toronto: McGraw-Hill Ryerson, 1974.

CICOUREL, A., and KITSUSE, J. I. *The Educational Decisionmakers.* Indianapolis: Bobbs-Merrill, 1963.

CLAIRMONT, D. H. J. *Deviance Among Indians and Eskimos in Aklavik, N.W.T.* Ottawa: The Queen's Printer, 1963.

CLARK, ANDREW HILL. *Acadia: The Geography of Early Nova Scotia to 1760.* Madison: University of Wisconsin Press, 1968.

CLARK, B. R. *The Open Door College.* New York: McGraw-Hill, 1960.

CLARK, E.; COOKE, D.; and FALLIS, G. "Socialization, Family Background and Secondary School", in R. M. Pike and E. Zurick, eds., *Socialization and Values in Canadian Society.* Vol. II. Toronto: McClelland and Stewart, 1975.

CLARK, S. D. *The Social Development of Canada.* Toronto: University of Toronto Press, 1942.

————. *Church and Sect in Canada.* Toronto: University of Toronto Press, 1948.

————. *The Developing Canadian Community.* Toronto: University of Toronto Press, 1962.

————. "The American Take Over of Canadian Sociology: Myth or Reality". Paper presented at the Atlantic Provinces Sociology and Anthropology Conference, Halifax, March 30, 1973.

CLEMENT, WALLACE. *The Canadian Corporate Elite: An Analysis of Economic Power.* Toronto: McClelland and Stewart, 1975.

CLIFFORD, N. K. "Religion and the Development of Canadian Society: An Historiographical Analysis", *Church History* 38 (December 1969): 506–23.

COBURN, DAVID. "Sociology and Sociologists in Canada: Problems and Prospects", in Jan J. Loubser, ed., *The Future of Sociology in Canada.* Montreal: Canadian Sociology and Anthropology Association, 1970.

COLEMAN, J. S. *Youth: Transition to Adulthood.* Report of the Panel on Youth of the Presidential Advisory Commission. Chicago: University of Chicago Press, 1974.

COLLINS, RANDALL. "Functional and Conflict Theories of Educational Stratification", *American Sociological Review* 36 (1971): 1002–19.

————. "Where Are Educational Requirements for Employment Highest?" *Sociology of Education* 47 (1974): 419–42.

COOPER, DAVID. *The Death of the Family.* Baltimore: Penguin, 1971.

CORBETT, D. C. *Canada's Immigration Policy.* Toronto: University of Toronto Press, 1957.

COTTAM, JEAN. *Canadian Universities: American Takeover of the Mind?* Toronto: Gall, 1974.

COURTNEY, JOHN C. *The Selection of National Party Leaders in Canada.* Toronto: Macmillan, 1973.

COUSINEAU, D. F., and VEEVERS, J. E. "Incarceration as a Response to Crime: The Utilization of Canadian Prisons", *The Canadian Journal of Criminology and Corrections* 14 (1972): 10–31.

CRICHTON, ROBERT. *The Great Imposter*. New York: Random House, 1959.
CRYSDALE, STEWART. *The Industrial Struggle and Protestant Ethics in Canada*. Toronto: Ryerson, 1961.
———. *The Changing Church in Canada*. Toronto: The Board of Evangelism and Social Service, 1965.
———. "Workers' Families and Education in a Downtown Community", in K. Ishwaran, ed., *The Canadian Family*. Toronto: Holt, Rinehart and Winston, 1971.
———, and BEATTIE, C. *Sociology Canada: An Introductory Text*. Toronto: Butterworth, 1973.
CRUIKSHANK, JULIE. "Matrifocal Families in the Canadian North", in K. Ishwaran, ed., *The Canadian Family*. Toronto: Holt, Rinehart and Winston, 1971.
CUNEO, C. J., and CURTIS, J. E. "Quebec Separatism: An Analysis of Determinants Within Social Class Levels", *The Canadian Review of Sociology and Anthropology* 11 (February 1974): 1–29.
———. "Social Ascription in the Educational and Occupational Status Attainment of Urban Canadian", *Canadian Review of Sociology and Anthropology*, 1975, in press.
CURTIS, J. E., and SCOTT, W. G. *Social Stratification in Canada*. Scarborough: Prentice-Hall, 1973.

DAHRENDORF, RALF. *Class and Class Conflict in Industrial Society*. Stanford: Stanford University Press, 1959.
DANZIGER, K. "Differences in Acculturation and Patterns of Socialization among Italian Immigrant Families", in R. Pike and E. Zurick, eds., *Socialization and Values in Canadian Society*. Vol. II. Toronto: McClelland and Stewart, 1975.
DAVIS, ARTHUR K. "Some Failings of Anglophone Academic Sociology in Canada", in J. J. Loubser, ed., *The Future of Sociology in Canada*. Montreal: Canadian Sociology and Anthropology Association, 1970.
———. "Canadian Society and History as Hinterland Versus Metropolis", in Richard J. Ossenberg, ed., *Canadian Society: Pluralism, Change, and Conflict*. Scarborough: Prentice-Hall, 1971.
DAVIS, J. "Learning the Norm of Universalism: The Effect of School Attendance", in R. Pike and E. Zurick, eds., *Socialization and Values in Canadian Society*. Vol. II. Toronto: McClelland and Stewart, 1975.
DAVIS, K., and MOORE, W. E. "Some Principles of Stratification", *American Sociological Review* 10 (1945): 242–49.
DAVIS, M., and KRAUTER, J. F. *The Other Canadians: Profiles of Six Minorities*. Toronto: Methuen, 1961.
DAWSON, C. A., and YOUNGE, E. R. *Pioneering in the Prairie Provinces: The Social Side of the Settlement Process*. Toronto: Macmillan, 1940.
DAWSON, R. M., and WARD, N. *The Government of Canada*. Revised. Toronto: University of Toronto Press, 1970.
DEATON, RICK. "The Fiscal Crisis of the State", *Our Generation* 8, No. 4 (1972).
DEMERATH, N. J. III. *Social Class in American Protestantism*. Chicago: Rand McNally, 1965.
———, and HAMMOND, P. E. *Religion in Social Context*. New York: Random House, 1969.
DENIS, A. B. "CEGEP Students: Varieties in Socialization Experience", in R. Pike and E. Zurick, eds., *Socialization and Values in Canadian Society*. Vol. II. Toronto: McClelland and Stewart, 1975.
DENTON, F. T., and OSTRY, S. *Historical Estimates of the Canadian Labour Force*. 1961 Census Monograph. Ottawa: The Queen's Printer, 1967.

DOCTOR X. *The Intern.* New York: Harper and Row, 1965.

DOFNY, J., and RIOUX, M. "Social Class in French Canada", in M. Rioux and Y. Martin, eds., *French-Canadian Society.* Vol. I. Toronto: McClelland and Stewart, 1964.

DOSMAN, EDGAR. *Indians: The Urban Dilemma.* Toronto: McClelland and Stewart, 1972.

DOZIER, EDWARD P. "Problem Drinking among American Indians", *Quarterly Journal of Studies in Alcohol* 27 (1960): 72–87.

DRACHE, DANIEL, ed. *Quebec—Only the Beginning.* Toronto: New Press, 1972.

DRAKE, M. *Population and Society in Norway, 1735–1865.* Cambridge: Cambridge University Press, 1969.

DREEBEN, R. *On What Is Learned in School.* Reading, Mass.: Addison Wesley, 1968.

DRIEDGER, L., and CHURCH, G. "Residential Segregation and Institutional Completeness: A Comparison of Ethnic Minorities", *Canadian Review of Sociology and Anthropology* 11 (February 1974): 30–52.

DUNCAN, OTIS D. "A Socio-Economic Index for All Occupations", in Albert J. Reiss, ed., *Occupations and Social Status.* New York: The Free Press, 1961.

DURKHEIM, E. *The Elementary Forms of the Religious Life.* New York: The Free Press, 1915.

———. *Education and Society.* New York: The Free Press, 1956. (First published 1906–11.)

EFFRAT, ANDREW, ed. *Perspectives in Political Sociology.* New York: Bobbs-Merrill, 1973.

EICHLER, M. "Women as Personal Dependents . . .", in M. Stephenson, ed., *Women in Canada.* Toronto: New Press, 1973.

ELGEE, W. H. *The Social Teachings of the Canadian Churches.* Toronto: Ryerson, 1964.

ELKIN, FREDERICK. *The Family in Canada.* Ottawa: The Vanier Institute of the Family, 1964.

———. "Communications Media and Identity Formation in Canada", in B. Singer, ed., *Communications in Canadian Society.* Toronto: Copp Clark, 1972.

ELLIOTT, JEAN LEONARD, ed., *Minority Canadians: Immigrant Groups.* Scarborough: Prentice-Hall, 1971.

ENGLEMANN, F., and SCHWARTZ, M. *Political Parties and the Canadian Social Structure.* Scarborough: Prentice-Hall, 1967.

———. *Canadian Political Parties: Origin, Character, Impact.* Scarborough: Prentice-Hall, 1975.

ENROTH, R.; ERICSON, E. E.; and PETERS, C. B. *The Jesus People: Old-Time Religion in the Age of Aquarius.* Grand Rapids: Eerdmans, 1972.

ESHLEMAN, ROSS J. *The Family: An Introduction.* Boston: Allyn and Bacon, 1974.

ETZIONI, AMITAI. *A Comparative Analysis of Complex Organizations.* New York: The Free Press, 1961.

EYLANDS, V. J. *Lutherans in Canada.* Winnipeg: Columbia Press, 1945.

FAGUY, P. A. "The Canadian Penal System of the Seventies", *Canadian Journal of Criminology and Corrections* 15 (1973): 7–12.

FALARDEAU, J. C. "The Parish as an Institutional Type", *The Canadian Journal of Economics and Political Science* 15 (1949): 354–67.

———. "The Seventeenth-Century Parish in French Canada", in M. Rioux and Y. Martin, eds., *French-Canadian Society.* Toronto/Montreal: McClelland and Stewart, 1964.

FARBER, BERNARD. *Family: Organization and Interaction*. San Francisco: Chandler, 1964.

FELDMAN, L. D., and GOLDRICK, M. D., eds. *Politics and Government of Urban Canada: Selected Readings*. Toronto: Methuen, 1972.

FORCESE, D., and RICHER, S. *Issues in Canadian Society: An Introduction to Sociology*. Scarborough: Prentice-Hall, 1975.

FORNATARO, J. V. "Canadian Prisons Today", in W. T. McGrath, ed., *Crime and Its Treatment in Canada*. Toronto: Macmillan, 1965.

FRANK, A. G. *Capitalism and Underdevelopment in Latin America*. New York: Monthly Review Press, 1967.

FREITAG, W. "Lutheran Tradition in Canada", in J. W. Grant, ed., *The Churches and the Canadian Experience*. Toronto: Ryerson, 1963.

FRIEDENBERG, E. Z. "The Function of the School in Social Homeostasis", *Canadian Review of Sociology and Anthropology* 7, No. 1 (February 1970): 5–16.

Gallup Poll of Canada. *Toronto Daily Star*, March 2, 1970.

GARIGUE, PHILIPPE. "French Canadian Kinship and Urban Life", *American Anthropologist* 58 (1956). References are made to the reprinted version in K. Ishwaran, ed., *The Canadian Family*. Toronto: Holt, Rinehart and Winston, 1971.

———. *La Vie Familiale des Canadiens Français*. Montreal: University of Montreal Press, 1962. Reference is made to an English translation of certain sections of this book. "The French Canadian Family", in B. Blishen *et al.*, eds., *Canadian Society*. 3rd ed. Toronto: Macmillan, 1968.

———. *L'Option Politique du Canada Français*. Montreal: Edition du Levrier, 1963.

———. "Change and Continuity in Rural French Canada", in M. Rioux and Y. Martin, eds., *French-Canadian Society*. Toronto/Montreal: McClelland and Stewart, 1964.

GARRY, CARL. "The Asbestos Strike and Social Change in Quebec", in W. E. Mann, ed., *Social and Cultural Change in Canada*. Vol. I. Toronto: Copp Clark, 1970.

GEORGE, M. V. *Internal Migration in Canada*. 1961 Census Monograph. Ottawa: The Queen's Printer, 1970.

———. An Interview with Glennis Zilm, "Birth Rates in Canada Lowest Ever", *Winnipeg Free Press*, March 3, 1973.

GINGERICH, O. *The Amish of Canada*. Waterloo, Ont.: Conrad Press, 1972.

GLOCK, C. Y., and STARK, R. *Religion and Society in Tension*. Chicago: Rand McNally, 1965.

GOBLOT, E. "Cultural Education as a Middle Class Enclave", in E. Burns and T. Burns, eds., *Sociology of Literature and Drama*. Harmondsworth: Penguin, 1973.

GODFREY, D., and WATKINS, M., eds., *Gordon to Watkins to You*. Toronto: New Press, 1970.

GOODE, W. J. "The Theoretical Importance of Love", *American Sociological Review* 24 (1959)

GORDON, MILTON. *Assimilation in American Life*. New York: Oxford University Press, 1964.

GORDON, WALTER L. *A Choice for Canada*. Toronto: McClelland and Stewart, 1966.

GOUSSE, CLAUDE. "Réflexions sur l'Avenir de la Sociologie au Québec", in J. J. Loubser, ed., *The Future of Sociology in Canada*. Montreal: The Canadian Sociology and Anthropology Association, 1970.

GRAHAM, E. "Schoolmarms and Early Teaching in Ontario", in *Women at Work: Ontario, 1850–1930*. Toronto: Canadian Women's Educational Press, 1974.

GRAICUNAS, V. A. "Relationships in Organization", in L. Gulick and L. Urwick, eds., *Papers on the Science of Administration*. 3rd ed. New York: Institute of Public Administration, 1937.

GRANT, GEORGE P. *Lament for a Nation*. Toronto: McClelland and Stewart, 1965.

GRANT, J. W., ed. *The Churches and the Canadian Experience*. Toronto: Ryerson, 1963.

Gray Report. A Citizen's Guide to the Gray Report. Toronto: New Press, 1971.

————. *Foreign Direct Investment in Canada*. Ottawa: The Queen's Printer, 1972.

GREELEY, A. M. *The Denominational Society*. London: Scott, Foresman, 1972.

GREENFIELD, S. "Love and Marriage in Modern America: A Functional Analysis", *Sociological Quarterly* 6 (1965).

GRINDSTAFF, C. F.; BOYDELL, C.; and WHITEHEAD, P. C. *Population Issues in Canada*. Toronto: Holt, Rinehart and Winston, 1971.

GUINDON, H. "Social Unrest, Social Class, and Quebec's Bureaucratic Revolution", in Hugh Thorburn, ed., *Party Politics in Canada*. Scarborough: Prentice-Hall, 1967.

GURR, TED ROBERT. *Why Men Rebel*. Princeton: Princeton University Press, 1970.

HALL, O., and MACFARLANE, B. *Transition from School to Work*. Ottawa: Department of Labour, 1962.

HALL, RICHARD H. "The Concept of Bureaucracy: An Empirical Assessment", *The American Journal of Sociology* 69 (July 1963).

HAMBLIN, ROBERT L. "Mathematical Experimentation and Sociological Theory: A Critical Analysis", *Sociometry* 34 (1971): 423–52.

HAMILTON, CHARLES V. "Blacks and Mass Media", *Columbia Forum*, Winter 1971.

HAMILTON, RICHARD H. *Class and Politics in the United States*. New York: John Wiley, 1972.

HANS, N. *Comparative Education: A Study of Educational Factors and Traditions*. 3rd ed. London: Routledge and Kegan Paul, 1958.

HARDING, JAMES. "Canada's Indians: A Powerless Minority", in J. Harp and J. R. Hofley, eds., *Poverty in Canada*. Scarborough: Prentice-Hall, 1971.

HARGREAVES, D. *Social Relations in a Secondary School*. London: Routledge and Kegan Paul, 1968.

Harvard Educational Review. *Science, Heritability and I.Q.* Cambridge, Mass.: Harvard Educational Review, 1969.

HARVEY, E. *Educational Systems and the Labour Market*. Don Mills: Longman, 1974.

HARVEY, T. G.; HUNTER-HARVEY, S. K.; and VANCE, G. "Nationalist Sentiment Among Canadian Adolescents: The Prevalence and Social Correlates of Nationalistic Feelings", in E. Zurick and R. Pike, eds., *Socialization and Values in Canadian Society*. Vol. I. Toronto: McClelland and Stewart, 1975.

HASKELL, M. R., and YABLONSKY, L. *Criminology, Crime and Criminality*. Chicago: Rand McNally, 1974.

HATT, P. K.; FARR, N. L.; and WEINSTEIN, E. "Types of Population Balance", *American Sociological Review* 20, No. 11 (February 1955): 14–21.

HAVEL, J. E. "Some Effects of the Introduction of a Policy of Bilingualism in the Polyglot Community of Sudbury", *Canadian Review of Sociology and Anthropology* 9, No. 1 (1972): 57–71.

HAWKINS, F. *Canada and Immigration*. Montreal: McGill-Queen's University Press, 1972.

HEAP, JAMES L., ed. *Everybody's Canada: The Vertical Mosaic Reviewed and Re-Examined*. Toronto: Burns and MacEachern, 1974.

HECHTER, MICHAEL. "Review of 'The Modern World-System' by I. Wallerstein", *Contemporary Sociology* 4 (1975): 217–22.

HEDLEY, R. A., and WARBURTON, T. R. "The Role of National Courses in the Teaching and Development of Sociology: The Canadian Case", *Sociological Review* 21, No. 2 (1973).

HEENEY, A. D. P. "Mackenzie King and the Cabinet Secretariat", *Canadian Public Administration* 3 (September 1967): 366–75.

HEER, DAVID M. "The Trend of Interfaith Marriages in Canada: 1922–1957", *American Sociological Review* 27 (1962): 245–50. References in Chapter 8 are to the reprinted version in K. Ishwaran, ed., *The Canadian Family*. Toronto: Holt, Rinehart and Winston, 1971.

———. "The Measurement and Bases of Family Power: An Overview", *Marriage and Family Living* 25 (1963).

HENRIPIN, JACQUES. *Trends and Factors of Fertility in Canada*. 1961 Census Monograph. Ottawa: The Queen's Printer, 1972.

———. "Quebec and the Demographic Dilemma of French Canadian Society", in Dale C. Thomson, ed., *Quebec Society and Politics: Views from the Inside*. Toronto: McClelland and Stewart, 1973.

HENRY, FRANCES. *Forgotten Canadians: The Blacks of Nova Scotia*. Don Mills: Longman, 1973.

HENRY, J. "Docility, or Giving Teacher What She Wants", *The Journal of Social Issues* 2 (1955): 33–41.

HENSHEL, ANNE-MARIE. "Swinging: A Study of Decision-Making in Marriage", *American Journal of Sociology* 78, No. 4 (1973).

HERBERG, W. *Protestant-Catholic-Jew*. New York: Doubleday, 1960.

HERTZLER, J. O. *The Crisis in World Population*. Lincoln: University of Nebraska Press, 1956.

HILL, R., and HANSEN, D. A. "Identification of Conceptual Frameworks Utilized in Family Study", *Marriage and Family Living* 22 (1960).

HILLER, H. H. "The New Theology and the Sociology of Religion", *The Canadian Review of Sociology and Anthropology* 6 (August 1969): 179–87.

HOBART, CHARLES W. "Eskimo Education in the Canadian Arctic", *Canadian Review of Sociology and Anthropology* 7, No. 1 (February 1970): 49–69.

———. "Sexual Permissiveness in Young Canadians: A Study of Attitudes and Behavior", in C. Boydell, C. F. Grindstaff, and P. C. Whitehead, eds., *Deviant Behavior and Societal Reaction*. Toronto: Holt, Rinehart and Winston, 1972.

———. "Attitude Toward Parenthood Among Canadian Young People", *Journal of Marriage and the Family* 35, No. 1 (1973).

———, and BRANT, C. S. "Eskimo Education, Danish and Canadian", *Canadian Review of Sociology and Anthropology* 3, No. 2 (May 1966): 47–66.

HODGETTS, A. B. *What Culture? What Heritage?* Toronto: Ontario Institute for Studies in Education and Prentice-Hall, 1965 and 1968.

HODGETTS, J. E., et al. *The Biography of an Institution*. Montreal: McGill-Queen's University Press, 1972.

HOGARTH, J. "Towards a Model of Sentencing Behaviour", in C. L. Boydell, P. C. Whitehead, and C. F. Grindstaff, eds., *The Administration of Criminal Justice in Canada*. Toronto: Holt, Rinehart and Winston, 1974.

HOLDAWAY, E. A. "What Topics Are Discussed at School Board Meetings?" *School Progress* 39, No. 4 (April 1970). Reprinted in H. A. Stevenson et al., eds., *The Best of Times, The Worst of Times: Contemporary Issues in Canadian Education*. Toronto: Holt, Rinehart and Winston, 1972.

HONIGMANN, J., and HONIGMANN, I. *Eskimo Townsmen*. Ottawa: Canadian Research Centre for Anthropology, University of Ottawa, 1965.

HOROWITZ, GAD. "Conservatism, Liberalism, and Socialism in Canada: An Interpretation", *Canadian Journal of Economics and Social Science* 32 (May 1966): 144–71.

HOSTETLOR, J. A., and HUNTINGTON, G. E. *The Hutterites in North America.* New York: Holt, Rinehart and Winston, 1967.

HUGHES, D. R., and KALLEN, E. *The Anatomy of Racism: Canadian Dimensions.* Montreal: Harvest House, 1974.

HUNT, MORTON. *Sexual Behavior in the 1970's.* Chicago: Playboy Press, 1974.

HURD, W. B. *Origin, Birthplace, Nationality and Language of the Canadian People.* Census Monograph, 1921 Census of Canada, Dominion Bureau of Statistics. Ottawa: The King's Printer, 1929.

————. *Racial Origins and Nativity of the Canadian People.* Census Monograph, 1931 Census of Canada. Vol. XIII. Dominion Bureau of Statistics. Ottawa: The King's Printer, 1942.

————. *Ethnic Origin and Nativity of the Canadian People.* Census Monograph, 1941 Census of Canada, Dominion Bureau of Statistics. Ottawa: The Queen's Printer, n.d.

INNIS, H. A. *Empire and Communications.* Toronto: Oxford University Press, 1950.

IRVING, J. A. *The Social Credit Movement in Alberta.* Toronto: University of Toronto Press, 1959.

ISHWARAN, K. "The Canadian Family: An Overview", "Calvinism and Social Behavior in a Dutch Canadian Community", and "Family and Community Among the Dutch Canadians", all in K. Ishwaran, ed., *The Canadian Family.* Toronto: Holt, Rinehart and Winston, 1971.

JACOBSON, HELGA E. "The Family in Canada: Some Problems and Questions", in K. Ishwaran, ed., *The Canadian Family.* Toronto: Holt, Rinehart and Winston, 1971.

JENCKS, C., *et al. Inequality: A Reassessment of the Effect of Family and Schooling in America.* New York: Basic Books, 1972.

JENNESS, DIAMOND. *Indians of Canada. Bulletin of the Canada Department of Mines,* No. 65. Ottawa: Native Museum of Canada, 1932.

JENSEN, A. R. "How Much Can We Boost I.Q. and Scholastic Achievement?" *Harvard Educational Review* 39, No. 1 (1969): 1–123.

DE JOCAS, Y., and ROCHER, G. "Inter-Generation Occupational Mobility in the Province of Quebec", *Canadian Journal of Economics and Political Science* 23 (1957): 58–66.

JOHNSON, A. W. "The Treasury Board of Canada and the Machinery of Government in the 1970s", *Canadian Journal of Political Science* 4 (September 1971): 346–66.

————. "Planning, Programming and Budgeting in Canada", *Public Administration Review* 33 (January–February 1973): 23–31.

JOHNSON, LEO A. "The Development of Class in Canada in the Twentieth Century", in G. Teeple, ed., *Capitalism and the National Question in Canada.* Toronto: University of Toronto Press, 1972.

————. *Incomes, Disparity and Impoverishment in Canada Since World War II.* Toronto: New Bytown Press, 1973.

————. *Poverty in Wealth: The Capitalist Labour Market and Income Distribution in Canada.* Toronto: New Hogtown Press, 1974.

JOHNSTONE, JOHN C. *Young People's Images of Canadian Society: An Opinion Survey of Canadian Youth 13–20 Years of Age.* Study No. 2, Royal Commission on Bilingualism and Biculturalism. Ottawa: Information Canada, 1969.

JONES, F. E. "The Social Origins of High School Teachers in a Canadian City", in B. Blishen *et al.*, eds., *Canadian Society*. 3rd ed. Toronto: Macmillan, 1968.
————, and SELBY, J. "School Performance and Social Class", in T. J. Ryan, ed., *Poverty and the Child: A Canadian Study*. Toronto: McGraw-Hill Ryerson, 1972.
JONES, RICHARD. *Community in Crisis: French-Canadian Nationalism in Perspective*. Toronto: McClelland and Stewart, 1972.
JOY, R. J. *Languages in Conflict*. Toronto/Montreal: McClelland and Stewart, 1972.

KALBACH, W. E. *The Impact of Immigration on Canada's Population*. Ottawa: The Queen's Printer, 1970.
————. "Propensities for Intermarriage in Canada as Reflected in the Ethnic Origins of Native-born Husbands and Their Wives: 1961 and 1971". Paper presented at the annual meeting of the Canadian Sociology and Anthropology Association, Toronto, August 24, 1974.
————, and MCVEY, W. W. *The Demographic Bases of Canadian Society*. Toronto: McGraw-Hill, 1971.
KATZ, M. B. *The Hamilton Project, Interim Reports*. Working Paper No. 26. Toronto: Ontario Institute for Studies in Education (mimeo), 1969, 1970.
KELLY, W. H. "The Police", in W. T. McGrath, ed., *Crime and Its Treatment in Canada*. Toronto: Macmillan, 1965.
KELNER, M. "Ethnic Penetration into Toronto's Elite Structure", *Canadian Review of Sociology and Anthropology* 7 (May 1970).
KEYFITZ, NATHAN. "The Growth of Canadian Population", *Population Studies* 4 (June 1950): 47–63.
————. "Canadians and Canadiens", *Queen's Quarterly* 70, No. 1 (Winter 1973–74): 163–82.
KIERKENDAL, LESTER A. *Premarital Sexual Intercourse and Interpersonal Relations*. New York: Julian Press, 1961.
KING, A. J. C. "Ethnicity and School Adjustment", *Canadian Review of Sociology and Anthropology* 5 (1968): 84–91.
————. "Teachers and Students: A Preliminary Analysis of Collective Reciprocity", *Canadian Review of Sociology and Anthropology* 7, No. 1 (February 1970): 35–48.
KINSEY, ALFRED C., *et al. The Sexual Behavior in the Human Female*. New York: W. B. Saunders, 1953.
KIRKPATRICK, A. M. "After-Care and the Prisoners' Aid Societies", in W. T. McGrath, ed., *Crime and Its Treatment in Canada*. Toronto: Macmillan, 1965.
KOHL, SEENA. "The Family in a Post-Frontier Society", in K. Ishwaran, ed., *The Canadian Family*. Toronto: Holt, Rinehart and Winston, 1971.
————, and BENNETT, J. "Succession to Family Enterprises and Migration of Young People in a Canadian Agricultural Community", in K. Ishwaran, ed., *The Canadian Family*. Toronto: Holt, Rinehart and Winston, 1971.
KUBAT, D., and THORNTON, D. *A Statistical Profile of Canadian Society*. Toronto: McGraw-Hill Ryerson, 1974.
KUZEL, P., and KRISHANAN, P. "Changing Patterns of Remarriage in Canada: 1961–1966", *Journal of Comparative Family Studies* 4, No. 2 (1973).

LACEY, C. *Hightown Grammar*. Manchester: Manchester University Press, 1970.
LACOSTE, NORBERT. "The Catholic Church in Quebec: Adapting to Change", in D. C. Thomson, ed., *Quebec Society and Politics: Views from the Inside*. Toronto: McClelland and Stewart, 1973.
LAI, VIVIEN. "The New Chinese Immigrants in Toronto", in Jean Leonard Elliott,

ed., *Minority Canadians: Immigrant Groups.* Scarborough: Prentice-Hall, 1970.
LAMBERT, W. E., and TUCKER, G. R. *Psychology Today* 7 (September 1973): 89–95.
LAMY, PAUL G. "Political Socialization of French and English Canadian Youth: Socialization into Discord", in E. Zurick and R. Pike, eds., *Socialization and Values in Canadian Society.* Vol. I. Toronto: McClelland and Stewart, 1975.
LANE, DAVID. *The End of Inequality.* Harmondsworth: Penguin, 1971.
LANGLOIS, G. *Histoire de la Population Canadienne Française.* Appendice II. Montreal: Editions Albert Lévesque, 1934.
LANGTON, KENNETH P. *Political Socialization.* Toronto: Oxford University Press, 1969.
LANPHIER, C. M., and MORRIS, R. N. "Structural Aspects of Differences in Income Between Anglophones and Francophones", *Canadian Review of Sociology and Anthropology* 11 (February 1974): 53–66.
LATOUCHE, DANIEL. "The Independence Option: Ideological and Empirical Elements", in Dale C. Thomson, ed., *Quebec Society and Politics: Views from the Inside.* Toronto: McClelland and Stewart, 1973.
LATOWSKY, EVELYN. "Family Life Styles and Jewish Culture", in K. Ishwaran, ed., *The Canadian Family.* Toronto: Holt, Rinehart and Winston, 1971.
———. "Parenthood—The Basis of Social Structure", in V. F. Calverton and S. D. Schmalhausen, eds., *The New Generation.* London: Macauley, 1971.
LAWR, D., and GIDNEY, R., eds. *Educating Canadians: A Documentary History of Public Education.* Toronto: Van Nostrand Reinhold, 1973.
LAXER, JAMES. "Introduction to the Political Economy of Canada", in R. Laxer, ed., *(Canada) Ltd.: The Political Economy of Dependency.* Toronto: McClelland and Stewart, 1973a.
———. "Canadian Manufacturing and U.S. Trade Policy", in R. Laxer, ed., *(Canada) Ltd.: The Political Economy of Dependency.* Toronto: McClelland and Stewart, 1973b.
———. *Canada's Energy Crisis.* Toronto: James Lewis and Samuel, 1974.
LAXER, ROBERT, ed. *(Canada) Ltd.: The Political Economy of Dependency.* Toronto: McClelland and Stewart, 1973.
LAZARSFELD, P. F.; BERELSON, B.; and GAUDET, H. *The People's Choice.* New York: Duell, Sloan, and Pierce, 1944.
LEMERT, EDWIN. "The Use of Alcohol in Three Salish Tribes", *Quarterly Journal of Studies in Alcohol* 19 (1958): 99–109.
LENSKI, GERHARD E. *Power and Privilege: A Theory of Social Stratification.* New York: McGraw-Hill, 1966.
LÉVESQUE, RENÉ. *An Option for Quebec.* Toronto: McClelland and Stewart, 1968.
LEVITT, KARI. *Silent Surrender: The Multinational Corporation in Canada.* Toronto: Macmillan, 1970.
———. "Political Disintegration", in A. Rotstein and G. Lax, eds., *Independence: The Canadian Challenge.* Toronto: McClelland and Stewart, 1972.
LIEBERSON, STANLEY. *Language and Ethnic Relations in Canada.* New York: John Wiley, 1970.
LIPSET, SEYMOUR M. *The First New Nation: The United States in Historical and Comparative Perspective.* New York: Basic Books, 1963.
———. "Revolution and Counterrevolution: The United States and Canada", in O. Kruhlok, R. Schultz, and S. I. Pobihushchy, eds., *The Canadian Political Process: A Reader.* Toronto: Holt, Rinehart and Winston, 1970.
———; TROW, M. A.; and COLEMAN, J. S. *Union Democracy: The Internal Politics of the International Typographical Union.* Glencoe, Ill.: The Free Press, 1956.
LIPTON, CHARLES. "Canadian Unionism", in G. Teeple, ed., *Capitalism and the National Question in Canada.* Toronto: University of Toronto Press, 1972.

508   INTRODUCTION TO CANADIAN SOCIETY

LOCKHART, ALEXANDER. "Future Failures: The Unanticipated Consequences of Educational Planning", in R. Pike and E. Zurick, eds., *Socialization and Values in Canadian Society*. Vol. II. Toronto: McClelland and Stewart, 1975.

LORIMER, JAMES. *A Citizen's Guide to City Politics*. Toronto: James Lewis and Samuel, 1972.

LUMSDEN, IAN, ed. *Close the 49th Parallel, etc.: The Americanization of Canada*. Toronto: The University of Toronto Press, 1970.

LUNDBERG, G. A.; SCHRAG, C. C.; and LARSEN, O. N. *Sociology*. New York: Harper and Brothers, 1958.

LYDEN, F. J., and MILLER, E. G., eds. *Planning, Programming, Budgeting: A System Approach to Management. Appendix: U.S. Bureau of the Budget Bulletin to the Heads of Executive Departments and Establishments of Planning-Programming-Budgeting, Bulletin 66-3, 1965*. Chicago: Markham Publishing, 1968.

MACCOBY, E. E., and JACKLIN, C. N. *The Psychology of Sex Differences*. Stanford, Calif.: Stanford University Press, 1974.

MACKINNON, F. *The Politics of Education*. Toronto: University of Toronto Press, 1960.

MACLEOD, A. J. "Criminal Legislation", in W. T. McGrath, ed., *Crime and Its Treatment in Canada*. Toronto: Macmillan, 1965.

MACPHERSON, C. B. "The Social Sciences" in Julian Park, ed., *The Culture of Contemporary Canada*. Toronto: Ryerson, 1957.

———. *Democratic Theory: Essays in Retrieval*. London: Oxford University Press, 1973.

MADELEY, ST. JOHN. "Probation", in W. T. McGrath, ed., *Crime and Its Treatment in Canada*. Toronto: Macmillan, 1965.

MAHEU, ROBERT. *Les Francophones du Canada, 1941–1991*. Montreal: Editions Parti Pres, 1970.

MALLORY, JAMES R. *The Structure of Canadian Government*. Toronto: Macmillan, 1971.

MANGALAM, J. J. "Toward an International Perspective for the Growth and Development of Sociology in Canada", in J. Loubser, ed., *The Future of Sociology in Canada*. Montreal: The Canadian Sociology and Anthropology Association, 1970.

Manitoba. Department of Health and Social Development. *The Rise of the Sparrow: A Paper on Corrections in Manitoba*. Winnipeg, 1972.

———. Department of Health and Social Development. *Probation Services*. Winnipeg, 1972.

MANN, W. E. *Sect, Cult and Church in Manitoba*. Toronto: University of Toronto Press, 1955.

———. "The Canadian Church Union, 1925", in N. Ehrenstrom and W. G. Muelder, eds., *Institutionalism and Church Unity*. Association Press, 1963.

———. "Canadian Trends in Premarital Behavior", *Bulletin*. The Council for Social Service, 198 (1967).

———. "Non-Conformist Sexual Behavior on the Canadian Campus", in W. E. Mann, ed., *Deviant Behavior in Canada*. Toronto: Social Science Publishers, 1968.

———. "Sex at York University", in W. E. Mann, ed., *Underside of Toronto*. Toronto: McClelland and Stewart, 1970.

MANZER, RONALD. *Canada: A Socio-Political Report*. Toronto: McGraw-Hill Ryerson, 1974.

MARCHAK, M. PATRICIA. *Ideological Perspectives on Canada*. Toronto: McGraw-Hill Ryerson, 1975.

MARCHETTI, V. L., and MARKS, J. D. *The C.I.A. and the Cult of Intelligence*. New York: Knopf, 1974.

Marketing. November 25, 1960.

MARSDEN, L. R. *Population Probe*. Toronto: Copp Clark, 1972.

MARUNCHAK, MICHAEL H. *The Ukrainian Canadians: A History*. Winnipeg: Winnipeg Ukrainian Free Academy of Sciences, 1970.

MARX, KARL. *Value, Price and Profit*. New York: International Publishers, 1935.

————. *The German Ideology*. London: Lawrence and Wishart, 1965.

————, and ENGELS, F. *Manifesto of the Communist Party*. New York: International Publishers, 1932.

————. *The German Ideology*. New York: International Publishers, 1963.

MASLOVE, ALLAN M. *The Pattern of Taxation in Canada*. Ottawa: Information Canada, 1972.

MASSON, J. K., and ANDERSON, J. D. *Emerging Party Politics in Urban Canada*. Toronto: McClelland and Stewart, 1972.

MATHEWS, ROBIN. "Canadian Culture and the Liberal Ideology", in R. Laxer, ed., *(Canada) Ltd.: The Political Economy of Dependency*. Toronto: McClelland and Stewart, 1973.

————, and STEELE, J. *The Struggle for Canadian Universities*. Toronto: New Press, 1969.

MAUSS, HEINZ. *A Short History of Sociology*. New York: The Citadel Press, 1966.

MAXWELL, M. P., and MAXWELL, J. D. "Boarding School: Social Control, Space and Identity", in D. K. Davies and K. Herman, eds., *Social Space: Canadian Perspectives*. Toronto: New Press, 1971.

MAYKOVICH, M. K. "Ethnic Variation in Success Value", in R. Pike and E. Zurick, eds., *Socialization and Values in Canadian Society*. Toronto: McClelland and Stewart, 1975.

MCCORMACK, THELMA. "Social Theory and the Mass Media", *Canadian Journal of Economics and Political Science* 27, No. 4 (1961): 479–87.

————. "Folk Culture and the Mass Media", *European Journal of Sociology* 10 (1969): 220–37.

MCDAIRMID, G., and PRATT, D. *Teaching Prejudice: A Content Analysis of Social Studies Textbooks Authorized for Use in Ontario*. Toronto: Ontario Institute for Studies in Education, 1971.

MCDONALD, L. "Religion and Voting: A Study of the 1968 Canadian Federal Election in Ontario", *Canadian Review of Sociology and Anthropology* 6 (1969): 429–41.

MCDOUGALL, D. M. "Immigration into Canada, 1851–1920", *Canadian Journal of Economics and Political Science* 27, No. 2 (May 1961): 162–75.

MCDOUGALL, ROBERT L. "The Dodo and the Cruising Auk: Class in Canadian Literature", in Eli Mandel, ed., *Contexts of Canadian Criticism*. Chicago: University of Chicago Press, 1971.

MCELROY, A. "Ethnic Identity and Modernization: The Biculturation of Baffin Island Inuit Children", in R. Pike and E. Zurick, eds., *Socialization and Values in Canadian Society*. Vol. II. Toronto: McClelland and Stewart, 1975.

MCLUHAN, MARSHALL. *Understanding Media*. Toronto: McGraw-Hill, 1964.

MCNAUGHT, CARLETON. *Canada Gets the News*. Toronto: Ryerson, 1940.

MCNEIL, J. L. "Egerton Ryerson, Founder of Canadian (English-Speaking) Education", in R. S. Patterson *et al.*, eds., *Profiles of Canadian Educators*. Toronto: D. C. Heath, 1974.

510   INTRODUCTION TO CANADIAN SOCIETY

MEAD, MARGARET. *Sex and Temperament in Three Primitive Societies*. London: Routledge and Kegan Paul, 1935.

———. *Growing Up in New Guinea*. Harmondsworth: Penguin, 1942.

MEALING, S. R. "The Concept of Social Class and the Interpretation of Canadian History", *The Canadian Historical Review* 46 (1965): 201–18.

MEISEL, JOHN. "Religious Affiliation and Electoral Behaviour: A Case Study", *Canadian Journal of Economics and Political Science* 22 (November 1956): 481–96.

———. "Foreword", in John Porter, *The Vertical Mosaic: An Analysis of Social Class and Power in Canada*. Toronto: University of Toronto Press, 1965.

———. *Working Papers on Canadian Politics*. Montreal: McGill-Queen's University Press, 1972.

MELTZ, NOAH M. *Manpower in Canada, 1931 to 1961*. Ottawa: Department of Manpower and Immigration, 1968.

MEYER, PAUL. *Administrative Organization: A Comparative Study of Public Administration*. London: Stevens and Sons, 1957.

MILBURN, G., and HERBERT, J. *National Consciousness and the Curriculum: The Canadian Case*. Toronto: Ontario Institute for Studies in Education, 1975.

MILIBAND, RALPH. *The State in Capitalist Society*. London: Quartet, 1969.

MILLER, F. P. "Parole", in W. T. McGrath, ed., *Crime and Its Treatment in Canada*. Toronto: Macmillan, 1965.

MILLETT, D. "The Orthodox Church: Ukrainian, Greek and Syrian", in J. L. Elliott, ed., *Minority Canadians 2: Immigrant Groups*. Scarborough: Prentice-Hall, 1971.

MILNER, H., and MILNER, S. H. *The Decolonization of Quebec: An Analysis of Left-Wing Nationalism*. Toronto: McClelland and Stewart, 1973.

MOIR, J. S. *Church and State in Canada West*. Toronto: University of Toronto Press, 1959.

MOL, J. J. "Churches and Immigrants Research Group for European Migration Problems", *Bulletin* 9 (May 1961): 1–80.

MOREUX, COLETTE. *Fin d'une Réligion?* Montreal: Les Presses de l'Université de Montréal, 1969.

———. "The End of a Religion", in G. A. Gold and M. A. Tremblay, eds., *Communities and Culture in French Canada*. Toronto/Montreal: Holt, Rinehart and Winston, 1973.

MORF, G. *Le Terrorisme Québecois*. Montreal: Les Editions de l'Homme, 1970.

MORROW, E. L. *Church Union in Canada*. Toronto: Thomas Allen, 1923.

MUNROE, D. *The Organization and Administration of Education in Canada*. Ottawa: Information Canada, 1974.

MUSGROVE, F. "Population Changes and the Status of the Young", in *Youth and the Social Order*. London: Routledge and Kegan Paul, 1964. Reprinted in P. W. Musgrave, ed., *Sociology, History and Education*. London: Methuen, 1970.

NAEGELE, KASPAR D. "Canadian Society: Some Reflections", in B. Blishen *et al.*, eds., *Canadian Society*. Toronto: Macmillan, 1961.

NAYLOR, R. T. "The Rise and Fall of the Third Commercial Empire of the St. Lawrence", in G. Teeple, ed., *Capitalism and the National Question in Canada*. Toronto: University of Toronto Press, 1972.

NEILL, A. S. *Summerhill: A Radical Approach to Childrearing*. New York: Hart, 1960.

NETT, E. "The Socio-Psychological Effects on The Family of the Women's Movement", *Canadian Home Economics Association Journal*, 1975.

NEWLAND, CHESTER A. "Collective Agreement Concepts: Applications in Govern-

ment", *Public Administration Review* 38 (March–April 1968): 117–26.
NIEBUHR, R. *The Social Sources of Denominationalism.* New York: The World Publishing Company, 1957.
NORTHOVER, W. E. "Variations in Belief among Roman Catholics", in C. Beattie and S. Crysdale, eds., *Sociology Canada.* Scarborough: Butterworth, 1974.

O'DEA, T. F. *The Sociology of Religion.* Englewood Cliffs, N.J.: Prentice-Hall, 1966.
OGBURN, W. F. *Social Change.* New York: Dell Publishing, 1966.
OGMUNDSON, RICK. "Social Class and Canadian Politics: A Reinterpretation". Doctoral Dissertation, Sociology Department, University of Michigan, 1972.
———. "Party Class Images and the Class Vote in Canada", *American Sociological Review* 40 (August 1975a), in press.
———. "On the Use of Party Image Variables to Measure the Political Distinctiveness of a Class Vote: The Canadian Case", *Canadian Journal of Sociology* 1 (1975b), in press.
———. "Mass-Elite Linkages and Class Issues in Canada", *Canadian Review of Sociology and Anthropology* 13 (1976a), in press.
———. "On the Measurement of Party Class Positions: The Case of Canadian Political Parties at the Federal Level", *Canadian Review of Sociology and Anthropology* 13 (1976b), in press.
O'NEIL, JOHN. "Facts, Myths, and the Nationalist Platitude", *The Canadian Journal of Sociology* 1, No. 1 (1975).
Ontario, Provincial Committee on the Aims and Objectives of Education in the Schools of Ontario. *Living and Learning.* Hall-Dennis Report. Toronto: Ontario Department of Education, 1968.
The Ontario Teacher. Vol. 1, p. 156. Cited in Graham, 1974, p. 171.
OSSENBERG, RICHARD J. "Social Pluralism in Quebec: Continuity, Change and Conflict", in R. J. Ossenberg, ed., *Canadian Society.* Scarborough: Prentice-Hall, 1971.
OSTRY, SYLVIA. *The Occupational Composition of the Canadian Labour Force.* 1961 Census Monograph. Ottawa: The Queen's Printer, 1967.
———. *The Female Worker in Canada.* 1961 Census Monograph. Ottawa: The Queen's Printer, 1968.
O'TOOLE, ROGER. "A Consideration of 'Sect' as an Exclusively Religious Concept: Notes on Underground Traditions in the Study of Sectarianism". Unpublished paper, University of Toronto, 1971.

PACKARD, VANCE. *The Sexual Wilderness.* New York: Pocket Books, 1968.
PALTIEL, KHAYYAM ZEV. *Political Party Financing in Canada.* Toronto: McGraw-Hill, 1970.
PARK, L. C., and PARK, F. W. *Anatomy of Big Business.* Toronto: James Lewis and Samuel, 1962, 1973.
PARSONS, TALCOTT. "The School as a Social System: Some of Its Functions in American Society", *Harvard Educational Review* 29, No. 4 (Fall 1959): 297–318.
———. "Kinship in the Contemporary United States", *American Anthropologist* 43 (1942).
———. "Christianity and Modern Industrial Society", in E. A. Tiryakian, ed., *Sociological Theory, Values, and Sociocultural Change.* New York: The Free Press, 1963.
———, and BALES, R. F. *Family: Socialization and Interaction Process.* New York: The Free Press, 1955.
PATTERSON, E. PALMER. *The Canadian Indian: A History Since 1500.* Don Mills: Collier-Macmillan, 1972.

PERLMAN, DANIEL. "The Sexual Standards of Canadian University Students". Unpublished paper, 1971.
PETER, KARL. "The Hutterite Family", in K. Ishwaran, ed., *The Canadian Family.* Toronto: Holt, Rinehart and Winston, 1971.
PETERSEN, WILLIAM. "The Ideological Background of Canada's Immigration", in B. Blishen *et al.*, eds., *Canadian Society.* Toronto: Macmillan, 1955.
PHILLIPS, C. E. *The Development of Education in Canada.* Toronto: Gage, 1957.
PIDDINGTON, RALPH. "A Study of French-Canadian Kinship", in K. Ishwaran, ed., *The Canadian Family.* Toronto: Holt, Rinehart and Winston, 1971.
PIKE, ROBERT M. *Who Doesn't Get to University—and Why: A Study on Accessibility to Higher Education in Canada.* Ottawa: Association of Universities and Colleges of Canada, 1970.
———. "Introduction and Overview", in R. Pike and E. Zurick, eds., *Socialization and Values in Canadian Society.* Vol. II. Toronto: McClelland and Stewart, 1975.
———, and ZURICK, E. "Preface", in R. Pike and E. Zurick, eds., *Socialization and Values in Canadian Society.* Toronto: McClelland and Stewart, 1975.
PINARD, MAURICE. "Working Class Politics: An Interpretation of the Quebec Case", *Canadian Review of Sociology and Anthropology* 7 (May 1970): 87–109.
PINEO, PETER C. "The Extended Family in a Working Class Area of Hamilton", in B. Blishen *et al.*, eds., *Canadian Society.* 3rd ed. Toronto: Macmillan, 1971.
———, and PORTER, J. "Occupational Prestige in Canada", *Canadian Review of Sociology and Anthropology* 4 (1967): 24–40.
PLUNKETT, T. J. "Structural Reform of Local Government in Canada", *Public Administration Review* 33 (January–February 1973): 40–51.
PODOLUK, JENNY R. *Incomes of Canadians.* 1961 Census Monograph. Ottawa: The Queen's Printer, 1968.
PORTER, JOHN. "The Economic Elite and Social Structure in Canada", *Canadian Journal of Economics and Political Science* 23 (1957).
———. *The Vertical Mosaic: An Analysis of Social Class and Power in Canada.* Toronto: University of Toronto Press, 1965.
———. "Canadian Character in the Twentieth Century", *Annals of the American Academy of Political and Social Science* 370 (March 1967): 48–56.
———. *Canadian Social Structure: A Statistical Profile.* Toronto: McClelland and Stewart, 1969.
———. "The Democratization of Canadian Universities and the Need for a National System", *Minerva*, Vol. 3 (July 1970): 325–33, 338–42, 355–56. Reprinted in H. A. Stevenson *et al.*, eds., *The Best of Times, The Worst of Times.*
PORTER, M. P.; PORTER, J.; and BLISHEN, B. R. *Does Money Matter? Prospects for Higher Education.* Toronto: Institute for Behavioural Research, York University, 1973.
POWELL, ALAN, ed. *The City: Attacking Modern Myths.* Toronto: McClelland and Stewart, 1972.
PRATT, DAVID. "The Social Role of School Textbooks in Canada", in E. Zurick and R. Pike, eds., *Socialization and Values in Canadian Society.* Vol. I. Toronto: McClelland and Stewart, 1975.
PRESTHUS, ROBERT. *Elite Accommodation in Canadian Politics.* Cambridge: Cambridge University Press, 1973.
PYKE, S. W. "Children's Literature: Conceptions of Sex Roles", in R. Pike and E. Zurick, eds., *Socialization and Values in Canadian Society.* Vol. II. Toronto: McClelland and Stewart, 1975.

RAE, DOUGLAS W. *The Political Consequences of Electoral Laws.* New Haven, Conn.: Yale University Press, 1967.

RAMSEY, C. A., and WRIGHT, E. N. *Grade Nine Programme Replacement: Non-Canadian Born Students.* Toronto: Research Dept., Board of Education, 1969.

RAMU, G. N. "Sexual Attitudes and Behavior of University of Manitoba Students". Unpublished paper, 1973.

REGENSTREIF, S. P. "Group Perceptions and the Vote: Some Avenues of Opinion Formation in the 1962 Campaign", in J. Meisel, ed., *Papers on the 1962 Election.* Toronto: University of Toronto Press, 1974.

REILLY, WAYNE C. "Political Attitudes Among Law Students in Quebec", *Canadian Journal of Political Science* 4 (1973): 122–31.

REISS, IRA. *Premarital Sexual Standards in America.* New York: The Free Press, 1970.

———. *Social Context of Sexual Permissiveness.* New York: The Free Press, 1967.

REITZ, J. "Language and Ethnic Community Survival", *The Canadian Review of Sociology and Anthropology.* Special Issue in Honour of the VIII World Congress of Sociologists. Toronto: University of Toronto Press, August 1974.

RESNICK, PHILIP. "Canadian Defence Policy and the American Empire", in I. Lumsden, ed., *Close the 49th Parallel, etc.: The Americanization of Canada.* Toronto: University of Toronto Press, 1970.

REYNAUD, ANDRE. *The Canadian Economic System.* Toronto: Macmillan, 1967.

RICHERT, JEAN PIERRE. "The Impact of Ethnicity on the Perception of Heroes and Historical Symbols", *Canadian Review of Sociology and Anthropology* 11 (May 1974): 156–63.

RICHMOND, ANTHONY H. *Post-War Immigrants in Canada.* Toronto: University of Toronto Press, 1967.

RIOUX, MARCEL. *Quebec in Question.* Toronto: James Lewis and Samuel, 1971.

———. "The Development of Ideologies in Quebec", G. A. Gold and M. A. Tremblay, ed., *Communities and Culture in French Canada.* Toronto/Montreal: Holt, Rinehart and Winston, 1973.

ROBBINS, J. E. "Home and Family Background of Ottawa Public School Children in Relation to Their I.Q.'s", *Canadian Journal of Psychology* 2 (March 1948): 35–41.

ROBERTSON, HEATHER. "Give Us Back Our Airwaves", *Maclean's,* June 1973, p. 88.

ROBIN, MARTIN, ed., *Canadian Provincial Politics.* Scarborough: Prentice-Hall, 1972.

ROBSON, R. A. A., and LAPOINTE, M. *A Comparison of Men's and Women's Salaries and Employment Fringe Benefits in the Academic Profession.* Studies of the Royal Commission on the Status of Women, No. 1. Ottawa: Information Canada, 1971.

ROCHER, GUY. *A General Introduction to Sociology: A Theoretical Perspective.* Toronto: Macmillan, 1972.

———. "Formal Education: The Issue of Opportunity", in D. Forcese and S. Richer, eds., *Issues in Canadian Society.* Scarborough: Prentice-Hall, 1975.

———, and BÉLANGER, P., eds. *École et Société au Québec: Éléments d'une Sociologie de l'Éducation.* Montreal: Editions HMH, 1970.

ROHMER, RICHARD. *The Arctic Imperative: An Overview of the Energy Crisis.* Toronto: McClelland and Stewart, 1973.

ROSE, R., and URWIN, D. "Social Cohesion, Political Parties and Strains in Regimes", in M. Dogan and R. Rose, eds., *European Politics: A Reader.* Boston: Little, Brown, 1971.

ROSENTHAL, R., and JACOBSEN, L. *Pygmalion in the Classroom: Teacher Expectation and Pupils' Intellectual Development.* New York: Holt, Rinehart and Winston, 1968.

ROSENBERG, L. *Canada's Jews: A Social and Economic Study of the Jews in Canada.* Montreal: Bureau of Social and Economic Research, Canadian Jewish Congress, 1939.

ROSSI, A. "Transition to Parenthood", *Journal of Marriage and the Family* 30 (1968).

ROSSIDES, D. W. *Society as a Functional Process: An Introduction to Sociology.* Toronto: McGraw-Hill, 1968.

ROTSTEIN, A., and LAX, G., eds. *Independence: The Canadian Challenge.* Toronto: Committee for an Independent Canada, 1972.

———. *Getting It Back: A Program for Canadian Independence.* Toronto: Clarke Irwin, 1974.

RYAN, S. "The Adult Court", in W. T. McGrath, ed., *Crime and Its Treatment in Canada.* Toronto: Macmillan, 1965.

RYDER, N. B. "Components of Canadian Population Growth", *Population Index* 20, No. 2 (1954): 71–80.

RYERSON, E. "Special Report to the Governor and Legislature of 1847", in J. G. Hodgins, ed., *Documentary History of Education in Upper Canada.* Vol. 7. Toronto, 1896–1910. (Printed in Lawr and Gidney, eds., *Educating Canadians.*)

SAMPSON, ANTHONY. *The Sovereign State of ITT.* Greenwich, Conn.: Fawcett, 1973.

SCHINDELER, F., and HOFFMAN, D. "Theological and Political Conservatism: Variations in Attitudes Among Clergymen of One Denomination", *Canadian Journal of Political Science* 1 (December 1968).

SCHLESINGER, BENJAMIN. "Remarriage as Family Reorganization for Divorced Persons", in K. Ishwaran, ed., *The Canadian Family.* Toronto: Holt, Rinehart and Winston, 1971.

———. *Families.* Toronto: McGraw-Hill Ryerson, 1972.

SCHMITT, DAVID R. "Magnitude Measures of Economic and Educational Status", *Sociological Quarterly* 6 (1965): 387–91.

SCHWARTZ, MILDRED. *Public Opinion and Canadian Identity.* Berkeley: University of California Press, 1967.

———. "Canadian Voting Behaviour", in R. Rose, ed., *Electoral Behaviour: A Comparative Handbook.* New York: Macmillan, 1974.

———. "Politics: The Issue of Citizenship", in D. Forcese and S. Richer, eds., *Issues in Canadian Society: An Introduction to Sociology.* Scarborough: Prentice-Hall, 1975.

SCHWARZ, A. "Autopsie d'une Alienation; La Jeunesse Amérindienne du Nord Canadien", in R. Pike and E. Zurick, eds., *Socialization and Values in Canadian Society.* Vol. II. Toronto: McClelland and Stewart, 1975.

SCOTT, R. B. Y., and VLASTOS, G., eds. *Toward the Christian Revolution.* Chicago: Willett Clarke, 1936.

SEELEY, J.; SIM, R. A.; and LOOSELY, E. W. *Crestwood Heights: A Study of the Culture of Suburban Life.* New York: John Wiley, 1956, and Toronto: University of Toronto Press, 1956.

SÉVIGNY, R. "Religious Experience Among Quebec Youth", in C. Beattie and S. Crysdale, eds., *Sociology Canada.* Scarborough: Butterworth, 1974.

SHIBUTANI, T., and KWAN, K. W. *Ethnic Stratification.* New York: Macmillan, 1965.

SHORTT, A., and MALCOLM, D. "Memorandum on Improvements Required in the Dominion Civil Service", *Borden Papers*, Vol. 229, 128577-93. Cited in J. Hodgetts *et al.*, *The Biography of an Institution.* Montreal: McGill-Queen's University Press, 1972, p. 35.

SILCOX, C. E. *Church Union in Canada: Its Causes and Consequences.* New York: Institute of Social and Religious Research, 1933.

SILVERMAN, R. A., and TEEVAN, J. J. "Measuring Crime and Delinquency", in R. Silverman and J. Teevan, eds., *Crime in Canadian Society.* Toronto: Butterworth, 1975.

SIMON, HERBERT A. *Administrative Behavior.* 2nd ed. New York: The Free Press, 1957.

SINDELL, P. "Some Discontinuities in the Enculturation of the Mistassini Cree Children", in N. A. Chance, ed., *Conflict and Culture: Problems of Developmental Change Among The Cree.* Ottawa: Canadian Research Centre for Anthropology, 1968.

SINGER, BENJAMIN D. "American Invasion of the Mass Media in Canada", in C. L. Boydell, C. K. Grindstaff, and P. C. Whitehead, eds., *Critical Issues in Canadian Society.* Toronto: Holt, Rinehart and Winston, 1971.

SINGER, MILTON. "Cultural Values in India's Economic Development", *Annals of the American Academy of Political and Social Science* 305 (1956).

————. "Review of Max Weber's *The Religion of India*", *American Anthropologist* 63 (1961).

————. "Religion and Social Change in India: The Max Weber Thesis, Phase Three", *Economic Development and Cultural Change* 14, No. 4 (1966).

SKOGSTAD, G. "Adolescent Political Alienation", in E. Zurick and R. Pike, eds., *Socialization and Values in Canadian Society.* Vol. I. Toronto: McClelland and Stewart, 1975.

SLATER, P. "Parental Role Differentiation", in R. Coser, ed., *The Family: Its Structures and Functions.* New York: St. Martin's Press, 1974.

SMILEY, DONALD V. "Must Canadian Political Science Be a Miniature Replica?" *Journal of Canadian Studies* 9, No. 1 (1974).

SPETZ, S. N. "Criminal Court Procedure", in C. L. Boydell, P. C. Whitehead, and C. F. Grindstaff, eds., *The Administration of Criminal Justice in Canada.* Toronto: Holt, Rinehart and Winston, 1974.

STARK, R., and GLOCK, C. Y. *American Piety: The Nature of Religious Commitment.* Los Angeles: University of California Press, 1968.

STEELE, J., and MATHEWS, R. "The Universities: Takeover of the Mind", in I. Lumsden, ed., *Close the 49th Parallel, etc.* Toronto: University of Toronto Press, 1970.

STEVENSON, H. A., *et al.*, eds. *The Best of Times, The Worst of Times: Contemporary Issues in Canadian Education.* Toronto: Holt, Rinehart and Winston, 1972.

STINCHCOMBE, ARTHUR L. "Bureaucratic and Craft Administration of Production: A Comparative Study", *Administrative Science Quarterly* 4 (June 1959): 168–87.

STOLK, MARY. *The Battered Child in Canada.* Toronto: McClelland and Stewart, 1972.

STOLZMAN, J., and GAMBERG, H. "The National Question and Canadian Sociology", *The Canadian Journal of Sociology* 1, No. 1 (1975).

STONE, L. O. *Urban Development in Canada.* 1961 Census Monograph. Ottawa: The Queen's Printer, 1967.

————. *Migration in Canada: Regional Aspects.* 1961 Census Monograph. Ottawa: The Queen's Printer, 1970.

STREET, T. G. *Canada's Parole System.* Ottawa: Information Canada, 1972.

SUTHERLAND, E. H., and CRESSEY, D. *Principles of Criminology.* New York: J. B. Lippincott, 1966.

SVALASTOGA, KAARE. *Social Differentiation.* New York: McKay, 1965.

SYKES, GRESHAM. "The Structure of Authority", *Public Opinion Quarterly* 17 (Spring 1953): 147–49.

TEEPLE, GARY, ed. *Capitalism and the National Question in Canada*. Toronto: University of Toronto Press, 1972.
————. " 'Liberals in a Hurry': Socialism and the CCF–NDP", in G. Teeple, ed., *Capitalism and the National Question in Canada*, 1972.
THOMSON, DALE C., ed. *Quebec Society and Politics: Views from the Inside*. Toronto: McClelland and Stewart, 1973.
TOMEH, A. K. *The Family and Sex Roles*. Toronto: Holt, Rinehart and Winston, 1975.
TROELTSCH, E. *The Social Teachings of the Christian Churches*. New York: Harper and Row, 1960.
TRUDEAU, PIERRE ELLIOTT. *Federalism and the French Canadians*. Toronto: Macmillan, 1968.
TRUMAN, TOM. "A Critique of Seymour M. Lipset's Article, 'Value Differences, Absolute or Relative: The English-Speaking Democracies' ", *Canadian Journal of Political Science* 4 (1971): 497–525.
TURNER, R. H. "Sponsored and Contest Mobility and the School System", *American Sociological Review* 25 (December 1960): 855–67.

United States of America. Population Reference Bureau. *1973 World Population Data Sheet*. Washington, D.C., 1973.
————. United States President's Commission on Law Enforcement and the Administration of Justice. *Task Force Report: Science and Technology*. Washington, D.C.: U.S. Government Printing Office, 1967.
————. United States Bureau of the Census. *Statistical Abstract of the United States, 1973*. Washingon, D.C., 1973.
University of Toronto. Faculty of Education. *Student Handbook*. 1972.

VALLEE, FRANK G. "The Emerging Northern Mosaic", in R. J. Ossenberg, ed., *Canadian Society: Pluralism, Change and Conflict*. Scarborough: Prentice-Hall, 1971.
————. "Multi-Ethnic Societies: The Issues of Identity and Equality", in D. Forcese and S. Richer, eds., *Issues in Canadian Society*. Scarborough: Prentice-Hall, 1975.
————, and SHULMAN, N. "The Viability of French Groupings Outside Quebec", in M. Wade, ed., *Regionalism in the Canadian Community, 1867–1967*. Toronto: University of Toronto Press, 1969.
VALLIÈRES, PIERRE. *White Niggers of America*. Toronto: McClelland and Stewart, 1971.
VAN DEN BERGHE, PIERRE L. *Race and Racism*. New York: John Wiley and Sons, 1967.
VAN LOON, RICHARD J. "Political Participation in Canada: The 1965 Election", in C. Beattie and S. Crysdale, eds., *Sociology Canada: Readings*. Toronto: Butterworth, 1974.
————, and WHITTINGTON, M. S. *The Canadian Political System: Environment, Structure and Process*. Toronto: McGraw-Hill, 1971.
Vanier Institute of the Family. *Canadian Resources on the Family*. Ottawa: Vanier Institute of the Family, 1972.
VEEVERS, J. E. "The Social Meanings of Parenthood", *Psychiatry* 36 (1973).
VILE, M. J. C. *The Structure of American Federalism*. London: Oxford University Press, 1961.

WAKIL, PARVEEZ S. "On the Question of Developing a Sociology of Canadian Family: A Methodological Statement", *Canadian Review of Sociology and*

Anthropology 7, No. 2 (1970).

——. "Marriage and the Family in Canada", in K. Ishwaran, ed., *The Canadian Family*. Toronto: Holt, Rinehart and Winston, 1971.

WALLER, I., and CHAN, J. "Prison Use: A Canadian and International Comparison", *Criminal Law Quarterly* 17 (1975): 47–71.

Wahn Report. The Eleventh Report of the Standing Committee on External Affairs and National Defence Respecting Canada-U.S. Relations. Ottawa: The Queen's Printer, 1970.

WALLERSTEIN, IMMANUEL. *The Modern World-System: Capitalist Agriculture and the Origins of the European World-Economy in the Sixteenth Century*. New York: Academic Press, 1974.

WALSH, H. H. *The Christian Church in Canada*. Toronto: Ryerson, 1956.

——. *The Church in the French Era*. Toronto: Ryerson, 1966.

WARNER, W. L.; MEEKER, M.; and EELLS, K. *Social Class in America*. New York: Harper, 1960.

WARNOCK, JOHN W. *Partner to Behemoth: The Military Policy of a Satellite Canada*. Toronto: New Press, 1970.

WATKINS, MEL. "Resources and Underdevelopment", in R. Laxer, ed., *(Canada) Ltd.: The Political Economy of Dependency*. Toronto: McClelland and Stewart, 1973.

Watkins Report. Foreign Ownership and the Structure of Canadian Industry: Report of the Task Force on the Structure of Canadian Industry. Ottawa: The Queen's Printer, 1968.

WEBER, MAX. *The Theory of Social and Economic Organization*. London: Hodge (references in Chap. 4); New York: Oxford University Press (references in Chap. 11); 1947.

——. *From Max Weber: Essays in Sociology*, eds. H. H. Gerth and C. W. Mills. London: Routledge and Kegan Paul, 1948.

——. *The Protestant Ethic and the Spirit of Capitalism*. London: Allen and Unwin (references in Chap. 3); New York: Scribner's (references in Chap 9); 1958.

WEITZMAN, L. J., et al. "Sex Role Socialization in Picture Books for Preschool Children", *American Journal of Sociology* 77, No. 6 (May 1972): 1125–50.

WHITE, W. L.; WAGENBERG, R. N.; and NELSON, R. C. *Introduction to Canadian Politics and Government*. Toronto: Holt, Rinehart and Winston, 1972.

WHITEHURST, R., and PLANT, B. "A Comparison of Canadian and American University Students' References Groups, Alienation, and Attitudes Towards Marriage", *International Journal of the Family Sociology*, el 1 (1971). Reprinted in W. E. Mann, ed., *Canada: A Sociological Profile*. Toronto: Copp Clark, 1971.

WHYTE, D. R. "Religion and the Rural Church", in M. A. Tremblay and W. J. Anderson, eds., *Rural Canada in Transition*. Ottawa: Agricultural Economics Research Council of Canada, 1966.

WIENER, NORBERT. *The Human Use of Human Beings*. New York: Doubleday, 1954.

——. *Cybernetics*. Boston: M.I.T. Press, 1961.

WILSON, B. R. *Religion in Secular Society*. London: C. A. Watts, 1966.

——. *Religious Sects*. Toronto/New York: McGraw-Hill, 1970.

WILSON, D. J. *The Church Grows in Canada*. Toronto: Ryerson, 1966.

WINKS, ROBIN W. "Negro School Segregation in Ontario and Nova Scotia", *Canadian Historical Review* 50 (June 1969): 164–91.

——. *Blacks in Canada*. Montreal: McGill-Queen's University Press, 1970.

WOLCOTT, HARRY F. *A Kwatiutl Village and School*. New York: Holt, Rinehart and Winston, 1967.

WOLFF, WILLIAM B. "Organizational Constructs: An Approach to Understanding

Organizations", in P. M. Dauten, Jr., ed., *Current Issues and Emerging Concepts in Management*. Boston: Houghton Mifflin, 1962.
WOYTINSKY, W. S., and WOYTINSKY, E. S. *World Population and Production*. New York: The Twentieth Century Fund, 1953.
WRIGLEY, E. A. *Population and History*. Toronto: McGraw-Hill, 1969.
WRONG, DENNIS. *Population and Society*. 3rd ed. New York: Random House, 1967.

YINGER, M. J. *The Scientific Study of Religion*. New York: Macmillan, 1970.

ZELDITCH, M. "Role Differentiation in the Nuclear Family: A Comparative Study", in T. Parsons and R. F. Bales, eds., *Family: Socialization and Interaction Process*. New York: The Free Press, 1955.
ZENTNER, HARRY. "Parental Behavior and Student Attitudes Towards High School Graduation Among Indian and Non-Indian Students in Oregon and Alberta", *Alberta Journal of Educational Research* 8 (December 1966): 211–19.
ZURICK, ELIA T. "Children and Political Socialization", in K. Ishwaran, ed., *The Canadian Family*. Toronto: Holt, Rinehart and Winston, 1971.
———. "Introduction and Overview", in E. Zurick and R. Pike, eds., *Socialization and Values in Canadian Society*. Vol. I. Toronto: McClelland and Stewart, 1975.
ZUR-MUEHLEN, MAX VON. "The PhD Dilemma in Canada: A Case Study", in S. Ostry, ed., *Canadian Higher Education in the Seventies*. Ottawa: Economic Council of Canada, 1972.

Author Index

Adams, I., 131, 166, 313
Adler-Karlsson, G., 165
Alford, R., 166, 186
Allen, R., 389
Allingham, J. D., 118
Allmand, W., 281
Anderson, G. M., 388
Anderson, J. D., 157
Anderson, M., 296
Anderson, O., 159
Arafat, I., 341
Ares, R., 245
Astrachan, A., 13
Atwood, M., 431
Axworthy, L., 157

Bales, R. F., 311
Ball, W., 169
Barclay, H., 309, 372
Bartell, G., 342
Beattie, C., 146, 147, 200, 232
Beck, J. M., 157, 186, 206
Bèlanger, P. W., 423
Bell, D., 194
Bell, E. H., 293
Bell, R., 334
Bellah, R., 386
Bendix, R., 112, 115
Bennett, J. W., 427
Berg, I., 138
Berger, P., 350, 352, 378, 392
Bernstein, B., 427
Berry, B., 246
Bertrand, A., 253
Bettelheim, B., 314
Bhatt, G. S., 355
Bibby, R. W., 313
Bienvenue, R. M., 4, 156, 237
Blishen, B., 406
Bloch, H. A., 275

Blood, R. O., 319
Bocking, R. C., 158, 164, 165
Boissevain, J., 239, 412
Bottomore, T., 117
Bourgeault, P., 159
Bowland, J. G., 463
Boydell, C. L., 269
Brant, C. S., 220, 412
Braroe, N. W., 240
Brazeau, J., 233
Breton, R., 181, 215, 217, 240, 315, 423, 424, 426, 430, 493
Brinkerhoff, M., 313
Brody, H., 229, 230, 240
Brown, L., 185, 205
Butler, D., 187

Cairns, A. C., 157, 187
Campbell, A., 185
Campbell, C., 178
Campbell, K. G., 175, 187, 203
Campbell, M., 248
Camu, P., 22
Cardinal, H., 214, 248
Carlos, S., 396
Caron, A., 180
Chan, J., 275
Chimbos, P. D., 333
Christian, W., 178
Church, G., 221
Cicourel, A., 425
Clairmont, D. H., 413
Clark, A. H., 215
Clark, E., 424
Clark, S. D., 356, 357, 480, 481, 482, 483, 485, 486, 487, 488, 493
Clement, W., 123, 126, 127, 128, 131, 149, 157, 180, 188, 189, 192, 193, 194, 196, 198, 200, 202, 204, 208

Clifford, N., 350
Coburn, D., 485, 486, 489, 493
Coleman, J. S., 434
Collins, R., 137, 138
Comte, A., 349
Connidis, I. A., 269
Cottam, J., 181, 182
Courtenay, J. C., 201
Cousineau, D. F., 274, 275, 276, 278, 279
Cressey, D., 275
Cruikshank, J., 310
Crysdale, S., 320, 377, 378, 389, 390, 394, 395
Cuneo, C. J., 149, 150, 151, 249
Curtis, J. E., 112, 149, 150, 151, 249

Dahrendorf, R., 113, 115, 117
Davis, A. K., 150, 160, 486, 493
Davis, J., 428
Davis, Kingsley, 114
Davis, M., 411, 412
Dawson, C. A., 383, 493
Dawson, R. M., 157, 450
Deaton, R., 131
Demerath, N. J., 377
Denis, A. B., 419
Denton, F. T., 28, 30
Dofny, J., 150
Dosman, E., 227, 228, 229, 230, 239
Dozier, E. P., 229
Drache, D., 195
Drake, M., 21
Dreeben, R., 429
Driedger, Leo, 221
Duncan, O. D., 128
Durkheim, E., 349, 352, 385
Duval, R., 423

Effrat, A., 157
Eichler, M., 347
Elgee, W. H., 382, 383
Elkin, F., 94, 297, 298, 300, 306, 309, 326, 343

Elliott, J. L., 238
Englemann, F., 172, 173, 187, 192
Engles, F., 113, 115
Enroth, R., 384
Eshleman, R., 328–9
Etzioni, A., 204
Eylands, V. J., 375

Faguy, P. A., 280
Falardeau, C. P., 378, 382
Farber, B., 300, 301, 322
Feldman, I. D., 157
Forcese, D., 481, 483, 484, 491
Fornataro, J. V., 276
Frank, G., 171
Friedenberg, E. Z., 408
Freitag, W., 375

Gamberg, H., 492, 493, 494
Garigue, P., 248, 297, 309, 312, 315, 318, 323, 344, 386
Garry, C., 388
Gaudet, R., 350
Geis, G., 275
George, P. M., 307
Gidny, R., 414
Gillies, J. M., 157
Gingerich, O., 386
Glock, C. Y., 379, 390
Goblot, E., 434
Godfrey, B., 165
Goldrick, M., 157
Goode, W. J., 329
Gordon, M., 226, 240
Gordon, W., 165
Graicunas, V. A., 463
Grant, G. P., 165, 179, 200, 206
Grant, J. W., 375
Greenfield, S., 329
Grindstaff, C. F., 217
Grosman, B., 258, 262, 263, 264
Guindon, H., 179
Gurr, T. R., 246
Guyat, D. E., 307

Hall, O., 320
Hall, R. H., 440
Hamblin, R. L., 138
Hamilton, C. V., 97
Hamilton, R. H., 187
Hansen, D. A., 301
Harding, J., 236–7
Hargreaves, D., 424, 430
Hartt, P., 255
Harvey, E., 408
Harvey, T. G., 431
Haskell, M. R., 255
Hatt, P. K., 21
Heap, J., 126, 188
Hechter, M., 170
Hedley, R. A., 489
Heeney, A. D. P., 451
Heer, D., 319, 332
Henripin, J., 34, 35, 45, 60, 171
Henry, F., 216
Henry, J., 429
Henshel, A., 342
Herberg, W., 386
Herbert, J., 432
Hertzler, J. O., 13
Hill, R., 301
Hiller, H. H., 5, 9, 294, 393
Hobart, C., 220, 306, 334, 335, 341, 412, 413
Hodgetts, J. E., 181, 430, 431, 458
Hoffman, D., 387
Hogarth, J., 269
Holdaway, E. A., 433
Honigman, J., 238
Horowitz, G., 177
Hostetler, J. A., 300
Hughes, D. R., 218
Hughes, E. C., 493
Hunt, M., 342
Hunter, A., 2, 4, 406
Huntington, G. E., 300
Hurd, B., 38, 39

Innis, H., 86, 87

Irving, J. A., 389
Ishwaran, K., 296, 297, 298, 300, 309, 312, 318, 332

Jacklin, C. N., 426
Jacobson, H., 298
Jenness, D., 214
Johnson, A. W., 453
Johnson, L. A., 131, 160
Johnstone, J. C., 181, 409
Jones, F. E., 433
Jones, R., 379
Joy, R. J., 245, 409, 410

Kalbach, W. E., 2, 9, 15, 16, 17, 20, 31, 39, 47, 48, 151, 169, 216, 217, 241, 304, 312, 326, 331
Kallen, E., 218
Katz, M. B., 402
Kelley, W. H., 257
Keyfitz, N., 22, 248
Kierans, E., 165
King, A. J. C., 426, 432
Kirkendal, L., 334
Kirkpatrick, A. M., 288, 290
Kitsuse, J. I., 424
Kohl, S., 310, 311, 427
Krauter, J. F., 411, 412
Krishnan, P., 339
Kubat, D., 50, 345
Kuzel, P., 339
Kwan, K. W., 212, 237, 240, 247

Lacey, C., 424, 430
Lacoste, N., 386
Lai, V., 239
Lamy, P. G., 181
Langton, K. P., 317
Lanphier, C. M., 147, 232
Lapointe, M., 141
Latif, A. H., 237
Latouche, D., 249
Latowsky, E., 309, 312, 331
Lawr, D., 414

Lax, G., 165
Laxer, J., 158, 162, 165, 171, 183
Lazarsfeld, P., 185
Lemert, E., 229
Lenski, G., 115
Lévesque, R., 170, 209
Levitt, K., 124, 165, 170, 203
Lieberson, S., 69, 245
Lipset, S., 112, 115, 150, 444
Lipton, C., 121
Lockhart, A., 164
Lorimer, J., 157
Lumsden, I., 178
Lundberg, G., 155
Lyden, F. J., 470

Maccoby, E. E., 426
McCormack, T., 2, 3, 9, 90, 92
MacDonald, J. C., 315
McDonald, L., 387, 388
McDougall, D. M., 22, 180
McElroy, A., 412
McFarland, B., 320
McGrath, W. T., 254
Mackinnon, F., 434
Macleod, A. J., 254
McLuhan, M., 86, 87, 90
McNaught, C., 104
McNeill, J. L., 403
Macpherson, C., 176, 479, 481, 482, 486, 493
McVey, W. W., 15, 16, 17, 20, 31, 151, 217, 304, 326, 331
Madeley, St. John, 272
Maheu, R., 245
Malcolm, D., 456
Mallory, J. R., 157
Mann, W. E., 334, 335, 374, 387, 482, 493
Manzer, R., 172, 181, 183, 184, 189, 195, 219
Marchak, M., 177, 193, 203, 205, 206, 426
Marchett, V. L., 206

Marks, J. D., 206
Marunchak, M. H., 372
Marx, K., 113, 115, 116, 117, 349, 378, 379
Maslow, A., 131
Masson, J. K., 157
Mathews, R., 169, 178, 432
Mauss, H., 481
Maxwell, J. D., 428
Maxwell, M. P., 428
Mealing, S. R., 180
Meisel, J., 185, 186, 387, 388
Meltz, N., 132, 137
Milburn, G., 432
Miliband, R., 114, 117
Miller, E. G., 470
Miller, F. P., 283
Millett, D., 372
Milner, H., 170, 249, 381
Milner, S. H., 170, 249, 381
Moir, J. S., 383
Mol, J. J., 372
Moore, W., 114
Moreux, C., 248, 386
Morf, G., 249
Morris, R., 147, 232
Morro, E. L., 374
Munro, D., 415
Musgrove, F., 408

Naegele, K., 150
Naylor, R. T., 157, 192, 194
Neill, A. S., 434
Nett, E. M., 345, 346
Newland, C. A., 472
Niebuhr, R., 354–5
Northover, W. E., 393

O'Dea, T., 351
Ogburn, W. F., 86
Ogmundson, R., 2, 3, 155, 166, 184, 187
O'Neill, J., 493
Ossenberg, R., 231

Ostry, S., 28, 29, 30, 31, 120, 139, 140
O'Toole, R., 355

Packard, V., 334, 335
Paltiel, K., 202
Park, F., 123, 124
Park, L., 123, 124
Parsons, T., 298, 311, 323, 391
Patterson, E. P., 214
Perlman, D., 334, 335
Peterson, W., 216
Phillips, C. E., 403
Piddington, R., 323
Pike, R., 181, 320, 430
Pinard, M., 187, 240
Pineo, P., 134, 135, 323, 324
Plant, B., 340, 341
Plunkett, T. J., 460
Podoluk, J., 129, 139
Porter, J., 117, 123, 124, 125, 126, 127, 128, 130, 134, 135, 144, 149, 151, 166, 168, 171, 181, 187, 188, 190, 191, 196, 197, 199, 200, 201, 204, 207, 208, 209, 215, 220, 231, 232, 314, 317, 380, 381, 406, 418, 422, 424, 425, 426, 427, 428, 432
Powell, A., 157
Pratt, D., 181
Presthus, R., 184, 199, 200

Rae, W., 184
Ramsey, C. A., 427
Ramu, G. N., 5, 7, 176, 293, 335, 341
Regenstreif, S. P., 388
Reitz, J., 69
Reilly, W. C., 181
Reiss, I., 333, 334
Resnick, P., 205
Reynaud, A., 192
Richer, S., 481, 483, 484, 491
Richert, J. P., 219, 430
Richmond, A., 216, 231
Rioux, M., 150, 167, 215, 249, 386

Robbins, J. E., 157, 166
Roberts, R. W., 307
Robin, M., 174
Robson, R. A. A., 141
Rocher, G., 486
Rohmer, R., 158, 165
Rose, R., 166, 171
Rosenberg, L., 369
Rossi, A., 312
Rossides, D. W., 481
Rotstein, A., 165
Ryan, S., 263, 264, 266, 267
Ryder, N. B., 22
Ryerson, E., 402, 403

Sampson, A., 206
Santos, C. R., 6, 7, 294
Schindeler, F., 387
Schlesinger, B., 296, 339
Schmidt, D. R., 132
Schwartz, M., 165, 172, 173, 174, 184, 186, 187, 192
Scott, R. B. Y., 389
Scott, W. G., 112
Seely, J., 318, 323
Sévigny, R., 393
Shibutani, T., 212, 237, 240, 247
Shortt, A., 456
Shulman, N., 225
Silcox, C. E., 375
Silverman, R. A., 275, 276
Simon, H. A., 463
Singer, B. B., 182
Singer, M., 480
Sirjamaki, J., 293
Skogstad, G., 431
Slater, P., 312
Smiley, D. V., 198
Spencer, B. G., 232
Spetz, S. N., 264
Stark, R., 379, 390
Steele, J., 182, 432
Stinchcombe, A. L., 439
Stokes, D., 187

Stolk, M., 315
Stolzman, J., 492, 493, 494
Stone, L. O., 16, 19
Street, T. G., 284
Stryckman, P., 350
Sutherland, E. H., 275
Svalastoga, K., 114
Sykes, G., 447
Synge, J., 4, 294

Teeple, G., 123, 195
Teevan, J. J., 275, 276
Thomas, W. I., 4
Thomson, D. C., 170
Thornton, D., 52, 345
Tomeh, A. K., 312, 342
Troeltsch, E., 354
Trudeau, P. E., 184
Truman, T., 150
Turner, R. H., 407

Urwin, D., 166, 171

Vallee, F. G., 225, 238
Vallières, P., 167, 249
Van den Berghe, P., 212, 218
Van Loon, R. J., 157, 162, 182, 183,
    185, 200, 201
Veevers, J. E., 274, 275, 276, 278,
    279, 306
Vile, M. J. C., 448
Vincent, C., 307
Vlastos, G., 389

Wakil, P., 296, 326, 327
Waller, I., 275
Wallerstein, I., 170
Walsh, H. H., 350, 355, 382
Warburton, T. R., 489
Ward, N., 157, 450
Warner, W. L., 131
Warnock, J. W., 205, 206
Watkins, M., 159, 162, 165, 195, 203
Weber, M., 87, 114, 349, 380, 391
Weitzman, L. J., 429
White, W. L., 160, 181
Whitehurst, R., 340, 341
Whittington, M., 157
Whyte, D. R., 395, 396
Wiener, N., 79
Wilson, B., 350, 355, 359, 367
Winks, R. W., 231
Wolfe, D. M., 319
Wolff, W. B., 439
Woytinsky, E. S., 14
Woytinsky, W. S., 14
Wright, E. N., 427
Wrigley, E. A., 14

Yablonsky, L., 255
Yinger, M., 38, 352, 356, 392
Yorburg, B., 341
Younge, E. R., 383

Zelditch, M., 311
Zentner, H., 239
Zurick, E., 179, 180, 181, 317, 318
Zur-Muehlen, M. V., 182

Subject Index

Acculturation, 237–9
Administrative bilingualism, 468–9
After-care agencies
  history of, 288
  work of, 289
Aird Report, 95
Archambault Report, 279, 280
Assimilation, 237–46
  linguistic, 242–5
  primary-group relationship,
    239–40
  secondary relationship, 239–40
  structural integration, 239–42
Authority, 114

Biculturalism
  demographic dimensions, 31–48
  ethnic dimensions, 218–20
Bilingualism
  administrative aspects, 468–9
  demographic aspects, 34–8
  threats to, 36–8
Birth rate, crude, 305–6
British North America Act, 256, 263,
    266, 276, 415, 443
Bureaucracy
  characteristics of, 440–1
  definition of, 439
  governmental, 443–6
  hierarchical nature of, 441
  informal structure of, 442–3
  non-governmental, 443–6
  as organizational construct, 439
  political setting of, 447–9
  power and responsibility, 473–6
  rules of, 441–2
Bureaucracy, federal
  changes in, 468–72
  geographic dispersion of, 461–4
  growth of, 459–61

  personal processes in, 464–8
  types of appointments, 465–6

Canadian newspapers, 104–5
  underground newspapers, 109
Canadian sociology, 7, 488, 490
  internationalization of, 490
  nationalization of, 490
  See also Sociology of Canada
Child abuse, 315
Church-sect
  in Canada, 355–8
  discussion of, 354–5
  hypothesis, 354–5
  See also Religion
Class, social, 112, 226
  bourgeoisie, 116
  Canadian class structure, 117–28
  dominant, 113
  education and, 423–5
  political behaviour and, 166–8
  proletariat, 116
  religious affiliation and, 377
  subordinant, 113
  working class, 119–22
Collective bargaining, 457, 471–3
Commissioner of Penitentiaries, 277
Communication
  as cultural phenomenon, 79
  language, role of, 82–3
  social causation, 86–8
  social inequality, 83–6
  social institution, 89–110
  social policy and, 109–10
  social structure, 82–3
  study of, 78–80
  technology of, 86–7
  verbal and non-verbal, 80–2
Confederation, 15, 16
Consensus, 252

Correctional institutions, 274–82
  definition of, 276
  organization of, 276
Crime, definition of, 254
Criminal Code, 270
Criminal, definition of, 255
Criminal-court system
  adult, 265–8
  functions of, 268–9
  organization of, 267–8
Criminal-justice system, 253
  function of, 253
  organization of, 253
Crown prosecutor, functions of,
  263–4
Culture, definition of, 401
Cultural diversity and change,
  demographic profiles, 48–74
Cultural lag, 86

Demographic transition, 11–30.
  theory, 21, 22
Demography
  and political behaviour, 168–9
  and religion, 358–63
Department of the Solicitor General,
  276–7
Deutsch Commission, 410
Divorce, 336–42
  grounds for, 338–40
  rate of, 337–40

Economic relations, with United
  States, 162
Ecumenism, 373–6
  in Canada, 374
  definition of, 373
Education system, control of, 414–16
Education in Canada
  achievement and ethnicity, 426–7
  aspirations by class, 425–6
  British and French, 410–11
  colleges in Quebec, 419
  Doukhobor, 412

elitist approach, 407–8
expenditure for, 417
historical development, 402–14
mental ability and, 423
national awareness and, 431–2
native, 412–13
in 19th century, 403–4
occupation and, 422
populist approach, 407–8
post-secondary, 405–12
power and control of, 432–4
social class and, 423–5
socialization function of, 428–32
streaming in, 430
in 20th century, 404–5
Elite
  business, 191–4
  comporador, 127, 128
  composition of, 189–90
  defensive, 202–6
  educational, 198–9
  ideological, 196–9
  judicial, 200–1
  labour, 194–6
  political, 201–3
  power structure of, 188–209
  public service, 199–200
  recruitment of, 189–90
  religious, 197
  structure and organization, 128–32
Endogamy, ethnic, 38–40, 241–2,
  330–2
Ethclass, 226
Ethnic consciousness, 248
Ethnic diversity, 213–26
Ethnic group
  charter groups, 214–16, 230–1
  definition of, 201
  intergroup differences, 232–7
  other ethnic groups, 216–17, 231–2
  size and distribution, 217–18
  stratification, 226–37
Ethnic institutions, 218
Ethnic religions, 372

Ethnicity
  changes in diversity, 59, 60
  distribution by province, 53, 54,
    66, 68
  education and, 409–14
  educational achievement and,
    426–7
  marriage and, 330–2
  religion and, 367–73
  variations in demographic
    distribution, 50–4
Executive power, 449
Exogamy, 241–2

Family
  in Canada, 298
  Canadian, 298
  census, 298–9
  conceptual framework, 301–4
  culture, 301–4
  decision making, 318–19
  definition of, 297–8, 299–300
  functions of, 304–21
    educational, 319–20
    political, 316–17
    primary, 304
    reproductive, 305–8
    secondary, 304
    socialization, 308–9
    status placement, 313–14
  identity, 309–10
  locus of political power, 316
  occupation, 310–11
  of one nation, 301
  political actions of, 316
  of procreation, 301
  role transmission, 311–12
Family life in Canada, research on,
  295–7
Fateaux Report, 279, 280, 284
Federal departments, 458–9
Federalism, 448
Fertility
  ethnic and cultural factors, 56–8

by ethnic groups, 34, 60–2
French, 32–4
by religion, 58, 59
Folkways, 252
French Canadians, value system of,
  219
Friendship groupings, 240–1

Gaol, definition of, 276
Glassco Royal Commission, 457
Government, system of, 133–74
Great Revival, 357

Habitant family, 355–6
Hinterland and metropolis, 160,
  165–6
Household
  census, 298, 299
  definition of, 297–8

Identity
  ethnic, 215, 229
  function of the family, 309
Immigration, 21, 22
  British migration, 31–2
  effects of age and sex on, 27, 28
Incarceration, objectives of, 278
Income
  by ethnic group, 148
  by occupation, 133
  selected, 134
  by sex, 133
Institutional completeness, 220–1
Intermarriage, 241–2, 330–2

John Howard Society, 288, 291

Kin
  affinal, 302
  bilateral, 321
  lineal, 302
  matrilineal, 321
  patrilineal, 321

Kinship residence
  matrilocal, 321
  neolocal, 322
  patrilocal, 321
Kinship structure, 321–4

Labour force
  changes in, 28–30
  by education, 137, 142
  by ethnic group, 145, 146
  female participation in, 30, 344–6
  by occupation, 29, 120, 122, 137,
    141, 142, 145, 146
  by sex, 29, 118
Labour theory of value, 116
Language
  communications, role of, 82–3
  and education, 408–14
  retention of culture, 68–74
  social inequality, 84–5
Laws, 252
Law enforcement, 256–62
  See also Police
Living together, 341

Manitoba government
  Dept. of Health and Social
    Development, 281
  Probation Service, 272
Marginal adaptation, 231
Marginality, 240–1
Marriage
  age differential, 327
  age of, 326–8
  critical attitude toward, 340–2
  definition of, 324
  demographic profiles, 325–9
  marriage rates, 325–6
Mass media
  capitalism, relation to, 102–4
  censorship in, 98–9
  characteristics of, 89–92
  class identity, 96–8
  dysfunction, sources of, 98–104

information in, 93
  integrative function of, 92–6
  ownership of, 100–2
Massey Report, 95
Mate selection, factors in, 329–36
Mate swapping, 341–2
Mobility, social, 149, 151
  contest, 407
  through education, 407
  sponsored, 407
  vertical, 114
Monocratic organization, 445–7
Mores, 252
Mortality, 62, 63
Multiculturalism, 4

National Film Board Act, 95
National identity, mass media, 94–6
National Parole Board, 284–90
  composition of, 284
  jurisdiction of, 284
  policies of, 284–5
National Parole Service, 290–1
Native people, 214, 227–30
New Light Movement, 356, 357

Orderly replacement, 301–3
Ouimet Report, 254, 258, 270, 271,
    272, 273, 278, 280, 282, 288

Parent Commission, 406, 419
Parole, 282–91
  definition of, 282
  eligibility, 285
  parole, full, 286
  parole, day, 286
  procedures, 285
  supervision, 286–7
Patriarchy, 303
Plea bargaining, 264
Police, 256–62
  functions of, 258–9
  recruitment, 260
  training, 261

trends in work, 260
Political behaviour
  and Canadian geography and
    natural resources, 158–9
  and culture, 171–2
  ethnic heterogeneity, 169–71
  ideology and, 176–8
  linguistic heterogeneity, 169–71
  mass, 175–88
  regional economic relationships,
    159–62
  religious heterogeneity, 169–71
Political participation, 183–4
Polycratic organization, 445–7
Population
  by age and sex, 24–7
  English-French contrasts, 40–8
  by ethnic components, 55, 56, 146
  by highest level of education, 146
  by official language, 35
  percentage married, 35
  provinces, 18
  by religious components, 55, 56
  vital rates, 23
Population growth
  natural increase, 16–20
  New France, 15
  patterns of change, 22–4
  world, 12–16
Poverty, rate by family size, 130–1
Power, 111
Premarital sex, 333–5
Prestige, 111
  score for selected occupations, 135
Prima facie case, 268
Prime Minister, role of, 449–50
Principle of exclusion, 298
Prison, definition of, 275
  See also Correctional institutions
Privy Council, 450–2
Probation
  adult, 269–74
  breach of, 274
  conditions of, 273

definition of, 270
"Profane" in religion, 352
Prosecution, 262–5
Provincial and regional disparity,
  indicators, 161
Public Service Commission, 456–8

Race, definition of, 212–13
Recidivism in Canadian prisons, 278
Release of prisoners
  earned remission, 282
  methods for, 282–7
  remission, 282
  statutory remission, 282
  temporary absence, 282
  See also Parole
Religion, 349–97
  colonialism and, 382–4
  conservative function of, 385–8
  definition of, 350–1
  ethnicity and, 367–73, 379–81
  organization of, 353–76
  regional distribution, 363–6
  social change and, 384–96
  social class and, 379–81
  social stratification and, 376–84
  urbanization and, 395–6
Remission Service, 283
Royal Canadian Mounted Police,
  functions of, 257–8
Royal Commission on Bilingualism
  and Biculturalism, 125, 215,
  216, 219, 221, 223, 225, 231,
  245, 380–1, 409, 410

"Sacred" in religion, 352
Salvation Army, 283, 288
Schools, 415–16
  enrolment, 416
  federal, 416
  organization, 415–16
  private, 411
  public, 415–16
Secessionist Movement, 248–50

Secularization, 390–5
  definition of, 391–2
Sex roles
  family structure and, 342–6
  marriage, impact on, 346–7
  traditional patterns, 342–4
Social conflict, 246–50
  social change and the emergence
    of, 247–8
Social control, 252
Socialization
  definition of, 401
  political, 179–82, 317–18
Social structure, 9
Social system, definition of, 253
Sociology in Canada, 481–90
  American influence, 484–8
  French and English differences,
    488–9
  origins of, 481–5
Sociology of Canada, 7, 488, 491–4
Special Senate Committee on
    Poverty, 129–30
Status
  achieved, 113

ascribed, 113, 313–14
Canadian structure, 128–48
group, 113
Stratification, social
  definition of, 112
  ethnicity and, 143–8
  functional theory of, 114
  origins of, 114, 115
  positional, 129–39
  recruitment, 139–48
  religion and, 376–84
  sex and, 139–43

Territorial church, 357, 358
Ticket of Leave Act, 283
Treasury Board, 452–5

Universal permanent availability, 5,
    302, 303, 325, 328
Urbanization, 16–19
  religion and, 395–6

Voting behaviour, 185–8

Zero population growth, 308